Strategic Management and International Business Policies for Maintaining Competitive Advantage

Ailson J. De Moraes
Royal Holloway University of London, UK

A volume in the Advances in Business Strategy
and Competitive Advantage (ABSCA) Book Series

Published in the United States of America by
  IGI Global
  Business Science Reference (an imprint of IGI Global)
  701 E. Chocolate Avenue
  Hershey PA, USA 17033
  Tel: 717-533-8845
  Fax: 717-533-8661
  E-mail: cust@igi-global.com
  Web site: http://www.igi-global.com

                        Library of Congress Cataloging-in-Publication Data

Names: Moraes, Ailson de, editor.
Title: Strategic management and international business policies for
  maintaining competitive advantage / edited by Ailson De Moraes.
Description: Hershey, PA : Business Science Reference, [2023] | Includes
  bibliographical references and index.
Identifiers: LCCN 2022047392 (print) | LCCN 2022047393 (ebook) | ISBN
  9781668468456 (hardcover) | ISBN 9781668468463 (paperback) | ISBN
  9781668468470 (ebook)
Subjects: LCSH: International business enterprises--Management. | Strategic
  planning.
Classification: LCC HD62.4 .S78 2023 (print) | LCC HD62.4 (ebook) | DDC
  658/.049--dc23/eng/20221125
LC record available at https://lccn.loc.gov/2022047392
LC ebook record available at https://lccn.loc.gov/2022047393

This book is published in the IGI Global book series Advances in Business Strategy and Competitive Advantage (ABSCA) (ISSN: 2327-3429; eISSN: 2327-3437)

British Cataloguing in Publication Data
A Cataloguing in Publication record for this book is available from the British Library.
All work contributed to this book is new, previously-unpublished material. The views expressed in this book are those of the authors, but not necessarily of the publisher.
For electronic access to this publication, please contact: eresources@igi-global.com.

Advances in Business Strategy and Competitive Advantage (ABSCA) Book Series

Patricia Ordóñez de Pablos
Universidad de Oviedo, Spain

ISSN:2327-3429
EISSN:2327-3437

MISSION

Business entities are constantly seeking new ways through which to gain advantage over their competitors and strengthen their position within the business environment. With competition at an all-time high due to technological advancements allowing for competition on a global scale, firms continue to seek new ways through which to improve and strengthen their business processes, procedures, and profitability.

The **Advances in Business Strategy and Competitive Advantage (ABSCA) Book Series** is a timely series responding to the high demand for state-of-the-art research on how business strategies are created, implemented and re-designed to meet the demands of globalized competitive markets. With a focus on local and global challenges, business opportunities and the needs of society, the **ABSCA** encourages scientific discourse on doing business and managing information technologies for the creation of sustainable competitive advantage.

COVERAGE

- Customer-Orientation Strategy
- Strategic Alliances
- Value Creation
- Co-operative Strategies
- Ethics and Business Strategy
- Cost Leadership Strategy
- Business Models
- Value Chain
- Foreign Investment Decision Process
- Differentiation Strategy

IGI Global is currently accepting manuscripts for publication within this series. To submit a proposal for a volume in this series, please contact our Acquisition Editors at Acquisitions@igi-global.com or visit: http://www.igi-global.com/publish/.

Titles in this Series

For a list of additional titles in this series, please visit: http://www.igi-global.com/book-series/advances-business-strategy-competitive-advantage/73672

Digital Natives as a Disruptive Force in Asian Businesses and Societies
Omkar Dastane (UCSI Graduate Business School, UCSI University, Malaysia) Aini Aman (Universiti Kebangsaan Malaysia, Malaysia) and Nurhizam Safie Bin Mohd Satar (Universiti Kebangsaan Malaysia, Malaysia)
Business Science Reference • © 2023 • 322pp • H/C (ISBN: 9781668467824) • US $250.00

Handbook of Research on Sustainable Consumption and Production for Greener Economies
Richa Goel (Symbiosis International University, India) and Sukanta Kumar Baral (Indira Gandhi National Tribal University, India)
Business Science Reference • © 2023 • 481pp • H/C (ISBN: 9781668489697) • US $295.00

Cases on the Resurgence of Emerging Businesses
Shefali Saluja (Chitkara Business School, Chitkara University, India) Dhiresh Kulshrestha (Chitkara Business School, Chitkara University, India) and Sandhir Sharma (Chitkara Business School, Chitkara University, India)
Business Science Reference • © 2023 • 316pp • H/C (ISBN: 9781668484883) • US $265.00

Handbook of Research on Sustainability Challenges in the Wine Industry
Bartolomé Marco-Lajara (University of Alicante, Spain) Armand Gilinsky (Sonoma State University, USA) Javier Martínez-Falcó (University of Alicante, Spain & Stellenbosch University, South Africa) and Eduardo Sánchez-García (University of Alicante, Spain)
Business Science Reference • © 2023 • 435pp • H/C (ISBN: 9781668469422) • US $295.00

Opportunities and Challenges of Business 5.0 in Emerging Markets
Sumesh Dadwal (Northumbria University, UK) Pawan Kumar (Lovely Professional University, India) Rajesh Verma (Lovely Professional University, India) and Gursimranjit Singh (Lovely Professional University, India)
Business Science Reference • © 2023 • 357pp • H/C (ISBN: 9781668464038) • US $250.00

Embracing Business Sustainability Through Innovation and Creativity in the Service Sector
Pankaj Kumar Tyagi (Chandigarh University, India) Vipin Nadda (University of Sunderland, UK) Vishal Bharti (Chandigarh University, India) and Ebru Kemer (Niğde Ömer Halisdemir University, Turkey)
Business Science Reference • © 2023 • 329pp • H/C (ISBN: 9781668467329) • US $250.00

701 East Chocolate Avenue, Hershey, PA 17033, USA
Tel: 717-533-8845 x100 • Fax: 717-533-8661
E-Mail: cust@igi-global.com • www.igi-global.com

Table of Contents

Detailed Table of Contents

Chapter 1
Corporate Governance: The Role of Board of Directors in the Strategic Planning Process of
Organizations 1
>   *Michael Anibal Altamirano, King Graduate School, USA*
>   *Ameil A. Sloley, King Graduate School, USA*

Corporate governance is a system of controlled activities that act as a form of stewardship for organizations. Governance is represented by a board of directors, which balance the interest of stakeholders and company performance through the evaluation of internal processes such as organizational mission and vision, establishing core values, review of strategic planning process, assessment of organizational policies, hiring and compensation of senior executives, promoting diversity and inclusion, appraisal of executive leadership performance, and self-governance. Boards operate autonomously as they uphold their fiduciary obligations to the company and monitor and control corporate accountabilities. For boards to be effective, they should adhere to the highest standards of integrity while being objective in the delegation of their duties. This chapter offers a perspective of corporate governance and its relative relation, the strategic planning process, while explaining the complexity of organizational boards of directors.

Chapter 2
Internationalization Strategies: Circumventing the Liability of Newness – A Case Study of
Irregular Internationalization Paths 12
>   *Beatriz Clarinha, University of Aveiro, Portugal*
>   *Diana Cunha, University of Aveiro, Portugal*
>   *Francisca Sá, University of Aveiro, Portugal*
>   *António Carrizo Moreira, University of Aveiro, Portugal*

This chapter analyzes the internationalization process of an irregular exporter and seeks to perceive the internationalization theory that explains the company over this international path. Some of the most studied internationalization models that explain the rapid internationalization process were reviewed in order to compare the main characteristics of each theory. Methodologically the chapter uses primary data, obtained from an interview, complemented by the analysis of secondary data. A synthesis table seeks to summarize the characteristics of the internationalization process of each of the four theories analyzed.

Chapter 3

Organizational leaders design and incorporate business models or processes to gain competitive advantage. These business models or methods detail how the organization operates to gain a competitive advantage and ultimately increase shareholders' wealth. Some business models incorporate unethical leadership and business practices at the expense of corporate social responsibility (CSR). The exclusion of CSR often eradicates stakeholders' value, leading to numerous unsustainable results. The disregard for CSR drives consequences inclusive of but limited to climate change, forced and child labor, poor workplace conditions, irreversible depletion of natural resources, gender inequality, absence of diversity and inclusion, pollution, and using tainted supply chains. Organizational leadership must transform business models to achieve sustainability. The lack of established frameworks and policing bodies to monitor organizations hinder the global thrust toward sustainable development growth.

Chapter 4

In light of the COVID-19 pandemic that shook the world, both multinational enterprises (MNEs) and small and medium enterprises (SMEs) have to learn and manage faster, better, and smarter to stay sustainable and remain competitive. This chapter emphasizes the need for a rethought, reimagined, redesigned, reinvented, reengineered, and rejuvenated waterfall approach in managing predictive projects to modern project management, using the six As in design thinking, to meet the clarion call with an agile mindset.

Today's hyper-competitive business environment calls for alignment among all organisational aspects for the attainment of sustainable competitive advantage. The capital structure of firms is merely one of these aspects and comprises two primary types of funding: equity and debt. Given the diverse characteristics these possess, there isn't a single debt-to-equity ratio that works for all firms or even the same firm at different stages. To support firm objectives, this must be determined with respect to the firm's competitive position, stage of maturity, shareholder and management requirements, and the wider environment. This chapter will first review some key attributes of both equity and debt and then discuss various determinants that can impact a mix of the two and ultimately the firm's capital structure to support its competitive position.

Erdinç Koç, Bingol University, Turkey
Seda İşgüzar, Malatya Turgut Ozal University, Turkey

Having a competitive advantage is vital for companies trying to survive in an intensely competitive environment. In this study, the effect of innovation orientation and service provider experience on competitive advantage, which is examined in the context of resource-based view and relational view theory, is examined. Data have been collected from the top managers of 222 firms operating in the tourism sector in Turkey. The findings showed that innovation orientation and service provider experience increased competitive advantage. At the same time, it has been observed that the competitive advantage increases as the service provider experience increases. Finally, it has found that service provider experience has a mediating role in the relationship between innovation orientation and competitive advantage. The study is important in terms of revealing that the use of different competitive strategies together produces good results in the process of discovering different strategic elements that can provide sustainable competitive advantage.

Jesús Barrena-Martínez, University of Cádiz, Spain
Macarena López-Fernández, University of Cádiz, Spain
Pedro M. Romero-Fernández, University of Cádiz, Spain
Margarita Ruiz-Rodriguez, University of Cádiz, Spain

Contributing to sustainability no longer remains an optional activity. Institutional pressures exert a major influence on organisations towards the adoption of sustainability. However, the literature shows how these pressures are necessary but remain insufficient. This chapter focuses on how there is a certain organisational discretion regarding the refusal to merely conform by going further than strictly required (strategic commitment to sustainability). In this respect, the human resources (HR) manager acquires a crucial role in this process as an institutional entrepreneur. A qualitative study is also carried out with which it is intended to understand this process of institutionalisation in a real case study. The results of the interview with the HR manager show the proactivity acquired on assuming the role of institutional entrepreneur: an aspect that has favoured not only the awareness and institutionalisation of sustainability at a strategic level, but also the culture, processes, practices, and services that include this management philosophy.

discussing the implications of sustainable development agendas for strategic sustainability, the chapter also reviews two case studies of organisations that have successfully adopted sustainability into their strategic value propositions. Finally, it discusses Raworth's framework as a model for reinterpreting strategic sustainability management in the Anthropocene.

Chapter 14

The pharmaceutical industry's route to market had historically been based on sales teams interacting with key healthcare practitioners (HCPs) in their place of work. The COVID-19 pandemic forced an immediate reinvention of the pharmaceutical industry's entire sales strategy to protect multimillion dollar investments in new treatments and the essential feedback loop between the pharmaceutical industry and HCPs. Virtual and digital solutions were quickly put in place, demonstrating how such a radical strategic pivot is not only possible but can have unexpected benefits. The author is a pharmaceutical industry professional, and this chapter is based on his personal experiences of the industry's strategic response and the limited amount of published research available. The author concludes that leveraging new digital engagement strategies with the industry and optimizing external stakeholder relationships will be key to success in the industry's next normal.

Chapter 15

Small and medium-sized enterprises (SMEs) suffer persistent challenges due to global market competition, time limits to respond strategically, talent retention, productivity, and uncompetitive operational expenses. Enhancing employee performance (EP) then becomes critical in defining SME success. The purpose of this study is to evaluate the influence of strategic management (SM) and leadership capabilities (LC) on EP and recommend solutions to improve EP. The function of employee engagement (EE) as a mediator between interactions involving LC, SM, and EP is also investigated. A quantitative research method was employed by collecting empirical data of employees working with Malaysian SMEs. Analysis including reliability and normality assessments, confirmatory factor analysis, and structural equation modelling with AMOS 22 were carried out. According to the data, SM exerts a positive and substantial impact on EP. In the context of Malaysian SMEs, the novel findings provide a strong reason for the use of SM, emphasising the need to strengthen managers' knowledge in SM capabilities.

In the research, data were obtained from 200 different senior managers. As a result of the analysis, it was concluded that the attitudes of senior managers in Türkiye, the general level of trust similar to the general structure in Türkiye, and the rate of civic participation are low. In this respect, in the context of weak and strong ties, which is the first type of social capital, it is seen that senior managers in Türkiye have weak and strong ties at a low level. Finally, it was concluded that senior managers in Türkiye are higher than all other types of social capital in terms of structural social capital based on the existence of network structures between individuals and conceptual social capital, which is a more abstract part of social capital and is representative of trust, norms, and common discourses.

Existential crises question the organization's readiness to withstand uncertainties. Geopolitics and natural disruptions have changed human behavior into a "new normal." In improving business continuity, HEIs must strategically deal with operating models, resilience, and agility and be better prepared for disruptions. Typical HEI reactions of online home TLR lack addressing the human capacity/capability needs, technologies/infrastructure, academic/student services support, and TLR evaluation/assessments that cover the HEI broader approach of education values, systems, mechanisms and pedagogies, and student outcomes assurance. It includes HEI human, infor, and organizational capital capacities and capabilities of these systems. Being resilient and agile calls for faster decision-making focused on HEI priorities. This chapter addresses the HEI strategic readiness through a strategic organizational readiness model (SORM) managing the HEI organization readiness. The SORM evolves around the HEI six thematic systems, with resilience and agility as vital analytical and assessment parameters.

Preface

Welcome to *Strategic Management and International Business Policies for Maintaining Competitive Advantage*. In today's rapidly changing and discontinuous business environment, organizations face immense challenges in maintaining their competitive edge. It is crucial for businesses to adopt strategic management practices and develop key business policies to navigate the complexities and uncertainties of the global marketplace.

This edited reference book aims to provide comprehensive insights into the field of strategic management and international business policies. We have carefully curated a collection of chapters written by renowned experts, practitioners, and academics, offering diverse perspectives and practical strategies to address the dynamic nature of modern business.

We begin by acknowledging the significant contributions of esteemed scholars such as Michael Porter, who introduced the fundamental concepts of competitive strategy, competitive forces, and competitive advantage. While these concepts still hold relevance today, we recognize the evolving relationship between business organizations and society. Increasingly, organizations are taking a proactive role in addressing wider societal issues and integrating sustainability into their strategies.

In this book, we emphasize the importance of sustainable competitive advantages, continuous improvement, and innovation in achieving enduring success. We delve into the complexities of the global business environment, where executives must navigate numerous variables and interdependencies that impact decision-making. Our aim is to equip readers with the knowledge and tools to make informed choices, minimizing unintended consequences and maximizing positive outcomes.

This book serves as a guide for individuals studying business strategy, helping them avoid acting without sufficient information and analysis. By implementing the appropriate business policies and strategies, organizations can proactively shape their own future and exert control over their destiny. We firmly believe that strategy should not be limited to a reactive approach but should empower organizations to initiate and influence activities in their turbulent business environment.

Our research and insights contribute to the growing body of knowledge in strategic management and international business policies. While traditional approaches focused on strategic choice, we highlight the significance of the process itself in implementing successful strategies. This book aims to bridge theory and practice, benefiting students pursuing management and international business degrees, as well as practitioners, entrepreneurs, managers, executives, and academics.

The chapters included cover a wide range of topics, addressing key questions such as the relevance of strategy in a complex business environment, the strategic decision-making process amidst turbulence, the role of corporate governance, and the factors influencing the micro and macro environment. We delve into creating and sustaining international business policies for maintaining competitive advantage and explore the potential of these policies to overcome business inertia.

Additionally, we examine strategic offensives, the complexities of competing across national borders, organizational transformation, hybrid strategies for competitive advantage, and the pursuit of business sustainability in a complex environment. Finally, we explore strategic flexibility, competitive advantage in the 21st century, and navigating the new competitive landscape.

We hope that this book serves as a valuable resource, empowering readers with the knowledge and tools to navigate the complexities of strategic management and international business policies. It is our sincere belief that by embracing these principles, organizations can thrive and shape their own destinies in today's turbulent business environment.

Below is a short summary of the topics covered in each of the chapters of this book.

An Introduction on the History of Strategy Concepts and the Relevance for Strategic Management and International Business Policies

In today's globalized and fiercely competitive business landscape, organizations are constantly seeking ways to gain and sustain a competitive advantage. The dynamic nature of the international business environment, coupled with evolving market trends, technological advancements, and changing customer preferences, poses significant challenges for businesses worldwide. It is imperative for organizations to adopt a strategic approach and implement effective international business policies to stay ahead in the race.

This book delves into the realm of strategic management and international business policies, focusing on their crucial role in maintaining a competitive advantage in the global marketplace. The purpose of this preface is to provide an overview of the topics covered in this book, highlight their relevance, and set the stage for the exploration of strategic management principles and international business policies.

Chapter 1. Corporate Governance: The Role of Board of Directors in the Strategic Planning Process of Organizations

Understanding the history of strategy helps boards of directors gain insights into the evolution of strategic thinking and practices. By examining past strategies, boards can learn from successful and unsuccessful approaches, informing their role in the strategic planning process. Historical knowledge allows boards to provide valuable guidance, challenge assumptions, and ensure effective oversight, thus contributing to the organization's competitive advantage.

Chapter 2. Internationalization Strategies: Circumventing the Liability of Newness: A Case Study of Irregular Internationalization Path

The history of strategy offers valuable insights into internationalization strategies employed by organizations over time. By studying irregular internationalization paths taken by organizations, researchers can identify patterns, challenges, and opportunities. This knowledge helps organizations develop effective internationalization strategies that circumvent the liability of newness, minimize risks, and leverage the experiences of others, ultimately contributing to their competitive advantage in the global marketplace.

Chapter 3. Organizational Transformation: The Way to Sustainability

Examining the history of strategy provides a rich understanding of organizational transformation processes. By studying successful transformations, organizations can learn from the strategies employed, identify critical success factors, and understand the challenges faced. This historical knowledge informs the development of effective transformation strategies that align with sustainability principles, enhance competitiveness, and ensure long-term success.

Chapter 4. Modern Project Management for Successful Execution of Investment Strategy

The history of strategy highlights the importance of effective project management in executing investment strategies. By analyzing past projects, organizations can identify best practices, lessons learned, and project management methodologies that have yielded successful outcomes. This historical perspective informs the development of modern project management approaches, enabling organizations to execute their investment strategies efficiently and achieve a competitive advantage.

Chapter 5. The Role of Capital Structure in Achieving Competitive Advantage for Firms in a Global Context

The history of strategy provides insights into the capital structure decisions made by successful firms in different eras and contexts. By studying past capital structure strategies and their impact on competitive advantage, researchers can identify patterns, trade-offs, and optimal approaches. This knowledge informs firms' decision-making processes, enabling them to develop capital structures that enhance their competitive advantage in a global context.

Chapter 6. Can Innovation Orientation and Service Provider Experience Gain Competitive Advantage for Firms?

The history of strategy reveals the importance of innovation orientation and service provider experience in gaining a competitive advantage. By examining past strategies of innovative firms and service providers, researchers can identify the factors that contribute to their success. This historical knowledge guides organizations in fostering an innovation-oriented culture, leveraging service provider experience, and ultimately gaining a competitive edge through superior offerings and customer experiences.

Chapter 7. Institutionalization of Sustainability: The HR Manager as a Strategic Entrepreneur in its Adoption

The history of strategy sheds light on the institutionalization of sustainability practices within organizations. By studying the strategic efforts of HR managers in promoting sustainability over time, researchers can understand the challenges, enablers, and best practices associated with its adoption. This historical understanding guides HR managers in becoming strategic entrepreneurs, driving the institutionalization of sustainability practices and contributing to the organization's competitive advantage.

These connections illustrate how the history of strategy intersects with various topics, providing valuable insights and guiding organizations and researchers in making informed decisions, formulating effective strategies, and ultimately maintaining a competitive advantage in their respective domains.

Chapter 8. Organizational Opportunities Through Digital and Social-Media Marketing

The history of strategy provides a retrospective view of the evolution of marketing practices, including the emergence of digital and social-media marketing. By studying the strategies employed by organizations in leveraging digital and social media over time, researchers can identify effective approaches, trends, and customer preferences. This historical knowledge informs organizations' digital marketing strategies, enabling them to capitalize on opportunities, engage with their target audience, and maintain a competitive advantage in the digital era.

Chapter 9. Maintaining Global Competitiveness Even in a Period of Global Crisis: The Perspective of Small Economies

The history of strategy provides insights into how small economies have maintained their global competitiveness during times of crisis. By studying past strategies adopted by successful small economies, researchers can identify resilience factors, adaptability measures, and innovative approaches. This historical understanding informs small economies' strategic decision-making processes, enabling them to navigate global crises effectively, preserve their competitive advantage, and seize new opportunities.

Chapter 10. Incorporating Sustainability into Strategic Management for Maintaining Competitive Advantage: The Requisite Holism of Process, Institutional, and Instrumental Dimensions

The history of strategy highlights the evolution of sustainability considerations in strategic management. By examining past strategies, organizations can understand how sustainability has transformed from a peripheral concern to a central aspect of strategic decision-making. This historical perspective informs the integration of sustainability into organizations' strategic management processes, ensuring a holistic approach that aligns with societal expectations, enhances brand reputation, and contributes to long-term competitive advantage.

Chapter 11. Competing Across National Borders

The history of strategy provides insights into how organizations have competed across national borders throughout different time periods. By studying past strategies of multinational corporations, researchers can identify factors that contribute to successful international competition. This historical knowledge informs organizations' cross-border strategies, enabling them to navigate diverse markets, address cultural nuances, and leverage global opportunities while maintaining a competitive advantage.

Chapter 12. Productive-Technological Capabilities, Development, and National Sovereignty: Old and New Challenges for Brazil

The history of strategy sheds light on the challenges and opportunities faced by nations in developing productive-technological capabilities. By analyzing past strategies employed by countries like Brazil, researchers can understand the drivers of success and the obstacles encountered. This historical perspective guides policymakers and organizations in formulating strategies to enhance productive-technological capabilities, safeguard national sovereignty, and maintain a competitive advantage in an increasingly interconnected world.

Chapter 13. Strategic Sustainability in the Anthropocene

The history of strategy provides insights into how organizations have responded to environmental challenges and sustainability concerns over time. By examining past strategies, organizations can learn from successes and failures in achieving strategic sustainability. This historical understanding informs the development of strategies that mitigate environmental impact, embrace circular economy principles, and ensure long-term viability, thus contributing to a competitive advantage in the Anthropocene era.

Chapter 14. Reinventing Strategic Execution in the Pharmaceutical Industry

The history of strategy in the pharmaceutical industry offers valuable lessons in strategic execution. By studying past strategic initiatives and their outcomes, researchers can identify critical success factors, implementation challenges, and areas for improvement. This historical knowledge informs the reinvention of strategic execution approaches.

Chapter 15. Augmenting Performance through Strategic Management and Leadership Capabilities: Implications for Small and Medium-Scale Enterprises

The history of strategy provides insights into the strategic management and leadership capabilities that have driven the performance of small and medium-scale enterprises (SMEs) over time. By studying successful SMEs and their strategies, researchers can identify the key competencies and leadership approaches that have contributed to their competitive advantage. This historical knowledge informs the development of strategic management and leadership capabilities in SMEs, enabling them to enhance performance, adapt to changing environments, and seize growth opportunities.

Chapter 16. Types of Social Capital in the Context of Company Managers: A Field Study for Policies to Maintain Competitive Advantage in Turkey

The discontinuation and turbulent nature of business environments make it crucial for organizations to adopt strategic management practices and develop key business policies to be alert to environmental changes. Organizational competitiveness has become the center of strategic management literature as an explanation for organizational success. However, in the past two decades, there has been a shift in the nature of the relationship between business organizations and society, with business organizations increasingly playing a more proactive role in wider societal issues.

Let us now take a step back to examine the history of strategy. This will help us to understand how strategy has evolved and how managers nowadays can adopt the best approach when formulating international business policies for maintaining competitive advantage despite the turbulent global environment nowadays.

The History of Strategy

All firms have strategies even if, at the extreme, the strategy is no more than to adopt a reactive response to market challenges and do what seems best for survival at a particular time. A positive strategy, however, requires 'a sense of purpose'. Military strategy goes back at least to Sun Tsu's Art of War in 500 BC, but the term 'strategy' or strategic management has a relatively short history in the business field. Strategic management is not used in the academic business school lexicon much before the 1960s, and even more recently the area of study can often be seen masquerading under the title of Business Policy, or in the case of this book International Business Policies for Maintaining Competitive Advantage.

The 1950s

The military strategy of the 1950s, particularly influenced by the experiences of World War II and the Cold War, also contributed to the development of strategic management. Concepts such as contingency planning, competitive analysis, and situational awareness from military strategy found application in the business context. The idea of aligning resources, assessing competitive advantages, and anticipating future challenges became important considerations for organizational strategists.

In the 1950s there was a group of Harvard professors who propagated the concept of Corporate Strategy by interacting with corporate boards and encouraging them to think 'outside the box' in terms of what they were, and what they were trying to achieve, e.g. "Are we a hi-tech company or a transportation company?"

At the same time in the public sector Robert McNamara was busy introducing Programme Planning and Budgeting (PPB) to the US Department of Defence, who were used to resource allocation by means of lobbying and an absence of performance measures.

In 1954, Peter Drucker published his influential book, "The Practice of Management," which emphasized the importance of strategic thinking and management. Drucker argued that effective management required a systematic and purposeful approach, with a focus on setting objectives, analyzing the business environment, making strategic choices, and aligning organizational resources. His work laid the groundwork for modern management practices and highlighted the strategic dimension of management.

The 1950s marked a significant period in the history of strategic management, with the emergence of key ideas and frameworks that laid the foundation for modern strategic thinking. During this decade, scholars and practitioners began to shift their focus from purely operational and tactical concerns to a more strategic approach to managing organizations.

adoption of a distinctive and sustainable strategy. Operational effectiveness and efficiency mean performing similar activities better than rivals perform them; a successful strategy means performing different activities from rivals or performing similar activities in different ways (Porter 1996, p. 62). As Porter (1996) argues, firms need to re- focus their attention on the main components of strategy: performing unique activities, choosing a strategic position, making trade-offs that underlie sustainability, and optimizing the fit of an entire system of activities. Successful, sustainable strategy is forged by managers willing to make difficult choices to preserve their companies' unique activities.

Analyzing Strategy

The strategy literature contains numerous conceptual frameworks, models, tools and techniques designed to help senior management understand and analyze these dimensions of strategy. Mintzberg identifies ten, Johnson six, Whittington four, and Chaffee three, as we see later in this topic.

Many have different names to describe similar approaches e.g. linear, classical, planning or adaptive, emergent, logical incremental. They advocate particular kinds of solution to particular kinds of problem and specify courses of action. Others are descriptive of what often happens in practice. They aim to add to our understanding of how strategies are formulated and implemented.

The position adopted is that every corporation can be considered to be unique. Corporations have their own in- ternal strengths and weaknesses and confront particular opportunities and threats. These are partly derived from the historical legacies of past strategic decisions and realized strategies and partly derived from the forces which operate in new and changing competitive environments, and also critically from the exercise of strategic choice by top management.

In the highly competitive global business landscape, organizations face the challenge of maintaining a competitive advantage. Strategy analysis and international business policies play a vital role in this endeavor by providing frameworks and guidelines for effective decision-making and policy implementation. Strategy analysis involves assessing internal and external factors, understanding market dynamics, and identifying strategic opportunities and risks. International business policies focus on addressing the challenges and opportunities of the international market, including cultural differences, market selection, entry modes, and policy implementation. By effectively analyzing strategy and international business policies, organizations can develop a strategic roadmap that aligns their resources, capabilities, and goals with the changing global landscape, enabling them to maintain a competitive advantage.

Unique Circumstances

Competitive environments differ, from industry to industry and country to country, and corporations differ from one another in their internal characteristics. Therefore, it is impossible to offer any universally guaranteed prescriptions for competitive success. All that can be said with certainty is that most of the models in the literature can offer insights of greater or lesser relevance to any given case.

The international business world is a complex one. Despite the exhortations of consultants to keep things simple, managers know that in reality international business management is not simple. International business policies play a critical role in maintaining a competitive advantage in diverse and dynamic competitive environments. These policies encompass a range of strategic decisions and actions taken by organizations operating in international markets to effectively navigate the challenges and capitalize on opportunities.

Introduction

Strategic management can be defined as the art and science of formulating, implementing, and evaluating cross-functional decisions that enable an organization to achieve its objectives. As this definition implies, strategic management focuses on integrating management, marketing, finance and accounting, production and operations, research and development, and information systems to achieve organizational success. The term strategic management in this text is used synonymously with the term strategic planning. The latter term is more often used in the business world, whereas the former is often used in academia. Sometimes the term strategic management is used to refer to strategy formulation, implementation, and evaluation and strategic planning referring only to strategy formulation. The purpose of strategic management is to exploit and create new and different opportunities for tomorrow; long-range planning, in contrast, tries to optimize for tomorrow the trends of today.

Strategic management is concerned with the processes by which management plans and coordinates the use of business resources, with the general objective of securing or maintaining a competitive advantage. Corporate strategic management, in both domestic and international settings, generally has three dimensions. The first is strategy process, whereby strategy formulation may be conceived as a process with a policy outcome. The second dimension is strategy content, concerned with the foundations upon which successful corporate strategy decisions can be developed. The third facet of corporate strategic management is context, wherein the particular internal characteristics of corporations and their external competitive environments must be understood in order to formulate successful strategies and maintaining competitive strategy.

There are numerous conceptual frameworks, theoretical models and analytical tools designed to help management understand and analyse these dimensions of strategy in terms of international business policies in different areas. This book deals with some of these, particularly those that may be of most relevance in an international context. It will be of particular value to individuals employed in organisations undergoing strategic change, and those involved in the implementation of business policy in highly competitive environments.

THE STRATEGY CONCEPT

Operational Effectiveness and Competitiveness

Operational effectiveness does not necessarily translate into sustainable profitability. The root of many companies' competitive problems is their failure to distinguish between operational efficiency and the

The history of strategy reveals the importance of social capital in the context of company managers and its impact on competitive advantage. By examining past strategies and practices in Turkey, researchers can identify the types of social capital that have been leveraged by successful companies. This historical understanding informs the formulation of policies and practices that foster social capital among managers, facilitating knowledge sharing, collaboration, and networking, which in turn contribute to maintaining a competitive advantage.

Chapter 17. New Normal HEI: Strategic Organizational Readiness Model

The history of strategy in higher education institutions (HEIs) provides insights into how these institutions have adapted to changing circumstances and embraced strategic organizational readiness. By studying the strategies adopted by HEIs in response to disruptive events or transitions, researchers can identify the organizational capabilities and readiness factors that have enabled successful adaptation. This historical perspective informs the development of a strategic organizational readiness model for HEIs, facilitating their agility, responsiveness, and competitive advantage in the "new normal" landscape.

These connections demonstrate how the history of strategy informs and influences a wide range of topics, from corporate governance to sustainability, digital marketing to cross-border competition, and leadership capabilities to organizational readiness. By drawing upon historical insights, organizations and researchers can learn from past successes and failures, shape their strategies and decision-making processes, and ultimately enhance their competitive advantage in a dynamic and evolving business environment.

The insights presented in this book are not only relevant to business practitioners and executives but also to researchers and students in the field of strategic management. By embracing the diverse perspectives and practical knowledge shared within these pages, readers can enhance their strategic thinking, decision-making abilities, and ultimately contribute to the success of their organizations.

We hope that this book serves as a valuable resource, providing guidance and inspiration to those seeking to navigate the complex landscape of strategic management and international business policies. We invite you to embark on this journey with us as we explore the intricacies of maintaining competitive advantage in an ever-changing global business environment.

Ailson J. De Moraes
Royal Holloway University of London, UK

Industry Life Cycle

The concept of the industry life cycle gained attention during the 1970s. Scholars such as Richard Foster and William Abernathy explored the stages of growth and decline that industries undergo, highlighting the need for firms to adapt their strategies accordingly. Understanding the industry life cycle helped organizations anticipate and respond to changes in market demand, competition, and technological advancements (Foster, 1986; Abernathy and Utterback, 1978).

Strategic Management Process

The 1970s saw the refinement and codification of the strategic management process. Scholars like Henry Mintzberg, Richard Rumelt, and James Brian Quinn focused on the stages of strategic management, including analysis, formulation, implementation, and evaluation. Their works contributed to a more structured and systematic approach to strategic decision-making within organizations. (Mintzberg et al., 1998; Rumelt et al., 1994; Quinn, 1980).

Globalization and International Strategy

The 1970s witnessed an increase in globalization, prompting scholars to explore the complexities of international strategy. Raymond Vernon's product life cycle theory, John Dunning's eclectic paradigm, and Alan Rugman's internalization theory provided insights into the strategies firms adopt when entering and competing in international markets. These theories helped organizations navigate the challenges and opportunities of globalization. (Vernon, 1966; Dunning, 1977; Rugman, 1980).

The 1980s marked a significant period in the field of strategic management, characterized by new perspectives, approaches, and frameworks that shaped strategic thinking and practices. This decade witnessed the continued evolution of strategic management theory and its application in diverse industries. The history of strategy in the 1980s:

Strategic Alliances and Joint Ventures

The 1980s saw a rise in strategic alliances and joint ventures as organizations sought collaborative approaches to gain a competitive advantage. Scholars such as Yves L. Doz and Gary Hamel explored the benefits and challenges of forming strategic alliances, emphasizing the importance of partner selection, cooperation, and value creation. Their works shed light on the strategic implications of collaboration in a rapidly changing business environment (Doz and Hamel, 1998).

Core Competencies

The concept of core competencies gained prominence in the 1980s, thanks to the work of C.K. Prahalad and Gary Hamel. They argued that organizations should focus on developing and leveraging their unique capabilities and expertise to achieve a sustainable competitive advantage. The identification and nurturing of core competencies became crucial for firms aiming to differentiate themselves in the marketplace (Prahalad and Hamel, 1990).

Strategic Change and Turnaround

The 1980s witnessed a heightened focus on strategic change and turnaround strategies as organizations faced increased market turbulence and competitive pressures. Scholars such as Donald C. Hambrick and Michael A. Hitt explored the dynamics of strategic change, turnaround management, and the factors that contribute to organizational decline and recovery. Their research provided insights into the strategies and approaches organizations can adopt to revitalize their performance (Hambrick and D'Aveni, 1988; Hitt and Ireland, 1985).

Strategic Entrepreneurship

The concept of strategic entrepreneurship emerged in the 1980s, integrating strategic management principles with entrepreneurial actions. Scholars such as Howard H. Stevenson and William A. Sahlman explored the role of entrepreneurial behavior in identifying and exploiting opportunities, managing risks, and achieving competitive advantage. Their work shed light on the relationship between entrepreneurship and strategic management (Stevenson and Gumpert, 1985; Sahlman, 1990).

Globalization and Global Strategy

With the increasing globalization of markets, scholars explored the complexities of global strategy during the 1980s. The works of scholars like Kenichi Ohmae and Christopher A. Bartlett and Sumantra Ghoshal focused on multinational corporations' strategies for competing globally, managing global operations, and balancing local responsiveness with global integration. Their research provided valuable insights into the challenges and opportunities of operating in a globalized business environment (Ohmae, 1985; Bartlett and Ghoshal, 1989).

The 1990s witnessed significant developments in the field of strategic management, characterized by the emergence of new concepts, approaches, and frameworks. This decade marked a period of globalization, technological advancements, and evolving market dynamics, which influenced strategic thinking and practices. The history of strategy in the 1990s:

Dynamic Capabilities

The concept of dynamic capabilities gained prominence in the 1990s as scholars sought to understand how organizations adapt and renew their resources and capabilities to maintain a competitive advantage. David J. Teece, Gary Pisano, and Amy Shuen contributed to this field, emphasizing the importance of a firm's ability to sense, seize, and transform resources to respond to environmental changes and market opportunities. The notion of dynamic capabilities emphasized the need for strategic flexibility and agility (Teece et al., 1997; Pisano and Teece, 1994).

Knowledge Management and Intellectual Capital

The 1990s marked a growing recognition of the strategic value of knowledge and intellectual capital within organizations. Scholars such as Ikujiro Nonaka and Thomas A. Stewart explored the role of knowledge creation, transfer, and utilization in driving innovation and competitive advantage. The focus on knowledge management highlighted the importance of capturing, sharing, and leveraging knowledge as a strategic resource (Nonaka and Takeuchi, 1995; Stewart, 1997).

E-Business and Digital Strategy

The advent of the internet and digital technologies in the 1990s brought about significant changes in the business landscape. Scholars and practitioners began exploring the strategic implications of e-business and digital strategy. Michael E. Porter's work on competitive advantage in the digital era and Michael J. Earl's research on digital transformation provided insights into leveraging digital technologies to create value, reach new markets, and enhance customer experiences (Porter, 2001; Earl, 1996).

Strategic Alliances and Networks

The 1990s witnessed a continued focus on strategic alliances and networks as organizations sought collaborative strategies to enhance their competitiveness. Scholars like Andrew Campbell and Goold, Marcus Alexander explored the dynamics of strategic alliances, emphasizing the importance of partner selection, relationship management, and value creation through networked strategies. The study of strategic alliances and networks shed light on the complexities of interorganizational collaborations in a globalized business environment (Campbell and Goold, 1999).

Balanced Scorecard

The balanced scorecard, introduced by Robert Kaplan and David Norton in the 1990s, gained popularity as a strategic management tool. The balanced scorecard emphasized the importance of a balanced set of performance measures, beyond financial indicators, to assess organizational performance. This framework facilitated the alignment of strategic objectives, key performance indicators, and targets across different levels of an organization, enhancing strategic execution and performance management (Kaplan and Norton, 1996).

The 21st century has brought about significant shifts in the field of strategic management, shaped by technological advancements, globalization, sustainability concerns, and changing market dynamics. This period has witnessed the emergence of new concepts, frameworks, and approaches to strategy. The history of strategy in the 21st century up to nowadays:

Disruptive Innovation and Business Models

The concept of disruptive innovation gained prominence in the 21st century, thanks to the work of Clayton M. Christensen. His research highlighted how disruptive technologies and business models can reshape industries and create new market opportunities. The focus shifted from incremental innovation to radical innovation that challenges existing business models (Christensen, 2003).

Open Innovation and Co-Creation

Scholars such as Henry Chesbrough popularized the concept of open innovation, emphasizing the importance of leveraging external knowledge and collaborating with external partners in the innovation process. This shift encouraged organizations to embrace a more collaborative and inclusive approach to innovation, involving customers, suppliers, and other stakeholders in the co-creation of value (Chesbrough, 2003).

Strategic Agility and Ambidexterity

The 21st century saw an increased emphasis on strategic agility and ambidexterity as organizations sought to adapt to rapid changes and uncertainties. Scholars like Charles A. O'Reilly III and Michael L. Tushman explored how organizations can balance exploration and exploitation activities to simultaneously pursue innovation and efficiency. This concept highlighted the importance of agility and flexibility in strategy formulation and execution (O'Reilly and Tushman, 2013).

Digital Transformation and Strategy

The pervasive influence of digital technologies in the 21st century necessitated a focus on digital transformation. Scholars like George S. Day and Peter Weill examined the strategic implications of digitalization, exploring how organizations can leverage technology to transform their business models, enhance customer experiences, and gain a competitive edge. The integration of digital strategy became crucial for organizations across industries (Day and Schoemaker, 2016; Weill and Woerner, 2018).

Sustainability and Corporate Social Responsibility

The 21st century marked an increased awareness of sustainability and corporate social responsibility (CSR) in strategic management. Scholars like Stuart L. Hart and C.K. Prahalad explored the concept of the "bottom of the pyramid," highlighting the potential for businesses to create social and environmental value while pursuing economic success. This focus on sustainability and CSR reflected a growing recognition of the importance of long-term societal and environmental considerations in strategy formulation (Hart, 2005; Prahalad, 2006).

Strategy in the Age of Artificial Intelligence

The 21st century has witnessed the rise of artificial intelligence (AI) and its impact on strategic management. Scholars and practitioners have explored how AI can transform various aspects of strategy, including data analytics, decision-making, customer insights, and process automation. The integration of AI in strategy has the potential to enhance organizational performance, competitive advantage, and innovation (Brynjolfsson and McAfee, 2017; Iansiti and Lakhani, 2020).

Strategic Resilience and Risk Management

With the increasing complexity and volatility of the business environment, strategic resilience and risk management have gained importance. Scholars like Nassim Nicholas Taleb and Andrew Zolli have examined strategies for organizations to build resilience, adapt to shocks, and navigate uncertainties. The focus on strategic resilience highlights the need for organizations to anticipate and proactively respond to potential disruptions and risks (Taleb, 2010; Zolli and Healy, 2012).

Globalization and International Strategy

Globalization has continued to shape strategic management in the 21st century. Scholars like Pankaj Ghemawat and Yves Doz have explored the challenges and opportunities associated with international strategy, emphasizing the need for organizations to adapt their strategies to different cultural, economic, and political contexts. The study of globalization and international strategy provides insights into how organizations can expand into new markets, leverage global resources, and manage cross-border operations (Ghemawat, 2007; Doz and Kosonen, 2010).

Strategy Execution and Organizational Change

The focus on strategy execution and organizational change has gained prominence in the 21st century. Scholars such as John P. Kotter and Larry E. Greiner have explored the dynamics of organizational change, providing frameworks and strategies to effectively implement and sustain strategic initiatives. The emphasis on strategy execution highlights the importance of aligning organizational structure, culture, and processes to support strategic objectives (Kotter, 1996; Greiner, 1998).

Behavioural Strategy

The field of strategic management has increasingly recognized the influence of human behaviour on strategic decision-making and outcomes. Scholars like Dan Lovallo and Richard P. Rumelt have examined cognitive biases, decision-making processes, and the role of emotions in shaping strategy. The integration of behavioural insights into strategic management offers a deeper understanding of how individuals and groups make strategic choices and the implications for organizational performance (Lovallo and Kahneman, 2003; Rumelt, 2011).

The 21st century has brought about transformative changes in the field of strategic management. The emergence of disruptive innovation, digital transformation, sustainability concerns, and global dynamics has influenced the way organizations formulate and execute strategies. The works mentioned in the bibliography provide a foundation for further exploration of the concepts, theories, and frameworks that have shaped strategic management in this dynamic era.

The study of strategy in the 21st century continues to evolve as organizations navigate the complexities of a rapidly changing business landscape. By embracing new perspectives, leveraging technology, and considering societal and environmental impact, organizations can enhance their competitive advantage and drive long-term success. In this book the study of strategy is identified by several approaches and some cases based on the relevance of the history of strategy for strategic management and international business policies for maintaining competitive advantage.

The history of strategy holds great relevance for strategic management and international business policies in maintaining competitive advantage. Understanding the historical evolution of strategic thinking and practices provides valuable insights into the foundations, challenges, and successes of strategic management. The relevance of history in the context of maintaining competitive advantage can be explained as following:

Learning from Past Strategies

Examining historical strategies allows organizations to learn from both successful and unsuccessful endeavours. By understanding the strategies employed by industry leaders or competitors in the past, organizations can gain insights into effective approaches and potential pitfalls. This knowledge can inform the formulation of current strategies and help organizations make informed decisions to maintain a competitive edge.

Adapting to Changing Business Environment

The history of strategy highlights the importance of adapting to the changing business environment. Over time, industries have undergone significant transformations due to technological advancements, globalization, regulatory changes, and shifts in customer preferences. By studying how strategies have evolved in response to such changes, organizations can identify patterns and principles that can guide them in navigating similar challenges in the present and future.

Avoiding Repetition of Mistakes

History serves as a valuable teacher by offering lessons from past mistakes. By examining the failures and shortcomings of previous strategies, organizations can identify common pitfalls and avoid repeating them. This proactive approach to learning from history can save valuable resources, minimize risks, and enhance the chances of success in developing effective strategies.

Shaping Long-Term Perspectives

Understanding the historical context of strategy development helps organizations develop a long-term perspective. By examining the strategic decisions and outcomes of organizations over time, they can assess the sustainability and durability of various strategies. This broader view enables organizations to anticipate industry shifts, emerging trends, and potential disruptors, allowing them to shape their strategies accordingly to maintain a competitive advantage over the long term.

Embracing Continual Innovation

The history of strategy demonstrates the need for continual innovation to stay competitive. Organizations that have consistently adapted, evolved, and embraced innovation have fared better in maintaining a competitive advantage. By studying the historical progression of innovative strategies, organizations can gain insights into the importance of fostering a culture of innovation, exploring new opportunities, and staying ahead of market trends.

Global Perspective and International Business

The history of strategy provides a global perspective on the evolution of international business. By examining the strategies employed by multinational corporations, understanding the impact of globalization, and considering the historical context of international trade and market dynamics, organizations can shape their international business policies. This knowledge helps organizations navigate cross-cultural complexities, identify market entry strategies, and build effective international alliances and partnerships.

The history of strategy serves as a valuable resource for strategic management and international business policies aimed at maintaining competitive advantage. Learning from past strategies, adapting to changing environments, avoiding mistakes, shaping long-term perspectives, embracing innovation, and understanding the global context all contribute to the effective formulation and execution of strategies. By leveraging historical insights, organizations can enhance their strategic decision-making processes and position themselves for sustained success in a highly competitive business landscape. The concepts of strategy and the relevance of history in strategic management and international business policies are intricately connected and essential for maintaining a competitive advantage. The history of strategy provides valuable lessons, insights, and perspectives that guide organizations in formulating and executing effective strategies to stay ahead in a dynamic and competitive business landscape.

By studying the historical evolution of strategic thinking and practices, organizations can learn from past strategies, both successful and unsuccessful, to inform their current decision-making processes. Understanding the strategies employed by industry leaders or competitors in the past enables organizations to identify effective approaches, potential pitfalls, and industry patterns that can shape their strategies and maintain a competitive edge.

The history of strategy also helps organizations adapt to the changing business environment. By examining how strategies have evolved in response to technological advancements, globalization, customer preferences, and regulatory changes, organizations gain valuable insights into navigating similar challenges in the present and future. This knowledge allows them to proactively adapt their strategies and seize emerging opportunities while minimizing risks.

Furthermore, the history of strategy helps organizations avoid repeating mistakes. By examining past failures and shortcomings, organizations can identify common pitfalls and develop strategies that mitigate such risks. This learning from history approach enables organizations to save valuable resources, make informed decisions, and increase the likelihood of successful outcomes.

A long-term perspective is crucial for maintaining a competitive advantage, and the history of strategy provides the context for shaping this perspective. By studying the strategic decisions and outcomes of organizations over time, organizations can assess the sustainability and durability of various strategies. This broader view helps them anticipate industry shifts, emerging trends, and potential disruptors, enabling them to shape their strategies accordingly and stay ahead of the competition.

In addition, the history of strategy emphasizes the importance of continual innovation. By examining the progression of innovative strategies over time, organizations understand the necessity of fostering a culture of innovation, exploring new opportunities, and staying ahead of market trends. This mindset allows them to proactively innovate and adapt to evolving customer needs, maintaining a competitive advantage in the face of rapid changes.

Lastly, the history of strategy provides a global perspective and is particularly relevant for international business policies. By examining the strategies employed by multinational corporations and understanding the historical context of international trade and market dynamics, organizations can shape their international business policies effectively. This knowledge enables them to navigate cross-cultural complexities, identify market entry strategies, and build fruitful international alliances and partnerships.

In conclusion, the study of strategy concepts and the relevance of the history of strategy are invaluable for strategic management and international business policies. By leveraging historical insights, organizations can enhance their strategic decision-making processes, adapt to changes, avoid pitfalls, maintain a long-term perspective, foster innovation, and effectively navigate the global business landscape, ultimately enabling them to maintain a competitive advantage and drive sustained success.

REFERENCES

Abernathy, W. J., & Utterback, J. M. (1978). Patterns of Industrial Innovation. *Technology Review*, *80*(7), 40–47.

Andrews, K. R. (1987). *The Concept of Corporate Strategy*. Richard D. Irwin.

Ansoff, H. I. (1965). *Corporate Strategy: An Analytic Approach to Business Policy for Growth and Expansion*. McGraw-Hill.

Ansoff, I. (1957). Strategies for Diversification. *Harvard Business Review*, *35*(5), 113–124.

Bartlett, C. A., & Ghoshal, S. (1989). *Managing Across Borders: The Transnational Solution*. Harvard Business School Press.

BCG (Boston Consulting Group). (1970). *Perspectives on Experience*. The Boston Consulting Group.

Campbell, A., & Goold, M. (1999). *Strategy Alliance: Managing Through Interorganizational Collaboration*. Oxford University Press.

Chesbrough, H. W. (2003). *Open Innovation: The New Imperative for Creating and Profiting from Technology*. Harvard Business School Press.

Christensen, C. M. (2003). *The Innovator's Dilemma: When New Technologies Cause Great Firms to Fail*. Harvard Business Review Press.

Cyert, R. M., & March, J. G. (1963). *A Behavioral Theory of the Firm*. Prentice-Hall.

Day, G. S., & Schoemaker, P. J. H. (2016). *Peripheral Vision: Detecting the Weak Signals That Will Make or Break Your Company*. Harvard Business Review Press.

Doz, Y. L., & Hamel, G. (1998). *Alliance Advantage: The Art of Creating Value Through Partnering*. Harvard Business School Press.

Dunning, J. H. (1977). Trade, Location of Economic Activity, and the Multinational Enterprise: A Search for an Eclectic Approach. In B. Ohlin, P. O. Hesselborn, & P. M. Wijkman (Eds.), *The International Allocation of Economic Activity* (pp. 395–418). Macmillan. doi:10.1007/978-1-349-03196-2_38

Earl, M. J. (1996). The New and Old Economies: A Strategic Perspective. In R. W. Zmud (Ed.), *Framing the Domains of IT Management: Projecting the Future Through the Past* (pp. 127–148). Pinnaflex Educational Resources.

Foster, R. N. (1986). *Innovation: The Attacker's Advantage*. Summit Books. doi:10.1007/978-3-322-83742-4

Hambrick, D. C., & D'Aveni, R. A. (1988). Large Corporate Failures as Downward Spirals. *Administrative Science Quarterly*, *33*(1), 1–23. doi:10.2307/2392853

Hart, S. L. (2005). *Capitalism at the Crossroads: Aligning Business, Earth, and Humanity*. Wharton School Publishing.

Henderson, B. D. (1970). *The Product Portfolio*. Perspectives on Experience. The Boston Consulting Group.

Hitt, M. A., & Ireland, R. D. (1985). Corporate Distinctive Competence: Strategy, Industry, and Performance. *Strategic Management Journal, 6*(3), 273–293. doi:10.1002mj.4250060307

Kaplan, R. S., & Norton, D. P. (1996). *The Balanced Scorecard: Translating Strategy into Action*. Harvard Business School Press.

Learned, E. P., Christensen, C. R., Andrews, K. R., & Guth, W. D. (1969). *Business Policy: Text and Cases*. Richard D. Irwin.

Mintzberg, H. (1978). Patterns in Strategy Formation. *Management Science, 24*(9), 934–948. doi:10.1287/mnsc.24.9.934

Mintzberg, H., Ahlstrand, B., & Lampel, J. (1998). *Strategy Safari: A Guided Tour through the Wilds of Strategic Management*. Free Press.

Nonaka, I., & Takeuchi, H. (1995). *The Knowledge-Creating Company: How Japanese Companies Create the Dynamics of Innovation*. Oxford University Press.

O'Reilly, C. A. III, & Tushman, M. L. (2013). Organizational Ambidexterity: Past, Present, and Future. *The Academy of Management Perspectives, 27*(4), 324–338. doi:10.5465/amp.2013.0025

Porter, M. E. (1979). How Competitive Forces Shape Strategy. *Harvard Business Review, 57*(2), 137–145. PMID:18271320

Prahalad, C. K. (2006). *The Fortune at the Bottom of the Pyramid: Eradicating Poverty Through Profits*. Pearson Prentice.

Rumelt, R. P., Schendel, D. E., & Teece, D. J. (1994). *Fundamental Issues in Strategy: A Research Agenda*. Harvard Business School Press.

Selznick, P. (1957). *Leadership in Administration: A Sociological Interpretation*. Harper & Row.

Williamson, O. E. (1967). Hierarchical Control and Optimum Firm Size. *Journal of Political Economy, 75*(2), 123–138. doi:10.1086/259258

Chapter 1
Corporate Governance:
The Role of Board of Directors in the Strategic Planning Process of Organizations

Michael Anibal Altamirano
King Graduate School, USA

Ameil A. Sloley
King Graduate School, USA

ABSTRACT

Corporate governance is a system of controlled activities that act as a form of stewardship for organizations. Governance is represented by a board of directors, which balance the interest of stakeholders and company performance through the evaluation of internal processes such as organizational mission and vision, establishing core values, review of strategic planning process, assessment of organizational policies, hiring and compensation of senior executives, promoting diversity and inclusion, appraisal of executive leadership performance, and self-governance. Boards operate autonomously as they uphold their fiduciary obligations to the company and monitor and control corporate accountabilities. For boards to be effective, they should adhere to the highest standards of integrity while being objective in the delegation of their duties. This chapter offers a perspective of corporate governance and its relative relation, the strategic planning process, while explaining the complexity of organizational boards of directors.

INTRODUCTION

Corporate governance is an organizational system of rules, policies, and best practices that firm's put in place to oversee vision, strategy, and control. Corporate governance principally involves inclusive stakeholders, both the internal and external environments such as customers, shareholders, organizational leadership, suppliers, financiers, the government(s), and the community immersed in and around the firm (Al-Fazari, 2020). This chapter will focus on the overarching role of board of directors in the strategic

DOI: 10.4018/978-1-6684-6845-6.ch001

planning process of organizations. The authors of this proposal, serve as board members in the for-profit and non-profit sectors. They have applied knowledge and proficiency of the strategic management process.

A board of directors is a consortium of individuals elected to represent the shareholders and best interests of organizations. Globally, all public companies are required to have a board of directors (Nuryana & Surjandari, 2019); whereas private and non-profit companies are not required to, but often have a board in place (Pizzi, Rosati, & Venturelli, 2021). The relationship between the board and stakeholders forms in a trust, legal, an ethical obligation often referred to as a fiduciary responsibility (Schanzenbach & Sitkoff, 2020). It is important to note that a board, does not immerse itself in the day-to-day activities of organizations. They serve to counsel organizational leaders and look after stakeholder interests. This service often includes:

- Provide organizational direction through
  - Mission
  - Vision
  - Goals
  - Core values
  - Evaluation of strategic plan
- Establish board and organization-wide policies
- Hiring and setting compensation of the CEO/President/Executive Directors
- Evaluate the performance of the CEO/President/Executive Director
- Abide by fiduciary duties of protecting organizational assets, investments, and corporate social responsibility
- Ensuring the firm's success through continuous monitoring and control

CORPORATE GOVERNANCE AND DIRECTION

Boards are formed through a system of nominations and elections. The nominating committee, a sub-committee of the board of directors, will meet with and vet a candidate that has been nominated, upon finding the candidate appropriate, the committee presents & endorses the candidate's nomination at a formal board meeting, at that time, stakeholders will have an opportunity to vote on the candidate's admission to the board. Investors also have the power to nominate a board candidate, often when seeking to change the direction or policies established by boards (Castellanos & George, 2020).

Once boards are formed and functioning in productive comportments, they take on the more active role, as strategic advisors to the organization. They do so by allocating resources, identifying priority issues, approving mission and vision statements, establishing goals, objectives, and values (Mayer, 2021), and allocating funds to best support the strategic plan. This creates two functions, the approval of the strategic plan and the continuous review of the plan until a new one is formulated, usually every 1-3 years (Mikalef, et al, 2020).

Strategic Planning is the process of developing a business strategy. It involves the formulation and implementation of plans that will guide the firm's actions to achieve its goals and objectives. Committees are formed for strategic planning; the group should include board members, senior and middle management, staff members and other stakeholder representatives (Kabeyi, 2019). The process requires an assessment of the status and firm's performance and should be directly related to its goals. The process will assist the organization with answering the following questions:

- Where are we now? This is an internal and external environmental assessment and where priority issues are identified
- Where do we want to be? This includes the Organizational vision, mission, goals, and objectives
- How will we get there? This is a strategic plan that will map out the intention for the organization
- Whom must do what, by when? This will focus on those involved in carrying out the plan
- How are we doing? This is an ongoing review of the strategic plan

Working as a collective, the board is vital in its role of reviewing the firm's progress and changing strategies when warranted (Knight, Daymond, & Paroutis, 2020). The staff generates the information for review along with a reporting of their performance assessment. It is significant to note, that the information gathered should include data from external stakeholders, such as vendors, investors, and analysts. From outside the firm, the community will have a unique perspective on not only the company, but also the industry in which the company operates; this may reveal useful insights on the outlook of the industry. Essential to the strategic planning process, is a SWOT Analysis (Strengths, Weaknesses, Opportunities, and Threats). Companies use the SWOT analysis, as it provides a 360° view of the business, it indicates what the company does well, and it identifies and highlights areas for improvement (Palomares, et al, 2021). SWOT represents aspects of both the internal and external environments of the organization. Strategic Planning is a continuous and time-consuming process, that requires firms to be committed and flexible in its willingness to change, to be successful, or as is required by societal changes/influence (external threat).

The internal factors of SWOT, strengths and weaknesses are crucial to the organization's operations; as it involves the allocation of human and financial resources, methods, and strategies for daily operations all of which will affect the achievement of goals. It is important, as unlike the other components of SWOT, the organization can take immediate action to correct and improve their weaknesses (Deshpande, 2019); they have total control over these areas. The external components opportunities and threats can a bit more challenging and are often unpredictable. The company should be prepared to find and capitalize upon opportunities, while identifying and neutralizing threats. Ideally, the external components include political, economic, social values, and technological trends. Once the SWOT analysis is completed, it should then be recorded, and the results presented to the committee for review and discussion; this should be done prior to the start of the strategic planning process. The committee must determine how to address critical issues and how to handle any discrepancies in the data among the leadership of the organization as it relates to the firms' goals (Fischer, et al, 2020).

Consider the Strategic Planning Process, a Roadmap

- It provides clear and defined action items and improves the chance for an organization's success
- It will help to get your team aligned with the organization's goals, mission and vision
- It will provide better understanding of industry trends that could impact the organization
- It will help to identify and evaluate the best methods to use to accomplish the organization's goals
- It helps to develop an implementation process to keep you and the team accountable

The board of directors should be thought of as the conscience of an organization, as such it is imperative that they participate in the strategic planning process, where successful direction of the firm's operations will yield positive results for not only the firm but for all its stakeholders. Involvement of the Board also provides for the organization - an extended group of related industry experts who can provide information, cooperatively, mentor and guide the organization's leadership (Garcia Meca & Palacio, 2018).

As boards navigate through the continuous strategic planning process, they often must address unexpected issues that can often derail best-laid plans. Issues include public relations problems, issues related to corporate social responsibility, ineffective or incapacitated CEO/President, global or domestic crisis, social issues such as diversity, equity and inclusion, and employee related issues such as stress, anxiety, motivation, and burnout (Lopez-Fernandez, 2018). The board's ability to successfully guide the organization through the navigation of these issues will largely depend on a history of trust and cohesion between the firm's leadership and the board.

POLICY MAKERS

The principal duty of board of directors is to act in the best interest of the organization, by overseeing and counseling executive leadership along with serving and protecting the needs of stakeholders (Boivie, et al, 2021). These responsibilities function to provide boards with reasonable procedures in their fiduciary roles as caretakers of organizations. Corporate policy is created as a means of measuring corporate success. Subsequently, boards are governed by their policies, they help to create and review the programs that govern the organization. Members of the board review pertinent materials prior to arranged meetings, and they are expected to attend and participate in meetings, normally four times a year. In times of organizational crises, boards will hold emergency meeting, where the evidence of the crisis are discussed in a formal manner. Within boards, are also committees formed to serve and oversee specific areas within the organization. Directors, as stewards, uphold and promote the highest standards of ethical conduct (Pucheta-Martinez & Gallego-Alvarez, 2019). Through their working efforts with executive leaders, they help to create a positive organizational culture and bring leaders that understand and buy-into said culture. Boards will self-govern their overall performance, vote on re-electing members, and consider the nomination of new members (Kabeyi, 2020).

Board Responsibilities

Board of directors nurture relationships with executive leaders and outside advisors in an effort to help guide organizations to success. They receive regular progress reports and informational materials prior to meetings. The purpose of the meetings is to review progress and financial information, evaluate new organizational initiatives, and provide counseling and feedback to executive leaders (Hoppmann, Naegele, & Girod, 2019).

The composition of boards varies but share several common attributes. Most boards consist of independent directors, these are outside professionals that do not have a conflicting interest with the organization (Aluchna, Mahadeo, & Kaminski, 2020). The smaller percentage of board members consists of the CEO/President of the company and other key executives; the size of boards can range between 9 and 18 members. Leadership within the board of directors involves a chair, or lead director who is initially nominated and placed in position by majority vote. This position of elected leadership is periodic and boards will vote to continue or change leadership based on their agreed upon by-laws. Responsibilities include:

- Organize and provide meeting agendas
- Ensuring board diversity
- Presiding over organized meetings and executive sessions
- Updating information from executive sessions to CEO/President
- Reporting to directors response from CEO/President
- Serving as liaison between board and the organization
- Reviewing and approving all information sent to the board
- Scheduling of board and committee meetings
- Be available to consult and communicate with major shareholders

It is paramount for the board chair to promote diversity within the board and throughout the organization, starting with the executive leaders. Discrimination in the workplace is a global crisis, diversity, equity, and inclusion should be an integral part of corporate governance. In 2019, women made up 18% of board membership and people of under-represented backgrounds accounted for 29% in 2017 (Yilmaz, et al, 2022). The percentages for executive leaders are even less, but there is a striking correlation between diversity and productivity. According to Hunt et al. (2018):

Companies in the top-quartile for gender diversity on their executive teams were 21% more likely to have above-average profitability than companies in the fourth quartile. For ethnic/cultural diversity, top-quartile companies were 33% more likely to outperform on profitability.

This presents an opportunity for corporate governors to embrace and promote diversity efforts within the board of directors and throughout the organization (Gromley, et al, 2021). It is an endeavor of organizational significance, and ultimately all organizational culture is established through the modeled behavior of executive leaders (Kortsch, Bashenkhaeva, & Kauffeld, 2022).

LEADERSHIP RECRUITMENT

Recruitment is a vital responsibility for all organizations. Ideally, organizations place concerted effort into onboarding talent that meshes with the organizational culture and adds value to the organizational mission (Haromszeki, 2022). Unfortunately, many firms fail to recruit effectively. From an internal perspective, organizations recruit talent to fill vacancies, aid in efficiency, and help increase productivity. Externally, recruitment efforts are affected by several factors including the economy, the political climate, and socio-cultural trends. Hiring the right talent helps organizations reach financial and growth goals whereas, failing to recruit or hiring the wrong talent will result in financial loss and lost confidence among stakeholders (Stahl, et al, 2020).

Recruiters

The responsibility of board of directors is to provide oversight in the recruitment of executive leadership, as well as evaluate, monitor, and compensate new executive hires (Boivie, et al, 2021). Modern boards focus primarily on the hiring of CEOs and Presidents. The function of recruiting and hiring leadership can be complicated and can take some time because the selection must always be right. Obviously, hiring the right organizational leader is a matter of perspective. Two circumstances drive the need to hire a new leader, an impending resignation or termination. A resignation will usually afford a board a significant amount of time to formulate a plan and a search committee. Whereas, a termination will often result in the naming of an interim CEO/President in an effort conduct a proper leadership search. The interim leader should be a carefully considered appointment, as the leader selected must be capable of stabilizing the company amidst the turmoil and trauma of a leadership termination (Sechrest, 2020).

The board must have a clear understanding of the organizational culture and mission and not select a candidate that is counter-intuitive to the values of the organization. Depending on the circumstance, the search can take anywhere from three to seven months. The board committee, tasked with hiring will usually use an executive search firm. An executive search firm is a company that specializes in assisting to place qualified leadership candidates in high-ranking executive positions (Baldo, Valle, & Olivas-Lujan, 2019). The executive search firm will normally find the candidate(s) that match the specific parameters, laid out by the board's recruiting committee. The ideal candidate(s) should meet the specific qualifications, core competencies, and values that best represent the firm. Careful consideration is placed on diversity, experience, and a proven record of accomplishment. Normally, at the CEO level, most candidates are usually well educated and possess graduate degrees or higher.

Compensation

Compensation of executive leaders is in a constant state of flux. Average numbers tend to rise every year. Most CEO salaries are to be over $1million (U.S.) per year, not including various bonuses and incentives (Lovett, Rasheed, & Hou, 2022). The eventual compensation numbers are based on varying factors such as the candidates proven record, candidate's demands, company affordability, and the current industry average. While numbers can seem exorbitant, investors will analyze the eventual payoff of compensation, because as long as the company continues to grow after a hire and share values rise, investors will see compensation decisions in their favor (Chapas & Chassagnon, 2021). Firms will continue to justify executive compensation numbers as "pay for performance". This concept is easy for many to understand, but it also implies the risk involved in hiring a new executive leader.

A base salary, as generous as it sometimes is, is usually not enough to bring in the best possible talent; organizations will often add bonuses, stock options, and perquisites (Wang, et al, 2021). These operate as incentives for executives to perform at optimum levels. A correlation can be made between overall company performance and the performance of the CEO. Performance evaluation often stems from financial measures such as profit growth, revenue growth, return on equity, and stock price (You, et al, 2020). These are simple quantifiable measures. Active boards will create a balanced scorecard to measure all outcomes related to executive performance.

Executive compensation is not an exact science. Factors like industry trends and a candidate's proven record of accomplishment weigh heavily on the eventual decision. Stakeholders understand the risk/

reward aspect of compensation decisions (Choi & Suh, 2019). The executive compensation package should inevitably motivate leaders to perform optimally and in the best interest of stakeholder.

EVALUATING EXECUTIVE PERFORMANCE

Once an organization leader is on boarded, board of directors are tasked with evaluating that executive's performance in order to determine contract renewals and yearly increases to salaries and bonuses (Wijethilake & Ekanayake, 2020). Performance evaluations can be ongoing, and both formal, and informal. The main purpose of the evaluations is to provide feedback. Executive leaders should expect to report progress to boards of directors and provide open channels of communication with board members. The purpose of feedback and all communication is to be constructive and transparent. Transparency is an important aspect of integrity in business. Transparency establishes trust between executive leaders and board members.

Once a year a formal evaluation is conducted where executive leaders will submit a self-appraisal to the board. Self-appraisals are based on varying performance factors that measure if goals and objectives were met and determine future goals and objectives (Zyung & Shi, 2022). The evaluation gives the executive leader an opportunity to highlight their accomplishments. Boards of directors consider the self-evaluation as an important aspect of the appraisal. The board will provide thorough feedback during a formal meeting with the executive leader, where they reference every section of the self-evaluation, as well as comment on any other areas the board deems important.

Key Factors of the Executive Performance Evaluation

- Achievement of goals and objectives
- Upcoming goals
- Overall performance of duties and responsibilities
- Additional performance factors
- Improvement and development plans set conjointly with executive and board of directors

After a successful evaluation by the board of directors, executive leaders will often receive an increase to their wages and bonus incentives. If the evaluation is not acceptable, most boards will not waste time in terminating a contract and will begin the search for a replacement. When evaluating overall executive leader performance, boards will consider steady improvement of the company in all aspects of profit, stock prices, productivity, and reputation (Osiichuk, 2022). A bad quarter, or even a bad year may not be enough to terminate a contract, unless the results are calamitous. Usually, terminations are the result of overall collective issues that result in a failure to perform.

FIDUCIARY DUTIES OF BOARD OF DIRECTORS

The fiduciary responsibilities of a board of directors are grounded in loyalty to the organization. They carry out their duties as stewards of community trust in an objective, ethical, and efficient manner. Their primary responsibility is to act in the best interest of the company they represent and not seek benefit for themselves. Their agenda must be driven by what is best for the organization and stakeholders. Their decisions are then weighed carefully as to not place the company at risk (Hill, 2020).

All board members must fully understand their duties and obligations as directors. When members fail to carry out their fiduciary duties they place the company's reputation in jeopardy and face expulsion from the board (Attenborough, 2020). A breach of fiduciary duty can result from a director committing explicit acts of mismanagement, failing to meet the explicit obligations of outlined as a board member, and the commitment of a legal or ethical violation (McGee, 2020). Any act by a board, or member, that has adverse impact on the company's reputation, organizational management, and overall company condition is considered a breach.

MONITORING AND CONTROL

A common practice of strategic management is monitoring the strategic plan in order control progress in a productive manner. Controlling a strategic plan begins with the initial planning phases of environmental assessment, and reviewing the current mission, vision, core values, and goals and objectives (Merendino & Melville, 2019). The methodology of these phases is deliberate and ultimately results in a current strategic plan. Throughout the strategic planning process, active board of directors, along with executive leadership, monitor the progress of the planning and ultimate strategic direction (Zhou, Owusu-Ansah, & Maggina, 2018). Boards of directors provide objective feedback focused on helping the organization succeed and grow. Once a strategic plan is in place, the board will continue to monitor progress in order to control positive outcomes. If plans falter, the board and executive leaders will suggest slight adjustments or drastic changes to the strategic plan. In order for strategy to be effective, their needs to be direct involvement and monitoring by executive stakeholders; in order to determine if strategic goals and objectives are clear, realistic, measurable, and are being met.

CONCLUSION

Corporate governance is critically important for the overall success of an organization. It provides a system of monitoring from an impartial group of directors that serve a fiduciary responsibility to the organization. The organization and responsibilities of the board are complex, but well-coordinated, starting with the chair and placement of external and internal board members. Boards are self-governed by an approved set of bylaws that outline their ethical and fiduciary responsibilities to the company. Through their responsibilities they are directly involved in the hiring and setting compensation of senior executives, nominating and voting in new board members, and the stewardship of organization.

REFERENCES

Al Fazari, H. (2020). Higher education in the Arab world: governance and management from the perspective of Oman and Sohar university. In *Higher Education in the Arab World* (pp. 279–295). Springer. doi:10.1007/978-3-030-58153-4_11

Pucheta-Martínez, M. C., & Gallego-Álvarez, I. (2019). An international approach of the relationship between board attributes and the disclosure of corporate social responsibility issues. *Corporate Social Responsibility and Environmental Management, 26*(3), 612–627. doi:10.1002/csr.1707

Schanzenbach, M. M., & Sitkoff, R. H. (2020). Reconciling fiduciary duty and social conscience: The law and economics of ESG investing by a trustee. *Stanford Law Review, 72*, 381.

Sechrest, T. (2020). The Interim Leader: Organizational Considerations Before the Permanent Leader Arrives. *Journal of Leadership, Accountability and Ethics, 17*(4).

Stahl, G. K., Brewster, C. J., Collings, D. G., & Hajro, A. (2020). Enhancing the role of human resource management in corporate sustainability and social responsibility: A multi-stakeholder, multidimensional approach to HRM. *Human Resource Management Review, 30*(3), 100708. doi:10.1016/j.hrmr.2019.100708

Wang, H. C., Fang, C. C., Lou, Y. I., & Zhaohui Xu, R. (2021). Determinants of CEO bonus compensation. *Financial Internet Quarterly 'e-Finanse', 17*(3).

Wijethilake, C., & Ekanayake, A. (2020). CEO duality and firm performance: The moderating roles of CEO informal power and board involvements. *Social Responsibility Journal.*

Yilmaz, M. K., Hacioglu, U., Tatoglu, E., Aksoy, M., & Duran, S. (2022). Measuring the impact of board gender and cultural diversity on corporate governance and social performance: evidence from emerging markets. *Economic Research-Ekonomska Istraživanja*, 1-35.

Zhou, H., Owusu-Ansah, S., & Maggina, A. (2018). Board of directors, audit committee, and firm performance: Evidence from Greece. *Journal of International Accounting, Auditing & Taxation, 31*, 20–36. doi:10.1016/j.intaccudtax.2018.03.002

Zyung, J. D., & Shi, W. (2022). In retrospect: The influence of chief executive officers' historical relative pay on overconfidence. *Strategic Organization, 20*(3), 627–651. doi:10.1177/14761270211004891

Chapter 2
Internationalization Strategies:
Circumventing the Liability of Newness – A Case Study of Irregular Internationalization Paths

Beatriz Clarinha
University of Aveiro, Portugal

Diana Cunha
University of Aveiro, Portugal

Francisca Sá
University of Aveiro, Portugal

António Carrizo Moreira
University of Aveiro, Portugal

ABSTRACT

This chapter analyzes the internationalization process of an irregular exporter and seeks to perceive the internationalization theory that explains the company over this international path. Some of the most studied internationalization models that explain the rapid internationalization process were reviewed in order to compare the main characteristics of each theory. Methodologically the chapter uses primary data, obtained from an interview, complemented by the analysis of secondary data. A synthesis table seeks to summarize the characteristics of the internationalization process of each of the four theories analyzed.

DOI: 10.4018/978-1-6684-6845-6.ch002

INTRODUCTION

The globalization process has driven firms' internationalization (Ietto-Gillies, 2012; Ribau et al., 2015). Normally, Small and Medium-sized Enterprises (SMEs) seek to exploit their competitive advantages in overseas markets involving exporting activities as the main outward internationalization modes of entry (Ribau et al., 2018; Stanisauskaite & Kock, 2016). However, with the globalization process, firms have been changing their international behavior according to the dramatic socioeconomic shifts in the international environment. As a result of the increasing international competition, several models and theories of internationalization have been used to categorize firms' behaviors in international markets, namely SMEs.

Nowadays, the international environment is complex, since SMEs and multinationals are increasingly adopting various forms of internationalization strategies (Ribau et al., 2015) that aim to: "serve global markets, rapidly deploy new products in several countries, or adapt their brands to global/multidomestic environments" (Ribau et al., 2015, p. 529).

Naturally, the concept of internationalization has evolved over time and varies depending on the area under study. Moreover, it depends on firm-based factors, such as size, age, management mode, among others (Paul & Sánchez-Morcilio, 2019; Ribau et al., 2015; 2018). Briefly, internationalization can be described as the process of increasing involvement in international operations, that is, increasing activities in foreign markets (Calof & Beamish, 1995).

According to the literature, international expansion represents an opportunity for company's growth and added value creation, particularly for SMEs. Indeed, companies that enter international markets usually increase their technological and market knowledge, improve their performance, and become more innovative. In this way, they also become stronger competitors in domestic markets (Engelman et al., 2015).

Ribau et al. (2015) offer an evolutionary schematic perspective of the main internationalization theories, foci and assumptions following a historical perspective. Paul & Sánchez-Morcilio (2019) defend that the internationalization process is conservative and predictable. As such, it is possible to claim that behavioral theories emerged as more or less predictable explaining the internationalization of SMEs.

Several models have been put forward to explain the internationalization path followed by SMEs—born globals (BGs), born regionals (BRs) or born again globals (BAGs)—as an alternative to the traditional Uppsala model in order to explain the scale, scope, and speed of internationalization. As the internationalization path can hardly be explained by a single theory, the aim of this chapter is to, based on a single case study known as CASTLE—which for confidentiality reasons its name cannot be disclosed—, discuss the characteristics of the internationalization of CASTLE and identify the typology of internationalization that fits CASTLE the most. For that, four internationalization models are going to be used to understand CASTLE internationalization path—Uppsala model, BGs, BRs, and BAGs—to identify the one that resembles the most to CASTLE's. CASTLE's characteristics are unique as the company started to expand abroad right from its inception and, nowadays, is present in all continents. In this sense, several topics will be addressed and discussed, such as: the modes of entry abroad, the main internationalization drivers and barriers when entering foreign markets. Moreover, the four internationalization modes are analyzed using CASTLE's internationalization path, reasons for internationalizing, modes of entry and speed of internationalization, among others.

An important assumption for all studies on this type of small and medium-sized companies is their resource constraints (Hånell & Nordman, 2019). However, managers and/or founders have an indispensable and preponderant role in networking so that they enhance their internationalization paths, showing that companies with international entrepreneurial orientation seek international markets taking on risky, proactive and innovative behaviors that underpin their rapid internationalization process (Coviello, 2015). Nevertheless, more important than entrepreneurial orientation is adaptation of the firm as markets change dramatically.

Based on a case study, this book chapter seeks to explore the following research questions:

1. How did the company take advantage of the globalization process and embraced the opportunities in the international arena?
2. How has the company evolved in international markets and has adapted to swift changes?
3. What determinants motivated this rapid and early internationalization process and the subsequent adaptation process?
4. What are the main theories – Uppsala model, Born Global, Born Regional or Born-again Global – that can explain the internationalization process of the company?

This document is structured as follows: after the introduction, Section 2 presents the literature review. Section 3 describes the methodology adopted. In Section 4 the general presentation of the company chosen is done. Section 5 addresses the main results obtained from the interview and data analyzed. In Section 6 the results are discussed. Finally, in section 7 the main conclusions drawn from this work are shown.

LITERATURE REVIEW

Uppsala Model

The internationalization of SMEs is a multifaceted theme as it involves different topics and contexts in which SMEs operate (Ribau et al., 2018). Although this area of research has been extensively analyzed in the last decades, the Uppsala Model is recognized as the most used one addressing the internationalization of SMEs (Ribau et al., 2015; 2018). This model depicts the internationalization of SMEs as a gradual process in which companies internationalize based on the market knowledge they have and the more knowledge they internationalize the more committed they are to leverage further the internationalization process. As such, this model depends on the company's internal characteristics but also on the contextual characteristics that influence companies in the international path.

The revised version of the original Uppsala model adds the business networks' perspective and their implications. If the original Uppsala model was based on the assumption that developing knowledge was fundamental to the firm's internationalization, Johanson and Vahlne (2009) revised the model incorporating business networks and previous management team relationships as essential to generate new essential knowledge for the internationalization process, i.e., the concept of relationship-specific knowledge generated through inter-organizational interactions are important to generate heterogeneous capabilities and resources. As such, companies may follow resource-seeking or market-seeking behaviors to evolve in their international paths.

Born Globals

The globalization of the world economy brought about not only global markets, but global competition as well (Zander, McDougall-Covin, & Rose, 2015), creating examples of companies with rapid internationalization processes in the early stages of the firm's internationalization process (Ribau et al., 2015). This firms, Born Globals (BGs), expand to international markets, taking advantage of both new global contextual conditions and new needs, which are based on rapid internationalization approaches (Covielo, 2015; Ribau et al., 2015; Weerawardena et al., 2007).

BGs stand out for having: a global vision from the beginning of their business activity, managers with international market orientation as well as prior international experience, and strong capabilities (Ribau et al., 2015).

Since they were already born operating in international markets, BGs do not normally follow the typical linear internationalization process proposed by the Uppsala model (Ribau et al., 2015). Clearly, BGs are focused on how early they become international, rather than how they serve the local market and are characterized by their proactive international strategy (Oviatt & McDougall, 1994).

Born Again Globals

Born Again Globals are known for being well-established in their domestic markets with no motivation to begin the internationalization process (Bell et al., 2001), but as soon as they implement some strategic changes, they may adopt an international focus (Schueffel et al., 2014). Also known as late internationalizers, they usually change their internationalization perspective when they go through "critical incidents" such as reformulation of the management team, the focal firm being acquired by a competitor, acquisition of a firm with international operations, and customer influence, among others (Bell et al., 2001).

Born Again Globals usually begin their internationalization process incrementally (Baum et al., 2015) with the main motivation for entering external markets being to exploit new resources and networks (Bell et al., 2003). As such, Born Again Globals are present in a low number of foreign markets, and have a high institutional and cultural distance from foreign markets (Baum et al., 2015).

Born Regionals

The internationalization of BRs is very similar to that of Born Globals as they internationalize soon after their inception. However, they focus their international activities on a geographical area that is very similar to the contextual characteristics that they face in their country of origin (Baum et al., 2015; Lopez et al., 2009). The main reasons behind this path is that the companies tend to exploit some specific competitive advantages in its region and the need to operate in vast international markets is very limited (Baum et al., 2015).

Born Regionals are less likely to be learning oriented towards, as they are focused on their geographical proximity (Baum et al., 2011). BGs and BRs are closely related, being the main difference between them the number of countries they serve (Lopez et al., 2009).

Entry Modes

When a company begins to consider the possibility of going international, there are several aspects to which it should pay the greatest attention so that the process runs with as few difficulties and objections as possible. There are numerous ways of entering foreign markets, and most suitable mode of entry for a given market is only one of these aspects. This choice implies making several decisions that may affect the company, and, for this, it is necessary to know and understand the characteristics of a given market/country, since "it is difficult to understand the business environment in a country without studying the current political system and institutions, government policies, and a variety of data and other information on the country's economy" (Zeqiri & Angelova, 2011, p. 573), as well as aspects related to the culture, demography and history of that country. Thus, a company seeking to internationalize needs to assess the factors that play a significant role during the decision-making process for market selection and then proceed to choose the entry mode that best suits that market (Zeqiri & Angelova, 2011).

The modes of entry into a foreign market fall into three major groups: (A) export; (B) contractual forms; and (C) foreign direct investment. Exporting can occur in three distinct types: direct, indirect and own. Contractual forms can take many forms, the most important of which are: licensing, franchising and strategic alliances. Regarding foreign direct investment, this can occur through the acquisition of an existing company or the creation of a new subsidiary (Armstrong & Sweeney, 1994).

Naturally, each mode has its advantages and disadvantages, but a company will be more attracted to a specific mode depending on its nature, background and experience, strategic objectives, and resources (Zeqiri & Angelova, 2011). In the following, these different modes of entry into a foreign market will be briefly analyzed.

A.   Export

In exporting, goods are sold in a country other than the one where they are manufactured (country of origin). This is a traditional method of reaching foreign markets and is the simplest, fastest and most common way to do this. In this case, there is no need for the company to invest in a foreign country because exporting does not require the goods to be produced in the destination country. Most of the costs associated with exporting take the form of marketing expenses (Zeqiri & Angelova, 2011).

As stated earlier, exporting can take on three different types (Gabrielsson et al., 2002). In the direct export mode, the producing firm handles export activities directly with the first intermediary located in the target country, which will take care of the distribution of the products (examples: importers, agents and distributors). The indirect export mode exists when another company located in the domestic market performs export activities on behalf of the producing company (examples: trading company or subcontractor) (Gabrielsson et al., 2002). Finally, the own export type occurs when the company uses its own assets and knowledge network and there is no domestic or foreign intermediary between the company and the final customer. The producer's own export team is involved in sales activities to serve end customers and is in charge of sales promotion, customer acquisition and product distribution. Examples are online sales (website orders) or mail orders (Gabrielsson et al., 2002).

B.   Contractual Forms

Contractual forms allow companies to collaborate with their counterparty. Thus, costs are shared and they can specialize even more in their skills and gain more knowledge about the market. The main contractual forms are (Zeqiri & Angelova, 2011): licensing, franchising, and strategic alliances. A license agreement is a commercial agreement between a licensor who has a competitive advantage/monopoly position (e.g. a patent, a trademark, a design, copyright, a manufacturing capability) of which it has the exclusive right, which prevents others from exploiting the idea, design, etc., and a licensee who pays a fee in exchange for the rights to use the intangible asset and possibly technical assistance (e.g. pays a royalty per unit produced). Franchising is an entry mode quite similar to licensing: it is also a contractual arrangement whereby, upon payment of a royalty fee by the franchisee to the franchisor, the latter grants the franchisee the right to use an already developed and tested business concept, including the trademark, products/services, marketing, etc., in order to ensure the success of the franchisee's business. The difference from the licensing mode is that the franchisee must abide by certain rules given by the franchisor (Zeqiri & Angelova, 2011). Alliances represent an agreement between two companies that come together to develop a certain project, operate jointly in a certain market, etc. Typically, alliances are about entering a market and sharing risk, rewards and technology to achieve a common goal, which requires reciprocity, mutual efforts and acting together (Zeqiri & Angelova, 2011).

C.   Foreign Direct Investment

Foreign Direct Investment (FDI) is the direct ownership of facilities in the destination market/country. It involves capital, technology and personnel. Direct ownership provides a high degree of control in operations and the ability to learn more about consumers, the competitive environment and the market in general. However, it requires a high level of resources and a high degree of commitment. FDI can be done by acquiring an existing company or creating a new subsidiary (Zeqiri & Angelova, 2011).

Facilitators to Enter International Markets

One of the factors that facilitates the entry of a company into overseas markets is the so-called international orientation. This factor concerns the entrepreneurial vision and vocation of the owner or manager of a company to internationalize it (Deprey et al., 2012). This managerial international orientation may stem from: his/her international work experience, which may enable him/her to become aware of the opportunities that exist in foreign markets (Hutchinson et al., 2007); the length and extent of the trips managers have spent abroad, whether studying or working (the longer in time and the more extensive his/her stay abroad has been, the greater the orientation); his/her foreign language skills; and his/her understanding of cultures other than his own (Deprey et al., 2012).

Technology may be another relevant factor in facilitating firms' entry into international markets. However, the effects of technology on internationalization vary depending on the area in which the firm operates, being more important in some sectors than in others. Technology can therefore be a source of competitive advantage in the internationalization process and fundamental to entry modes. For example, companies can make use of the Internet and communication technologies to develop a virtual presence, which gives them immediate and low-cost access to foreign markets, reducing geographical distance and facilitating interaction with potential international clients. Technology also makes it possible to operate from the home country, but also travel abroad as needed (Deprey et al., 2012).

A third factor that can facilitate firms' internationalization is their degree of specialization in market niches, i.e., the adaptation of products to specific markets. That is to say that meeting customer needs by tailoring goods and services to small segments can represent a source of competitive advantage in foreign markets (Deprey et al., 2012). In fact, providing appropriately focused and customized products and services for niche markets is essential in the internationalization process of companies. To prove this, based on a study revealing that in six of the nine companies investigated, the specialization "is an important reason for their distinctiveness and attraction to international clients, many with whom they have long-standing relationships" Deprey et al. (2012, p. 1617).

Finally, what can be considered the factor that most favors the entry of companies into foreign markets is networks. Networks are important for several stages of the internationalization process, from the identification and exploitation of market opportunities to the growth and establishment of the company in international markets. Networks can be classified as: business networks (also called formal), which refer to relationships with other business actors; and social networks (also called informal), which allude to social contacts with friends and family (Andersson et al., 2018; Ojala, 2009).

On one hand, relationships and networks represent key tools for gaining access to market-relevant information and other material and immaterial resources (Andersson et al., 2018). Moreover, networks can not only help overcome internal resource deficiencies but also enable access to knowledge and experience absent within the firm (Hutchinson et al., 2006; Ribau et al., 2019). Indeed, by working more closely with other firms, it is possible to obtain, combine and share expertise, resources and knowledge, as well as coproduce additional knowledge in ways that would not be possible if a firm operated independently (Welch et al., 1998). On the other hand, when faced with uncertainty when entering new markets, firms can draw on contacts and connections with others firms of the network to minimize risk (Zain & Ng, 2006). Deprey et al. (2012) further highlight the important role that networks play in helping to "determine which ways to enter abroad and, to a lesser extent, which markets to enter" (p. 1611).

Barriers to Entering International Markets

When a company enters international markets, some obstacles hinder this process and create failures in operations, causing the company to have large financial losses and giving rise to negative attitudes toward internationalization (Al-Hyari et al., 2012). Thus, companies must know how to overcome them to be successful in these markets.

There is a wide variety of aspects that can be considered barriers to the internationalization of companies, one of them being the lack of financial resources (Roy et al., 2016). The fact that companies do not have enough financial resources to be present abroad and to export their products is an obstacle that prevents many companies from going down this path (Al-Hyari et al., 2012). Although there is the possibility of receiving government support for these situations, some governments do not provide it and those that do so are rarely enough to help all the companies that need it. With this lack of government support, it becomes impossible for many of them to reach the international market. In addition to the lack of support from the government, political risk, corruption and the laws of each country are all obstacles for companies to enter various countries (Roy et al., 2016).

Culture can be presented as either a benefit or a problem to the entry into several markets. As an obstacle, it represents the cultural distance that exists between different countries and the different languages spoken in them. Thus, it is important that companies have a good knowledge of the culture and language of the markets they intend to enter, so that they can adapt better and be well-regarded by future partners/distributors (Roy et al., 2016).

The insecurity of the logistics process, the costs that it can represent, as well as the price difference between companies and their competitors, must be taken into consideration in order to remain competitive and survive in these markets (Al-Hyari et al., 2012).

METHODOLOGY

As the case study method allows the analysis of specific situations, this chapter was based on a Portuguese firm—CASTLE—that is an internationalized company, with a clear position in the market that has had an adaptive strategy in international markets. The case study is based on a qualitative analysis of the previous knowledge of the firm gained from public presentations, the sound brand name it has on the market and an interview carried out with CASTLE's CEO.

CASTLE produces a broad range of products—luxury perfumed soaps, solid shampoos and conditioners, hand and body gel, body lotion, hand cream, shaving products, eau de toilette, travel packs, among others—for the premium market. It started its production activities as a sourcing company to supply luxury perfumed soaps for an American brand. After an initial success, CASTLE needed to muddle through this competitive market and created its own brand after losing its anchor in the American market. This company was selected as it allows the analysis of several theories that support the internationalization process firms go through with new empirical results drawn from specific situations under analysis. Moreover, this case study also allows the investigation of particular contextual phenomena that influences the firm's positioning and evolution and the interpretation of retrospective information that supports theoretical and practical insights (Eisenhardt, 1989; Ribau et al., 2019; Yin, 2014). Furthermore, the case study method is particularly appropriate to analyze a dynamic perspective over time involving a complex nonlinear internationalization process (Durão & Moreira, 2019; Vissak & Francioni, 2013; Silva & Moreira, 2019).

CASTLE was selected based on a theoretical sampling approach, which involves the selection of business cases that meet several important aspects under analysis (Patton, 2015): (a) being involved in a nonlinear internationalization process; (b) the participation in the provision of B2B and B2C markets; (c) having core activities in the luxury market; and (d) actively seeking to increase the international market segment.

Based on the qualitative nature of the research, a semi-structured interview was arranged with CASTLE's CEO to collect data. This interview took place in June 2022 and lasted around one hour. This semi-structured interview aimed at obtaining insightful primary information from the interviewee regarding the history of the company, the internationalization strategy—motivations, timings, sales volume and exports percentages—, main markets where the company operates and how the company has managed to adapt to those markets. In order to complement the information obtained, secondary information from public sources—firm's website, public presentations, information from industrial associations, among others—complemented primary data obtained during the interview, supporting triangulation of information, validity and reliability (Eisenhardt, 1989). Moreover, all information was complemented by a visit to CASTLE's premises, which also helped the interviewers to break the ice and the interviewee to feel more comfortable while speaking in his own environment. In order not to interfere with the messages carried out by the interviewee, the interviewers kept an unobtrusive presence, not interfering with the on-going events and activities. After the interview, the researchers' impressions were summarized for subsequent analysis.

To ease the interviewing process, the researchers started by explaining the objectives of the research, guaranteeing the interviewee total anonymity. The interview script was developed to explore the firm's internationalization path, its importance for the firm, and how the firm managed to serve different types of markets abroad in such a competitive market. After obtaining information and data from all the possible sources, it was possible to transcribe all information into a single case story.

COMPANY PRESENTATION

CASTLE was founded in 1999 by Aquiles Barros, Porto, Portugal. Originally, it was the result of a challenge proposed to the founder to create a soap production company, exclusively for an American brand and in 2000 CASTLE started this production with only six workers. In 2003, the company lost its only client and was faced with one of the most important decisions in its history: close doors or risk continuing. At that time, CASTLE chose to continue its production for other American brands and for large Spanish company, until 2006.

In that year, the company decided to start producing its own brands, creating a product brand with the same name of the company, in 2007, Portus Cale. Until 2008 it exported 100% of its production. It was in 2008 that CASTLE started to sell its products in Portugal, CASTLE's country of origin, followed later by exports to several other countries. Nowadays, the brand is present on all continents and its exports represent about 80% of the sales volume.

Although the company started producing its own brands, that did not stop it from continuing to produce for other brands worldwide. Even today CASTLE produces for major global brands, based mainly in the USA. CASTLE does not position itself as a simple soap company: it sells gifts, luxury soaps as well as products for the body and the home.

At present, it operates with about 150 employees, with a single production plant in Portugal, and is characterized as a company that, because of the price and the quality of its products, sells affordable luxury. The hand-packed products allow the company to have a connection with all the items it produces, valuing the work of employees. A dedicated team is exactly what CASTLE considers to be the secret to its success.

To serve all the countries in which it is present, CASTLE adopts a standardization strategy, meaning that it produces and distributes the same products to all the countries. Therefore, the company tries to keep up with the trends, both in Portugal and abroad, in order to create products that satisfy and surprise its customers.

CASTLE operates in the B2B market—because it distributes its products to other stores, which then sell them, and manufactures products for other brands—and in the B2C (business to consumer) sector, because it sells its products in its own stores, both physical and online.

RESULTS

Currently, CASTLE has around 150 employees hired directly by the company. However, this number varies according to the time of year, for example: during the Christmas season, the number goes up.

Regarding the turnover, in 2021, the company invoiced 14 million euros, which reflects a trend of continuous growth, although, due to the Covid-19 pandemic, in 2020 there was a drop in growth.

Over the years there has been a change in CASTLE's marketing strategy: initially, they did not make advertisements, which meant they did not work with paid advertising. They did occasional actions with influencers and worked with some agencies, although it was something sporadic. At this moment, the company is reorganizing its marketing strategy and is working with an external agency to promote products, namely through advertisements on social networks. Those ads occur, mostly, when new products are launched, as was the case of the latest launch of Portus Cale—White Crane. In addition, at specific times, such as Christmas, they look to create new events, where they invite influencers and public figures, so they make their followers aware of the products and the brand, promoting them. At the same time, the company also seeks to establish contact with direct customers and promote the brand as much as possible, in a measured way, as it is a company that does not want to be everywhere at once, but rather intends to choose and manage customers (helping them grow with them) while showcasing the core of the brand: traditional, hand-packed products in Portugal. It is a gradual change that is still being designed and that involves changing the approach they use towards the market: a strong presence on social networks, greater contact with influencers, the creation of two of their own shops at El Corte Inglés, which is a major department store—with one shop in Porto and the other one in Lisbon.

In terms of competitors, Claus Porto, belonging to the Ach. Brito group, is considered CASTLE's biggest national competitor, followed by Benamôr. Internationally, *L'Occitane en Provance* stands out.

CASTLE's main product brand is present in the four corners of the world (see Figure 1), with the European continent being the most evident one. Here, Great Britain appears as one of the company's main markets, but it also has a vast presence in countries like Ireland, Spain and France. For many years, Portugal was not one of CASTLE's key markets; nevertheless, today, it is undoubtedly one of its vital clients.

On the other side of the world, Southeast Asia has been one of CASTLE's great bets, and Hong Kong is the market most explored by the company. CASTLE is also strongly inserted in the American continent, with the USA representing one of its most important clients. It has also been registering significant growth in Canada.

CASTLE is also growing considerably in South America and has a more tenuous presence in Oceania and Africa. The latter is a market that CASTLE finds more difficult to enter due to the lesser means of some countries. The company thus recognizes that its products are not of easy access to everyone due to the premium price.

The choice of which countries to enter was based on a variety of reasons. The one that may be considered the main reason is the fact that, from very early on, one of CASTLE's main goals has been to expand internationally. As already mentioned, the company was born to produce soaps for an American brand. Even after losing this client, CASTLE chose to continue to export to the USA, since it already had experience in that market and, therefore, knew how the export process worked in that country.

As far as Great Britain is concerned, and as in several European countries, its entry was natural since these were markets in which it made sense for CASTLE to be present. Furthermore, the existence of good contacts allowed the entry of the company into the British market. Even though the United Kingdom's exit from the European Union in 2020 made things a little more difficult in terms of bureaucracy, the business continued successfully. Entry into the Southeast Asian market was also favored through contacts with people from those countries, and these relationships are still maintained today.

Figure 1. CASTLE in the world

On the other hand, the assiduity in international fairs, namely those that take place annually in Italy and France—*Cosmoprof* and *Maison & Objet* respectively—, has enabled CASTLE to enter these markets, which is mainly through contacts that the commercial team receives (besides the prospection that is a tiny part, since there are more people contacting them than the other way around). Most contacts come from these European fairs, but they are also present in some others outside Europe. The fact that these countries are very open to the beauty and cosmetic industry was also essential to facilitate the entry of the company.

In terms of objectives/projects, currently, CASTLE's purpose is not to increase the number of markets where they are present but to grow in the markets where they already are present. The reason for this is they think that if there is enormous accessibility, the brand will be discredited. In addition, by increasing production exponentially, it would be difficult for them to continue to be what they are, traditionally working by hand. Clients are chosen carefully, as it is intended that beyond the business itself, a solid and lasting relationship is maintained. Thus, they aim to grow more in the Spanish market, developing their presence in the Iberian market. Besides that, the German market is another goal. Although they place a lot of barriers to the entry of foreign products, Germans are extremely loyal customers because, from the moment they trust the brand and its quality, they have the habit of recommending it, which is very important for companies that are starting to enter these countries.

As a project for the future, CASTLE intends to consolidate its presence in the Asian market, which they consider to be an interesting market, but also one of slow penetration due to the nature of the Asian culture in which it is necessary to build a relationship before the negotiation itself. However, after gaining that trust in the partner, it becomes a long-lasting relationship that brings great advantages to those who do business with these countries. The justification given during the interview for the desire to be present in Asia has several points: (1) because the countries of the Asian continent give great importance to personal health and beauty care; (2) because it is a very appealing market that is little explored by Portuguese companies; (3) because it is a very malleable market that offers great opportunities to companies like CASTLE by accepting new products with different materials; (4) because of a demographic reason since they are highly populated countries; and (5) because despite being very demanding clients, they do not mind spending, for example, 100€ on cream if they know it is worth it.

In fact, the interviewee mentioned that they already have some presence in Asia: they have some distributors in South Korea, Japan and China, some pop-up shops (shops opened for a specific purpose, managed by CASTLE or by its suppliers and which, after some time, may or may not remain in the same place or even close), namely in Hong-Kong.

In total, CASTLE exports around 80% of its production. Naturally, the most popular products vary from market to market. Generally speaking, the collections that are top sales abroad, especially on the European and American continents, are Ruby Red, which is inspired by the so well-known Port Wine, and Gold & Blue, inspired by traditional Portuguese tiles. In Asia, White Crane stands out, a collection inspired precisely by Asia. In Portugal, the *Sardinha* [sardine] collection is particularly appreciated for its underlying cultural issue.

Alongside this, it should be noted that CASTLE operates in two distinct ways: it has its own brands but it also produces for some foreign brands. The latter arises through clients who contact the company with a concept for a collection in mind but do not have the means to produce it. In the past, sales to foreign brands represented a large percentage of the company's exports; today it is the company's own brands that are most sought after by nationals and internationals.

Until now, CASTLE has entered the foreign market only through exportation. It is known that the company sells its products abroad through its website (online shop) and through the physical points of sale of its distributors because the company does not have its own shop abroad. In this sense, to distribute to the points of sale, CASTLE works with logistics companies. There is therefore no other intermediary between the company and the client, either nationally or internationally. So that this whole process runs smoothly and satisfies all the parties, CASTLE carefully assesses all the companies that want to be their distributors so that it does not harm the distributors they already have. The shops present in foreign countries are normally located in more sophisticated commercial areas with a high level of affluence, which serve an upper-middle/high-class public, and aesthetically suit the image that CASTLE wants to transmit to its clients.

For CASTLE, it is a matter of pride to show foreign countries what is made in Portugal and the people that make it. In this way, it is clear the importance the company gives to its employees, who wrap millions of soaps per year by hand, since, by choice, they do not have machines for that purpose. In addition, Portugal is considered a fashionable country, so making culture and traditions known through cosmetics is something that attracts people.

However, entering certain foreign markets has its obstacles, particularly at the legal level. In the USA, for example, CASTLE cannot export some products (e.g., diffusers) because above a certain level of alcohol the items are not accepted, at least not by air. As for China, trademark registrations are complex, so some companies trying to enter this market find out that the trademarks have already been registered. Besides this, CASTLE needs to have some adaptation capacity to meet deadlines and rationalize everything so that the products do not lose their quality and characteristics during the export process. It is also necessary to take into account that markets change, as well as the way consumers view products.

For CASTLE, it is fundamental to establish contact networks before entering markets, and this is something that greatly facilitates entry into them. In fact, the solid relationships that the company still maintains today with the big markets are part of its internationalization strategy and arose before entering the countries in question.

In some cases, the relationships established between CASTLE and its distributors are managed by companies, such as in Spain. In this country, CASTLE has a company that helps them do market management, which facilitates the distribution of their products. In other markets/countries, the company's relationships are mostly based on advice, contacts or people who know people. In rarer but also possible cases, some relationships have arisen purely by chance.

In this last situation, the interviewee gave the example of the beginning of a relationship in which the director of one of the company's departments, during a visit to Porto, met a man from Hong Kong trying to buy a train ticket and decided to help him. During this moment, they talked about several topics, including CASTLE. So, through this interaction, a business opportunity arose and became a reality and, nowadays, this man's company is the main distributor of CASTLE products in Hong Kong. Taking this into consideration, it can be said that some CASTLE relationships have opened international opportunities that were not planned.

Generally speaking, the internationalization strategy of the company has remained the same over time, with the presence at international fairs being highlighted, as it is possible to make CASTLE known to countries all over the world. Missing, for example, *Maison & Objet*, in Paris, will certainly have an economic and commercial impact on the company. To date, CASTLE has not exited any foreign markets, which shows that the internationalization strategy has worked relatively well, and, for this reason, the company does not intend to change it.

CASTLE generally adopts a standardization strategy because, as they are present in many countries, it would be complicated, both in terms of logistics and product management, to adapt all the products to each country, or even to create different products for each one. However, there are occasional cases of product adaptation, although these are minimal. They try to follow trends and be ahead of competitors to create collections that reflect the cultural and aesthetic context of the time, not only in Portugal but also abroad. An example of this is the White Crane collection which mixes Portuguese ceramics with Asian influences.

According to the interviewee, the biggest difference between Portugal and the other countries where they operate is the fact that Portugal is more traditional and reserved. However, this is not a negative factor, as CASTLE has products to serve this type of client. Nevertheless, it is necessary to adjust its production a little in order to globalize it so that it can serve all markets, and this constitutes a challenge for the company.

Given these differences, CASTLE needs to be able to adapt to them. So, the company has distributors in the countries where it operates with whom they are in constant contact in order to be the link between CASTLE and the clients in all the countries, for example, the distributor can explain more effectively to the clients why there is a sardine-shaped product. This way of business makes it much easier for the company to connect with its customers. If CASTLE itself made this connection, it would not work so well.

CASTLE does not have any subsidiary established abroad, either in production or in the commercial or financial department, so it relies only on its distributors, as has already been mentioned. It is not the company's intention to establish any subsidiary abroad soon, in other words, it is not part of the company's strategy at the moment. So, it can be said that all CASTLE products are produced in Portugal; only some components of the products may not be made in the country of origin, for example, the palm oil that is used to produce soaps. However, the final CASTLE product is 100% made in Portugal.

In the words of the interviewee, the founder did not accept the challenge of creating the company thinking that, later, this would be his life's work. He simply accepted it thinking that it was a temporary project, created with the well-defined purpose of producing exclusively for the American brand, and so he never imagined the global reach that the brand would have. Having said this, the interviewee believes that the company was not born "global", although it later registered a global reach. However, this subject will be discussed in more detail below.

DISCUSSION

CASTLE's Positioning in Internationalization Models

As it was founded with the purpose of creating products exclusively for a foreign customer, CASTLE has been an international company since its inception. However, its internationalization is considered passive, because the company was subcontracted to sell its products abroad for several years, and did not try to internationalize by itself as generally happens. Therefore, this company started opposite to normal: it started selling abroad first and, only later, in 2008, it focused on the domestic market. For this reason, it can be said that it had an irregular internationalization process.

CASTLE is an example that internationalization is not always a unidirectional, linear and incremental process in which companies first focus on the domestic market for a while, and only then expand internationally, as Carlos et al. (2021) mention.

In order to understand CASTLE's position with regard to the internationalization model, table 1 was prepared, adapting the "yes" or "no" answers taking into account CASTLE's internationalization process. Thus, in table 1, a comparison is made and a parallel is established between several internationalization models: Uppsala, BG, BAG and BR.

Concerning the moment of internationalization, and as explained above, CASTLE could be considered a Born Global or a Born Regional since its internationalization started right at the beginning. However, it would be a passive Born Global or a passive Born Regional, since internationalization was not the objective for the creation of the company; it emerged naturally, when responding to a proposed challenge, as will be discussed below. Thus, and for the reasons already explained, the Uppsala Model does not fit CASTLE's internationalization strategy in this topic.

Regarding the motivations for internationalization, the objective for the establishment of the company was not the search for resources or the search for the market, nor the internationalization, since this was only to respond to a challenge launched to the founder of CASTLE. Therefore, the Uppsala Model and the Born Global perspective are excluded here. However, the following must be taken into account:

- Depending on the moment under analysis, the Born Again Global perspective can be considered: the moment of creation of the company did not result from a "critical incident", but the moment when the first customer stopped being interested in the products (leaving CASTLE without any customers) can actually be considered a "critical incident" because it forced the company to re-think its strategy in order to survive.

- Likewise, depending on the moment under analysis, the BR perspective can also be considered: it can be said that in the first phase, the motivation for internationalization was not market search, as the company was subcontracted on an exclusive basis, but the direction that the company took later did lead it to search for other markets.

Regarding the volume of sales abroad, CASTLE always registered more than 25% of sales abroad in relation to the total turnover, both in its initial phase (when it exported 100%) and after its "strategic change", from the moment it started selling to the domestic market, which currently represents around 20%, against the 80% of the volume of sales abroad. Thus, any of the models fits CASTLE's situation in this subject.

Concerning the presence in international markets, CASTLE did not limit its presence exclusively to foreign markets geographically and/or culturally close or distant. Therefore, its presence is considered global since it can be found both in nearby markets and geographically and culturally distant markets. In this way, the Born Global perspective is the only one that fits the company in this topic.

As far as the speed of internationalization is concerned, it can be considered fast in the first phase of the company, since it started selling abroad right from the beginning. However, the company later went through a lethargic period: after the American client cancel the contract, CASTLE was from 2003 to 2008 selling only to American brands and to Zara Home (as mentioned by the interviewee). From 2008 onwards, there was a sudden and rapid internationalization, as CASTLE started selling to several markets at the same time. For this reason, the Uppsala Model and the Born Again Global are the ones that do not fit CASTLE's position.

Finally, regarding the company's entry modes abroad, exports stand out but also local networks which, through contacts, allowed CASTLE to enter more easily in some of the markets. Because of this, the Born Global and the Born Regional perspectives reflect the company's situation on this topic.

With this analysis, we can conclude that there is no typology in which CASTLE fits perfectly since none of the typologies analyzed in table 1 fully reflects the company's path and situation. CASTLE has a unique and somewhat unusual internationalization process and, therefore, calls into question the theories proposed in the literature. However, the closest model would be Born Global, in a passive way, although in terms of resources and internal competences the company does not fulfill these requirements.

Table 1. CASTLE's positioning in internationalization models

Characteristics	Uppsala Model	Born Global	Born Again Global	Born Regionals
Moment of internationalization	After developing the domestic market	Up to three years after the start of operations	No time limit, but normally late internationalization	Up to three years after the start of operations
	No	Yes	No	Yes
Motivations for internationalization	Search for resources and market	It is the initial objective for the creation of the company	As a result of "critical incidents"	Market search
	No	No	Initially—No Later—Yes	Initially—No Later—Yes
Sales volume abroad	No established rule	More than 25% of turnover	More than 25% of turnover in the three years following the strategic change	More than 25% of turnover
	Yes	Yes	Yes	Yes
Presence in international markets	Foreign markets geographically and/or culturally close	Global markets	Foreign markets geographically and/or culturally close	Foreign markets geographically and/or culturally close
	No	Yes	No	No
Speed of internationalization	Slow and incremental	Fast	Fast and sudden internationalization after a lethargic period. Several markets at the same time	Fast
	No	Yes	No	Yes
Entry modes	Low export commitment and gradual evolutionary perspective. First exports, then foreign presence	Export and local networks	Acquisition of distribution and/or market subsidiaries	Exports and local networks
	No	Yes	No	Yes

CASTLE's Motives to Internationalize

CASTLE's motives for entering international markets can be considered reactive or proactive, depending on the moment to which it refers. At first, in 2003, when the company lost the only customer to whom it sold, the reasons for internationalization were reactive. This is because CASTLE was forced to look for new customers (otherwise, it would not be able to survive) so internationalization was not directly desired by the company: it had to react to the situation it was faced with. In the second moment, when CASTLE had already established itself in the domestic market while working for world brands, the reasons to continue to internationalize and expand to new countries are considered proactive. In fact, at that time, the company was looking to further ensure its place in global markets, as well as to increase sales and market share.

CASTLE's Entry Modes

Until today, CASTLE entered the international market exclusively through exports, which represent around 80% of the company's sales volume. We also know that CASTLE sells its products to foreign countries in two ways: through the online store on the company's website, and through physical points of sale in the countries where it is present. Considering the distinction made in the framework section on what direct, indirect and own export modes are, we can say that CASTLE uses:

- Own export mode when it comes to online sales, as the company is responsible for promoting and distributing the products, establishing a direct relationship with the customer;
- Indirect export mode when it comes to exports to points of sale since the distributors are the ones who own the products, that is, they are the intermediaries between the company and the final customer and are responsible for the export process.

Facilitators for CASTLE's Entry Into International Markets

The factor that undoubtedly facilitates CASTLE's entry into foreign markets is the networks. As already mentioned, the interviewee stated that in some markets, networks effectively play a crucial role in the company's internationalization strategy, as they help to reduce risks. The solid relationships that the company maintains in these markets took place even before it entered them. In addition, it is known that the existing networks are essentially social, having emerged through personal knowledge and advice from close people. The situation that occurred at the train station in Porto—in which one of the company's members met the one who is now a CASTLE partner in Hong Kong—is a good example of a network that began as social and that, later, extended to business.

CASTLE's Standardization Strategy

According to CASTLE, Portugal is a traditional and reserved country, while other countries are more open to globalization. In this way, the products that CASTLE develops are suitable for all markets (that is, it follows a standardization strategy), as there is a need to globalize the products so that they can be distributed all over the world. However, if the company created products according to the market in which it would distribute them, that is, if it opted for an adaptation strategy, it could attract more customers, increasing its annual revenue.

As pointed out by the interviewee during the interview, this process would be very laborious and would require great flexibility from the company, which, given its size, would not be possible. In this way, the implementation of subsidiaries around the world would allow CASTLE to explore the possibility of adapting products, since the efforts would be shared, and each subsidiary would be responsible for developing and producing the products that suit its market.

Possibilities for the Future

As already mentioned, CASTLE does not have any subsidiaries abroad, which has both positive and negative consequences for the company. In fact, not having subsidiaries allows the company for greater control of the products, since all production is in one place and there is a greater personal approach to all orders placed with CASTLE due, for example, to the handmade packaging of all soaps. The reception of the components to produce the products is also facilitated since they are all directed to the same place, without the need to manage other deliveries, which can increase costs.

On the other hand, if the company had subsidiaries in strategic countries, it would facilitate different situations. By implementing a production subsidiary, for example in the USA, Canada or in a European country (as they are CASTLE's biggest markets), the distribution of products to countries close to these would be easier, with a reduction in distribution costs. If there were subsidiaries of the commercial department abroad, it would be possible to have closer and more dedicated contact with the distributors, as there would be face-to-face contact with them more often, strengthening relationships.

CASTLE adopted the strategy of supplying its products abroad through resellers, which facilitates its entry into different markets. However, it would also be beneficial for CASTLE to open its own stores abroad, giving customers the possibility to have a more personal experience with the brand. However, if the company switched to this strategy, it would be liable to lose its distributors, as they would become a competitor to them. If that happened, CASTLE might not be able to survive in the international market. Therefore, the current strategy is considered the best to maintain, as they have distributors responsible for selling their products and they reach international customers with their own brand through online sales and physical points of sale.

CONCLUSION

This chapter analyzes the internal and external context of CASTLE, as well as its international strategic formulation, based on an qualitative methodology. In conclusion, we must emphasize the crucial importance of networks and relationships as a facilitator of entry into international markets, which was verified in the case of CASTLE: first, by the knowledge that CASTLE's founder had of the American entrepreneur who challenged him to create the company, and, subsequently with the contacts that were established, some of them by mere chance, and which allowed easier entry into various markets (for example, the moment when a CASTLE employee helped a Chinese gentleman buy a ticket at a train station, which resulted in a Chinese client for CASTLE).

Another conclusion is that, at the moment, CASTLE's only way of entering foreign markets is through exports. Exports account for a large percentage of sales volume since the company only sells 20% of what it produces for the domestic market, and the remaining 80% is destined for export abroad.

As for the accessibility of products, these are available in their own stores in Portugal and in resellers' stores both in Portugal and abroad, as well as in the online store in a large number of countries. It is also concluded that CASTLE has opted for a strategy of standardization of products, all of which are produced in the country of origin.

CASTLE is, as analyzed, a company with a very particular development process, what causes some difficulties to its characterization in terms of Internationalization Model. For this reason, the main conclusion that we reached with this work is that internationalization is not always a linear process that all companies follow, and therefore it is not always possible to fit a company into one of the internationalization model typologies found in the literature, as is the case with CASTLE.

The objective of this chapter was to analyze CASTLE internationalization strategy and confront four different typologies regarding international path the company has followed. As a result of the literature review of the most suitable internationalization models—Uppsala Model, Born Global, Born Again

Global and Born Regional—it is possible to claim that the internationalization path that resembles the most with CASTLE's characteristics, is the Born Global. However, it is possible to argue that the internationalization process was irregular and adaptive over time and no single typology fits theory perfectly. Moreover, the Born Again Global is the typology that less fits CASTLE international path. This conclusion is based on the analysis of the interview and other secondary data that were summarized on table 1, based on the matching of characteristics of the firm's internationalization process and the information obtained during the research process.

The case study carried out took into account the theoretical models that resemble the most with CASTLE's characteristics and its learning paths and plans for the future. It is clear that theory hardly fits CASTLE situation as theories tend to be explanatory and the identification of the reality needs to be confronted with the theory under analysis and the firm's internationalization behavior.

REFERENCES

Al-Hyari, K., Al-Weshah, G., & Alnsour, M. (2012). Barriers to internationalisation in SMEs: Evidence from Jordan. *Marketing Intelligence & Planning, 30*(2), 188–211. doi:10.1108/02634501211211975

Andersson, S., Evers, N., & Gliga, G. (2018). Entrepreneurial marketing and born global internationalisation in China. *Qualitative Market Research, 21*(2), 202–231. doi:10.1108/QMR-11-2016-0115

Armstrong, R. W., & Sweeney, J. (1994). Industry type, culture, mode of entry and perceptions of international marketing ethics problems: A cross-cultural comparison. *Journal of Business Ethics, 13*(10), 775–785. doi:10.1007/BF00876258

Baum, M., Schwens, C., & Kabst, R. (2015). A latent class analysis of small firms' internationalization patterns. *Journal of World Business, 50*(4), 754–768. doi:10.1016/j.jwb.2015.03.001

Bell, J., McNaughton, R., Young, S., & Crick, D. (2003). Towards an Integrative Model of Small Firms Internationalisation. *Journal of International Entrepreneurship, 1*(4), 339–362. doi:10.1023/A:1025629424041

Calof, J. L., & Beamish, P. W. (1995). Adapting to foreign markets: Explaining internationalization. *International Business Review, 4*(2), 115–131. doi:10.1016/0969-5931(95)00001-G

Carlos, C. T., de Jesus, N. B., Henriques, R. N., & Moreira, A. C. (2021). Challenges of the Internationalization Process: A Case Study of a Knowledge-Intensive Service Company. In A. Moreira (Ed.), *Cases on Internationalization Challenges for SMEs* (pp. 65–82). IGI Global. doi:10.4018/978-1-7998-4387-0.ch004

Coviello, N. (2015). Re-thinking research on born globals. *Journal of International Business Studies, 46*(1), 17–26. doi:10.1057/jibs.2014.59

Deprey, B., Lloyd-Reason, L., & Ibeh, K. I. N. (2012). The internationalisation of small- and medium-sized management consultancies: An exploratory study of key facilitating factors. *Service Industries Journal, 32*(10), 1609–1621. doi:10.1080/02642069.2012.665899

Durão, V., & Moreira, A. C. (2019). Critical and inhibiting success factors in inter-organizational networks: A case study. In S. Teixeira & J. Ferreira (Eds.), *Multilevel Approach to Competitiveness in the Global Tourism Industry* (pp. 63–86). IGI Global.

Eisenhardt, K. M. (1989). Building theories from case study research. *Academy of Management Review*, *14*(4), 532–550. doi:10.2307/258557

Engelman, R., Zen, A. C., & Fracasso, E. M. (2015). The Impact of the Incubator on the Internationalization of Firms. *Journal of Technology Management & Innovation*, *10*(1), 29–39. doi:10.4067/S0718-27242015000100003

Gabrielsson, M., Kirpalani, V. H. M., & Luostarinen, R. (2002). Multiple channel strategies in the european personal computer industry. *Journal of International Marketing*, *10*(3), 73–95. doi:10.1509/jimk.10.3.73.19542

Hutchinson, K., Alexander, N., Quinn, B., & Doherty, A. M. (2007). Internationalization motives and facilitating factors: Qualitative evidence from smaller specialist retailers. *Journal of International Marketing*, *15*(3), 96–122. doi:10.1509/jimk.15.3.96

Hutchinson, K., Quinn, B., & Alexander, N. (2006). SME retailer internationalisation: Case study evidence from British retailers. *International Marketing Review*, *23*(1), 25–53. doi:10.1108/02651330610646287

Ietto-Gillies, G. (2012). *Transnational Corporations: Fragmentation Amidst Integration*. Routeldge.

Lopez, L. E., Kundu, S. K., & Ciravegna, L. (2009). Born global or born regional? Evidence from an exploratory study in the Costa Rican software industry. *Journal of International Business Studies*, *40*(7), 1228–1238. doi:10.1057/jibs.2008.69

Ojala, A. (2009). Internationalization of knowledge-intensive SMEs: The role of network relationships in the entry to a psychically distant market. *International Business Review*, *18*(1), 50–59. doi:10.1016/j.ibusrev.2008.10.002

Oviatt, B., & McDougall, P. (1994). Toward a theory of international new ventures. *Journal of International Business Studies*, *25*(1), 45–64. doi:10.1057/palgrave.jibs.8490193

Patton, M. Q. (2015). *Qualitative Evaluation and Research Methods*. Sage.

Paul, J., & Sánchez-Morcilio, R. (2019). Toward a new model for firm internationalization: Conservative, predictable, and pacemaker companies and markets. *Canadian Journal of Administrative Sciences*, *36*(3), 336–349. doi:10.1002/cjas.1512

Ribau, C. P., Moreira, A. C., & Raposo, M. (2015). Internationalisation of the firm theories: A schematic synthesis. *International Journal of Business and Globalisation*, *15*(4), 528–554. doi:10.1504/IJBG.2015.072535

Ribau, C. P., Moreira, A. C., & Raposo, M. (2018). SME internationalization research: Mapping the state of the art. *Canadian Journal of Administrative Sciences*, *35*(2), 280–303. doi:10.1002/cjas.1419

Ribau, C. P., Moreira, A. C., & Raposo, M. (2019). Multidyadic relationships: A multi-stage perspective. *Global Business and Economics Review*, *21*(6), 732–755. doi:10.1504/GBER.2019.102553

Roy, A., Sekhar, C., & Vyas, V. (2016). Barriers to internationalization: A study of small and medium enterprises in India. *Journal of International Entrepreneurship, 14*(4), 513–538. doi:10.100710843-016-0187-7

Schueffel, P., Baldegger, R., & Amann, W. (2014). Behavioral patterns in born-again global firms. *Multinational Business Review, 22*(4), 418–441. doi:10.1108/MBR-06-2014-0029

Silva, P., & Moreira, A. C. (2019). Subsidiary survival: A case study from the Portuguese electronics industry. *Review of International Business and Strategy, 29*(3), 226–252. doi:10.1108/RIBS-10-2018-0094

Stanisauskaite, V., & Kock, S. (2016). The dynamic development of international entrepreneurial networks. In H. Etemad, S. Denicolai, B. Hagen, & A. Zucchella (Eds.), *The changing global economy and its impact on international entrepreneurship* (pp. 119–135). Edward Elgar. doi:10.4337/9781783479849.00012

Vissak, T., & Francioni, B. (2013). Serial nonlinear internationalization in practice: A case study. *International Business Review, 22*(6), 951–962. doi:10.1016/j.ibusrev.2013.01.010

Weerawardena, J., Mort, G. S., Liesch, P. W., & Knight, G. (2007). Conceptualizing accelerated internationalization in the born global firm: A dynamic capabilities perspective. *Journal of World Business, 42*(3), 294–306. doi:10.1016/j.jwb.2007.04.004

Welch, D. E., Welch, L. S., Young, L. C., & Wilkinson, I. F. (1998). The importance of networks in export promotion: Policy issues. *Journal of International Marketing, 6*(4), 66–82. doi:10.1177/1069031X9800600409

Yin, R. (2014). *Case Study Research. Design and Methods.* Sage.

Zain, M., & Ng, S. I. (2006). The impacts of network relationships on SMEs' internationalization process. *Thunderbird International Business Review, 48*(2), 183–205. doi:10.1002/tie.20092

Zander, I., McDougall-Covin, P., & Rose, E. (2015). Born globals and international business: Evolution of a field of research. *Journal of International Business Studies, 46*(1), 27–35. doi:10.1057/jibs.2014.60

Zekiri, J., & Angelova, B. (2011). Factors that influence entry mode choice in foreign markets. *European Journal of Soil Science, 22*(4), 572–584.

ADDITIONAL READING

Moreira, A. C., & Alves, C. (2016). Commitment-trust dynamics in the internationalization process: A case study of market entry in the Brazilian market. In Information Resources Management Association (Ed.), International Business: Concepts, Methodologies, Tools, and Applications, (Volume 3, Chapter 57, pp. 1206-1229). IGI Global. doi:10.4018/978-1-4666-9814-7.ch057

Moreira, A. C., Silva, P., Mota, J. H., & Gadim, H. (2019). De-internationalization of SMEs: A Case Study. In A. C. Moreira & P. Silva (Eds.), *Handbook of Research on Corporate Restructuring and Globalization* (pp. 143–169). IGI Global. doi:10.4018/978-1-5225-8906-8.ch007

Mota, J. H., & Moreira, A. C. (2017). Determinants of the capital structure of Portuguese firms with investments in Angola. *Suid-Afrikaanse Tydskrif vir Ekonomiese en Bestuurswetenskappe*, *20*(1), a885. doi:10.4102ajems.v20i1.885

Ribau, C. P., Moreira, A. C., & Raposo, M. (2017). Export performance and the internationalisation of SMEs. *International Journal of Entrepreneurship and Small Business*, *30*(2), 214–240. doi:10.1504/IJESB.2017.081438

Ribau, C. P., Moreira, A. C., & Raposo, M. (2018a). Categorising the internationalisation of SMEs with social network analysis. *International Journal of Entrepreneurship and Small Business*, *35*(1), 57–80. doi:10.1504/IJESB.2018.094264

Ribau, C. P., Moreira, A. C., & Raposo, M. (2018b). Internacionalização de PME no Continente Americano: Revisão da Literatura. *Innovar (Universidad Nacional de Colombia)*, *28*(67), 59–73. doi:10.15446/innovar.v28n67.68613

Ribau, C. P., Moreira, A. C., & Raposo, M. (2019). The role of exploitative and exploratory innovation in export performance: An analysis of plastics industry SMEs. *European Journal of International Management*, *13*(2), 224–246. doi:10.1504/EJIM.2019.098149

KEY TERMS AND DEFINITIONS

Globalization: A global trend aimed at integrating economies, finances, trades, and communications is often depicted as the absence of trade restrictions among countries, which are eliminated through worldwide free trade deals and agreements between nations. This movement entails expanding from local and narrow-minded viewpoints to a more expansive perspective of a world that is interconnected and interdependent, with unhindered movement of capital, goods, and services across international borders, thereby leading to increased investment prospects.

Internationalization: The phenomenon of businesses expanding their presence in global markets through a deliberate strategy is known as internationalization. This strategy involves firms choosing to enter foreign markets in order to compete. Such internationalization typically involves transactions of goods, services, or resources between two or more firms or organizations situated in different countries.

Internationalization Process: The path a company takes as it moves from operating within a domestic market to targeting a specific foreign market involves various entry modes such as exports, foreign direct investment (FDI), franchising, and others, which can significantly impact the company's subsequent trajectory and the costs associated with internationalization. The two primary theories that explain this process are the Uppsala model and the network-based approach.

Uppsala Model: One of the highly debated dynamic theories in the Nordic School and International Business Studies pertains to the internationalization process of companies. Known as the Uppsala model, it elucidates the learning process of organizations and the influence of such learning on the companies' international expansion. This theory posits that a company's internationalization journey is gradual, progressing from non-regular exports to the eventual establishment of overseas entities.

Chapter 3
Organizational Transformation:
The Way to Sustainability

B. Anthony Brown
Independent Researcher, USA

Keri L. Heitner
Walden University, USA

ABSTRACT

Organizational leaders design and incorporate business models or processes to gain competitive advantage. These business models or methods detail how the organization operates to gain a competitive advantage and ultimately increase shareholders' wealth. Some business models incorporate unethical leadership and business practices at the expense of corporate social responsibility (CSR). The exclusion of CSR often eradicates stakeholders' value, leading to numerous unsustainable results. The disregard for CSR drives consequences inclusive of but limited to climate change, forced and child labor, poor workplace conditions, irreversible depletion of natural resources, gender inequality, absence of diversity and inclusion, pollution, and using tainted supply chains. Organizational leadership must transform business models to achieve sustainability. The lack of established frameworks and policing bodies to monitor organizations hinder the global thrust toward sustainable development growth.

INTRODUCTION

Organizational leaders often perform an organizational transformation to create organizational agility (Butler & Surace, 2015), especially strategic agility in hyper-competitive industries (Lewis et al., 2014). Organizational transformation can be in the form of planned or managed change, the difference being who executed the transformation process (Levy & Merry, 1986). Levy and Merry (1986) attributed planned transformation to external agents collaborating with organizational leadership; organizational leaders executed and managed transformation.

Organizational sustainability or sustainable development is growth that satisfies the present generation's requirements without adversely affecting future generations' ability to meet their needs (IISD,

DOI: 10.4018/978-1-6684-6845-6.ch003

n.d.; Wilkinson et al., 2001). Hence, organizational sustainability became relevant as a mode of business operation where corporate leaders must seek to satisfy current needs without disrupting the markets of the future (Boudreau & Ramstad, 2005). To promote organizational sustainability, leaders may attempt to orchestrate and drive a business model that generates holistic values consistent with the hyped long-term conservation and augmentation of financial, environmental, and social capital (Wales, 2013). In line with Wales (2013), promoting economic, environmental, and social capital is corporate social responsibility ([CSR], Aguinis & Glavas, 2012; Doane, 2005; Raimi et al., 2015); triple bottom line ([TBL], Slaper & Hall, 2011; The Economist, 2009); and the resurrected theme: environmental, social governance ([ESG], Maxwell, 2022; Munro & Van Drunen, 2022).

For some corporations, organizational sustainability is often solely verbally espoused but not featured as part of the corporate business model (Adler et al., 2008). To promote and maintain organizational sustainability, leaders must foster an organic organizational culture that generates holistic values in harmony with the long-term conservation and augmentation of financial, environmental, and social capital (Wales, 2013). Leaders must be more transparent with their business practices and do more than greenwashing (Adler et al., 2008, p. 144). There is a growing need for organizational leadersh to transform their shareholders' based business models into stakeholders' business process cultures. The new sustainable business model must consider environmental impacts such as climate change and effects on employees such as employee on-the-job deaths, including suicides, injuries, and layoffs (Barry, 2022; J. Chan, 2013; Flammer et al., 2021; Haiken, 2014; Maxwell, 2022).

In this chapter, we examine organizational transformation as a viable way to achieve sustainability. The purpose of this chapter is to review the benefits and challenges of transforming existing (shareholders') organizational business models to sustainable (stakeholders' oriented) business models, the roles and practicality of self-monitoring and self-reporting systems such as ESG, and any differences that exist by geographic location (the United States or international), industry sector, and size of the organization.

REVIEW OF THE LITERATURE AND LITERATURE SEARCH STRATEGY

Hammer (1990) coined and presented business process reengineering (BPR) as a business process transformation concept. The thrust of BPR is (a) disbanding legacy rules and practices, (b) exnovation, and (c) introduction of innovative processes versus automating ancient practices (Hammer, 1990). As a business process transformation concept, BPR focuses on transformation to increase process efficiency, with cost, growth, and control being secondary to quality, innovation, speed, and service (Gazova et al., 2016; Hammer, 1990). BPR, as a business process transformation concept, had no consideration for concepts such as TBL, CSR, ESG, and sustainability. BPR attracted mixed definitions and reviews (O'Neill & Sohal, 1999) and allowed for the birth of other process improvement concepts.

Subsequent process and quality improvement practices for the production and service industries included but were not limited to total quality management ([TQM], Pantouvakis & Psomas, 2016), business process management ([BPM], Hammer, 2015), enterprise resource planning ([ERP], AboAbdo et al., 2019; Addo-Tenkorang, 2011), just in time (JIT) lean management (Milewski, 2022), Motorola's six sigma (Chakraborty & Tan, 2012) and 'The Toyota Way' (Marksberry, 2011; Tsukada, 2013). As organization leaders discovered new ways to improve process efficiency, the cost of production decreased, allowing production volume to increase along with shareholders' wealth. Increased production volume necessitated (a) an increase in raw material supplies, (b) more and larger supply chains, and (c), subsequently, larger labor forces all around. None of the aforementioned business process modification concepts incorporated a CSR, TBL, or ESG organizational sustainability chromosome.

Sustainability surfaced in the 1980s and definitively in 1987, in the United Nations ([UN], 1987) Brundtland Commission Report. The definition adopted by the UN was and remains "sustainable development is the development that meets the needs of the present without compromising the ability of future generations to meet their own needs' (UN, 1987, p. 41). With time, social, human or cultural, economic, and environmental emerged as the four pillars of sustainability (Marco, 2021; RMIT University, 2017). Later literature condensed social, human, or cultural into *social* only and focused on environmental, social, and economic – the now-driven ESG concept.

The ESG concept has been around for years and recently re-emerged as a buzz theme (Maxwell, 2022). ESG denotes the three key factors (social and environmental performance and financial performance) considered when measuring the return performance of an investment in a business or company, considering sustainability and ethical impact (Daugaard, 2020). The incorporation of ESG to create sustainable business models (SBM) has gained new traction as organizational leadership appears to seek *new* responsibility ways to create a seamless relationship between environmental performance and social and financial performance (Kluza et al., 2021). However, measuring and reporting ESG is challenging as (a) the responsibility lies with leadership to use specific metrics to measure their organization's ESG compliance and impact (Haklová et al., 2020; Rajesh, 2020); and (b) the responsibility of voluntary self-monitoring and self-reporting leaves room for data manipulation (Fiaschi et al., 2020). Furthermore, the shareholders of some corporations remain resistive to disclosing the impact of their business model on the environment and social capital (Flammer et al., 2021; Munro & Van Drunen, 2022).

Scholars and practitioners provided copious literature on corporate social responsibility (CSR), similar to ESG (Doane, 2005). Leaders must practice corporate environmental and social responsibility while harvesting profits (Carroll, 1991; Doane, 2005; Raimi et al., 2015; Schwab, 2008). Doane (2005) explained that as a voluntary self-regulating process, CSR is promoted as a tool to address from labor guidelines and human rights violations to the reduction of greenhouse gas (GHG) emissions. Myths also plague CSR as an unconventional approach. Two of these myths are leaders' ethical performance improves with voluntary self-monitoring and self-reporting and that regulations and management systems will change corporate shareholders' behavior (Doane, 2005).

The triple bottom line (TBL) is another framework parallel to CSR and ESG (Elkington, 2004; Slaper & Hall, 2011). TBL, coined by Elkington (2004) in 1994, was introduced as an accounting framework encompassing three elements of performance: social, environmental, and financial – identical to ESG. Elkington posited that TBL differs from traditional reporting formats as TBL includes the ecological (or environmental) and social components missing from conventional accounting reporting. (Elkington, 2004; Slaper & Hall, 2011). Adding the social and ecological facets to the financial dimension earned TBL the theme of the three Ps: people, planet, and profits or the 3Ps.

The literature search process involved conducting searches of key terms and assessing the references associated with the results. The key search terms included but were not limited to business models, corporate social responsibility, triple bottom line, environmental, social, and governance; business process re-engineering, business process management, total quality management, just in time, six sigma, the Toyota way, innovation, exnovation, ethics, corporate ethics, climate change, global warming, greenwashing, sustainable development goals, shareholders' wealth, and stakeholders' value.

CASE DESCRIPTION

The overarching theme of sustainability translates to embracing significant changes in how humans treat the planet to avert irreparable damage. Organizational sustainability encompasses organization leadership's ability to maintain a trade-off between current economic demands and the future requirements of the environment (McCloy, 2019; UN, n.d.-d; Wales, 2013). Thus, organizational sustainability is becoming an inevitable corporate and global priority as the infinite quest for dominance over the biosphere is replaced by the challenge of achieving ecological balance (Wilkinson et al., 2001). In corporate and policy frameworks, leaders' sustainability business models must maintain a business process continuously over time to (a) avoid the exhaustion of natural or physical resources, so that said resources will remain available for the long term and (b) subsequently suppress climate change (UN, n.d.-f).

Between September 25 to 27, 2015, all UN Member States present at the United Nations Headquarters in New York adopted a shared blueprint for peace and prosperity for people and the planet for the present and the future (UN, n.d.-d). The blueprint incorporated 17 sustainable development goals (SDGs). The objective of the UN Member States' established 2030 Agenda for Sustainable Development is that by 2030, the world would be transformed into one governed by sustainability, incorporating (a) people, (b) planet, (c) prosperity, (d) peace, and (e) partnership (United Nations [UN], n.d.-f). The first three tenets of the UN 2030 Agenda for Sustainable Development mirror the 3Ps of the TBL concept. As The UN Member states advocate the 2030 Agenda for Sustainable Development, in line with achieving the 17 SDGs are (a) retarding climate change, (b) reduction in ocean abuse, and (c) deforestation (UN, n.d.-d).

On December 12, 2015, the United Nations Framework Convention on Climate Change (UNFCCC) adopted the 2015 Paris Agreement (UN, n.d.-c, n.d.-e). The 1992 UNFCCC report indicated that climate change is a change of climate attributed directly or indirectly to human activity that alters the composition of the global atmosphere, in addition to natural climate variability observed over comparable periods. Subsequently, the primary objective of the UNFCCC's 2015 Paris Agreement is to maintain, for this century, a global temperature rise well below 2 °C and as close as possible to 1.5 °C above pre-industrial levels (connect4climate, n.d.; UN, n.d.-a). The UNFCCC is recognized as the principal international, intergovernmental forum for negotiating the global response to climate change.

The definition of climate change adapted for this chapter is the long-term adverse shifts in the recordings of weather patterns such as temperature, precipitation, and wind patterns (UN, n.d.-g; U.S. Geological Survey [USGS], n.d.). The measurement of global earth temperature reveled that in 2017 the Earth's temperature was 1 °C higher than in the 1800s preindustrial era (Dietz et al., 2020). Presently, the Earth's overall temperature is approximately 1.1°C above said 1800s preindustrial period, with the warmest period, recorded being 2011 to 2020 (UN, n.d.-g). The increase in the Earth's temperature, known as global warming, is attributed to the global increase in GHG emissions (USGS, n.d.). GHG emissions comprise carbon-based gases emitted from fossil fuels, for example, coal, oil, and gas for global commercial production, emissions from motor vehicles, land clearing causing deforestation, and methane emissions from garbage landfills (UN, n.d.-g).

The UNFCCC's Paris Agreement signaled the reorientation towards a net-zero emissions world, making the implementation of the Paris Agreement crucial for the achievement of the UN's (17 SDGs) 2030 Agenda for Sustainable Development, and to subsequently retard climate change (UN, n.d.-e). Climate change also constitutes desertification caused by deforestation, polar ice caps melting, unusually increased floodings, and increasingly more intensive storm systems with longer storm seasons. (UN, n.d.-g). Other adverse consequences are that homes and entire communities are at risk due to rising sea levels, water scarcity, droughts, famines, and food insecurity, especially in developing nations (Berchin et al., 2017; Flammer et al., 2021; UN, n.d.-g). These adverse consequences promulgate an increase in displaced persons or climate refugees due to climate change (Berchin et al., 2017; Flammer et al., 2021; UN, n.d.-g). Within the 2030 Agenda for Sustainable Development, the tenets of one or more of the 17 SDGs correlate with alleviating these issues.

However, climate change is not the only consequence of global warming driven by unsustainable business practices. The Paris Agreement also explicitly recognized that sustainable production and consumption patterns would play a pivotal role in addressing climate change (connect4climate, n.d.; UN, n.d.-e). Unsustainable business processes give rise to or include poor working conditions, health issues arising from poor working environments, unemployment, questionable supply chain process and associated child and enslaved person (forced) labor; workplace gender inequality propagating the glass ceiling effect, resource procurement resulting in biodiversity loss, water scarcity, and deforestation and corporate financial maleficence resulting in employee pension erosion. Again, within the 2030 Agenda for Sustainable Development, one or more of the 17 SDGs are designed to tackle these issues.

Benefits of Transforming to Sustainable Business Models

While there are 17 SDGs, in this section, the focus will be on the benefits that could be derived from transforming unsustainable business models and activities (as listed in the last paragraph) by adapting the SDGs designed to transform the business model or practices to sustainable ones. The key SDGs for examination in this section are: (a) SDG 4 - ensure inclusive and equitable quality education and promote lifelong learning opportunities for all, (b) SDG 5 - achieve gender equality and empower all women and girls, (c) SDG 6 – Ensure availability and sustainable management of water and sanitation for all, and (d) SDG 8 - promote sustained, inclusive and sustainable economic growth, full and productive employment and decent work for all.

SDG 4: Ensure Inclusive and Equitable Quality Education and Promote Lifelong Learning Opportunities for All

Globally, more than 30% of the 160 million child laborers do not attend schools ((International Labour Organization [ILO], 2021). This exclusion contravenes SDG 4 - ensure inclusive and equitable quality education and promote lifelong learning opportunities for all (ILO, 2021). The COVID-19 pandemic resulted in school closures, thus driving some 8.6 million more children into child labor situations – some work in mines with their parents as the parent did not wish to leave their children unsupervised at home (ILO, 2021). ILO reports cited that once in employment, the resumption of education post-COVID-19 pandemic lockdown proved difficult for many (ILO, 2021).

SDG 5: Achieve Gender Equality and Empower All Women and Girls

Of the 6.3 million persons engaged in forced commercial sexual exploitation, women and girls account for 4.9 million or 77.8% of those persons (ILO, 2022b, 2022a). The 2022 ILO report on forced labor and forced marriages cited that in 2021, an estimated 22 million people were living in forced marriage (ILO, 2022b). Women and girls as young as 9 accounted for more than two-thirds or an estimated 14.9 million persons in forced marriages (ILO, 2022b). Women and girls in forced marriage are highly susceptible to violence, abuse, sexual exploitation, and other forms of forced labor (ILO, 2022b). Forced marriage as a form of modern slavery is a global issue in developed and developing nations, straddling nearly all socio-economic, cultural, and religious frontiers (ILO, 2022b).

Collectively, 19.8 million women and girls either admitted into commercial sexual exploitation or bonded in forced marriages, if not rescued and liberated, may (a) never experience the benefits of SDG 4 - ensure inclusive and equitable quality education and promote lifelong learning opportunities (ILO, 2021, 2022b). Additionally, these disenfranchised women may never experience being educated as a fundamental human right and subsequently make meaningful economic contributions in a world already dwarfed by the insufficient presence of Diversity and Inclusion (Kapur, 2019; Koengkan et al., 2022).

Education at the basic level of reading, writing, and numeracy is fundamental to lifelong learning opportunities, which women and girls are often deprived of (UN, n.d.-b). Denying young girls of education is often the precursor for the proliferation of lifelong gender inequality. The consequences usually range from future adulthood and personal and family poverty to stymied national economies (especially in developing nations); and collectively uneven global economic growth (Esen & Seren, 2021; Koengkan et al., 2022). Aside from forced labor, child labor, and forced marriage, numerous factors prohibit educating girls who grow up to become uneducated women (Kapur, 2019). Factors include but are not limited to poverty, traditional practices, and lack of proper school infrastructure (Kapur, 2019).

Poverty adversely affects gender equality and education (Kapur, 2019). Boys and girls born to impoverished parents often struggle with less-than-average health and malnutrition (American Association of University Women [AAUW], 2020). They make their debut appearance at the school gates already at a disadvantage – if the girls make it to school. Overcrowded and inadequate school facilities, such as lack of proper infrastructure, including toilets, are challenging issues. Even with free and public education, other associated costs are unaffordable to parents. Insufficient and lack of trained and qualified teachers, no money for lunch and transportation (considering that many children may not have food at home), and inadequate textbooks and stationery are but some of the challenges encountered during the schooling years (Walker et al., 2019). Girls who somehow make it through the school gates are often withdrawn before or at the expense of a bother, marking a dismal end to what could have been a stellar future (Walker et al., 2019).

Traditional practices often engulfed in poverty in developing nations are critical drivers of educational gender inequity (ILO, 2022b). In many parts of the world, family or cultural tradition bears the perception that girls hold little or no economic value for their own families and society (ILO, 2022b). Subsequently, girls' only value is their future role as mothers and wives; formal education for girls is of no value for them to succeed in their future roles as mothers and wives. Due to poverty and scarce resources, in families with children of both gender, the future part of a son is often one of patriarchal values - to ascend to head of the family (ILO, 2022b). The son's predestined future role is a preconceived notion of superior earning potential making his formal education a priority over that of his sister(s) (ILO, 2022b). Thus in many nations and cultures the default decision (and solution) due to poverty is to formally educate sons and train daughters at home to become future homemakers.The preceding is a generational loop for millions of the world's poorest girls whose stellar future is replaced by a life of struggle probably inclusive of child labor, graduating to forced labor due to the absence of education.

The Glass Ceiling and Salary Disparities

Many girls who attained proper formal education up to the tertiary level mature into permanently marginalized women of the infamous *minority* society club as they struggle to secure suitable employment opportunities in their respective professional fields (Chisholm-Burns et al., 2017; Ezzedeen et al., 2015). In both developed and developing nations, women remain discriminated against regarding promotions to the management and executive management levels. Often they are denied empowerment opportunities as they are repeatedly passed over for promotions to the "C" Suite – chief executive officer (CEO), chief financial officer (CFO), and chief operations officer (COO). Women rarely break through the notorious *glass ceiling* – a colloquial term that refers to that upper limit above which many women never ascend to reach the "C" suite despite their superior capabilities compared to men in the same organization in identical, lower, or even higher positions (Cook & Glass, 2014; Wesarat & Mathew, 2017).

For example, the 2022 list of Fortune 500 companies comprises a paltry 4.8% of women CEO on a list of 500 corporations spanning countries, including the United States, Germany, the United Kingdom, and China (Hinchliffe, 2022b). The women CEO numbered 44 and worked for United States corporations – a figure dubbed a record high for women CEOs (Hinchliffe, 2022a). While considered a significant achievement, there was not much to celebrate in the *global women in leadership biosphere* considering that (a) the Fortune 500 listing began in 1955, (b) 1972 saw the first Fortune 500 woman CEO, and (c) the 2021 listing recorded the first two black women CEO – a year when women CEO represented only 4.1% of total Fortune 500 CEOs. Globally and particularly in developing nations including Latin America and the Caribbean (LAC), workplace gender bias blatantly replaces Diversity and Inclusion (Ayman & Korabik, 2010), as senior-level leadership covertly and overtly excludes women of all ethnicity, race, and culture from having a say in corporate decision-making matters and expressing their viewpoints and perspectives (B. A. Brown & Heitner, 2022; Eagly & Chin, 2010).

The gender salary gap remains a valid contentious matter (Abendroth et al., 2017). Due to gender inequality, globally, women earn lower wages than men performing similar roles in the same organization (Nopo, 2012; Wiler et al., 2022). The gender salary disparity phenomenon straddles all nations. Today in the United States, a woman earns 83 cents for every dollar a man earns, compared to 82.3 cents in 2019, suggesting a slight and insufficient closure of the gender salary disparity (AAUW, 2020). The gap continues and widens in retirement as women receive 70 cents for every dollar a man gets (AAUW, 2020). The fact that women earn lower salaries than men allows for lower pension and social security contributions, thus the widened difference in the retirement era (AAUW, 2020).

The data in the preceding paragraph did not account for the COVID-19 pandemic. Furthermore, research indicates that the pandemic negatively impacted women's employment security more adversely than men, especially in developing nations, as in the LAC (B. A. Brown & Heitner, 2022). Outside the workplace, discrimination and gender inequality continue as women classified as minorities based on gender, race, and ethnicity are discouraged from participating in social, economic, cultural, and political activities and are often denied the right to own property (Kapur, 2019; UN, n.d.-b).

The success of the Paris Agreement and the UN 2030 Agenda for Sustainable Development requires an immense amount of human resources – girls and women on a global, colossal scale, as Diversity, Inclusion, and culture matter (Downey et al., 2015; Farndale et al., 2015). Thus the fundamental benefit of educating girls is eliminating gender inequality, as achieving gender equality sets the stage for the equal participation of more girls and women of all ages globally. Empowering girls and women allows for more decision-makers' involvement, especially regarding race, ethnicity, and culture (Heitner, 2018), required to propel the changes set out in the Paris Agreement and the UN 2030 Agenda for Sustainable Development. There is a need for corporate and international assistance to alleviate the inequities surrounding educating girls. Corporate leadership needs to transform its business models and conventional thinking to address gender bias and the gender salary gaps in the workplace to improve corporate success like TBL and CSR (Chung, 2015; The International Economy, 2017). A benefit of transforming business processes regarding paying fair wages to women is improved TBL and for women to make better contributions towards their pension and enjoy a decent retirement as eligible men do.

SDG 6: Ensure Availability and Sustainable Management of Water and Sanitation for All

Approximately 99% of all liquid freshwater on Earth is groundwater (UN, 2022a, 2022b). Groundwater is rainfalls seeping through the Earth's surface and accumulating deep underground in porous spaces, cracks, and crevices, forming a collective aquifer (Denchak, 2022). Despite surface water availability, such as rivers, lakes, and oceans, groundwater has the most extraordinary capacity to provide global nations with immense socio-economic and environmental benefits, including climate change adaptation and SDG achievement (UN, 2022a).

Agriculture, inclusive of irrigation and livestock rearing, accounts for 70% of water use worldwide and over 40% in many Organisation for Economic Co-operation and Development (OECD) countries, making agriculture the most significant consumption of groundwater and surface water (Khokhar, 2017; OECD, n.d.) Human settlement constitutes the second-largest consumption of groundwater. Groundwater (a) accounts for approximately 49% of the total volume of water for global domestic consumption, (b) serves as the sole source of drinking water for the vast majority of the global rural population without public or private supply systems, and (c) constitutes approximately 25% of all water used for supplying 38% of land irrigated globally (UN, 2022a). For reference, (a) groundwater constitutes approximately 40% of potable water in the United States (Denchak, 2022), (b) Asia and the Pacific consume 60% of the world's groundwater, while (c) groundwater comprises 30% of all freshwater usage in the LAC (UN, 2022a).

Industrial use, such as commercial production, then mining constitutes the third largest groundwater consumption. For example, in the trending realms of renewable energy, lithium is a mined mineral used in the production of batteries used in electric vehicles and storing solar power for green facilities. Currently, the largest mined lithium deposits come from developing South American nations, mainly Bolivia, Chile, and Argentina (Campbell, 2022). The next biggest lithium-producing country is the United States, followed closely by Australia and China, with minute deposits in Zimbabwe, Brazil, and Portugal, the only European nation (Campbell, 2022; Penn et al., 2021). The lithium mining and extraction process requires water evaporation via evaporation ponds accounting for approximately 21 million liters per day, resulting in a behemoth of 2.2 million liters (2,200 tons) of water to produce just one ton of lithium (Campbell, 2022). Due to the massive amounts of water required for lithium mining in Chile, there is an ongoing scarcity of water and multiple community water-related conflicts, particularly in Toconao in northern Chile (Campbell, 2022).

Undoubtedly, the three primary uses of groundwater are the significant sources of its pollution (UN, 2022a). Rainfall flowing into groundwater and surface water takes with it farm and livestock waste, pathogens, carcinogens, traces of insecticides, herbicides, and fungicides; nitrates from fertilizer and enriched nutrients causing eutrophication in lakes and reservoirs (McPhillips, 2019; UN, 2015, 2022a,

2022b; WHO, 2022). Some developing nations do not have proper sanitation and toilets, making open defecation a norm (McPhillips, 2019; WHO, 2022). Consequently, untreated sewage (wastewater) makes its way into both surface water and groundwater either via rainwater runoff or direct dumping into surface waters which ultimately seeps into groundwater (McPhillips, 2019; WHO, 2022). Documented evidence of industrial groundwater pollution includes General Electric's (GE) overt pollution of Newg York's Hudson River. Over a period spannng 30 years ending in 1977, GE pumped wastewater from two manufacturing plants into the Hudson River, resulting groundwater contamination (Environmental Protection Agency [EPA], 2022a; National Oceanic and Atmospheric Administration [NOAA], 2015).

Access to clean water is a fundamental, non-negotiable human right (UN, n.d.-b). However, in 2005 while Nestlé flourished as the largest producer of bottled water, the incumbent CEO Peter Brabeck-Letmathe presented opposing views (Emery, 2018). While speaking on water privatization, he declared that (a) it is an extreme solution to believe that human beings should have a right to water and (b) water like food-stuff water should have a market value (Andrei, 2017; Confino, 2013; Emery, 2018). In the 1970s, Nestlé aggressively promoted their baby powdered milk formula over breastfeeding in developing nations, especially African nations, without access to clean water and sanitation (Andrei, 2017). Nestlé is a reoccurring decimal regarding lack of CSR towards customers and known association with supply chains involving modern slavery and the worst forms of child labor (Andrei, 2017; Kelly, 2016; NORC, 2020).

Groundwater is the key source of domestic water supply globally, and its pollution affects everyone as all wastewater has the potential to seep into and contaminate groundwater. According to the WHO (2022), globally, approximately 829,000 persons die annually from diarrhea as a result of unsafe drinking water, sanitation, and hand hygiene. The UN (2015 cited that (a) 2 million tons of sewage and other effluents drain into the world's waters daily and (b) annually unsafe water accounts for more deaths than all forms of violence, including war combined. Organizational transformation to shift from unsustainable to sustainable business models is imminently required of corporations that (a) intentionally or otherwise cause the discharge wastewater in a manner that could contaminate the world's groundwater as once contaminated groundwater may remain contaminated forever (UN, 2022a). The governments of the requisite nations also need to act fast and provide proper sanitation infrastructure to end open defecation and implement appropriate sewage treatment facilities.

Globally, the reliance on groundwater abstracted for human consumption will only increase, predominantly due to rising water demand by all sectors and increasing variation in rainfall patterns climate change (UN, 2022b). Consequently, corporations globally relying on groundwater for agriculture, production, and mining must exhibit responsible groundwater consumption. The current groundwater storage depletion rate is at its fastest as today's intensive abstraction rate far exceeds its recharge rate (UN, 2022a). Additionally, climate change results in severe adverse rainfall variations to former rainfall patterns, which exacerbates the retarded recharge rate of groundwater aquifers (Denchak, 2022; UN, 2015). Researchers projected that by 2050 the global population would reach 9 billion people, requiring an estimated 50% increase in demand for agricultural products such as food, and feed relative to 2012 levels (Khokhar, 2017; UN, 2022b). This 2050 projected demand will require a 15% increase in groundwater abstraction (Khokhar, 2017; UN, 2022a).

There are immense benefits in transforming to sustainable organizational practices incorporating responsible consumption, mainly responsible consumption of groundwater. Water, particularly groundwater, is vital to poverty aversion, eliminating water and food insecurities, creating decent jobs, socioeconomic development, and the resilience of societies and economies to climate change (UN, 2015,

2022a). Sustainable organizational practices incorporating responsible consumption provide further benefits inclusive not limited to (a) reducing and preventing droughts, (b) preventing groundwater conflicts between communities, (c) preventing rapid depletion of groundwater aquifers, and (d) averting land collapsing in regions with landscape and soil types susceptible to deformation in response to variations in groundwater pressure (UN, 2022a, pp. 34–35).

Sustainability (based on the 17 SDGs) emphasizes responsible consumption today to preserve resources for future needs and requires immediate and intense attention from all sectors. Organizational transformation to shift from unsustainable to sustainable business models regarding groundwater consumption and preservation is imminently required of corporations and governments that (a) intentionally or otherwise cause the discharge of wastewater in a manner that could contaminate the world's groundwater and (b) exhibit irresponsible consumption of groundwater (UN, 2022a).

SDG 8: Promote Sustained, Inclusive, and Sustainable Economic Growth, Full and Productive Employment, and Decent Work for All

SDG 8 target 7 is to end child labor in all its forms by 2025 and eliminate forced labor, modern slavery, and human trafficking by 2030 (UN, n.d.-b, 2019). Johnson (2015) posited that there are more than 20 million victims of human trafficking. Trafficking in people or human trafficking intersects with forced labor, child labor, and the worst forms of child labor, forced marriages, commercial sexual exploitation, and modern slavery (ILO, 2022b, 2022a). According to the ILO (2022a, 2022b) 2021 global estimates report, (a) a total of 49.6 million people were living in modern slavery, (b) 27.6 million of that 49.6 million people were engaged in forced labor, and (c) 17.3 million of the said total were subjected to exploitation in the private sector. The report further cited that forced commercial sexual exploitation accounted for 6.3 million persons, of which women and girls account for 4.9 million of those in forced commercial sexual exploitation (ILO, 2022b, 2022a).

In this chapter, forced labor refers to all persons admitted into labor involuntarily by coercion, violence, deception, destitution, or threat. Specific reference to such persons as laborers below age 18 will take on the term child labor or forced child labor. Forced labor punctuates industries such as services (for example, hotels and spas but excludes domestic working), manufacturing, construction, agriculture, fishing, domestic working, quarry and mining, commercial sexual exploitation, begging, and other illicit activities (UN, 2019). For example, while fighting child labor lawsuits in Ivory Coast, Nestlé admitted to sourcing fish for its cat food line from the Thailand fishing industry – one known for human trafficking and slave labor (Kelly, 2016). Thus forced labor, even for persons 18 years and older, is a deterrent to promoting sustained, inclusive, and sustainable economic growth, full and productive employment, and decent work for all (ILO, 2022b, 2022a; Johnson, 2015).

The increased poverty climate proliferated by the COVID-19 pandemic, especially in developing nations, created job losses and increased destitution (ILO, 2022a, 2022b; UN, 2019). Destitution ushers in vulnerability allowing poverty-stricken persons to fall prey to coercion and false promises of a better life, thus increasing human trafficking, forced marriages for both genders below age 18, forced labor, and the worst forms of child labor (ILO, 2022a, 2022b; UN, 2019). If not extracted from forced marriages and slave labor, such persons may never realize their full potential and have decent employment outside modern slavery (ILO, 2022a). Another deterrent to promoting sustained, inclusive and sustainable economic growth, full and productive employment, and decent work for all in developing nations is child labor (ILO, 2021, 2022c; Johnson, 2015; Paikah et al., 2021). According to the ILO (2022c), more than 160 million children serve as child laborers.

The ILO 1973 Minimum age Convention sets the standard for the minimum age for persons admitted for employment (ILO, n.d.-a, n.d.-b, n.d.-c). Under article 2 of the Worst Forms of Child Labour Convention, 1999 (No. 182), ILO (n.d.-b, n.d.-c) defined a child as a person below the age of 18. The ILO (n.d.-a) also set other age standards where persons below age 18 can be admitted for light work in cases where the economy and educational facilities are insufficiently developed. Under article 3 of the Minimum Age Convention, 1973 (No. 138), 18 is the minimum age at which a person can be admitted for any type of hazardous employment which can potentially endanger the health, safety, or morals of young persons (ILO, n.d.-a).

The ILO (2021) 2020 estimates showed that 63 million girls and 97 million boys aged 5 to 17 years are admitted to child labor globally. Of the total 160 million children (meaning 1 in every 10 children) aged 5 to 17 years admitted in child labor, (a) 79 million (nearly half) work as children in hazardous environments which directly endangers their health, safety, and moral development and (b) 3.3 million of these children are forced child laborers (ILO, 2021, 2022b). While the ILO report indicated improvements in the most affected areas, such as Asia, the Pacific, and Latin America, the numbers consistently increased in sub-Saharan African nations – the region with child labor numbers exceeding the rest of the world combined (ILO, 2021). The ILO (2021) recorded a summary increase of 168 million child laborers aged 5 to 11 years in 2020 compared to 2016 and estimated that due to poverty proliferated by the COVID-19 pandemic, an additional 8.9 million children will be in child labor by the end of 2022. While child labor can be intergenerational – passed down through families as a traditional means of employment, there is still harm to children. (alliance8.7, 2022).

While agriculture accounts for the highest rate of child labor (forced, intergenerational, or otherwise), child labor is also evident in hazardous mining, commercial sexual exploitation, manufacturing, forced marriages, domestic street peddling, begging, and working in kiosks and shops (Andrei, 2017; Fetuga et al., 2005; ILO, 2021). Child labor is associated with the African nation of Côte d'Ivoire (Ivory Coast) supply chains, from which Nestlé procures its cocoa to manufacture chocolate (Andrei, 2017; Clarke, 2015). Cadbury chocolate manufacturers are associated with child labor in cocoa farms in Ghana (Hinch, 2018; Rowselle, 2022). Child labor in the Ghanian and Ivory Coast cocoa growing industry is classified among the worst forms of child labor (in hazardous employment) as children use sharp machetes and often sustain accidental self-inflicted wounds and (b) children laborers on some farms in the Ivory Coast are trafficked from Burkina Faso, Guinea, and Mali and forced into labor (Rowselle, 2022; Sisso, 2019; U.S. Department of Labor [DOL], n.d.).

Apple, Google, Dell, Microsoft, and Tesla have been named as defendants in lawsuits for their complicit actions regarding the death of forced child laborers in cobalt mines in the Democratic Republic of the Congo (DRC) (Amnesty International, 2016; Kelly, 2019). While these companies may not own the cobalt mines, the lawsuit detailed that the corporations aided and abetted the tainted supply chains of mining companies by knowingly procuring the cobalt, which is a crucial component in batteries for their products (Kelly, 2019). Engaging children under age 18 in mining operations, resulting in severe injuries and death, qualifies as the worst form of child labor (DOL, n.d.).

The admission of children into (forced) child labor by default excludes over 30% of said child laborers from schools which eventually contravenes SDG 4 - ensuring inclusive and equitable quality education and promoting lifelong learning opportunities for all (ILO, 2021). The benefit of achieving SDG target 8.7 is the liberation of enslaved people so they can attain and experience full and productive employment and decent work. The contravention of SDG 4 is further exacerbated by a perpetuation of adult forced, or slavery labor (ILO, 2022a, 2022b; Johnson, 2015) as children admitted in some of the worst forms of child labor often become adults still engaged in forced labor (ILO, 2022c). Nestlé (subconsciously) recognized the loss of childhood and irreparable endangering of young persons' health, safety, or morals and initiated a program to pay an incentive to Ivory Coast and Ghanaian cocoa farmers to not engage in child labor, thus keeping children in schools and away from the cocoa farms (Allen, 2022).

Challenges With Implementing Sustainable Business Models

For organizational sustainability to be of merit, some tenets must be worth protecting, renewing, or restoring. Thus, protecting and ensuring a balance between environmental care, social well-being, and economic growth with constant ethical dimensions for the present and future illustrates the primary reason for driving organizational sustainability (Wilkinson et al., 2001). The ethically infused environmental care, social well-being, and economic growth posited by Wilkinson et al. (2001) echo the tenets of ESG. Consequently, sustainability and sustainability growth, as declared in the UN 2030 Agenda for Sustainable Development and based on the reduction of GHG emissions from global industrialization, deforestation, and other factors listed as part of the 17 SDGs, weighs heavily on organizational business process transformation.

Subsequently, meeting the 2030 Agenda for Sustainable Development will require transforming organizational business processes across countless corporations in developed and developing nations constituting the UN Member States. Transformation to a sustainable organizational culture will require eliminating old practices, infrastructures, and unsustainable technologies (Heyen et al., 2017; Kimberly, 1981). Hence, beyond the challenges of merging shareholders' and shareholder's values (Baumfield, 2016; Gelles & Yaffe-Bellany, 2019; Vinten, 2001) or transforming existing (shareholders') organizational business models to sustainable (stakeholders') business models (Baumfield, 2016), there are multiple challenges associated with creating and sustaining organizational sustainability. Some challenges are unethical leadership, unethical supply chain systems, availability of requisite technology in many developing nations, ESG implementation, monitoring and reporting within organizations, and the economic status of developing countries within the UN Member States.

To best understand the holistic benefits of complying with the Paris Agreement and the UN 2030 Agenda for Sustainable Development, it is necessary to reference past and ongoing examples of corporations' unsustainable business practices contradicting the Paris Agreement and the UN 2030 Agenda for Sustainable Development. Examples of corporate leaders' unethical transgressions, disregard for social responsibility and SDG include Monsanto's Agent Orange, cancer-linked Aspartame, and controversial dairy cow hormone (Anderson & Kariss-Nix, 2014); and Nestle's (a) denying knowledge of child labor in cocoa supply chains in Africa but admitting involvement in slave labor in Thailand's fishing industry, (b) promoting baby powdered milk formula over breastfeeding in developing nations without access to clean water, and (c) stating that access to clean water is not a public right (Andrei, 2017; Kelly, 2016). Others include the Challenger disaster (Hoke, 2013; Robison, 2002; Werhane, 1991), the cleanup fiasco post the Exxon Valdez grounding (Bowen & Power, 1993; Holusha, 1989), General Electric's polluting the Hudson River (EPA, 2022a), and Martha Stewart's cooking the books (Lomax, 2003). The 2008 global financial crisis (Bridgman, 2010), mass employee suicides at Apple's Foxconn assembly division (J. Chan, 2013; Lucas et al., 2013), Volkswagen's admitted cheating on vehicle emissions testings (Hotten, 2015; Plungis, 2015) and confirmed racial discrimination and poor working conditions at Tesla

(Barry, 2022) reflect corporate leaders who repeatedly abused their (espoused) commitment to ethical behavior and corporate social responsibility (CSR).

Stakeholders

Stakeholders are those persons and entities who impact or are impacted by the shareholders' business models without whom the corporations would cease to exist (Baumfield, 2016; Freeman, 2010). Thus, stakeholders include the environment, employees, customers, supply chains, distributors, trade unions, and surrounding communities. Considering that there is copious literature espousing that organizational sustainability requires a perfect marriage between shareholders' and stakeholders' values, there should be a genuine thrust for organizational transformation toward sustainability. Furthermore, there are several frameworks (ESG, CSR, TBL) for use to assist in merging the social and environmental dimensions with the existing financial dimension of current business models. The advent of climate change due to existing (shareholder-dominant) business models and the regulatory bodies globally pushing for ESG reporting on sustainable business activities signifies an urgency for transformation from conventional to sustainable business models.

There is a munificence of benefits from supply chain operators as (manufacturing) stakeholders (operating as a business) embracing CSR, TBL, ESG, and working to fulfill the Paris Agreement and the UN 2030 Agenda for Sustainable Development. Using (a) several research models, (b) variables such as cost-sharing and profit-sharing, and (c) forced labor as a *negative CSR parameter*, researchers concluded that (as a benefit when forced labor is involved in supply chains, a reduction in forced labor by both retailer and the manufacturer (implementing CSR), increases overall profitability for both the retailer and the manufacturer (Mahdiraji et al., 2020).

Additional benefits based on research conclusions to note are (a) based on profit-sharing contract as a variable, the highest overall profit is realized when manufacturers undertake the leadership role in driving CSR, and (b) sensitivity analysis confirmed that the desired situation of the profitability of the retailer to be higher than that of the manufacturer occurs when the forced labor ratio between manufacturer and retailer approaches zero (Mahdiraji et al., 2020). The fact that the highest overall profit is realized when manufacturers undertake the leadership role in driving CSR should not be confounding, as the manufacturers can advocate CSR, TBL, and ESG in their organization but choose to use their available capacity to do the opposite. Again without effective legislative governance, the supply chain operators.

SDG 8 target 5 aims to achieve productive employment, decent work for all persons with disabilities, and equal pay for work of equal value. Given all the known benefits of embracing CSR, TBL, and ESG, a significant challenge to achieving sustainability in stakeholder operations is the ongoing proliferation of the engrained lack of human rights, labor, environmental and ethical practices, particularly in supply chains in developed nations with little or no labor laws. In 2010, Foxconn Technology Group, the multinational corporation (MNC) Taiwanese plant, produced more than 40% of the world's electronics (J. Chan, 2013; Lucas et al., 2013). Foxconn's largest plant, Foxconn City, was home to manufacturing Apple products (Lucas et al., 2013). In 2010, 18 migrant Chinese employees aged 17 to 25 attempted suicide by jumping from buildings at Foxconn facilities. Fourteen died, while four survived with many crippling (lifetime) injuries (J. Chan, 2013; Lucas et al., 2013). The response was (a) erecting suicide nets, (b) barricading the windows, and (c) employees signing a no-suicide pledge disclaimer clause (J. Chan, 2013). The reason for the mass suicide attempts was employees cited that they lost dignity and face based on employer treatment – standing still in front of coworkers for a time equal to that which an employee reported late (Jones, 2010); or cleaning toilets without glove as punishment for making errors on the production line (Lucas et al., 2013, pp. 91–92). An undercover investigation detailed that profit maximization, punishment, and public humiliation were synonyms for Foxconn's culture and employee dignity was irrelevant (J. Chan, 2013). While Apple does not own Foxconn City, Foxconn City as an Apple partner, was the largest producer and supplier of Apple electronics.

Digressing to another industry in a separate developing nation Bangladesh which hosts apparel manufacturing sweat-shops for nearly all international garment retailers, is (a) the second largest apparel exporter after China, (b) employs some 3.2 million workers, chiefly women across more than 5,000 factories, and (c) pays the lowest minimum wage in the world (Manik & Yardley, 2012, 2013). On November 24, 2012, a fire at Tazrene Fashion, a modern slavery sweatshop without fire sprinklers, blocked fire escapes and iron grilles on many windows, killed 112 persons, with 53 burned beyond recognition (Manik & Yardley, 2012). By April 24, 2013, and again in Bangladesh, the eight-story garment factory complex Rana Plaza building collapsed, claiming 1,134 lives and critically injuring more than one thousand (G. Brown, 2015; Kasperkevic, 2016; Manik & Yardley, 2013). The owners of the collapsed Rana plaza violated building codes as they illegally constructed the four upper floors without permits, and the building foundation was substandard (E. Chan, 2021; Manik & Yardley, 2013).

Bangladesh is one of the countless developing nations exploited by MNCs, especially in the garment manufacturing industry. Guatemala (Hoskins & Mayorga, 2020), Honduras (Cuevas, 1996), Indonesia (IndustriALL, 2016), Jamaica (James, 1988), Cambodia, India, Egypt, and most of the Middle East and North Africa (MENA) region (E. Chan, 2021; Kasperkevic, 2016), punctuates the long, grim history of *host government allowed MNC exploitation* for profit over dignity, CSR, TBL and ESG in the apparel manufacturing industry. Exploitation involving less than minimum wages, overt sexual harassment, extended working hours, punishment, workplace bullying, forced overtime, dismissals without payment of earned wages and benefits, reduction of salary for making errors, near impossible quotas, insufficient rest breaks, threats of termination, lack of access to drinking water causing fainting from dehydration, and denial of sick leave characterizes modern slavery sweatshops (Cuevas, 1996; James, 1988; Kasperkevic, 2016; Lucas et al., 2013). Exploitation also occurs in other industries, as a reference in (a) child labor on cocoa farms in Ghana (Hinch, 2018; Rowselle, 2022); (b) child labor on cocoa farms in Côte d'Ivoire (Andrei, 2017; Clarke, 2015) using trafficked children (DOL, n.d.; Rowselle, 2022; Sisso, 2019); (c) cobalt mining in DRC (Amnesty International, 2016; Kelly, 2019); and (d) modern slave labor at Foxconn (Chibber, 2012; Lucas et al., 2013).

Like any MNC, supply chain operators, as independent stakeholders (whether small, medium, or large enterprises), have a duty of care to enforce CSR, TBL, and ESG for the protection and growth of their employees, which subsequently leads to higher profitability (Mahdiraji et al., 2020) and alleviation of poverty (Raimi et al., 2015). However, without effective legislation in impoverished nations, supply chains operate in the name of growing the local economy (Bresnahan, 2020). While stakeholders, particularly in supply chain operations, seemingly operate with impunity, regulations, and restrictions, there is a bigger picture regarding the lack of CSR while using antiquated principles involving forced labor, corruption, bribery, and lack of transparency to achieve excessively high production quotas leading to mega profits (Transparency International, 2007, 2017, 2022). Transparency International cited that the most impoverished countries experience the most exploitation and are ranked low on the corruption perceptions index (CPI), indicating high levels of corruption and an evident continuous strong correlation between corruption and poverty (Transparency International, 2007). The MNC (retailer) typically headquartered in developed nations continuously ranks /placed high on the CPI list indicating minimal corruption. ESG compliance, corruption, bribery, and transparency regarding MNCs will be discussed in the following section.

Shareholders and MNC Unethical Practices

Organizations predominantly stay in business to maximize shareholders' wealth (Bakan, 2005). Corporate shareholders generally consist of persons at the senior level and the board of directors charged with the governance of the corporation and external entities with financial stakes in the said corporation (Lazonick & O'Sullivan, 2002). According to Bakan (2005) and Lazonick and O'Sullivan (2020), the concept of the retention of financial earnings to reinvest in the organization for corporate growth, without regard for how the corporation's business model impacts environmental and social capital, characterizes the maximization of shareholders' wealth. Lazonick and O'Sullivan further stated that in the 1980s and more so in the 1990s, creating shareholders' wealth transitioned from retention and reinvestment to downsizing and redistribute as organizational leadership (a) reduced labor force and classified the cost savings as corporate equity, (b) used revenues for business expansion versus the use of revenues to buy back stocks and pay dividends, and (c) awarded senior managers with stock options and higher salaries. Shareholders, MNC, and international brands will be used interchangeably in this chapter.

ESG symbolizes the three key factors (social and environmental performance and financial performance) considered when measuring the return performance of an investment in a business or company, reflecting sustainability and ethical impact (Daugaard, 2020). According to Kluza et al. (2020), the incorporation of ESG to create SBM is a requisite for organizational leadership as they seek *new* responsible ways to create a seamless relationship between environmental performance and social and financial performance. Sustainable production includes responsible consumption and clean and renewable energy use (UN, n.d.-b). On May 17, 2021, Tesla, the worlds leading electric vehicle (EV) producer (Cole, 2022) and self-proclaimed advocate for pioneering the world's transition to sustainable energy (Tesla, 2021), lost its place on the S&P 500 ESG Index (Barry, 2022; Dorn, 2022).

Launched in 2019 and dedicated to companies excelling at ESG issues, the S&P 500 ESG Index allows investors to choose between companies based on their robust commitment to ESG goals (Barry, 2022). Using market capitalization as the datum, the S&P 500 ESG Index evaluates the stock value of some major corporations listed in the United States that meet specific sustainability criteria (Barry, 2022). According to Dorn (2022), though Tesla may be committed to eliminating fossil fuel-powered vehicles to drive sustainability development when scrutinized through a wider ESG lens, Tesla fell behind its sector peers. Areas Tesla floundered and collapsed on, resulting in declining criteria level rankings, included but were not limited to lack of (a) a low carbon strategy that focuses on companies' strategies to reduce the carbon intensity of its car portfolio and (b) the corporation's codes of business conduct regarding the implementation of transparent reporting on infractions and the existence of anti-competitive behavior, corruption and bribery cases (Dorn, 2022). See (Dorn, 2022; Sanchez, 2022) for ESG scoring criteria and evaluation methodology.

Of even more significant concern, which aided in Tesla's declining criteria level ratings relative to its sector peers, are two issues that contravene multiple SDGs and corresponding targets. Firstly, on February 9, 2022, California's civil rights agency, the Department of Fair Employment and Housing (DFEH), filed a civil action against Tesla, Inc. (Alim, 2022; Wipper et al., 2022). The civil action encompassed claims of racial harassment, racial discrimination, retaliation, and Tesla's failure to prevent discrimination, harassment, and retaliation against Black and African American workers at Tesla's California Fremont facility (Alim, 2022; Dorn, 2022; Wipper et al., 2022, pp. 12–18). According to the civil action, daily, Black and African American employees endured repeated offensive racial slurs inclusive of the use of the "N" word and graffiti inclusive of hangman's noose and swastikas on the walls of shared employee spaces (Wipper et al., 2022, pp. 12–14). At the Fremont plant, Black and African American workers are over-represented in Tesla's contract workforce, accounting for circa 3% and 20% of professionals and factory operatives, respectively (Wipper et al., 2022, p. 4). Still, Black or African Americans did not comprise the executive team (Wipper et al., 2022, p. 4).

Secondly, in the year leading up to June 2022, there were some 273 motor vehicle accidents involving the use of the onboard driver-assistance systems (autopilot) in Tesla's vehicles (Siddiqui et al., 2022). Tesla drew fierce criticism for handling the National Highway Traffic Safety Administration investigation regarding the multiple deaths and injuries sustained in the accidents (Barry, 2022; Dorn, 2022; Laing, 2022; Siddiqui et al., 2022). Additionally, there are employee reports of modern slavery sweatshop-like working conditions at Tesla's Fremont plant (Berman, 2020). While corporations such as Chevron, Johnson & Johnson, Berkshire Hathaway, Wells Fargo and Co., Home Depot, and Meta, among others, lost their place on the May 2022 rebalancing of the S&P 500 ESG Index, Tesla is featured in this chapter on organizational transformation to achieve sustainability, for its espoused objective to "accelerate the world's transition to sustainable energy" and for being the world leading produce of alternately powered vehicles (Barry, 2022; Dorn, 2022; Tesla, 2021).

Tesla losing its place on the S&P 500 ESG Index because Tesla corporation's lack of codes of business conduct regarding the implementation the transparent reporting on infractions and the existence of anti-competitive and behavior corruption and bribery cases (Dorn, 2022); weighs heavily on true sustainability relative to its sector peers. For example, the United Nations Global Compact (UNGC) Ten Principles (UN, 2016) forms the foundation of the S&P 500 ESG Index scoring criteria. The UNGC Ten Principles highlights 10 sustainable criteria in four categories, and all principles connect with several of the 17 SDGs (UN, 2016, p. 6). The four categories are (a) human rights (principles 1 and 2), (b) labor (principles 3 to 6), (c) environment (principles 7 to 9), and (d) business ethics (principle 10) (Sanchez, 2022; UN, 2016). Stepping away from the civil actions in Fremont, California, while Tesla was not named in acts of corruption and bribery cases, there are causes for concerns regarding their known association and complicity regarding child labor in cobalt mines in the DRC (Amnesty International, 2016; Kelly, 2019) and the water-intensive extraction of lithium (Benchmark, 2022; Campbell, 2022), critical components used in manufacturing the Tesla batteries.

Aside from breaches of good human rights, environmental, and labor practices, another persistent challenge with implementing sustainable business practices is the lack of shareholders (MNCs) accountability, disclosure, and transparency regarding their business practices. This challenge usually surfaces when profits precede CSR, TBL, and ESG at home in their developed nation, especially in the least developed territories involving supply chains (Transparency International, 2007, 2017, 2022). For example, on November 24, 2012, the Tazrene Fashion fire in Bangladesh revealed a crucial flaw regarding the lack of transparency in the global garment supply chain (Manik & Yardley, 2013). United States retailers Walmart and Sears indicated they were unaware that Tazrene Fashion manufactured their apparel (Manik & Yardley, 2012, 2013). They maintained that their suppliers surreptitiously subcontracted the jobs, which exposed flaws in monitoring the industry's global apparel supply chain: (Manik & Yardley, 2012, 2013).

Post the April 24, 2013, Rana Plaza collapse in Bangladesh, web sites, customs records, clothing labels, production records, and other documents recovered in the ruins alluded to multiple international retailers and brands using the Rana Plaza as a supply chain for manufacturing their garments (Kasperkevic, 2016; Manik & Yardley, 2013). According to Kasperkevic (2016) and Manik and Yardley (2013), some international brands (and parent countries) that used Rana Plaza in Bangladesh before its collapse included Mango (Spain), Primark (Ireland) Walmart (United States), C&A (Netherland, Belgium, and Germany), Benetton (Italy), Cato Fashions (United States), H&M (Sweden), Gap (United States). The lack of accountability, disclosure, and transparency from the Tazrene fire engulfed the Rana Plaza collapse. When asked about a document detailing cutting specifications for an order from Benetton, a spokesman for the Benetton Group denied any connection to the Rana Plaza (Manik & Yardley, 2013). He equivocally stated that no factory in Rana Plaza supplied Benetton Group or any of its brands (Manik & Yardley, 2013).

Subsequently, some international retailers (MNCs) forged an independent, legally binding agreement with local trade unions known as the accord on fire and building safety in Bangladesh (Accord, 2018; Sainato, 2022). The purpose of the accord was for both parties to collaborate and provide a safe and healthy garment and textile industry in Bangladesh (Accord, 2018; Kasperkevic, 2016; Sainato, 2022). Walmart never signed on to the Bangladesh legally binding accord and opted to partner with Gap to create a voluntary organization called the Alliance for Bangladesh Worker Safety (Kasperkevic, 2016). At the time or writing this chapter, H&M, Benetton, and Mango signed the accord, but neither Walmart nor Gap did (Sainato, 2022). Independent probes into Walmart's supply chain process revealed a lack of transparency, making it difficult to hold the company accountable, especially since Walmart does not publicly disclose its supply chain facilities (Kasperkevic, 2016).

Walmart, Sears, and Benetton would not be the only MNCs, retailers, or stakeholders to exhibit a lack of (a) accountability, (b) disclosure, (c) transparency, and (d) CSR or deny knowledge of and involvement when breaches of human rights, labor, environmental, or business ethics are unearthed. To date, Nestlé and Cargill still challenge lawsuits, and (a) deny knowledge of child labor on Côte d'Ivoire cocoa farms, (b) denied aiding and abetting forced labor in cocoa supply chains in Africa, and (c) declared that they are not proprietors of the cocoa farms engaged in child and forced labor (Balch, 2020a, 2020b; NORC, 2020). In the case of Dell being named as a defendant in a law suit for affiliation with child labor in DRC cobalt mining, Dell declared they have never knowingly engaged supply chains involving any form of involuntary labor, child labor, or duplicitous employment practices (Kelly, 2019). At the same time, the United Kingdom-based Glencore owners of said cobalt mines declared that Glencore does not tolerate any form of a child, forced, or compulsory labor (Kelly, 2019) – which neither confirms nor denies knowledge of child or forced labor activities in their cobalt mines.

The practice of denying affiliation with questionable supply chains while taking a hands-off approach also involved Nike. In 2001 the director exhibited the brash attitude that Nike does not own the supply chain manufacturers, so Nike has *no control over whatever happens there* (Macintyre, 2014). Some defenders of sweatshop labor contend that sweatshops and other forms of low-wage opportunities provided by MNCs or foreign direct investment (FDI) benefit the host population (Bresnahan, 2020). According to the sweatshop defenders, irrespective of the less-than-minimum wages paid, job opportunities would otherwise not be available without the intervention of the MNCs (Bresnahan, 2020). Furthermore, MNCs appear to adhere to the philosophy of the "Non-Worseness claim," which suggests that any less than minimum wage from sweatshops is still better than nothing. Even if a host nation implements regulations to improve working conditions and salaries, the MNC can relocate operations to other places conducive to their needs (Berkey, 2021; Bresnahan, 2020). Collective bargaining is always near non-existent, and often the supply chain operators cited that they cannot pay better wages and provide better working conditions as the MNCs pay low prices (James, 1988; Manik & Yardley, 2012, 2013).

Without the host government's approval, MNCs do not enter and operate in any sovereign territory (host country) or source supplies. The granting of government approval thus makes the host country (for example, Bangaladesh), by all means, a stakeholder providing a supply chain service to the MNC. While MNCs or the host country's supply chains servicing the MNC's operations have no obligations to hire local workers, to think that exploitation by MNCs or their regional supply chain operators is expected because the host nation employees voluntarily accepted the job is simply accepting that MNCs thrives on the destitution of host nations – which is unacceptable (Transparency International, 2007). According to Johnson (2015), corporate attorneys are responsible for steering senior-level leadership toward effectively managing supply chains. Thus, Nike, Nestlé, Cargill, and all other MNCs and international brands have a responsibility involving a duty of care applying CSR, TBL, and ESG, and not to exploit due tho the host country's vulnerability and destitution (Berkey, 2021). Kelly (2019) indicated that filed court documentation stated that MNCs like Apple, Dell, Microsoft, Google, and Tesla possess the authority and resources to manage their cobalt supply chains and that their failure to do so contributed to the deaths and injuries suffered by their clients.

The arrival of MNCs signals multiple new job opportunities, increased import and export revenues, and a fresh injection of foreign currency and infrastructural development from the MNC investing a percentage of their earnings into the host nation's economy (Bresnahan, 2020). However, the narrative often reads differently regarding investing profits in a host country, considering that African cocoa farmers received circa a minuscule 6% of the global chocolate industry's total revenues (Balch, 2020b). Thus the elite list of wealthy and least corrupt (as per the CPI) nations - predominantly in Europe, North America East Asia, continuously showboat their relatively clean public sectors, empowered by a robust conflict of interest and freedom of information protocols, political stability, with a civil society free to exercise speech and oversight (Transparency International, 2007, 2017, 2022). With all the assumed entitlement, many MNCs from these least corrupt nations do not practice their home customs while operating in developing countries where bribery often becomes a part of conducting business (Transparency International, 2007).

Consequently, critics argued that the issue of exploitation in host countries, whether by the MNC alone, or MNC in tandem with their host county supply chains, goes well beyond the MNC and supply chains (Manik & Yardley, 2013). Transparency International (2007) concurred with Manik and Yardley 2013. They cited that corruption is at the roots of MNCs sustaining hegemonic tendencies in developing host nations as monies for bribes flows from MNCs based in the world's wealthiest countries down to high-level public officials in impoverished developing countries. The host country's government is often unwilling to address the exploitation due to their ingrained dependency on foreign exchange, (b) jobs created, and (c) fear of the MNC relocating to another country (Manik & Yardley, 2013).

Technology Concerns

The objective of SDG 9 is to build resilient infrastructure, promote inclusive and sustainable industrialization and foster innovation by 2030. Transformation to sustainable organizational cultures will require exnovation or the intended termination of old practices, infrastructures, and unsustainable technologies (Heyen et al., 2017; Kimberly, 1981). In this chapter, exnovation applies to the intentional abandonment of business processes and technology not compliant with ESG protocols. Exnovation can be immediate or executed on a phased basis, allowing organizational leaders to embrace new ways of thinking. The reduction of green house gasses (GHG) by the exnovation of fossil fuel energy use must be on a phased basis as a sudden change to an alternate source of energy for production may not be sustainable and could prove disastrous for an organization (Krüger & Pellicer-Sifres, 2020). While exnovations could prove manageable for MNCs headquartered in developed nations, the majority of the re-orientation lies with upgrading and building resilience in small and medium enterprises in developing countries with (a) antiquated or inadequate infrastructure and processes or (b) neither infrastructure nor processes. Thus with great reason, the objective of SDG 9 (regarding developing industries, innovation, and infrastructure by 2030) made multiple specific references to least developed countries, African countries, landlocked developing countries, and small island developing states.

As discussed previously, organizational transformation for sustainability requires a seamless integration between the Paris Agreement and the UN 2030 Agenda for Sustainable Development (UN, n.d.-a). Building resilient infrastructures, promoting inclusive and sustainable industrialization, and fostering innovation, will require intervention at all levels in virtually every industry – (a) agriculture; (b) mining; (c) fishing; (d) forestry, (e) construction; (f) financial including affordable credit allowing for the integration impoverished nations into global value chains and markets; (g) information and communications technology (ICT); (h) manufacturing industrialization enhancement to significantly reduce unemployment and increase gross domestic product (GDP) via the implementation of clean, renewable, and environmentally friendly technologies and industrial processes; and (i) scientific research (UN, n.d.-b).

Thus, the achievement of SDG 9 will require that developed nations and MNCs alike (a) introduce existing technology (such as internet, agricultural and mineral mining) to many developing nations that are currently not exposed to such new/different forms of technology and in some cases where required (b) share (proprietary or patented) technology for example in research and development, (ICT), medical research, agriculture, security, and law enforcement. With lack of trust listed as the primary barrier to industrial sharing economies (Govindan et al., 2020); the primary concern is the willingness of private and public sectors in developed nations and MNCs listed and unlisted, to share technological (proprietary and patented) expertise that possibly forms part of their success, to other less developed nations (seen as future competitors).

Technology Components

By virtue of (a) the UN 2030 Agenda for Sustainable Development and (b) the composition of the 17 SDGs, extensive organizational transformation is required to achieve sustainability, more so in developing nations compared to developed nations (UN, n.d.-b) – even for a component considered as basic domestic broadband internet access. For example, SDG 9 target 8 was to significantly increase access to ICT and provide universal and affordable access to the internet in the least developed countries by 2020. However, during the COVID-19 pandemic and referencing only the Latin America and the Caribbean region, less than 50% of domestic households had access to broadband internet, stymied by a 27% digital divide between urban and rural areas (B. A. Brown & Heitner, 2022; Inter-American Development Bank [IDB], 2020). Fifty percent of domestic broadband internet access in Latin America and the Caribbean is low compared to 86.3% in the OECD member states (B. A. Brown & Heitner, 2022; Ortuño, 2020). Given the multitude and magnitude of innovation and exnovation required, especially for the least developed countries, transformation to attain sustainability will require (a) multiple technology components and (b) partial to entire process changes across multiple industries, currently employing unsustainable practices. Using renewable and clean energy sources to reduce GHG will be a pivotal aspect of the innovation (Tesla, 2021).

Management and Organizational Concerns

Management's primary concern with organizational transformation for sustainability and ESG centers on (a) reporting ESG and (b) the metrics and methodologies ESG monitoring organizations employ when assessing corporate ESG performance to subsequently assign ESG scores and rankings (Flammer et al., 2021; Haklová et al., 2020; Kerber & Jin, 2022; Munro & Van Drunen, 2022; Rajesh, 2020). S&P, Morgan Stanley Capital International, Bloomberg LP, Sustainalytics unit of Morningstar Inc., and PricewaterhouseCoopers are among some 160 entities that provide support for corporations desirous of managing their risks, returns, and climate change impact while becoming ESG compliant or are also rating agencies (Morgan Stanley Capital International [MSCI], 2022; PricewaterhouseCoopers [PwC], 2022). MSCI, S&P, and Sustainalytics are ESG rating companies; however, MSCI is the largest ESG rating company (Simpson et al., 2021).

Measuring and reporting ESG is challenging as (a) the responsibility lies with leadership to use specific metrics to measure their organization's ESG compliance and climate impact (Haklová et al., 2020; Rajesh, 2020); and (b) the responsibility of voluntary self-monitoring and self-reporting leaves room for data omission and manipulation (Fiaschi et al., 2020; Flammer et al., 2021). Using what is termed as *check box type ESG reporting checklists*, leadership operates on a don't ask, don't tell basis, thus being at liberty to circumvent disclosing data regarding GHG emissions, supply chain and raw material sourcing, climate change vulnerability, Diversity, Inclusion, and equity; labor management, and business ethics when self-reporting their corporate ESG performance (Jonsdottir et al., 2022; Simpson et al., 2021). Furthermore, the shareholders of some corporations remain resistant to disclosing the impact of their business model on the environment and social capital (Flammer et al., 2021; Munro & Van Drunen, 2022). While very little is known about how investors use ESG information for investing, the self-reported data may suffer from compromised materiality, accuracy, and reliability for investors relying on ESG data (Amel-Zadeh & Serafeim, 2018; Jonsdottir et al., 2022). Thus, self-reported data, possibly deficient in materiality, accuracy, and reliability, get analyzed by ESG rating entities using controversial metrics and methodologies to assess corporate ESG performance to subsequently assign ESG scores and rankings (Flammer et al., 2021; Haklová et al., 2020; Kerber & Jin, 2022; Munro & Van Drunen, 2022; Rajesh, 2020).

Upon learning of Tesla's removal from the S&P 500 ESG Index. Tesla's CEOs retorted that ESG is a scam (Barry, 2022; Kerber & Jin, 2022). Tesla's CEO also voiced that ESG monitoring and ranking agencies favor corporations that marginally adjust their business processes while their negative impact on climate change increases, as he referenced (a) the inclusion of six oil companies on the S&P 500 ESG Index with oil company Exxon Mobil being ranked among the top 10 best ESG compliant companies on said list and (b) the admission of new-comer oil refiner Phillips 66 to said S&P 500 ESG Index (Barry, 2022; Kerber & Jin, 2022). In response, Margaret Dorn, the S&P Dow Jones Indices' head of ESG indices for North America, declared that the ESG Index serves to provide a more accurate representation of a corporation's CSR commitments versus what is espoused on its website (Barry, 2022; Kerber & Jin, 2022). Dorn added that (a) the S&P 500 ESG prioritizes a corporation's business practices across all key ESG dimensions over the company's mission statement and face value and (b) Tesla's lack of disclosures relative to industry peers should concern investors interested in evaluating the company across ESG criteria (Kerber & Jin, 2022).

But there exists an ongoing controversy regarding ESG metrics. Previously Tesla CEO reiterated that ESG's failure to focus on the company's real-world impact on environmental and societal capital makes the ESG evaluation methodologies *fundamentally flawed* (Barry, 2022; Tesla, 2021). Tesla's CEO allegation of fundamentally flawed ESG evaluation and processes attracted much support, resulting in a snowballing of equal sentiments from other critics, citing ad hoc practices and inconsistencies in the ESG metrics employed by particularly MSCI (Quinson, 2022; Simpson et al., 2021; Tesla, 2021). The ESG critics vehemently advocated that ESG metrics and evaluation criteria (incorrectly) focus on investment risks and returns (corporate bottom line growth) versus focusing on real-world impact (Quinson, 2022; Simpson et al., 2021; Tesla, 2021).

For example, Simpson et al. (2021) cited that in 2019, (a) fast food giant McDonald's Corporation's generated 54 million tons of GHG, reflecting a 7% increase over the preceding 4 years, while (b) their (beef) supply chain generated more GHG emissions than Hungary or Portugal. Nonetheless, on April 23, 2022, owing to recalculations by MSCI, McDonald's earned a ratings upgrade as MSCI *rewarded* the company's environmental practices - installing recycle bins around certain areas in the United Kingdom and France as they (McDonald's) could receive cautions for not recycling (Simpson et al., 2021). Simpson et al. concluded that in this assessment regarding McDonald's, which is similar to all others, MSCI only focused on if environmental issues (recycling in this instance) had the potential to harm the company. Subsequently, mitigation of risks to the planet (GHG emissions) was purely incidental.

In other instances, Simpson et al. (2021) gleaned from MSCI's reports featuring their evaluation methodologies and metrics that water stress speaks to if a community has sufficient water supply to support a corporation, not if the corporation is creating stress on the community's water supply with 32% of environmental upgrades granted on this MSCI's rationalization of water stress. Further inspection of MSCI's records revealed (a) 51 rating upgrades issued based on corporate adoption of ethics and corporate behavior policies for bans on existing criminal activities such as bribery and money laundering, (b) 35 reports indicating corporations receiving rating upgrades for implementing the conducting an annual employee survey that might reduce turnover, and (c) 23 rating upgrades issued to diverse corporations for implementing data protection guidelines, including companies whose core business data or software management or production (Simpson et al., 2021). Critics deemed MSCI's metrics as greenwashing and supporting corporate greenwashing (Quinson, 2022; Simpson et al., 2021), especially that implementing and reporting the most elementary business practices punctuated 71% of the rating upgrades examined.

How Feasible is Organizational Transformation for Sustainability?

Considering (a) the 17 SDGs and associated targets of the UN 2030 Agenda for Sustainable Development and (b) Merriam-Webster's definition of feasible as being capable of being dealt with successfully, sustainability-driven by organizational transformation may not be feasible by the end of the year 2030. For example, in 2020, during the COVID-19 pandemic and referencing only the Latin America and the Caribbean region, less than 50% of domestic households had access to broadband internet, stymied by a 27% digital divide between urban and rural areas (B. A. Brown & Heitner, 2022; Inter-American Development Bank [IDB], 2020). The preceding data is vital for mentioning as the aim of SDG 9 target 8 is to significantly increase access to information and communications technology and strive to provide universal and affordable access to the Internet in the least developed countries by 2020 (UN, n.d.-b).

Additionally, many other generational and persistently ongoing issues contravene the tenets of ESG, as outlined earlier in this chapter. The problems mentioned earlier apparently propagate without host country government intervention, including but not limited to the continued exponential growth in (a) groundwater shortages due to excessive abstraction and pollution, (b) trafficking and child labor in global supply chains resulting in children, particularly girls not receiving an education, (c) trafficking and forced labor and forced marriages, (d) modern slavery work environments, and (e) MNCs lack of accountability, disclosure and transparency relative their industry peers (Barry, 2022; Dorn, 2022; ILO, 2021, 2022b; UN, 2022a). The feasibility of organizational transformation drive sustainability materializing even post 2030, will require collaborative intercession at the (host country) government legally binding policy-making level, or other levels, beyond and outside the preview of the UN and investors investing in ESG funds offered by MSCI and S&P 500 ESG (Kerber & Jin, 2022).

Furthermore, the unfeasibility of organizational transformation as a means to sustainability will persist for as long as MNC leadership and critics deem there are no incentives for the shift toward sustainable development. The lack of incentive hinges on controversies surrounding ESG monitoring, ad hoc evaluation metrics, and subsequent rating level upgrades from ESG monitoring entities (Quinson, 2022; Simpson et al., 2021; Tesla, 2021). Some critics and at least one CEO still interrogate the (a) favorable ESG ratings of conventional vehicle manufacturers using *ESG check box checklists to improve their production process* while continuously producing GHG-emitting conventional fossil fuel vehicles, (b) one fast food MNC receiving favorable ratings for installing recycle bins at undisclosed locations in Europe, and (c) multiple corporations receiving inexplicable rating upgrades for documenting the fulfillment of the most rudimentary of corporate governance expectations (Quinson, 2022; Simpson et al., 2021; Tesla, 2021).

Several ESG-focused fund management agencies hold portfolios for oil, weapons manufacturing, and mining corporations – industries considered antithetical to ESG tenets (Quinson, 2022). For example, MSCI, the largest ESG rating entity and portfolio fund management firm, traded the largest ESG-focused exchange-traded fund (Barry, 2022; Quinson, 2022). The iShares ESG Aware MSCI USA ETF (ESGU) fund, valued at $22.9 billion at the time of trading, contained circa 3.1% of its assets invested in the oil and gas industry, the sector dubbed as the leader in accelerating climate change (Barry, 2022; Quinson, 2022). Additionally, before Russia declared war on Ukraine, of the estimated 4,800 ESG funds representing more than $2.7 trillion in total assets, ESG funds held $8.3 billion in Russian assets, including government bonds and other Russian company investments (Marsh & Schwartzkopff, 2022; Quinson, 2022). Tesla's CEO and some bewildered critics alike concurred that *sustainable investing* is typically about sustaining corporations (Barry, 2022; Simpson et al., 2021; Tesla, 2021), while other critics seek insights into the role ESG data play in investment decisions and challenges faced if any, with incorporating said ESG data in their investment decision making (Amel-Zadeh & Serafeim, 2018).

The inconclusiveness and duplicity surrounding ESG metrics and methodologies, amalgamated with some categories of portfolios traded by ESG rating entities, could indicate that some ESG fund managers' interest lies in selling ESG-focused exchange-traded fund portfolios (investment risks and returns) versus real-world impact (Quinson, 2022; Simpson et al., 2021; Tesla, 2021). While the organizational transformation to achieve sustainability and become ESG-compliant is necessary, ESG is not about *ESG-washing and ticking checkboxes on an ESG checklist* to provide big data analytics for investors (Quinson, 2022; Simpson et al., 2021; Tesla, 2021). The transformation aims to address and comply with the Paris Agreement and the UN 2030 Agenda for Sustainable Development in a realistic time frame (Quinson, 2022). The issues in this section added to the fact that corporations can buy carbon credits to offset their corporate carbon footprints (ClimateTrade, 2022); will always create corridors for excuses from MNC leadership to avoid transformation and thus keep sustainability driven by organizational transformation unfeasible.

SOLUTIONS AND RECOMMENDATIONS

While there is a current understanding that organizations predominantly stay in business to maximize shareholders' wealth (Bakan, 2005), organizational transformation remains the viable route to global sustainable development. As such, in this section, the solutions and recommendations presented will not focus on ESG data as a tool for investment decision-making, which would, in part, speak to the board governance aspect of ESG (Quinson, 2022; Simpson et al., 2021). The solutions and recommendations presented regarding organizational transformation driving sustainable development will be based on the original tenets of CSR and TBL. Regarding ESG as an overarching concept, the focus will be on (a) environmental as encompassing GHG emissions, water abstraction, waste management, and groundwater pollution; supply chain management and raw material sourcing, and climate change vulnerability; (b) social comprising of labor management, Diversity and Inclusion, gender equality, and community relations; and (c) governance making specific reference to business ethics, while encapsulating board governance, and intellectual property protection. In essence, while the real world impact of renewable and clean energy products from coprporations are equally commendable as they are important, the (environmental, social, and governance) cost incurred to produce these real world impact must be considered and accounted for.

The solutions and recommendations that could aid the realization of the Paris Agreement and some of the 17 SDGs and their related targets of the UN 2030 Agenda for Sustainable Development based on best practices are outlined below.

Formulating and Enforcing International Legislations and Legally Binding Agreements

Achieving fulfillment of the UN 2030 Agenda for Sustainable Development must be approached from a different angle involving legally binding approaches wherever possible. For example, the European Union (EU) and 192 countries accepted the Paris Agreement, a legally binding international treaty that entered into force on 4 November 4, 2016. (UN, n.d.-d). The UN 2030 Agenda for Sustainable Development is not legally binding (UN, n.d.-e). Stemming from the UN 2030 Agenda for Sustainable Development 17 SDGs are a host of ESG-washing conundrums, spiraling into massive stock-picking traded-fund management portfolios (Quinson, 2022; Simpson et al., 2021), none of which focuses on either real-world impact (climate change) or the actual cost of creating real-world impact. Without a proper system of reporting, monitoring, rating, and the accompanying factors of legal implications, conditionality, and sanctions for non-compliance, achieving sustainable development will remain in a state of fluidity.

Regarding the EU position on minority protection, Sasse (2008) questioned the possibility of measuring compliance when conditionality is in flux. Sasse further interrogated the meaning of compliance in a constructed norm like minority protection. For this chapter and leaning on Sasse, what does ESG compliance mean in the sense of a constructed norm like organizational transformation to achieve sustainable development that lacks an internal (UN) consensus, a firm legal base, and clear benchmarks, standard metrics and is used flexibly over time (Sasse, 2008)? The authors of this chapter further concurred with Sasse by emphasizing that the absence of the preceding factors gives way to weak and fluctuating interpretations for conditionality and subsequent compliance (regarding ESG).

Legislation must be binding, comprehensive, and vehemently implemented and monitored. For example, the September 2001 signing of the Harkin Engel Protocol to reduce the worst forms of child labor by 70% across the cocoa industry of Côte d'Ivoire and Ghana by 2020 (ILO, 2011; International

Cocoa Initiative, 2021). Thus, by specifying the *worst forms of child labor*, Harkin Engel Protocol covers a child harvesting cocoa pods with a machete on an African cocoa farm, but not the child serving water on said African cocoa farm. In September 2011, ADM, Barry Callebaut, Cargill, Ferrero, The Hershey Company, Kraft Foods, Mars, Incorporated, and Nestlé constituted a group of eight that pledged US$2 million to a new public-private partnership (PPP) with the ILO to combat child labor in cocoa growing communities in Ghana and. Again, this collaboration was voluntary, not legally binding. On September 13, 2010, several dignitaries from the United States, Côte d'Ivoire, and Ghana met and signed a *Declaration of Joint Action* to support the implementation of the Harkin-Engel Protocol.

The requirement for clearly defined comprehensive binding legislations with a firm legal base and conditionalities increases as corporations and the justice system may exact interpretations as per discretion. Referencing the Alien Tort Statute (ATS) enacted in 1789 by the First Congress and signed into law by George Washington (Balch, 2020a; EarthRights International, 2022). The ATS is a U. S. law that allows non-American citizens to file lawsuits in United States federal courts for various breaches of international law (Cornell Law School, 2022; EarthRights International, 2022). MNCs Nestlé and Cargill implicated in child labor supply chains had lawsuits filed against them for aiding and abetting forced labor on African cocoa farms (Balch, 2020a). According to Balch (2020a), both MNCs indicated that they were not liable under the ATS. The U. S. Supreme Court ruled that plaintiffs cannot use the ATS for human rights matters against corporations for acts committed in a foreign territory because the defendant corporation operates within the United States (Balch, 2020a).

While the African cocoa supply chain was featured here, there is also the pending court case regarding the worst forms of child in cobalt mining in DRC (Kelly, 2019). Basically, in the absence of legal mechanisms to hold MNCs and supply chain operators accountable when they operate in unsustainable ways, they will continue to operate in an unsustainable manner. Referencing the legally binding agreement Between MNCs and local trade unions, *the accord on fire and building safety in Bangladesh* (Accord, 2018; Sainato, 2022). Walmart never signed on to the Bangladesh legally binding accord and opted to partner with Gap to create a voluntary organization called the Alliance for Bangladesh Worker Safety (Kasperkevic, 2016). Giving MNCs the latitude to sign or not sign a legally binding agreement may not exact a morally satisfactory response. Consequently, legislations, contracts, and agendas must, where possible, be legally binding with a firm legal base and clear benchmarks, comprehensive with standard metrics that lack flexibility for varied interpretations. If transgressors involved in child labor and forced labor cannot be apprehended before and during the act, then there should be mechanisms to prosecute then when apprehended even though apprehension is after the fact.

Corporate Wrongdoing Index

Critics and researchers relentlessly question the position of ESG data in investment decisions, any associated limitations, and any consensus on overcoming them while incorporating said ESG data into their investment decision-making process (Amel-Zadeh & Serafeim, 2018). Some researchers advocate that there should be specific metrics and methodologies for measuring and reporting corporate unethical behavior or *a corporate wrongdoing index* as much as their espoused metrics for measuring ESG-washing (Fiaschi et al., 2020). The corporate wrongdoing index would perfect areas the ESG index failed. According to Fiaschi et al. (2020) the areas are (a) temporal consistency covering the exact date when the misconduct occurred and (b) absolute transparency in the scoring of corporate involvement in wrongful business conduct as ESG uses codified data. The existence of a corporate wrongdoing index giving (a) accurate date of wrongdoing occurrence, (b) the constituencies (environmental, social, or governance) breached; and (c) a transparent metric for rating the occurrence of corporate wrongdoing would act as a deterrence. Additionally, having precise information from a corporate wrongdoing index to correlate with an ESG index should make a better tool for investment advisors.

Host Country Government Managing MNCs and Supply Chains

The arrival of MNCs, whether for labor, resources, or both, proliferates the grand impression of increased employment, economic growth, increased exports, technology sharing, knowledge and skills transfer, poverty alleviation, retained profits for host nation infrastructural development, and introduction to new standards in anti-pollution standards (Bresnahan, 2020; Ferdausy & Rahman, 2009). Instead, the reality of corruption, employee exploitation, tax evasion, the outflow of profits, environmental pollution, prevention of autonomous development, unethical supply chains, and health and safety risks replaces previous expectations (Bresnahan, 2020; Ferdausy & Rahman, 2009).

Transparency International (2007) cited that corruption is at the roots of MNCs sustaining hegemonic tendencies in developing host nations as monies for bribes flows from MNCs based in the world's wealthiest countries down to high-level public officials in impoverished developing countries. The host country's government is often unwilling to address the exploitation due to their entrenched dependency on the MNC and fear of the MNC relocating to another country, thus increasing the unemployment rate (Manik & Yardley, 2013). Host country governments must start evaluating the cost of MNCs operating in their nations (Hoskins & Mayorga, 2020). While the MNC creates jobs, the non-worseness clause must never be accepted as a job not paying a living wage is not worth the life of citizens (Bresnahan, 2020).

Often the resources (lithium, cobalt, cocoa beans, etc.) required by the MNC is located in developing nations without the technical expertise for extracting and harvesting (Amnesty International, 2016; Balch, 2020b; Hinch, 2018; Kelly, 2019). Cost reduction by way of child and forced labor using bare hands or primitive tools are typical in supply chain labor, as complicit MNCs deny affiliation and knowledge of the atrocities (Amnesty International, 2016; Balch, 2020b; Hinch, 2018; Kelly, 2019). Corporate attorneys have the resources to guide their board of directors regarding supply chain management (Johnson, 2015). Host nation governments must protect their citizens, especially children, from exploitation (Hoskins & Mayorga, 2020; Transparency International, 2007, 2017, 2022).

Host country governments must enter into contracts with MNCs that benefit their nation (Ferdausy & Rahman, 2009). The respective government of Chile, with the world's largest supply of lithium; DRC, with the world's most extensive cobalt; and Côte d'Ivoire and Ghana, with the world's best cocoa beans, are in positions to negotiate better agreements with MNCs. Infrastructures such as schools, hospitals, improved roads, water, assistance with acquiring clean and renewable energy for electrical supply, technology sharing, transfer of skills and knowledge, and a form of *sudden death departure host nation tax* for abrupt exit should be negotiated into the contracts as applicable. The construction of modern schools would allow girls to become educated and reduce the gender inequity gap (Esen & Seren, 2021; Walker et al., 2019). The contractual arrangements must be thoroughly managed, and MNCs must be held accountable accordingly.

While the International Apparel Federation (IAF), established in 1972, still exists, through digital age networking, developing nations should collaborate and create an international apparel manufacturing coalition for developing nations. Based on website information, the IAF is headquartered in the Netherlands – a developed nation listed as the eighth least corrupt country on the Transparency International 2021 CPI since 2016, but (b) home of international brand C&A that used Rana Plaza at the time the building collapse in Bangladesh (Manik & Yardley, 2013; Transparency International, 2022). Thus developing nations need a holistic body created by themselves, for themselves. Should managing MNCs become a collective practice of developing nations, especially those with premium and unique resources and skills, then MNCs will lose the liberty of casually relocating to other countries deemed more accepting of their atrocities.

Teaching Ethics in Business Schools

Cordeiro (2003) posited that business ethics was on the decline and the only solution to having ethical managers is to teach ethics as a course to graduate students in business schools. Cordeiro mentioned multiple unethical practices, such as Mitsubishi, Sears, and President Clinton. The authors of this chapter added for popular reference (a) Martha Stewart's cooking the books (Lomax, 2003), (b) for breach of trust and creating mass impoverishment - the 2008 global financial crisis where millions of people lost their pensions and investments due to poor decision making by fund managers (Bridgman, 2010); (c) for challenges with sustainable development and climate change - Volkswagen's admitted cheating on vehicle emissions testings (Hotten, 2015; Plungis, 2015); and (d) for poor labor management and not disclosing business ethics – Tesla for focusing only on what they interpret as the *real-world impact* of their sustainable development but not the cost of achieving said real-world impact (Kelly, 2019; Kerber & Jin, 2022; Laing, 2022; Wipper et al., 2022, 2022). While no training may provide leadership with the conviction to not harm others, the authors concur that at least exposure to the knowledge consequences of unethical practices in business school could make a difference in the real-world.

Paying Living Wages and Removing Gender Salary Gap

In Guatemala, the minimum wage for the garment manufacturing sector is US$374.00 (£330.00) per month, but union reports indicated some employees received as little as US$205.00 (£181.00) per month (Hoskins & Mayorga, 2020). The living wage in Guatemala is US$770.00 (£680.00) per month (Hoskins & Mayorga, 2020). In the DRC, children with primitive tools digging for cobalt rocks in dark, underground tunnels earn as little as $2.00 (£1.50) per day. In Bangladesh, at the time of the November 2012 Tazrene Fashion Fire and the April 2013 collapse of Rana Plaza, reports indicated that the minimum wage for garment workers was approximately US$37.00 monthly (Manik & Yardley, 2013). Today in 2022, the monthly minimum wage in Bangladesh is US$14.80 for all sectors except the garment industry, where the minimum wage is US$52.31 per month (Minimum-Wage.org, 2022). The minimum wage in Bangladesh has a 5-year increase schedule, but the last adjustment was on December 1, 2013. In 2019 the average daily earnings for a farmer in Côte d'Ivoire was approximately 85 cents (74 pence) (Adams, 2019).

Like many other industries, the garment industry has a higher percentage of women employees than men (Hoskins & Mayorga, 2020; Manik & Yardley, 2013). The fact that women earn lower salaries than men allows for lower pension and social security contributions, thus the widened difference in the retirement era (AAUW, 2020). Paying fair wages to women will enable them to contribute better to their pensions and enjoy a decent retirement as eligible men do. Governments, MNCs, and supply chains are responsible for removing gender salary gaps and paying equitable living wages as such wages alleviate poverty, reduce the gender salary gap, and improve CSR and TBL (Barford et al., 2022; Carr et al., 2021).

Increase Remote and Hybrid Working in Corporations

Globally in 2020, fossil fuel usage in all forms of transportation (sea, air, and road combined) (a) accounted for16.2% of total GHG emissions, while road transportation alone (cars, buses, motorcycles, and commercial freight movers) accounted for 11.9% of total global GHG emissions (Ritchie, 2020). Notably, passenger travel (cars, buses, and motorcycles) contributed 60% of road transport emissions (International Energy Agency [IEA], 2022; Ritchie, 2020). According to the EPA (2022b), in 2020, in the United States, transportation (sea, air, and road combined) was the largest producer of GHG emissions, accounting for 27% of all GHG emissions. The EPA also reported that 2020 GHG emissions from transportation reflected a 13% reduction compared to 2019, primarily due to the COVID-19 pandemic and increased restrictions that led to reduced travel. Additionally, GHG emissions, specifically from passenger transportation, decreased by 16% for the same period and reason (EPA, 2022b). Researchers in China revealed that China's air quality improved during the COVID-19 lockdown (Zhou et al., 2022). However, a sharp increase in energy consumption accompanied the reopening of the economy, and GHG emissions surged to pre-lock-down levels (Zhou et al., 2022).

Considering that the UNFCCC's 2015 Paris Agreement is to maintain, for this century, a global temperature rises well below 2 °C and as close as possible to 1.5 °C above pre-industrial levels (connect4climate, n.d.; UN, n.d.-a), remote and hybrid working would reduce the volume of passenger transportation and subsequently the volume of GHG emissions. While not all jobs, especially in developed nations, can be worked remotely (B. A. Brown & Heitner, 2022), employers, where possible, must maintain or resume remote and hybrid work. Many corporations built resilience while their employees worked from home during the global lockdown and should operate on the acquired resilience versus resuming pre-pandemic back-to-work mode.

Groundwater Governance

Researchers estimated that by 2050, feeding the planet's 9 billion inhabitants will require an estimated 50% increase in agricultural production and a 15% increase in water abstraction demand relative to 2012 levels (Khokhar, 2017; UN, 2022a). To coincide with the UN 2030 Agenda for Sustainable Development, the projected increased agricultural productivity must be accomplished using sustainable escalation of groundwater abstraction while lessening agricultural production's environmental and water footprints (UN, 2022a). To best control future groundwater abstraction, it may be necessary to control the location and volume of water abstractions from aquifers, especially for commercial use (UN, 2022a). Control mechanisms could include but are not limited to (a) regulatory involving the need for government permits for abstractions, (b) market-based by applying tariffs for abstraction or incentives to corporations practicing good groundwater conservation practices or for facilitating the implementation of new technologies, and practice to preserve groundwater, (c) create awareness on the importance of changing to a sustainable attitude towards groundwater consumption, and (d) monitoring and sanctioning to pressure commercial groundwater users to adjust their groundwater requirements to varying aquifer condition(UN, 2022a).

CONCLUSION

Simultaneously addressing the Paris Agreement and the 2030 Agenda for Sustainable Development is the most effective approach to enable countries to achieve their SDGs and targets efficiently and quickly (UN, n.d.-a). Considering the objectives of the Paris Agreement and the UN 2030 Agenda for Sustainable Development, a high degree of global sustainability could be achieved with their adaptation (UN, n.d.-f, n.d.-d). Health, jobs, supply chains, and homes are at risk as rising sea levels, water scarcity, droughts, famines, and food insecurity in developing nations remain ongoing concerns and phenomena. Reduction in GHG emissions from unsustainable business and other practices would reduce the development and promulgation of these adverse concerns brought on by climate change (Berchin et al., 2017; Flammer et al., 2021; UN, n.d.-g).

Researchers also demonstrated that developing nations' gross domestic product (GDP) has decreased while private consumption increases with a decrease in investments (de Bandt et al., 2021; Kompas et al., 2018). Economic calculations on the potential damage of climate change may be severely under-estimated (Kompas et al., 2018, p. 1153). Organizational transformation must begin at an accelerated pace to begin driving sustainability. Whether CSR, ESG, or TBL, these three concepts add social and environmental responsibilities to the (often seemingly lone) existing organizational commitment or purpose – maximization of shareholders' wealth via financial investment and production. The inclusion of the social and environmental dimensions for ensuring corporate sustainability based on responsible business processes fuels continuously the debate regarding shareholders' value versus stakeholders' value (Baumfield, 2016; Freeman, 2010; Lockhart & Taitoko, 2005; Mitchell et al., 1997; Vinten, 2001). History has shown that the wealthiest lack the moral compass to do what is right even with conditionality or consequences, let alone the absence of one or both, as evidenced by the disregard for CSR and human rights in the workplace. The 2021 CPI shows that top-scoring countries' complacency has been detrimental to global anti-corruption efforts and now to their affairs (Transparency International, 2022).

The matter of child and forced labor requires additional and international intervention. Extant literature exists on the subject matter, but merely a regurgitation of the number of forced child labor of the worst form, forced labor, human trafficking, forced marriages, modern slavery girls and women forced into the sex trade have increased for years on end. While in bondage, these girls and women remain without education. Suppose these girls (and women) cannot receive an education which is a fundamental human right, or be business models liberated. In that case, the thrust of the SDGs and their relevant targets regarding eliminating atrocities against women and gender inequality must be realized.

The voluntary self-monitoring and self-reporting components do not create incentives for organizational CSR compliance (Doane, 2005). While CSR and ESG have common espoused goals of corporate sustainability and transparency, CSR compliance (like ESG compliance) remains voluntary (Munro & Van Drunen, 2022). Regulators in some sectors continue petitioning their respective governments for mandatory ESG compliance and reporting, the regulating sectors for other countries are still formulating ESG frameworks, while some fund management and rating agencies sell ESG-incorporated portfolios (Fiaschi et al., 2020; Munro & Van Drunen, 2022; Quinson, 2022; Simpson et al., 2021).

While corporations clamor to be their industry's leader in providing sustainable development, the authors recommend that corporate leadership consider the actual cost of sustainability in conjunction with the real-world impact. China refines more than 60% of lithium, 75% of cobalt, and 96% of manganese mined globally, and by the end of 2022, China will produce more than 70% of electric vehicle batteries (Benchmark, 2022). Of note, the addition of cobalt and manganese here is vital as the unsustainable mining of these minerals poses a grave threat to health, life, and the environment and contravenes the aims of the Paris agreement and the UN 2030 Agenda for Sustainable Development (Benchmark, 2022; Campbell, 2022; Duka et al., 2011; Kelly, 2019; Penn et al., 2021). From chocolate to renewable energy, the lives and dignity of all involved in sustainable development matter.

REFERENCES

Abendroth, A.-K., Melzer, S., Kalev, A., & Tomaskovic-Devey, D. (2017). Women at work: Women's access to power and the gender earnings gap. *Industrial & Labor Relations Review*, *70*(1), 190–222. doi:10.1177/0019793916668530

AboAbdo, S., Aldhoiena, A., & Al-Amrib, H. (2019). Implementing enterprise resource planning (ERP) system in a large construction company in KSA. *Procedia Computer Science*, *164*, 463–470. doi:10.1016/j.procs.2019.12.207

Accord. (2018). *The Bangladesh accord on fire and building safety*. https://bangladeshaccord.org/

Adams, T. (2019, February 24). From bean to bar in Ivory Coast, a country built on cocoa. *The Guardian*. https://www.theguardian.com/global-development/2019/feb/24/ivory-coast-cocoa-farmers-fairtrade-fortnight-women-farmers-trade-justice

Addo-Tenkorang, R. (2011). Enterprise resource planning (ERP). *Computers in Industry*, 9.

Adler, P. S., Forbes, L. C., & Willmott, H. C. (2008). *Critical management studies*. https://www.research-gate.net/publication/264808848_Critical_Management_Studies

Aguinis, H., & Glavas, A. (2012). What we know and don't know about corporate social responsibility: A review and research agenda. *Journal of Management*, *38*(4), 932–968. doi:10.1177/0149206311436079

Alim, F. (2022). DFEH Sues Tesla, Inc. For race discrimination and harassment. *Civil Action*, *006830*(No. 22CV), 1.

Allen, A. (2022, January 27). *Nestlé to pay cocoa farmers to keep children in school*. Supply Management. https://www.cips.org/supply-management/news/2022/january/nestle-to-pay-cocoa-farmers-to-keep-children-in-school/

alliance8.7. (2022). *Breaking the cycle of intergenerational child labour in the Philippines—How Eron escaped the gold mine*. https://www.alliance87.org/interactive/philippines/

Amel-Zadeh, A., & Serafeim, G. (2018). Why and how investors use ESG information: Evidence from a global survey. *Financial Analysts Journal*, *74*(3), 87–103. doi:10.2469/faj.v74.n3.2

American Association of University Women. (2020). *The simple truth about the gender pay gap: AAUW report*. https://www.aauw.org/resources/research/simple-truth/

Amnesty International. (2016). *Exposed: Child labour behind smart phone and electric car batteries*. https://www.amnesty.org/en/latest/news/2016/01/Child-labour-behind-smart-phone-and-electric-car-batteries/

Anderson, L., & Kariss-Nix, B. (2014, March 4). Why does everyone hate Monsanto? *Modern Farmer.* https://modernfarmer.com/2014/03/monsantos-good-bad-pr-problem/

Andrei, M. (2017, May 19). Why Nestle is one of the most hated companies in the world. *ZME Science.* https://www.zmescience.com/science/nestle-company-pollution-children/

Ayman, R., & Korabik, K. (2010). Leadership why gender and culture matter. *The American Psychologist, 65*(3), 157–170. doi:10.1037/a0018806 PMID:20350015

Bakan, J. (2005). *The corporation: The pathological pursuit of profit and power.* Free Press.

Balch, O. (2020a, August 5). US could become 'safe haven' for corporate abusers, activists warn. *The Guardian.* https://www.theguardian.com/global-development/2020/aug/05/us-could-become-safe-haven-for-corporate-abusers-activists-warn

Balch, O. (2020b, October 20). Chocolate industry slammed for failure to crack down on child labour. *The Guardian.* https://www.theguardian.com/global-development/2020/oct/20/chocolate-industry-slammed-for-failure-to-crack-down-on-child-labour

BarfordA.GilbertR.BealesA.ZorilaM.NelsonJ.(2022).*The case for living wages: How to improve business performance and tackle poverty.* Apollo - University of Cambridge Repository. doi:10.17863/CAM.80370

Barry, E. (2022, May 25). Why Tesla CEO Elon Musk is calling ESG a "scam." *Time.* https://time.com/6180638/tesla-esg-index-musk/

Baumfield, V. S. (2016). Stakeholder theory from a management perspective: Bridging the shareholder/stakeholder divide. *Australian Journal of Corporate Law, 31*, 23.

Benchmark. (2022, October 3). Infographic: China's lithium ion battery supply chain dominance. *Benchmark.* https://www.benchmarkminerals.com/membership/chinas-lithium-ion-battery-supply-chain-dominance/

Berchin, I. I., Valduga, I. B., Garcia, J., & de Andrade Guerra, J. B. S. O. (2017). Climate change and forced migrations: An effort towards recognizing climate refugees. *Geoforum, 84*, 147–150. doi:10.1016/j.geoforum.2017.06.022

Berkey, B. (2021). Sweatshops, structural injustice, and the wrong of exploitation: Why multinational corporations have positive duties to the global poor. *Journal of Business Ethics, 169*(1), 43–56. Advance online publication. doi:10.100710551-019-04299-1

Berman, B. (2020, May 21). Tesla employees fear unsafe conditions at factory, call it 'modern-day sweatshop.' *Electrek.* https://electrek.co/2020/05/21/tesla-employees-fear-unsafe-conditions-at-factory-call-it-modern-day-sweatshop/

Boudreau, J. W., & Ramstad, P. M. (2005). Talentship, talent segmentation, and sustainability: A new HR decision science paradigm for a new strategy definition. *Human Resource Management, 44*(2), 129–136. doi:10.1002/hrm.20054

Bowen, M. G., & Power, F. C. (1993). The moral manager: Communicative ethics and the Exxon Valdez disaster. *Business Ethics Quarterly, 3*(2), 97–115. doi:10.2307/3857366

Bresnahan, C. O. (2020, September 13). *Multinational corporations in developing countries.* The Borgen Project. https://borgenproject.org/multinational-corporations-in-developing-countries/

Bridgman, T. (2010). Beyond the manager's moral dilemma: Rethinking the "ideal-type" business ethics case. *Journal of Business Ethics, 94*(S2), 311–322. doi:10.100710551-011-0759-3

Brown, B. A., & Heitner, K. L. (2022). Worker response to the rapid changes caused by disruptive innovation: Managing a remote workforce without any training or preparation. In R. Hynes, C. Aquino, & J. Hauer (Eds.), *Multidisciplinary approach to diversity and inclusion in the COVID-19-era workplace* (pp. 189–205). IGI Global. doi:10.4018/978-1-7998-8827-7.ch011

Brown, G. (2015). Bangladesh: Currently the worst, but possibly the future's best. *New Solutions, 24*(4), 469–473. doi:10.2190/NS.24.4.b PMID:25816164

Butler, B., & Surace, K. (2015). Call for organisational agility in the emergent sector of the service industry. *Journal of Business and Management, 10,* 4–14.

Campbell, M. (2022, February 1). *South America's "lithium fields" reveal the dark side of electric cars.* https://www.euronews.com/green/2022/02/01/south-america-s-lithium-fields-reveal-the-dark-side-of-our-electric-future

Carr, S., Young-Hauser, A., Hodgetts, D., Schmidt, W., Moran, L., Haar, J., Parker, J., Arrowsmith, J., & Jones, H. (2021). Research update: How decent wages transform qualities of living—by affording escape from working poverty trap. *Journal of Sustainability Research, 3*(2). Advance online publication. doi:10.20900/jsr20210012

Carroll, A. B. (1991). The pyramid of corporate social responsibility: Toward the moral management of organizational stakeholders. *Business Horizons, 34*(4), 39–48. doi:10.1016/0007-6813(91)90005-G

Chakraborty, A., & Tan, K. C. (2012). Case study analysis of Six Sigma implementation in service organisations. *Business Process Management Journal, 18*(6), 992–1019. doi:10.1108/14637151211283384

Chan, E. (2021, April). *It has been 8 years since the Rana Plaza disaster. What's changed?* British Vogue. https://vogue-int-rocket.prod.cni.digital/rana-plaza-garment-workers

Chan, J. (2013). A suicide survivor: The life of a Chinese worker. *New Technology, Work and Employment, 28*(2), 84–99. doi:10.1111/ntwe.12007

Chibber, K. (2012, September 24). Foxconn: "Hidden dragon" out in the open. *BBC News.* https://www.bbc.com/news/business-19699156

Chisholm-Burns, M. A., Spivey, C. A., Hagemann, T., & Josephson, M. A. (2017). Women in leadership and the bewildering glass ceiling. *American Journal of Health-System Pharmacy, 74*(5), 312–324. doi:10.2146/ajhp160930 PMID:28122701

Chung, D. J. (2015). How to really motivate salespeople: New research challenges conventional wisdom about the best ways to pay your team. *Harvard Business Review, 4,* 54.

Clarke, J. S. (2015, September 2). Child labour on Nestlé farms: Chocolate giant's problems continue. *The Guardian.* https://www.theguardian.com/global-development-professionals-network/2015/sep/02/child-labour-on-nestle-farms-chocolate-giants-problems-continue

Cole, C. (2022, April 27). *Who's winning America's electric vehicle race?* CNET. https://www.cnet.com/roadshow/news/american-electric-vehicle-analysis/

Confino, J. (2013, February 4). Nestlé's Peter Brabeck: Our attitude towards water needs to change. *The Guardian.* https://www.theguardian.com/sustainable-business/nestle-peter-brabeck-attitude-water-change-stewardship

connect4climate. (n.d.). *2030 Agenda and Paris Agreement: Best achieved together.* https://www.con-nect4climate.org/infographics/2030-agenda-and-paris-agreement-best-achieved-together-klimalog-bmz

Cook, A., & Glass, C. (2014). Above the glass ceiling: When are women and racial/ethnic minorities promoted to CEO? *Strategic Management Journal, 35*(7), 1080–1089. doi:10.1002mj.2161

Cornell Law School. (2022, June). *Alien Tort Statute.* LII / Legal Information Institute. https://www.law.cornell.edu/wex/alien_tort_statute

Cuevas, F. (1996, July 16). In Honduras, "sweatshop" wages better than nothing for many workers. *AP News.* https://apnews.com/article/fb4d8d420e730a16623275241409a11b

Daugaard, D. (2020). Emerging new themes in environmental, social and governance investing: A systematic literature review. *Accounting and Finance, 60*(2), 1501–1530. doi:10.1111/acfi.12479

de Bandt, O., Jacolin, L., & Thibault, L. (2021). Climate change in developing countries: Global warming effects, transmission channels and adaptation policies. SSRN *Electronic Journal, 68.* doi:10.2139/ssrn.3888112

Denchak, M. (2022, April 18). *Water pollution: Everything you need to know.* NRDC. https://www.nrdc.org/stories/water-pollution-everything-you-need-know

Dietz, T., Shwom, R. L., & Whitley, C. T. (2020). *Climate change and society.* Academic Press.

Doane, D. (2005). Beyond corporate social responsibility: Minnows, mammoths and markets. *Futures, 37*(2), 215–229. doi:10.1016/j.futures.2004.03.028

Dorn, M. (2022, May 17). *The (re)balancing act of the S&P 500 esg index.* https://www.indexologyblog.com/2022/05/17/the-rebalancing-act-of-the-sp-500-esg-index/

Downey, S. N., van der Werff, L., Thomas, K. M., & Plaut, V. C. (2015). The role of diversity practices and inclusion in promoting trust and employee engagement. *Journal of Applied Social Psychology, 45*(1), 35–44. doi:10.1111/jasp.12273

Eagly, A. H., & Chin, J. L. (2010). Diversity and leadership in a changing world. *The American Psychologist, 65*(3), 216–224. doi:10.1037/a0018957 PMID:20350020

EarthRights International. (2022). *Alien Tort Statute.* EarthRights International. https://earthrights.org/litigation-and-legal-advocacy/legal-strategies/alien-tort-statute/

Elkington, J. (2004). Enter the tripple bottom line. In *The tripple bottom line: Does it all add up?* (1st ed.). Routledge.

Emery, D. (2018). *Did the ceo of Nestlé say water is not a human right?* https://www.snopes.com/fact-check/nestle-ceo-water-not-human-right/

Environmental Protection Agency. (2022a, April 9). *Hudson River cleanup* [Overviews and factsheets]. https://www.epa.gov/hudsonriverpcbs/hudson-river-cleanup

Environmental Protection Agency. (2022b, August 5). *Sources of greenhouse gas emissions* [Overviews and factsheets]. https://www.epa.gov/ghgemissions/sources-greenhouse-gas-emissions

Esen, Ö., & Seren, G. Y. (2021). The impact of gender inequality in education and employment on economic performance in Turkey: Evidence from a cointegration approach. *Equality, Diversity and Inclusion, 41*(4), 592–607. doi:10.1108/EDI-04-2021-0099

Ezzedeen, S. R., Budworth, M.-H., & Baker, S. D. (2015). The glass ceiling and executive careers still an issue for pre-career women. *Journal of Career Development, 42*(5), 355–369. doi:10.1177/0894845314566943

Farndale, E., Biron, M., Briscoe, D. R., & Raghuram, S. (2015). A global perspective on diversity and inclusion in work organisations. *International Journal of Human Resource Management, 26*(6), 677–687. doi:10.1080/09585192.2014.991511

Ferdausy, S., & Rahman, S. (2009). *Impact of multinational corporations on developing countries.* Academic Press.

Fetuga, B. M., Njokama, F. O., & Olowu, A. O. (2005). Prevalence, types and demographic features of child labour among school children in Nigeria. *BMC International Health and Human Rights, 5*(1), 2. doi:10.1186/1472-698X-5-2 PMID:15743516

Fiaschi, D., Giuliani, E., Nieri, F., & Salvati, N. (2020). How bad is your company? Measuring corporate wrongdoing beyond the magic of ESG metrics | Elsevier Enhanced Reader. *Business Horizons, 63*(3), 287–299. doi:10.1016/j.bushor.2019.09.004

Flammer, C., Toffel, M. W., & Viswanathan, K. (2021). Shareholder activism and firms' voluntary disclosure of climate change risks. *Strategic Management Journal, 42*(10), 62. doi:10.1002mj.3313

Freeman, R. E. (2010). *Strategic management: A stakeholder approach.* Cambridge University Press. doi:10.1017/CBO9781139192675

Gazova, A., Papulova, Z., & Papula, J. (2016). The application of concepts and methods based on process approach to increase business process efficiency. *Procedia Economics and Finance, 39*, 197–205. doi:10.1016/S2212-5671(16)30284-2

Gelles, D., & Yaffe-Bellany, D. (2019). Shareholder value is no longer everything, top c.e.o.s say. *The New York Times*, 11.

Govindan, K., Shankar, K. M., & Kannan, D. (2020). Achieving sustainable development goals through identifying and analyzing barriers to industrial sharing economy: A framework development. *International Journal of Production Economics, 227*, 107575. doi:10.1016/j.ijpe.2019.107575

Haiken, M. (2014). More than 10,000 suicides tied to economic crisis, study says. *Forbes*. https://www. forbes.com/sites/melaniehaiken/2014/06/12/more-than-10000-suicides-tied-to-economic-crisis-study-says/

Haklová, D., Gallovič, M., & Vitálošová, E. (2020, August 20). *ESG reporting and preparation of a sustainability report*. https://www.pwc.com/sk/en/environmental-social-and-corporate-governance-esg/esg-reporting.html

Hammer, M. (1990, July 1). Reengineering work: Don't automate, obliterate. *Harvard Business Review*. https://hbr.org/1990/07/reengineering-work-dont-automate-obliterate

Hammer, M. (2015). What is business process management? In J. vom Brocke & M. Rosemann (Eds.), *Handbook on business process management 1: Introduction, methods, and information systems* (pp. 3–16). Springer. doi:10.1007/978-3-642-45100-3_1

Heitner, K. L. (2018). Race, ethnicity, and religion in the workplace. In C. T. E. de Aquino & R. W. Robertson (Eds.), *Diversity and inclusion in the global workplace: Aligning initiatives with strategic business goals* (pp. 49–67). Springer International Publishing. doi:10.1007/978-3-319-54993-4_3

Heyen, D., Hermwille, L., & Wehnert, T. (2017). Out of the comfort zone! Governing the exnovation of unsustainable technologies and practices. *Gaia (Heidelberg)*, *26*(4), 326–331. doi:10.14512/gaia.26.4.9

Hinch, R. (2018). Chocolate, slavery, forced labour, child labour and the state. In *A Handbook of food crime* (pp. 77–92). Policy Press. doi:10.2307/j.ctt22rbk9t.10

Hinchliffe, E. (2022a, May 23). Roz Brewer, Thasunda Brown Duckett, Karen Lynch make up record number of female Fortune 500 CEOs. *Fortune*. https://fortune.com/2022/05/23/female-ceos-fortune-500-2022-women-record-high-karen-lynch-sarah-nash/

Hinchliffe, E. (2022b, August 23). Female CEOs run just 4.8% of the Fortune Global 500. *Fortune*. https://fortune.com/2022/08/03/female-ceos-global-500-thyssenkrupp-martina-merz-cvs-karen-lynch/

Hoke, T. (2013). Corporate culture in support of engineering ethics. *Civil Engineering, 83*(9), 46–47.

Holusha, J. (1989, April 21). Exxon's public-relations problem. *The New York Times*. https://www. nytimes.com/1989/04/21/business/exxon-s-public-relations-problem.html

Hoskins, T., & Mayorga, J. (2020, August 6). Covid outbreak exposes dire conditions at Guatemala factory making US brands. *The Guardian*. https://www.theguardian.com/global-development/2020/aug/06/covid-outbreak-exposes-dire-conditions-at-guatemala-factory-making-us-brands

Hotten, R. (2015, December 10). Volkswagen: The scandal explained. *BBC News*. https://www.bbc. com/news/business-34324772

Industri, A. L. L. (2016, July 20). *Indonesia: Low wages in the textile and garment industry undermine workers' rights*. IndustriALL. https://www.industriall-union.org/indonesia-low-wages-in-the-textile-and-garment-industry-undermine-workers-rights

Inter-American Development Bank. (2020). *Internet para todos: Helping Latin America log on*. https://www.iadb.org/en/improvinglives/internet-para-todos-helping-latin-america-log

International Cocoa Initiative. (2021). *Harkin Engel protocol*. https://www.cocoainitiative.org/knowledge-hub/resources/harkin-engel-protocol

International Energy Agency. (2022). *Transport sector CO2 emissions by mode in the sustainable development scenario, 2000-2030 – charts – data & statistics*. https://www.iea.org/data-and-statistics/charts/transport-sector-co2-emissions-by-mode-in-the-sustainable-development-scenario-2000-2030

International Institute for Sustainable Development. (n.d.). *Sustainable development*. Author. https://www.iisd.org/mission-and-goals/sustainable-development

International Labour Organization. (2011, August 7). *Africa: Child labor in cocoa fields/ Harkin-Engel Protocol* [Document]. https://www.ilo.org/washington/areas/elimination-of-the-worst-forms-of-child-labor/WCMS_159486/lang--en/index.htm

International Labour Organization. (2021). *Child Labour: Global estimates 2020, trends and the road forward* [Report]. http://www.ilo.org/ipec/Informationresources/WCMS_797515/lang--en/index.htm

International Labour Organization. (2022a). *Forced labour, modern slavery and human trafficking*. https://www.ilo.org/global/topics/forced-labour/lang--en/index.htm

International Labour Organization. (2022b). *Global estimates of modern slavery: Forced labour and forced marriage*. International Labour Office., doi:10.54394/CHUI5986

International Labour Organization. (2022c, September 28). *Impact stories: From child labour and forced labour to dreams of a better future*. https://www.ilo.org/global/topics/child-labour/news/WCMS_835919/lang--en/index.htm

International Labour Organization. (n.d.-a). *Convention C138—Minimum age convention, 1973 (No. 138)*. https://www.ilo.org/dyn/normlex/en/f?p=NORMLEXPUB:12100:NO:12100:P12100_ILO_CODE:C138:NO

International Labour Organization. (n.d.-b). *Convention C182—Worst forms of child labour convention, 1999 (No. 182)*. https://www.ilo.org/dyn/normlex/en/f?p=NORMLEXPUB:12100:NO:12100:P12100_ILO_CODE:C182:NO

International Labour Organization. (n.d.-c). *The worst forms of child labour (IPEC)*. https://www.ilo.org/ipec/Campaignandadvocacy/Youthinaction/C182-Youth-orientated/worstforms/lang--en/index.htm

James, C. (1988, April 5). *Jamaican government probing free zone working conditions*. https://www.joc.com/maritime-news/jamaican-government-probing-free-zone-working-conditions_19880405.html

Johnson, E. C. Jr. (2015, September 22). Business lawyers are in a unique position to help their clients identify supply-chain risks involving labor trafficking and child labor. *Business Lawyer, 70*(4), 1083.

Jones, R. (2010, May 29). Something rotten at Apple's core? Shocking toll of suicides at iPad factory in China revealed. *Daily Mail Online*. https://www.dailymail.co.uk/news/article-1282481/iPad-factory-suicides-China.html

Jonsdottir, B., Sigurjonsson, T. O., Johannsdottir, L., & Wendt, S. (2022). Barriers to using ESG data for investment decisions. *Sustainability (Basel), 14*(9), 5157. doi:10.3390u14095157

Kapur, R. (2019). Gender inequality in education. *International Journal of Transformations in Business Management, 9*(1). https://www.researchgate.net/publication/334162862_Gender_Inequality_in_Education.

Kasperkevic, J. (2016, May 31). Rana Plaza collapse: Workplace dangers persist three years later, reports find. *The Guardian.* https://www.theguardian.com/business/2016/may/31/rana-plaza-bangladesh-collapse-fashion-working-conditions

Kelly, A. (2016, February 1). Nestlé admits slavery in Thailand while fighting child labour lawsuit in Ivory Coast. *The Guardian.* https://www.theguardian.com/sustainable-business/2016/feb/01/nestle-slavery-thailand-fighting-child-labour-lawsuit-ivory-coast

Kelly, A. (2019). Apple and Google named in US lawsuit over Congolese child cobalt mining deaths. *The Guardian*, 5.

Kerber, R., & Jin, H. (2022, May 19). Tesla cut from S&P 500 ESG Index, and Elon Musk tweets his fury. *Reuters.* https://www.reuters.com/business/sustainable-business/tesla-removed-sp-500-esg-index-autopilot-discrimination-concerns-2022-05-18/

Khokhar, T. (2017, March 22). *Chart: Globally, 70% of freshwater is used for agriculture.* https://blogs.worldbank.org/opendata/chart-globally-70-freshwater-used-agriculture

Kimberly, J. R. (1981). Managerial innovation. Handbook of Organizational Design, 1(84), 104.

Kluza, K., Zioło, M., & Spoz, A. (2021). Innovation and environmental, social, and governance factors influencing sustainable business models—Meta-analysis. *Journal of Cleaner Production, 303*, 14. doi:10.1016/j.jclepro.2021.127015

Koengkan, M., Fuinhas, J. A., Belucio, M., Kazemzadeh, E., Poveda, Y. E. M., Alavijeh, N. K., & Santiago, R. (2022). The consequences of gender inequality on Latin America's economic growth: Macroeconomic evidence. *Sexes, 3*(3), 3. Advance online publication. doi:10.3390exes3030030

Kompas, T., Pham, V. H., & Che, T. N. (2018). The effects of climate change on GDP by country and the global economic gains from complying with the Paris Climate Accord. *Earth's Future, 6*(8), 1153–1173. doi:10.1029/2018EF000922

Krüger, T., & Pellicer-Sifres, V. (2020). From innovations to exnovations. Conflicts, (de-) politicization processes, and power relations are key in analysing the ecological crisis. *Innovation (Abingdon), 33*(2), 115–123. doi:10.1080/13511610.2020.1733936

Laing, K. (2022, May 18). Fatal Tesla model s crash in California prompts federal probe. *Bloomberg. Com.* https://www.bloomberg.com/news/articles/2022-05-18/fatal-tesla-model-s-crash-in-california-prompts-federal-probe

Lazonick, W., & O'Sullivan, M. (2002). Maximizing shareholder value: A new ideology for corporate governance. In Corporate governance and sustainable prosperity (pp. 11–36). doi:10.1057/9780230523739_2

Levy, A., & Merry, U. (1986). *Organizational transformation: Approaches, strategies, theories.* Greenwood Publishing Group.

Lewis, M. W., Andriopoulos, C., & Smith, W. K. (2014). Paradoxical leadership to enable strategic agility. *California Management Review*, *56*(3), 58–77. doi:10.1525/cmr.2014.56.3.58

Lockhart, J. C., & Taitoko, M. (2005). An examination of shareholder–stakeholder governance tension: A case study of the collapses of Ansett Holdings and Air New Zealand. In C. R. Lehman, T. Tinker, B. Merino, & M. Neimark (Eds.), *Corporate governance: Does any size fit?* (Vol. 11, pp. 223–246). Emerald Group Publishing Limited. doi:10.1016/S1041-7060(05)11010-4

Lomax, S. (2003). Cooking the Books. *Business and Economic Review*, *49*(3), 3.

Lucas, K., Kang, D., & Li, Z. (2013). Workplace dignity in a total institution: Examining the experiences of Foxconn's migrant workforce. *Journal of Business Ethics*, *114*(1), 91–106. doi:10.100710551-012-1328-0

Macintyre, D. (2014, July 8). *10 major clothing brands caught in shocking sweatshop scandals*. TheRichest. https://www.therichest.com/rich-list/most-shocking/10-major-clothing-brands-caught-in-shocking-sweatshop-scandals/

Mahdiraji, H. A., Hafeez, K., Jafarnejad, A., & Rezayar, A. (2020). An analysis of the impact of negative CSR 'forced labour' parameter on the profitability of supply chain contracts. *Journal of Cleaner Production*, *271*, 122274. doi:10.1016/j.jclepro.2020.122274

Manik, J. A., & Yardley, J. (2012, December 17). Bangladesh finds gross negligence in factory fire. *The New York Times*. https://www.nytimes.com/2012/12/18/world/asia/bangladesh-factory-fire-caused-by-gross-negligence.html

Manik, J. A., & Yardley, J. (2013, April 24). Building collapse in Bangladesh leaves scores dead. *The New York Times*, 1–4.

Marco. (2021, March 6). Sustainable business models: 4 pillars to social enterprises sustainability. *Social Business Design*. https://socialbusinessdesign.org/sustainable-business-models-4-pillars-for-sustainability-in-social-enterprises/

Marksberry, P. (2011). The Toyota Way—A quantitative approach. *International Journal of Lean Six Sigma*, *2*(2), 132–150. doi:10.1108/20401461111135028

Marsh, A., & Schwartzkopff, F. (2022, March 8). Esg funds had $8.3 billion in Russia assets right before war. *Bloomberg*. https://www.bloomberg.com/news/articles/2022-03-08/esg-funds-had-8-3-billion-in-russia-assets-right-before-the-war

Maxwell, N. (2022, January 25). *Esg: What is it and why has it become so popular?* https://skybound-wealth.co.uk/blog/esg-what-is-it-and-why-has-it-become-so-popular

McCloy, J. (2019, October 16). *What is sustainability? 13 examples to integrate into your life*. https://greencoast.org/sustainability/

McPhillips, D. (2019, December 19). 10 countries with the worst drinking water. *US News & World Report*. www.usnews.com/news/best-countries/slideshows/10-countries-with-the-worst-water-supply

Milewski, D. (2022). Managerial and economical aspects of the just-in-time system "lean management in the time of pandemic.". *Sustainability (Basel)*, *14*(3), 1204. doi:10.3390u14031204

Minimum-Wage.org. (2022). *Bangladesh minimum wage—World minimum wage rates 2022.* https://www.minimum-wage.org/international/bangladesh

Mitchell, R. K., Agle, B. R., & Wood, D. J. (1997). Toward a theory of stakeholder identification and salience: Defining the principle of who and what really counts. *Academy of Management Review, 22*(4), 853–886. doi:10.2307/259247

Morgan Stanley Capital International. (2022). *Powering better investment decisions.* https://www.msci.com/

Munro, M., & Van Drunen, G. (2022, January 5). 2022 will prove a pivotal year for ESG reporting. *Corporate Compliance Insights.* https://www.corporatecomplianceinsights.com/2022-will-prove-a-pivotal-year-for-esg-reporting/

National Oceanic and Atmospheric Administration. (2015, September 3). *Hudson River Trustees determine injury to groundwater: Damage assessment, remediation, and restoration program.* https://darrp.noaa.gov/hazardous-waste/hudson-river-trustees-determine-injury-groundwater

Nopo, H. (2012). *New century, old disparities: Gender and ethnic earnings gaps in Latin America and the Caribbean.* World Bank Publications. doi:10.1596/978-0-8213-8686-6

NORC. (2020, October 19). *Increase in hazardous child labor in cocoa production amid an expansion of cocoa farming in Côte d'Ivoire and Ghana.* https://www.norc.org/NewsEventsPublications/PressReleases/Pages/increase-in-hazardous-child-labor-in-cocoa-production-amid-an-expansion-of-cocoa-farming-in-cote-d'ivoire-and-ghana.aspx

O'Neill, P., & Sohal, A. S. (1999). Business process reengineering a review of recent literature. *Technovation, 19*(9), 571–581. doi:10.1016/S0166-4972(99)00059-0

Organisation for Economic Co-operation and Development. (n.d.). *Water and agriculture.* https://www.oecd.org/agriculture/topics/water-and-agriculture/

Ortuño, C. I. (2020, June). *COVID-19 and digital inclusion in Latin America and the Caribbean: A connectivity and access problem.* http://www.sela.org/en/press/articles/a/64488/covid-19-digital-inclusion-in-latin-america-and-the-caribbean

Paikah, N., Ruslan, A., Riza, M., & Sakharina, K. (2021). Implementation of government responsibility in fulfillment of child labor education rights in work relationships. *Design Engineering (London), 6,* 15.

Pantouvakis, A., & Psomas, E. (2016). Exploring total quality management applications under uncertainty: A research agenda for the shipping industry. *Maritime Economics & Logistics.* Advance online publication. doi:10.1057/mel.2015.6

Penn, I., Lipton, E., & Angotti-Jones, G. (2021, May 6). The lithium gold rush: Inside the race to power electric vehicles. *The New York Times.* https://www.nytimes.com/2021/05/06/business/lithium-mining-race.html

Plungis, J. (2015, September 18). *Volkswagen admits to cheating on U.S. emissions tests.* Bloomberg. https://www.bloomberg.com/news/articles/2015-09-18/epa-says-volkswagon-software-circumvented-car-emissions-testing

PricewaterhouseCoopers. (2022). *ESG reporting services.* https://www.pwc.com/us/en/services/esg/esg-reporting.html

Quinson, T. (2022, March 16). Greenwashing is increasingly making ESG moot. *Bloomberg.* https://www.bloomberg.com/news/articles/2022-03-16/greenwashing-is-increasingly-making-esg-investing-moot-green-insight

Raimi, L., Akhuemonkhan, I., & Ogunjirin, O. D. (2015). Corporate social responsibility and entrepreneurship (csre): Antidotes to poverty, insecurity and underdevelopment in Nigeria. *Social Responsibility Journal, 11*(1), 81–56. doi:10.1108/SRJ-11-2012-0138

Rajesh, R. (2020). Exploring the sustainability performances of firms using environmental, social, and governance scores. *Journal of Cleaner Production, 247,* 119600. doi:10.1016/j.jclepro.2019.119600

Ritchie, H. (2020, September 18). *Sector by sector: Where do global greenhouse gas emissions come from?* https://ourworldindata.org/ghg-emissions-by-sector

RMIT University. (2017). *The four pillars of sustainability.* https://www.futurelearn.com/info/blog

Robison, W. (2002). Representation and misrepresentation: Tufte and the Morton Thiokol engineers on the Challenger. *Science and Engineering Ethics, 8*(1), 59–81. doi:10.100711948-002-0033-2 PMID:11840958

Rowselle, J. (2022, April 5). *Cadbury attacked over children handling machetes on cocoa farms.* Supply Management. https://www.cips.org/supply-management/news/2022/april/cadbury-attacked-over-children-handling-machetes-on-cocoa-farms/

Sainato, M. (2022, September 23). 'Give workers an equal seat': Pressure builds for Levi's to protect factory employees. *The Guardian.* https://www.theguardian.com/global-development/2022/sep/23/levis-garment-workers-bangladesh-pakistan-international-accord-health-safety

Sanchez, M. (2022, April 27). *What is new in S&P ESG Indices?* https://www.indexologyblog.com/2022/04/27/what-is-new-in-sp-esg-indices/

Sasse, G. (2008). The politics of EU conditionality: The norm of minority protection during and beyond EU accession. *Journal of European Public Policy, 15*(6), 842–860. doi:10.1080/13501760802196580

Schwab, K. (2008). Global corporate citizenship—Working with governments and civil society. *Foreign Affairs, 87*(1), 107–118.

Siddiqui, F., Lerman, R., & Merrill, J. B. (2022, June 15). Teslas running autopilot involved in 273 crashes reported since last year. *Washington Post.* https://www.washingtonpost.com/technology/2022/06/15/tesla-autopilot-crashes/

Simpson, C., Rathi, A., & Kishan, S. (2021, December 10). The ESG mirage. *Bloomberg.* https://www.bloomberg.com/graphics/2021-what-is-esg-investing-msci-ratings-focus-on-corporate-bottom-line/

Sisso, S. M. R. M. (2019). The impact of innovations in the fight against trafficking, exploitation and child labor in Cote D'Ivoire. *Journal of Law, Policy and Globalization, 88,* 101. https://doi.org/DOI:10.7176/JLPG

Slaper, T. F., & Hall, T. J. (2011). *The triple bottom line: What is it and how does it work?* https://www.ibrc.indiana.edu/ibr/2011/spring/article2.html

Tesla. (2021). *Impact report 2021.* https://www.tesla.com/ns_videos/2021-tesla-impact-report.pdf

The Economist. (2009, November 17). Triple bottom line. *The Economist.* https://www.economist.com/node/14301663

The International Economy. (2017). Does the conventional wisdom about productivity need to be reconsidered? *International Economy*, 8–27.

Transparency International. (2007). *Persistent corruption in low-income countries requires global action.* https://www.transparency.org/news/pressrelease/20070925_persistent_corruption_in_low_income_countries_requires_global_acti

Transparency International. (2017). *Corruption perceptions index 2016.* https://www.transparency.org/news/feature/corruption_perceptions_index_2016

Transparency International. (2022). *2021 corruption perceptions index.* https://www.transparency.org/en/cpi/2021

Tsukada, O. (2013). Global dissemination of the Toyota Way in sales and marketing. *Journal of Knowledge Globalization, 6*(3), 53–76.

UN. (n.d.-b). *#Envision2030: 17 goals to transform the world for persons with disabilities.* https://www.un.org/development/desa/disabilities/envision2030.html

UN. (n.d.-e). *The Paris agreement.* https://www.un.org/en/climatechange/paris-agreement

United Nations. (1987). *Report of the world commission on environment and development: Our common future.* http://www.un-documents.net/our-common-future.pdf

United Nations. (2015). *International decade for action "water for life" 2005-2015. Focus areas: Water quality.* https://www.un.org/waterforlifedecade/quality.shtml

United Nations. (2016). *The UN Global Compact ten principles and the sustainable development goals: Connecting, crucially.* https://www.unglobalcompact.org/library/4281

United Nations. (2019). *Ending child labour, forced labour and human trafficking in global supply chains* [Report]. http://www.ilo.org/ipec/Informationresources/WCMS_716930/lang--en/index.htm

United Nations. (2022a). *The United Nations world water development report 2022: Groundwater: Making the invisible visible.* https://unesdoc.unesco.org/in/documentViewer.xhtml?v=2.1.196&id=p:usmarcdef_0000380721&file=/in/rest/annotationSVC/DownloadWatermarkedAttachment/attach_import_602c40dc-c87b-4245-bda0-25a445e0b1fb%3F_%3D380721eng.pdf&updateUrl=updateUrl7305&ark=/ark:/48223/pf0000380721/PDF/380721eng.pdf.multi&fullScreen=true&locale=en#WWDR%202022%20EN%20report%20master.indd%3A.286494%3A3457

United Nations. (2022b, March 21). *Un world water development report 2022.* UN. https://www.unwater.org/publications/un-world-water-development-report-2022

United Nations. (n.d.-a). *Action on climate and SDGs*. https://unfccc.int/topics/action-on-climate-and-sdgs/action-on-climate-and-sdgs

United Nations. (n.d.-c). *Key aspects of the Paris Agreement*. https://unfccc.int/most-requested/key-aspects-of-the-paris-agreement

United Nations. (n.d.-d). *The 17 goals | sustainable development*. https://sdgs.un.org/goals

United Nations. (n.d.-f). *Transforming our world: The 2030 agenda for sustainable development*. https://sdgs.un.org/2030agenda

United Nations. (n.d.-g). *What is climate change?* https://www.un.org/en/climatechange/what-is-climate-change

U.S. Department of Labor. (n.d.). *Findings on the worst forms of child labor—Côte d'Ivoire*. https://www.dol.gov/agencies/ilab/resources/reports/child-labor/cote-divoire

U.S. Geological Survey. (n.d.). *What is the difference between global warming and climate change?* https://www.usgs.gov/faqs/what-difference-between-global-warming-and-climate-change

Vinten, G. (2001). Shareholder versus stakeholder – is there a governance dilemma? *Corporate Governance*, *9*(1), 36–47. doi:10.1111/1467-8683.00224

Wales, T. (2013). *Organizational sustainability: What is it, and why does it matter?* Academic Press.

Walker, J., Pearce, C., Boe, K., & Lawson, M. (2019). *The power of education to fight inequality: How increasing educational equality and quality is crucial to fighting economic and gender inequality*. Oxfam. doi:10.21201/2019.4931

Werhane, P. H. (1991). Engineers and management: The challenge of the Challenger incident. *Journal of Business Ethics*, *10*(8), 605–616. doi:10.1007/BF00382880

Wesarat, P., & Mathew, J. (2017). Theoretical Framework of Glass Ceiling. *Paradigm, 21*(1), 21–30. doi:10.1177/0971890717700533

Wiler, J. L., Wendel, S. K., Rounds, K., McGowan, B., & Baird, J. (2022). Salary disparities based on gender in academic emergency medicine leadership. *Academic Emergency Medicine*, *29*(3), 286–293. doi:10.1111/acem.14404 PMID:34689369

Wilkinson, A., Hill, M., & Gollan, P. (2001). The sustainability debate. *International Journal of Operations & Production Management*, *21*(12), 1492–1502. doi:10.1108/01443570110410865

Wipper, J. L., McKenna, A., & Thanasombat, S. (2022). *DFEH-vs-Tesla* (Civil Action No. 22CV006830). https://calcivilrights.ca.gov/wp-content/uploads/sites/32/2022/02/DFEH-vs-Tesla.pdf

World Health Organization. (2022). *Water, sanitation and hygiene (WASH)*. https://www.who.int/health-topics/water-sanitation-and-hygiene-wash

Zhou, M., Hu, T., Zhang, W., Wang, Q., Kong, L., Zhou, M., Rao, P., Peng, W., Chen, X., & Song, X. (2022). COVID-19 pandemic: Impacts on air quality and economy before, during and after lockdown in China in 2020. *Environmental Technology*, 1–11. doi:10.1080/09593330.2022.2049894 PMID:35244530

KEY TERMS AND DEFINITIONS

Business Model: A corporation's plan for making a profit. The method typically entails a pre-defined strategy for providing goods or services to an identified market.

Child Labor: Any work that deprives children of their childhood, potential, and dignity and harms physical and mental development. It is defined by the ILO Minimum Age Convention, 1973 (No. 138), and the Worst Forms of Child Labour Convention, 1999 (No. 182), and by the United Nations Convention on the Rights of the Child.

Climate Change: The long-term adverse shifts in the recordings of weather patterns such as temperature, precipitation, and wind patterns.

Forced Labor: Is defined by the ILO Forced Labour Convention, 1930 (No. 29), as "all work or service that is exacted from any person under the menace of penalty and for which the said person has not offered himself voluntarily."

Global Warming: The increase in the Earth's temperature attributed to the global increase in GHG emissions such as carbon-based gases emitted from the uses of fossil fuels, emissions from motor vehicles, land clearing causing deforestation, and methane emissions from garbage landfills.

Greenwashing: Leadership's attempts to deceive consumers by portraying false information on sustainable aspects of a product or the company to overshadow the company's involvement in environmentally damaging practices.

Hybrid Working: A form of work schedule that allows employees to work predominantly away from a traditional office environment and only in the office on a scheduled or as-needed basis.

Sustainability: Sustainability or sustainable development is conscientious growth that requires a balance between satisfying present and future requirements to not adversely affect the ability of future generations to meet their needs,

Chapter 4
Modern Project Management for Successful Execution of Investment Strategy

Chan Kah Chee

(iD) https://orcid.org/0000-0002-9925-7783

Wholistic Institute of Lifelong Learning (WILL), Singapore

ABSTRACT

In light of the COVID-19 pandemic that shook the world, both multinational enterprises (MNEs) and small and medium enterprises (SMEs) have to learn and manage faster, better, and smarter to stay sustainable and remain competitive. This chapter emphasizes the need for a rethought, reimagined, redesigned, re-invented, reengineered, and rejuvenated waterfall approach in managing predictive projects to modern project management, using the six As in design thinking, to meet the clarion call with an agile mindset.

INTRODUCTION

Modern project management (MPM) is a design thinking process of converting investment strategy into a portfolio of prioritised programs and projects to be implemented by the right people with the right process, using the right planet, to achieve the right profit for the right purpose.

This chapter focuses on why MPM is vital for developing and nurturing a high-performance culture, what the benefits are, and how design thinking ensures the successful implementation of investment strategy via prioritised projects. The conclusion of this chapter concurs with the Project Management Institute's 6th Edition (2017) and 7th Edition (2021), of "Body of Knowledge". This says that MPM aligns strategic, business, and operation strategies to accomplish unified goals, objectives and targets (key performance indicators) that are intertwined and inseparable."

Organisational culture is the way we work. The goal is to build and nurture a culture of excellent performance. This means supreme execution capability, which needs to be hard for others to emulate. Senior management should be committed to project management as a common language for non-routine

DOI: 10.4018/978-1-6684-6845-6.ch004

work (Chan, 2016). The criteria for this should be added value with minimum risk. This commitment makes it easier to align goals and objectives and keep the focus throughout the organisation.

According to Christensen (2011), innovation strategy implementation has different levels - lightweight for efficiency projects, mediumweight for sustaining the project, and heavyweight for transformative projects. This will make ambitious targets for shareholders, which need to be SMART (specific, measurable, accountable, realistic and time-bound).

Although most lightweight projects are related to innovation for efficiency, SMEs will benefit from modern project management (MPM). Multinational Enterprise (MNE) investments are associated with mediumweight and heavyweight projects for sustainability and transformative innovation.

MODERN PROJECT MANAGEMENT

MPM brings individual competence, project team capacity, and ultimately organisational capability to achieve excellence in execution despite constant change. Business conditions have been Volatile, Uncertain, Complex and Ambiguous since the 1980s, when Bennis & Nanus (1985) coined the acronym 'VUCA'. The process continues: Industry 4.0, the digital business transformation economy, is in transition to Industry 5.0 (Santhi & Muthuswany, 2023; Xu, Lu, et.al., 2021). Learning must keep pace, so must be at least equal to the rate of change, and preferably faster. ©Project-Based Accelerated Action Learning (©PBAAL) makes an excellent basis for steady and highly relevant learning.

Technology puts all leaders, of a company, industry or nation, at the same starting point for VUCA competition. It's a case of survival of the fittest, and the savviest (Moore, 2015, 2013, 2008). All organisations, of any size, need an innovation strategy, and the right people to implement it. They must have enough discipline to carry it through, using the right process and the right tools. These are also known as 'planet', i.e., the Internet of Things (IOT) including information & communications technology (ICT), and this speeds things up. When this works well, the results are faster and better, which helps to beat the competition.

The first and most crucial step is to improve employer-employee engagement, to gain mutual trust and empower everyone at all levels to do their jobs. Without trust, they may compete against each other, or minimise their efforts. MPM encourages teams to work together, cross-fertilising their ideas and reinforcing each other. Individuals improve their competence, teams increase capacity, organisations grow in synergy and business value. The ultimate goal is transformation into a high-performance culture that is hard to copy or steal.

Figure 1 shows that the successful implementation of an investment strategy depends on an organisational culture of performance and its capability to perform. This will lead to excellence in execution.

Figure 1. MPM for successful implementation of investment strategy

Build to Last Through the 6 Rs of Modern Project Management

It is important to build good foundations, so that the enterprise will last through difficult times, and unknown-unknown risks. These are the risks that you do not know are coming, and more than that, you do not know that the risk exists. One huge example of this is the covid pandemic, which has created a new "normal".

The Six Rs

To build to last, (Collins, 2019; Collins & Porras, 1994) there are six Rs to apply to the innovation of projects:

- **Rethink:** The new way of working (WOW) for routine, non-routine, and digital work using a disciplined agile approach (Ambler & Lines, 2022).
- **Reimagine:** 40% of routine work will be replaced by artificial intelligence (AI) and digital technology (Schwab & Davis, 2018).
- **Redesign:** 60% of non-routine work with higher business value-added for multitasking will be carried out as project work in the global business supply chain (Nieto-Rodriguez, 2021).
- **Reinvent:** Changing the way we think, work, behave, and perform in the transformation roadmap of Industry 4.0 in transition to Industry 5.0 is inevitable (Martin, 2022; Grant, 2021).
- **Reengineer:** With four types of modern technology – Internet AI, business AI, perception AI, and autonomy AI, is often used (Lee & Chen, 2021; Lee, 2018).
- **Rejuvenate:** With future skills and competence to surpass the competition with four types of power: communications power, expert power, adaptive power, and sustainable power, for competitive advantage (Chen & Chan, 2022).

Figure 2. The imperative of unifying the six Rs and project leadership to succeed
Source: Adapted from Deborah (2020) and Deborah et al. (2007).

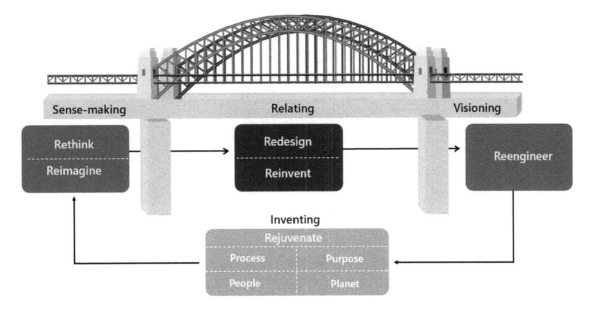

Figure 2 depicts the imperative of combining six Rs and the project leadership paradigm to build competitive credibility. This is vital in order to succeed in the new normal.

There is a bridge to cross. The input is sense-making leadership, which is a challenge. There is a need to rethink and reimagine how to convert investment strategy into prioritised projects.

When crossing the bridge, it is essential to meet expectations, using relating or servant leadership to collaborate with internal and external stakeholders.

A *stakeholder* is anyone who has an influence on the success or failure of an endeavour or project. Thus, it is imperative to redesign and reinvent stakeholder value management for win-win or mutual benefits relationship building or rapport. This has to take into account the latest information and communication technology, which may replace face-to-face interaction.

The objective or output is to reengineer visioning leadership to transform or improve continuously to stay afloat and beat the competition.

The essence of inventing meticulously is to rejuvenate lessons learnt, to avoid repeating the same mistakes. Learning by doing brings tacit knowledge, which bridges the gap between theory and practice (Pfeffer, 2022; Sutton & Pfeffer, 1999). When this learning if project-based, as in PBAAL, this learning is accelerated. Communication and collaboration transform tacit knowledge into explicit knowledge, which can be further transformed into organisational assets for educating and training. Investing in MPM brings synergy, improving the following whole-brain thinking skills (Pink, 2006). Thus, PBAAL ensures that the learning process equals or exceeds the rate of change in the VUCA business ecosystem. Then the rate of learning accelerates, and spreads through the organisation faster. It can all link up with technology and the IoT as a communication strategy.

Practical Steps 1: Organisations can close the knowing/doing gap by holding brief daily meetings – just 15 minutes to pinpoint any obstacles, and giving someone responsibility to remove those barriers. MPM is a hybrid of agile and predictive project management. Lessons learnt can be updated daily

Figure 3. Change agent needs 11 project leadership interpersonal skills

instead of at the end of each deliverable. This builds in continuous improvements. A cycle of plan-do-study-act, carried out faithfully, can win stakeholder trust and engagement. This is also applicable to virtual teams using IoT.

Table 1 presents the 11 interpersonal skills that an effective key change agent needs—the rationale for making projects into "a school for leaders." There needs to be a reliable barometer for measuring the quality of a leader. Clark et al. (1994) suggests using a leadership scorecard or successful track record in managing projects of different complexity and cultural diversity. For example:

Lightweight (cross-functional) – efficient innovation

Mediumweight (cross-borders or turn key projects) – sustaining innovation

Heavyweight (crisis or turnaround projects) – transformative innovation.

Because leadership is a process of influencing a group or team in accomplishing common goals an apples-to-apples comparison of leadership can be made. A project cuts across different departments or multicultural organisations (internal or external), so resources can be borrowed. The leadership role is 90% to communicate, connect, and get things done quickly.

Figure 3 shows 11 project leadership interpersonal skills. The change agent needs these to be proficient in (PMI, 2017).

The choice to transform from good to great is "do or die," in line with the paradigm shift by changing the ways we think, work, behave, and perform (Chan and Lim, 2021).

This section highlights the essence of communications power in developing and nurturing expert, adaptive, and sustainable power through PBAAL. Unifying the six Rs eliminates the risk of complacency. There needs to be a pipeline of agile project leaders in the new normal. All this is important for successful digital business transformation in the era of transition from Industry 4.0 in to Industry 5.0 (Speculand, Chen and Chan, 2023; Ng and Chan, 2023, 2022).

Table 1. Eleven elements of project leadership interpersonal skills

Interpersonal Skills	Description
Leadership	Communicating the vision and inspiring the project team to achieve high performance
Team building	Helping a group of individuals with a common goal to work interdependently with each other
Motivating	Creating an environment to meet project objectives while offering maximum self-satisfaction related to what people value most
Facilitating	Building trust across the project team and other key stakeholders through effective team leadership
Communicating to connect	Being aware of the communication styles of other parties, cultural differences, relationships, personalities and the overall context of the situation
Decision making	Applying the four decision styles—*command*, *consultation*, *consensus*, and *random* (e.g., a coin toss)—to make decisions individually or involve the project team
Managing conflict	Identifying causes of conflict and managing them, minimising negative impacts
Negotiating	Conferring with others to collaborate or reach an agreement
Coaching	Developing the project team to higher levels of competency and performance
Influencing	Getting others to cooperate towards common goals and project objectives with minimum resistance to change
Political and cultural awareness	Understanding and capitalising on cultural differences to create an environment of mutual trust and a win–win atmosphere

Why Is MPM Important for Success?

MPM is one of the core competencies of every manager to attain the highest business value and lowest risk for investment strategies, by implementing prioritised projects. Work can be divided into routine and non-routine work.

Routine work adds less business value. It is repetitive, needs less skill and fewer decisions. It can be outsourced for cheaper, faster, or better results. It can also be automated in light of the digital business transformation economy.

MPM is a common language for non-routine work that requires a project team. Problems will inevitably arise; changes will have to be made and strategies formed. The team needs a thorough understanding of underlying principles, the likely effects of any adjustments and how to add value. Any decisions made need to be "SMART" – (*specific*, *measurable*, *accountable*, *realistic*, and *time-bound*). The intended outcome is increased productivity, higher profit margin, resource savings from better cost control, better time management without scope creep, enhanced customer satisfaction and repeat orders. If achieved, these positive outcomes will establish or reinforce brand loyalty and improve reputation inside and outside the market segment, creating global brand leadership.

Practical Steps 2: Every organisation has a unique way of manging projects. The ISO 21500:2021 standard is a guide for project, program, and portfolio management. It does not provide best practice. Professional bodies for project management, such as The Project Management Institute (PMI) of the USA, has two standards – in the sixth and seventh edition of PMBOK (Project Management Body of Knowledge) endorsed by ANSI (America National Standard Institute). PMI provides certification for professional project managers who are proficient with best practice. Although project managers may be from different organisations, being PMP certified provides a common ground and language.

The overall effect is sustainable competitive advantage when change is the only constant. With MPM, teams have agile mindsets, they expect change, and resistance is supplanted by adaptability and willingness to find new solutions.

Whole-Brain Thinking Skills

Along with collaboration and problem-solving, comes synergy, an extension of cooperative effort. Investing in MPM brings synergy, improving the following whole-brain thinking skills (Pink, 2006).

- Holistic thinking for enhancing the ability to integrate – leads to clarity in planning
- Systems thinking for enhancing the ability to implement – leads to effective monitoring (of people) and control (of processes)
- Critical thinking for enhancing the ability to innovate – leads to effective decision-making
- Lateral thinking for enhancing the ability to improve continuously – leads to effective communication through empathy to gain consensus or support

MPM should become a common language for international and global business. In a similar vein, English is an official common language for international business. Figure 4 shows the strategic, business, and operations value chain effect of MPM across the whole organisation. It enhances individual competence and project team capacity and eventually becomes organisational capability for excellence in execution. However, the organisational capability to perform has to pass through five stages of development before nurturing a high-performance culture, from ad hoc through to continual improvement - Figure 5. Its supreme execution capability improves the total productivity of the five Ms (manpower, money, machines, materials, method) for a competitive edge of cost, quality, speed, dependability, and flexibility.

Practical Steps 3: Organisations have the ability to execute simple-to-complex projects that mature with planned change. Some are overly ambitious and carry on with projects that have failed at the implementation stage. Organisational capability cannot be higher than the competence levels of employees and teams, who have to work in tandem with the demands of the project and the pace of learning. Strategy and execution gaps will result in overrun in schedule, cost, and scope creep. An example is the Airbus A380, delayed by 1.5 years, resulting in Euro few billion losses.

Figure 4. Total value chain effect of modern project management

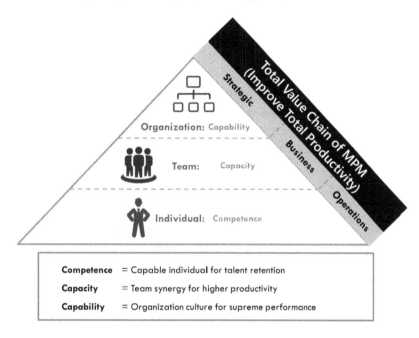

Figure 5. Five stages of organisational development to reach maturity of excellence in execution

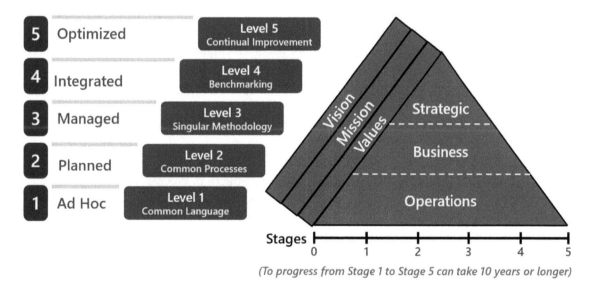

Why Make MPM the School for Leadership?

MPM involves people working together and learning from each other, combining organisational development with self-development. This could be called a 'school for leadership'.

Leadership is the process in which a person (manager) influences a team towards common goals and objectives. A leader's ability, regardless of management hierarchy and seniority, can be measured using projects of different sizes and complexity – lightweight, mediumweight, or heavyweight.

Lightweight projects have a cross-functional team, takes a few months to a maximum of three years to complete, and stays within a certain budget.

A six-sigma improvement project is considered a *lightweight project.*

M*ediumweight projects* can be turnkey projects managed by a multinational cross-functional (diverse) teams from different vendors, contractors, and suppliers. There is a higher budget and more attention from senior management. It may take up to five years to complete.

Examples are condominiums, public housing, and new and improved education systems.

Heavyweight projects, such as constructing rapid mass transportation systems, could take up to 25 years. They are high-profile and need the attention of top management, investors, and regulators. Adept stakeholder value management is essential. Different levels of complexity and diversity of projects can reflect on the types and quality of leadership—a key indicator of a proficient business leader.

*Heavyweight projects come in m*any shapes, sizes, and complexity, e.g., crisis turnaround. For example, an Indonesian conglomerate had a debt of USD 14 billion. They needed a turnaround strategy to show that ongoing projects could finance the loan and eventually generate enough cash flow to rejuvenate and grow the business.

Who Is Responsible for Project Implementation?

Making projects the school for leaders should be ubiquitous and permeate the whole organisation. Effective leaders influence groups towards accomplishing agreed goals and objectives. This is made possible through facilitation planning, enabling the workforce to take ownership of the process. This cultivates a strong sense of discipline in execution and accountability.

Being a change agent is one of the roles of senior management, and every manager should strive to overcome resistance to change. MPM pulls (encourages) rather than pushes (compels) people to change. It is a people partnership for a win-win outcome - human aspects of managing projects.

Why Is High-Performance Culture the Root of Excellence in Execution?

Every organisation needs to derive an implementable investment strategy. A pragmatic approach is to convert the strategy into projects, using the right people and the right process, enhancing productivity with the right tools and technologies (planet). This results in the best unit cost (business value project supply chain). Everyone wins.

The capability of an organisation can be measured by how well it can sustain quality, speed, flexibility and reliability for transient competitive advantage. Other necessities are competence in integrating and coordination of people, process and planet, to achieve or exceed return on investment (ROI), being on-cost, on-quality, and on schedule. It should meet performance targets and expectations of all stakeholders. All of these depend on the quality of leadership. When an enterprise succeeds it will attract further funds as other companies cannot compete. This may extend to other nations, bringing more foreign investment.

Why MPM Enhances Competencies

MPM enhances four inseparable competences

- Knowledge
- Skills
- Action
- Attitude

These are also linked to the four whole-brain thinking skills.

- Holistic thinking – integrating ideas, concepts, processes, planet, technology

Putting the pieces together for effective planning

- Systems thinking – converting strategies into portfolio of prioritised projects, selecting highest value and lowest risk to secure supreme ROIs

Putting the right pieces in the right place for effective monitoring and control

- Critical thinking – transforming complex and expensive products or services into simple and affordable ones (disruption innovation)

Replacing obsolete or redundant pieces with new or improved ones for effective decision-making

- Lateral thinking – improving continuously, gaining consensus through good communication

Creating pieces to solve problems from different perspectives

- These four thinking abilities combined with PBAAL will bring synergy and impactful outcomes.

Figure 6 captures one of the key benefits of MPM, to enhance the ability to integrate, implement, innovate, and improve continuously for sustainability.

Why MPM Fits the 80/20 Principle

The *80/20 principle* focuses on 20% of the key activities that have a positive impact on 80% of business revenue. This applies in many different situations, and it works, especially in a project-driven environment. If project managers focus on 20% of the activities on the critical path, this empowers the project team to implement the remaining 80% (non-critical activities). In this way, they can manage up to five projects of similar capacity and complexity. This will significantly improve the productivity of the five Ms. Christensen et al. (2015) concurred, saying that innovation strategy is 50% transforming, 30% sustaining, and 20% efficiency. Thus, transforming plus sustaining equals 80%, and so is worth 80% of the total investment. The 80/20 principle is a pragmatic tool for prioritising investment strategy.

Figure 6. Four thinking abilities in MPM

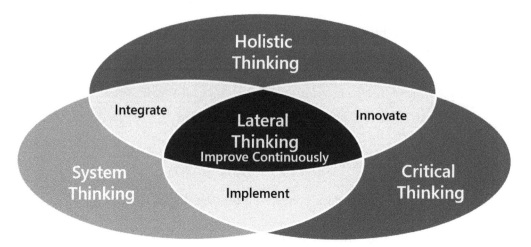

Benefits of MPM

MPM (as a common language for higher business value) enables the alignment of strategy (portfolio) with business (programs) and operations (projects), by prioritizing investments in critical resources. This is done by converting strategy into prioritized projects applying the 80/20 principle for its successful implementation (investment incorporating enterprise risk governance). Managing strategic risk and projects is achieved through facilitated workshops with key stakeholders present to plan cohesively for proficiency and clarity. To attain discipline in execution, one ownership is fixed for each process.

- MPM increases productivity and capacity, although the impact of individual competence is limited. Even supreme capability from individuals and teams must be unified to gain the full benefit of each. This will bring a culture of high performance and a synergistic impact on total productivity gained from critical resources.
- For example, some enterprises can only carry out lightweight efficiency projects. Others can manage up to mediumweight sustaining projects. A high-performance culture organization can drive heavyweight transforming projects, such as digital business transformation. These organizations can outsource medium and lightweight projects to contractors. Thus, organizational execution capability is optimized.

Practical Steps 4: To keep overheads down (also known as indirect or fixed costs to minimum essentials). MNEs and conglomerates outsource lightweight and mediumweight projects to main or subcontractors. They must be capable of completing the work to meet the required product quality specifications - on-scope, on-schedule, and on-cost for win-win benefits/profit margins.

- MPM has the unique and transient competitive advantage of being adept in project leadership throughout the whole company and industry. This makes a benchmark for its maturity in supreme execution capability.

Figure 7. MPM changes from pyramid to a value stream S–I–O–M model

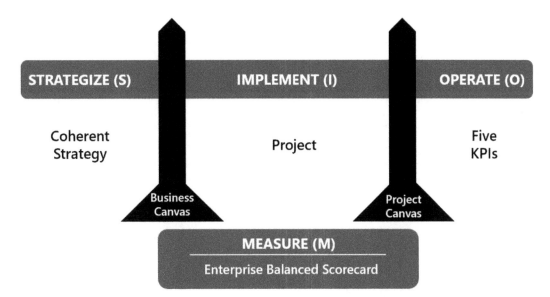

- MPM should not be limited to companies. It should permeate the whole education system (from primary to tertiary, and then organization ecosystems). There would be a massive impact if whole nations became project-driven through MPM as a common language for work. The barometer of organizational success is its leadership, as a process of developing and nurturing a pipeline of world-class agile project managers for foreign direct investments (FDIs), with the highest business value and lowest risks.

Practical Steps 5: Singapore has no natural resources. Without FDIs there will be no investment strategy for growth via projects. The consequence is no work to be done and thus, no jobs. The Singapore government subsidizes Singaporeans and permanent residents to study and develop project management competence. An incentive scheme with a discount of up to 60% of the course fee is offered to students working to qualify as project management professionals. To stay competitive, Singapore is a project-driven nation.

- Project-based lessons learnt are incremental and iterative processes, resulting in accelerated action learning to mitigate risk. MPM integrates and aligns strategic-business-operations objectives and converts investment strategy into strategic, business and project plans, considering environmental and social factors as well as governance. Its strategy fulfils three criteria of being unique, scalable, and hard to emulate. Anything less is unrealistic if the organization is to excel in VUCA world with its constant changes in the ecosystem.

For ability in execution, it is essential to flatten the pyramid to a process value stream organization structure using an S–I–O–M (Strategize–Implement–Operate–Measure) model depicted in Figure 7.

Practical Steps 6: Directive projectized organisation structure is often used to oversee key or critical projects where all the project managers report directly to the CEO as long as the project is active.

Figure 8. Project canvas
Source: Nieto-Rodriguez (2021)

Foundation	People			Creation		
Purpose **Why** are we doing the project?	**Sponsorship** **Who** is accountable for the project?	**Stakeholders** **Who** will benefit from and be affected by the project?	**Resources** **Who** will manage the project, and which skills are needed to deliver it?	**Deliverables** **What** will the project produce, build, or deliver?	**Plan** **How** and **when** will the work be carried out?	**Change** **How** will we engage stakeholders and manage the risks?
Investment How much will the project cost?				**Benefits** **What** benefits and impact will the project generate, and **how** will we know the project is successful?		

Upon successful completion of the project, the project team will be dissolved. They will return to their respective division or reassigned to other projects. This arrangement will not upset formal organisation structure. It will be easier to implement changes (Nieto-Rodriguez, 2022).

The outcome of strategizing is a coherent strategy:

- Operational excellence for a cost advantage
- Product leadership for a performance advantage
- Customer solution for an experience advantage
- Value innovation for a value-for-money advantage

Figure 9. Predictive or waterfall project management of the five Ws and two Hs

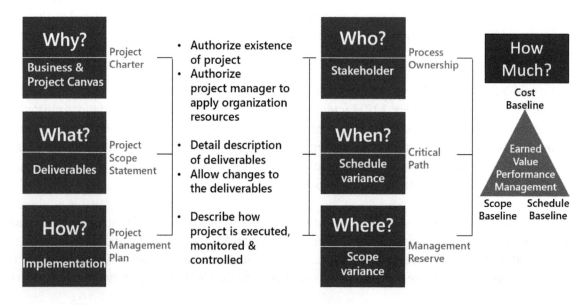

Figure 10. Eight domains of PMBOK, 7th Edition
Source: PMI (2021)

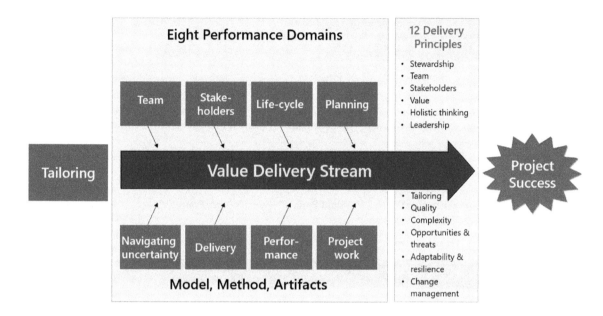

It is essential to focus on one of the coherent strategies. The business canvas is used to ascertain the attractiveness of the business case or proposition (Osterwalder & Pigneur, 2010). Next is to convert the coherent strategy into a prioritized project to justify the benefits. The project canvas is used for benefits analysis (Nieto-Rodriguez, 2021). The sequence is business canvas followed by project canvas, depicted in Figure 8.

For implementation, the common methods are predictive, hybrid, and adaptive (including iterative, incremental and agile).

Figure 9 captures the essence of a predictive or waterfall project methodology.

Figure 10 summarizes eight knowledge domains from the 7th edition of the *Project Management Body of Knowledge* from the Project Management Institute.

Operations are measured by five key performance indicators:

- Cost
- Quality
- Speed
- Dependability
- Flexibility - Agile project scope and predictive project cost are flexible and can be changed. Scope, cost and schedule cannot be changed.

An enterprise-balanced scorecard functions as a closed-loop system to measure planned targets versus actual performance. The four key performance areas are:

- Innovation and growth to enhance staff competence from PBAAL

Figure 11. Evolution of project management over five decades

PURPOSE	Evolution of Project Management from 1970s to beyond 2020s			
	1.0	2.0	3.0	4.0
Process	Implement	Integrate	Innovate	Improve Continuously
People	Junior Management	Middle & Junior Management	Senior, Middle, Junior Management	Key Stakeholders *(Internal & External)*
Planet *(Technology)*	Faster	Better	Faster, Better, Cheaper	Faster, Better, Smarter
Management Approach	Left Brain	Right Brain	Whole-Brain	©Project-Based Accelerated Action Learning
Strategy	Process-Driven	Customer-Driven	Agile-Driven	Human Capital & Digital-Driven
Era	1970s	1990s	2000s	> 2020s

(Source: Dr KC Chan)

Figure 12. Purpose, project, people, and profit of MPM

Learning equals or exceeds the rate of change.

Figure 13. Innovation strategy as a pipeline of critical resources for enterprises

Design Thinking for MPM is to convert investment strategy into a portfolio of prioritized programs & projects

- Internal business processes for speed through digital business transformation to replace routine work with automation.
- Stakeholder value management, influencing their expectations through win-win relationships and providing a good experience for customer retention.
- Sustainable financial performance by optimization and reinforcement of competitive cost advantage for revenue growth, profitability, and liquidity to stay afloat.
- Hindsight gained from MPM is useful for investment strategy. Success depends on the amalgamation of people for discipline, process for ability, and planet for speed in execution.

See Figure 11 for the evolution of MPM.

Figure 12 shows the intertwined and interdependent elements of project, people, and purpose. This incorporates environmental and social factors. The aim is to increase profits by being faster (speed and dependability), better (quality), and smarter (cost and flexibility).

MPM helps to find clarity when planning between projects. When making the plan care should be taken that it aligns with strategic and business objectives, and that resources are allocated appropriately.

Figure 13 shows a way of using design thinking, arranging the concerns into boxes according to the time needed to complete the project.

- Box 1 (short-term, < 3 years): managing the present projects
- Box 2 (mid-term, < 6 years): selectively dropping some of the low business value-adding or irrelevant projects
- Box 3 (long-term, ≥ 10 years): creating projects for the future

Figure 14. The 6 As of design thinking for MPM

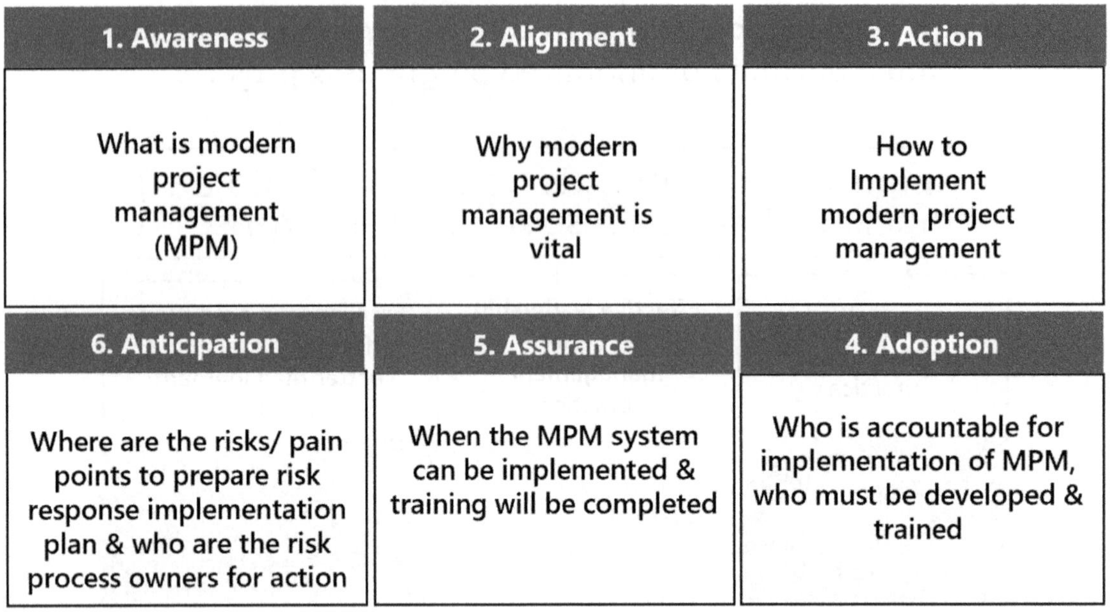

1. Awareness	2. Alignment	3. Action
What is modern project management (MPM)	Why modern project management is vital	How to Implement modern project management
6. Anticipation	**5. Assurance**	**4. Adoption**
Where are the risks/ pain points to prepare risk response implementation plan & who are the risk process owners for action	When the MPM system can be implemented & training will be completed	Who is accountable for implementation of MPM, who must be developed & trained

In this way, strategic business-operation objectives for the allocation of critical resources to projects can be fully aligned to achieve total productivity of resources. This means the five Ms (manpower, money, machines, materials, method). Artificial intelligence may also be used.

It is essential to use a projectized office *of strategy innovation management* (OSIM). This differs from a traditional *project management office* (PMO), which plays a supportive or centralized role with limited influence because the CEO is not directly involved. By contrast, an OSIM operates at a strategic level in collaboration with executives to ensure projects and portfolio activities are acting for the benefit of the overall business. The CEO, doubling as a CPO (chief project officer), is most effective in the execution of investment strategy by allocating the five Ms into a portfolio of prioritized programs and projects. There are different levels of innovation according to the weight level of the project (Nieto-Rodriguez, 2021; Christensen, Hall, et. al., 2016). Lightweight projects need to be efficient, mediumweight sustainable, and heavyweight projects transformative.

The Design Thinking Approach to Modern Project Management

Figure 14 captures the essence of MPM using the six As of design thinking as follows.

- **Awareness:** What, why, how, when, where, who, and how much an enterprise can benefit from MPM.
- **Alignment:** Concept, competence, and connections, where PBAAL equals or exceeds the rate of change in the VUCA business environment, regionally, internationally, and globally.
- **Action:** The nine-box total solutions (see Figure 17) to execute the investment strategy by converting it into strategically acceptable, financially sensible, and tactically viable projects.

- **Adoption:** How to overcome resistance to change by focusing on the 80/20 rule for stakeholders' transition change management.
- **Assurance:** How to ensure that the strategic goals, business objectives, and operational targets are tracked and managed to achieve the required project KPIs (key performance indicators) as part of corporate governance for investments.
- **Anticipation of Risks:**

What are the pain points that can escalate into a crisis?

What is the risk-response strategy to mitigate known-unknown risks, like the trade friction between USA and China?

What is the workaround strategy for unknown-unknown risks like the COVID-19 pandemic?

The rest of this chapter expands on each of these As in turn.

Briefly, awareness of all issues is an essential start-point for any project. The many threads have to be aligned for the whole project to work. Then action is necessary to convert the plan into viable projects. The strategy has to be adopted and resistance avoided. There needs to be assurance that the necessary work will be done to make the project successful. All along the way there has to be anticipation so that any slip-ups along the way are quickly detected and rectified.

Awareness

Future skills must permeate the whole organization to achieve business excellence. Design thinking for the total solutions approach to MPM is a coherent strategy that connects strategic, business, and operations endeavours. These can then move in tandem by transforming strategically acceptable investment into financially sensible business results and tactically viable productivity performance.

The five whys of design thinking are cemented in Figure 15.

Figure 15. The Five whys of modern project management

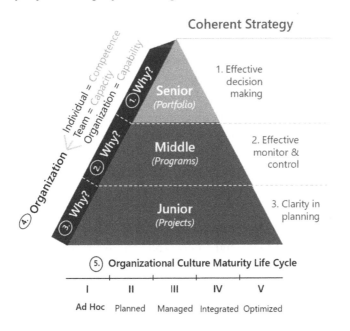

Why Are Effective Decision-Making Skills Crucial for Senior Management?

The investment strategy must be acceptable at the strategic level. This means converting the strategy into a portfolio of prioritized programs and projects. A total solutions design thinking approach helps to achieve a chain effect of financial good sense and tactical viability. This should meet the project requirements and the stakeholder expectations to beat the competition.

Why Are Effective Monitoring and Controlling Crucial for Middle Management?

Middle management needs to keep checking that the investment strategy stays on track and is steadily geared to achieving the objectives. Programs are prioritized projects invested in different parts of the world where benefits can only be obtained through synergistic outcomes, not by managing them individually. In better practice, programs are managed on a regional basis because of cultural proximity. The accrued benefits are measured by performance indicators (PIs) for each region, as follows:

- Regional revenue growth
- Market share
- Retention of key account customers
- Profitability
- Liquidity

The cross-subsidizing effect between projects across the region is used to sustain a fast-growth strategy—applying profits to maintain businesses that are not making money from highly lucrative programs or projects. This mid to long-term business strategy is to minimise risk while maintaining a resilient and strong business presence. Organizational adversity capital is reflected in its sustainable power to beat the competition, gaining from speed or a first-mover advantage when businesses start to turn around.

Why Is Clarity in Planning Crucial for Junior Management?

Investments are prioritised at the senior management level. Then they are converted into a portfolio of prioritized programs or projects for execution at middle management level. The junior level is accountable for the successful implementation of the project through process ownership. Each process must have only one owner. Everyone is accountable for completing the task on-schedule, on-cost, and on-scope, meeting stakeholder expectations and quality requirements for operational excellence advantage. People (i.e., process owners) must have discipline in execution.

Why Is It Crucial for the Organization to Be Wholly Responsible to Key Stakeholders?

Successful completion requires that the project is delivered on-scope (the right specifications or requirements), on-schedule (delivery promise), and on-cost (budget) to accomplish the agreed ROI (return-on-investment). This demands clarity in planning, process ownership at every stage, and steady self-discipline Project teams must have the right training, the right tools, and the right techniques for speedy progress.

There are three factors that make an effective barometer to measure an organization's execution capability:

- Competence of people as individuals
- Process of building team spirit or synergy (teamwork that transforms individual competence into team capacity)
- Tools (also known as planet) to provide for speed in execution

These factors make a coherent strategy for unifying people, process, and planet, focusing on the right business objectives. There are four common coherent strategies:

- Operational excellence for best cost
- Product leadership for best performance
- Stakeholder satisfaction for best solutions
- Value innovation for best value

Why Is It Crucial to Know the Current Phase in the Organizational Culture Maturity Life Cycle?

Every organization needs to go through five phases of development to reach maturity level.

1. Ad Hoc Phase: Unconscious Incompetence

You do not know that you do not know the intricacies of the business: New start-ups with a few entrepreneurial-minded people, loyalty and warmth towards each other, and little formality push the business for fast growth. Typical skills are problem-solving techniques and project management methodology to create a common language for work.

2. Planned Phase: Conscious Incompetence

You know that you do not know: The enterprise is growing and needs guidelines. There is too much firefighting, and priorities are unclear. Common processes are necessary for improving productivity, through using and optimizing resources and proper documentation. ISO 9000, 14000, and 18000, as appropriate. Typical systems are systems thinking for rationalization (80/20 rule) and standardization (total quality management).

3. Managed Phase: Conscious Competence

You know that you know: Too many meetings, too much paperwork caused by excessive monitoring and control and a low-risk attitude. Losing touch with customers due to closely assigned roles and responsibilities. Building empires requires a balance between positive and negative politics. Developing and implementing key performance indicators (KPIs) to ensure human resources are rewarded and incentivized to create business value-add for the enterprise.

4.   The Integrated Phase: Unconscious Competence

When you do not know that you know: The enterprise has developed and installed clear management systems. There is consistent behaviour due to organizational culture which upholds organizational values, with specialist and talented staff to build unique products and services. There is a commitment to formalize and integrate every aspect of management planning, coordinating, and controlling, from the strategic level to the business and operations levels. Benchmarking against better practice becomes the norm in pursuit of world-class quality products or services in business excellence. Typical skills are holistic thinking and critical thinking.

5.   Optimized Phase: Mastery

Continuous innovation on what you know: Employees are given more autonomy. There is positive management of change, more concern about training, developing and coaching future leaders, equipping them with the right skills and competence to strive and thrive beyond world-class performance. They can then inspire and nurture talented human resources to transform them into human capital with a sense of belonging and corporate ownership. They can then cope with the demands of digital business transformation in Industry 4.0 in transition to Industry 5.0.

This phase involves evidence-based lean management unified with six-sigma, modern business analytics techniques for expert power, communications power, adaptive power, and sustainable power to stay in the league. Design thinking skills are needed for unifying lateral, holistic, systems, critical and lateral thinking for disruptive innovation of a product, service, or solution, embracing artificial intelligence capabilities.

Table 2 presents the five Ws and two Hs of the benefits of MPM prior to the alignment process of understanding the concept, competence, and connections of MPM. This alignment is necessary to stay relevant, as is the ability to thrive and strive in the VUCA globalized economy.

Table 2. Overview of modern project management (the five Ws and two Hs)

Element	Modern Project Management
What (scope)	Enable alignment of strategic, business and project objectives to organisation innovation strategy.
Why (purpose)	Ensure projects are strategically acceptable, financially sensible, and tactically viable.
How (process)	People-driven six As process
Who (people)	Projectized structure for PBAAL in which each team member reports directly to CEO
When (schedule)	SMEs go through the five stages of transition to reach maturity
Where (pain points)	Ability to integrate, implement, innovate, and improve continuously to stay on-schedule, on-cost, and on-scope (quality)
How much (benefits)	PBAAL exceeds the rate of change
PBAAL	Make projects the school for leaders using light-, medium- and heavy-weight projects

Clark et al. (1994) advocated making "projects the school for leaders". Projects give valuable lessons in how to bring the strategy to fruition. Bridging the strategy and execution gap involves four types of competence – the ability to *integrate*, *implement*, *innovate*, and *improve* continuously (Chan, 2016).

A project manager plays the role of a key change agent. This requires excellent communication power to connect with internal and external stakeholders and enhance their soft skills. If this is done well, it unifies management, leadership, and entrepreneurship for a paradigm shift (Chen & Chan, 2022). Change will happen expeditiously when we start with changing the way we think–a common sense panacea but seldom used.

Alignment

Figure 16 depicts the links between concept, competence, and connections of design thinking for MPM using a Venn diagram. The concept of MPM is to craft an innovation strategy with the right competence by developing individuals and project teams. They will have the capacity to achieve organizational execution capability for supreme performance to beat the competition. To stay relevant and attain sustainable competitive advantage, MNEs and SMEs have to change the way they think, work, behave, and perform. Otherwise, they are in peril of extinction.

Figure 16. Design thinking of MPM concept, competence, and connections

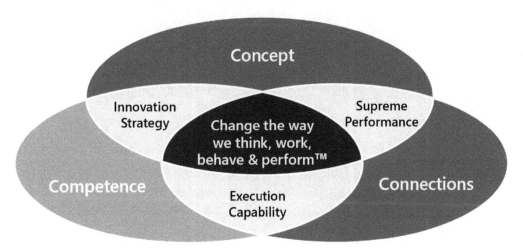

Action

Revisit Figure 13 for the pipeline of projects to support the innovation strategy prioritized into Box 1, Box 2, and Box 3 projects over the last decade. Figure 17 shows the next step. Derive a nine-box solution for managing the paradigm shift for transition change management to cope with the new normal caused by the pandemic. This will become a known-unknown residual risk and part of our ecosystem.

Figure 17 shows the connections between the MPM concept, its framework, and the associated process. This macro approach is crucial in establishing total systems management of the project prior to its initiation. The concept of MPM gives a systematic and proven methodology ensuring successful implementation of projects resulting in the greatest business value creation, risk-minimization, or cost reduction, i.e., the resultant benefits.

Adoption

It is a well-known fact that only 10% of soundly formulated strategies are effectively and efficiently executed (Kaplan & Norton, 2008). More alarmingly, it is apparent that many companies are disappointed by the lack of success in key aspects of their innovation projects, with only 10% achieving great success in profit-critical criteria such as meeting target margins, planned volumes, or market share. Companies should pay heed to the advice of Dwight D. Eisenhower: "Plans are nothing. Planning is everything." This axiom is especially valid in this concept-based artificial intelligent economy or the age of digital business transformation.

Figure 17. Nine-box solution for transition change management for better practice in MPM

Purpose:	People:	Process:	Create Value
• Define the purpose of the project in quantifiable terms • Define the primary & secondary objectives of the project	• Form the right team of Sponsor(s), Owner, Team Leader, Members/ Specialists (If a key person is missing, the chance of success is reduced)	• Ensure that the process map & the business processes are available for analysis • Check the steps in the project life cycle	
Scope:	**Support:**	**Schedule:**	Minimize Risk
• The scope should be focused & not overly ambitious or covers too wide an area • Develop the "Is" & "Is Not" of your project scope	• Ensure that project is supported by top/ senior management in terms of time & resources & within the scope	• List process sequence to determine the critical path in the Gantt Chart • Define clearly Starting & Closing Points	
Strategy:	**Structure:**	**Systems:** Types of deliverables:	Reduce Cost
• Strategy is a solution to achieve the purpose • Strategy should make the process more effective / efficient • Strategy should result as a system/ deliverables	• Establish the organizing & working committee structure for validation, verification & smooth management of the project	• Management Information System • Materials Control System • Process Improvement System Compare in quantifiable terms before & after system implementation	

One of the main reasons behind failed strategy is the way the CEO communicates strategic intent. A sure-fire way to get resistance is trying to force it down the hierarchy. Often CEOs call a company-wide meeting to inform people of decisions made, with unrealistic key performance indicators. The CEO then walks away thinking the job is done.

They have really missed the strategic reality, i.e., a strategy must be supported by the right people (project management team), process and planet (tools or technologies). As purported by Senge, "people don't resist change; they resist being changed."

Figure 18. Prioritization of available resources is good practice in MPM

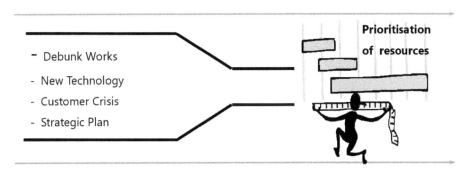

One better way to encourage buy-in or support from any change management project is to manage it as a pipeline. Critical resources can be prioritized using the three-box concept. by prioritizing critical resources using the three-box concept:

- Box 1 – manage the present project
- Box 2 – select the important parts of the project, drop anything that's outdated or not performing well.
- Box 3 – create the future using MPM

Figure 18 highlights the imperative of bottleneck areas in investment strategy implementation via projects. Thus, critical resources are prioritized based on the highest business value and lowest risk.

Figure 19. Unified concept of MPM

Bottlenecks are inevitable in every organisation because of limited resources, residue and secondary risks caused by unknown-unknown factors, e.g., covid pandemic. A turnaround strategy to cope with a risk response needs to prioritise using acceptance criteria based on impact (quantitative analysis) and probability of occurrence (qualitative analysis) – strategic management of risks for project governance.

Figure 19 shows the unified concept of MPM that links ideation to the vision of an enterprise and its environment.

- The investment strategy is converted into a portfolio of prioritized programs and projects.
- The successful execution of the strategy and its performance are measured using an enterprise-balanced scorecard with germane metrics.
- The right key performance indicators (KPIs) for monitoring and control of people (for innovation and growth), process (for continuous improvement in internal business processes), and planet (to track and manage customer satisfaction and financial performance). (Stanford certified project manager course materials, 2011).

Assurance

By thinking through all the resources needed and charting these to plan and control progress, we can produce a complete tool of better management to ensure the project succeeds. Value creation perhaps has less to do with the process of MPM itself than the work to establish the project definition document or canvas. This is crucial to answering the detailed questions in the nine-box solution. This definition is the formal and agreed connection between the strategic requirement for change and the means by which that change will be put into effect. It recognizes the constraints around the project and where it fits into the bigger business picture.

Anticipation

There are many ways to minimize risk, Unpleasant surprises can be avoided by defining all tasks and their duration, relationships, resources MPM allows for alternative priorities to be set and different balances of resources to be used to recover from delays.

This means adopting an agile mindset. The agile mindset is comprised of eight principles, seven promises, and eight guidelines (Ambler & Lines, 2022), summarized below.

Eight Principles

- Delight customers
- Be awesome
- Context counts
- Be pragmatic
- Choice is good
- Optimize flow
- Organize around products and services
- Enterprise awareness

Figure 20. Overview of modern project management

Seven Promises

- Create psychological safety and embrace diversity
- Accelerate value realization
- Collaborate proactively
- Make all work and workflow visible
- Improve predictability
- Keep workloads within capacity
- Improve continuously

Eight Guidelines

- Validate our learnings
- Apply design thinking
- Attend to relationships through the value stream
- Create effective environments that foster joy
- Change culture by improving the system
- Create semi-autonomous self-organizing teams
- Adopt measures to improve outcomes
- Leverage and enhance organization assets

CONCLUSION

MPM starts from the strategic level and is aligned and inextricably linked to the enterprise business and operations objectives. The key components are shown in Figure 20. The investment strategy is implemented via a prioritized project by a cross-functional team comprised of the right people, applying the right process, and using the right planet, across the whole organization.

The strategy is also converted into short-term, mid-term or long-term investment solutions. Projects are defined by scope or specification, schedule, and cost for comparison, making it is easier to perform apple-to-apple financial justifications. The project is exposed to strategic, business, and operational risks. They are classified as key risk areas, key risk indicators, and key performance indicators for monitoring and control.

The MPM system is designed and built to enhance the ability to integrate, implement, innovate, and continuously improve lightweight, medium weight, and heavyweight projects for total productivity. Thus, MPM is strategic enterprise project management.

REFERENCES

Ambler, S. W., & Lines, M. (2022). *Choose your WOW: A disciplined agile approach to optimizing your way of working*. Project Management Institute.

Bennis, W., & Nanus, B. (1985). *Leaders: Strategies for Taking Charge*. Academic Press.

Chan, K. C. (2016). Project management as core competence for all managers. *International Journal of Professional Management*, *11*(3), 1–4.

Chan, K. C. (2020). *Design thinking for strategic enterprise project management* [Conference session]. International Project Management Conference: Beyond Projects—Embracing the New Era.

Chan, K. C., & Lim, W. P. (2021). Paradigm Shift: Changing the way we think, work, behave and perform. *International Journal of Professional Management*, *13*(3), 1–10.

Chen, J., & Chan, K. C. (2022). Intelligent innovation strategy: Beyond world class manufacturing. *Tsinghua Business Review*, *2022*(May), 1–20.

Christensen, C. (2011). *The innovator's dilemma: The revolutionary book that will change the way you do business*. Harper Business. doi:10.15358/9783800642816

Christensen, C., Hall, T., Dillon, K., & Duncan David, S. (2016). Know your customers' jobs to be done. *Harvard Business Review*, *94*(9), 54–62.

Christensen, C., Raynor, M., & McDonald, R. (2015). What is disruptive innovation? *Harvard Business Review*, *2015*(December), 1–11. PMID:17183796

Clark, K. B., Bowen, H. K., Halloway, C. H., & Wheelwright, S. (1994). Make projects the school for leaders. *Harvard Business Review*, *1994*(September–October).

Collins, J. (2019). *Turning the flywheel: A monograph to accompany Good to Great*. Harper Business.

Collins, J., & Porras, J. I. (1994). *Build to last: Successful habits of visionary companies (Good to Great)*. Harper Business.

Deborah, A. (2020). *Thriving in uncertainty: 5 leadership activities for a nimble response*. MIT Sloan Executive Education Blog.

Deborah, A., Malone, T., Orlikowski, W. J., & Senge, P. M. (2007). In praise of the incomplete leader. *Harvard Business Review*, *2007*(February).

Ghemawat, P. (2018). *Redefining global strategy: Crossing borders in a world where differences still matter*. Harvard Business Review Press.

Grant, A. (2021). *Think again: The power of knowing what you don't know*. Penguin Random House.

Kaplan, R., & Norton, D. (2008). *The premium execution: Linking strategy to operations for competitive advantage*. Harvard Business School.

Lee, K.-F. (2018). AI super-powers: China, Silicon Valley, and the new world order. Houghton-Mifflin Harcourt.

Martin, R. L. (2022). *A new way to think*. Harvard Business Review Press.

Moore, G. A. (2008). *Dealing with Darwin: How great companies innovate at every phase of their evolution*. Portfolio.

Moore, G. A. (2013). *Crossing the chasm* (3rd ed.). Harper Business.

Moore, G. A. (2015). *Zone to win: Organizing to compete in an age of disruption*. Diversion Books.

Ng & Chan. (2022). Digital transformation paradigm shift for enterprise agility. *International Journal of Professional Management, 17*(1), 1–11.

Ng & Chan. (2023). Stakeholder value management for successful digital business transformation. *International Journal of Professional Management, 18*(1), 1–11.

Nieto-Rodriguez, A. (2021). The project economy has arrived. *Harvard Business Review*, *99*(6), 38–45.

Nieto-Rodriguez, A., (2022). The rise of the chief project officer. *Harvard Business Review*, 1-9.

Osterwalder, A., & Pigneur, Y. (2010). *Business model generation*. John Wiley and Sons.

Pfeffer, J. (2022). *Seven rules of power*. Swift Press.

Pink, D. (2006). *A whole new mind: Why right-brainers will rule the future*. Penguin.

Project Management Institute. (2017). *Project management body of knowledge* (6th ed.). Author.

Project Management Institute. (2021). *Project management body of knowledge* (7th ed.). Author.

Santhi, A. R., & Muthuswamy, P. (2023). Industry 5.0 or Industry 4.OS? Introduction to Industry 4.0 and a Peek into the Prospective Industry 5.0 Technologies. *International Journal on Interactive Design and Manufacturing*, *2023*(17), 947–979. doi:10.100712008-023-01217-8

Schwab, K., & Davis, N. (2018). *Shaping the future of the fourth industrial revolution: A guide to building a better world.* Random House.

Speculand, Jin, & Chan. (2022). Excellence in execution of digital strategy: story of DBS (the world's best bank). *International Journal of Professional Management, 17*(5), 1–7.

Sutton, R., & Pfeffer, J. (1999). *The knowing and doing gap: How smart companies turn knowledge into action.* Harvard Business Review Press.

Xu, X. (2021). *Journal of Manufacturing Systems, 61*(October), 530–535. doi:10.1016/j.jmsy.2021.10.006

Chapter 5
The Role of Capital Structure in Achieving Competitive Advantage for Firms in a Global Context

Georgi Danov

Independent Researcher, UK

ABSTRACT

Today's hyper-competitive business environment calls for alignment among all organisational aspects for the attainment of sustainable competitive advantage. The capital structure of firms is merely one of these aspects and comprises two primary types of funding: equity and debt. Given the diverse characteristics these possess, there isn't a single debt-to-equity ratio that works for all firms or even the same firm at different stages. To support firm objectives, this must be determined with respect to the firm's competitive position, stage of maturity, shareholder and management requirements, and the wider environment. This chapter will first review some key attributes of both equity and debt and then discuss various determinants that can impact a mix of the two and ultimately the firm's capital structure to support its competitive position.

1. INTRODUCTION

We often discuss the speed of current technological developments, as evidenced by an ever-growing number of new products and features that pop up seemingly on a daily basis and revolutionise how we live. It is astounding to consider how much the world has changed over the last 50 or 100 years, so much more than it had in the thousands of years prior. It was only in 1903 when the Wright brothers successfully completed the first self-propelled airplane flight, which lasted a mere 12 seconds. Yet, look at us now: sending robotised spacecrafts to roam the galaxy and land on Mars, for example. This gigantic evolutionary leap is more than evident. What is *not* so visible at face value, however, is this revolution in other aspects in life: such as the proliferation of how we do business. We've become increasingly cre-

DOI: 10.4018/978-1-6684-6845-6.ch005

ative in our business models and how we can profit from technological advancements, the explosion of social media, infrastructure improvements and globalisation as a whole. All of these have significantly increased the level of sophistication of modern businesses and the intensity of market competition. Consider car manufacturers, for example. When Ford introduced the assembly line and started producing its famous Model T, the firm was predominantly preoccupied with producing cars in the shortest possible time and in the most efficient manner: one colour, one ideal production method, one assembly line, one business model. It was all about productivity and cost. While these remain important considerations, modern car manufacturers must now adopt a holistic business perspective: considering global supply chains that leverage hundreds of suppliers and intermediaries, the most efficient way to finance new factories, squeezing funding costs by fractions of a percent, advanced marketing strategies that not only reach consumers but also influence consumer behaviour (using carefully selected colours, musical tones, visuals, etc.) and sophisticated psychological models to elicit an ideal response. Likewise, early 20th century car manufacturers were obliged to consider competition from other car brands, bikes and motorcycles alone. Today, they must compete against not only these but also aviation, scooters, dense public transport networks, video conferencing and the forthcoming metaverse: which will reduce one's physical presence in a target location, stifling the need for vehicles to move people from one place to the other.

At face value, primary business principles remain the same: stay close to your customers, deliver marketable products, and improve efficiency so you can compete effectively. Yet, there is so much more to this today than ever before, with companies leveraging blockchain, big data, super-sophisticated statistical analyses and psychology to a once-unimaginable extent. Yes, companies are fighting extra hard to gain a competitive advantage in any way possible.

It is also important to note that the state of the world economy has changed dramatically over the last few decades. Most markets are now in a mature state and saturated with dozens or hundreds of competitors, fighting tooth and nail for market share. This is a dramatic change compared to the fast-growing economies and industries of 20th century when there was so much untapped potential and rising sales could mask operational inefficiencies and waste that many firms experienced in their non-core operations. It isn't until business goes bad and sales, market share and profits begin to drop that firms start worrying about slack and prioritise scarcer resources for projects that promise the highest return on investment.

In this hyper-competitive 21st century environment, it is no longer sufficient to move one's production or service centres to low-cost locations, mass advertise, develop a superior product and/or adopt more efficient distribution channels. While these are still important, not a single one offers firms a sustainable competitive edge in isolation. Rather, *all* components grounded in organisation, strategy, product offerings and corporate functions must work together as a well-oiled machine: with each cog performing a specific function in a precise way to support overall machine functioning and thus ensure effective operation. One such cog is a lean, efficient capital structure. Management decisions considering how to finance assets and future firm growth must be made with respect to strategy, growth prospects, existing debt levels, the industry in which a firm operates, and signals that decisions send to the market and its wider environment—among other things. This makes capital structure a deliberate and highly complex consideration; dedicated departments within larger companies that focus on assessing the optimal mix in fact highlight its strategic importance. No longer a marginalised peripheral activity, capital structure is a central consideration that in some cases can determine the very survivability of the firm itself.

The primary purpose of this chapter is to review the role of capital structure in achieving a sustainable competitive advantage for firms. We will first cover some of the basics including the definition of capital structure, its main components such as equity and debt and their key attributes. We will then examine the cost of capital, which is impacted by capital structure and the weighted average cost of capital (WACC) as a measure of this. Finally, primary chapter contents will emphasise the various factors that influence a company's decision to utilise equity or debt: considering various angles including structure and competition, firm-specific considerations, external factors that sometimes arise and practical limitations that perhaps impact all of these.

2. WHAT IS CAPITAL STRUCTURE?

Let's start with a brief definition of what capital structure is. While this varies slightly among sources, it is generally defined as the mix of equity and debt a firm uses to finance its assets and operations. An efficient capital structure is one, which minimises financing costs. In theory, this is quite intuitive. Money itself has a cost and is in limited supply, and a firm increases its value by investing in profitable projects and operations whose return is higher than the cost of capital required to finance them. The lower the cost, the higher the potential profit. What is *not* so simple, however, is how to achieve this cost-efficient capital structure.

In general, a firm has two broad sources of financing: equity and debt. It is worth noting that retained earnings feed into equity and while this is the cheapest source, this chapter will focus primarily on external sources. So, a company facing future growth opportunities must often make decisions on how to finance the same by using retained earnings, issuing equity or taking on more debt (either via loans or bond issuance).

3. WHY DOES CAPITAL STRUCTURE MATTER?

When discussing capital structure, we must mention the seminal Modigliani-Miller (M&M) Theorem (Modigliani & Miller, 1958). Back in 1958, Noble laureates Franco Modigliani and Merton Miller contended that the value of a firm was independent of its capital structure: with the theoretical justification based on the principle of no arbitrage and the assumption of efficient markets. It suggests that in employing some simplifying assumptions (e.g., no taxes or financial distress costs), it is irrelevant if a firm finances operations via equity or debt.

While this work is massively influential in the field of corporate finance, many of these assumptions are unrealistic in the real world. Taxes are real, financial distress costs are real, financial markets are not fully efficient, there is often information asymmetry between the knowledge of company management and shareholders, etc. As a result, modern corporate finance theories often examine capital structure as having implications on firm profitability and its potential to increase firm value. A multitude of reasons feed into this; in this chapter, we will review some of the more common causes. First and foremost, capital structure impacts a firm's capital expenses (i.e., how much it costs to obtain financing). Secondly, it alters cash flows: which in turn affects a firm's liquidity position, its ability to respond to competitive pressures and current/future profitability. Thirdly, it sends signals to firm's shareholders and the wider market regarding its financial health and valuation. Fourthly, it impacts the governance model, reporting and disclosures a firm is subjected to. Each of these is reviewed in more detail later on in the chapter, but it is worth examining key attributes and principles of both equity and debt before diving in.

3.1. Equity and Its Primary Attributes

Equity refers to a stake in a company or a financial asset taken by an investor in exchange of capital. By purchasing firm equity, an investor purchases a claim on its assets as well as its future profitability. Different types of equity include ordinary shares (also known as common stock), preferred shares of various classes—which can have different attributes—and convertible equity, which can be converted to common stock at a later time. In this chapter, we will only consider ordinary shares—by far the most common type—for simplicity purposes. The main advantage of equity issuance for a company is that capital need not be repaid: unlike taking out a loan or issuing a bond. It also does not subject the firm to fixed interest or coupon payments, which can put a strain on its income stream. Companies can of course decide to issue dividends, but these are discretionary on ordinary shares and are thereby sometimes not paid out unless the company decides to do so. The global equity market is huge. For perspective, the combined global equity issuance for 2021 alone (excluding any secondary market trading) stood at USD 1.07 trillion (Shimokawa, 2022). Yet, this is merely a fraction of the global equity market capitalisation, which as of June 2022 stood at an eye-watering USD 105 trillion according to Statista (Statista, 2022).

While the above are significant advantages from a company's perspective, this does not infer equity capital is free. Investors will only hold equity if they believe they can reap benefits in the future, in line with their estimated rate of return. The riskier a company is perceived to be, the higher the return investors expect for incurring the additional risk of holding its equity. It does, however, entitle investors to receive a share of future profitability, which could be significant for firms in a growth stage or those with profitable opportunities ahead in contrast with debt financing.

Another equity attribute is that it is inherently more expensive than debt (i.e., the return investors require for holding a company's stock is higher compared to the cost of debt). This is because debt repayment has a higher priority than equity in the event of a company default. Debt has first lien (i.e., the right over repayment or allocation of company assets in the event of trouble), which makes it safer from an investor perspective. In contrast, there is no commitment to ever repay equity investment: increasing the risk profile of the investment itself, for which investors demand an equity premium. This highlights one of the most fundamental relationships in finance: a positive correlation between risk and required return.

Additionally, when a firm makes capital decisions, it can rarely do so in isolation without regard to shareholder interests. It must be mindful of the impact this can have on existing shareholders as well as signals this sends to the market as a whole. Equity issuance is not always welcomed by existing shareholders, as it reduces share prices and dilutes their ownership (i.e., lowers their percentage claim on firm assets and future profits). It can also send a negative signal to the market that suggests the company is over-valued and alludes to information asymmetry between management and everyone else. Hence, companies must be careful when issuing new equity. We will examine this in more detail later on in the chapter. In October 2022, the Swiss financial group Credit Suisse experienced this first hand when raising $4 billion through equity. The financial giant was struggling with ongoing litigation and losses from some of its peripheral businesses for a period of time, culminating in a firm restructuring announcement in late October. Within a day the share price tumbled by just over 20% following multiple announcements: restructuring, capital raise and a 3rd quarter loss. While it is difficult to assess how much exactly each of these factors contributed to the fall, the loss announcement and direction of the restructuring were largely expected by analysts who followed the company closely, hence these would have been factored in the share price already.

3.2. Debt and Its Primary Attributes

Debt refers to firm borrowing with a promise to repay the borrowed money (principal) at a future point in time. Debt financing exists as one of two broad categories: loans and bonds, both of which have similar properties. These reflect a fixed-term commitment to repay borrowed funds with interest payments (in the case of bonds, a 'coupon') at regular intervals throughout its lifetime. This makes debt dangerous, as higher levels can increase financial leverage to the point that firms might struggle to keep up with the interest or coupon schedule and run into financial trouble. History has seen many firms default on their debt when competitive pressures mount, or markets slow down. The below graph—produced by global investment bank JP Morgan for the US economy—is an excellent illustration of this. It clearly shows the increased rate of default during economic downturns in the 21st century: ranging from the dot.com bubble to the 2008 financial crisis and most recently the COVID pandemic. While these are not solely attributable to financial leverage, the correlation becomes obvious when we transpose the increasing levels of debt observed during the same period. Please see Figure 1, which depicts high-yield default rates in the US plotted against periods of economic weakness.

Figure 1. US high-yield default rates

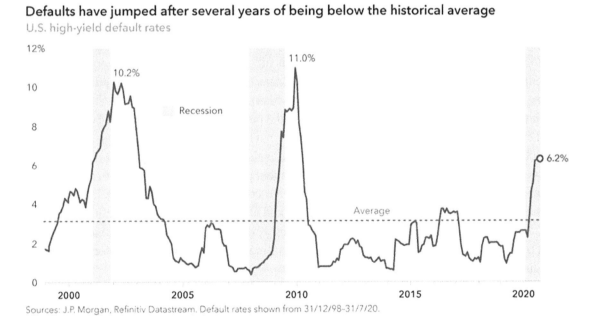

Defaults have jumped after several years of being below the historical average
U.S. high-yield default rates

Sources: J.P. Morgan, Refinitiv Datastream. Default rates shown from 31/12/98-31/7/20.

This begs the question: why do companies use debt? There are in fact several answers to this query. We spoke about the first lien lenders have on company assets if circumstances sour, which makes debt generally cheaper than equity. Another important benefit is its tax deductibility. Interest repayment hits the P&L and acts as a tax shield for firms, ultimately lowering their cost of capital and reducing taxes. This is sometimes particularly beneficial in jurisdictions with higher corporate tax rates, as the size of the tax shield is larger.

However, one must not only consider the immediate financial impact of capital structure on a company. What is particularly attractive about debt financing is that it is time-bound to the duration of the loan or maturity of the bond. Once this subsides, the lender has no claim on future firm profitability. So, when companies expect to grow and improve their profitability in the future, this limited commitment is welcomed by management: allowing for a larger proportion of earnings to be retained and reinvested. Similarly, while large equity holders sometimes have the power to exert control over the management and direction of a firm, this is generally not the case with lenders. While large lenders can impose specific firm conditions (e.g., the level of future borrowing and indebtedness), these provisions are not as pervasive as the influence large shareholders can exert.

All of these benefits help explain the vast amount of debt issued in the world, with S&P Global reporting the total value of 2021 corporate bond offerings hitting nearly USD 8 trillion: or almost eight times the combined value of equity issues for the same period (London at al., 2022).

4. EXTERNAL FINANCING METHODS

Before we discuss various factors impacting capital structure, it is worth reviewing different financing methods available to firms—as these lay the foundation for some topics explored later on in the chapter. For simplicity purposes, we will only review the primary categories and exclude some instruments with exhibit debt and equity features and niche products.

Both equity and bonds can be issued to the public and traded on recognised exchanges or sold privately to one or a small number of investors. Methods differ in their sophistication, cost and number of intermediaries involved in the process. We also have loans, which are privately sourced: most commonly from one or multiple banks (based on the size of the loan).

With respect to both equity and bonds, selling to the public is a complicated and expensive process. We will examine financing costs later on in the chapter, but for now, suffice it to say that issuing securities to the public and floating them on an exchange requires the involvement of a large number of sophisticated intermediaries, compliance and a series of stringent prerequisites: subjecting firms to much more governance and disclosures than required for a private company. While these offerings are complex, expensive and add significant operational constraints and overhead, the primary benefit is that they reach a wide range of potential investors. Needless to say, however, they are often prohibitively expensive for smaller firms or are sometimes unsuitable for those wanting to retain some level of information obscurity by remaining out of the public eye.

For those latter firms, private sales are sometimes more suitable or achievable. We can further distinguish between private placements within this category—which are often organised with the help of investment banks and offer securities to a small number of selected investors—and private sales to one or few identified investors such as angel investors or venture capitalists. Both types contain lesser information content compared to public offerings and are relatively inexpensive in comparison: making them more suitable for smaller firms or those wanting to avoid information disclosures. The downside for the firm, however, is that private sales limit the potential reach: especially when the firm attempts to identify investors without help from professional intermediaries (e.g., investment banks). While we're currently seeing an increase in platforms that can help match those in need of financing with those who can offer the same, these opportunities are still fairly limited.

Lastly, we have loans: the oldest method to obtain external funding, traceable back to 2,000 BC in ancient Mesopotamia when Sumerian farmers used loans to fund seeds and sustenance until harvest. Loans still remain a primary source of external financing for many companies, especially smaller ones or those located in countries with bank-oriented culture.

Regardless of the method pursued, however, one thing that is of paramount importance for the firm when raising additional funds, is the reason *why*. This sends signals to capital providers and in the case of public companies, the wider investor community, as to the stability and future growth opportunities of the firm. Capital raises, required to fund the firm's expansion into a new product, market segment or geographic area could signal to the market of strong future prospects and expected growth. This could prop up the share price, in return. Conversely, raising new capital to support ongoing operations or cover financial losses, could mean the company is running into trouble. This would send a negative signal to the market and the share price is expected to decline, as a result. Silicon Valley Bank, a top-20 US bank, endured the unfortunate fate of learning this the hard way in March 2023 when it found itself cash-strapped as a result of over-exposure to long-term fixed income instruments, combined with client withdrawals. In theory, these by themselves should not have brought the bank down (and certainly not as quickly as they did). The bank *could* have managed its liquidity woes behind closed doors but instead decided to attempt and raise $2.25 billion to shore up its balance sheet: immediately raising alarm bells among its clients, who grew concerned about their funds and rushed to pull out their money as part of a good old-fashioned bank run. Two days after the capital raise announcement and $42 billion in withdrawals later, US federal regulators announced they had seized control of the bank.

Private companies do not have public shareholders and do not attract as much analyst attention, so they are shielded by some of these considerations to an extent. However, the reasons why a firm needs to raise capital are still legitimate and capital providers are bound to ask these questions. The answers will have a major impact on willingness to lend/invest and the risk-premium required in return.

5. COST OF CAPITAL

Having laid the foundation and clarified some key concepts, let's delve into the cost of capital, how it is calculated and how it is influenced by capital structure.

The cost of capital is the minimum rate of return a company or project must generate before turning profitable. The lower the cost, the higher the potential return a firm can expect: hence boosting its value by delivering value-added projects. The weighted average cost of capital (WACC) calculation is one widely accepted method to determine the cost of capital in a straightforward manner:

WACC = (E/V x Re) + (D/V x Rd x (1-t)), where:

E and D = market value of firm equity and debt, respectivelyV= firm valueRe and Rd = cost of equity and debt, respectivelyt = tax

Mathematically, increasing the portion of debt in the capital structure reduces WACC due to its tax advantage. As a result, a cost structure financed fully by debt would arguably have the lowest cost of capital. Of course, things are never so simple in practice. The relationship between the debt portion of the firm and cost of debt is not linear. Given the financial strain of interest/coupon repayment on a company, there comes a point when further debt might become too heavy on the P&L: spelling financial trouble

Figure 2. WACC/leverage relationship

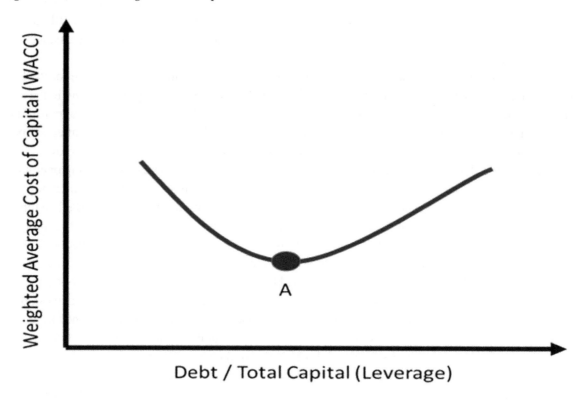

for the firm. In severe cases, this can even effectuate the demise of the firm itself. At this point, the increased risk of highly leveraged firms calls for a higher risk premium demanded by investors, which will drive up the cost of capital. The non-linear nature of this relationship is illustrated below in Figure 2.

Point A marks the optimal capital structure (i.e., the point where debt levels provide the maximum tax benefit before this advantage is eroded by the cost of financial distress). This begs the question: where exactly is Point A? What is the exact equity-to-debt ratio that maximises the capital structure? Unfortunately, like most things in business and finance, there is no single answer or a golden rule. Mature companies or those in particular industries (e.g., utilities) often have the capacity to bear more debt than others. As a rule of thumb, companies can monitor when a marginal increase in debt financing would start incurring higher costs (i.e., when the next round of debt financing would cost more than the previous one).

While the cost of financing is a major factor in choosing an optimal capital structure, many other factors related to firm strategy, the industry it operates in, growth stage, relative competitiveness, etc. are no less important in this decision. All factors considered, striking the right balance is more of an art than a science. We will examine some of these factors next across the following categories: structural and competitive factors, management considerations and external environment factors.

6. FACTORS INFLUENCING THE CAPITAL STRUCTURE

6.1. Structural and Competitive Factors

Though not an exhaustive list, some primary factors considered include:

Type of Industry: Companies in some industries are better equipped to support higher levels of financial leverage than others. As interest and coupon payments are naturally fixed and paid at regular intervals, debt financing is more suitable for firms with stable income streams. Utilities and companies that sell non-discretionary consumer goods are good examples given higher levels of insulation from fluctuations in economic activity or seasonal changes. On the flip side, a high level of debt is less suitable for firms with volatile or cyclical returns. In these cases, repayment is more easily supportable during strong or peak months but a real challenge when demand and earnings are low (a ski shop during the summer, for example).

Asset Structure: Another angle related to industry type is the asset structure of the firm. Firms with highly specific or intangible assets that have limited liquidation value in the event of default might have a preference towards equity. The nature of their assets—which makes their valuation more difficult and/or of limited utility to potential buyers—lowers their usefulness if a fire sale is required to meet specific financial obligations. On the other hand, some firms have a higher degree of general-purpose assets that are sometimes more valuable as collateral and able to retain their relative value if sold. A good example of the former are technological or pharmaceutical companies, which generally tend to have fewer tangible assets but rather rely heavily on intangibles (e.g., parents, R&D or branding) (Rajan & Zingales, 1995).

Size and Maturity: Similar to the industry argument, there is evidence that larger and more established companies are better equipped to support higher levels of debt. The rationale here is simple. Larger firms generally have more assets that can be liquidated if needed and also tend to be more diversified, which generally reduces their operating risk. These factors allow them to carry more debt compared to smaller firms that perhaps have a single revenue stream or fewer assets to liquidate if necessary (Titman & Wessels, 1998). The diversification factor is also known as the 'coinsurance effect.' While diversification is not necessarily limited to larger companies alone, as a general rule, this is more often observed among these compared to smaller outfits. The degree of correlation between the businesses is also important, as a high correlation suggests limited diversification benefits and hence a weaker ability to sustain debt.

While the above point addresses a firm's ability to support debt, the size and relative maturity of a firm can also impact its willingness to do so and its ability to access different types of financing. As we discussed earlier, a primary benefit of debt is that the firm's obligation ends when the loan is settled or the bond matures. Hence, lenders have no further claim on firm assets or income stream. This is sometimes an attractive feature for companies with significant growth potential, as lenders have no claim over future earnings: tilting the scale more towards debt, contrary to the argument above. It is also worth discussing the availability of funding for smaller firms that perhaps have no choice but to take out a loan if they cannot tap into equity markets.

Market Competition: While the above factors focus more on the firm itself, decisions are rarely made outside the context of the market and relative position a firm occupies in relation to other players. These are important considerations with respect to levels of output, pricing and marketing, as much as they are for the capital structure of the firm. Companies must be careful not to assume a disproportionately higher level of leverage in relation to their competitors unless they enjoy a dominant position or operate in a non-competitive (e.g., monopolistic or oligopolistic) industry. We have already mentioned the potential financial strain interest or coupon schedules can put on a firm. Should the profitability outlook of a firm worsen or fierce competition drive profit margins down, debt servicing can become an issue: potentially limiting a company's ability to increase investment levels and compete effectively with competitors, eroding its market share and overall competitiveness. This effect is often referred to as the 'market power cost of debt.' Choosing a capital structure that supports using sufficient levels of retained earnings as a buffer can offer a firm enough flexibility to manoeuvre, change direction or counter-attack if necessary—without jeopardising its survivability.

Leverage can also signal to competitors to turn up the heat if they sense a firm is already struggling and is cash-strapped. Engaging in predatory practices by slashing product prices is not unusual in this scenario, hence further aggravating the firm's position or—in extreme cases—driving it out of the market (Telser, 1966). Should a firm expect a pending drop in product demand, general levels or economic activity or an attack launched by a competitor, it's perhaps prudent to deleverage its capital structure by reducing debt levels and recapitalising with equity.

6.2. Management Considerations

While the previous section primarily discussed company factors and competitive pressures that can impact capital structure, this section will review some practical management considerations that can influence this decision.

Issuance Costs: Issuing additional equity or debt is not an easy or cheap process but one that involves the services of investment banks and various additional intermediaries. When issuing new equity, standard issuance costs (also known as 'flotation costs') include audit, legal and accounting fees, investment banking fees, fees paid to the stock exchange for listing shares, etc. On average, it is estimated that firms pay between 2% and 8% in flotation costs (Wallstreet Mojo, 2019), although estimates vary based on the source. For a company looking to raise £100 million in new equity, this equates to £2 to £8 million in issuance costs—which is not insignificant. There are two broad ways to account for these costs:

1. Incorporate them into the cost of capital
2. Adjust the cash flow

Using the first approach, the cost of equity is increased to factor in additional costs: ultimately boosting the cost of capital for the project. However, it is often argued that this approach tends to overstate the cost of capital as this is a one-off expense and should be treated as such.

The second approach deducts costs from the project cash flow, which is used to calculate the net present value (NPV). This is arguably the better approach, as it accounts for the one-time nature of the expense.

Similarly, the process of issuing bonds involves fees associated with underwriting, legal services, financial advisory and agency bond ratings, etc. These are consistent regardless of whether the issuing party is a corporation or government body. A University of California, Berkeley survey that assessed over 800 debt issues in the US estimated these costs amount to just over 1% of the bond issue principal amount (Joffe, 2015). While this was based on government bond issues alone and, admittedly, there were some significance variances from this estimated average, the cost of debt issue generally falls below that of equity.

Given significant costs associated with both equity and debt issues, raising further capital in capital markets requires significant consideration. All other factors aside, issuing debt securities is often cheaper. The differential becomes even more significant if we consider loans, the costs for which are insignificant in comparison.

Ownership: The desire of firm management to retain partial or full ownership of the firm is a critical determinant in the decision process. Equity financing requires the concession of ownership in exchange for capital infusion, but debt financing does not. This specific disparity is of great importance for private companies, especially smaller or family-owned businesses wherein giving up ownership is often an undesirable option. Perhaps there is an established family history, connection to a family sense of achievement or pride and/or major/sole source of income linked to the survival of the family that would make giving up ownership much more emotionally complex beyond just pure economic aspects of the transaction. The ownership factor is of lesser importance for public firms, which are owned by external investors (not necessarily fully). While the potential dilution of shareholding among existing investors should be considered for a 100% publicly owned company, there often isn't a majority personal stake by firm management that can trigger an emotional response. Thus, this decision is often made at arm's length.

Information Asymmetry: A large body of literature suggests firms prioritise sources of capital based on the level of information they divulge. This is often referred to as the 'pecking order theory,' initially suggested by Gordon Donaldson in 1961 (Donaldson, 1961) and later modified by Myers and Majluf (Myers & Majluf, 1984). According to this theory, firms give priority to the mode of financing with the least information content: suggesting the use of retained earnings as a first choice, followed by debt financing and equity issuance as a last resort. This is because equity issues require a vast number of disclosures to the investment community, reducing the information asymmetry management might wish to protect.

The underlying principle of this theory is that contrary to the efficient market hypothesis, a gap often exists between the level of information internal management possesses and what is known by the public. This gap is sometimes particularly large with respect to technological or pharmaceutical companies, whose assets are predominantly intangible in the form of R&D and patents and tend to be more secretive than others. That said, the issuance of debt can signal to the investment community that the management team is confident about the future of the company and/or believes its share price is undervalued. Conversely, the use of equity can send the opposite signal and apply downward pressure on equity due to beliefs that the firm is perhaps over-valued.

Agency Costs: One curious angle of the capital structure argument is that of agency costs incurred by shareholders. The theoretical grounds for this argument are built on the realisation that firm management is perhaps inclined to pursue their own value maximisation that can differ from shareholder interests. In 1976, Jensen and Meckling developed the so-called 'agency cost theory' based on this premise, arguing that agency costs can only be eliminated if company management and shareholders are the same party. In every other case, the interest of these parties will begin to diverge to an extent. One possible way to reduce these costs, they argued, is to introduce debt to the capital structure of the firm (Jensen & Meckling, 1976). In their view, the need to conform to the repayment schedule of the debt would introduce fiscal discipline for the management team and hence limit opportunistic behaviour on their part (e.g., the pursuit of low or no value-added projects or diversification opportunities).

6.3. Environmental Factors

The previous two sections largely reviewed the capital structure decision from the perspective of the firm or its management team. Companies, however, do not operate in a vacuum. Hence, it is important to also review some of the broader determinants that influence the decision: including interest rates, taxes and the regulatory landscape.

Interest Rate Levels: This is an obvious factor, as interest rates are a key component of every loan or bond product (zero-coupon bonds are an obvious exception as they do not pay coupons, although interest rates are still used to calculate the bond price). As these products pay out interest or coupons, their levels are determined by current interest rates. The higher the reference interest rates, the higher the interest/coupon on the debt product to entice lenders to lend money to the firm: consequently boosting the cost of these products in a high-interest rate environment. At the time of this writing in late 2022/early 2023, we are seeing this very phenomenon play out before our eyes as central banks around the world raise interest rates to curb borrowing and, as a result, spending to reign in unusually high inflation. While this is a relatively hostile environment to operate in and market conditions are unfavourable for both equity and debt financing, the implicit cost of capital associated with equity financing is perhaps considered a more palatable route. Conversely, when interest rates are low, explicit borrowing costs would be lower for firms: presenting a more opportune time to consider loans or bonds.

Taxes: This is another self-explanatory factor impacting the equity vs debt-financing decision, as it is a direct input into the WACC calculation. Earlier in the chapter, we spoke about how the tax deductibility of interest rates offers a tax shield. The higher the tax rates in a country, the larger the size of the shield: making debt financing a more lucrative alternative to equity. Here, we will only consider taxes from the perspective of the firm. Yet, it is worth noting that the tax environment also affects investor preference of equity over debt (or vice versa) and is thus perhaps a route companies would consider exploring: making the offering more appealing to investors.

Regulatory Framework and Investor Protection: Not unlike the wider market economy, efficient capital market functioning is founded on an effective regulatory and legal framework. Investors—regardless of their target asset class investment objectives—would have little incentive to invest if they don't believe sufficient protection is offered or local regulation is conducive to doing business in the spirit of the market economy and supremacy of the law. Hence, bankruptcy law, investor protection and regulations promoting market transparency and stability play a crucial role in creating a fair business and financial environment. Conversely, a lack thereof hinders the development of efficient capital markets and consequently limits a firm's ability to finance its operations via public offerings. In such an environment, companies needing extra capital have little choice but to rely on bank loans: leveraging their capital structures in the process.

As a general rule, strong legal and regulatory frameworks are conducive to doing business and supporting capital market growth: regardless of the legal system type. However, a significant volume of research explores the relationship between the type of legal system (civil law-based vs common law-based) and the relative dependency on bank or market-based funding. While research on the topic dates back to 20th century, more recently, the Bank of International Settlement (BIS) found that common law systems favour the development of market-based finance due to a higher degree of protection offered to holders of equity and debt securities (Gambacorta et al., 2014). A good example of a common law economy is the US, where banks were found to provide only around 20% of overall funding to companies. In contrast, research suggests that civil law-based economies (such as France and many other countries in continental Europe) tend to have higher levels of bank loan utilisation.

7. HOW CAN WE KNOW IF OUR CAPITAL STRUCTURE IS UNFAVOURABLE?

There isn't a single mix of equity and debt that is best for all companies or even the same company at different points in time. Likewise, a golden rule doesn't exist as to how much debt a firm should carry, nor is this a one-time exercise. It is rather a matter of dynamic monitoring and re-assessment throughout the life of the firm while considering all factors discussed above.

It is also fair to say that it is virtually impossible for all factors to point towards the same answer (i.e., whether to finance the next capital-intensive project with debt or equity). These will often conflict, which is what makes this decision highly complex. However, one must keep in mind some practical considerations based on everything we have covered thus far:

- Is the next round of debt financing more expensive than the previous one, suggesting a higher risk of default that will push the WACC higher, all other things being equal?
- Is the firm struggling to meet interest/coupon schedule demands?
- Is the firm experiencing or likely to experience a liquidity squeeze if it assumes more debt?
- Will the decision limit the firm's ability to respond to market/competitive pressures?
- Does the firm's capital structure consider the current prevalent state of the economy (e.g., level of economic activity, interest rates or inflation, among other key economic indicators)?

Management *can* and *should* access and assess all of these information points. Some external indicators are also perhaps useful for management (as well as other stakeholders), including the premium charged for credit default swaps (CDS) on firm bonds or ratings assigned by rating agencies. These indicators consider overall firm risk (not necessarily limited to its capital structure) and are useful to monitor as they'll likely reflect a decline in the firm's capital or liquidity position.

8. LIMITATIONS TO CONSIDER

Thus far, this chapter has principally focused on factors affecting firm preference or the ability to support varying levels of financial leverage in relation to equity. Now we will introduce some practical limitations that can limit one's ability to access specific types of financing and hence impact the capital structure.

Capital market development and sophistication are crucial for supporting an efficient capital structure. If we define efficient structure as the right mixture of equity and debt, achieving this is dependent on gaining access to sources of both equity and debt. Since private offerings of equity and debt limit financing opportunities for a firm, public offerings are sometimes quite beneficial.

However, as we covered earlier, public offerings—whether an initial public offering (IPO) or a secondary option—are dependent on the availability of liquid markets that draw enough investor interest and have a complex network of sophisticated intermediaries (agent banks, exchanges, rating agencies, legal firms, custodians, etc.).

Many developing economies tend to have underdeveloped capital markets, lacking the infrastructure, knowledge base and regulatory and legal framework to promote the efficient functioning of these capital markets. Likewise, they often lack the support network of intermediaries and agents required to facilitate transactions.

On the flip side, while selling equity or bonds is a complex transaction, this process has one simple, fundamental prerequisite akin to selling any other product: a customer who wants to buy. The investor base typically comprises two large groups: institutional and retail investors. The former is represented by mutual, hedge or pension funds or insurance companies, which are often very sophisticated and command large pools of money. The latter group comprises non-professional investors who usually trade on their own accounts, commanding much smaller money pools and lacking relative sophistication. A sufficient pool of investors within a market is, of course, paramount for selling one's equity or bonds: which is where market size plays an important role as well. The larger the market size, the larger the investor base (arguably).

Take Bulgaria, for example. This country has one stock exchange—the Bulgarian Stock Exchange (BSE) —based in the capital Sofia. There are fewer than 400 companies currently listed, with a total market capitalisation of almost USD 17 billion (Sustainable Stock Exchanges, 2019). By comparison, the London Stock Exchange (LSE)—one of the largest exchanges in the world—has a combined market capitalisation for all companies listed of over USD 4 trillion, spread across roughly 2,000 companies (Statista, 2020). A vast difference thus exists between the size of these two markets, but what is even more curious is the case of their trading volume. For the entire *month* of August 2022, there were just over 4,500 transactions on BSE (BSE, 2022) compared to a *daily* average of 660,000 for LSE. The low liquidity of BSE trading is a significant impediment to raising the desired additional capital a firm might need.

9. CONCLUSION

All firms need capital if they are to continue growing or to diversify or simply remain competitive. This is a fundamental principle of managing a company. In the last few decades, however, the roles of corporate finance and capital structure specifically have grown exponentially from previously marginalised functions to strategically important roles and even sources of competitive advantage. Larger organisations now realise the importance of having a lean and efficient capital structure and employ large and sophisticated finance departments that use complex analyses to determine the right mixture of equity and debt: aligned to the wider company strategy, competitive position in the industry, management team objectives and the wider operational environment. This highlights the importance of capital structure as a complex and deliberate component of corporate life.

For many markets and industries, the days of rapid growth with plenty of untapped potential and enough demand for everyone are long gone following decades of growth, technological revolutions and intense market competition. Companies can no longer afford to be wasteful or careless with their spending, relying on strong market growth to compensate and pick up the slack. It is a new world out there: one driven by discipline, holistic thinking and alignment across all aspects of organisational life if a firm is to remain competitive. While the development of new and improved products and services, more efficient production and distribution channels and an understating of customer needs remain as important as ever, the era of scarcity has brought forward the 'softer' and previously marginalised aspects of corporate functioning: including the role of capital structure.

Determining the right capital structure is not a simple matter. It has a major impact on the cost of capital of the firm, which is directly related to the profitability of a project or the firm as a whole. Like most things in business and finance, there is no golden rule as to how much equity or debt is right for a firm. This is determined by factors like the type of the business, its stage of development, nature of the income stream, assess base and not least the risk appetite of the management team, among other things. All of these are intricately intertwined, determining the firm's ability to support increasing levels of financial leverage.

To the above, we can also add the firm's *willingness* to increase the equity or debt portion of capital. Increased levels of debt could limit firm's ability to respond to change, increased competition, or economic uncertainty, as well as future ability to grow. The capital structure also has a direct impact on ownership, management team aspirations and future performance. Hence, capital decisions are not only reactive in nature, a by-product of many other factors, they can be pro-active and deliberate, reflecting the objectives of the firm, as a master of its own destiny.

Lastly, we should not forget that even the largest company in the world, is a part of a wider ecosystem that exerts its influence on constituent firms. Interest rates, inflation, state of the economy, taxes, government policies and regulatory frameworks…all of these come together and steer the future course of the firm and as a result, have a major impact on capital structure decisions.

The real complexity in determining the right capital structure of a firm arises from the diversity of these factors and the signals each one sends…signals which are very often also contradictory. This makes achieving the right fit for a firm more of an art than a science and an incredibly complex process but getting it right can not only offer a competitive advantage but also impact the very survivability of the firm.

REFERENCES

Bse-sofia.bg. (2022). https://www.bse-sofia.bg/en/statistics

Donaldson, G. (1961). *Corporate debt capacity: A study of corporate debt policy and the determination of corporate debt capacity*. Academic Press.

Gambacorta, L., Yang, J., & Tsatsaronis, K. (2014). *Financial structure and growth*. BIS. https://www.bis.org/publ/qtrpdf/r_qt1403e.pdf

Jensen, M. C., & Meckling, W. H. (1976). Theory of the firm: Managerial behavior, agency costs and ownership structure. *Journal of Financial Economics, 3*(4), 305–360. doi:10.1016/0304-405X(76)90026-X

Joffe, M. (2015). *The Costs of Issuing Municipal Bonds Doubly Bound*. Haas Institute Berkeley Edu. https://haasinstitute.berkeley.edu/sites/default/files/haasinstituterefundamerica_doublybound_cost_of_issuingbonds_publish.pdf

London, D., Popoola, B., Wittstruck, N., York, N., & Paris, M. (2022). *Authors Sustainable Finance Global Sustainable Bond Issuance Likely To Fall In 2022*. https://www.spglobal.com/_assets/documents/ratings/research/101566504.pdf

Modigliani, F., & Miller, M. H. (1958). *The Cost of Capital, Corporation Finance and the Theory of Investment. The American Economic Review, 48(3)*. https://www.jstor.org/stable/1809766?origin=JSTOR-pdf

Myers, S. C., Majluf, N. S. (1984). Corporate financing and investment decisions when firms have information that investors do not have. *Journal of Financial Economics, 13*(2), 187–221. doi:10.1016/0304-405X(84)90023-0

Rajan, R. G., & Zingales, L. (1995). What Do We Know about Capital Structure? Evidence from International Data. *The Journal of Finance, 50*(5), 1421–1460. doi:10.1111/j.1540-6261.1995.tb05184.x

Shimokawa, K. (2022). *Equity & SPAC Issuance Drop Again, H1 2022 Figures Down Year over Year.* S&P Global. https://www.spglobal.com/marketintelligence/en/news-insights/blog/equity-spac-issuance-drop-again-h1-2022-figures-down-year-over-year

Statista. (2020). *Market value of firms on London Stock Exchange 2020.* Statista. https://www.statista.com/statistics/324578/market-value-of-companies-on-the-london-stock-exchange/

Statista. (2022). *Domestic equity market capitalization globally 2021.* Statista. https://www.statista.com/statistics/274490/global-value-of-share-holdings-since-2000/

Sustainable Stock Exchanges. (2019). *Bulgarian Stock Exchange: SSE Initiative.* https://sseinitiative.org/stock-exchange/bse-sofia/

Telser, L. G. (1966). Competition and the Long Purse. *The Journal of Law & Economics, 9,* 259–277. doi:10.1086/466627

Titman, S., & Wessels, R. (1988). The Determinants of Capital Structure Choice. *The Journal of Finance, 43*(1), 1–19. doi:10.1111/j.1540-6261.1988.tb02585.x

WallStreetMojo. (2019). *Flotation Cost.* Wallstreet Mojo. https://www.wallstreetmojo.com/flotation-cost/

Chapter 6
Can Innovation Orientation and Service Provider Experience Gain Competitive Advantage to Firms?

Erdinç Koç
Bingol University, Turkey

Seda İşgüzar
Malatya Turgut Ozal University, Turkey

ABSTRACT

Having a competitive advantage is vital for companies trying to survive in an intensely competitive environment. In this study, the effect of innovation orientation and service provider experience on competitive advantage, which is examined in the context of resource-based view and relational view theory, is examined. Data have been collected from the top managers of 222 firms operating in the tourism sector in Turkey. The findings showed that innovation orientation and service provider experience increased competitive advantage. At the same time, it has been observed that the competitive advantage increases as the service provider experience increases. Finally, it has found that service provider experience has a mediating role in the relationship between innovation orientation and competitive advantage. The study is important in terms of revealing that the use of different competitive strategies together produces good results in the process of discovering different strategic elements that can provide sustainable competitive advantage.

DOI: 10.4018/978-1-6684-6845-6.ch006

1. INTRODUCTION

Today, firms face global market conditions transformed by technological developments. In this environment, firms need to be innovative and adopt the right competitive strategies in order to protect their markets, increase their competitiveness, ensure long-term growth and survive, because in the global competitive environment, uncertainty prevails and everything changes very quickly. In addition, the time required for competitors to obtain similar resources and opportunities and to copy a good idea is considerably shorter. Every company that has a share in a market has a competitive strategy, whether explicitly stated or not. However, in the challenging competitive environment created by globalization, these firms should be able to discover different approaches and produce unique strategies that include their own specific conditions. In addition they should also be able to identify their shortcomings and perform appropriate revisions, be flexible and fast learning organizations. This study offers a hybrid strategy that will enable firms operating in the service sector to be more competitive, and focuses on two variables that can provide a competitive advantage.

So How?

The answer to this question is sought in the strategy literature. The area of strategic management tries to discover the basis of sustainable competitive advantage by starting from "why do some firms consistently outperform others?" question and offers different theoretical approaches for this. From a wide perspective, it can be said that there are two approaches in the related literature regarding the reasons why some firms are better in terms of performance (Barney and Clark, 2007).

Porter's (1981) position school, using the structure-behavior-performance (SCP) approach, is the first of these. According to this approach, the way to gain competitive advantage is to gain a good position in the industry. Competition is shaped by five competitive forces (potential competitors, bargaining power of buyers, bargaining power of suppliers, threat of substitute products/services, and competition among existing competitors in the industry). If the firm can restrict entry into sectors with various barriers, it can maintain its position and ensure sustainability (Porter 1981; Porter 1989; Porter 2008).

The second approach is the resource-based approach, which focuses on the distinctive capabilities and resources of the firm. These two approaches (position school and resources-based approach) are strategies known as cornerstones in the competition literature. The resource-based approach is thought to be an overarching structure for resource-based view, knowledge-based view, dynamic capabilities view, and relational view (Baum and Dobbin 2000). This study is theoretically built on the basis of resource-based view and relational view.

In the context of the resource-based approach, the most widely used theory in the literature is the resource-based view, which emerged with the work of Wernerfelt (1984) and whose basic concepts were created by researchers such as Barney (1986, 1991) and Peteraf (1993). This theory suggests that firms must have unique strategic resources in order to gain competitive advantage (Barney 1991). Barney hypothesizes that the resources involved are heterogeneously distributed, fixed (cannot easily move between firms), and thus firms with these resources can gain a long-term competitive advantage. Of course, in order for available resources to be seen as a capability, some critical properties must be met. These resources must be unique, rare, valuable, inimitable and non-substitutable (Barney and Hesterly 1999).

Another theory considered in the context of the resource-based approach is the relational view. The relational view, developed based on Social Network Theory, argues that inter-firm collaborations provide sustainable competitive advantage and bring relational gains. It suggests that different skills and resources acquire through the relationships established between firms. According to the relational view, these capabilities and resources are relation-specific and can be retained for a long time as a competitive advantage (Lavie 2006).

As mentioned, the resource-based and relational view tries to explain the sustainable competitive advantage by focusing on the strategic resources and relationships that the firm has. But having resources is not enough. These resources should be used effectively to innovate. From the beginning of the 1990s, when the resource-based view was introduced, the world has undergone a great change. The success of firms in maintaining their place in their markets has become more than ever related to how fast they can adapt to changing conditions and how innovative they are. Because digitalization has created an ever-changing, uncertain industry. By analyzing the assumptions of resource-based and relational view, comments on which resources can make a difference in the market and achieve long-term performance gains become importance. However, current strategies may not be enough to keep businesses afloat in crisis situations such as natural disasters, wars, and pandemics. In such cases, businesses may need to change their competitive advantage strategies to increase their resilience. Crises such as the Covid-19 pandemic and the Ukraine-Russia war have recently confronted businesses with this situation, disrupting the norms of the global market.

Especially during the prolonged Covid-19 pandemic, issues such as maintaining product and service production, preserving a healthy and safe workforce, addressing short and long-term challenges brought about by remote work, coping with supply chain disruptions, and achieving the most efficient results with minimal contact have come to the forefront, requiring innovative solutions to overcome them (Ambrogio et al. 2022).

The COVID-19 pandemic has led to many businesses worldwide shutting down or reducing their operations, resulting in many people becoming unemployed. For example, in the US, the unemployment rate rose to 14.8% in April 2020, the highest rate since 1948. The pandemic has caused production and supply chain disruptions in many industries, leading to delays in product releases and inventory shortages. Supply chain disruptions in various sectors such as clothing, food, vaccines, automobiles, and electronics have caused difficulties in getting products to the market and maintaining adequate inventory levels (CCSA 2020; CRS 2021).

The COVID-19 pandemic has caused contraction in all sectors that produce productions and services. Although there is no sector that was not affected by this crisis, the service industries that require intensive interaction with people, such as tourism, have experienced a higher contraction rate. In sectors where remote work is an alternative to face-to-face work, the situation has been relatively better. For example, while the manufacturing sector experienced a contraction of 19% during the peak of the first wave in the second quarter of 2020, the construction sector experienced a contraction of 15%, and sectors such as IT with white-collar workers who can work remotely experienced contractions of less than 10% (European Commission, 2021). The COVID-19 pandemic, which has had a significant impact on global economic and social systems, has forced companies to develop new strategies.

During this process, companies have had to become more dynamic, agile, and innovative, with significant changes in their business models. In addition, the presence of proactive measures has become more important than ever (Tronvoll et al 2020; Giritli Nygren and Olofsson 2020).

During this period, restaurants have started to work only with home delivery, and many retail stores have invested in e-commerce platforms. Educational institutions have provided online education to their students, and banks, software companies, etc. have switched to a remote working model. Of course, rapid steps towards digitization have been necessary to achieve all of these. The necessity to update and strengthen technological infrastructure has emerged. Companies that are already prepared for this have gained a greater competitive advantage, while those trying to make up for their shortcomings in this area have lost more time and money (Dash 2022; Ambrogio et. al. 2022). The Covid-19 restrictions imposed by China have also demonstrated the need for companies to not be dependent on a single geographic region. In addition, practices such as having backup suppliers to prevent production from stopping, effective inventory management, and the use of digital solutions that provide efficient information flow have become increasingly important (Ambrogio et. al. 2022).

All of these, along with the economic chaos that disrupts the economic balance, are also creative destructions that create opportunities for innovation (Schumpeter 1942). Companies must explore new ways to minimize risks and gain competitive advantage in these environments (McGrath and MacMillan 2009; Davison 2020). The identification of what kind of innovations can be made in products and services, how business models can be differentiated, and which activities create value or not, based on such determinations and implemented applications, brings economic stability back to businesses (Ambrogio et al. 2022). Therefore, companies that analyze the opportunities and threats brought by the relevant conditions well and have the flexibility to adapt to the current situation have been able to survive.

New competition rules usually emerge in such crisis periods and push companies to search for new transition ways. Especially the COVID-19 pandemic has accelerated the digital transformation of firms and this situation has provided firms with the opportunity to redesign their products, create digital alternatives and rethink their product/service distribution channels. Therefore, it is very important for businesses to discover what their skills are to adapt to the changing conditions they face (Tronvoll et al. 2020). Digitizing the firm, innovation capability, innovativeness in business processes, establishing strategic partnerships, and creating strategic positions in new ecosystems are extremely important (Seetharaman 2020; Al-Omoush, Simón-Moya and Sendra-García 2020).

From this point of view, the research focuses on the question: "is it possible to discover different resources that will provide sustainable competitive advantage in the context of resource-based view and relational view theory?" The answer is sought in the service industry. Because there is a period when economic activities started to be focused on the service sector and firms realized that they had to compete in service (Li et al., 2015). Increasing the volume of exports, providing foreign exchange inflow and employment opportunities, tourism has a great role in the economic growth of countries such as Turkey and Italy today. Competitiveness to be achieved in this field will contribute to the provision of sustainable development. It is important to determine the resources that will enable the firms operating in this sector to fight even in crisis environments such as pandemics and natural disasters. However, the sector that has been most affected by the Covid-19 pandemic is tourism. The closure of borders and travel restrictions imposed by countries have almost brought the tourism industry to a halt. For example, in Italy, the tourism industry lost 74 billion euros in 2020, which is equivalent to 4.2% of the country's gross domestic product. Similarly, the tourism industry in Turkey lost around 20 billion dollars in 2020 due to the pandemic (The Investment Office 2021). It is also important for companies operating in this sector to identify the resources that determine the advantages that will increase their resilience in crisis situations such as pandemics and natural disasters.

After this section, the descriptive information of the headings of competitive advantage, resource-based view, relational view, innovation orientation, service provider experience and the literature presenting the relationships between these headings are given. The methodology continued with the headings of findings. In the last section, conclusions and recommendations are presented.

2. LITERATURE

What is competitive advantage and sustainable competitive advantage? Adam Smith defines competition as the struggle of firms with each other in order to attract the attention of customers and gain their appreciation. Today, however, it is not possible to encounter any company or country that resists the idea that "competition is a necessity" (Porter and Harrigan, 1993). Because the global markets brought about by digitalization have forced firms to be much more competitive.

In order for a firm to say that it has a competitive advantage, it must create more economic value than rival firms. That is, if the firm can create more economic value in the product market than its marginal competitor, it has a competitive advantage (Peteraf and Barney 2003). The size of this advantage is equal to the difference between the economic value created by the firm and the economic value created by its competitors. So, is the competitive advantage sustainable?

What causes this question to be asked is again hidden in Barney's definition of competitive advantage. The comparison of the economic value created by the firm is made by taking its marginal competitor as a criterion. In other words, a decision is made by looking at what another competitor does, which has achieved the same competitive advantage. In today's competitive market, it does not take long for competitors to access and imitate a good idea, product or method. Therefore, having a competitive advantage does not guarantee consistent good performance. However, it can be said that a sustainable competitive advantage is achieved if current and future competitors cannot implement and copy the economic value-creating strategy of the firm (Barney, 1991).

Traditional economic theory takes a negative view of how long firms can maintain their competitive advantage. It argues that the competitive advantage gained by firms in competitive markets is far from sustainable, can be quickly identified and copied, and therefore short-lived. However, empirical studies by researchers such as McGahan and M. Porter (2003) have shown that competitive advantage can be sustained in some markets (Barney and Hesterly 2015).

The resource-based approach and the relational view theory, which define the elements that will provide sustainable competitive advantage to firms, are explained in more detail below.

Resource Based View

According to the resource-based view, competitive advantage depends on the unique resources and capabilities that the firm offers to the competition in its environment. It argues that firms with original resources will gain competitive advantage by acquiring strategic resources in the markets more effectively and efficiently than their competitors (Barney 1986).

The resource-based view has two basic assumptions. First, firms in an industry are not similar in terms of the strategic resources they control and the strategies they pursue. The second assumption is that the resources that businesses use to implement their competitive strategies are immobile, cannot be easily transferred and imitated. In summary, strategic resources in the industry are heterogeneous and fixed (Barney 1991). Many resources the firm has can provide competitive advantage; however, to gain a sustainable competitive advantage, these heterogeneous resources must be valuable, rare, inimitable and non-substitutable. Firms must look within to discover these resources and capabilities. According to Barney (1991), human capital, organizational capital and physical capital constitute the resources of firms. Features such as equipment, technology, geographical location used in a company are examples of physical capital. In particular, it refers to human capital such as the knowledge, experience, decision abilities, intelligence and intuition powers that managers and employees have in the company. Organizational culture, relations between employees, reporting structure, etc. qualifications are evaluated within the scope of organizational capital. Among these, resources that can meet four characteristics are considered to have the potential to provide sustainable competitive advantage. Obtaining a competitive advantage in a company does not guarantee that it will be sustainable, and a sustainable competitive advantage does not mean that it will be long-term. Structural differences that may occur in the sector may cause the loss of sustainable competitive advantage. This situation, which is described as "Schumpeterian Shocks" in the literature, requires firms to reevaluate their resources. In the digital age, where change takes place at a dizzying pace, this necessity makes itself felt even more. Firms have to constantly review and restructure their competitive strategies in order to gain and maintain competitive advantage. For this reason, it is very important for firms to discover new company resources that will enable them to survive in changing market conditions.

2.1 Relational View

The relational view argues that alliances with other firms and the relational returns that result from this alliance provide sustainable competitive advantage (Dyer and Singh 1998; Lavie 2006). The concept of relational returns refers to the extraordinary and relation-specific gains that are produced not by the firms themselves but as a result of the alliances they have established.

The relational view is an approach that uses and extends the assumptions of the resource-based view (Lavie 2006). According to the relational view, the relationship is a resource with competitive value for the partners (Balestrin & Zen, 2010). The cooperation of firms can take many forms, from commercial agreements to R&D partnerships and license agreements (Lavie, 2006). Through these relationships, firms can acquire relationship-specific abilities that are difficult to imitate.

Four mechanisms are used to generate relational returns. These are relationship-specific assets, information sharing routines, complementary resources, and effective governance (Dyer et al., 2018; Lavie, 2006, Dyer and Singh, 1998). Gains generated by relational returns generation and protection mechanisms create causal ambiguity for competitors. That is, the causal links between the relevant relational return and the sustainable competitive advantage cannot be understood by the competitors. Thus, this can result in an inimitable competitive advantage created only by the relevant relationship.

2.2 Innovation Orientation and Competitive Advantage

Resource-based view theory suggests that companies need to identify and use the most likely sustainable competitive advantage source of their controlled tangible and intangible assets for sustainable competitive power (Barney and Clark 2007; Caseiro and Coelho 2019). The search for competitive advantage should start with an analysis of the resources and capabilities that the company already possesses. It is crucial to discover the firm characteristics that can provide flexibility to the company during a crisis. Nowadays, companies' innovation capability and knowledge are seen as the key to competitiveness and economic growth. (Stock and Zacharias 2011; Piñeiro et al. 2020). Research on internal factors that would give competitive advantage to tourism SMEs during the Covid-19 pandemic revealed a positive relationship between innovation capability and competitive advantage (Feriady and Farliana 2022). Studies conducted during the pandemic process also revealed that innovative firms performed better than those that are not innovative, were able to survive longer, and grow economically. Firms with high innovation capacity can respond more quickly to constantly changing market conditions and maintain their competitive edge (Fiorentino, Longobardi and Scaletti 2020; Adam and Alarifi 2021). In addition, it is believed that the innovation orientation, which is expressed as a shared belief and understanding structure guiding and directing all the company's organizational strategies and actions, increasing the number of innovations, is a valuable internal resource for firms that ensures the successful development and implementation of innovations.

Innovation orientation can simply be defined as the tendency to accept and encourage an idea or behavior that is new to the firm (Ionescu and Ionescu 2015). Dobni (2010), on the other hand, defines innovation orientation as the intention to be innovative and the environment that will support innovation. Innovation orientation is a guiding principle that encourages and increases firm innovation, and ensures the creation and implementation of strategies for innovation (Siguaw, Simpson and Enz 2006). The innovation orientation leads the company to be constantly innovative. This increases the company's ability to adapt to the changing environment. Thus, the long-term survival of the company can be ensured. Therefore, it can be said that innovation orientation is actually a way of thinking and leadership (Siguaw, Simpson and Enz 2006). How open a firm is to new ideas, how willing it is to change the way it does business by adopting new technology, resources, talent or different administrative/information systems are related to the innovation tendency of that firm (Chen, Tsou and Huang 2009, Dobni 2010).

Some researchers argue that innovation is very important in order to gain and maintain a long-term competitive advantage; however, the most important thing is not the innovation itself, but the innovation process and how firms manage it (Stock and Zacharias 2011). In other words, competitive advantage is not innovation, but the firm's ability to continuously create competitive advantage based on innovation. Organizations with this ability not only anticipate market needs, but do so by creating an innovation orientation within the firm's culture. Firms with a high innovation orientation engage in value creation strategies (Siguaw, Simpson and Enz 2006). Firms with a high innovation orientation engage in value creation strategies. This situation moves firms beyond mere innovation and directs them to create an organizational culture that is open to innovative ideas and difference (Siguaw, Simpson and Enz 2006). For this reason, some researchers state that the success of a firm depends on its innovation orientation at the global level (Manu and Sriram 1996).

In addition, innovation orientation, which enables the successful development and execution of innovations, increases the number of innovations, guides and directs all organizational strategies and actions of the company, and is also expressed as a common belief and understanding structure, is considered to be a valuable internal resource for firms. Innovation orientation is a multi-information structure embedded in the company's formal and informal systems, behavior, competencies, processes, and many relationships from the individual belonging of the employees to the harmony between them. Besides, since it is hard to understand and copy exactly, specific to the relevant company. Therefore, when evaluated from a resource-based point of view, it can be said that innovation orientation has the characteristics that a valuable resource should have. In this regard, the following assumption has been made:

"Innovation orientation increases competitive advantage."

2.3 Service Provider Experience and Competitive Advantage

According to the relational view theory, the relational benefits brought by collaborations with other firms can lead to a competitive advantage. The embedded knowledge in partner firms represents social capital for the company. Especially the Covid-19 pandemic has been a process that has shown the need for firms to collaborate more (Peñarroya-Farell and Miralles 2022).

Because crises like the pandemic and the Russia-Ukraine war have shown companies that their own sustainability is only possible with the sustainability of their partners. During this process, there are empirical evidences that partner relationships and knowledge sharing established to seize as many new opportunities as possible, to overcome the crisis and to turn it into a growth opportunity, increase competitive advantage (Al-Omoush, Simón-Moya and Sendra-García 2020; Haider et al. 2023). Therefore, strategic collaborations by firms are seen as an effective resource in generating new ideas and solutions to overcome challenges (Li Gu and Song 2013; Faccin & Balestrin 2018). Hence, for a company to continue creating value in a connected world, it is necessary to have welfare partners (Lia, Gua and Songb 2013; Faccin and Balestrin 2018).

So, service provider selection plays an important role in co-production (Blazevic and Lievens 2008). These collaborations create resources that are difficult to imitate. It is thought that the more stable and permanent the business relationship history, the better the service innovation performance will be in the collaboration environment (Etgar 2008). In addition, the unique expertise or experience of the service provider with whom collaboration is established can increase the problem-solving capabilities and innovation of firms and provide them with the flexibility to adapt to changing conditions more quickly (Auh et al. 2007; Chen, Tsou and Huang 2009).

Therefore, it can be said that the business experience of the collaborating company can be a separate advantage for firms. Considering that competition has moved from the firm level to the supply chain level, these imitation and irreplaceable factors that the supply chain possesses can increase the competitive power of the relevant firms. This is because it is difficult to replicate and obtain both the relationships between companies and service providers and the relationships within the supply chain network of the relevant service provider.

Based on the relational perspective, it is predicted that the experience of the service provider within the supply chain can give companies a sustainable competitive advantage. In this regard, the following assumption is made:

"Service provider experience increases the competitive advantage."

2.4 The Mediating Role of Service Provider Experience on the Relationship Between Innovation Orientation and Competitive Advantage

Firms must innovate in order to protect their markets, ensure long-term growth and most importantly survive in turbulent environments. Especially in the 21st century, when economic activities have started to be service-centered rather than production-centered, firms have realized that they need to compete in service (Tapscott and Williams 2006). Therefore, how to improve service innovation through effective measures has become an important research topic (Wang, Jian and Zhao 2013).

Innovation is also done through co-production through interaction between suppliers (Huang, Li and Chen 2009). So today, co-production is another alternative to improve service innovation performance (Wang, Jian and Zhao 2013). It is known that cooperation, knowledge sharing and network connections between firms (Zach and Hill 2017) increase the innovative capabilities of the company and the level of innovation (Faems, Van Looy and Debackere 2005; Schilling and Phelps 2007). Collaborating with customers and firms in the service production process provides the firm with knowledge, resources, or capability to co-create value.

Innovation orientation, which is a measure of innovation capacity, is a necessary strategic approach and a driving force in order to overcome the difficulties encountered, absorb new developments and encourage organizational innovation. Being open to different technologies, business models, resources and capabilities is related to innovation orientation and service providers can determine businesses' innovation orientation, participate in their innovation activities, and provide the necessary resources for innovation. Also firms with high innovation orientation seek external sources, and create collaborative strategies such as joint ventures and alliances (Dobni 2010).

Taking all these into account, it is believed that collaborations with service providers that have high expertise and experience in providing knowledge, resources, or skills to the innovation process of firms with a high innovation orientation can increase their competitive advantage. Based on all of these, the following assumption has been made:

"There is meditaing role of service provider experience in the relationship between innovation orientation and competitive advantage."

Today, firms face a great competitive pressure. Past success and competitive advantage cannot guarantee future success. Therefore, the globalizing market requires the implementation of different competitive strategies. Firms try to find the best combination of internal and external resources to seize new business opportunities and increase their competitiveness. In this process, the discovery of new resources and talents can make firms more innovative and competitive compared to their competitors. In this context, it is important to consider innovation orientation as an internal resource and service provider experience as a relational return brought by cooperation and to examine whether it provides a competitive advantage.

3. METHODOLOGY

In this study, an application has been carried out whether service provider experience has a mediating role in the relationship between innovation orientation and competitive advantage. Hotel managers operating in Turkey constitute the population of the study. Although hotels are categorized by professional organizations and public authorities by considering different criteria, all hotels operating in Turkey are included in the study. An online survey link was sent to 1186 hotel managers via LinkedIn, reminder messages were sent, but feedback was received from 222 participants. When the number of responses reached is examined, it is understood that the rate of participation in the survey is 19%. The questionnaire form consists of two parts. In the first part, there are questions about descriptive statistics for the participants and the hotels they work at, while in the second part there are likert type scale items about the constructs. In the study, innovation orientation consists of 10 items, service provider experience consists of 5 items and competitive advantage consists of 7 items. Descriptive statistics and explanatory factor analysis were performed using SPSS 25 program, confirmatory factor analysis, discriminant validity and mediation analyzes were performed using Smart PLS. Of the research participants, 88 (39.6%) work as general managers and 27 (12.1%) as front office managers. 107 (48.1%) of the respondents stated that they have served in the position they have worked for 10 or more years. 119 (53.6) of the enterprises stated that they carry out activities with 9 or more service providers in the service production process. When the enterprises working with 5-8 service providers are included in this number, it is understood that 154 (69.3%) of the enterprises are in cooperation with more than five service providers. 77 (34.6%)

Table 1. Descriptive statistics

Position	N	%	Number of Staff	N	%
General Manager	88	39,6	0-9	17	7,6
Deputy General Manager	11	4,9	10-49	59	26,5
Human Resource Manager	15	6,7	50-249	79	35,5
Customer Relationship Manager	15	6,7	250 and above	67	30,1
Front Office Manager	27	12,1	Number of service providers		
Purchasing Manager	2	0,9	1	14	6,3
Sales-Marketing Manager	14	6,3	2-4	54	24,3
Technical Service Manager	8	3,6	5-8	35	15,7
Other	42	18,9	9 and above	119	53,6
Operating Time			Working time with service providers (year)		
0-3	31	13,9	0-3	44	19,8
3-5	21	9,4	3-5	45	20,2
5-10	63	28,3	5-10	77	34,6
10 and above	107	48,1	10 and above	56	25,2

of the enterprises declared that the period of cooperation with service providers is between 5-10 years. All of the descriptive statistics obtained in the study are shown in Table 1.

3.1 Reliability and Validity Analyses

In the study, reliability and validity analyses were carried out before examining the relationships between the constructs. Cronbach alpha and Composite Reliability values were examined in the reliability analyzes of the structures. As seen in Table 2. Cronbach's alpha values of the structures vary between 0.957 and 0.972, and Composite Reliability (CR) values between 0.959 and 0.972. In order to ensure internal consistency, Cronbach alpha and Composite Reliability values are required to be higher than 0.7 (Hair et al., 2013). When the values of the buildings are examined, it is seen that they are above the reference values.

Table 2. Overview of construct reliability and validity

	Cronbach's Alpha	Composite Reliability (CR)	Average Variance Extracted (AVE)
HSD	0.972	0.972	0.874
IO	0.969	0.972	0.759
RA	0.957	0.959	0.760

Exploratory factor analysis and confirmatory factor analysis were performed respectively within the scope of validity analysis. As seen in Table 2., the item loadings of the constructs are above 0.4 for EFA and 0.5 for DFA. The model fit indices obtained as a result of confirmatory factor analysis were

Table 3. Factor loadings in exploratory and confirmatory factor analysis

	EFA			DFA		
SPE1	0,820			0.906		
SPE2	0,844			0.934		
SPE3	0,824			0.950		
SPE4	0,838			0.946		
SPE5	0,822			0.937		
IO1		0,742			0.774	
IO2		0,813			0.937	
IO3		0,779			0.718	
IO4		0,846			0.921	
IO5		0,779			0.754	
IO6		0,702			0.899	
IO7		0,730			0.918	
IO8		0,785			0.953	
IO9		0,760			0.921	
IO10		0,764			0.879	
CA1			0,724			0.932
CA2			0,780			0.848
CA3			0,767			0.937
CA4			0,811			0.779
CA5			0,783			0.912
CA6			0,814			0.799
CA7			0,794			0.881

also found to be among acceptable values for SRMR (0.043), Chi-square (1.067) and NFI (0.843). In the research, VIF values were also examined to test whether there was a collinearity problem and it was seen that the values reached were between 1.00-2.165 and it can be stated that there was no collinearity problem because the values reached were below the reference value of 3.

Heterotrait-monotrait (HTMT) values were examined to test whether the constructs had discriminant validity. The fact that the HTMT values are lower than 0.85 indicates that the constructs have discriminant validity (Kline, 2011). When Table 4 is examined, it is seen that values between 0.718 and 0.762 have been reached and it can be stated that the constructs have discriminant validity.

Table 4. HTMT Results

	SPE	**IO**	**CA**
SPE			
IO	0,732		
CA	0,718	0,762	

3.2 Mediation Analysis

For mediation analysis, three variables, X, M and Y, must be present in the study. X is the independent variable while Y is the dependent variable. M is the mediator variable assumed to transmit the causal effect of X to Y (Agler & De Boeck, 2017). Baron and Kenny (1986) state that three conditions must be met in order for the mediation effect to be mentioned. The independent variable should have a significant effect on the dependent variable (1). The mediating variable should have a significant effect on the dependent variable (2). The independent variable should have a significant effect on the mediating variable (3). The hypotheses formed by considering these preconditions were tested within the scope of the study.

The preconditions were tested sequentially within the scope of the study. The effect of innovation orientation on competitive advantage is tested with hypothesis H1, the effect of service provider experience on competitive advantage H2 and the effect of innovation orientation on service provider experience with hypothesis H3. It has been determined that the path between innovation orientation and competitive advantage is 6,164, the path between service provider experience and competitive advantage is 3,954, and the path between innovation orientation and service provider experience is significant at the p<0.01 level

Figure 1. Structural model

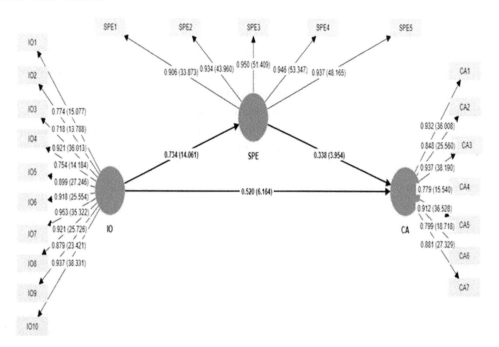

Table 5. Analyses of hypotheses

	Effect	Standard Deviation	T Statistics	P Values
SPE CA	0,338	0,085	3,954	0,000
IO SPE	0,734	0,052	14,061	0,000
IO CA	0,520	0,084	6,164	0,000
IO SPE CA	0,248	0,065	3,794	0,000

with 14,061 t values. All values related to the measurement model in which the relationships between the constructs are tested are shown in Figure 1.

It is seen from the analysis results that innovation orientation has a positive and significant effect on competitive advantage (β=0.520). In this respect, it can be stated that the H1 hypothesis is supported. It can be said that the H2 hypothesis is also supported by finding that service provider experience positively effects competitive advantage ($\beta = 0.338$). It can be stated that the H3 hypothesis is supported by the finding that innovation orientation has a positive and significant effect on the service provider experience ($\beta = 0.734$). It is stated that when the effect of the independent variable on the dependent variable is completely eliminated, there is full mediation, and when it decreases, there is partial mediation. The H4 hypothesis tests the mediating role of service provider experience in the effect of innovation orientation on competitive advantage. When the results are examined, the direct effect of innovation orientation on competitive advantage is 0.520, while the indirect effect of innovation orientation on competitive advantage is 0.248 when service provider experience is a mediating variable. All hypotheses have a t value of over 2.54 at the p<0.001 confidence level. The fact that the indirect effect achieved by including the mediator variable in the model is lower than the direct effect indicates the presence of a partial mediation effect.

4. CONCLUSION

In today's world where there is intense competition in almost every sector, the ability of businesses to maintain their competitive position and gain sustainable competitive advantage depends on having talents that foster innovation. When evaluated from a resource-based point of view, these capabilities, which are considered as intangible assets, are the elements that will give businesses a competitive advantage. These capabilities should also be the basis of the strategies that innovative enterprises will develop based on knowledge and customer-oriented. Innovation orientation is one of the important skills put forward in the development of proactive growth-based strategies. Innovation orientation also allows to define how innovative a business is. The increasing innovativeness of businesses allows to gain competitive advantage, as it is often stated in the literature. Within the scope of the study, the direct and indirect effects of innovation orientation on competitive advantage were examined and it was tried to contribute to the relevant literature with the results obtained. According to the results, it is understood that innovation orientation has a direct effect on competitive advantage. This result was reported by Iriyanto et al. (2021) coincides with the studies. Considering the mediating role of service provider experience, the indirect effect of innovation orientation on competitive advantage is also examined in the study. When the results were examined, it was concluded that the service provider experience had a mediating role.

This study has some limitations. The study was carried out with the data collected in the hotel services sector, which is one of the sub-divisions of the service sector. In future studies, analyzes can be carried out by collecting data from different sub-sectors of the service sector or from a sample that can represent the service sector as a whole. In the study, the mediating role of service provider experience in the relationship between innovation orientation and competitive advantage was examined. In future studies, the mediator or regulatory role of different variables in the relationship between innovation orientation and competitive advantage can be investigated.

REFERENCES

Adam, N. A., & Alarifi, G. (2021). Innovation practices for survival of small and medium enterprises (SMEs) in the COVID-19 times: The role of external support. *Journal of Innovation and Entrepreneurship*, *10*(1), 15. doi:10.118613731-021-00156-6 PMID:34075328

Agler, R., & De Boeck, P. (2017). On the Interpretation and Use of the Mediation: Multiple Perspectives on Mediation Analysis. *Frontiers in Psychology*, *8*, 1984. doi:10.3389/fpsyg.2017.01984 PMID:29187828

Al-Omoush, K. S., Simón-Moya, V., & Sendra-García, J. (2020). The impact of social capital and collaborative knowledge creation on e-business proactiveness and organizational agility in responding to the COVID-19 crisis. *Journal of Innovation & Knowledge*, *5*(4), 279–288. doi:10.1016/j.jik.2020.10.002

Ambrogio, G., Filice, L., Longo, F., & Padovano, A. (2022). Workforce and supply chain disruption as a digital and technological innovation opportunity for resilient manufacturing systems in the COVID-19 pandemic. *Computers & Industrial Engineering*, *169*, 108158. doi:10.1016/j.cie.2022.108158 PMID:35431410

Auh, S., Bell, S. J., McLeod, C. S., & Shih, E. (2007). Co-production and customer loyalty in financial services. *Journal of Retailing*, *83*(3), 359–370. doi:10.1016/j.jretai.2007.03.001

Balestrin, A., Verschoore, J. R., Perucia, A. (2014). The relational view of strategy: Empirical evidence from business cooperation networks. *Revista de Administração e Contabilidade de Unisinos, 11*.

Barney, J. B. (1986). Strategic factor markets: Expectations, luck and business strategy. *Management Science*, *32*(10), 1231–1241. doi:10.1287/mnsc.32.10.1231

Barney, J. B. (1991). Firm resources and sustained competitive advantage. *Journal of Management*, *17*(1), 99–120. doi:10.1177/014920639101700108

Barney, J. B., & Clark, D. N. (2007). *Resource-Based Theory, Creating and Sustaining Competitive Advantage*. Oxford University Press.

Barney, J. B., & Hesterly, W. (1999). Organizational Economics: Understanding the Relationship Between Organizations and Economic Analysis, Studying Organization: Theory and Method. Sage Publication.

Baron, R. M., & David, A. K. (1986). The Moderator-Mediator Variable Distinction in Social Psychological Research: Conceptual, Strategic and Statistical Considerations. *Journal of Personality and Social Psychology*, *51*(6), 1173–1182. doi:10.1037/0022-3514.51.6.1173 PMID:3806354

Baum, J. A. C., & Dobbin, F. (2000). *Economics meets sociology in strategic management*. JAI Press. doi:10.1016/S0742-3322(2000)17

Blazevic, V., & Lievens, A. (2008). Managing innovation through customer coproduced knowledge in electronic services: An exploratory study. *Journal of the Academy of Marketing Science, 36*(1), 138–151. doi:10.100711747-007-0064-y

Caseiro, N., & Coelho, A. (2019). The Influence of Business Intelligence Capacity, Network Learning and Innovativeness on Startups Performance. *Journal of Innovation & Knowledge, 4*(3), 139–145. doi:10.1016/j.jik.2018.03.009

CCSA. (2020). *How Covid-19 is changing the world: A statistical perspective volume II*. https://unstats.un.org/unsd/ccsa/documents/covid19-report-ccsa_vol2.pdf

Chen, S.-J., Tsou, H. T., & Huang, A. J.-H. (2009). Service delivery innovation: Antecedents and impact on firm performance. *Journal of Service Research, 12*(1), 36–55. doi:10.1177/1094670509338619

CRS (Congressional Research Service). (2021). *Unemployment rates during the Covid-19 pandemic*. https://crsreports.congress.gov/product/pdf/R/R46554/9

DashB. (2022). Remote work and innovation during this covid-19 pandemic: an employers' challenge. *International Journal of Computer Science & Information Technology, 14*(2). https://ssrn.com/abstract=4341103

Davison, R. M. (2020). The transformative potential of disruptions: A viewpoint. *International Journal of Information Management, 55*, 102149. doi:10.1016/j.ijinfomgt.2020.102149 PMID:32836628

Dobni, C. B. (2010). The relationship between an innovation orientation and competitive strategy. *International Journal of Innovation Management, 14*(2), 331–357. doi:10.1142/S1363919610002660

Dursun, İ. (2021). Michael Porter ve Jay Barney'in Rekabet Üstünlüğü ile İlgili Yaklaşımlarının Değerlendirilmesi. *Akademik Hassasiyetler, 8*(15), 189–208.

Dyer, J. H., & Singh, H. (1998). The relational view: Cooperative strategy and sources of interorganizational competitive advantage. *Academy of Management Review, 23*(4), 660–679. doi:10.2307/259056

Dyer, J. H., Singh, H., & Hesterly, W. S. (2018). The relational view revisited: A dynamic perspective on value creation and value capture. *Strategic Management Journal, 39*(12), 3140–3162. doi:10.1002mj.2785

Etgar, M. (2008). A descriptive Model of the Consumer Co-Production process. *Journal of the Academy of Marketing Science, 36*(1), 97–108. doi:10.100711747-007-0061-1

European Commission. (2021). *The sectoral impact of the Covid-19 crisis*. https://www.consilium.europa.eu/media/48767/eg-note-sectoral-impact_fin.pdf

Faccin, K., & Balestrin, A. (2018). The dynamics of collaborative practices for knowledge creation in joint R&D projects. *Journal of Engineering and Technology Management, 48*, 28–43. doi:10.1016/j.jengtecman.2018.04.001

Faems, D., Van Looy, B., & Debackere, K. (2005). Interorganizational Collaboration and Innovation: Toward A Portfolio approach. *Journal of Product Innovation Management, 22*(3), 238–250. doi:10.1111/j.0737-6782.2005.00120.x

Feriady, M., & Farliana, N. (2022). Model of Innovation Capability and Competitive Advantage of Tourism SMEs During Covid-19 Pandemic. *Economic Education Analysis Journal*, *11*(3), 274–283. doi:10.15294/eeaj.v11i3.61666

Fiorentino, R., Longobardi, S., & Scaletti, A. (2021). The early growth of start-ups: Innovation matters. Evidence from Italy. *European Journal of Innovation Management*, *24*(5), 1525–1546. doi:10.1108/EJIM-02-2020-0057

Giritli Nygren, K., & Olofsson, A. (2020). Managing the Covid-19 pandemic through individual responsibility: The consequences of a world risk society and enhanced ethopolitics. *Journal of Risk Research*, *23*(7-8), 1031–1035. doi:10.1080/13669877.2020.1756382

Haider, M., Shannon, R., Moschis, G. P., & Autio, E. (2023). How has the covid-19 crisis transformed entrepreneurs into sustainable leaders? *Sustainability (Basel)*, *15*(6), 5358. doi:10.3390u15065358

Hair, J. F., Hult, T. G. M., Ringle, C. M., & Sarstedt, M. (2013). *A Primer on Partial Least Squares Structural Equation Modeling (PLS-SEM)*. Sage Publications.

Huang, Y. K., Li, E. Y., & Chen, J. S. (2009). Information Synergy as the Catalyst Between Information Technology Capability and Innovativeness: Empirical Evidence from the Financial Service Sector. *Information Research*, *14*(1).

Ionescu, A., & Ionescu, C. (2015). The relationship between the innovation orientation and organization's performance in Romania. *Romanian Journal of Economics*, *40*(49), 299–312.

Iriyanto, S., Suharnomo, S., Hidayat, M. T., & Anas, M. (2021). Do Intangible Assets and Innovation Orientation Influence Competitive Advantages? A Case Study of SMEs in Indonesia. *Universal Journal of Accounting and Finance*, *9*(1), 105–115. doi:10.13189/ujaf.2021.090111

Kline, R. B. (2011). *Principles and Practice of Structural Equation Modeling* (3rd ed.). Guilford Press.

Lavie, D. (2006). The competitive advantage of interconnected firms: An extension of the resource-based view. *Academy of Management Review*, *31*(3), 638–658. doi:10.5465/amr.2006.21318922

Li, M., Liu, Y., Zhang, L., & Jian, Z. (2015). The impacts of internal innovation orientation and external co-production on service innovation performance. *2015 International Conference on Logistics, Informatics and Service Sciences (LISS)*, 1-6. 10.1109/LISS.2015.7369755

Lia, G., Gua, Y.-G., & Songb, Z.-H. (2013). Evolution of cooperation on heterogeneous supply networks. *International Journal of Production Research*, *51*(13), 3894–3902. doi:10.1080/00207543.2012.754968

Manu, F. A., & Sriram, V. (1996). Innovation, marketing strategy, environment, and performance. *Journal of Business Research*, *35*(1), 79–91. doi:10.1016/0148-2963(95)00056-9

McGahan, A., & Porter, M. (2003). The emergence and sustainability of abnormal profits. *Strategic Organization*, *1*(1), 79–108. doi:10.1177/1476127003001001219

McGrath, R., & MacMillan, I. C. (2009). *Discovery-Driven Growth Seize Opportunity. A Breackthrough Provess to Reduce Risk and Seize Opportunity*. Harvard Business Press.

Peñarroya-Farell, M., & Miralles, F. (2022). Business model adaptation to the covid-19 crisis: Strategic response of the spanish cultural and creative firms. *Journal of Open Innovation, 8*(1), 39. doi:10.3390/joitmc8010039

Peteraf, M. (1993). The Cornerstones of Competitive Advantage: A Resource-Based View. *Strategic Management Journal, 14*(3), 179-191.

Porter, M. E. (1981). The contributions of industrial organization to strategic management. *Academy of Management Review, 6*(4), 609–620. doi:10.2307/257639

Porter, M. E. (1989). How competitive forces shape strategy. Readings in Strategic Management, 133-143.

Porter, M. E. (2008). The five competitive forces that shape strategy. *Harvard Business Review, 86*(1), 78–93. PMID:18271320

Schilling, M. A., & Phelps, C. C. (2007). Interfirm collaboration networks: The impact of large-scale network structure on firm innovation. *Management Science, 53*(7), 1113–1126. doi:10.1287/mnsc.1060.0624

Schumpeter, J. A. (1942). Capitalism, socialism and democracy (3rd ed.). George Allen and Unwin.

Seetharaman, P. (2020). Business models shifts: Impact of Covid-19. *International Journal of Information Management, 54*, 102173. doi:10.1016/j.ijinfomgt.2020.102173 PMID:32834338

Siguaw, J. A., Simpson, P. M., & Enz, C. A. (2006). Conceptualizing innovation orientation: A framework for study and integration of innovation research. *Journal of Product Innovation Management, 23*(6), 556–574. doi:10.1111/j.1540-5885.2006.00224.x

Stock, R. M., & Zacharias, N. A. (2011). Patterns and performance outcomes of innovation orientation. *Journal of the Academy of Marketing Science, 39*(6), 870–888. doi:10.100711747-010-0225-2

Tapscott, D., & Williams, A. D. (2006). *Wikinomics: How Mass Collaboration Changes Everything.* Portfolio Hardcover.

The Investment Office of the Presidency of the Republic of Türkiye. (2021). *Tourism sector in Türkiye.* https://www.invest.gov.tr/en/library/publications/lists/investpublications/tourism-industry.pdf

Tronvoll, B., Sklyar, A., Sörhammar, D., & Kowalkowski, C. (2020). Transformational shifts through digital servitization. *Industrial Marketing Management, 89*, 293–305. doi:10.1016/j.indmarman.2020.02.005

Wang, C., Jian, Z., & Zhao, X. (2013). Effects of co-production and innovation orientation on relationship property and service innovation. *2013 10th International Conference on Service Systems and Service Management*, 237-242. 10.1109/ICSSSM.2013.6602512

Werlang, N. B., & Rossetto, C. R. (2019). The effects of organizational learning and innovativeness on organizational performance in the service provision sector. *Gestão & Produção, 26*(3), e3641. doi:10.1590/0104-530x3641-19

Wernerfelt, B. (1984). A Resource-Based View of the Firm. Strategic Management Journal, 5(1), 171-180.

Zach, F. J., & Hill, T. L. (2017). Network, knowledge and relationship impacts on innovation in tourism destinations. *Tourism Management, 62*, 196–207. doi:10.1016/j.tourman.2017.04.001

Chapter 7
Institutionalisation of Sustainability:
The HR Manager as a Strategic Entrepreneur in Its Adoption

Jesús Barrena-Martínez
University of Cádiz, Spain

Macarena López-Fernández
University of Cádiz, Spain

Pedro M. Romero-Fernández
University of Cádiz, Spain

Margarita Ruiz-Rodriguez
University of Cádiz, Spain

ABSTRACT

Contributing to sustainability no longer remains an optional activity. Institutional pressures exert a major influence on organisations towards the adoption of sustainability. However, the literature shows how these pressures are necessary but remain insufficient. This chapter focuses on how there is a certain organisational discretion regarding the refusal to merely conform by going further than strictly required (strategic commitment to sustainability). In this respect, the human resources (HR) manager acquires a crucial role in this process as an institutional entrepreneur. A qualitative study is also carried out with which it is intended to understand this process of institutionalisation in a real case study. The results of the interview with the HR manager show the proactivity acquired on assuming the role of institutional entrepreneur: an aspect that has favoured not only the awareness and institutionalisation of sustainability at a strategic level, but also the culture, processes, practices, and services that include this management philosophy.

DOI: 10.4018/978-1-6684-6845-6.ch007

INTRODUCTION

Sustainable development, understood as "developments that meet the needs of the present without compromising the ability of future generations to meet their own needs" (WCED, 1987, p. 43), has emerged as an unavoidable priority, and pushed organisations to incorporate it into their business management. Companies are institutions with great influence in shaping society. They form the economic engine that sustains society, with a power that makes them not only an economic entity, but also a business model that serves as an example to guarantee economic, social, and environmental balance (*Triple Bottom Line*, Elkington, 1998). For this reason, organisations are increasingly required to be responsible for their actions, and to be consistent with the decisions they make.

From the considerations of the Institutional Theory, the theoretical approach that supports this chapter, organisations are directly affected by the society in which they carry out their activity, which constitutes an aspect that determines their behaviour (Powell & DiMaggio, 1991). From an outside-in perspective, companies must respond to external pressures, because as they know this would imply achieving legitimacy, acceptance, and, consequently, their survival in the market. According to this classic argument of institutional theory, with the same institutional pressures, organisations will adopt similar strategies and practices (without any differentiation), that are accepted as legitimate and widespread in their field, in order to guarantee their survival.

However, it cannot be forgotten that each organisation is embedded in an internal institutional structure (Greenwood & Hinings, 1993) and hence there is the possibility that organisations respond in their own way to institutional pressures, by going beyond compliance with the environment: this is known as *organisational discretion* (Oliver, 1991). Thus, organisations under the same pressures may respond differently, by committing themselves, in this case, to a greater or lesser extent to sustainability. In this respect, the institutional perspective transfers the degree to which a company contributes to sustainability to the micro-organisational sphere, which depends largely on the commitment they acquire at a strategic level. Contributing to sustainability would imply its institutionalisation, since it reflected in organisational processes and behaviour.

This chapter focuses on this aspect. Given that the adoption of sustainability by organisations is a discretionary activity in which intervene not only the institutional pressures but also technical influences (organisational capacity), two main challenges are tackled: (a) the provision of a theoretical framework that explains how organisations institutionalise sustainability in their strategies, processes, and activities; and (b) the presentation of evidence, through study, of the role that the HR manager plays as an institutional entrepreneur in the adoption, development, and management of sustainability.

To this end, on the one hand, the institutionalisation model will be taken into consideration (Bar-Haim & Karassin, 2018; Scott, 1995), which integrates concepts of neo-institutionalism into the intra-organisational sphere, while on the other hand, the concept of institutional entrepreneur is studied (Battilana, 2006; DiMaggio, 1988), which highlights the importance that managerial discretion acquires in this process. Together, these concepts provide a theoretical foundation that enables an in-depth analysis of the relationship between the organisation and its environment, as well as, at a strategic level, an analysis within the organisation itself (Lewis et al., 2019).

The structure of the chapter is divided into six sections. Firstly, it is explained how organisational discretion helps to incorporate sustainability at a strategic level. Second, from an intra-organisational perspective, the process of institutionalising sustainability in the organisation is given in detail, as is the role of the institutional entrepreneur in this process. Specifically, it is justified why the Human Resources

Management (HRM) can and should acquire this role of institutional entrepreneur, thereby leading to the institutionalisation of sustainability.

INSTITUTIONAL PRESSURES FOR SUSTAINABILITY (IPS) AND ORGANISATIONAL DISCRETION

Is there a standardised organisational response to sustainability development?

Traditionally, institutional theory has highlighted the influence that the environment exerts on organisations that conditions their behaviour (Oliver, 1991). Broadly speaking, their arguments establish that, with the same institutional pressures, organisations adopt identical strategies and practices accepted as legitimate by society, in order to guarantee their survival. In this respect, regarding *Institutional Pressures for Sustainability* (IPS) organisations imitate similar actions in terms of sustainability to those developed by other successful companies in the market, thereby becoming isomorphic with said companies (Powell & DiMaggio, 1991). According to the institutional theory, this response will allow them, among other aspects, to be rewarded with legitimacy, and to attain resources and long-term survival in the market (DiMaggio & Powell, 1983).

This premise that obviates the possibility that organisations can respond in their own way to institutional pressures has been widely criticised in the literature, leading to institutional theory being labelled as *deterministic* (Goodstein, 1994). The reason is that not all organisations respond to institutional pressures in the same way, since a number resist or evade external isomorphic pressure. In other words, they do not passively adapt to their environments (Covaleski & Dirsmith, 1988; Judge & Zeithaml, 1992). Along these lines, there are many authors who defend the existence of both acceptance and resistance to change (Hitt & Tyler, 1991; Oliver, 1991; Pache & Santos, 2010), by incorporating elements of the strategic-choice approach into their work (Weick, 1969). They demonstrate that organisations have the ability to interpret their environment and respond to relatively fixed restrictions, by actively modifying the elements of the external context (Covaleski & Dirsmith, 1988; Judge & Zeithaml, 1992). This perspective has been defined in the literature as *voluntarist* (Goodstein, 1994), assuming that "organizations are active in creating and defining institutional demands" (Scheid-Cook, 1992, p. 537). Deterministic criticism towards institutional theory is overcome by including the consideration that organisational activity is not only the result of a conformity (or isomorphism) with the existing institutional demands in the environment, but that the internal capacity of the organisations working against these demands must also be taken into account. However, it is important not to fall into the confusion of perceiving determinism and voluntarism as opposite positions, but as ends of a continuum (Gopalakrishnan & Dugal, 1998). This interval enables different organisational responses to be made based on the degree of strategic choice that companies are granted by the environmental conditions (Gopalakrishnan & Dugal, 1998). An argument that transferred to the topic of sustainability, will allow us to understand why organisations can adopt their own response to IPS that differs from that of their competitors.

Along these lines, Hrebiniak & Joyce (1985), among others, proposed a typology of organisational adaptation to the environment, based on four behaviours (Natural Selection, Differentiation, Strategic Choice, and Undifferentiated Choice), which enable the way in which organisations experience a certain degree of freedom to be demonstrated, even though they are restricted by the environment. They also state that it is a dynamic process (circular), resulting from the relationship between organisation and environment, and that both strategic choice and determinism are cause and consequence of each other.

Supporting this approach, the contribution by Oliver (1991) presents a turning point in the development of institutional theory. In fact, it proposes a typology of strategic responses or behaviours that organisations can show the institutional pressure, which vary from active resistance to passive compliance. Thus, institutional pressure can cause acquiescence, comprise, avoidance, defiance, or manipulation, due to the strategic choice made in defence of organisational interests (Oliver 1991).

By making the use of these arguments to the implementation of sustainability in organisations, the question becomes: Do organisations adapt to the institutional context to obtain legitimacy and survive, or do they develop their own response? That is, *is there a pre-established organisational response or, in contrast, does it develop despite IPS?*

Based on the above arguments, the choices and organisational capacity regarding sustainability are neither deterministic nor pure voluntarist. Organisations develop their own strategic choice towards sustainability, although within the pressures imposed by their institutional environments. Through the specific configuration of their organisational structures and systems, they support, to a different degree and in a different way, the ideas, values, and corporate beliefs that define them towards sustainability. In the words of Greenwood & Hinings (1993), organisations have their own *"interpretative scheme"*; each one, it could be said depends on the degree of commitment acquired at a strategic level with sustainability. In this respect, it is crucial to underline that there is an opportunity to go beyond that which is established by the IPS, and beyond the acceptance and incorporation of sustainability at a strategic level, in its processes and behaviours.

However, *on what will it depend that organisations have a greater degree of commitment to sustainability at a strategic level?* From among the numerous internal variables that can influence the incorporation of sustainability at a strategic level, the strategic criteria of the management (Judge & Zeithaml, 1992) must be underlined, given that both institutional and strategic considerations are reflected in decision-making (Goodstein, 1994; Judge & Zeithaml, 1992). And, as Judge & Zeithaml (1992) specify, managerial involvement can be *"an institutional response or a strategic adaptation to external pressures"* (Judge & Zeithaml, 1992, p. 787). Therefore, the organisation's response to IPS is a function of their nature, but also of the degree to which they are represented within the organisation in the form of meaning, objectives, functions, and processes: the organisational core system (Pache & Santos, 2010).

THE INTRA-ORGANISATIONAL SCOPE IN THE INSTITUTIONALISATION OF SUSTAINABILITY

Every organisation is composed of an organisational structure. Laughlin (1991) considers it to be made up of design archetype, sub-systems, and the interpretive scheme. On *sub-systems* or tangible organisational elements, two less tangible dimensions provide them with meaning. These are the design archetype (represented by the organisational structure, decision processes, communication systems, and human resources), and the interpretive scheme, in which the mission (purpose for direction and action), the culture (beliefs, values, and organisational norms) and the paradigms (rules that maintain the lower levels) are found. These are a set of elements that must be maintained in continuous balance and be consistent with each other (Greenwood & Hinings, 1993). This organisational model was adapted by Scott (1995). According to this model, the organisation is an interpretive scheme that consists of a set of quasi-stable systems or structures and human actions. By ignoring any of these aspects, underlines Scott, the adoption of a partial and non-holistic view would be implied.

A good understanding of the organisational structure acquires great importance since organisations are not only shaped by institutional pressures but also by technical aspects (organisational dynamics) (Phillips et al., 2000). The separation between the external and technical aspects would generate situations of inconsistency, obstacles, and/or a slowing down of the attainment of any objective, which, in this case, involves the incorporation of sustainability into the organisation processes. Hence, contributing to sustainability requires its institutionalisation, that is, its incorporation at all levels of the organisational structure.

How does this process occur? Institutionalising sustainability requires introducing it into certain elements of the organisational structure and systems. Kikulis et al. (1995) state that, at a minimum, sustainability should be incorporated into *"some aspects of organizational structure and operation that are more susceptible or resistant to change"* (p. 68), these are the so-called high-impact systems, which are made up of *"those structural elements that have a great impact on organizational design coherence"* (Kikulis et al., 1995, p. 72). Returning to the conception of the organisation presented by Laughlin (1991) and later adapted by Scott (1995), the incorporation of sustainability at the intra-organisational level would require its incorporation in the structural part that supports the ideas, values, and beliefs, that is, in the interpretative scheme (Greenwood & Hinings, 1993). However, this would imply addressing a process of change in the organisations. Such a process, according to Robertson et al. (1993), would be determined by making adaptations and/or modifications in a series of variables called *"manipulable"*, which would determine and guide the behaviour of the members of the organisation. These variables would be defined by: *formal elements or organising arrangements, social factors, technology, and physical setting*. According to Robertson et al. (1993), social factors can be understood as the "individual and group characteristics of the people in an organization, their patterns and processes of interaction, and the organizational culture" (p. 620).

Along these same lines, Greenwood & Hinings (1996) emphasise the *characterisation of intra-organisational dynamics* as the variable that will determine the acceptance, rejection, acceleration, or slowdown of the change process. In other words, they consider that organisations are heterogeneous entities, with their own internal dynamics, in which there are groups with different objectives, power, and interests, with different capacities to address change processes, and with schemes of different values. A set of dynamics that show how the incorporation of sustainability in organisations, despite being a process of choice initiated by the pressures of the environment, requires a technical nature. Thus, the contribution to sustainability will only occur when the pressures of the institutional context are combined, with greater or lesser intensity, with the organisational dynamics that act as a trigger and accelerate the process of change. Along these same lines, Beckert (1999) highlights the role that *intra-organisational agency* and *power* acquires in this process of institutionalisation. Organisational actors that hold power act by managing the process of change in the organisation according to their interests. These acquire a strategic nature because success in the institutionalisation process depends to a great extent on these actors. Nevertheless, the effects are sometimes opposite and the intra-organisational agency violates the existing institutional rules. However, how is it possible that the actors try to act based on their interests, if the structures and strategies are shaped by the institutional context? DiMaggio (1988) points out as the main cause the power of the agents "agents who have an interest in specific institutional structures and who command resources which can be applied to influence institutionalised rules, either by committing those resources to the support of existing institutions or by using them for the creation of new institutions" (DiMaggio, 1988, p. 15).

In addition to the above variables, Fiol & O'Connor (2002) add that within organisations two key aspects act as a barrier or as a facilitator of change processes: emotion and cognition. They state that the emotions derived from the cognitive assessment that an actor makes (in this case, regarding the incorporation of sustainability in the organisational strategy) influence the reasoning capacity and the processing of information, thereby determining the decision for or against the incorporation of sustainability into business strategy.

However, all the aforementioned variables are not disconnected. Pache & Santos (2010) integrate the possible strategic responses to institutional demands and pay special attention to the role played by intra-organisational dynamics. In this triangle, they especially focus on the agency theory and strategic choice and highlight how organisations commit themselves at a strategic level to institutional demands depending on the degree to which their agents diverge or conflict.

This process of tensions and contradictions in different areas and aspects at the organisational level must be channelled and managed by a corporate area with a strategic and transversal nature. The question lies in not only who or what area will have the capacity to assume the role of interpreting the environment and have the appropriate rationality and discretion to incorporate the commitment to sustainability at a strategic level and spread it throughout the organisation. In other words, who will act as an *institutional entrepreneur*, and identify possibilities to create and transform institutions towards a new business model.

THE HUMAN RESOURCES MANAGER AS AN INSTITUTIONAL ENTREPRENEUR IN THE ACCOMPLISHMENT OF SUSTAINABILITY

Throughout this work, the evolution experienced by institutional theory has been aimed at expanding its levels of application, from the macro to the micro level, including the individual aspect with the agency theory considerations (Lewis et al., 2019). This process implies that the traditional conception of organisational passivity regarding institutional pressures must be questioned. The concept that describes this organisational change, beyond external pressures, has been called organisational institutionalisation, which is "the purposive action on individual and organizations aimed at creating, maintaining and disrupting institutions" (Lawrence & Suddaby, 2006, p. 215).

However, institutionalisation implies organisational change and requires the active intervention of a person/department that mobilises resources in the implementation of divergent changes and assumes the challenge of changing the established institutional order (Battilana et al., 2009). It is DiMaggio (1988), based on Eisenstadt (1980), who gives this figure the name of *institutional entrepreneur* to highlight the role of the actors who actively intervene in institutional change. More specifically, actors are seen as capable of addressing the disconnection of the organisation from its social context and acting to change it. This, as has been mentioned, implies introducing the foundations of active agency in institutional theory. In fact, "the paradox of embedded agency" (Seo & Creed, 2002), since, effectively, it is a paradox that organisational actors try to act according to their interests within an institutional environment, in which they are immersed, which shapes strategies, structures and behaviours. The deterministic consideration traditionally attributed to institutional theory is therefore rejected.

Initially, the institutional entrepreneur has been conceived as an agent who, based on their interests and, therefore, by default, changes the acceptances taken for granted in organisations. This does not mean that institutional entrepreneurship is a disruptive concept, but rather the opposite: a continuous process that must be present in all the practices and actions of the organisation. Institutional entrepreneurship is understood as "the activities of actors who have an interest in particular institutional arrangements and who leverage resources to create new institutions or to transform existing ones" (Maguire et al., 2004, p. 657). In other words, institutional entrepreneurs are those who mobilise resources to initiate and actively participate in the implementation of organisational changes, thereby assuming the challenge of modifying the established institutional order (Battilana et al., 2009; Ren & Jackson, 2020). Due to their key position in the company hierarchy, this consideration grants managers the possibility of acting as promoters, thereby preventing, to a certain extent, the organisation from being completely shaped by the institutional context in which it is integrated (Battilana, 2006). The state of the institutional context in which the organisation sometimes finds itself can present tensions, divergences, contradictions, and/or conflicts therein, this being the opportunity that the manager takes advantage of with power, intention, social position, and resources to champion change (Colombero et al., 2021). Institutional entrepreneurs are, therefore, organised actors with sufficient resources to identify possibilities, and to create and transform institutions.

Regarding the incorporation of sustainability in organisations, Greenwood et al. (2015) consider that sustainability is an institutional prescription that organisational actors comply with to different degrees. In this respect, they propose two possible positions: one that leans towards the organisational leaders' role exercising a primordial role; and, another opposing position, which advocates a secondary role, in which managerial intervention is not decisive in the creation and institutionalisation of these ideas and behaviours in organisations. The predominant position advocates the former position, whereby managers are paramount, have the ability to go beyond the IPS, and can decide discretionally. They also understand how to carry out the adoption, diffusion, and implementation of organisational change throughout the organisation.

But *what leads managers to initiate these changes towards sustainability?* Rothenberg (2007), based on the work of Greenwood & Hinings (1996), Beckert (1999), and Seo & Creed (2002), establishes that the main factors that influence the proactive behaviour of the manager include: the power held by said manager within the organisation, the relationship between institutional and technical pressures, and the prominence of these pressures. In a complementary way, Kump (2021) establishes that the personal values of the manager are also critical for their behaviour, although when they face threats from the environment, they may encounter conflicts of values and various tensions between the implementation of sustainable changes and the desire to comply with organisational goals and results. Thus, it is established that managers mobilise to promote change towards sustainability when they consider that the company is susceptible, vulnerable, to environmental threats, when the perceived benefits of the change outweigh the obstacles, or when there is an external signal that requires it. It is at this point that managers assume the role of precipitators of organisational change towards sustainability (Kump, 2021).

Although it is essential to understand what justifies the role of institutional entrepreneur towards the integration of sustainability, it is also interesting to ascertain *who is responsible for or assumes that institutional role within the organisation*. Authors, such as Porter & Kramer (2006), maintain that, in order to commit to and contribute to sustainability at the organisational level, it is not possible to develop actions in isolation from different departments or specific organisational areas, and it is necessary to manage these actions transversally, in order to create shared value. Managing sustainability across the board requires an institutional entrepreneur who fosters communication, collaboration, and the commitment of all stakeholders and organisational functions. Within the organisation chart, it is considered indispensable to exercise this figure of institutional entrepreneur, given the strategic situation reached by the human resources department, since it is a strategic body linked to senior management, with transversal capacity, which provides relationship and knowledge systems, and supplies the company with a specific and specialised vision, in accordance with its strategic objectives.

A PwC study (2022) conducted on managers of 1,640 listed companies concludes that, sustainability actions have traditionally been linked to the marketing department, due to the commercial actions that characterize it; however, this management has changed radically. Currently, sustainability management is led by a Chief Sustainability Officer (CSO), who appears in the organisation chart of the company and manages the interests of managers, employees, customers, and shareholders, in order to minimise environmental, social, and economic aspects within the company, and to satisfy the needs of these interest groups. The CSO addresses how sustainability must extend beyond specific actions that strengthen the brand. Sustainability must be integrated into the organisation's strategy by taking on an ever-increasing relevance in day-to-day activities and in corporate reports. However, and despite the importance that this figure acquires, the results of PwC (2022) also conclude that the role of the CSO continues to be largely inactive, due to the limited power granted to it in terms of decision-making, compared to the power wielded by other directors.

The question that arises, given the strategic and transversal nature of the human resources department, is *should the role of the CSO be developed by the human resources manager?* The institutional entrepreneur, from the human resources management, would lead this interaction between external pressure and internal organisational processes regarding sustainability. This aspect can present an opportunity not only to achieve better organisational results, but also to enrich the role of HRM in organisations. The challenges inherent to organisational sustainability are transcendental and require managers who are active and proactive to go beyond the traditional role of agent of change and adopt the role of institutional entrepreneur. HRM systems (human resources strategies, policies, and practices) are the instruments to promote such change. As institutional entrepreneurs, HRM professionals can shape the decision-making and actions of organisational members through their HRM orientations as well as their interactions with executives, middle managers, and employees. By crossing boundaries, they can collaborate with a wide range of external stakeholders to shape the institutional logic of the broader context in which the organisation is embedded. The knowledge, skills, resources, and capabilities of HRM professionals clearly render them institutional entrepreneurs.

The aforementioned approaches are outlined in the following conceptual model (see Figure 1), which describes the process of institutionalising sustainability in an organisation. In this figure, the focus is on the role of institutional entrepreneur that the human resources manager assumes for the adoption and dissemination of sustainability in the organisation, based on their special strategic position therein. As a manager, this individual takes on the active challenge of participating in the formation of the company's identity and contributes to its transversal development in the processes, especially when the organisation does not adopt a position of passive acceptance determined by institutional pressure, but instead chooses to design its own active response. It is at this point that the human resources department can intervene by playing a leadership role in this process and can contribute to its dissemination among stakeholders through human resources policies, practices, and processes. This design of the organisation's response to a commitment to sustainability not only provokes internal repercussions, but also implies the possibility of the organisation acting as an external disseminating agent, thereby becoming a pioneer and an example for other companies in the institutionalisation and transversal development of sustainability.

Figure 1.

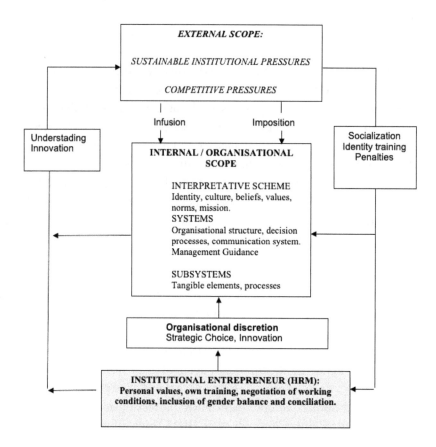

METHOD

In order to contrast the aforementioned approaches, it is shown below, through a qualitative study of the multiservice company Mayse S.L., how this organisation carries out the previously described process of institutionalisation of sustainability, and ascertains whether the profile of institutional entrepreneur in the figure of the human resources manager facilitates this process.

Specifically, the case method has been chosen by combining various data collection methods, since this method not only has the ability to explain the how and why of a given phenomenon, but it can also enable the collection and measurement of behaviours and the collection of information that is not only verbal (Yin, 1994).

In order to overcome the limitations and biases attributed to this methodology, that is, the possible subjectivity of the researcher, and the reliability of the results, two interviewers have been incorporated in this work for the sake of greater objectivity. Regarding the representativeness and scientific generalisation of the results obtained, Yin (1994, p. 21) states that, "case studies, like experiments, are generalizable to theoretical propositions and not to the universal population." In this respect, the generalisation would not be statistical but analytical, since the intention is to generalise the theory (Yin, 1994). The importance of choosing a single case with an exploratory nature is therefore defended.

For the contextualisation of the company Maintenance and Services (Mayse S.L.), its main activity is to provide "building, industrial, and office cleaning services" nationwide. This is a family business that has approximately 150 employees, of which 11 belong to administrative staff and management positions.

This company has been selected because it belongs to a context in which fundamentally regulatory, as well as competitive, institutional pressures predominate, which have conditioned its evolution. These constitute a set of pressures that are especially evident when facing contract-bidding processes. Furthermore, Mayse S.L. is undergoing a process of incorporating sustainability induced by regulatory institutional pressure, common to the entire activity sector.

To address the investigation, the objectives to be achieved were established beforehand, the person designated to interview was contacted, and the questions to be discussed in the meeting were sent to the interviewee. The personal interview, of a structured and open nature, was conducted with the person in charge of human resources, which enabled the broader vision of the institutionalisation process of sustainability that this organisation was implementing.

After the interview, all the information extracted was transcribed and, finally, it was analysed descriptively. The results obtained were subsequently linked to the theoretical framework that supports the institutionalisation process of sustainability, in a procedure that, according to the "pattern marching" formula (Yin, 1994), advocates the "induced" study.

RESULTS

The transcript of the interview has been incorporated in Appendix I.

The results obtained from the interview with the human resources department of Mayse S.L., whose main activity is focused on developing multi-service and logistics activities in companies and public bodies that are labour-intensive, show that the company plays an active/proactive role towards incorporating sustainability at a strategic level.

Institutional pressures have been a determining factor for its initial consideration, but the company demonstrates that it has gone beyond merely conforming to the demands of the environment, by gradually and naturally committing itself to sustainability at a strategic level, thereby making it an element of his identity.

This commitment to sustainability is reflected in numerous activities, processes and behaviours that make up the daily life of the organisation. An example of this can be seen in the use of ecological products in the services it offers. Initially, the main doubt held by the company lay in the level of acceptance by customers that these products could enjoy, since the price of an organic product is higher than that of a traditional product. However, and despite this uncertainty, the company has fought for the market to understand that the use of this type of ecological product forms an essential part of the company and shows a true reflection of its corporate values. However, the head of human resources states that, despite the effort made by the company to demonstrate its commitment to sustainability, it is sometimes difficult to maintain this belief, leading to a certain insecurity regarding its use. The person in charge of human resources explains that this feeling is largely due to the fact that private companies only notice an increase in maintenance and service contracts, and fail to value the certifications and compliance with sustainable standards that the company presents. However, from Mayse S.L. it is defended that in the long run these costs result in an improvement in occupational health, reduction in work accidents and sick leave (allergies, respiratory problems, injuries, etc.) which, consequently leads to a reduction in costs that are not appreciated a priori.

At the level of public institutions, Mayse S.L. emphasise that the situation is completely the reverse. There is greater pressure and obligation in their requirements towards sustainability, since the tenders or contracts are evaluated by Governmental Organisations (Local City Councils or at the level of the Autonomous Community) in terms of scores based on the level of certificates held regarding sustainability standards in its processes and activities.

Given the comments made, the head of human resources stresses that Mayse S.L. maintains its commitment to sustainability. It incorporates sustainability into its day-to-day activities, not due to coercive, mimetic, and/or regulatory pressures, but rather because it is an essential part of its corporate values. Thus, another example is presented by the manager, this time focused on the adoption of measures of human resources, whose main objective is to improve the quality of life of employees, although most of these actions are the result of negotiation with the company board. Among these measures, it is worth highlighting those referring to gender diversity in all job positions, and the company has even developed its own equality plan and promoted conciliation actions in an effort to reduce work absenteeism and to maintain a motivated workforce with high productivity and excellent levels of work safety. Along these lines, she mentions how, ever since the health crisis triggered by Covid-19, the company has maintained a hybrid model of both face-to-face working practices and teleworking, which has resulted in greater employee satisfaction. In her company philosophy, they are committed to young and trained talent, and offer a work model that enables them to retain these new generations. The person in charge of Mayse S.L. is confident of the positive effect that these efforts will exert on the organisational results in improving the number and quality of the bids obtained.

Regarding the role played by the human resources department in the institutionalisation of sustainability, the head of human resources expresses her support for this premise. She believes that, in her case, the fact that it is a family business has positively favoured the incorporation of sustainability at a strategic level, by fostering the inter-relationship between the management team and staff. This circumstance, together with her personality, her values, and her concern for sustainability, she considers to constitute the determining factors that can classify her as an institutional entrepreneur in this process of institutionalising sustainability in Mayse S.L.

To conclude, the interviewee expresses her personal opinion on where Mayse S.L. stands regarding the level of contribution to sustainability compared to other companies in the sector. In this respect, the head of human resources considers their company to be pioneers at the level of sustainable development and SMEs. This opinion is substantiated by the awards they have received in terms of occupational risk prevention and the set of measures they have developed towards social integration, the adoption of conciliation measures (adopting adapted work shifts), gender (pursuing objectives of equality), and training (as one of the main ways of disseminating sustainability among the workforce). Furthermore, she underlines that the company contributes to sustainability in its *triple bottom line*: (i) at the environmental level, by relying on an ecological product in the long term; (ii) at the social level, by developing personnel management under a socially responsible orientation; and (iii) at the economic level, with job creation.

However, the head of human resources clarifies that the circumstances of the Covid-19 have caused greater demands not only for chemical products and sanitation, but also in the logistics, and in the cleaning and maintenance processes, which has made it difficult to incorporate sustainability in the use of organic products.

CONCLUSIONS AND DISCUSSIONS

From the framework of institutional theory, this work has presented the change that the consideration of the internal institutionalisation of sustainability implies in organisations and the strategic role acquired by the figure of the institutional entrepreneur. The argument is based on the consideration that the inclusion/institutionalisation of sustainability in organisations requires a body linked to general management and strategic decision-making, and should also be of a transversal nature, so that it can promote and facilitate changes that can break away from the dominant institutional logic. The actors who allocate resources to initiate and implement such divergent changes are the so-called institutional entrepreneurs (Battilana et al., 2009), a figure that has been revealed through the results of the interview, as being assumed by the human resources manager of Mayse S.L.

Organisational sustainability therefore requires professionals capable of identifying opportunities, mobilising allies, stimulating the creation of a new vision, and consolidating new institutional logic, by changing norms, rules, routines, and values that balance economic, social, and environmental performance (Ren & Jackson, 2020). An institutional entrepreneur leads the interaction between external pressures and internal organisational processes for sustainability, which, for human resources management, represents the opportunity to enrich their role in organisations.

The results of the case study in Mayse S.L. have provided evidence and perceptions of a manager of human resources, operations, and occupational-risk prevention, with approximately 20 years of experience, that enrich the theoretical discussion carried out. Among the most outstanding conclusions, it is worth highlighting the proactive role of the human resources manager as an institutional entrepreneur, the necessary synergies that must be carried out for a correct integration of sustainability in a transversal way, and the additional commitment that the organisation acquires with this concept that goes far beyond that prompted by institutional pressure. The commitment to training at all organisational levels in terms of sustainability, together with the commitment of management in decision-making on aspects that imply improvements in the economic, social, and environmental dimensions, also constitute outstanding and necessary aspects for the correct institutionalisation of sustainability.

REFERENCES

Bar-Haim, A., & Karassin, O. (2018). A multilevel model of responsibility towards employees as a dimension of corporate social responsibility. *Journal of Management and Sustainability*, 8(1), 1–15. doi:10.5539/jms.v8n3p1

Battilana, J. (2006). Agency and institutions: The enabling role of individuals' social position. *Organization*, 13(5), 653–676. doi:10.1177/1350508406067008

Battilana, J., Leca, B., & Boxenbaum, E. (2009). How Actors Change Institutions: Towards a Theory of institutional entrepreneurship. *The Academy of Management Annals*, 3(1), 65–107. doi:10.5465/19416520903053598

Beckert, J. (1999). Agency, Entrepreneurs, and Institutional Change. The Role of Strategic Choice and Institutionalized Practices in Organizations. *Organization Studies*, 20(5), 777–799. doi:10.1177/0170840699205004

Colombero, S., Duymedjian, R., & Boutinot, A. (2021). The embedded-agency paradox revisited: Discussing Deleuze and Guattari's concept of becoming for institutional entrepreneurship. *Scandinavian Journal of Management, 37*(1), 101142. doi:10.1016/j.scaman.2021.101142

Covaleski, M. A., & Dirsmith, M. W. (1988). An institutional perspective on the rise, social transformation, and fall of a university budget category. *Administrative Science Quarterly, 33*(4), 562–587. doi:10.2307/2392644

DiMaggio, P. J. (1988). Interest and agency in institutional theory. In L. G. Zucker (Ed.), *Institutional patterns and organizations: Culture and environment* (pp. 147–161). Ballinger.

DiMaggio, P. J., & Powell, W. W. (1983). The iron cage revisited: Institutional isomorphism and collective rationality in organizational fields. *American Sociological Review, 48*(2), 147–160. doi:10.2307/2095101

Eisenstadt, S. N. (1980). Cultural orientations, institutional entrepreneurs, and social change: Comparative analysis of traditional civilizations. *American Journal of Sociology, 85*(4), 840–869. doi:10.1086/227091

Elkington, J. (1998). Partnerships from cannibals with forks: The triple bottom line of 21st-century business. *Environmental Quality Management, 8*(1), 37–51. doi:10.1002/tqem.3310080106

Fiol, C. M., & O'Connor, E. J. (2002). When hot and cold collide in radical change processes: Lessons from community development. *Organization Science, 13*(5), 532–546. doi:10.1287/orsc.13.5.532.7812

Goodstein, J. D. (1994). Institutional pressures and strategic responsiveness: Employer involvement in work-family issues. *Academy of Management Journal, 37*(2), 350–382. doi:10.2307/256833

Gopalakrishnan, S., & Dugal, M. (1998). Strategic choice versus environmental determinism: A debate revisited. *The International Journal of Organizational Analysis, 6*(2), 146–164. doi:10.1108/eb028882

Greenwood, R., & Hinings, C. R. (1993). Understanding Strategic Change: The Contribution of Archetypes. *Academy of Management Journal, 36*(5), 1052–1081. doi:10.2307/256645

Greenwood, R., & Hinings, C. R. (1996). Understanding Radical Organizational Change: Bringing Together the Old and the New Institutionalism. *Academy of Management Review, 21*(4), 1022–1054. doi:10.2307/259163

Greenwood, R., Jennings, P. D., & Hinings, B. (2015). Sustainability and organizational change: An institutional perspective. *Leading sustainable change: An organizational perspective*, 323-55. doi:10.1093/acprof:oso/9780198704072.003.0013

Hitt, M. A., & Tyler, B. B. (1991). Strategic decision models: Integrating different perspectives. *Strategic Management Journal, 12*(5), 327–351. doi:10.1002mj.4250120502

Hrebiniak, L. G., & Joyce, W. F. (1985). Organizational adaptation: Strategic choice and environmental determinism. *Administrative Science Quarterly, 30*(3), 336–349. doi:10.2307/2392666

Judge, W. Q. Jr, & Zeithaml, C. P. (1992). Institutional and strategic choice perspectives on board involvement in the strategic decision process. *Academy of Management Journal, 35*(4), 766–794. doi:10.2307/256315 PMID:10122320

Kikulis, L. M., Slack, T., & Hinings, C. R. (1995). Sector-specific patterns of organizational design change. *Journal of Management Studies, 32*(1), 67–100. doi:10.1111/j.1467-6486.1995.tb00646.x

Kump, B. (2021). When do threats mobilize managers for organizational change toward sustainability? An environmental belief model. *Business Strategy and the Environment, 30*(5), 2713–2726. doi:10.1002/bse.2773

Laughlin, R. C. (1991). Environmental disturbances and organizational transitions and transformations: Some alternative models. *Organization Studies, 12*(2), 209–232. doi:10.1177/017084069101200203

Lawrence, T. B., & Suddaby, R. (2006). Institutions and institutional work. The Sage handbook of organization studies, 215-254. doi:10.4135/9781848608030.n7

Lewis, A. C., Cardy, R. L., & Huang, L. S. (2019). Institutional theory and HRM: A new look. *Human Resource Management Review, 29*(3), 316–335. doi:10.1016/j.hrmr.2018.07.006

Maguire, S., Hardy, C., & Lawrence, T. B. (2004). Institutional entrepreneurship in emerging fields: HIV/AIDS treatment advocacy in Canada. *Academy of Management Journal, 47*(5), 657–679. doi:10.2307/20159610

Oliver, C. (1991). Strategic responses to institutional processes. *Academy of Management Review, 16*(1), 145–179. doi:10.2307/258610

Pache, A. C., & Santos, F. (2010). When worlds collide: The internal dynamics of organizational responses to conflicting institutional demands. *Academy of Management Review, 35*(3), 455–476. doi:10.5465/AMR.2010.51142368

Phillips, N., Lawrence, T. B., & Hardy, C. (2000). Inter-organizational collaboration and the dynamics of institutional fields. *Journal of Management Studies, 37*(1), 23–43. doi:10.1111/1467-6486.00171

Porter, M. E., & Kramer, M. R. (2006). The link between competitive advantage and corporate social responsibility. *Harvard Business Review, 84*(12), 78–92. PMID:17183795

Powell, W. W., & DiMaggio, P. J. (1991). *The New Institutionalism in Organizational Analysis*. University of Chicago Press. doi:10.7208/chicago/9780226185941.001.0001

PriceWaterhouseCoopers. (2022). *Empowered Chief Sustainability Officers. The key to remaining credible and competitive.* https://www.strategyand.pwc.com/de/en/unique-solutions/sustainable-impact-made-real/empowered-chief-sustainability-officers.html

Ren, S., & Jackson, S. E. (2020). HRM institutional entrepreneurship for sustainable business organizations. *Human Resource Management Review, 30*(3), 100691. doi:10.1016/j.hrmr.2019.100691

Robertson, P. J., Roberts, D. R., & Porras, J. I. (1993). Dynamics of planned organizational change: Assessing empirical support for a theoretical model. *Academy of Management Journal, 36*(3), 619–634. doi:10.2307/256595

Rothenberg, S. (2007). Environmental managers as institutional entrepreneurs: The influence of institutional and technical pressures on waste management. *Journal of Business Research*, *60*(7), 749–757. doi:10.1016/j.jbusres.2007.02.017

Scheid-Cook, T. L. (1992). Organizational enactments and conformity to environmental prescriptions. *Human Relations*, *45*(6), 537–554. doi:10.1177/001872679204500601

Scott, W. R. (1995). *Institutions and organizations*. Sage Publications.

Seo, M. G., & Creed, W. D. (2002). Institutional contradictions, praxis, and institutional change: A dialectical perspective. *Academy of Management Review*, *27*(2), 222–247. doi:10.2307/4134353

Weick, K. (1969). The social psychology of organizing. Reading, MA: Addison.

World Commission on Environment and Development. (1987). *Our Common Future Oxford*. Oxford University Press.

Yin, R. K. (1994). Discovering the future of the case study. Method in evaluation research. *Evaluation Practice*, *15*(3), 283–290. doi:10.1016/0886-1633(94)90023-X

APPENDIX I: COMPLETE INTERVIEW

Company: MAYSE SL
HR manager: Ms. Encarnación Díaz
Webpage: https://www.maysesl.com
RESEARCH AIM: To explain the influence that institutional pressures exert towards the adoption of sustainability, and to highlight the role that the HR manager plays as an institutional entrepreneur in the adoption, development, and management of sustainability.
METHOD: Case study, interview with HR manager.

1. Institutional Pressures for Sustainability. Did the institutional pressures from legislation, certification bodies, and government lead Mayse S.L. to consider sustainability? If so, provide an example.

Institutional pressures are a starting point for the incorporation of sustainability into the organisation. However, Mayse S.L. goes further. The greatest institutional pressures towards sustainability come from tenders in public companies, in which there are objective criteria referring to the contribution to sustainability by our organisation that are subject to being rated by the evaluating administrations. Examples of these requirements are given in equality plans and sustainability reports, which must be in force at the time of bidding. At the private company level, only certain multinationals demand commitments or requirements with sustainability, but these are scarce.

2. Organisational discretion (flexibility to make decisions on sustainability). Does Mayse S.L. have its own different response to sustainability pressures regarding other companies in the sector? In other words, is Mayse S.L. considered a sector leader/pioneer in the introduction of sustainability? In this case, provide an example.

As an SME and family business, we have many economic restrictions compared to large companies that operate in the national territory, and hence are unable to access most subsidies and state aid. However, in the SME category, I think we can be considered pioneers in terms of sustainable decisions in its three areas (economic, social, and environmental). The company recently received an award from the Autonomous Community for the prevention of occupational risks carried out by the company, and, in addition, our company stands out thanks to the set of measures that are implemented regarding the well-being of the workforce.

3. Introduction of sustainability at a strategic level in Mayse S.L. Is Mayse S.L. active in the creation and definition of behaviours, culture, and practices that achieve its sustainability? Please provide an example.

As the HR manager, HR are strategic for company. The company has made a major effort in the design of training, equality plans, and union dialogue in order to handle the social and economic impact. There is also great concern about the environment and the use of ecological products. Likewise, sustainability is integrated into design and project management depending on the duration of projects. The strategic and sustainable philosophy is more 1widely introduced in projects and contracts of greater duration (two/ four years) than those of only one year.

4. Conflicts/ synergies to incorporate sustainability at a strategic level. Are conflicts and tensions generated between different departments and/or people, or are there synergies when it comes to understanding and responding to pressures towards sustainability? Provide an example.

Due to differences between departments, a lot of work lies ahead in terms of finding a single and united approach in favour of sustainability. Since Mayse S.L. is *a family company, the manager, who has extensive experience in the sector, undergoes new pressures, such as sustainability, and, when making decisions, it is important that there is confidence and guarantees in investments in sustainability both at the level of manager and of other management bodies. However, the fact that* Mayse S.L. *is a small family business helps us to a great extent, as is shown and communicated through all the measures that are implemented. An example of this is in the reduction of working hours, which, in the long term, is more viable both for the workers, since it improves their satisfaction with the company, and for the company, since there are fewer requests for extra days off, it reduces absenteeism, and improves the involvement and sense of belonging of the workers. The person in charge concludes that there are discrepancies between the different family generations, who harbour different thoughts on issues of effectiveness and economic results.*

5. The profile of the human resources manager and the involvement of the management team towards the institutionalisation of Sustainability. Do you consider that your personal involvement or your values have been decisive in the company's degree of commitment to sustainability? Provide an example.

My involvement as head of human resources and that of the directors and administrators in office is 100%. This translates into daily and continuous training regarding our contribution to sustainability, which is also carried out from day one for new employees. Moreover, I believe that my personality, values, and concern for sustainability have been determining factors.

6. Awareness of Mayse SL regarding sustainability. In your opinion, which agents have contributed most to shaping the company's sustainable awareness? The influence of specific stakeholders, the influence of managers (power to make decisions), or that of employees (pressure for better quality of life/ remuneration)?

There is widespread awareness in the company, but it is not an easy process since there are major differences in age and the jobs are very diverse, and this entails the need for continuous training in sustainability issues. However, maintaining a level of sustainability is a continuous task, which does not stop (learning new uses for products, reduction of chemical substances, etc.), in order to act in a more responsible and sustainable way.

Are the Sustainable Development Goals SDGs part of the essence of the company, its identity, and culture? Are the SDGs strategic in nature and do they encompass all organisational levels and processes?

Regarding the SDGs, although there is no real commitment to each specific objective, commitment does exist at a general level. However, I am sure that Mayse S.L. makes a significant contribution to sustainability through its involvement in this management philosophy. Furthermore, it is a process that has been carried out naturally and not imposed by the pressures of society. It is a great challenge, because for many stakeholders the economic aspect continues to prevail in relation to the social and environmental dimensions.

7. Relationship between the Human Resources' function and Sustainability in Mayse S.L. Has the human resources' function collaborated in the incorporation and dissemination of the SDGs in the company? How?

Training, employment relationships, and the incorporation of specialised technicians are the main tools that the human resources' function uses in order to be able to carry out the challenge of incorporating sustainability in Mayse S.L. Only through synergies between people and departments can the challenge of incorporating sustainability be tackled effectively.

Does Mayse have a Chief Sustainability Officer (CSO), or is this figure assumed by the human resources manager?

In Mayse S.L., this figure does not exist, but if it did, the person in charge of human resources would be the most appropriate figure to carry out this function.

To finalise the interview, the person in charge is asked whether the assumption of various functions (operations, human resources, risk prevention) implies having a broader vision and a multidisciplinary profile, consistent with that of the institutional entrepreneur, and whether these values are kept outside of their working life.

I am committed to sustainability as a philosophy of management and life: outside the office it is something natural and desired, it gives me a broader vision than that of the company's operations, and of its dealings with staff and unions. These values began to be instilled in me from the most basic educational levels, which boosts my awareness of society regarding the importance of sustainability.

Chapter 8
Organizational Opportunities Through Digital and Social Media Marketing

K. Pradeep Reddy
SAGE University, Bhopal, India

Venkateswarlu Chandu
Koneru Lakshmaiah Education Foundation, India

B. Shifaly
The Hindu College MBA, Machilipatnam, India

Bhavana Likhitkar
LNCT, Bhopal, India

Amala Gangula
IBPS, India

ABSTRACT

The internet and social-media have altered customer behaviour as well as the methods in which businesses operate. Organizations may benefit from digital and social-media marketing (DSMM) by lowering expenses, increasing brand-recognition, and increasing revenues. However, poor electronic word-of-mouth as well as obtrusive and unpleasant online-brand presence poses substantial obstacles. This chapter brings together the aggregate wisdom of various renowned experts on DSMM concerns. This study provides a significant and prompt contribution to both practitioners and investigators in the context of issues and challenges, highlighting the shortcomings of the existing research, identifying research gaps, and developing questions and propositions that can help promote knowledge in the area of DSMM promotions.

DOI: 10.4018/978-1-6684-6845-6.ch008

1. INTRODUCTION

The internet, social-media, smartphone applications, and other digital-communications tools have become commonplace for billions of people worldwide. According to January 2020 data, "4.54 billion" individuals are found to be active users of internet, accounting for '59 percent' of the worldwide populace (Statista, 2020). Social-media has become an essential part of many people's life throughout the globe, and people are also spending more-time online seeking for information, purchasing 'products and services', interacting with other customers about their experiences, and connecting with businesses. Organizations have responded to this shift in customers'behaviour by using "digital and social-media marketing (DSMM)" strategies into their company (Stephen, 2016).

Organizations may greatly benefit from incorporating social-media marketing into their overall business strategy (Abed et al., 2015; Abed et al., 2016; Rathore et al., 2016; Shareef et al., 2019). Companies may use social-media to engage with their consumers, raise brand-recognition, influence consumer-attitudes, get-feedback, enhance current goods and services, and promote revenues (Kapoor et al., 2018; Lal et al., 2020).Dwivedi et al. (2021) have provided a detailed narrative on key-aspects as well as perspectives on more specific-issues such as artificial intelligence, virtual world's sales promotion, virtual goods governance, cellphone advertising and marketing, "business-to-business (B2B)" marketing, "electronic word-of-mouth (e-WOM)", and moral questions.

Because to the collapse of conventional communication channels and societal reliance on brick-and-mortar operations, businesses must seek best practices in digital and social media marketing strategies in order to keep and expand market-shares (Schultz and Peltier, 2013). Significant problems exist for organisations building their social media strategy and goals in the context of a new reality of increasing consumer power and enhanced knowledge of cultural and societal standards (Kietzmann et al., 2011). This study brings together various renowned experts' aggregate perspectives to examine the substantial-prospects, difficulties, and future research agenda linked to key-components of online sales-promotion.

This paper's observations address a wide range of DSMM themes, reflecting the perspectives of different viewpoints. The study is an important and timely contribution to the literature, providing crucial insight to researchers in the progress of knowledge in this marketing arena. As the digital and social media marketing business evolves and takes its place as an important and critical component of an organization's marketing strategy, this topic is positioned as a timely addition to the literature. The remainder of this article is arranged as follows. Section 2 provides an overview of current controversies and overarching topics in the literature with the viewpoints of many professionals on DSMM. Section 3 covers the challenges in DSMM, and the fourth section concludes with limitations and future research directions.

2. LITERATURE

The available literature on DSMM was summarized in this section, and each subject from a review of the literature has been discussed. The studies in this section were found by searching the "Scopus database" using the keywords "social-media", "digital marketing", and "social-media marketing". This method was comparable to that employed in current review publications on a variety of significant issues (Dwivedi et al., 2019, Marriott et al., 2017). According to Dwivedi et al. (2021), the overall subjects were separated into four key parameters: environmental aspects, organisational aspects, marketing aspects, and outcome-based aspects (Table 1).

Table 1. Different significant aspects in DSMM

Parameters	Sources
Environmental aspects	Alam et al. (2019); Arora et al. (2019); Gaber et al. (2019); Islam et al. (2018); Kim and Jang (2019); Mandal (2019); and Seoand Park (2018)
Organizational aspects	Ballestar et al. (2019); Gil-Gonz´alez et al. (2018); Miklosik et al. (2019); Ritz et al. (2019); Roumieh et al. (2018); and Vermeer et al. (2019)
Marketing aspects	Ang et al. (2018); Hutchins and Rodriguez (2018); Kang and Park (2018); Parsons and Lepkowska-White (2018); and Teo (2019)
Outcome-based aspects	Ahmed et al. (2019); Aswani et al. (2018); Ibrahim and Aljarah (2018); Morra et al. (2018); Shanahan et al. (2019); Stojanovic et al. (2018); Tarnovskaya and Biedenbach (2018); and Wong et al. (2018)

The amount of time spent online and the various activities carried out utilising digital devices are referred to as "screen time (ST)" (DataReportal, 2020). Pandya and Lodha (2021) found dramatic enhancement in ST during COVID-19. There was however mixed repercussions of prolonged ST use and a muddled understanding between healthy and unhealthy social-connectedness via digital-media, the suggestions for negative consequences on mental-health warrant a strict need for instilling healthy digital-habits, especially given that digitization was there to stay and develop with period. The usage of digital technology has increased dramatically during the previous two decades. It has increased human exposure to prolonged screen time, which is becoming increasingly problematic. Digital technology is the use of electronic equipment to store, create, or analyse data; it also promotes communication and virtual interactions on social media platforms that use the internet (Vizcaino et al., 2020). Computers, laptops, palmtops, smartphones, tablets, and other similar devices with screens are examples of electronic gadgets. They serve as a means of communication, virtual exchanges, and interpersonal connectivity. Humans require social interaction to function. Furthermore, social interaction improves mental health. Because of the COVID-19 pandemic, digital networks have become the sole way for individuals to retain socio-emotional connections (Kanekar and Sharma, 2020). Digital technology influences how individuals utilise digital devices to preserve or avoid social relationships, as well as how much time they devote to virtual social connectivity (Antonucci et al., 2017).

2.1 Environmental Aspects

The environment in which businesses function has been greatly impacted by the development and adoption of digital technology. Studies in this area are primarily concerned with how digital marketing and "electronic word-of-mouth (e-WOM)" communications have changed consumer behaviour and customer relations. Technology advancements and the widespread usage of handheld devices have drastically altered consumer behaviour, which has a direct impact on how we communicate, utilise social commerce to make decisions, and conduct online business (Hossain et al., 2019). The growing use of digital marketing and social-media has altered attitudes of customers about online purchasing, resulting in increased market dominance for e-commerce-centric businesses (Komodromos et al., 2018). Customer behaviour has also been impacted by the rising number of shopping channels (Hossain et al., 2020), resulting in an increasingly dispersed consumer purchasing experiences. Utilizing mobile-tools, buying-tools, proximity-services, and digital-wallets has made mobile-channels the standard, and is now ingrained in customers' everyday life. These factors all influence the customer satisfaction (Shukla and Nigam, 2018).

It is critical to determine user demands, as well as their thoughts and attitudes toward various types of advertising and communications, just as it is in conventional marketing. According to Girondaand Korgaonkar(2018), invasiveness, confidentiality control, relative advantage, and individual creativeness all had a direct influence on a consumer's behavioral intent regarding personal information. The research by Abou-Elgheit (2018) highlighted the significance of comprehending shifting consumer behaviour from a larger perspective, despite the fact that many studies in the literature depend on customers from wealthy nations. The study performed marketing through social-media in Egypt, recognizing the significance of cognitive, emotions, experiences, and personal traits that might influence consumers' decision-making and confidence in internet shopping. Their study argued that organisations' social-media marketing initiatives should take into account demographical, geographical, regional, and behavioural target groups.

2.2 Organizational Aspects

Organizations have used a variety of ways in the usage of digital and social media marketing, with corporations displaying diverse views toward social-media strategy. Matikiti et al. (2018) investigated the factors that influence the attitudes of South African travel businesses and tour operators. The study discovered that there are both internal and external variables impacting attitude by using questionnaires gathered from 150 agencies. Internal variables include management support and managers' educational-level. External variables include competition pressure, perceived advantages, and perceived ease of use. Canovi and Pucciarelli (2019) conducted research on the attitudes of mini-bar businesses regarding social-media marketing. According to their report, while the majority of vineyard owners acknowledge the social, economic, and emotional benefits of social-media, they are far from fully utilizing it.

According to the literature, attitudes toward social media differ based on the size and kind of firm. Social-media is perceived by B2B organizations as having lower overall-efficacy as a marketing medium and as being less crucial for relationship development than traditional communication-formats (Iankova et al., 2019). Organizations employ a variety of technologies to analyze and capture data from social-media, as well as manage multi-channel communications. Companies, on the other hand, frequently lack enough awareness of emerging-technologies such as "Artificial Intelligence (AI)", with many organizations demonstrating poor-levels of "adoption and exploitation" of "Machine Learning (ML)" analytical-tools (Duan et al., 2019). Companies might utilize these technologies to automate the curating of brand-related social-media photos (Tous et al., 2018), as well as to discover more successful targeting in promotional-marketing (Takahashi, 2019).

2.3 Marketing Aspects

For social-media marketing, businesses employ a variety of social media channels, including Facebook, Twitter, Snapchat, and others. The platforms used are determined by the target-audience and the marketing-plan. Chen and Lee (2018) looked at the usage of Snapchat for social-media marketing with a focus on young customers. According to the survey findings, Snapchat represented the most intimate, informal, and dynamic platform that provided information to users, sociability, and amusement. According to the survey, youngsters appear to have a favourable view regarding Snapchat, with comparable emotions toward buying behaviour and companies marketed platforms. Tafesse and Wien (2018) examined various business strategies, including transformational - where the experience and identity of the focal brand exhibits desirable psychological characteristics; informational - presents factual product; service information in clear terms; and interactional - where social media advertising cultivates ongoing interactions with customers and message strategies.

Kusumasondjaja (2018) discovered that valued-advertisements were more commonly replied to than informational messaging. For informational appeal, Twitter was more successful. According to the results, Facebook seemed best adapted for infotainment postings, while Instagram was preferable for interactive material integrating insightful and interesting attractions. On Instagram and Facebook interactive types of advertisements with mixed appeals received the most responses, while a self-oriented message with informative appeal received the least. Advertisers care about the characteristics of social-media messages. Hwang et al. (2018), for example, applied motivation theory in a tourist environment to suggest that complete, usefulness, versatility, timeliness of the argumentation, excellence, and reliability of brand trust all have a beneficial influence on the user's pleasure. Customers may therefore be more likely to visit the website again and buy the tourism-related item as a result, which in turn can impact user intention. Incorporating comedy and emotions can increase customer interaction, according to Lee et al. (2018), who examined 106,316 Facebook messages from 782 businesses.

2.4 Outcome-Based Aspects

The implications of DSMM may have both beneficial and bad consequences for businesses. According to earlier investigations, the social-media marketing improves customer's loyalty (Hanaysha, 2018), and buying-intent (Alansari et al., 2018). Social-media, according to studies, may have a big impact on customer loyalty, brand sustainability, and company performance (Veseli-Kurtishi, 2018). As per Syrdal and Briggs (2018), engagement should be treated as a cognitive mental state distinct from participatory action, which includes enjoying and sharing information. While the bulk of researches focus on the impact of DSMM on commercial-businesses, some studies focus on non-profit outcomes. Smith (2018) investigated how non-profit organizations used Twitter and Facebook as well as the results and effects on user engagement, and came to the conclusion that people react differently to social-media activities across platforms. Organizations must examine the bad results and consequent implications of DSMM.

3. CHALLENGES IN DSMM

Lack of relevant conceptions and validated-measures (Cooper et al., 2019) to examine prospective models of how social-media usage affects consuming habits is one of the difficulties in doing research on social-media marketing. Adapting current-scales for the social-media environment is possible, but it is not always effective (Tran et al., 2019). The present scales do not adequately capture and assess the complexities of social-media. There is presently no scale that measures the extent of perceived connectivity via social-media among a person and others, as well as perceived connectivity via social-media among a person and a business. Investigating these connections as well as the linkages between perceived connectivity and behavioural outcomes like brand-awareness, e-WOM intentions, and buying behaviour would be intriguing. One suggestion for future study is the creation of scales related to social-media and it's potential.

Change is a continuous in social-media platforms because they are in permanent beta-phase, which is the ongoing introduction of new functionality. This makes researching social-media marketing and the analytics linked with social-media difficult. Other measures that might be beneficial emerge on social-media, even while some social-media metrics may remain constant, such the followers' quantity, views, and shares, respectively.For instance, social-media influencers—also referred to as influencers are people who have the power to sway others by suggesting and endorsing "products and services on social-media". By 2022, the influencer selling market is predicted to be worth "$15 billion" (Schomer, 2019), and measures like customer-influence impacts, stickiness-indices, and customer-influence values (Kumar andMirchandani, 2012) have become crucial in identifying potential influencers to spread the word about the brand, raise brand awareness, and encourage online dialogues about the company. Another issue to be concerned about is the decline in organic reach, which is the amount of individuals who have viewed the material at no expense to the advertiser (Tutenand Solomon, 2018).Aside from the constant evolution of current social-media platforms, another source of concern is the creation of new social-media platforms. New social-media platforms emerge, gaining popularity and new followers, giving both possibilities and problems for DSMM. Because the various DSMM platforms may have diverse capacities for companies to communicate with individuals, the marketing managers must learn to adapt successful platform's utilization forconsumers'reach. In order to generate customer-leads and improve consumer-engagement, possibly new marketing-techniques for the new DSMM platforms need to be developed. The novel DSMM platforms also present opportunities for additional research for academicians in researching DSMM, such as potentially comparing the different platforms, exploring how and why individuals may use the various social-media for distinct purposes, and establishing or reconfiguring metrics for assessing the investment returns.

4. CONCLUSION

The current study gives a variety of perspectives on DSMM. The experts' viewpoint includes basic views of this subject as well as perspectives on more specialized concerns such as AI, augmented reality marketing, digital content management, mobile advertising and marketing B2B-marketing, and aspects pertaining to the morality and the negative outlook of DSMM. Each essential feature provides personal perspective and experience on specific themes that represent many of the current disputes in academic and practitioner-focused investigations. It was obvious that businesses must utilize social-media marketing strategically to target new audiences given how-pervasive social-media is in consumers' lives. However, because of the absence of validated-scales, frequent changes in social-media platforms (even developing platforms), and the use of social-network analysis, the social-media marketing provides different problems for both scholars and practitioners.

It was clear that important parts of the existing literature on DSMM advocate future-studies that look at diverse-platforms, different user types, their individual characteristics, and analysis of culture-difference. These highlighted gaps might possibly serve as the foundation for various lines of future-studies in this area of study. This study offered significant and timely contributions to practitioners in the form of issues and opportunities,, as well as limitations of the research, shortfalls, queries, and/or proposals that can lead to better understanding as well as insights within the domain of DSMM by bringing together the findings from current research on DSMM and various views from experts.

REFERENCES

Abed, S. S., Dwivedi, Y. K., & Williams, M. D. (2015). Social media as a bridge to e-commerce adoption in SMEs: A systematic literature review. *The Marketing Review*, *15*(1), 39–57. doi:10.1362/14693 4715X14267608178686

Abed, S. S., Dwivedi, Y. K., & Williams, M. D. (2016). Social commerce as a business tool in Saudi Arabia's SMEs. *International Journal of Indian Culture and Business Management*, *13*(1), 1–19. doi:10.1504/IJICBM.2016.077634

Abou-Elgheit, E. (2018). Understanding Egypt's emerging social shoppers. *Middle East Journal of Management*, *5*(3), 207–270. doi:10.1504/MEJM.2018.093611

Ahmed, R. R., Streimikiene, D., Berchtold, G., Vveinhardt, J., Channar, Z. A., & Soomro, R. H. (2019). Effectiveness of online digital media advertising as a strategic tool for building brand sustainability: Evidence from FMCGs and services sectors of Pakistan. *Sustainability (Basel)*, *11*(12), 3436. doi:10.3390u11123436

Alam, M. S. A., Wang, D., & Waheed, A. (2019). Impact of digital marketing on consumers' impulsive online buying tendencies with intervening effect of gender and education: B2C emerging promotional tools. *International Journal of Enterprise Information Systems*, *15*(3), 44–59. doi:10.4018/IJEIS.2019070103

Alansari, M. T., Velikova, N., & Jai, T. (2018). Marketing effectiveness of hotel Twitter accounts: The case of Saudi Arabia. *Journal of Hospitality and Tourism Technology*, *9*(1), 63–77. doi:10.1108/JHTT-09-2017-0096

Ang, T., Wei, S., & Anaza, N. A. (2018). Livestreamingvs pre-recorded: How social viewing strategies impact consumers' viewing experiences and behavioral intentions. *European Journal of Marketing*, *52*(9-10), 2075–2104. doi:10.1108/EJM-09-2017-0576

Antonucci, T. C., Ajrouch, K. J., & Manalel, J. A. (2017). Social Relations and Technology: Continuity, Context, and Change. *Innovation in Aging*, *1*(3), igx029. Advance online publication. doi:10.1093/geroni/igx029 PMID:29795794

Arora, A., Bansal, S., Kandpal, C., Aswani, R., & Dwivedi, Y. K. (2019). Measuring social media influencer index-insights from facebook, Twitter and Instagram. *Journal of Retailing and Consumer Services*, *49*, 86–101. doi:10.1016/j.jretconser.2019.03.012

Aswani, R., Kar, A. K., Ilavarasan, P. V., & Dwivedi, Y. K. (2018). Search engine marketing is not all gold: Insights from Twitter and SEOClerks. *International Journal of Information Management*, *38*(1), 107–116. doi:10.1016/j.ijinfomgt.2017.07.005

Ballestar, M. T., Grau-Carles, P., & Sainz, J. (2019). Predicting customer quality in e-commerce social networks: A machine learning approach. *Review of Managerial Science*, *13*(3), 589–603. doi:10.100711846-018-0316-x

Canovi, M., & Pucciarelli, F. (2019). Social media marketing in wine tourism: Winery owners' perceptions. *Journal of Travel & Tourism Marketing*, *36*(6), 653–664. doi:10.1080/10548408.2019.1624241

Chen, H., & Lee, Y. J. (2018). Is Snapchat a good place to advertise? How media characteristics influence college-aged young consumers' receptivity of Snapchat advertising. *International Journal of Mobile Communications, 16*(6), 697–714. doi:10.1504/IJMC.2018.095129

Cooper, T., Stavros, C., & Dobele, A. R. (2019). Domains of influence: Exploring negative sentiment in social media. *Journal of Product and Brand Management, 28*(5), 684–699. doi:10.1108/JPBM-03-2018-1820

DataReportal. (2020). *Digital: 2020 Global Digital Overview* [Internet]. Available at: https://datareportal.com/reports/digital-2020-global-digital-overview

Duan, Y., Edwards, J. S., & Dwivedi, Y. K. (2019). Artificial intelligence for decision making in the era of Big Data–evolution, challenges and research agenda. *International Journal of Information Management, 48*, 63–71. doi:10.1016/j.ijinfomgt.2019.01.021

Dwivedi, Y. K., Ismagilova, E., Hughes, D. L., Carlson, J., Filieri, R., Jacobson, J., Jain, V., Karjaluoto, H., Kefi, H., Krishen, A. S., Kumar, V., Rahman, M. M., Raman, R., Rauschnabel, P. A., Rowley, J., Salo, J., Tran, G. A., & Wang, Y. (2021). Setting the future of digital and social media marketing research: Perspectives and research propositions. *International Journal of Information Management, 59*, 102168. doi:10.1016/j.ijinfomgt.2020.102168

Dwivedi, Y. K., Ismagilova, E., Rana, N. P., & Weerakkody, V. (2019). Use of social media by b2b companies: Systematic literature review and suggestions for future research. *Conference on e-Business, e-Services and e-Society*, 345-355. 10.1007/978-3-030-29374-1_28

Gaber, H. R., Wright, L. T., &Kooli, K. (2019). Consumer attitudes towards Instagram advertisements in Egypt: The role of the perceived advertising value and personalization. *Cogent Business & Management, 6*(1).

Gil-Gonz'alez, A. B., Blanco-Mateos, A. L., De la Prieta, F., & de Luis-Reboredo, A. (2018). Study of competition in the textile sector by twitter social network analysis. *GECONTEC: RevistaInternacional de Gesti´on del Conocimiento y la Tecnología, 6*(1), 101–117.

Gironda, J. T., & Korgaonkar, P. K. (2018). iSpy? Tailored versus invasive ads and consumers' perceptions of personalized advertising. *Electronic Commerce Research and Applications, 29*, 64–77. doi:10.1016/j.elerap.2018.03.007

Hanaysha, J. R. (2018). Customer retention and the mediating role of perceived value in retail industry. *World Journal of Entrepreneurship, Management and Sustainable Development, 14*(1), 2–24. doi:10.1108/WJEMSD-06-2017-0035

Hossain, T. M. T., Akter, S., Kattiyapornpong, U., & Dwivedi, Y. (2020). Reconceptualizing integration quality dynamics for omnichannel marketing. *Industrial Marketing Management, 87*, 225–241. Advance online publication. doi:10.1016/j.indmarman.2019.12.006

Hossain, T. M. T., Akter, S., Kattiyapornpong, U., & Dwivedi, Y. K. (2019). Multichannel integration quality: A systematic review and agenda for future research. *Journal of Retailing and Consumer Services, 49*, 154–163. doi:10.1016/j.jretconser.2019.03.019

Hutchins, J., & Rodriguez, D. X. (2018). The soft side of branding: Leveraging emotional intelligence. *Journal of Business and Industrial Marketing*, *33*(1), 117–125. doi:10.1108/JBIM-02-2017-0053

Hwang, J., Park, S., & Woo, M. (2018). Understanding user experiences of online travel review websites for hotel booking behaviours: An investigation of a dual motivation theory. *Asia Pacific Journal of Tourism Research*, *23*(4), 359–372. doi:10.1080/10941665.2018.1444648

Iankova, S., Davies, I., Archer-Brown, C., Marder, B., & Yau, A. (2019). A comparison of social media marketing between B2B, B2C and mixed business models. *Industrial Marketing Management*, *81*, 169–179. doi:10.1016/j.indmarman.2018.01.001

Ibrahim, B., & Aljarah, A. (2018). Dataset of relationships among social media marketing activities, brand loyalty, revisit intention. Evidence from the hospitality industry in Northern Cyprus. *Data in Brief*, *21*, 1823–1828. doi:10.1016/j.dib.2018.11.024 PMID:30519601

Islam, J. U., Rahman, Z., & Hollebeek, L. D. (2018). Consumer engagement in online brand communities: A solicitation of congruity theory. *Internet Research*, *28*(1), 23–45. doi:10.1108/IntR-09-2016-0279

Kanekar, A., & Sharma, M. (2020). COVID-19 and Mental Well-Being: Guidance on the Application of Behavioral and Positive Well-Being Strategies. *Health Care*, *8*(3), 336. doi:10.3390/healthcare8030336 PMID:32932613

Kang, M. Y., & Park, B. (2018). Sustainable corporate social media marketing based on message structural features: Firm size plays a significant role as a moderator. *Sustainability (Basel)*, *10*(4), 1167. doi:10.3390u10041167

Kapoor, K. K., Tamilmani, K., Rana, N. P., Patil, P., Dwivedi, Y. K., & Nerur, S. (2018). Advances in social media research: Past, present and future. *Information Systems Frontiers*, *20*(3), 531–558. doi:10.100710796-017-9810-y

Kietzmann, J. H., Hermkens, K., McCarthy, I. P., & Silvestre, B. S. (2011). Social media? Get serious! Understanding the functional building blocks of social media. *Business Horizons*, *54*(3), 241–251. doi:10.1016/j.bushor.2011.01.005

Kim, D., & Jang, S. S. (2019). The psychological and motivational aspects of restaurant experience sharing behavior on social networking sites. *Service Business*, *13*(1), 25–49. doi:10.100711628-018-0367-8

Komodromos, M., Papaioannou, T., & Adamu, M. A. (2018). Influence of online retailers' social media marketing strategies on students' perceptions towards e-shopping: A qualitative study. *International Journal of Technology Enhanced Learning*, *10*(3), 218–234. doi:10.1504/IJTEL.2018.092705

Kumar, V., & Mirchandani, R. (2012). Increasing the ROI of social media marketing. *MIT Sloan Management Review*, *54*(1), 55–61.

Kusumasondjaja, S. (2018). The roles of message appeals and orientation on social media brand communication effectiveness. *Asia Pacific Journal of Marketing and Logistics*, *30*(4), 1135–1158. doi:10.1108/APJML-10-2017-0267

Lal, B., Ismagilova, E., Dwivedi, Y. K., & Kwayu, S. (2020). *Return on investment in social media marketing: Literature review and suggestions for future research. In Digital and social media marketing*. Springer.

Lee, D., Hosanagar, K., & Nair, H. S. (2018). Advertising content and consumer engagement on social media: Evidence from Facebook. *Management Science, 64*(11), 5105–5131. doi:10.1287/mnsc.2017.2902

Mandal, P. C. (2019). Public policy issues in direct and digital marketing–Concerns and initiatives: Public policy in direct and digital marketing. *International Journal of Public Administration in the Digital Age, 6*(4), 54–71. doi:10.4018/IJPADA.2019100105

Marriott, H., Williams, M., & Dwivedi, Y. (2017). What do we know about consumer m-shopping behaviour? *International Journal of Retail & Distribution Management, 45*(6), 568–586. doi:10.1108/IJRDM-09-2016-0164

Matikiti, R., Mpinganjira, M., & Roberts-Lombard, M. (2018). Application of the technology acceptance model and the technology-organisation-environment model to examine social media marketing use in the South African tourism industry. *South African Journal of Information Management, 20*(1), 1–12. doi:10.4102ajim.v20i1.790

Miklosik, A., Kuchta, M., Evans, N., & Zak, S. (2019). Towards the adoption of machine learning-based analytical tools in digital marketing. *IEEE Access : Practical Innovations, Open Solutions, 7*, 85705–85718. doi:10.1109/ACCESS.2019.2924425

Morra, M. C., Gelosa, V., Ceruti, F., & Mazzucchelli, A. (2018). Original or counterfeit luxury fashion brands? The effect of social media on purchase intention. *Journal of Global Fashion Marketing, 9*(1), 24–39. doi:10.1080/20932685.2017.1399079

Pandya, A., & Lodha, P. (2021). Social Connectedness, Excessive Screen Time During COVID-19 and Mental Health: A Review of Current Evidence. *Front. Hum. Dyn, 3*, 684137. doi:10.3389/fhumd.2021.684137

Parsons, A. L., & Lepkowska-White, E. (2018). Social media marketing management: A conceptual framework. *Journal of Internet Commerce, 17*(2), 81–95. doi:10.1080/15332861.2018.1433910

Rathore, A. K., Ilavarasan, P. V., & Dwivedi, Y. K. (2016). Social media content and product co-creation: An emerging paradigm. *Journal of Enterprise Information Management, 29*(1), 7–18. doi:10.1108/JEIM-06-2015-0047

Ritz, W., Wolf, M., & McQuitty, S. (2019). Digital marketing adoption and success for small businesses. *Journal of Research in Interactive Marketing, 13*(2), 179–203. doi:10.1108/JRIM-04-2018-0062

Roumieh, A., Garg, L., Gupta, V., & Singh, G. (2018). E-marketing strategies for islamic banking: A case based study. *Journal of Global Information Management, 26*(4), 67–91. doi:10.4018/JGIM.2018100105

Schomer, A. (2019). *Influencer marketing: State of the social media influencer market in 2020*. Business insider. https://www.businessinsider.com/influencer-marketing-report

Schultz, D. E., & Peltier, J. J. (2013). Social media's slippery slope: Challenges, opportunities and future research directions. *Journal of Research in Interactive Marketing, 7*(2), 86–99. doi:10.1108/JRIM-12-2012-0054

Seo, E. J., & Park, J. W. (2018). A study on the effects of social media marketing activities on brand equity and customer response in the airline industry. *Journal of Air Transport Management, 66*, 36–41. doi:10.1016/j.jairtraman.2017.09.014

Shanahan, T., Tran, T. P., & Taylor, E. C. (2019). Getting to know you: Social media personalization as a means of enhancing brand loyalty and perceived quality. *Journal of Retailing and Consumer Services, 47*, 57–65. doi:10.1016/j.jretconser.2018.10.007

Shareef, M. A., Mukerji, B., Dwivedi, Y. K., Rana, N. P., & Islam, R. (2019). Social media marketing: Comparative effect of advertisement sources. *Journal of Retailing and Consumer Services, 46*, 58–69. doi:10.1016/j.jretconser.2017.11.001

Shukla, P. S., & Nigam, P. V. (2018). E-shopping using mobile apps and the emerging consumer in the digital age of retail hyper personalization: An insight. *Pacific Business Review International, 10*(10), 131–139.

Smith, J. N. (2018). The social network? Nonprofit constituent engagement through social media. *Journal of Nonprofit & Public Sector Marketing, 30*(3), 294–316. doi:10.1080/10495142.2018.1452821

Statista. (2020). *Global digital population as of January 2020*. Available at https://www. statista.com/statistics/617136/digital-population-worldwide/

Stephen, A. T. (2016). The role of digital and social media marketing in consumer behavior. *Current Opinion in Psychology, 10*, 17–21. doi:10.1016/j.copsyc.2015.10.016

Stojanovic, I., Andreu, L., & Curras-Perez, R. (2018). Effects of the intensity of use of social media on brand equity. *European Journal of Management and Business Economics, 27*(1), 83–100. doi:10.1108/EJMBE-11-2017-0049

Syrdal, H. A., & Briggs, E. (2018). Engagement with social media content: A qualitative exploration. *Journal of Marketing Theory and Practice, 26*(1-2), 4–22. doi:10.1080/10696679.2017.1389243

Tafesse, W., & Wien, A. (2018). Using message strategy to drive consumer behavioral engagement on social media. *Journal of Consumer Marketing, 35*(3), 241–253. doi:10.1108/JCM-08-2016-1905

Takahashi, J. (2019). Consumer behavior DNA for realizing flexible digital marketing. *Fujitsu Scientific and Technical Journal, 55*(1), 27–31.

Tarnovskaya, V., & Biedenbach, G. (2018). Corporate rebranding failure and brand meanings in the digital environment. *Marketing Intelligence & Planning, 36*(4), 455–469. doi:10.1108/MIP-09-2017-0192

Teo, D. (2019). *Differences in perceptions and attitudes of Singaporean female football fans towards football marketing. In Gender and diversity: Concepts, methodologies, tools, and applications*. IGI Global.

Tous, R., Gomez, M., Poveda, J., Cruz, L., Wust, O., Makni, M., & Ayguad'e, E. (2018). Automated curation of brand-related social media images with deep learning. *Multimedia Tools and Applications, 77*(20), 27123–27142. doi:10.100711042-018-5910-z

Tran, G. A., Yazdanparast, A., & Strutton, D. (2019). An examination of the impact of consumers' social media connectedness to celebrity endorsers on purchase intentions for endorsed products. In American Marketing Association Summer Educators' Conference. Talk Presented at 2019 American Marketing Association Summer Educators.

Tuten, T. L., & Solomon, M. R. (2018). *Social media marketing* (3rd ed.). Sage Publications, Ltd.

Vermeer, S. A., Araujo, T., Bernritter, S. F., & van Noort, G. (2019). Seeing the wood for the trees: How machine learning can help firms in identifying relevant electronic word-of-mouth in social media. *International Journal of Research in Marketing*, *36*(3), 492–508. doi:10.1016/j.ijresmar.2019.01.010

Veseli-Kurtishi, T. (2018). Social media as a tool for the sustainability of small and medium businesses in Macedonia. *European Journal of Sustainable Development*, *7*(4), 262–262. doi:10.14207/ejsd.2018.v7n4p262

Vizcaino, M., Buman, M., DesRoches, T., & Wharton, C. (2020). From TVs to Tablets: The Relation between Device-specific Screen Time and Health-Related Behaviors and Characteristics. *BMC Public Health*, *20*(1), 1–10. doi:10.118612889-020-09410-0 PMID:32847553

Wong, P., Lee, D., & Ng, P. M. (2018). Online search for information about universities: A Hong Kong study. *International Journal of Educational Management*, *32*(3), 511–524. doi:10.1108/IJEM-12-2016-0268

Chapter 9
Maintaining Global Competitiveness Even in a Period of Global Crisis:
The Perspective of Small Economies

Drago Dubrovski

 https://orcid.org/0000-0001-9753-9552

International School for Social and Business Studies, Slovenia

ABSTRACT

In the context of the intense, extensive, radical, and dynamic changes that occur during global crises, strategic management needs to find such development solutions that will enable a company to do its best in such a turbulent environment and maintain or even improve global competitiveness. Deglobalisation and de-internationalisation for businesses in smaller economies can only be temporary, because strategic management in these companies must develop new means and ways to achieve a successful business in such a situation. Therefore, the key task of strategic management is to create a business model. A simplified correlation study between the largest Slovenian companies and major exporters shows the strong export orientation of Slovenian companies even during the COVID-19 pandemic.

INTRODUCTION

The increasing intensity and dynamism of unpredictable events and developments both in a company (or other profit or non-profit, private or multinational, production or service, individual and independent or related and dependent, smaller or larger, newly created or traditional organisation) and, in its environment, e.g., the global financial crisis in 2008–2013 and the epidemiological crisis in 2020–2021, have an impact on the increased difficulty and complexity of ensuring sufficient competitiveness and consequently the existence and development of companies (i.e., organisations). It is therefore not surprising that crises are already an inseparable part of modern business. However, solving a crisis situation or preventing its occurrence requires substantial changes or a renewal of a company which, as a rule, can only be achieved

DOI: 10.4018/978-1-6684-6845-6.ch009

through radical methods of changing existing structures, processes, strategies, and business models. All of this has an important and inevitable impact on the theory and practice of modern management. This article deals with the hypothesis that strategic management in small economies must find new business models for further successful participation in international trade, as de-internationalisation cannot be a solution.

GLOBAL CRISES

The extent of the crisis is simultaneously reflected in several areas, making it a complex or multidimensional phenomenon affecting the economic, social, traditional, psychological, and legal aspects. A crisis can therefore have many various dimensions. From an economic standpoint, there are global financial or economic crises, crises of related economies or regions, national economic crises, industry crises and corporate crises. All crises create a distressing, uncertain and worrisome situation, which endangers property as well as people, and influences established business and life flows, which is why we want to resolve this situation as soon as possible. Crises in the wider socioeconomic environment directly or indirectly affect the position of individual companies or other organisations, which may be more or less connected with the broader scope of the crisis. A crisis in one sector may have a significant negative impact on companies in completely different sectors. A crisis can impact any company (Crandall & Mensah, 2008) even if, at a certain time, the company is efficient in a fast-growing and high-potential industry, as the crisis can be caused by reasons which are not directly connected to the same industry.

A crisis is a short-lived, undesirable and critical situation in a company, which directly threatens the achievement of the objectives of the participants of this company and its continued existence and development, which is due to the intertwined and simultaneous operation of both external and internal causes (Dubrovski, 2022, p. 64; cf. Crandall et al., 2014, p. 3; James & Wooten, 2010, p. 17; Roux-Dufort, 2003; Saleh, 2016, p. 21).

The crisis is inextricably linked with modern companies. With the rise in the complexity of companies that are interactively connected with different social spheres and their involvement in global business, the potential for crisis is only exacerbated and the range of causes that can lead to a crisis is expanding. If we add all the other crises to this area, then today, a crisis in business is as "inevitable as death and taxes" (Fink, 1986, p. 67). A crisis is, therefore, not exceptional or completely unusual, as it is an integral part of the life cycle of companies or businesses, which can also be affected by completely unpredictable events (the COVID-19 pandemic). A crisis solves the accumulated economic imbalances, and these are an inseparable part of economic life at both macro- and micro- levels. The viral crisis in 2020 was a complete novelty at the time, as the modern economy had not faced such effects, and defence against it is all the more difficult because it first affected the individual and only then the companies (in case of an economic and financial crisis, the impact is reversed).

Thus, in modern times, we are talking about global crises. Globalisation is a multidimensional process consisting of economic, political, legal, and cultural components and involving countries, organisations and individuals. In business terms, globalisation is a state of international trade, investment, financial and human flows, increasingly joined by evermore regions, countries and companies, as well as products, services, technologies, knowledge or information. This forms a global market, which is still marked by certain specific local characteristics. Through the globalisation of international business, i.e., global internationalisation, which blurs clear borders between countries and regional areas and consequently alters the traditional definition of the geographical origin of a product or service, the dimensions of competitive processes are also changing. Today, globalisation is an inevitable point of view for organisations to take into account, regardless of the level of their internationalisation, their market appearance or the economic or even non-economic field in which they operate (cf. Fuchs, 2022, p. 16). Competition is intensifying in all (i.e., global) markets, so, local (i.e., national or regional) competitiveness alone would not suffice as far as trade (i.e., import) opportunities for survival and development are concerned. Globalisation namely requires global competitiveness, even in times of global crisis, and modern strategic management has to deal with this.

CONTEMPORARY STRATEGIC MANAGEMENT

Strategic Management and Modern Business Environment

When we associate the concept and content of management with the operation of the organisation in such a way that it can achieve the objectives set on the basis of the coordinated interests of the participants, we come to the connection of management with strategy, i.e., strategic management. Strategic management is a process of creative design, selection and implementation of development possibilities that significantly influence the long-term performance of the organisation by setting guidelines for its operation and by creating consistency between the underlying capabilities of the organisation and the environment in which it operates (cf. Crandall et al., 2014, p. 3; Dubrovski, 2018, p. 41). Strategic management means the strategic direction of the organisation in such a way as to achieve the objectives set, which includes the design and integration of the mission, vision, medium- and long-term goals, strategies to achieve objectives and the organisation's policy in the business model, through which the organisation creates value for itself and participants in the given environment and perceived risks.

Strategic management thus faces at least the following characteristics of the modern environment and business:

- The operation of an individual company must not conflict with the basic characteristics of the common macro trend of today's environment (internationalisation, flexibility, digitalisation, marketing, innovation), and it is most advantageous if it is completely consistent with them, which means that the company must take into account, when setting the vision and strategic direction to ensure continued existence and development, in addition to new products and services and technological and production processes, the constant development of new management approaches and methods (a survey covering 99 Slovenian companies of various sizes and activities found that R&D companies on average allocate 16% of their annual revenue from sales, the level of innovation is 36%, and 20% of companies integrate start-ups in their development; Ugovšek, 2020);
- At the same time, the contemporary company is lean, agile, dynamic, flattened, virtual, networked, modular, adaptive, project-oriented, digitised, intelligent and constantly learning, as it contains the characteristics of all the listed tags;
- Changes in the modern business environment in all areas are extremely dynamic, turbulent and unpredictable, which requires permanent adaptation of a company through the preparation and implementation of both active and reactive, evolutionary and revolutionary ways of renewing the company;

- The development of the modern environment is not predictable and linear but is based on a wide variety of events and phenomena, for which it is often impossible to find the right cause-and-effect relationship (i.e., causality), which makes it difficult for managers to plan long-term development;
- The dynamic change of the environment and the unpredictable changes require modern management to be constantly ready to implement changes through a three-stage model (monitoring developments and changes in the environment of the company, transferring current and future environmental characteristics to the company's strategies, models, processes and structures, implementing changes in the operation of the company on the basis of recorded and involved changes in the environment) so that a company can adapt to the changes in the environment;
- In a dialectic way, changes bring new quality (i.e., the negation of negation), and routine decisions based on similar past events are becoming less useful, with decisions of analytical and even more intuitive character coming to the forefront when solutions are sought outside established thinking frameworks on the basis of innovative and creative approaches;
- Many business models which could constitute a fundamental framework for decision-making in particular past situations are (no longer) useful due to the numerous limitations and unrealistic assumptions underlying the models; in modern business conditions, past (archaic) management models, approaches, styles and competences (i.e., skills, knowledge, and abilities) are not sufficient, so new, often completely innovative ones, need to be developed;
- On the one hand, the extreme intensity of changes in the macro- and micro-level environments, and on the other hand, the uselessness narrowed applicability of past models, methods, procedures and approaches puts management in an extremely demanding position, because in conditions of incomplete information, risk and uncertainty, when it is not possible to rely on past practice (i.e., routine) readymade plans, they need to make the best decisions, often radical and made under time pressure; and
- This is why the role and complexity of management (i.e., in the complex chaotic context) are increasing, while the progress of information and communication technology and forecasting models of the future do not replace the management but are only helpful and supportive; moreover, due to the exceptional progress of various technologies and the extent of the information available, often unregulated even contradictory, the subjective assessment of management, which includes social, environmental and ethical responsibility, is of vital importance.

Strategic management takes strategic decisions on which the future of the organisation depends. Strategic guidance within strategic management is the key to ensuring that the organisation is ready to meet tomorrow's challenges (Aljuhmani & Emeagwali, 2017). From this perspective, strategic decisions concern (Johnson et al., pp. 6–11):

- The orientation of the organisation in the long term,
- The performance of activities,
- Achieving a competitive advantage,
- Getting to know and responding to the competitive environment in which the organisation develops, positioning and selecting assets,
- The exploitation of the organisation's assets and competences,
- The business model,

- Resource acquisition, control, and allocation (financial, human, physical, technological, commercial, and relational), and
- The influence and power of interest groups.

The four key characteristics of strategic management are derived from the above (Smith & Kennedy, 2012, p. 15):

- It should be aimed at achieving the goals of the entire organisation (not only at a particular part, organisational logic versus individual),
- It makes decisions by involving different groups of participants (not just the selected ones),
- It integrates short-term and long-term aspects (not just one the other), and
- It chooses a compromise between efficiency and performance.

The key task of strategic management is to create a business model with which an organisation can ensure its further existence and competitive development, which is one of the fundamental objectives of the organisation. The modern environment, in which relationships and situations can change very rapidly, requires constant and close monitoring, transfer of these changes to the company, and preparation of measures to defend advance the company's position. This process must be automatic and permanent, and no passivity is allowed.

Strategic Management and Confrontation With Crises

A crisis in a company cannot always be predicted, as it can arise due to sudden external events (e.g., COVID-19 pandemic and the bullwhip effect in supply chain systems). However, research has shown that companies that have had different crisis scenarios to deal with certain extreme adverse events have responded more successfully to the crisis. Some organisations already belong to the areas for which there is a high degree of probability of the onset of a crisis (e.g., defence and security institutions and organisations, and organisations in the field of safeguarding and protection of people and property). Mitroff and Alpaslan (2003) found that only 5–25% of *Fortune* 500 companies have contingency plans (called *proactive companies*), while more than 75% are not ready to deal with unexpected crises (called *reactive companies*). Even a good plan of action in the event of a crisis, the consequences of which have already taken place, cannot foresee the development of all the events and the necessary action. Therefore, it is true that businesses need to pay more attention to preventing their occurrence than planning to exit it.

Potential crises, in which virtually every organisation finds itself, cannot be prevented as every business is risk-linked (e.g., in strategic, financial, operational, commercial, technical aspects). However, the methods of strategic management can prevent the emergence of a tougher situation, which would already be the onset of an acute crisis. In this way, companies are developing resilience to survive in a potential crisis and to act in uncertainty.

Continuous adjustment of corporate structures, systems and processes will help maintain the level of competitiveness of the offer operations and at the same time anticipate potential critical (crisis) points in the development of a company to prepare for them and either eliminate them limit their negative impact. In this way, strategic management can be an important tool in the fight against potential crises. Organisations have started to pay greater attention to their risk management (Spano & Zagaria, 2022, p. 35).

However, a crisis may also be caused by sudden external causes that could not be predicted and prepared for. The more turbulent, competitive, sensitive, and unpredictable the environment of a sectmarket area is, the greater the proportion of the impact of precisely these unpredictable and sudden external causes of crises. If, in the course of business, we have learned automatic behaviour based on strategic management principles and three-step actions (monitoring, transferring, implementing) from which our core capabilities, key factors of success, strengths and weaknesses, and threats and opportunities clearly emerge, in critical moments, we will find the most favourable solutions faster. Otherwise, we will be paralysed by a confused and usually shocking situation. In addition to knowledge of the content of strategic management, knowledge of the principles and procedures of company management in extremely difficult conditions crisis management will be of great help.

Due to the extraordinary dynamism and complexity of a company's environment as well as its internal structures, the management must therefore devote sufficient time to strategic planning and management. A company uses strategic planning for (Mintzberg, 1994, pp. 16–19): coordinating activities, securing the future, achieving rational operation, and controlling operations. However, since this requires, on the one hand, sufficient knowledge and familiarity with the methods of strategic management, management often leaves strategic issues unresolved, as they should be dealt with "when the time is right," and on the other hand, much needed time is lost to performing fully operational matters which should be delegated to lower middle management, the effect of which is often even inversely proportional to the time and energy invested. In this way, concern for short-term measures the so-called policy of extinguishing the fire prevails in a company, which does not mean preventing a crisis, but on the contrary, often even leads to it.

Practice shows that, as a company approaches crisis situations, management increasingly dedicates more time to daily operational situational tasks (e.g., securing cash on the day of payment of a salary, finding available funds to pay a matured debt instalment opening a letter of credit, technical resolution of complaints, etc.), which have the character of individual immediate operation without a defined direction. The more a company falls into a crisis, the higher the proportion of short-term operational measures, which, however, do not usually have a common denomination or direction.

Some of the reasons why management devotes too little time to strategic activities in the company are:

- A lack of competence and experience in both the management function and the methods and techniques used in strategic planning and implementation;
- A lack of vision;
- An escape to areas where errors are not fatal are less likely to occur;
- An escape to areas where there are several routine tasks (less creative and innovative operation);
- Giving priority to daily tasks and trusting that strategy will develop from these by itself;
- Perceiving the crisis situation as an objective fact(which occurred on the basis of subjective factors); and
- Weak competence among lower and middle management (resulting in taking over their tasks).

Strategic management (guidance and planning of the functioning of organisations), therefore, refers to the resolution of existential and developmental issues of a company, in which, instead of routine decisions, a greater scope is taken up by intuitive and analytical decisions. It follows from the above that abandoning (neglecting, underestimating) the role and importance of strategic planning can be very risky, even rapidly leading to a serious threat to the company (i.e., a crisis). Since strategic planning and direction fall within the domain of top management, planning and implementation of company strategy and policy constitute some of the significant internal causes of crises, since effective strategic planning and strategic management are the best means against corporate crises..

The development discontinuities discussed, which result from changes in the local and global environment of companies, have a significant impact on the theory and practice of modern management, and in particular on the characteristics and peculiarities of crisis management, where they present the current starting points for crisis management and achieving the renewal of business companies.

From the point of view of management bearers of strategic business decisions in the organisation, a crisis brings extraordinary and unusual conditions, which, due to the criticality of the moment, require very quick business decisions, and these must be as correct as possible, since corrections are usually not possible, so a crisis inevitably exposes the management aspect as well. Emergency situations generally represent an unusual situation, in which it is not possible to use tried and tested routine decisions, because management is encountering new situations (at least in this way) for the first time, perhaps less often. Even companies in crisis must be managed and cannot be left to automatic fate the course of events without corrective measures, and we have to strive for them to reach that state again in which the goals of the participants can be realised, because a crisis is often an integral part of the life cycle of an organisation, which arises from an extremely wide range of possible causes. According to this background, in addition to ongoing development issues, modern strategic management must also conceptually and substantively integrate the area of crisis management in the period of prevention of their occurrence and duration and the recovery from the crisis as permanent content and one of the key tasks.

ACHIEVING GLOBAL COMPETITIVENESS EVEN IN TIMES OF CRISIS

The Factors of Global Competitiveness

Strategic management literature and practice indicate that companies achieve competitive advantages based on established and implemented business models (Verhoef & Bijmolt, 2019). Competition is defined by the business conduct of co-suppliers (co-demanders) in the market by market competition between multiple providers (multiple demanders), so it is perceived as the endeavour of two more persons companies to achieve the same numerically limited goal in the same a similar field.

The means of competition cannot be the product service itself but the mode of placing (marketing and sales) of this product. The passive comparison of two products alone does not represent the process of competition; market competition is the active use of methods means of marketing for this product. Competition is a constant struggle between companies to achieve a comparative advantage in assets that will bring a competitive market position for certain market segments and, consequently, above-average financial success (Hunt, 2000, p. 138). Competitive advantage is a unique market position the company manages to develop and defend against competitors, which can be viewed from three perspectives: the *internal aspect* (focusing on the resources of the company and creating strategies that competitors cannot imitate), the *dynamic aspect* (focusing on opportunities, developing unique resources and the ability to create breakthrough changes), and the *external aspect* (focusing on the company's industry, occupying a position that enables the exploitation of opportunities; Breznik, 2018).

If we transfer the concept of competitiveness to global business, then it must be defined in terms of those characteristics that affect the intensity and orientation of a country's international trade. In this case, the concepts of competitiveness and comparative competitive advantages are synonyms. This means that a country will achieve the highest level of competitiveness if it makes the most of its comparative advantages in international trade. This is the widest and most abstract unit of competitiveness, the expression of which is the success of exchange of products, services, and knowledge with foreign countries (refers to the general reputation of the state and the reputation of its products, the judgments that consumers have about a particular country, perceptions of products as a whole). A narrower, equally derived unit of competitiveness refers to an individual entity manufacturer (provider).

A fundamental, original, and concrete unit of competitiveness is the competitiveness of a particular product service. Nevertheless, some, like Lloyd-Reason and Wall (2000, p. xx) have defined the competitiveness of the national economy as a separate unit. The competitiveness of a country is the degree to which a country, under free and competitive market conditions, can produce products and services that meet the requirements of international markets, while simultaneously maintaining and expanding the real incomes of its inhabitants. Thus, there are three levels of competitiveness, the first two being abstract and derived from a third concrete unit:

- The competitiveness of the national economy (the country of origin of the product the service);
- The competitiveness of the company between companies in the same national economy (domestic competitiveness) outside (international competitiveness); and
- The competitiveness of the product service (the ability of the product to compete successfully in a particular market at a particular time).

Of course, there is interaction and dependence between all levels of competitiveness. The foundation represents a single product (service), which consists of an assortment (programme) of the company, and the volume of interesting export products is a prerequisite for the effective integration of the national economy into an international exchange. The competitiveness of the national economy is thus built from the competitiveness of individual products and services and therefore represents abstract competitiveness. However, since the economy of a country appears externally as a unified whole and represents an actual and potential supplier demander on the world market, it directs its operations and implements measures that are most acceptable for such an economic system. The measures (sociopolitical and economic) that are (are not) adopted at the national level have, however, different effects on the competitive ability of individual companies individual products. Thus, this is about the feedback effect on the basic unit: the product.

There is a similar relationship between the company and the product. The corporate brand the reputation of the company in the general and professional public can have a decisive influence on the positioning of an individual product. The design policy of the product by forming the appropriate length, width and depth of the assortment affects a greater lesser possibility of selling a particular product in this assortment (Figure 1).

The production of luxury goods in countries with low labour costs can destroy the value of a highly positioned brand, even if the quality is undisputed. If a particular product is, in whole in part, e.g., produced in China, it is highly likely that such products will be cheaper for clients. However, when the client wants to resell such a product to his customers, the export of a product of Chinese origin may be a burden, which will lower its sales (i.e., export) price increase import charges. In such cases, it is necessary to weigh between potentially more expensive products in the country of origin a country with a higher level of perceived national economic competitiveness, which will allow higher sales prices to be achieved, on the one hand, and on the other hand, cost attractive production in a country with lower

Figure 1. The mutual influence of individuals levels of competitiveness

labour costs, which will lower production costs but, at the same time, will weaken market position and lower sales prices due to perception of the origin of the product. Various studies have found that consumers often use the image of the producer's country to judge the quality of an individual product (cf. Gürhan-Canli & Maheswaran, 2000; Tse & Lee, 1993).

Competitiveness factors are generally divided into price and non-price factors. Among the *price factors* of competitiveness at the level of the national economy are the most important costs (i.e., cost competitiveness) and the direct expression of them: prices (i.e., price competitiveness). This includes measures of internal and external intervention (protectionism and interventionism), which maintain deliberately regulate cost–price ratios. *Non-price factors* include: the general climate for the quality of products and services within the national economy, the state of scientific research activities (e.g., technological development, inventiveness, and innovation), marketing as a generally established business mentality and activity, the financing, credit and insurance systems in international trade, the development of the standardisation system at all levels (i.e., the harmonisation of national standards with international and industry standards), organisation and efficiency of foreign trade activity, general compatibility of export programmes with target markets, political and economic reputation of the country, its producers and products, competitive corporate and tax law, flexibility and the ability to respond quickly and correctly to foreign trade policies on protectionist measures in individual markets, timely and properly secured industrial property rights, efficiency of the public sector, implementation and assistance in the transformation of companies, and the development and spread of the information system within the national economy and its connection with international systems.

Factors of (un)competitiveness of the national economy include burdening an otherwise very good quality product with excessive costs in such a way that its competitive advantage, which is driven by quality, is lost. When exporting certain products of greater value (e.g., mechanical engineering, investment goods), the possibility of crediting the buyer will be extremely important. The economic policy measures will burden the situation of the once successful export product.

Among the factors of the company's competitiveness of the connected business system, it is possible to classify the possible establishment of the corporate brand under which existing and new products and services are marketed, when such a brand already sets a better starting point. Such different involvement of the company in wider business systems will enable the company's product to have a better market position within such a business system. Strategic purchasing and sales alliances and partnerships can have a decisive impact on purchasing and sales conditions. Successful corporate (national) lobbying (i.e., influencing decision-makers) can put a product project in a significantly better position. Involvement of a country in this that integration can constitute a direct advantage obstacle (e.g., envisaged high customs duties quantitative limits). The competitiveness of an individual product is influenced by the company's business policy, which can pay more attention to a particular product (e.g., in quality, marketing, delivery time) burden it with fewer costs (compensated by higher prices for other products markets), and such different business as a relationship with external participants. Company mergers and takeovers have impact the concentration of industries, with increasingly fewer business systems overseeing an ever-increasing sectoral share. A company that is not included in these business systems may have significant problems in the positioning of its product (the purchase of strategic components and raw materials) even if the product has undeniable quality, deliverability, reasonable price and sufficient marketing activities.

To the greatest extent possible, the position of the product on the market will depend on its own competitiveness factors, which are already treated as a prerequisite of any global market activities. A competitive product (the offer programme) is normally defined as a product for which the increased demand (sales volume) has a counterproductive effect on the volume of demand for another product. The main factors defining its competitive ability level of competitiveness are all characteristics of the offer package (i.e., tangible and intangible components), in particular, price and other sales conditions, quality in all dimensions, deliverability (delivery ability in time and space), and focused marketing activities aimed at a specific product service. A product that boasts superior quality, reasonable sales price, exemplary delivery ability, and sufficient marketing support should, as a rule (in theory), be the market leader. Often, due to the closure of distribution channels the oligopolistic position of buyers, it is not possible to place such a product on the market. The synergy and impact of all the above factors of competitiveness, however, constitute the aggregate competitiveness of each product on the global market (Figure 2).

Figure 2. Competitive position of the product in the global market

Dimensions of Global Competitive Struggle

Competition is the process of market competition between several suppliers between several demanders, in which competitors strive simultaneously in the same similar field for the same, albeit numerically limited, goal. Therefore, new competitors do not expand the field of competition but, within the boundaries of the same field, try to obtain a larger share for themselves, which will only be possible by taking over the shares of other competitors. However, the process of competition takes place not only between producers (providers) of the same kind of products services within the same industry but also in other areas, in which it is about obtaining greater benefits at the expense of worsening the position of other participants (Porter, 1985, p. 8; Porter, 1980, p. 4).

While the competition from suppliers of similar products within the same industry is the most recognisable to market participants, much less known even unknown competition comes from products manufactured from other materials, with different technology and cost structure, and with different offer components, and these products perform the same function as the product of the first branch (e.g., power tools belonging to the electrical industry versus hand tools originating from the metalworking branch, Lego blocks versus another form of children's entertainment, classic cameras versus digital technology, a plastic bottle can versus a glass bottle, eye lens versus glasses, cardboard versus plastic packaging). This competition may be significantly more dangerous for the existence and development of companies in the first sector, as it comes from an area which is normally not known to the first industry.

On the other hand, due to the dynamism of the global market, the life cycles of companies, technological and general progress, new, until then unknown competitors (newcomers) are constantly entering the markets, occupying taking over the existing market shares of the participants. If new players enter the market, then at that moment, everyone has certain competitive advantages. Otherwise, they would not be able to enter the market. Anyone entering the market as a new entrant has at least a temporary particular attraction in the offer, which will deprive existing players of a larger smaller piece of market share.

Additionally, there is also market competition in an otherwise vertical connection, which can mean a redistribution of the previous benefits among the participants in the connection if individual members of the chain (e.g., traders producers) increase their bargaining power for various reasons. The so-called redistribution of benefits, therefore, depends on the newly established negotiation possibilities. A company can improve its negotiating position if it acquires competitive (i.e., parallel new) suppliers and customers, which in practice can be quite a challenging and long-term task (especially in B2B). To the five directions of competition mentioned, Johnson et al. (2005, p. 124) add a sixth, called *state power*, where the main competitive weapon is the ability to lobby.

Therefore, competition does not only take place within the same industry between providers of comparable products but also in other directions, which does not allow even the slightest passivity in strategic management (cf. Moon, 2022, p. 7). Competitive action through appropriate measures must therefore be directed in all directions (e.g., acquisition of new customers and suppliers, differentiated and innovative supply, investment in research and development, and support services for existing customers,), bearing in mind that competition is also continuously active and aims to improve its position at the expense of worsening the position of its customers. Taking into account the already discussed changes in the environment and the impact of globalisation, the (global) competition is intensifying in all directions.

D'Aveni (1994) points out that instead of seeking long-term and ongoing advantages, the development of temporary advantages that arise at the moment must be prioritised (e.g., a company may launch a new product, win a new market, introduce a new business model). The extreme dynamism of competition and changes in the environment do not allow for the acquisition of permanent competitive advantages, but only occasional and temporary ones, so development activities need to be continuously carried out. This also makes long-term planning less useful, since it is not possible to predict the general development competition practices. However, achieving a competitive advantage is only possible when the company's assets are valuable, rare, imperfectly imitable, and imperfectly replaceable (Gouthier & Schmid, 2003). One of the greatest challenges for managers is always the correct identification and exploitation of business opportunities in fast-moving conditions. In a context of extreme uncertainty, key factors of market success and prolonged competitive advantages lie in the development and growth of superior organisational means (potentials) that combine the skills and knowledge of employees and determine specific heuristics for finding and solving problems (Seifert & Hadida, 2008, p. 294).

The competitive struggle is therefore intensifying across all markets; local (i.e., national regional) competitiveness alone is no longer enough in case of open commercial (import) opportunities for survival and development. Globalisation pressures (including the liberalisation of international trade) therefore require the achievement of global competitiveness, but at some stage, the company itself, no matter how efficient it is either on the revenue side (e.g., increasing market share and developing new products, markets, technologies, and approaches) and on the cost side (including all types of rationalisation), cannot achieve it to the extent needed to be able to successfully compete with groups of related companies (cf. Gessler, 2021, p. 145), that take advantage of the synergistic advantages (i.e., the notion that "2 + 2 = 5") arising from partnership cooperation. To ensure continued existence and faster development, growth is often insufficient with regard to its own resources (i.e., organic, internal growth)—in that case, partnership links with other companies are not only opportunities but also a necessity.

Globalisation and efforts to achieve sufficient global competitiveness result in a concentration of assets and capabilities (potentials), resulting in an increase in the volume of tangible and intangible assets per individual business system (i.e., group of companies) and a reduction in the number of independent companies competing in each industry. Consequently, this means that industrial and service industries are becoming increasingly capital concentrated and business integrated when the number of individual participants in the market is reduced, which, through capital links, are becoming larger are acting as strategically non-proprietary groups of companies. In the economic sphere, concentration is the process of increasing equity based on the combination of existing individual equity of companies, so that they lose their independence, while the economic power of the newly formed entity increases. Integration, however, is a form of company integration aimed at greater unity in business cooperation and does not necessarily lead to the loss of autonomy of the legal entities that form it. In fact, the past model of atomistic competition open competition of a large number of individual companies is increasingly disappearing, and it is replaced by a model of market rivalry between groups of companies networks of companies linked by ownership and interest. Network competition occurs from the networks of related companies competition between networks related groups of companies.

Industrial sectors (formed from related industries) can be highly concentrated and located in different phases of the concentration cycle (Vizjak, 2008, p. 32), from low-concentrated industries (e.g., real estate, services, insurance, banking, and trade), medium-concentrated industries (e.g., raw materials, energy and chemistry, informatics, communication and entertainment, and construction) to highly concentrated industries (e.g., pharmaceuticals, aerospace, and defence). The time the industries need to pass the entire concentration process and reach the maximum concentration level is, on average, 25 years. In the process of concentration, the industries go through four distinctive phases: the opening phase, the economies of scale phase, the focus phase, and the balancing phase. In this respect, some conclusions reached by the Kearney consulting company can be very important: with the process of globalisation, the concentration of industries, which are becoming global anyway, affects all companies, and thus also the long-term strategies and strategic decision-making of companies.

The purpose of increased concentration of companies their resources capabilities is to achieve with joint efforts such a level of competitiveness that will enable the participants in the global market to achieve a satisfactory level of development. Globalisation, therefore, leads to concentration, as well as asymmetrical and unstable oligopolies, systems based on product industry standards and products based on accepted global standards (Ramu, 1997, p. 46). In each country, capital pooling activities are always subject to strict legal regulation (restriction), which aims to prevent the reduction of competition caused by capital connections. Competition rules are aimed at ensuring fair and undistorted competition in the market economy and creating a single market. The purpose of anti-monopoly legislation is, therefore, to ensure the competitiveness of the economy by prohibiting the activities of companies that reduce could reduce the level of competition. Individual countries envisage different solutions in their national legislations, taking into account the realisation that the answer to the problems of capitalism is competition rather than corporatism (i.e., the formation of large business groups).

Achieving sufficient competitiveness is a more complex and demanding task in a global business than simply designing price and currency ratios and preparing the related measures. In particular, this becomes more complex in a period of global crises, which, given their varying intensity across sectors and industries, makes the formulation of satisfactory competitiveness much more complicated. Thus, in order to maintain improve their market position, companies have to change their business models partially completely, which is otherwise a key task of strategic management.

Maintaining and Increasing Competitiveness in a Period of Global Crisis With Improved Business Models

The business model defines how an organisation creates value (or benefit) for target customers in its business processes with a unique combination of programmes (e.g., products, services, knowledge, capital, information, technology for target participants), sales conditions (i.e., terms of trade), distribution channels and promotion, and with a unique combination of tangible and intangible assets in its business processes. Thereby, the organisation achieves its own basic goal and, indirectly, the goals of the participants of the organisation.

The business model, simplified and aggregated (Wirtz, 2019, p. 13), shows how a particular company in a given competitive environment meets the specific needs of the consumer in the target market at a certain point and at a certain time (Chernev, 2017). A business model reveals how the company adds its own contribution to the value of the final product service throughout the entire chain of adding value to input materials and initial services. A business model is a materialisation of strategic ideas through a constructive comparison of various factors (Jablonski, 2020, p. 21–22). Since a company receives payments through the successful sale of its products services in which profit is formed after deducting costs, an integral part of a business model is also the so-called *profit formula* (Johnson, 2018, p. 28; Nambisan & Luo, 2022, p. 138) achieving the highest added value through the entire product's lifetime. There are four elements of a business model: its content, its structure, its governance, and its value logic (Amit & Zott, 2021, p. 88). There is no business model that would always function in all situations, since it must take into account the understanding of key organisational elements and their joint operation, and therefore different business models are used during the different stages of the development of an organisation. Business models are complex systems, and they are only as good as their implementation (Bock & George, 2018, p. 40). In larger organisations, there may be several business models that co-exist and are synergetic (p. 184).

A business model contains numerous options at the core levels of functioning of the company, while these options shape a special practice and behaviour of the company. Since this practice is, in principle, invisible and rarely expressed explicitly, we are often not even aware of the model used. There are no best business models but rather a decision on the selection of possibilities suitable for a particular environment (Birkinshaw & Goddard, 2009). An idea is not yet a business model. Out of 3,000 ideas, 300 are developed into a project idea, of which 125 are developed into a smaller project, of which, in turn, nine are developed into a development project, of which 1.7, on average, are developed into products available on the market, and of which only one becomes a commercial success (Wildemann, 2017, p. 9). Over time, business models become more resistant to change (Christensen et al., 2016).

As described in previous chapters, due in part to the impact of globalisation and accelerated technological development, with an emphasis on information communication technology (i.e., digitalisation), companies must start thinking about new business models, which is a challenge for strategic management. In such a business situation, the new, modern business model can be based on (Wildemann, 2017, p. 8): (a) customer needs and innovation (e.g., specialised services, highest quality, and flexible modular offerings); (b) differentiation from the competition (e.g., proximity to customers, partnership, best market solution, the best price–service ratio); (c) key assets core competencies (technological know-how, long-term knowledge of customers, system-process know-how); and (d) an architecture for value creation (e.g., focusing on core capabilities and intelligent networking).

Research has shown that there has been a strong increase in interest in building, maintaining, and changing business models, as 70% of companies are trying to create innovative business models and 98% modify existing business models, according to a 2009 study (Casadesus-Masanell & Ricart, 2011). Interest in business models, as measured by published articles, increased from only a few in 1980 to more than 2,500 in 2018 (Amit & Zott, 2021, p. 5). New business models mostly come from (Wildemann, 2017, p. 9): product and programme development (57%), technology development (25%), the market (15%), and large leaps (turns). However, the introduction of a new model, which is not a linear process, but rather an iterative process of discovering ideas and transforming them into a model (Chernev, 2017), nevertheless requires a certain amount of time and takes place at several stages (Johnson, 2018, p. 152): discovery and creation of ideas (i.e., incubation) and concept development (over 1–3 years), design and acceleration (over 2–5 years), and transition and implementation (over 1–3 years). The level of failure when it comes to modifying existing business models is extremely high (even up to 70%), while the condition needed to plan the change is the already mentioned so-called holistic (helicopter) approach (Hendrickx, 2015). The most common mistakes in the design of business models are: (a) a lack of focus on the strategic aspect of operation, (b) each business model not being suitable for every company, (c) neglecting competition, and (d) static analysis.

Introducing new and changing existing business models to ensure the competitiveness of supply on the global market can be done by methods of evolutionary revolutionary changing that require different approaches, the rule being that when major changes in the business model's content are required when the company's competition backlog is higher when the company is in an acute crisis is threatened by it in the near future, when the company has not kept up with technological and general changes in time, the company has set itself an aggressive development policy. Revolutionary methods of changing business models will require sacrifice and are, on the whole, more expensive and significantly riskier, but in the cases described, there is simply no alternative. Achieving global competitiveness in a period of global crisis cannot be based on the same competencies as in a period of stable conditions. Strategic management needs to find new ways and means to provide value for customers, even in crisis situations, on the basis of an adapted new business model.

EMPIRICAL FINDINGS ON EXPORT ORIENTATION IN A PERIOD OF GLOBAL CRISIS: THE CASE OF SLOVENIA

In addition to some previous research (2010, 2016, 2020), which mainly looked at changing business models to maintain sufficient competitiveness in companies in difficulty (distressed companies), the empirical part of the paper examined another important correlation that characterises smaller economies (e.g., Slovenia), which must inevitably be embedded in global business, since the local market cannot guarantee existence and development without international trade and investment (in Slovenia, export of goods and services comprised 57.3% of GDP in 2009 and already 83.6% in 2021). During a period of global crisis, as a consequence of limiting trading closing borders, only larger economies with sufficient purchasing, sales, investment, and financial markets can survive maintain basic competitiveness, often at the cost of increased costs, reduced employment and poorer availability of all types of goods and services.

International business plays a particular role in the context of international economic and overall development (Martin, 2021, p. 3). The face of international business activities is changing, but it has always been changing; within the setting, ample opportunities exist for companies to develop a global footprint (p. 13). The research question in this discussion is whether, in a period of global crises strategic management of companies of such countries, smaller economies can act by focusing only on the local market and de-internationalising their operations. Through a simplified survey, we established whether the largest Slovenian companies, which are also among the best, could possibly build their global competitiveness in a period of global crisis on de-internationalisation, have nevertheless acted intensively on global markets, although they had to radically change their business models.

The simplified analysis covered the 101 largest Slovenian companies in 2021 (called the *TOP 101*), which contribute 62% of export revenues and 47% of profits; the added value of which, per employee, is 26% above the Slovenian average (*Finance*, 2022). The TOP 101 includes companies that have achieved at least EUR 40 million in revenue, have more than five employees and at least EUR 10 million in assets; however, branches, financial and holding companies, state funds and those that have not published data have not been taken into account. The TOP 101 ranking was based on the consideration of several indicators: sales revenue, EBITDA, capital, assets, and the number of employees. The rank was determined by the sum of the individual indexes in relation to the best one according to each indicator. The second list included the best companies in 2021 that operated profitably in the last three years, recording revenue growth and EBITDA compared to the previous year, taking into account also ROA, ROE, EBIT, and added value per employee. The third list is represented by the largest Slovenian exporters in 2020, with a ranking according to the export turnover achieved (TOP exporters).

For the purposes of this paper, we have summarised the ranking of the largest Slovenian companies according to the explained methodology of *Finance* magazine (2022), to which we have added information on the achieved rank in terms of business performance and exports. Thus, the list excludes those companies that are either state-owned (e.g., infrastructure companies), are non-profit is subsidised (e.g., postal services) or, depending on the activity they carry out, cannot be significant exporters (e.g., media,

Table 1. Export orientation of the largest companies in Slovenia in the period 2020–2021

Classification: Largest Companies	Company	Classification: Best Large Companies	Classification: Largest Exporters
1	Krka	70	1
3	Lek	62	4
4	Petrol	63	—
9	Gorenje	—	3
13	Revoz	—	2
14	Adria Mobil	8	6
15	Luka Koper	—	23
16	Impol	27	—
17	SIJ Acroni	—	8
20	LTH Castings	97	12
21	Hidria	26	17
24	Cinkarna Celje	21	20
26	Perutnina Ptuj	—	—
28	Mahle Electric Drives Slovenija	—	10
30	BSH Hišni aparati	72	7
32	Goodyear Dunlop Sava Tires	—	18
34	Helios TBLUS	71	15
35	Akrapovič	37	26
36	Talum Kidričevo	—	—
39	Hella Saturnus Slovenija	—	9
41	TAB	—	14
42	Unior	—	27
46	Pivovarna Laško Union	56	—
47	Atlantic Droga Kolinska	67	34
49	Domel	99	25
52	Količevo Karton	98	21
56	SIJ Metal Ravne	—	29
57	Fotona	—	75
61	Bia Separations	1	—
65	Danfoss Trata	13	33
66	Iskra	57	64
68	Interblock	—	—
69	Ljubljanske mlekarne	—	—
71	Kovintrade Celje	5	—
73	Tastepoint	15	48
74	Elrad Electronics	58	—

Continued on following page

Table 1. Continued

Classification: Largest Companies	Company	Classification: Best Large Companies	Classification: Largest Exporters
75	Inotherm	23	57
76	KolektEtra	—	32
77	Salonit Anhovo	87	—
78	Trelleborg Slovenija	—	41
79	ETI	—	37
81	Steklarna Hrastnik	19	65
82	Štore Steel	—	62
84	Intereuropa	—	—
91	Incom	54	49
92	TPV Automotive	—	54
93	Dinos	45	60
94	Iskraemeco	—	—
95	Contitech Slovenija	31	58
99	Žito	—	—
100	Weiler Abrasives	—	52

Note. From *Finance* (2022).

energy, utility, retail companies). Also excluded are tourist companies, which otherwise achieve a significant proportion of their revenues with foreign guests but do not record the data as exports (Table 1).

The comparison (see Table 1) shows that among the 51 largest Slovenian companies from the TOP 101 list, which have such an activity, whose products and services can be exported, there are 27 (52.9%) which are also among the best companies, and 37 (72.5%) which are also among the largest exporters. The largest Slovenian companies, half of which are also among the most successful, were clearly export-oriented even during the global crisis (COVID-19), and, at the same time, they are part of international strategic alliances capital connections. A more detailed comparison shows that many have had to change business models, taking into account digitalisation and progress in information and communication technology as well as safety and health protection requirements in order to maintain global competitiveness.

SOLUTIONS AND RECOMMENDATIONS

Global crises do indeed lead to deglobalisation, regionalization and geopolitical nationalism but this can only be temporary, because small economies such as Slovenia have no chance of surviving without integration into the world market. For smaller countries, de-internationalisation is not a solution in a period of global crisis (besides, "history suggests the path to taming inflation is through more international trade – not less"; James, 2023, p. 19)., but a partial or complete change in business models, with which strategic management needs to adapt to the new situation (e.g. global business models for the digital age; Nambisan & Luo, 2022, pp. 135). Therefore, strategic management cannot deviate from the internationalisation strategy, which is still a given framework of business, and must include among its permanent tasks the adaptation, modification renovation of business models that can continue to generate value for global market customers, regardless of the constraints of the global crisis. That is why organisational forms and characteristics and business models are being sought more and more and in an ever more innovative way, including on the basis of dynamic strategic thinking, which would enable the retention increase of existing competitive advantages and the creation of new competitive advantages in today's global market. New improved business models, which management can change with revolutionary evolutionary methods, are based on the achievements of information and communication technology, digital transformation and knowledge management, whose philosophical framework represents dynamic strategic thinking. "Responsibly managing international supply chains in the 21st century has become more complex and more important than ever" (Kilian-Yasin & Correa, 2021, p. 227). There are many possibilities for future research, especially by including a qualitative aspect of the internationalisation of the group of the most successful companies in a chosen area.

CONCLUSION

In a context of intense, extensive, radical, and dynamic changes, which also occur in the form of global crises, strategic management needs to find such development solutions that will enable a company to do its best in such a turbulent environment and maintain even improve global competitiveness. Small economies which, as a rule, cannot survive a global crisis through reverse internationalisation or de-internationalisation, the fight to retain global competitiveness in international trade, financial and investment flows in a global crisis is still inevitably, but with properly sophisticated business models, which must become a permanent task and content of strategic management. The simplified correlation study between the largest Slovenian companies and major exporters shows the strong export orientation of Slovenian companies even during the pandemic as a type of global crisis. Deglobalisation and de-internationalisation for businesses in smaller economies can only be temporary, because strategic management in these companies must develop new means and ways to achieve a successful business in such a situation. Therefore, the key task of strategic management is to create a business model that will consist of a unique combination of programmes (e.g., products, services, knowledge, capital, information, and technology for the target participants), sales conditions, distribution channels, and promotion, as well as creating value for target customers by applying a unique combination of assets in a competitive environment, thus enabling the company to achieve its own fundamental goal and, indirectly, the goals of the organisation's participants.

REFERENCES

Aljuhmani, H. Y., & Emeagwali, O. L. (2017). The roles of strategic planning in organizational crisis management: The case of Jordanian banking sector. *International Review of Management and Marketing*, *7*(3), 50–60.

Amit, R., & Zott, C. (2021). *Business model innovation strategy*. John Wiley & Sons. doi:10.1093/oso/9780190090883.003.0038

Birkinshaw, J., & Goddard, J. (2009). What is your management model? *MIT Sloan Management Review*, *50*(2), 81–90.

Bock, A. J., & George, G. (2018). *The business model book*. Pearson Education.

Breznik, L. (2018). Konkurenčna prednost–*o* čem sploh govorimo in kakšen je njen vpliv na uspešnost? *Izzivi managementu, 10*(2), 21–33.

Casadesus-Masanell, R., & Ricart, J. E. (2011). How to design a winning business model. *Harvard Business Review*, *89*(1–2), 101–107.

Chernev, A. (2017). *The business model: How to develop new products, create market value and make the competition irrelevant*. Cerebellum Press.

Christensen, C. M., Bartman, T., & van Bever, D. (2016). The hard truth about business model innovation. *MIT Sloan Management Review*, *58*(1), 30–40.

Crandall, W. R., & Mensah, E. C. (2008). Crisis management & sustainable development: A framework and proposed re-search agenda. *International Journal of Sustainable Strategic Management*, *1*(1), 16–24. doi:10.1504/IJSSM.2008.018124

Crandall, W. R., Parnell, J. A., & Spillan, J. E. (2014). Crisis management. *Sage (Atlanta, Ga.)*.

D'Aveni, R. A. (1994). *Hypercompetition*. The Free Press.

Dubrovski, D. (2010). Pomembnost ugotavljanja pravilnih vzrokov za nastanek podjetniške krize. *Management, 5*(1), 37–52.

Dubrovski, D. (2016). Handling corporate crises based on the correct analysis of its causes. *Journal of Financial Risk Management*, *5*(4), 264–280. doi:10.4236/jfrm.2016.54024

Dubrovski, D. (2018). *Management in organizacija*. International School for Social and Business Studies.

Dubrovski, D. (2020). Improved global competitiveness on the basis of new business models influenced by dynamic strategic thinking. In G. Andraz (Ed.), *Dynamic strategic thinking for improved competitiveness and performance* (pp. 271–288). IGI Global. doi:10.4018/978-1-7998-4552-2.ch011

Dubrovski, D. (2022). *Razsežnosti kriznega managementa*. International School for Social and Business Studies.

Finance. (2022). *Velikani slovenskega gospodarstva: največja podjetja v 2021*. https://manager.finance.si

Fink, S. (1986). *Crisis management*. Amacom.

Fuchs, M. (2022). *International management*. Springer. doi:10.1007/978-3-662-65870-3

Gessler, J.-Ch. (2021). Collaborative Practices of SMEs for the Purpose of Internationalization. In N. Tournois & Ph. Very (Eds.), *Open Internationalization Strategy* (pp. 131–145). Routledge. doi:10.4324/9781003095163-9

Gouthier, M., & Schmid, S. (2003). Customers and customer relationships in service firms: The perspective of the resource-based view. *Marketing Theory*, *3*(1), 119–143. doi:10.1177/1470593103003001007

Gürhan-Canli, Z., & Maheswaran, D. (2000). Cultural variations in country of origin effects. *JMR, Journal of Marketing Research, 37*(3), 309–317. doi:10.1509/jmkr.37.3.309.18778

Hendrickx, H. M. (2015). Business architect: A critical role in enterprise transformation. *Journal of Enterprise Transformation, 5*(1), 1–29. doi:10.1080/19488289.2014.893933

Hunt, S. D. (2000). A general theory of competition. *Sage (Atlanta, Ga.).*

Jablonski, A. (2020). Robustness in the business models of the organizations embedded in the circular economy. In B. Nogalski, A. A. Szpitter, A. Jablonski, & M. Jablonski (Eds.), *Networked business models in the circular economy* (pp. 19–53). IGI Global. doi:10.4018/978-1-5225-7850-5.ch002

James, E. H., & Wooten, L. P. (2010). *Leading under pressure.* Routledge.

James, H. (2023). *In defense of globalization.* International Monetary Fund.

Johnson, G., Scholes, K., Whittington, R., & Fréry, F. (2005). *Stratégique.* Pearson.

Johnson, M. W. (2018). *Reinvent your business model.* Harvard Business Review Press.

Kilian-Yasin, K., & Correa, R. (2021). Corporate social responsibility in international supply chains. In L. Martin (Ed.), *International business development* (pp. 223–246). Springer Gabler. doi:10.1007/978-3-658-33221-1_12

Lloyd-Reason, L., & Wall, S. (2000). *Dimensions of competitiveness.* Edward Elgar.

Martin, L. (2021). International business development in context–history, trends and realities. In L. Martin (Ed.), *International business development* (pp. 1–14). Springer Gabler. doi:10.1007/978-3-658-33221-1_1

Mintzberg, H. (1994). *The rise and fall of strategic planning.* Prentice Hall.

Mitroff, I. I., & Alpaslan, M. C. (2003). Preparing for evil. *Harvard Business Review, 81*(4), 109–115. PMID:12687925

Moon, H.-C. (2022). *Global business strategy.* World Scientific. doi:10.1142/12254

Nambisan, S., & Luo, Y. (2022). *The digital multinational.* The MIT Press. doi:10.7551/mitpress/13579.001.0001

Porter, M. E. (1980). *Competitive strategy.* The Free Press.

Porter, M. E. (1985). *Competitive advantage.* The Free Press.

Ramu, S. S. (1997). *Strategic alliances.* Response Books.

Roux-Dufort, C. (2003). *Gérer et decider en situation de crise.* Dunod.

Saleh, Y. D. (2016). *Crisis management.* Mill City Press.

Seifert, M., & Hadida, A. L. (2008). Strategic decisions in high-velocity contexts. In 21st century management: a reference handbook. Sage. doi:10.4135/9781412954006.n29

Smith, D. J., & Kennedy, J. W. (2012). *Contemporary strategic management.* North American Business Press.

Spano, R., & Zagaria, C. (2022). *Integrating performance management and enterprise risk management systems*. Emerald. doi:10.1108/9781801171519

Tse, D. K., & Lee, W. (1993). Removing negative country images: Effects of decomposition, branding, and product experience. *Journal of International Marketing, 1*(4), 25–48. doi:10.1177/1069031X9300100403

Ugovšek, A. (2020). Takšno je dejansko stanje inovativnosti v slovenskem gospodarstvo. *Glas gospodarstva, 2020*(December), 30–31.

Verhoef, P. C., & Bijmolt, T. H. A. (2019). Marketing perspectives on digital business models: A framework and overview of the special issue. *International Journal of Research in Marketing, 36*(3), 341–349. doi:10.1016/j.ijresmar.2019.08.001

Vizjak, A. (2008). *Competing against scale*. GV Založba.

Wildemann, H. (2017). *Neue Geschäftsmodelle in der Industrie 4.0*. TCW Transfer-Centrum.

Wirtz, B. W. (2019). *Digital business models*. Springer Nature. doi:10.1007/978-3-030-13005-3

KEY TERMS AND DEFINITIONS

Business Model: How an organisation creates value (or benefit) for target customers in its business processes with a unique combination of programmes, sales conditions, distribution channels and promotion, and with a unique combination of tangible and intangible assets in its business processes.

Competitiveness: Capability for global market rivalry.

Crisis: A short-lived, undesirable, and critical situation in a company (organisation), which directly threatens the achievement of the objectives of the participants of this company and its continued existence and development, which is due to the intertwined and simultaneous operation of both external and internal causes.

De-Internalisation: Reverse internationalisation, a reduction of the presence of companies in global trading, investment, and financial flows.

Globalisation: A state of international trade, investment, and financial and human flows, increasingly joined by ever more regions, countries, and companies, as well as products, services, technologies, knowledge, information.

Levels of Competitiveness: The competitiveness of the national economy (concerning the country of origin of the product the service), the competitiveness of the company between companies in the same national economy (*domestic competitiveness*) outside (*international competitiveness*), the competitiveness of the product service (i.e., the ability of the product to compete successfully in a particular market at a particular time).

Strategic Management: A process of creative design, selection and implementation of development possibilities that significantly influence the long-term performance of the organisation by setting guidelines fits operation and by creating consistency between the underlying capabilities of the organisation and the environment in which it operates.

Chapter 10
Incorporating Sustainability Into Strategic Management for Maintaining Competitive Advantage:
The Requisite Holism of Process, Institutional, and Instrumental Dimensions

Mojca Duh

https://orcid.org/0000-0002-2211-010X

Faculty of Economics and Business, University of Maribor, Slovenia

Tjaša Štrukelj

Faculty of Economics and Business, University of Maribor, Slovenia

ABSTRACT

The complex and turbulent contemporary business environment requires an understanding that considering sustainability challenges and issues in the strategic decision-making process is essential for building and maintaining a company's competitive advantage. The authors advocate that incorporating sustainability in the strategic planning process and developing sustainability strategies must be part of a company's transformation and reorientation to "a sustainability company." They explain the interdependences between the company's sustainability orientation, institutional solutions, and instrumental specifics and emphasize the requisite holism of process, institutional, and instrumental dimensions of strategic management for maintaining a company's competitive advantage. They conclude our chapter by presenting a model of interdependence of strategic management dimensions, sustainability, and competitive advantage of a company.

DOI: 10.4018/978-1-6684-6845-6.ch010

INTRODUCTION

Nowadays, the competitive environment surrounding companies is characterized by rapid changes and globalization (e.g., Ambrosini & Bowman, 2009; Baretto, 2010; Veršič et al., 2022) and caring consideration of the natural environment (Baumgartner & Rauter, 2017; Belak et al., 2014; Hahn & Tampe, 2021; Wheelen & Hunger, 2012; Štrukelj et al., 2020). Human industrial activity has caused severe environmental problems (e.g., climate changes, biodiversity loss, depletion of natural resources), which leads to the degradation of vital ecosystems (Hahn & Tampe, 2021; Walls et al., 2021).

In 1987, the World Commission on Environment and Development (WCED) attracted the wider public's attention with the term »sustainable development« in their report titled Our Common Future. Sustainable development was defined as development that "meets the needs of the present without compromising the ability of future generations to meet their own needs" (WCED, 1987, p. 24), aiming to secure intergenerational equity. The WCED emphasizes that sustainable development requires simultaneous consideration of three principles that present its foundations: environmental integrity, economic prosperity, and social equity (Bansal, 2005; WCED, 1987). The paradigm of sustainable development was addressed by the 2030 Agenda for Sustainable Development, which was adopted by all United Nations Member States in 2015. The 2030 Agenda addresses sustainability challenges through the 17 Sustainable Development Goals (SDGs). It also emphasizes the responsibility of every country to put effort into its development (i.e., which will enable people to live in peace and dignity, in a clean environment, and economic prosperity) and the need for joint efforts of all countries in addressing sustainability challenges. Most of these challenges can be solved only if all countries stand together to solve them (Agenda, 2015).

To reduce our adverse effects on the natural environment and society, we must change our industrial activity and practice sustainable production and consumption (Baumgartner & Rauter, 2017; Walls et al., 2021). Companies increasingly face pressure from various stakeholders to pay more attention to sustainability issues (Bansal & DesJardines, 2014; Meuer et al., 2020) and develop more sustainable strategies and business models (Fu et al., 2020; Hahn & Tampe, 2021). Companies should, in the process of using natural resources, consider the protection of the health of the planet Earth and the equitable distribution of the generated wealth to meet the needs of the present and future generations (Bansal & DesJardines, 2014). They should apply all three principles (i.e., environmental integrity, economic prosperity, and social equity) in their governance, management and functioning, inputs, and outputs to be considered as organizations striving for sustainability (Bansal, 2005; Štrukelj et al., 2020). Bansal and DesJardines (2014, p. 70) emphasize that sustainability »obliges firms to make intertemporal trade-offs to safeguard intergenerational equity«. According to the authors, sustainable companies successfully deal with temporal trade-offs in strategic decision-making, considering both the short and long term. Dyllick and Muff (2016) emphasize that »long-term aspects need to be given at least equal weight as short-term aspects« (p. 160) when sustainability issues are considered in strategic decisions. Companies' investments may not necessarily bring short-term returns but can create long-term benefits when sustainability is at stake (Bansal & DesJardines, 2014; Bertini et al., 2021). Even though there is a possibility of tensions between sustainability and profitability, companies need to address sustainability in their vision, mission, goals, strategies, and actions if they do not want to jeopardize their relationships with customers and investors (Bertini et al., 2021; Štrukelj et al., 2020). Companies with a fundamental and clear sustainability orientation (micro level) may positively impact the economy's and society's sustainable development (macro level). Only such a positive contribution to society and Planet Earth makes a company a sustainability business (Dyllick & Muff, 2016; Walls et al., 2016; Štrukelj et al., 2021). However, companies may also have a negative impact if their owners and leaders lack awareness of the importance of companies' sustainability orientation, decisions, and activities for sustainable development. Only sustainability awareness (Miller & Serafeim, 2014) and positive attitude of owners and leaders toward sustainability issues and concerns lead to positive (re)orientation of their companies toward sustainability (Dekker & Hasso, 2016; Roxas & Coetzer, 2012).

Recent research studies show that sustainability and social and environmental concerns have become important areas of companies' strategic decisions (Bertini et al., 2021; Dyllick & Muff, 2016; Hahn & Tampe, 2021; Walls et al., 2021). Therefore, sustainability strategies become necessary for maintaining competitive advantage (Dyllick & Muff, 2016; Walls et al., 2021) and making this area worth investigating. However, we lack research addressing the requisite holism of process, institutional and instrumental dimensions of strategic management when incorporating sustainability concerns in strategic decisions. We also lack research that examines the importance and effects of predefined sustainability vision, mission, purposes, goals, values, and culture in formulating and implementing sustainability strategies. Our research aim is to develop a model of interdependence of strategic management and sustainability, emphasizing the requisite holism of process, institutional and instrumental dimensions of sustainability in strategic management and the impact of sustainability efforts on maintaining the company's competitive advantage. As such, the model highlights the critical elements that should be considered by owners and leaders when integrating sustainability concerns and practices in their companies. We build our research on the concept of integral management (e.g., Belak et al., 2014), emphasizing the crucial influence of the coherence of strategic management with other dimensions and elements of governance and management on raising companies' awareness and commitment to sustainability (e.g., Baumgartner & Rauter, 2017). When examining the process dimension of strategic management, we limit ourselves to the strategic planning process in which the company's key stakeholders seek strategic opportunities and identify risks. At the same time, we consider internal strengths and weaknesses for dealing with sustainability challenges and formulating sustainability strategies. When discussing the institutional dimension of strategic management, the focus is on the central role of owners and business leaders (CEOs, top managers, and boards of directors) in solving sustainability challenges. Within the instrumental dimension, we focus on the role of the company's key stakeholders' values and beliefs and strategic management methods and tools when addressing sustainability challenges in strategic decisions.

The chapter is structured as follows: the first section is the introduction section outlining the problem addressed and defining the aim of the research. The second section presents strategic management from the following three dimensions: process, institutional and instrumental. In the third section, we discuss the sustainability concept and the required strategic reorientation of companies from "business as usual" to "a sustainability company", concentrating on sustainability strategies. The fourth section addresses the issues and solutions linked to incorporating sustainability in strategic planning. We advocate that incorporating sustainability in the strategic planning process must be part of maintaining the company's competitive advantage and reorientation and transformation into a sustainability company. In the fifth section, we discuss institutional and instrumental specifics in companies committed to sustainability by explaining the interdependences between the company's sustainability orientation, institutional solutions, and instrumental specifics and potential adaptation of strategic management tools and methods. In the sixth section, we present a model of interdependence of strategic management dimensions and sustainability, emphasizing the requisite holism of process, institutional and instrumental dimensions of strategic management for maintaining a company's competitive advantage. We believe that understanding the importance of the holistic incorporation of sustainability into strategic management is helpful, especially for all those stakeholders in companies who make strategic decisions that have consequences for maintaining competitive advantage and the well-being of today and future generations.

In the next chapter, we explain strategic management's process, institutional and instrumental dimensions. In the process dimension, we explain how the management process takes place, i.e. what decision-makers must do first and what they later do for the successful development of the company they lead. The institutional dimension explains who is in charge of this process, i.e. in what role are people responsible for the process decisions. The instrumental dimension refers to the possible ways that enable decision-makers to realize the given management process; it goes, for example, for management style and methods, which are instruments for defining the appropriate development of the company at the strategic management level.

PROCESS, INSTITUTIONAL AND INSTRUMENTAL DIMENSIONS OF STRATEGIC MANAGEMENT

Several definitions and concepts of strategic management can be found in the literature. For example, Wheelen and Hunger (2012) define strategic management as "a set of managerial decisions and actions that determines the long-run performance of a corporation" (p. 53). Their basic strategic management model consists of four elements: environmental (external and internal) scanning, strategy formulation, implementation, and evaluation and control. Similar »building blocks« can be found in several other concepts and models of strategic management (e.g., Hungenberg, 2001; Johnson et al., 2011; Lombriser & Abplanalp, 2005; Lynch, 2009). However, many of these models and concepts focus on the process dimension of strategic management and do not address other dimensions. We are convinced that strategic management should be understood broadly, and instrumental and institutional dimensions should be addressed besides the process dimension. In this section, we present strategic management from all three dimensions and build our presentation on the selected integral management model, the MER model of integral management (Belak & Duh, 2012; Belak et al., 2014). Models of integral management emphasize relations and interactions of strategic management with other elements of governance and management. More importantly, it demonstrates the importance of considering environmental conditions in decision-making.

The MER model of integral management (see Figure 1) presents the framework for explaining management's process, instrumental and institutional dimensions with a particular focus on strategic management. It provides a starting point for further exploration of incorporating sustainability into process, institutional and instrumental dimensions of strategic management in the following sections of this chapter. In our presentation, we focus on the inner circle in Figure 1, illustrating management in all three dimensions.

The process dimension of the MER Model is based on the idea that the management process has its hierarchy in which we proceed from the global and fundamental definitions of a company to the more detailed operational definitions (Figure 2). Therefore, three hierarchical levels should be distinguished: political, strategic, and operational. Similarly, Baumgartner and Rauter (2017) distinguish three relevant levels for corporate sustainability management: normative, strategic, and operational.

The highest political normative level is about looking for answers to questions "Why are we here?" and "Whose benefit does a company work for?". It is about deciding on vision, mission, purposes, and primary goals. These foundational definitions of a company should be communicated to internal and

Figure 1. The MER model of integral management
Source: Belak et al. (2014, p. 28)

external stakeholders, explaining what a company would like to become, the reasons for its existence, and the purpose of its functioning. The middle strategic level (strategic management) focuses on identifying strategic opportunities and threats, strengths and weaknesses, which are the basis for formulating strategies. Questions addressed at this level are: "What should an enterprise produce and how much?" and "How should this be produced?" Strategic management has a central role within the MER model of

Figure 2. Hierarchy of the proves dimension
Source: Belak et al. (2014, p. 65)

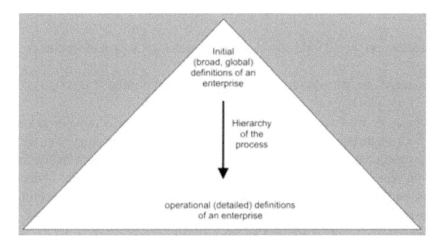

integral management as it is mainly about maintaining strategic potentials for the realization of vision, mission, purposes, and primary goals, thereby ensuring a company's existence and development and fulfilling expectations various stakeholders. The lowest operational level encompasses the resources planning and allocating and operational tasks, directly affecting strategy implementation. Decisions at this level should focus on the optimal implementation of changes necessary for the existence of a company and the optimal exploitation of the company's resources; decisions are not just operative but also tactical.

Planning as the basic management function is the "starting" activity in the management process and has to be carried out at all three hierarchical levels. In this chapter, we limit our discussion to strategic planning (i.e., planning on the strategic level), in which formulating strategies for achieving vision, mission, and goals is the main planning activity. Planning is followed by organizing and direct implementation; control, as the fourth basic management function, should not be seen as the last activity as it is required all the time and at all levels.

Central to the work of managers is the process of making decisions. Within the MER model, considerable attention is given to strategic decisions, which should be based on sound and comprehensive information on future developments in the company's external environment and cognitions of a company's internal strengths and weaknesses resulting from the organizational analysis. When formulating strategies and deciding on the best ones, leaders should consider different quantitative and qualitative selection criteria, among which we found as especially important the judgment on whether the selected strategy is in line with the company's vision and mission and contribute to the realization of the company's goals.

The institutional dimension of management provides solutions for the proper structure and organization of those involved in a company's decision-making process. The institutional solutions depend on many factors; the size and ownership of a company and the national legislation are among the most influential. As many institutional solutions are possible when considering previously mentioned factors, we provide a general solution that should be adapted to the specific (1) micro situation of a particular company (e.g., size, ownership, industry specifics, geographical dispersion) and (2) macro situation of a particular company (e.g., national legislation, economic situation, socio-political conditions). General institutional solution is based on the hierarchy of the management process; the following four major decision makers groups can be distinguished:

- Owners/shareholders who are the key decision makers at the political level make decisions about the company's vision, mission, purposes, and primary goals;
- Top management who decides about strategies and strategic allocation of resources at the strategic level;
- Middle management who decides about acquiring and exploitation of resources (i.e., on tactics), and
- First-line management who decides about the operative allocation of tasks.

In smaller companies, where an owner is also a manager, the majority of political and strategic decisions are made by a single person. In larger companies, the decision-making roles are divided among more persons (owners, managers at different levels, and departments). Personality traits, motivation, authority, and competencies of decision-makers significantly impact the "nature" of decisions made and influence owners' and managers' awareness of the requisite incorporation of sustainability into strategies.

Management as an instrumental system is a set of values, guiding principles, styles, techniques, and management methods. Values of owners and leaders, and the organizational culture in general, are given special attention as they have a crucial influence on all dimensions and activities of the management process. Therefore, they play an essential role in the company's transformation into a sustainability company (e.g., Bansal, 2005; Baumgartner & Rauter, 2017; Dekker & Hasso, 2016; Roxas & Coetzer, 2012).

In the next chapter, we discuss sustainability as a way of companies' strategic (re)orientation, which we found necessary for achieving and maintaining the company's competitive advantage in the market. First of all, we are researching the strategic reorientation of companies from an "old" business - business as usual to a "new" business - sustainability business. Next, we research how a company should integrate sustainability in strategies, i.e. in its strategic orientations, with which it achieves and maintains a competitive advantage in its industry on its market.

SUSTAINABILITY AS A STRATEGIC (RE)ORIENTATION OF COMPANIES

Strategic Reorientation of Companies From a Business as Usual to a Sustainability Company

A widely accepted understanding of sustainable development as the development that aims to meet the present generations' needs without compromising the future generations' needs (WCED, 1987) requires all members of society to act responsibly and make efforts towards sustainable development. Companies are also expected to act as responsible members of society, contributing to sustainable development due to their extensive impact on society, the economy, and the natural environment (Baumgartner & Rauter, 2017).

Academic interest in exploring company sustainability has increased significantly in the past two decades (Meuer et al., 2020; Hahn & Tampe, 2021). Consequently, different notions in the literature indicate incorporating sustainability concerns in companies' management and functioning. Bansal and DesJardines (2014) define »business sustainability« as »the ability of firms to respond to their short-term financial needs without compromising their (or others) ability to meet their future needs« (p.71). Hahn and Tampe (2021) claim that "business sustainability has been characterized as an essentially contested concept" (p. 457) since the common definition of business sustainability has not been agreed upon. The term "corporate sustainability" is also often found in the literature. In the opinion of Montiel & Delgado-Ceballos (2014), the first operationalization of the corporate sustainability construct was done by Bansal (2005), who defines sustainable corporate development as a three-dimensional construct based on (1) economic prosperity, (2) social equity, and (3) environmental integrity. However, many other definitions of corporate sustainability can be found in the literature. For example, Meuer et al. (2020) explored "corporate sustainability" definitions in influential and often-cited journals and found 33 original definitions of corporate sustainability. The analysis of these definitions shows a great variety in the understanding of the fundamental nature of corporate sustainability; it is considered as a company's "specific 'ability' 'capacity', or 'response' but also 'strategies and activities', 'products, policies, practices, or 'an approach', 'a concept' or 'a new paradigm'" (Meuer et al., 2020, p. 329). The lack of definitional clarity and approaches for operationalization and measuring corporate sustainability shows that corporate sustainability as a field is still evolving (Montiel & Delgado-Ceballos, 2014). We found for our further discussion in this chapter the "most useful" explanation of corporate sustainability as the three-dimensional construct encompassing economic, social, and environmental dimensions

(Bansal, 2005; Montiel & Delgado-Ceballos, 2014) referring to the initial WCED's (1987) definition of sustainable development.

In the opinion of Baumgartner and Rauter (2017), the main reason for deciding on sustainability as a strategic orientation of a company is "to reduce the negative environmental and social impacts of corporate activities while improving (or at least not reducing) the economic performance of the corporation" (p. 83). Implementing a sustainability orientation may positively influence other stakeholders and create benefits for the business community, society, and nature (Baumgartner & Rauter, 2017). Companies with a clear sustainability orientation are those that consider both the short- and long-term aspects in strategic and operative decisions (Bansal & DesJardines, 2014; Dyllick & Muff, 2016) and strive for a balance between the interests and needs of internal and external stakeholders (Baumgartner & Rauter, 2017).

Companies must address and consider sustainability issues when formulating their vision, mission, goals, strategies, and actions if they do not want to jeopardize their relationships with internal and external stakeholders (Bertini et al., 2021; Štrukelj et al., 2020). As pointed out by Meuer et al. (2020), managers "are becoming aware of the potential benefits of aligning operations with the principles of sustainable development" (p. 321). Companies increasingly consider and refer to sustainability, sustainability strategies, and/or sustainable development in their reports or websites (Montiel & Delgado-Ceballos, 2014). Most large corporations are involved in sustainability initiatives and have to report on environmental and social issues in their sustainability reports; corporate sustainability indices were created to evaluate companies. The European Union legally demands that large companies disclose nonfinancial statements in annual reports (Meuer et al., 2020).

Baumgartner and Rauter (2017) emphasize that attention should be given to relations between sustainability-related goals and other corporate goals as such relationships "can be complementary, competitive, or irrelevant" (p. 86). Companies define and follow environmental and social goals for two reasons. First, they may be forced to do so by the key stakeholders (e.g., owners, market stakeholders), and second, they may do that voluntarily. Companies' voluntary commitment to sustainability goals may be driven by ethical rationality (i.e., ethically motivated) or by economic rationality (i.e., expectations of economic benefits) (Baumgartner & Rauter, 2017).

Several authors (e.g., Bansal, 2005; Dyllick & Muff, 2016; Miller & Serafeim, 2014) suggest that the company's sustainability orientation and commitment develop gradually over time. Therefore, it is possible to identify key stages in this process. In the opinion of Dyllick and Muff (2016), this developmental process should be understood as »the transformation of business, moving from a business as usual to 'true business sustainability'" (p. 157). According to Miller and Serafeim (2014, p. 4), the stages represent »the degree to which sustainability is strategic and central to the organization«. By progressing through stages, companies improve the range of interactions with different stakeholders, undertake more complex responsibilities and strive towards adapting their business model to their sustainability goals. Stages present the reached level of sustainability awareness and implementation as a strategic and central orientation of a company. Very often, companies are at the first stage(s) only limited engaged with sustainability as they primarily focus on adapting their functioning to regulations. Such actions are not strategic, and sustainability is rarely integrated into strategies. The incorporation of sustainability issues in companies' strategies is »limited« to »transitional change aimed at improving existing organization practices or moving from existing practice to a new one" (Miller & Serafeim, 2014, p. 2). Many companies develop further and become more strategically focused on sustainability challenges and how to improve effectiveness and efficiency. Companies may remain at this stage for a longer time before evolving to the next stage, which can be due to their decision to wait until there is less uncertainty (Bansal, 2005). Some companies do not even reach the next stage at all. The next stage is much more transformative and innovative than the previous ones. Companies at this stage focus on innovation and reframe their corporate identities. They »aggressively innovate and capitalize on the rewards of sustainable development« (Bansal, 2005, p. 203). At this point, »sustainability tends to be integrated into the core business strategies« (Miller & Serafeim, 2014, p. 2). The leaders' efforts focus on developing systems, business models, operations, and procedures for maximizing long-term profitability while looking for solutions for societal problems and reducing harmful effects on the company's external environment (Miller & Serafeim, 2014).

In Miller and Serafeim's (2014) opinion, the initial incentive for sustainability-related changes results from endogenous and/or exogenous factors, which are both critical. Their research findings show that leaders' strong awareness of the requisite sustainability-related changes is an essential endogenous factor and is closely related to the exogenous factors of external engagement (e.g., of external activism or pressure from stakeholders). Bansal (2005) emphasizes that the probability of a company's commitment to sustainable development is higher when all three principles of sustainable development (i.e., environmental integrity, economic prosperity, and social equity) are congruent with the cultural norms and values of a company.

Integrating Sustainability in Strategies

The results of the large-scale survey among leaders conducted by Kiron et al. (2017) show that 90% of executives consider sustainability important, but only 60% of companies integrate sustainability into their strategies. Similarly, Circano (2014) reports that CEOs worldwide find sustainability necessary for companies' competitive position and survival, but not all companies incorporate sustainability into their corporate and business strategies. These findings show a relatively high level of sustainability awareness among managers, which is not followed by adequate decisions and measures or at least not in sufficient scope. Such a situation could also be due to the cognition of Baumgartner and Rauter (2017) that "the concept of sustainable development offers no clear guidance concerning which strategies, plans or activities need to be implemented" (p. 81). Meuer et al. (2020) call attention to several critics of corporate sustainability research, which does not provide a convincing explanation of "how firms can contribute to sustainable development" (p. 320) and how they can "effectively incorporate sustainable practices into their activities" (p. 320). We believe our research can contribute to a more comprehensive and explicit concept and explanation of integrating sustainability in strategic decisions and management and how this can help companies maintain competitive advantage and generate long-term benefits.

We find several definitions of a strategy in the literature and different classifications of strategies. Baumgartner and Rauter (2017) define a strategy as »a plan for attaining the defined goals under conditions of uncertainty" (p. 82). According to Wheelen and Hunger (2012, p. 67), a strategy should be "a comprehensive master plan that states how the corporation will achieve its mission and objectives. It maximizes competitive advantage and minimizes competitive disadvantage". Classification of three types of strategies is often found in the literature, and that are (e.g., Belak et al., 2014; Müller-Stewens & Lechner, 2005; Wheelen & Hunger, 2012): corporate, business, and functional strategies. Due to space limitations, we address only a corporate and a business strategy.

Corporate strategy defines the overall developmental direction of a whole company. Its formulation and implementation are of crucial importance not only for large multinational corporations but as well for smaller companies with a narrow portfolio of products and/or services (Müller-Stewens & Lechner,

2005; Wheelen & Hunger, 2012). When formulating a corporate strategy, a company should decide on three key issues (Belak et al., 2014; Wheelen & Hunger, 2012). The first refers to the company's overall developmental direction, which could be toward growth, stability, or decrease (retrenchment). It is a so-called directional strategy. Besides the overall direction, a company should decide whether to concentrate its functioning in the current industry or diversify in another industry. An essential part of a directional strategy is also a decision on whether a company will develop through internal or external development. The second issues refer to the industries and/or markets where a company offers its products and/or services. The third group of issues refers to managing and coordinating a company's activities and allocating resources (so-called parenting strategy).

Business strategy focuses on improving a company's competitive position within a particular industry or market segment. It is sometimes called a competitive strategy (Müller-Stewens & Lechner, 2005). The core of business strategy is the definition of ways of achieving a competitive advantage. A competitive advantage is understood as a company's or a business unit's ability to create value in a way that competitors cannot (Wheelen & Hunger, 2012). Two generic competitive strategies can be distinguished: lower cost and differentiation. A company's competitive advantage is defined by its competitive scope, which can be narrow (a market niche) or broad. Considering a competitive scope, companies "select" among four business strategies, and that is cost leadership or differentiation (broad competitive scope) or cost focus or differentiation focus (narrow competitive scope).

Dyllick and Muff (2016) claim that companies should »embed sustainability throughout the organization, including strategies and operations, governance and management processes, organizational structures and culture, as well as auditing and reporting systems" (p. 161). Several research studies emphasize the importance of incorporating sustainability concerns in strategies (O'Brien, 2018; Dyllick & Muff, 2016; Hahn & Tampe, 2021; Hart & Dowell, 2011; Walls et al., 2011). Sustainability-related strategies are necessary to be competitive today and even more so in the future (Dyllick & Muff, 2016; Hahn & Tampe, 2021; Walls et al., 2021). Not considering the natural environment in companies' strategies can present a severe obstacle to creating a competitive advantage (Hart & Dowell, 2011; Walls et al., 2011). Many companies have oriented toward a more proactive approach in addressing environmental issues due to regulatory changes and changes in leaders' perceptions and consumers' expectations (Walls at el., 2011). Walls et al. (2011) define an environmental strategy as "a set of initiatives that mitigate a firm's impact on the natural environment" (p. 73) and distinguish between reactive and proactive environmental strategies. According to the authors, reactive environmental strategies "address environmental issues when they arise as a result of the firm's activities", and proactive environmental strategies "emphasize prevention and are a unique combination of resources through which firms develop environmental capabilities" (Walls et al., 2011, p. 73). Hart and Dowell (2011) emphasize that leaders' understanding of sustainable development should not be limited to environmental issues but should also embed economic and social concerns. Sustainable development strategy "does not merely seek to do less environmental damage but, rather, to produce in a way that can be maintained indefinitely into the future" (p. 1466).

Similarly, Baumgartner and Rauter (2017) suggest that companies must consider their impact on society, the economy, and the natural environment and ways to reduce negative impacts. These considerations and solutions of a (more) sustainable company should be incorporated into the company's strategies. Companies may offer sustainable products and services to address specific demands of sustainability-oriented customers that help a company "to gain a selective advantage over its competitors" (Baumgartner & Rauter, 2017, p. 87). The authors distinguish between corporate sustainability strategies with an internal focus (introverted or conservative) and those with an external focus. The latter strategies are extroverted and visionary and may have a strong societal impact when improvements in terms of sustainability issues (i.e., economic, social, and environmental issues) are adequately addressed and incorporated into strategies. Successful implementation of such (sustainability) strategies benefits internal and external stakeholders and the planet Earth, which should be considered legitimate stakeholders (e.g., Stead & Stead, 2000).

Miller and Serafeim (2014) claim that strategies' nature and content depend on the achieved developmental stage of a company's sustainability awareness, commitment, and orientation (discussed previously in the text). Their research results show that companies develop generic sustainability strategies in the early stages of sustainability. In the later stages of sustainability, a company's strategy becomes more idiosyncratic (in terms of sustainability), customized to the requirements of different stakeholders, and based on the knowledge of conditions of present and future markets.

Baumgartner and Rauter (2017) believe that sustainability strategies in profit-oriented organizations are usually a subset of the corporate competitive strategy. According to the authors, the decision on sustainability strategy may be grounded in normative-ethical considerations, which means that sustainable development as a primary goal is motivated by ethical issues. On the other hand, the ground for sustainability strategy may be in (pure) economic rationality. In this case, the focus is on the economic advantages gained from improving sustainable behaviour. As pointed out by the authors, strategic decisions may well be grounded in normative-ethical considerations and economic rationality.

The above review of different views on sustainability strategies shows that authors share a joint opinion that sustainability concerns should be incorporated into strategies but without being clear on how this incorporation affects corporate strategy and business strategies. In the opinion of Baumgartner & Rauter (2017), sustainability strategies are a subset of a corporate strategy, and Walls et al. (2011) define environmental strategies as those addressing environmental issues. Rarely do the authors address the interdependence between strategies and vision, mission, and goals of a company regarding sustainability.

We believe that considering sustainability issues and incorporating sustainability is required in a corporate and business strategy. Sustainability strategies should not be viewed as a subset either of a corporate and neither of a business strategy. Considering all three pillars of sustainable development in strategic decisions is necessary for long-term successful value creation. Successful formulation and implementation of sustainability strategies depend on the company's stakeholders' awareness and comprehensive understanding of sustainability challenges, especially of key stakeholders (i.e., owners and managers). They should be aware of sustainable development's importance and contribution on the organisational, regional, and global levels to create well-being for all stakeholders and preserve the natural environment. It means that successfully implementing companies' strategies should create benefits for companies' owners and employees (i.e., internal stakeholders) and external stakeholders (e.g., customers, suppliers, banks, etc.). A sustainability vision, mission, and goals should be defined to make this happen as they present requisite preconditions for formulating sustainability corporate and business strategy.

Sustainability should be understood as an opportunity and a driver of innovation. Incorporating sustainability into strategies can positively affect competitiveness and lead to lower costs and higher revenues. Sustainability not only that can impact the products (design, production, costs) but can also positively affects brand value and a company's reputation (Carcano, 2014). Those companies that believe sustainability is an essential element of their strategies should explore sustainable products and processes that can improve environmental and social conditions (Placet et al., 2005). For example, Carcano (2014) studied sustainability and how it is incorporated into the strategic management of companies producing luxury products. Luxury products are high-priced, and only a few people can buy them. As "luxury positioning is associated with the creation of a social distance that, at first glance, it would seem irrelevant, or even contradictory, to the issue of sustainability" (Carcano, 2014, p. 37). However, the investigation of luxury companies and their strategic and management practice shows that these companies are intensely focused on their employees and take care of the environment and community. Research findings of Placet et al. (2005) show that innovation is a crucial element of sustainability-focused business strategy. When formulating such business strategies, a company should consider its core competencies, financial situation, skills, resources, and the sustainability challenges that a company faces. In the opinion of Placet et al. (2005), in the process of formulating a sustainability strategy, a company should (1) consider innovation in processes and products, (2) develop improved or new production processes with less harmful effects on the natural environment, (3) design improved or new environmentally friendly products, and (4) improve business processes by incorporating social and environmental considerations or even "invent brand-new industries devoted to improving environmental and social conditions" (p. 33).

Placet et al. (2005) emphasize that sustainability strategies should embed tri goals: environmental stewardship, social responsibility, and economic prosperity for a company and its stakeholders. These goals are interrelated and supportive. A company must carefully explore sustainability-related opportunities and threats to formulate a sustainability strategy. Such a sustainability strategy should be formulated that "transitions from traditional resource-intensive and volume-maximizing operations to an approach that uses fewer resources and maximizes both stakeholder and shareholder value requires leadership, commitment, planning, and innovation" (Placet et al., 2005, p. 33).

Even though tensions between sustainability and profitability exist and companies have experienced problems meeting sustainability goals, they must translate their sustainability commitments into actions. In the opinion of Bertini et al. (2021), companies are too often held back in realizing sustainability ideas as they build on the presumption that sustainability solutions would lead to higher investments and costs and, consequently, higher prices. However, as (1) consumers and other stakeholders are increasingly aware of sustainability issues, and (2) the growing number of companies have seen sustainability as a crucial part of long-term value creation, (3) maintaining a company's competitive advantage requires a proactive approach towards sustainability in strategic management. The next chapter explains incorporating sustainability in the strategic planning process.

INCORPORATING SUSTAINABILITY IN THE STRATEGIC PLANNING PROCESS

Sustainability strategic management as a process consists of a range of activities focused on establishing conditions for the sustainable development of a company. Basic as well as process functions have to be conducted. Planning, as one of the basic strategic management functions, begins with seeking strategic options, followed by formulating and evaluating strategies and preparing an implementation program. The process of seeking strategic options should include scanning the internal and external environment. The primary purpose of environmental scanning is the identification of (both internal and external) strategic factors, i.e. variables that will determine the development of a company in the future (Duh, 2018; Lombriser & Abplanalp, 2005; Müller-Stewens & Lechner, 2005; Wheelen & Hunger, 2012).

Companies must consider external opportunities, threats, and internal strengths and weaknesses when incorporating sustainability into strategies. Placet et al. (2005) emphasize that in the process of formulating strategies, managers should "realistically take into account both the drivers for sustainability and the impediments that may be encountered" (p. 40). Therefore, companies must integrate sustainability considerations into their strategic planning process (Baumgartner & Rauter, 2017).

Companies' external environment is characterized by numerous forces that seriously threaten sustainable development. It is estimated that by 2035 the world population will reach 8.6 billion, and the number of consumers will increase to 4 billion. Fast growth is predicted in emerging economies. Such growth will lead towards increasing demand for raw materials and energy. Global warming and rising sea levels have already negatively influenced agriculture and infrastructure. Urbanization has been continuing with unchanged speed and leading to the development of megacities in the developing world and is increasing the number of midsized cities in European countries. Fast technological development (ICT, biotechnologies, materials, mobile technologies, etc.) will lead to a hyperconnected world (European Commission, 2015).

A sustainability strategy requires careful study and analysis to fully understand sustainability-related opportunities and threats (Placet et al., 2005). Therefore, the strategic planning process is not easy and requires in-depth consideration of sustainability challenges. Managers committed to sustainability and finding it an essential element of corporate and business strategies should seek sustainable products and/or services and processes that will improve environmental and social conditions and simultaneously lead to preserving or improving profitability (Placet et al., 2005). As mentioned earlier, innovations are crucial. A sustainability strategy should consider the developments in a company's external environment and its specific situation. When formulating sustainability strategies the following should be done (Placet et al., 2005): (1) several options of sustainable development of a company should be taken into consideration; companies should explore a wide range of innovative and sustainability-related opportunities which can result in higher revenues, lower costs, higher value of products or in any other way contribute to the economic prosperity; (2) these options should be comprehensively consider from the environmental and social perspective – specific changes can reduce some environmental or social problems but can at the same time cause the new ones; (3) the company's stakeholders should be considered as well – a company has to identify its internal and external stakeholders when making strategic decisions; (4) financial risks and benefits should be considered, also risks and benefits of not innovating – competitors, suppliers, customers and new entrants in the company's industry may take market share by offering sustainable products and processes.

Scanning of the external environment is, therefore, of crucial importance for companies seeking optimal solutions for their sustainable development. Especially environmental uncertainty, which is defined by Wheelen and Hunger (2012) as "the degree of complexity plus the degree of change" (p. 146), requires managers to monitor rapid changes in the external environment constantly. The increasing number of global markets results in an increasing number and complexity of external strategic factors that companies must consider when making strategic decisions. Environmental uncertainty threatens managers as it hinders their ability to prepare long-range plans and make strategic decisions that enable companies to stay in equilibrium with their external environment. However, environmental uncertainty is also an opportunity as it opens new space for creativity and innovation (Wheelen & Hunger, 2012; Štrukelj et al., 2019; 2021).

Managers should identify and understand numerous variables in the company's natural, (broad) societal, and task environment. They have to scan the natural environment and variables in that environment which were in the past taken for granted and without any limitations (e.g., availability of fresh water and clean air). Every company has a particular impact on the natural environment. This impact is sometimes weak (e.g., excessive lighting in and on commercial buildings). At the same time, some other companies have substantial adverse effects on the natural environment due to their emissions and waste (Bansal, 2005). Due to global warming, conditions in the natural environment (e.g., sea level, weather, and climate) have become more and more uncertain, and for this reason, very difficult to predict. Managers should scan the natural environment for possible opportunities and threats and consider and rethink the effects of the company's activities on the natural environment. Both need to be addressed in making strategic decisions, and efforts should be made to reduce and prevent activities that have adverse and harmful effects on the natural environment (Wheelen & Hunger, 2012). Only such companies' efforts lead to implementing the environmental integrity principle (Bansal, 2005). Decisions and efforts focused on the ecologically and environmentally friendly functioning of a company should consider a company's outputs (i.e., products, services, waste, measures, and information), processes, capacities and structures, and inputs (e.g., raw materials, energy) (Belak et al., 2014; Stead & Stead, 2000). Thommen (2004) distinguishes among four target areas of companies' environmentally friendly functioning: (1) resources, (2) emissions, (3) waste, and (4) significant risks. Such requisite and sufficiently comprehensive treatment of the natural environment can help managers to identify the need for environmentally friendly products and services on the market (Duh, 2018; Wheelen & Hunger, 2012). For example, an important "source" of innovation can be the need for energy-sustainable buildings. According to the International Panel on Climate Change results, "30% of the energy used in buildings could be reduced with net economic benefits by 2030" (Action plan, 2008, p. 2).

Managers must also be aware of variables within a company's societal and task environment (e.g., Müller-Stewens & Lechner, 2005; Wheelen & Hunger, 2012). A task environment consists of elements or groups of stakeholders that directly impact a company and/or are affected by the company's activities. These groups of stakeholders are government, local communities, suppliers, competitors, customers, finance providers, unions, special interest groups, and trade associations. The task environment of a company is the industry in which a company functions (Duh, 2018; Wheelen & Hunger, 2012).

In a company's societal environment, we can identify those forces that have a long-term impact on a company. To better understand developmental trends in a company's societal environment, it is helpful to distinguish among several groups of forces. According to Wheelen and Hunger (2012), forces that impact several industries can be divided into the following groups: economic, technological, political, and sociocultural. Such division of forces in particular groups within a company's societal environment should be understood as a "tool" for identifying trends that might have a crucial impact on a company's performance and competitive positioning (e.g., Rüegg-Stürm, 2002). Such environmental segmentation is a valuable tool for managers. It enables them to understand environmental changes better and forecast future changes, phenomena, and trends.

In searching for strategic options and formulating strategies, a company should consider how to protect the natural environment and apply the principle of social equity as one of the preconditions for sustainable development. Bansal (2005) links the social equity principle with corporate social responsibility, which demands that companies "embrace the economic, legal, ethical, and discretionary expectations of all stakeholders" (p. 199) and not only of shareholders and investors. Therefore, during searching for strategic options and formulating strategies – managers must consider the expectations, needs and particular interests of stakeholders within and outside a company. It requires establishing and maintaining strong relationships with stakeholders' groups which can be achieved through transparent functioning, consideration of stakeholders' interest in the decision-making process, and equal distribution of wealth among relevant stakeholders. Bansal (2005) emphasizes that the integration of the social equity principle (as one of the preconditions for sustainable development) requires that companies adequately address and react to social issues such as "the decision not to employ child labour, not to produce socially unde-sirable products, and not to engage in relationships with unethical partners" (p. 199). For example, Gap International, one of the largest USA fashion companies, created a code of ethics according to which all Gap's suppliers must comply with all child-law regulations and laws (i.e., hiring, working hours, overtime, and working conditions). They must not employ workers that are under 14 years of age. After deciding on the code of ethics and introducing it into the practice, Gap did not cancel cooperation with suppliers that did not comply with the code's principle on child labour but instead asked suppliers to stop using child labour and involve these children in schools. They should pay them a regular salary for the whole schooling period and guarantee a job once they reach legal age. In one year of the code's validity, Gap cancelled cooperation with 23 suppliers that did not meet the standards required (Wheelen & Hunger, 2012). The report of the European Commission on the improvements regarding sustainable development shows that European companies increasingly integrate social and environmental issues and efforts in their activities and interactions with stakeholders voluntarily. There has been a considerable increase in the number of companies that introduced a system of environmental management in their practice. The number of EU eco-labels has also increased even though the market share of products with such labels is still relatively low (EC, 2011).

As the core of competitive advantage is "in the ability to identify and respond to environmental change well advance of competition" (Wheelen & Hunger, 2012, p. 156), an essential manager's task is to identify external strategic factors. An issue priority matrix can be a helpful approach in supporting managers to identify those critical trends in the natural, societal, and task environment that are considered to have a medium to a high probability of occurrence and a medium to a high probability of impact on a company (Wheelen & Hunger, 2012). The matrix helps managers decide which developments in a company's external environment to scan merely (low priority) and which developments they should monitor as strategic factors (high priority). Those factors recognized as a company's strategic factors are categorized into opportunities and threats (Wheelen & Hunger, 2012).

Scanning the external environment and identifying strategic factors regarding opportunities and threats is insufficient to formulate strategies to achieve and maintain a competitive advantage and sustainable development. Managers must be aware of a company's internal developmental capabilities and forces, which are internal strategic factors. Scanning a company's internal environment (also called internal scanning or organizational analysis) is aimed at identifying those internal strategic factors which are essential strengths and weaknesses of a company, especially in comparison with the present and/or potential key competitors. Several approaches to organizational analysis are well presented in the literature. Due to the limitations of the scope of this contribution, we are only indicating some potential starting points for exploring a company's internal environment. They can be in (e.g., Müller-Stewens & Lechner, 2005; Lombriser & Abplanalp, 2005; Wheelen & Hunger, 2012): resources, capabilities, competencies, and core competencies. For example, Wheelen and Hunger (2012) emphasize the importance of a resource-based approach to organizational analysis where a resource (e.g., tangible assets, a competency, a process, experiences, or knowledge) is a company's strength if it enables achieving and maintaining of a company's competitive advantage. A resource is a weakness when a company possesses or conducts a particular process poorly or even not at all, and its competitor possesses the required capabilities. Several authors (e.g., Martín-de Castro et al., 2011; Müller-Stewens & Lechner, 2005) emphasize that we should distinguish between material and nonmaterial resources due to the increasing importance of intellectual capital and knowledge for achieving a competitive advantage.

Companies' fast and successful responses to rapid and radical environmental changes are innovation and new knowledge that is a source of innovativeness of companies. Knowledge and the ability of a company to create new knowledge positively affect creativity, innovativeness, and required developments in a company (Nonaka et al., 2000). Knowledge and innovation are vital in coping with environmental challenges and striving to re-orientate a company from a business-as-usual to a sustainability company. Special attention is given to tacit knowledge in a company, which has more personal quality than explicit knowledge and is deeply rooted in someone's actions, ideals, values, and emotions. Therefore, tacit knowledge is hard to express or formalize (Nonaka, 1991, 1994; Nonaka & Takeuchi, 1995). Tacit knowledge can be an essential source of sustained competitive advantage if a company succeeds in collecting such knowledge and is accessible to all employees in a company, and at the same time difficult to transfer to other companies. Such knowledge is rooted in a specific context and refers to those elements that are difficult to observe and, therefore, such knowledge is difficult to imitate (Čater, 2011).

Formulation of strategies begins with situational analysis, during which we combine data, information, and cognitions acquired in scanning internal and external environments. Situational analysis is the process of "finding a strategic fit between external opportunities and internal strengths while working around external threats and internal weaknesses" (Wheelen & Hunger, 2012, p. 224). The formulation of corporate and business strategies is followed by selecting the best strategy. In this process, quantitative and qualitative criteria of selection should be applied. Namely, assessing a strategy only by using profit maximization and other quantitative performance criteria can lead to selecting a strategy that would create benefits only for owners. In such a case, the interests and benefits of other stakeholders would be neglected or given minimal consideration. Low importance also refers to a company's attitude towards the natural environment and its sustainability orientation.

Nevertheless, it is true also vice versa. For example, the decision of a company to use recycled materials in production may have a positive impact on reducing the adverse side effects of a company's activities on the natural environment. However, it can negatively affect dividends for shareholders (Wheelen & Hunger, 2012).

To avoid weighing the priorities of the interests of different stakeholders, a company needs to express its commitment to sustainability orientation clearly and embed its commitment to sustainability in foundational normative definitions of a company, that is, in its vision, mission, purposes, and primary goals. As sustainability also requires changes in company culture, defining the sustainability values a company stands for is essential in achieving such changes. A fundamental precondition for the reorientation of a company towards sustainability is, therefore, not only the formulation of sustainability strategies but also the integration of sustainability into a company's vision, mission, purposes, and primary goals. It requires that owners and managers understand the role of their company in society, particularly the role and impact of the company's operations on all three dimensions, so-called pillars of sustainable development. Wheelen and Hunger (2012) emphasize that we need a broad understanding of the sustainability concept and sustainable development. Therefore, it is helpful to consider the company's responsibilities. The authors cite Caroll's (1991, 2004) definition of four groups of responsibilities of a company's owners and managers, and that is economical, legal, ethical, and discretionary. The economic responsibilities of a company and its owners and managers are to produce goods and/or perform services that have value for society. This production and performance enable a company to settle its obligations to creditors and shareholders. Governments determine legal responsibilities with the provisions in laws that managers are expected to obey. Ethical responsibilities consist of respect for generally accepted beliefs and values about behaviour in society. Discretionary responsibilities are voluntary obligations and commitments of a company's owners and managers. Respecting and accepting all four responsibilities is necessary for sustainable development and a company's long-term survival and evolution. Clearly defined and expressed in implemented actions for preserving the natural environment may enable a company to realize higher product prices and greater brand loyalty. Such a company is attractive for potential employees looking for jobs in an environmentally friendly company and investors looking for long-term investment opportunities among environmentally responsible companies. Companies that are aware of their responsibilities towards the natural environment and realize them in practice have easier access to foreign markets characterized by high awareness of the importance of preserving the natural environment and companies' responsibilities (Wheelen & Hunger, 2012). We add that not only care for the natural environment but also consideration and integration of the other two pillars of sustainable development (i.e., social equity and economic prosperity) should be understood as responsibilities of owners and managers.

In this context, we should understand the proposition of Johnson et al. (2011) regarding the use of the following three performance criteria when evaluating and selecting strategies: (1) suitability – assessing whether a strategy responds to the identified internal and external strategic factors (opportunities, threats, strengths, weaknesses); (2) acceptability – assessing whether the strategy's performance outcomes meet stakeholders expectations (and not only expectations of shareholders and owners); (3) feasibility – assessing whether a strategy can be realized in practice. Several authors (e.g., Pučko, 2003; Wheelen & Hunger, 2012) emphasize suitability as one of the most crucial selection criteria. Only a strategy and (new or improved) outputs (products and/or services) that are recognized by customers as necessary and desirable lead to value creation (of course, costs, efficiency etc. should be considered) and contribute to economic prosperity. The value created is distributed to consumers through products and services, shareholders and owners through dividends and equity, and employees through payments for their work efforts (Bansal, 2005).

Formulation and selection of the best strategies are followed by developing a program of activities that turn strategies into actions and present an essential step in the strategy implementation process. According to Wheelen and Hunger (2012), preparing budgets and implementation procedures should be considered part of strategy implementation. We do not discuss the process of strategy implementation due to space limitations.

The next chapter examines strategic management institutional and instrumental dimensions and specifics in companies committed to sustainable development.

INSTITUTIONAL AND INSTRUMENTAL SPECIFICS IN COMPANIES COMMITTED TO SUSTAINABLE DEVELOPMENT

Institutional Dimension and Specifics

To become a sustainability business, a company's key stakeholders (owners, managers) should adopt a broad understanding of sustainability and put considerable efforts into creating shared value for the company, society, and nature (Dyllick & Muff, 2016; Walls et al., 2021). It is a fundamental condition for the reorientation of a company from "business as usual", which is based on purely economic logic (Dyllick & Muff, 2016), to "a sustainability company", also referred to as "business sustainability" (Bansal & DesJardines, 2014). The institutional dimension of management focuses on finding and determining the optimal structure and organization, required knowledge and competencies, authority, motivation, and personal characteristics of those involved in a company's decision-making process. A particular solution of the institutional dimension of management in a company depends on legislation and many other factors (e.g., legal form, the historical development of a company, industry specifics, a company's size, geographical dispersion, etc.) (Belak et al., 2014).

The institutional dimension is crucial for realizing a company's strategic sustainability orientation due to conflicting findings on the key stakeholders' (pro)active role regarding sustainability concerns. Dyllick and Muff (2016) report the increasing number of executives declaring that their companies' commitment to sustainability has grown in the past and is going to be more critical in the future. On the other hand, some other research findings (Bertini et al., 2021) show a higher probability of getting fired due to poor financial results for CEOs who strive for more sustainable practices than those who do not. Some other research studies show that CEOs of large USA companies do not incorporate sustainability issues in their strategic decisions. The topic of sustainability is addressed only in cases when CEOs are faced with direct pressure (Walls et al., 2021). According to Walls et al. (2021), heroic leaders are required to transform companies into "business beyond usual". As we focused in this chapter on strategic management and incorporating sustainability concerns in strategies and the strategic planning process, we built our investigation and discussion around the institutional dimension of strategic management. We primarily explore the central role of owners and top managers in solving sustainability challenges. Top managers make decisions on strategies and strategic allocation of resources, and there has to be consensus on the side of owners and shareholders in this respect. Other managers, employees, and workers of special departments are also involved in the strategic planning process. They are responsible for providing the required information, data, and forecasts to top managers in all steps of the strategic planning process. Top managers' knowledge and competencies, authority, motivation, and personal traits significantly affect their understanding of a company's challenges in the sustainable economy and crucially impact their attitude and commitment to sustainability (e.g., Miller & Serafeim, 2014). However, we should not underestimate the importance and impact of other staff involved in the strategic planning process. Their knowledge and competencies affect their understanding of a company's challenges in the sustainable economy, impacting their response to these challenges.

Different institutional solutions in companies with (re)orientation towards sustainability are found in the literature and practice. Several companies appointed Chief Sustainability Officers (CSOs) to their top management team as the driving "force" in the processes of formulating and implementing a company's sustainability strategy (Fu et al., 2020). Based on the research, Miller and Serafeim (2014) emphasize the crucial importance of introducing CSO to the top management team. In such a case, CSO has more power and can take care of integrating sustainability and sustainability goals in all decisions, also in decisions on a company's vision and strategies. CSO is a leader of changes necessary to realize a company's sustainability orientation. Fu et al. (2020) found in their research among large USA companies (i.e., S&P 500 firms) that the appointment and work of CSO have positive effects on the number of socially responsible actions of companies which increases while the number of socially irresponsible companies' activities decreases. This relationship becomes even more evident when a company has a sustainability committee. In companies with such a committee, sustainability challenges and sustainable development issues are more frequently discussed among managers. A sustainability committee provides help and support when the topic of sustainability is on the agenda and can positively contribute to the effectiveness of a company's sustainability initiatives. According to Miller and Serafeim (2014), the primary responsibility of a CSO is to take care of the company's realization of the sustainability orientation. They are involved in the formulation and implementation, and control of a sustainability strategy of a company. They follow and analyze business practices in this respect, explore social needs and propose strategies that integrate profitability and sustainable development of a company. Among CSOs' tasks and responsibilities are often stakeholder management, fostering a company's sustainability values and culture, and training employees about sustainable development and sustainability challenges.

The research findings of Miller and Serafeim (2014) show that the role of CSO in a company depends on the stage of progress toward sustainability. In the first stage, only a few companies have a person appointed as CSO or any similar position. In those companies with a CSO position, CSO has a relatively low level of authority. In the following stages, companies develop a CSO position with more authority compared to the first stage. The research findings also show that even companies that do not establish a CSO position have employees actively involved in a company's progress towards sustainability. These employees' titles, roles, and responsibilities vary across companies and stages. The success of CSOs in changing a company at every stage depends on their location, which should be close to the areas essential for implementing sustainability orientation.

As pointed out earlier, knowledge, competencies, authority, motivation, and personal traits of those involved in the strategic planning process, and especially of strategic decision-makers, influence the understanding of challenges a company has to deal with in the sustainable economy and, therefore significantly affect a company's response to these challenges. As pointed out by Hahn et al. (2014), managers should "simultaneously address widely diverging but interconnected concerns for the natural environment, social welfare, and economic prosperity" (p. 463). They are exposed to more information that they can successfully process. Therefore, they seek and select information following the relevance they assign to it based on their cognitive frame. The content of the cognitive frame presents everything that we know, assume, and believe about a particular field. So, through cognitive frames, "managers reduce complexity and ambiguity by selectively organizing and interpreting signals from the organizational context" (Hahn et al., 2014, p. 465). Therefore, several authors emphasize that managers responsible for sustainability (e.g., CSOs) must continuously monitor and learn from good sustainable practices and available external sources. Among their obligations is transferring sustainability knowledge to other managers and employees. The European Commission (European Commission, 2015) also emphasizes that education in general and the knowledge thus acquired is the basis for the development of social values, environmental awareness, innovation skills and capabilities, and other fundamental factors that shape the future of society.

Instrumental Dimension and Specifics

As introduced earlier in the text, the instrumental dimension in the MER model of integral management is about the place and role of values, entrepreneurial and managerial principles, styles, techniques, and methods for successful governance and management of a company, also for strategic management. Values of owners and leaders and the organizational culture, in general, are given special attention as they have a crucial influence on all dimensions and activities of the management process and therefore play an essential role in the company's transformation to a sustainability company.

Values and beliefs significantly influence individuals' sustainability awareness and commitment (Bansal, 2005; Dekker & Hasso, 2016; Roxas & Coetzer, 2012). Values of owners and leaders (CEOs, top managers, and boards of directors) embedded in the organizational culture impact the sustainability considerations in the strategic management process. The prevailing culture may welcome or resist integrating sustainability into a company's strategies (Baumgartner & Rauter, 2017). Stead and Stead

(2000) emphasize that the value system, which is based on sustainability, presents a sound (ethical) basis for the development of ecologically sensitive strategic management, which enables companies to meet the needs of the many "green" stakeholders who represent planet Earth in the business world. The level of sustainability awareness and commitment among owners and leaders, and in a company in general, impacts the definition of goals and formulation of strategies; ambitious sustainability goals and strategies are pursued in organizations with a high level of sustainability awareness and commitment (Baumgartner & Rauter, 2017; Štrukelj et al., 2022; Zdolšek et al., 2022).

An important place in the instrumental dimension has methods and techniques that can be applied in the management process. Companies may apply adapted or specific management methods to address environmental and social issues (e.g., sustainability balanced scorecards and environmental cost accounting) (Baumgartner & Rauter, 2017).

Monitoring, evaluating, and distributing information from the external and the internal environment to key people in a company is recognized as the crucial activity in the identification of opportunities and threats (i.e., external strategic factors) and strengths and weaknesses (i.e., internal strategic factors) in the process of planning the optimal developmental orientation of a company in the future. Identification of strategic factors and strategy formulation is more efficient and effective if we apply a range of methods and techniques of strategic management (Duh, 2018; Duh & Belak, 2014).

In the literature and practice, we find various methods and techniques for scanning a company's external environment and identifying external strategic factors as opportunities and threats (e.g., Duh & Belak, 2014; Wheelen & Hunger, 2012). Often described in the literature and applied in business practice is STEEP analysis (also called PESTEL analysis), whose fundamental purpose is scanning sociocultural, technological, economic, ecological, and political-legal forces. A widely accepted method for an analysis of a company's task environment is Porter's approach to industry analysis which some authors updated in the manner that they add one or more new forces to Porter's original forces, which are: the threat of new entrants, rivalry among existing firms, the threat of substitute products or services, bargaining power of buyers, and bargaining power of suppliers. The main idea behind analysing a company's task environment is that a company should know and understand the intensity of competition within its industry. This intensity level is defined by the previously described five forces (or even more forces in the adapted version of Porter's approach). A company has to explore and assess the importance of each of these forces for its success. The stronger these forces are, the fewer options a company has to raise prices and earn high profits.

Wheelen and Hunger (2012) add the sixth force to the original Porter's industry analysis, which is the relative power of other stakeholders. The power of interest groups that strive for a sustainable economy can significantly influence a company's sustainability commitments and, thus, its competitive position. In this context, we find stakeholder mapping (also called stakeholder analysis) a proper technique when a company considers integrating sustainability into the strategic planning process and strategies. Several authors (e.g., Johnson et al., 2011; Lombriser & Abplanalp, 2005; Müller-Stewens & Lechner, 2005; Stead & Stead, 2000) find this method to be an essential part of the investigation of a company's external environment. Stakeholder mapping helps a company recognize stakeholders' influences and understand their interests and expectations (their "stake") and power. A stakeholder is an individual or a group which can influence the company's decisions and activities and is affected by its activities. A stake of a particular stakeholder can come from the ownership interest, market interest, and/or political interest. A stakeholder's power has its "source" in the stakeholder's ownership rights and economic and/or political impact. The higher the power level, the greater the stakeholder's ability to affect a company's decision-making processes (Stead & Stead, 2000). Central to the stakeholder mapping approach is creating the power/interest matrix in which stakeholders are organized based on their power and the extent of their potential interest in the company's strategies (Johnson et al., 2011; Lombriser & Abplanalp, 2005). The matrix enables managers to recognize the most influential stakeholders in terms of their power and interests, and these are those stakeholders that will have a significant impact on strategic decisions in a company. In the context of sustainable development, Stead and Stead (2000) emphasize the recognition that the planet Earth is a legitimate stakeholder and that such strategic management should be designed to "efficiently and effectively serve the interests of the planet and its green representatives in the immediate business arena" (p. 313).

Among methods for scanning external environment is worth mentioning diverse forecasting techniques such as extrapolation, brainstorming, Delfi techniques, statistical modelling, and scenario writing (Duh, 2018; Duh & Belak, 2014; Müller-Stewens & Lechner, 2005; Wheelen & Hunger, 2012). These techniques are fundamental when identifying developmental trends, opportunities, threats, and risks in a rapidly changing environment. Kashmanian et al. (2011) suggest a scenario technique as one of the essential tools in formulating sustainability strategies. As part of preparing scenarios, managers ask themselves "what-if" questions with the aim of more long-term strategic thinking. Scenarios allow managers to test their assumptions, strategies, and plans. Several different scenarios can be created (e.g., optimistic, pessimistic, realistic) with the help of which managers can simulate different futures, possible challenges, and the company's response to them.

The purpose of scanning a company's internal environment (also called organizational analysis) is to identify internal strategic factors, which are strengths and weaknesses. Especially those internal strategic factors derived from comparisons with the current and potential competition are crucial for formulating the best strategies. Managers have to collect information on the structure, interdependence, and mode of operation of internal forces to assess its strengths (what a company is able and capable of doing) and weaknesses (the state or condition of lacking its strength) that hinder the company from achieving competitive advantages. Several methods and techniques can be supportive of this analytical process. Theory and practices often suggest value chain analysis, internal factors synthesis, resources and competencies analysis, and comparable analysis (Johnson et al., 2011; Lynch, 2009; Wheelen & Hunger, 2012). As emphasized by Müller-Stewens and Lechner (2005), there is no one "objectively correct" way. When selecting an approach and way of conducting organizational analysis, we have to decide on the "corestone" of our analysis. The "corestone" and starting point of organizational analysis can be in (Müller-Stewens & Lechner, 2005; Lombriser & Abplanalp, 2005; Wheelen & Hunger, 2012): resources, capabilities and competencies, and core and distinctive competencies.

Several methods and techniques were developed to conduct situational analysis at the beginning of the strategy formulation process (Duh, 2018; Duh & Belak, 2014; Müller-Stewens & Lechner, 2005; Wheelen & Hunger, 2012). The situational analysis aims to find "a strategic fit" between external opportunities and internal strengths while dealing with external threats and internal weaknesses. An often-applied approach in this process is SWOT analysis. Even though often used, there are several critics of SWOT analysis (e.g., it oversimplifies, generates long lists of factors without a clear focus, the same factor can be listed in two categories, etc.). Therefore, several changes and upgrades have been made to the original SWOT analysis concept. One is the SFAS matrix (i.e., strategic factors analysis summary matrix). The purpose of this matrix is to summarize external and internal strategic factors (Wheelen & Hunger, 2012) by assigning their weights (i.e., based on the factors' probable impact on the company's position) and ratings (i.e., a company's response to these factors). When creating the SFAS matrix, managers should consider the importance of the factor for the company's development performance and the company's ability to manage the factor successfully.

An essential step in the strategic planning process is assessing strategic options and selecting the best strategy. Among methods that can be applied in this process, we often find life cycle analysis, decision trees, financial analysis, and sensitivity analysis (e.g., Duh & Belak, 2014; Johnson et al., 2011). Quantitative and qualitative selection criteria can be applied when deciding on the best strategy. The (re)orientation of a company toward sustainability company requires adapting a combination of quantitative (e.g., profitability criteria) and qualitative criteria, with more substantial consideration of qualitative criteria. For example, decision-makers should consider whether the proposed strategy adequately responds to sustainability challenges and creates long-term benefits for shareholders and other company stakeholders.

The next chapter shows the model of interdependence of strategic management dimensions and sustainability for maintaining competitive advantage, emphasising the necessary consideration and integration of sustainability into all three dimensions of strategic management (process, institutional and instrumental dimension).

THE MODEL OF INTERDEPENDENCE OF STRATEGIC MANAGEMENT DIMENSIONS AND SUSTAINABILITY

Due to continuous changes in the business environment, companies must take care of such business (e) processes (governance, management, operations – implementation of the basic realization process) that will consider the need for sustainable development. This consideration should reflect on the company's and economies' needs and the needs of society and the environment (Štrukelj et al., 2020; Veršič et al., 2022).

The company's competitiveness became the key to explaining its success. Breakthrough insights in this area were pioneered by Porter (1980; 1985), who developed (1) the concept of business (competitive) strategy (operating either in a broad market or in a narrow (niche) market in a way that highlights either differentiation or low company costs), (2) an approach to industry analysis based on five competitive forces (mentioned earlier in the text), and (3) highlighted the importance of competitive advantage. All of Porter's concepts need to be upgraded in today's complex and unpredictable modern business environment. For companies to be resilient, they need to incorporate sustainability and sustainable development (see Section 3), which must be understood through the prism of strategic management and strategic planning processes (see Section 4). In the current business world, sustainability has become the only way to achieve a permanent competitive advantage for the company, as the wider society increasingly demands the sustainable orientation of the company. Companies must include sustainable aspects to achieve their competitive advantage, such as in the proposed sustainability strategy.

Moreover, that is why not only technological but also non-technological inventions and innovations have become a constant process of every company for its credibility and permanent, long-term business success achieving (Hahn & Tampe, 2021; Štrukelj et al., 2019; 2020; 2021; 2022; Zdolšek et al., 2022). The proposed model of interdependence of strategic management dimensions and sustainability incorporated these recognitions. It was developed to boost company competitiveness through the prism of sustainability (Figure 3). By following the developed recommendations of incorporating sustainability into vision, mission, purposes, primary goals, strategies, whole development, and business practice, owners and (top) managers of companies will be more successful in shaping the future of their

Figure 3. The proposed model of interdependence of strategic management dimensions and sustainability for maintaining competitive advantage

Unknown, known, ignored, and known, considered requirements of the environment about the sustainability of a company (including Porter's five competitive forces requirements)			
↓ Impact on a company			
Hierarchy of management process (including governance)	Incorporation of sustainability into all dimensions of strategic management		
	Process dimension	Institutional dimension	Instrumental dimension
Awareness and commitment to sustainability (normative political level) = preconditions for incorporation of sustainability in strategic management.	Fundamental reorientation to a sustainability company – conception, design, and selection of sustainability vision, mission, purposes, and primary goals.	Sustainability awareness and commitment of owners and shareholders.	Sustainability values, beliefs, and organizational culture.
↓ Preconditions for			
Strategic (re)orientation toward sustainability (strategic management level)	Searching for (strategic) development options and formulation of sustainability corporate and business strategies, structures, and implementation program.	Sustainability awareness and commitment of top managers, the role of chief sustainability officer (CSO).	Tools and methods for considering sustainability challenges in the strategic management process.
↓ The impact/cause of			
Gaining and maintaining competitive advantage via strategic flexibility and sustainability, and reorientation and transformation to a sustainability company.			

company through proactive, sustainability-oriented behaviour. Namely, we recognize the studied topic of incorporating sustainability into strategic management for a company's competitive advantages (the requisite holism of process, institutional and instrumental dimensions) as an important way of building strategic flexibility. Consequently, the company builds a competitive advantage, which is necessary for the survival and development of a company in the contemporary business environment.

Figure 3 illustrates the model in which consideration and integration of sustainability into all three dimensions of strategic management (process, institutional and instrumental) are presented. The model emphasizes the importance of defining a sustainability vision, mission, purposes, and primary goals as the precondition for formulating sustainability strategies. Sustainability values, beliefs, organizational culture, and sustainability awareness and commitment of a company's key stakeholders (owners, shareholders, managers) have an essential role in the company's reorientation towards sustainability. Environmental demands and requirements regarding companies' sustainability (including (and considering) Porter's five defined competitive forces) fundamentally impact companies' strategic management in all dimensions. In the process dimension, the incorporation of sustainability concerns in the strategic management process is addressed; more attention is given to the strategic planning process and sustainability strategies, among which a corporate and a business (competitive) strategy are considered. We believe that incorporating sustainability into the strategic planning process is a crucial element of the required changes for re-orientating a company from business as usual to a sustainability company. The model clearly shows the interdependencies between a company's sustainability orientation, process dimension, institutional solutions, and instrumental specifics and recommends potential adaptation of strategic management. The model shows the interdependence of strategic management dimensions and sustainability, illustrating the requisite holism of process, institutional and instrumental dimensions of sustainability in strategic management and the impact of sustainability efforts on maintaining the company's competitive advantage.

CONCLUSION

Sustainable development "requires" economic, environmental, and social development that allows the present and future generations to fulfil their needs. Companies play an essential role in the transition of societies towards sustainability as the final goal of sustainable development, that is, the state where principles of sustainable development have been accomplished.

Companies must incorporate sustainability into all dimensions of strategic management, that is, in the process, institutional and instrumental dimensions, to gain and maintain competitive advantage. A requisite precondition for that is sustainability awareness and commitment of the company's key stakeholders, sustainability organizational culture, and predefined sustainability vision, mission, purposes, and primary goals. In discussing the necessary strategic shift of companies from a business as usual to a sustainability company, we focus on sustainability strategies that must incorporate economic, societal, and environmental aspects. We emphasize that sustainability strategies should not be considered as a particular subgroup of a company's strategies. A company must address sustainability challenges in its corporate and business strategies. Understanding sustainability strategies demands that sustainability is embedded in all steps of the strategic planning process, which should be "supported" by competent and motivated managers and an adequate instrumental system. Integrating sustainability into the strategic planning process is vital for gaining and maintaining the company's competitive advantage and re-orientating and transforming into a sustainability company. The proposed model illustrates the requisite holism of process, institutional and instrumental dimensions of strategic management, and the interdependence between the company's sustainability orientation (vision, mission, purposes, primary goals, and strategies), institutional solutions (such as, for example, the inclusion of CSO in top management team) and instrumental specificities (importance of sustainability values, beliefs, organizational culture, and strategic planning tools and methods).

This chapter's contribution is based on both a scientific and a practical-professional basis. From a scientific point of view, we explained the integral concept of governance and management of the company, with a focus on strategic management. We also considered all three necessary aspects for requisite holism: process, institutional and instrumental dimensions. Next, we interdependently built on this research area with other sustainability-related research content. We connected sustainability with the sustainable development of the company. On this basis, we have developed a conceptual model of interdependence of strategic management dimensions and sustainability for maintaining the company's competitive advantage. The developed model uses concept-mapping logic, intended for use in practice, as it explains the relationships and connections between the elements included in it. The illustrative model is intended for direct use in practice. As a result, companies can improve their development and operations, achieve more competitive advantage and maintain it. All this strengthens economic development and brings benefits to society and nature. Based on the conducted research, we also developed several other recommendations for practice. A company's owners and (top) managers should try to influence its industry by systematically building their competitive advantage by integrating sustainability into their development, management, and operations. Many cases of good sustainability practices in companies can serve as guidelines and/or recommendations for all those companies that recognize sustainability as one of their primary goals and are nowadays looking for the best solutions for incorporating sustainability concerns in their "lives". Some of these cases are publicly available as the result of the Erasmus+ project Economics of Sustainability completed in 2022. They can be found in the online book with the same title, "Economics of Sustainability" (https://www.sbc.org.pl/dlibra/publication/614485/edition/578059/content) or in the gamification platform developed (https://econosteam.eu/gamification/).

An essential contribution of this chapter is in its advice for practice, in a way that is useful to (business) strategy creation and organization, which gives top managers additional recommendations on applied strategy making. Namely, when defining (business) strategy, top managers must start from the vision, mission and primary goals, where the general development directions are defined. When the need for company sustainability is included in the mission, top management decision-makers include it in the (business) strategy in such a way as to define through which development and what forms of company differentiation the company will achieve sustainability. These definitions of sustainable development must also be reflected in the company structures (e.g. the organizational structure must show the introduction of the chosen organizational form for the Chief Sustainability Officer, and the personnel structure must show when (in which year) we will hire him). Changes in other structures must also be visible (e.g. the technical-technological structure must show the purchase of new, more sustainable machines or software; maybe the ownership structure will change due to the new sustainable development orientation, etc.). Structures must follow strategies. The concretization of sustainability-oriented development decisions is further reflected through the company's development program, which defines which year it will introduce which aspect of sustainability in which strategic business area and how it will implement it. The development program is then concretized annually into action measures to achieve it.

If companies (1) design more appropriate, i.e., sustainability strategies for the modern, complex, and turbulent global environment and (2) the requirements for sustainability are implemented in the entire management process, they will gain both a competitive advantage and long-term success. Possibly it will also gain permanent financial and non-financial performance improvement. As there is a substantial impact on the public and the entire society demanding the sustainability orientation of companies, incorporating sustainability in management and operation is becoming a means for their success. The owners, therefore, gain both external and internal motivation for their orientation toward sustainability. External motivation results, for example, in a market that recognizes the company's sustainable orientation; therefore, customers buy their products/services, and the company is successful. Internal motivation results, for example, in their awareness that the company is a part of the mosaic of efforts to preserve the planet Earth for future generations.

We have developed some recommendations also for society. Each individual must realize that each of us has a personal responsibility to ensure the conditions for the survival of current and future generations. Our conduct must be responsible, also concerning companies. Suppose each of us demands sustainable business behaviour and buys only from companies that have included sustainability in their development and daily operations processes, their products, their attitude towards employees and other people, and nature. In that case, companies will be forced to embed sustainability into their "DNA". So, each of us and society as a whole must take responsibility for corporate social and environmental responsibility. It is necessary to raise the awareness of all stakeholders.

Additionally, we have developed some recommendations for economic policymakers. As representatives of the authorities, which must ensure the development and well-being of society, they must also be aware of the importance of not only the economic success of companies but also their success in terms of responsibility towards society and nature. Therefore, we suggest that policymakers impose obligations on companies arising from their economic but also social and environmental responsibilities. Appropriate legal regulations, educational systems, and raising awareness about the necessity of sustainable development can significantly contribute to critical changes in human behaviour, including companies.

ACKNOWLEDGEMENT

This work has been financially supported by the Slovenian Research Agency (research core funding No. P5–0023 "Entrepreneurship for Innovative Society" and research core funding No. BI–BA/19–20–001 "Analysis of the impact of using different teaching methods on the development of transversal competencies of students"), and the European Commission Erasmus+ program (grant No. 2019–1-PL01-KA203-065050 "Economics of Sustainability").

REFERENCES

Action Plan. (2008). *Communication from the Commission to the European Parliament, the Council, the European Economic and Social Committee and the Committee of the Regions on the Sustainable Consumption and Production and Sustainable Industrial Policy.* Retrieved October 18, 2021, from https://eur-lex.europa.eu/LexUriServ/LexUriServ.do?uri=COM:2008:0397:FIN:en:PDF

Agenda. (2015). *Transforming our World: The 2030 Agenda for Sustainable Development.* Retrieved March 22, 2023, from https://sdgs.un.org/publications/transforming-our-world-2030-agenda-sustainable-development-17981

Ambrosini, V., & Bowman, C. (2009). What are dynamic capabilities and are they useful construct in strategic management? *International Journal of Management Reviews, 11*(1), 29–49. doi:10.1111/j.1468-2370.2008.00251.x

Baković, Z. (2021). Za začetek pojdimo vsi skupaj v naravo. *Delo, 63*(253), 16.

Bansal, P. (2005). Evolving sustainability: A longitudinal study of corporate sustainable development. *Strategic Management Journal, 26*(3), 197–218. doi:10.1002mj.441

Bansal, P., & DesJardine, M. R. (2014). Business sustainability: It is about time. *Strategic Organization, 12*(1), 70–78. doi:10.1177/1476127013520265

Barreto, I. (2010). Dynamic Capabilities: A Review of Past Research and an Agenda for the Future. *Journal of Management, 36*(1), 256–280. doi:10.1177/0149206309350776

Baumgartner, R. J., & Rauter, R. (2017). Strategic perspectives of corporate sustainability management to develop a sustainable organization. *Journal of Cleaner Production, 140*(Part 1), 81–92.

Belak, J., Belak, J., & Duh, M. (2014). Integral management and governance: basic features of MER model. Saarbrücken: Lambert Academic Publishing.

Belak, J., & Duh, M. (2012). Integral management: Key success factors in the MER model. *Acta Polytechnica Hungarica, 9*(3), 5–26.

Bertini, M., Pineda, J., Petzke, A., & Izaret, J.-M. (2021). Can We Afford Sustainable Business? *MIT Sloan Management Review, 63*(1), 25–33.

Carcano, L. (2013, December). Strategic Management and Sustainability in Luxury Companies. *Journal of Corporate Citizenship, 52*(52), 36–54. doi:10.9774/GLEAF.4700.2013.de.00006

Caroll, A. B. (1991). The Pyramid of Corporate Social Responsibility: Toward the Moral Management of Organizational Stakeholders. *Business Horizons, 34*(4), 39–48. doi:10.1016/0007-6813(91)90005-G

Caroll, A. B. (2004). Managing Ethically with Global Stakeholders: A Present and Future Challenge. *The Academy of Management Perspectives, 18*(2), 114–120. doi:10.5465/ame.2004.13836269

Čater, T. (2011). Teorije osnov konkurenčne prednosti podjetja (Theories of basis of a compnay's competitve advantage). In T. Čater, M. Lahovnik, D. Pučko, & A. Rejc Buhovac (Eds.), Strateški management 2 (Strategic management 2) (pp. 29–58). Ljubljana: Ekonomska fakulteta, Enota za založništvo.

Dekker, J., & Hasso, T. (2016). Environmental Performance Focus in Private Family Firms: The Role of Social Embeddedness. *Journal of Business Ethics, 136*(2), 293–309. doi:10.100710551-014-2516-x

Duh, M., & Belak, J. (2014). The MER Model of integral management and governance: economic crisis and the applicability of management methods and techniques. In M. Duh, & J. Belak (Eds.), *Integral management and governance: empirical findings of MER model* (pp. 113–138). Saarbrücken: Lambert Academic Publishing.

Duh, M. (2018). *Upravljanje podjetja in strateški management [Corporate governance and strategic management]*. GV Založba.

Dyllick, T., & Muff, K. (2016). Clarifying the Meaning of Sustainable Business: Introducing a Typology from Business-as-Usual to True Business Sustainability. *Organization & Environment, 29*(2), 156–174. doi:10.1177/1086026615575176

EC. (2011). *Sustainable development in the European Union 2011: Monitoring report of the EU sustainable development strategy*. Retrieved October 12, 2022, from https://ec.europa.eu/eurostat/documents/3217494/5731705/224-EN-EN.PDF

European Commission. (2015). *2035 Paths Towards a Sustainable EU Economy*. Retrieved October 11, 2022, from https://publications.jrc.ec.europa.eu/repository/handle/JRC96826

Fu, R., Tang, Y., & Chen, G. (2020). Chief sustainability officers and corporate social (Ir) Responsibility. *Strategic Management Journal, 41*(4), 656–680. doi:10.1002mj.3113

Hahn, T., Preuss, L., Pinkse, J., & Figge, F. (2014). Cognitive frames in corporate sustainability: Managerial sensemaking with paradoxical and business case frames. *Academy of Management Review, 39*(4), 463–487. doi:10.5465/amr.2012.0341

Hahn, T., & Tampe, M. (2021). Strategies for regenerative business. *Strategic Organization, 19*(3), 456–477. doi:10.1177/1476127020979228

Hart, S. L., & Dowell, G. (2011). A Natural-Resource-Based View of the Firm: Fifteen Years After. *Journal of Management, 37*(5), 1464–1479. doi:10.1177/0149206310390219

Hungenberg, H. (2001). *Strategisches Management in Unternehmen. Ziele-Porzesse-Verfahren*. Gabler. doi:10.1007/978-3-322-94533-4

Johnson, G., Whittington, R., & Scholes, K. (2011). *Exploring Strategy: Text and Cases*. Prentice Hall, Pearson Education.

Kashmanian, R. M., Wells, R. P., & Keenan, C. (2011, Winter). Corporate Environmental Sustainability Strategy: Key Elements. *Journal of Corporate Citizenship, 2011*(44), 107–130. doi:10.9774/GLEAF.4700.2011.wi.00008

Kiron, D., Unruh, G., Reeves, M., Kruschwitz, N., Rubel, H., & ZumFelde, A. M. (2017, May). Corporate sustainability at a crossroads. Research report. *MIT Sloan Management Review*.

Lombriser, R., & Abplanalp, P. A. (2005). *Strategisches Management*. Versus Verlag.

Lynch, R. (2009). *Strategic Management*. Pearson Education.

Martín-de Castro, G., Delgado-Verde, M., López-Sáez, P., & Navas-López, J. E. (2011). Towards 'An Intellectual Capital-Based View of the Firm': Origins and Nature. *Journal of Business Ethics, 98*(4), 649–662. doi:10.100710551-010-0644-5

Meuer, J., Koelbel, J., & Hoffmann, V. H. (2020). On the Nature of Corporate Sustainability. *Organization & Environment, 33*(3), 319–341. doi:10.1177/1086026619850180

Miller, K. P., & Serafeim, G. (2014). *Chief sustainability officers: who are they and what do they do?* Working paper, Harvard Business School. Retrieved October 19, 2021, from Harvard Business School: https://dash.harvard.edu/bitstream/handle/1/13350441/15-011.pdf?sequence=1&isAllowed=y

Montiel, I., & Delgado-Ceballos, J. (2014). Defining and Measuring Corporate Sustainability: Are We There Yet? *Organization & Environment, 27*(2), 113–139. doi:10.1177/1086026614526413

Müller-Stewens, G., & Lechner, C. (2005). *Strategisches Management*. Schäffer-Poeschel Verlag.

Nonaka, I. (1991). The Knowledge-Creating Company. *Harvard Business Review*, *69*(6), 96–104.

Nonaka, I. (1994). A Dynamic Theory of Organizational Knowledge Creation. *Organization Science*, *5*(1), 14–37. doi:10.1287/orsc.5.1.14

Nonaka, I., & Takeuchi, H. (1995). *The Knowledge Creating Company*. Oxford University Press.

Nonaka, I., Toyama, R., & Konno, N. (2000). SECI, Ba and Leadership: A Unified Model of Dynamic Knowledge Creation. *Long Range Planning*, *33*(1), 5–34. doi:10.1016/S0024-6301(99)00115-6

O'Brien, G. (2018). Corporate Sustainability Officer: Looking for a seat at the table. *Business Ethics, The Magazine of Corporate Responsibility*. Retrieved June 14, 2022, from https://business-ethics.com/2018/01/28/13337-corporate-sustainability-officers-looking-for-a-seat-at-the-table/

Placet, M., Anderson, R., & Fowler, K. M. (2005). Strategies for sustainability. *Research Technology Management*, *48*(5), 32–41. doi:10.1080/08956308.2005.11657336

Porter, M. E. (1980). *Competitive Strategy*. The Free Press.

Porter, M. E. (1985). *Competitive Advantage. Creating and Sustaining Superior Performance*. The Free Press.

Pučko, D. (2003). *Strateško upravljanje* [Strategic management]. Ljubljana: Ekonomska fakulteta.

Roxas, B., & Coetzer, A. (2012). Institutional Environment, Managerial Attitudes and Environmental Sustainability Orientation of Small Firms. *Journal of Business Ethics*, *111*(4), 461–476. doi:10.100710551-012-1211-z

Rüeg-Stürm, J. (2002). *Das Neue St. Galler Management-Modell. Grundkategorien einer integrierte Managementlehre. Der HSG-Ansatz*. Haupt Verlag.

Stead, J. G., & Stead, E. (2000). Eco-Enterprise Strategy: Standing for Sustainability. *Journal of Business Ethics*, *24*(4), 313–329. doi:10.1023/A:1006188725928

Štrukelj, T., Nikolić, J., Zlatanović, D., & Sternad Zabukovšek, S. (2020). A Strategic Model for Sustainable Business Policy Development. *Sustainability (Basel)*, *12*(2), 1–28. doi:10.3390u12020526

Štrukelj, T., Taškar Beloglavec, S., Zdolšek, D., & Jagrič, V. (2022). Financial institutions' governance innovation and credibility strategy. In S. Grima, E. Özen, R. E. Dalli Gonzi (Eds.), Insurance and risk management for disruptions in social, economic and environmental systems: decision and control allocations within new domains of risk (pp. 233–255). Bingley: Emerald. Emerald studies in Finance, Insurance, and Risk Management.

Štrukelj, T., Zlatanović, D., Nikolić, J., & Sternad Zabukovšek, S. (2019). A cyber-systemic learning action approach towards selected students' competencies development. *Kybernetes*, *48*(7), 1516–1533. doi:10.1108/K-09-2018-0517

Štrukelj, T., Zlatanović, D., Nikolić, J., & Sternad Zabukovšek, S. (2021). The viable system model's support to social responsibility. *Kybernetes*, *50*(3), 812–835. doi:10.1108/K-12-2019-0860

Thommen, J.-P. (2004). *Lexikon der Betriebswirtschaft*. Versus Verlag.

Veršič, S., Tominc, P., & Štrukelj, T. (2022). SME Top Management Perception of Environmental Uncertainty and Gender Differences during COVID-19. *Sustainability, 14*(6), 3593 (1–33).

Walls, J. L., Phan, P. H., & Berrone, P. (2011). Measuring Environmental Strategy: Construct Development, Reliability, and Validity. *Business & Society, 50*(1), 71–115. doi:10.1177/0007650310394427

Walls, J. L., Salaiz, A., & Chiu, S.-C. (2021). Wanted: Heroic leaders to drive the transition to "business beyond usual". *Strategic Organization, 19*(3), 494–512. doi:10.1177/1476127020973379

WCED. (1987). *Our Common Future*. Report of the World Commission on Environment and Development. Retrieved October 1, 2021, from https://sustainabledevelopment.un.org/content/documents/5987our-common-future.pdf

Wheelen, T. L., & Hunger, J. D. (2012). *Strategic Management and Business Policy. Toward Global Sustainability*. Pearson Education.

Zdolšek, D., Jagrič, V., Štrukelj, T., & Taškar Beloglavec, S. (2022). The path towards international non-financial reporting framework. In S. Grima, E. Özen, I. Romānova (Eds.), Managing risk and decision making in times of economic distress, part B (pp. 37–60). Bingley: Emerald. doi:10.1108/S1569-37592022000108B032

Chapter 11
Competing Across National Borders

Sinfree Gono
Royal Holloway University of London, UK

ABSTRACT

Firms are epitomised as complex structural variables moulded by their environments, capabilities, and resources. For cross-border firms whose existence is typified by researchers as 'global commons' may no longer be governed by the rule of law but by their degree of geographical spread. These firms leverage their resources, experiences, and capabilities to access global markets beyond the comfort of local environments. This chapter focusses on firms foraying into international markets hence gives us an insight into their attempts at exploiting market power, accessing resources, and overcoming limitations of the home market by developing strategies that overcome the complexities of operating in a foreign market. The existence of institutional variations in these contexts call for a different set of capabilities and strategies that reside outside the firm's repertoire. Any failures by firm managers to understand the complexity of global markets and "raison d'être" of their internationalising will have wider strategic implications.

INTRODUCTION

Throughout history, international business literature has explored firms' willingness to enter markets outside of their traditional domestic safe spaces. Seeking to compete beyond domestic borders is driven by a variety of reasons; accessing new consumers and resources, economies of scale, exploiting of core competencies, and spreading business risk (Thompson et al., 2017). While there may be other reasons (see Landau et al., 2016 on using home country institutions as a leverage for internationalisation), firms (or their respective managers) are eager to know how to develop an integrated key global strategy lever that enhance their participation in an expanding market (Yip, 1989).

Whether a firm is adopting a global, transnational or multidomestic strategy (Parameswar and Dhir, 2016), managers face conflicting pressures on two fronts: local responsiveness vs efficiency gains from the need to globalise operations through standardisation (Thompson et al., 2017). A clear distinction here can be made between the firm and the market with the former signifying an entity whose birth is

DOI: 10.4018/978-1-6684-6845-6.ch011

denominated by geography (i.e., a UK, USA, etc., firm). The later spans the globe hence a 'global market'. For firms, foraying into international markets gives us an insight into their attempts at exploiting market power (i.e., strategising), access resources (Matthews, 2006; 2017) and overcome limitations of the home market (Chang and Pillania, 2010).

To harness competitiveness through superior performance, multinational enterprises (MNEs) have in the past adopted a centralised approach by making use of global strategies (Meyer et al., 2011); derived through complex interdependencies within and between multiple host locations compared to domestic firms that tend to operate in a single, most often protected, home market (Inkpen and Ramaswamy., 2005). The former fits a theoretical description of having "too much structure and too inflexible" (Davis et al., 2009). Notably, these complex market developments are not chance events, accelerations in market changes have been observed since the 1950s leading to global integration (Kobrin, 1991). Global integration has led to the rising prominence of multinational enterprises (MNEs) in the global economy (Dunning and Lundan, 2008). This has and continues to be driven by consumer demands made possible through a proliferation of E-Commerce.

The challenges for MNEs emanate from competition between firms as no longer constrained by national boundaries; the market domain has become dominated by innovative and aggressive competitors from a wide spectrum of global firms (Inkpen and Ramaswamy., 2005). With the eradication of trading barriers, firms increasingly look to compete in a single market, a global market. This has brought increased competition to firms' doorsteps in often difficult to define markets, lacking established rules of contact (Grimm et al., 2006). In pursuit of global competitiveness, several studies have shown that firm strategies are important guidelines for businesses seeking to compete (Graafland, Van de Ven, and Stoffele, 2003; Collis and Rukstad, 2008). Nevertheless, within the state of global business community driven by technology and innovation, existing models of strategy and competitive advantage appear not to address the dynamics of competition synonymised by ebbing and flowing of rivalry in global markets. For this reason, the author proposes that the differences in strategies for firms thriving in and across national boundaries require us to treat organisations as complex adaptive systems requiring agile strategies (Shams et al., 2021). To gain relevant insights into the nature of such firm strategies requires an understanding of divergent and convergent strategic tendencies at the centre of firm's interactions between its resource-based strategic posture[1] and variations in its external/global environment. Thus, this chapter examines the extent to which strategy-making by cross-border firms is often a multifaceted complex process beyond traditional internationalisation underpinnings. The following questions will be answered:

Why competing across national borders makes strategy making more complex? Can specific policies be implemented to guide the executives and the organisation?

LITERATURE REVIEW: STRATEGY, COMPLEXITY, AND POLICY

Strategy as a concept is not new; its origins lean on Chinese military history as articulated by Sun Tzu (McNeilly and McNeilly, 2012) and the strategy and tactics employed by the likes of Napoleon during his wars (Strachan., 2014). Since then, classical theorists have followed with the likes of Mintzberg et al (1998) beginning to use the strategy concept in the context of business and planning. This formed the basis of strategy that has become key for business executives.

Within this perspective, clearly the need to understand the determinants enabling firm managers to formulate a set of complex yet competitively driven strategies is critical. Nevertheless, it is important to remind ourselves that the insights seeking to understand strategic complexity may be confined to a single context where the firm is operating thus not fully reflect the strategy(ies) being pursued by the MNE on a global scale. In this case, the strategy is only a portion of the firm's strategic competitive gamut or strategy toolkits (Steinberg et al., 2020). These strategies may involve entering entirely new markets (Connelly et al., 2017).

Nevertheless, within the context of the firm, the role of strategy is viewed as about "shaping the future")., i.e., attaining desirable ends by using resources that a firm possess (McKeown, 2019). The term 'strategy' has been defined in a variety of forms, harbouring many meanings. It's safe to say it is 'overused, misunderstood, and misinterpreted'. Thompson et al. (2017) defined strategy as "consisting of an overarching direction set by managers, plus the competitive moves and business approaches that they are employing to compete successfully" (see page. 7). Authors such as Rumelt (2011), referred to attempts at defining "strategy" as a "broad guiding policy" being a mistake. The rational for this lies in strategy as being not just "what" you are trying to do, but also "why" and "how (to outcompete rivals)" you are doing it (Rumelt, 2011., Thompson et al., 2017).

THEORETICAL PERSPECTIVES ON FIRM COMPETITIVENESS

In seeking to understand competitiveness in the context of the firm, several attempts have been made in the past to articulate the theory of the firm (Coase, 1937; Penrose, 1959; and Barney, 2001). Penrose (1959) considered MNEs as a natural outcome of the pressures for growth hence our focus on cross-border firms. For this, one such theoretical framework is the Resource-based theory (RBT) which premises firms as "possessing different combinations or levels of strategic resources and capabilities" (Wernerfelt, 1984; Dierickx and Cool, 1989; Barney, 1991). While resources in themselves are important to the firm, the resource-based approach (RBT) fails to capture the essence of cross-border firm strategic complexities. Arguably, the belief in the RBT arises from an incessant historical focus on capabilities-based thinking which emphasises firm heterogeneity in opportunity sets (Teece, 2014).

Similarly, the role played by the eclectic paradigm (or OLI: ownership, location, internalisation) should not be negated. OLI paradigm is viewed as an integrative theoretical perspective of a multinational firm's diverse operational aspects (Dunning., 1977, Dunning and Lundan, 2008). Understanding of its three dimensions such as the 'internationalisation' dimension helps managers deal with the firm's extraterritoriality aspects. These have also been partially explored by Ghemawat's (2001) CAGE framework. Thus, it is relevant in informing managers intending on crafting cross border strategies to take account of a complex global arena.

Looking at Dunning's perspectives on internationalisation, ownership denotes a firms' competitive advantages by virtue of controlling strategic tangible and intangible assets: technology, machinery, physical structure, brand image, management skills, etc. (Dunning, 2001). Ownership-specific effects represented by the 'O' rests on the parent firm's spatially transferable intangible assets (Dunning, 2001). This represents those advantages gained by exploiting its ownership advantages internally by controlling its resources, reducing risk, and increasing its return (Dunning, 1998, 2000). By harnessing process and skills, firms can develop a complex strategy-making 'capability' better than others.

The other dimension of the OLI paradigm (the 'L') focusses on location advantages which despite the borderless nature of contemporary organisational competition remains relevant (see discussion on the importance of location in relation to Amazon, General Electric, Tesla's Giga factories, and Google by Florida and Adler., 2022). This owes its significance to the cluster concept popularised by Porter (1990) and Porter and Kramer (2006) who buttressed the continued relevance of location in competition and strategy, and as a source of the firm's competitive advantage (Porter, 1998; Porter and Kramer, 2019). For this and other reasons, globally, location has become and continues to be a key factor in the strategy equation.

Common among these theoretical perspectives is that they are ownership-based theories of the firm (Dunning and Lundan, 2008). However, in cross-border markets, there exist complex systems at multiple levels aided by interactions of a variety of firms in multiple contexts. Thus, the existence of institutional variations in these contexts call for a different set of capabilities and strategies that reside outside the firm's repertoire (Pisano, 2017). This perspective of strategy making has not received adequate attention, hence the focus of this chapter.

It is only ideal that the author puts cross-border firm complexities into perspective through the complexity theoretical lens (Anderson, 1999). In this perspective, the aim of the author is to expose the considerations that cross-border firm managers may need to do to untangle the complexity of the contexts the firm operates thereby putting themselves and their firms in a position to reasonably predict functional strategies for competitive advantage.

In contrast to the above discussion that premised a longstanding strategic approach in organisation theory on how firm resources and capabilities shape performance in dynamic environments to achieve competitive advantage, dealing with cross-border strategies requires a different approach that encompasses the complex yet nuanced challenges and opportunities. Managers should also pay attention to the foreign context where their firms are situated. This entails looking beyond the firm in crafting their strategies. In re-orienting themselves to new global operating environments, where strategies should be formulated to address rather practical and insightful direction for firms, managers should focus on the dynamics in each operational environment. In this case, understanding of traditional frameworks such as the Diamond of Competitive Advantage that rather espouses the virtues of competitiveness albeit from a country perspective is equally important. This model plays a role in understanding firm behaviour as its proximate environment shapes its competitiveness (Porter, 1990). This model's view of the nation contributes towards a firm managers' understanding of strategies as the set of contextual variables (i.e., factor, demand, related and supportive industries, firm strategy, structure, and rivalry conditions) all influence the competitive ability of firms (Grant, 1991).

COMPLEXITY AND CROSS-BORDER FIRMS

Prior studies on firm internationalisation efforts focussed on traditional forms of cross-border firms. These are regarded as stage models of internationalisation (from export activities to foreign direct investment) and the later structural forms of MNCs (the parent-subsidiary structure, the international division or worldwide product division) (Melin, 1992; Meyer et al., 2020). Unfortunately, these approaches fail to fully capture the complexity and strategy-making process phenomena that ensues modern cross-border organisations (Barney, 1991). In this perspective, you can argue that strategy can be viewed as either rational or incremental (Lindblom, 1959). However, this does not show clear dynamics enabling modern firms to attain competitiveness.

Another perspective presented by Mintzberg and Waters (1982), Mintzberg and McHugh (1985) and Burgelman (1994) views the role of competitive strategy as focussing on the effects of structure on performance, hence, the need for firm executives to attain a balance between "deliberate strategy" (i.e., top-down, and coordinated or constraining) and "emergent strategy" (i.e., bottom-up or less constraining). This brings to play the view by Porter (1980) who portrayed firm managers as analysts, whose strategic analysis equips them with deep knowledge of the environment. To this end, it is reasonable to assume development of firm strategies (or strategic positions) in new international markets as an emergent process as they respond to the challenges and opportunities in the market (Cunha and Cunha, 2006). Using this knowledge allows firms especially in new environments to adopt defensible competitive positions in the market structure (Porter, 1980), supported by the firm's valuable resources, i.e., a resource-based approach (Barney, 1991). Far from the ownership driven strategies and theoretical approaches, complexities faced by cross-border firms requires an understanding that considers the various issues faced by an MNE operating away from its home domain. This requires the use of complexity theory (Anderson, 1999).

COMPLEXITY THEORY

Organisation theory has lent a hand in providing some partial explanations on the behaviour of firms operating in complex cross-border environments. With the evolvement of technology, and firm innovativeness, global supply and value chains have become important mechanisms for competitiveness. The concept of flexibility, agility and supply chain embeddedness are a necessity for firms. Bringing these differing, yet complementary organisational tenets, it is fit that firms be viewed as complex structural variables moulded by their environments, capabilities, and resources. Similarly, firms have been described by Thompson (1967) as 'a set of interdependent parts' (see page 6). This equates to perceptions by Daft (1992, p. 15) who noted complexity with systems or activities within the organisation measured along a three-pronged dimension: Vertical organisational hierarchy, horizontal organisational structure, and complex spatial geographical location. These dimensions can be operationalised as complex systems that need to be dealt with concurrently by the organisation (Scott 1992). However, due to recent technological shifts that led firms towards a distributed or decentralised approach, each operational context is viewed as local by mimicking each firm's response to a given set of inputs rather than a centralised approach anchored on the domestic market axis. Pursuant to this, we view, complexity theory as an ideal framework relevant for cross-border MNEs that are often exposed to external changes that are more demanding than their internal changes (Anderson, 1999).

Clearly from the above discussion, strategy making for cross-border firms will be complex and can be viewed as being placed on the horns of dilemma as multiple embeddedness needs to be forged to blend the unique firm-level-specific advantages to location-specific competitiveness (Inkpen and Ramaswamy., 2005). An ideal strategy in this case is derived from balancing the global forces that require local domestic responsiveness (Meyer et al., 2011). Thus, the interplay between internal as well as contextual factors determine to a huge degree whether a strategy will succeed or fail. For this balance to be achieved, the underlying issues on MNEs and local contexts, need to "be 'externally embedded' within each local context while also being sufficiently 'internally embedded' within the MNE network" to derive global firm benefits (Meyer et al., 2011). Hence, crafting a relevant strategy requires managers to take view of elements that not just draw-in customers, but also allows the firm to attain a competitive edge that sets it apart from its rivals (Thompson et al., 2017).

Some prior studies have focussed much attention on deepening existing capabilities (firm-specific; Teece, 2022) that could be applied in defined and well-bounded domains (Cunha and Cunha, 2006). Others focussed on the location of the firm as espoused by various theories that engender tacit sources of advantage thus choosing one location in lieu of others (Mesquita, 2016). For firms competing across national boundaries, they have to deal with complex environments that need continuous adaptation to ever-evolving sensitivities (Church, 1999). If this is the case, can policies be formulated and implemented in response to these ever-changing and competing contours to avoid what Schumpeter (1934) referred to as creative destruction?

POLICY, STRATEGY, AND COMPETITIVENESS

"Institutions shape behaviour, but it is policy that changes behaviour" (Clegg, 2019). Firm-based and internationalisation theories, strategic (i.e., logic of the firm - Casadesus-Masanell and Ricart, 2010) and competitiveness underpinnings have been explored to a satisfactory depth; however, the field of policy, strategy, and competitiveness lacks a unifying theory. In attempting to explore this realm of cross-border firms, the author conceptualises them in duality; on one hand as entities that are part of a complex and uncontrollable environment (for example impact of political or economic events). On the other hand, they have an ability to influence competition, industry structure, consumers, regulators, etc. such as the likes of Apple, Microsoft, Facebook, and Amazon, hence a need for policy to encourage a level playing field. This is even more challenging for strategy where other firms' motive for cross-border activities is in line with national economic development policy not firm strategies (for example, the case of Chinese state-owned enterprises) (Wang et al., 2009). This forms the bedrock of the need to set policy as a guiding tool.

In the context of organisations, Lundan (2018) defined policy as referring to "*a change intentionally instigated by government to have an action upon the decision making and behaviour of firms within the international business domain*". Hence, its importance in the conception of strategy. One of the key perspectives in strategy is that through competitive actions firms attain a favourable market position. To sustain this position, firms attempt to "create, transfer, recombine, and exploit resources across multiple contexts" (Meyer et al., 2011); to match internal strengths with external opportunities, in a manner that complements the firm's strategies. This is the role of executives operating in a context governed by policies, in most instances quite different from their domestic countries.

Our view posits that, managers/strategists should consider the dynamics faced by their cross-border firms and that to be competitive they should place some capital on the complexities surrounding global markets whose existence in some contexts is not guided by rules. This points towards the use of rules or policies to enable firms to capture unpredictable opportunities. These markets may be synonymised with institutional voids that make decision making complex (Khanna and Palepu, 2013). Thus, like environmental sensing tools that provide firms with some strategic insights in new markets, our discussion contributes towards sharpening complexity theory (Andersen, 1999). In this perspective, this theory allows firms to attain benefits of formulating strategies that allow MNEs to exploit contextual opportunities in a wide array of markets. Thus our focus on the influence that government policies may have on the MNE and related but specific to firms, competition policies.

GOVERNMENT POLICIES

"Death and taxes are inexorable facts of existence. So is regulation" (Buckley, 2022). For both home and cross-border firms, governments can directly or indirectly influence the competitive arena of firms through investments in education, training, and infrastructure, among other factors not forgetting fiscal measures. Governments have also been known to contribute towards research and development (R&D) with some departments such as defence having the ability to produce viable commercial spin-offs (Grant, 1991). These investments in R&D stimulates innovation within the country.

Compared to open markets, conscious government policies encourage investment and economies of learning and scale (Johnson and Lundvall, 1994). Inevitably by stimulating investment, training, etc., the government's policies act towards stimulating competitive advantage through improvements to the four corners of Porter's (1990) national diamond framework. Additionally, firm strategies are further complicated when governments in foreign countries pursue economic nationalism (i.e., protective, and subsidised trade policies) and other restrictive policies that seek to protect domestic firms (Levitt, 1984).

The key issue to remember is whether incentive policy can work on the premise of encouraging changes in the locational behaviour of firms. It may be perceived as a waste of effort if government support is not targeted leading subsidising decisions that firms may have made already. These incentives may be political in nature hence may compromise strategic efficiencies by firms, creating a winner's curse (Patrick, 2016). Regardless, it is difficult to know the value of incentives [if any] to firms in the long term.

COMPETITION: ANTITRUST POLICY AND REGULATION OF COMPETITION

Markets globally are dominated by MNEs with consumers unable to separate domestic and international products due to the ubiquitous nature of consumption. In some contexts, international competition entails domestic monopolies created by mergers, and acquisitions are ineffective in creating and exercising market power (Grantt, 1991). This is the case in contexts such as the European Union (EU) where firms such as Google, Microsoft, etc. have received huge fines accused of having gone against the principles of fair competition (Financial Times, 2022). These nuanced and context specific challenges require that firm managers construct policy impact in formulating strategies. Though these policies could be viewed by huge firms as a curse, they may present firm strategies with a web of opportunity as they seek to recognise and build-in new realities in their strategic approaches in these new cross-border contexts. MNEs and their managers should instead seek these opportunities by developing new organisational responses, such as multi-domestic structures and cartelisation, to mitigate risk and capitalise on growth (Buckley, 2022).

The author notes the need for policy to guide strategy as relevant for firms operating in institutionally complex environments with a need for a wide variety of markets and product demands such as technical, manufacturing, regulatory, marketing, competition, etc. to capture an opportunity (Davis et al., 2009). This is more important as having some policy guidance for firms and their managers allows mitigation of divergent strategic errors simply by using policies/rules to guide the capture of opportunities especially in dynamic markets (Bingham, Eisenhardt and Furr, 2007).

The above discussion has clearly shown that firms operating across-borders denote presence in a wide array of countries, markets, and institutions, each of which has its own policies the list, and length of which differs from context to context. Inevitably, different policy frameworks will have huge implications for firm strategy(ies). This is not easy as cross-border firms face challenges of "institutional duality" arising out of operating across contexts with different national institutional frameworks (Holm, Decreton, Nell, and Klopf, 2017, Meyer and Li, 2022). Tied to this is the additional burden arising from home country institutional pressures stretching beyond national boundaries such as those faced by some Sub-Saharan and Chinese MNEs where respective governments involve themselves in matters concerning businesses. This, on occasion creates possible conflicts with pressures faced in the home market (Meyer and Thein, 2014; Stevens, Xie, and Peng, 2016). This may be compounded by the firm's home-country culture constituting a firm's administrative heritage (Bartlett and Ghoshal., 2002). While it may be difficult if not impossible to fully grasp global policy issues in each context, strategies may be formulated considering how each individual firm through their managers respond to market pressures (Buckley, 2022). Furthermore, to have a meaningful global strategy, firms or their managers must negotiate state policies which in most instances conflict across national boundaries and increase market and competitive pressures. Such is the nature of the global competition that MNEs encounter.

COMPETING IN THE AGE OF NO BORDERS

This chapter present some of the strategic complexities faced by cross-border firms. Teece (2022) viewed these firms as "border-spanning actors that are occasionally drafted as agents of state policy" as they face a more complicated future mainly because "what is strategic changes over time". This is compared to previous decades where firms could separate markets into domestic, regional, and international (Grimm et al., 2005). These decades' competitive realities demanded not only efficiency and high quality, but also fast cycle capability (Senge, 1990; Ulrich and Lake, 1990; Chakravarthy and Doz, 1992). Post this period, we saw a huge reduction in trade barriers allowing countries to trade hence competition between firms beyond national boundaries becoming increasingly prevalent and global.

Evidently, by the 2000's, advances in globalisation had taken hold with national/international distinctions eliminated (Teece, 2022). Though this presented an opportunity for domestic firms to explore beyond borders, inadvertently exposed firms to stiff competition in home-country markets. In operating in such marketing systems, strategy(ists) could view context as place-neutral apart from the likes of China and other emerging markets where institutional voids remain problematic.

New complex business dynamics not only demand efficiencies and capabilities (Stalk and Hout, 1990), and strategic flexibility (Womack, Jones, and Roos, 1990), but strategies that render old advantages obsolete by creating and sustaining competitive advantages to shield firms from losing their positions to competitors. This is in the knowledge that with time any firm competitive advantage will eventually be eroded (Ferrier et al., 1999); viewed by Schumpeter (1934) as the "a perennial gale of destructive advantage". Currently, with an ever-changing environmental context that is global in nature, firm strategy should be conceptualised as a critical firm process (Hammer and Champy, 1993). This will allow firms to respond not only to complex organisational needs and opportunities but also challenging and complex operating environment where the firm resides.

MANAGING COMPLEXITY OF MNES: A DISCUSSION IN CONTEXT

The focus of our discussion is on firm strategy with the lenses of complexity theory (Andersen, 1999) and that of complexity theory of strategy (Davis and Eisenhardt, 2005). Noting the premise of RBV (Barney, 2011) and the capabilities literature (Wernerfelt, 1984); the main thrust of our position is that contrary to traditional firms in the last few decades, the proliferation of technology, innovativeness and globalisation has had a huge implication on competitiveness for firms. To respond to these changes, organisations are continuously co-evolving to suit their environments in ways that diverge from classical paradigms and converge with the concepts best explained by the complexity theory which describe organisations as *"complex adaptive systems, ... that are sensitive to their environments"* (Cunha and Cunha, 2006) and *agile* (Shams et al., 2021).

Since the early conceptualisations of strategy as a concept, large organisations largely adopted a multidivisional form (M-form) structure delineated by both divisional and geographical forms (Hoskisson et al., 1994). The advent of technology and innovation driven environments has since witnessed new organisational forms which have evolved into large and complex entities (Inkpen and Ramaswamy, 2005). The internationalisation of firms as explained by Porter's (1990) Diamond model of competitive advantage demonstrates why some industries denominated in some nations are competitive when others might not (i.e., this gives us a single dimension perspective). Instead, firms may have to rely on what Teece (2020) referred to as the modified "double diamond" or "dual foundations" framework that reflects the influence of both home and host-country economies (Teece, 2022). Similarly, the location-premise popularised by Dunning (2008) continue to play a significant role in certain sectors such as manufacturing, as such location choices may continue to shape the firm's international footprint and geographic dispersion (Kafouros et al., 2022).

The desire and need to compete across national borders has exposed the conflicting location and integration pressures faced by global firms. Regardless of location advantages [or not], contemporary evidence clearly shows the need to accept that competition is more complex and evolves at speeds not experienced in the last few decades. This very aspect of location and strategy has driven the need to consider strategy complexity and the context of cross border firms. Consideration should also be paid to the importance of global supply and value chains, and in part driven by outsourcing of production supporting the growth of multinational corporations (Catterneo et al., 2010). This perception contributes to explaining the shift from a classic industrial system to a knowledge-based economy as all factors impact the competitiveness of a location hence strategy a firm may adopt. For this reason, we assert that such nuanced approaches to a firm's internationalisation efforts may change some of the fundamental dimensions upon which managers make complex strategic decisions.

BEYOND LOCATION

The author has considered strategies that are embedded in firm-centric capabilities (Ryan et al., 2012); and rely on the transfer of knowledge (O'Reilly et al., 2019) as benchmarks for best practices in creating new strategies geared for complex global competitiveness. Relying on approaches such as those formulated by Ghemawat (2001) that mainly premised competitiveness derived from distance, firm-centric resources (Barney, 2001) and location (Dunning, 2008), is not enough. Consideration that firm managers need to adopt new ways to harness global opportunities away from their domestic comfortable environments should be embraced. To do this they need to move away from strategies premised on MNE hierarchy and geocentric structure (Ghemawat, 2001; Hedlund, 2017). Reflecting on the main differences between these approaches, there is a tension between exploiting home generated competitive advantages and actively seeking advantages situated in the global spread of the firm (Hedlund, 2017). This presents complex choices that firms face when developing strategies of what they should do in-house versus what they should outsource (Mithas et al., 2014). The challenge for managers is formulating strategies that not only exploit internal firm resources but also tap into the opportunities in the global external environment of the firm. Bourgeois and Brodwin (1984) view this tension as representing the role played by firm strategies as that of the 'commander' [i.e., top-down approach] to that of the 'sponsor' where strategy emerges from bottom upwards which often requires approval by the top (Mintzberg, 1978).

The discussion above clearly demonstrated that it is possible for firms to find an optimal tension in aspects of their global business strategy and formulate strategies that seek to exploit resources that are within the firm (Barney, 2001), and the flexible exploration of new and distant resources that are external to the firm (Karim and Mitchell, 2000; Katila and Ahuja, 2002). This to a huge degree will neutralise complexities around strategy making. This perception marks a huge departure from observations by Inkpen and Rwamasamy (2005) who viewed the fundamentals of the strategy and organising processes of firms as invariant across both domestic and global firms. In this global arena, the industry environment of a firm bears a lot of influence on the degree to which strategic objectives converge or diverge from desired firm strategy. For this reason, the holds the view that to manage global firms, managers need to continually be adaptive.

From a conceptual perspective, a notable shift from a "classic industrial system to a knowledge-based economy" is here for us to see (Barton et al., 2017). Dunning (2014) talks of a gradual movement towards a world dominated by intellectual capital. The global arena is dominated by MNEs, and their connected global supply chains. Considering the competitiveness of a location premised by Dunning (2014) as one of the 'fundamental dimensions upon which firms make strategy decisions', MNE managers need to embrace and formulate strategies that address firm complexities beyond advantages that location offered.

IMPLICATIONS FOR MNES AND THEIR MANAGERS

There exists a lot of studies that have explored cross-border firm activities (Teece, 2022), cross-border strategy (Cunha and Cunha, 2006) and complexity (Andersen, 1999). What is common among these firms is that they are all contextually bound by laws existing within each context. What is different about the nature of these cross-border firms is their existence in what researchers may term the 'global commons" no longer governed by the rule of law (Jannace and Tiffany, 2019). Instead, they pander to masters located from their home countries such as China, Russia, etc. who seek to derive geopolitical and economic advantage from their home governments. Such type of cooperation of MNEs and governments has not been researched adequately in the context of strategy. This reflects firm-to-government competition hence the need for firm managers to not only prioritise global market environment but also the geo-politics existing in respective countries they operate.

THEORETICAL IMPLICATIONS

Over the last few decades, trade restrictions between and among countries have been gradually relaxed making it difficult to reconcile the classic approaches towards strategy formulation premised by location theorists. The increasing presence of MNEs whose cross-border activities have led to a shift in the internationalisation paradigm of firms could benefit from the adoption of a new framework that encompass strategic complexity and disruptions in global geopolitics. Considering that in formulating competitive strategies, firms must choose which actions they can (or can't) take, combine and re-combine to buttress the firm's competitive repertoire. This calls for the relevance of existing cross-border theories to be re-evaluated, and new ones devised encompassing geo-political contexts (Teece, 2022). This approach challenges singular approaches to seeking firm competitiveness as denoted by the efficiency-based theories of International Business and strategic management, dynamic capabilities (Teece and Pisano, 2003; Teece, 2014), and Dunning's (1980) eclectic paradigm for relevance.

This position is broadly in line with prior views that called into question the adequacy of many other theoretical frameworks: Resource-based theory (Beamish and Chakravarty, 2021), and Rugman's (1981) framework of firm-specific and country-specific advantages which should encompass the fusion of "firm" and "country" in the case of China. These frameworks if reformulated will take account of the dynamic nature of required strategies that advance and sustain competitive advantage in both domestic/local and cross-border markets.

CONCLUSION

It is without doubt that organisations have evolved from simply horizontal or vertically aligned institutions to more complex and adaptive systems that thrive in different environments. What has become clear is an increasing global consumer has attracted multinationals (MNEs) across many borders thereby challenging the notion of organisational size as being limited by geography or just a description of a global-few firms. This inevitably is exacerbated by mergers and acquisitions, firm re-organisations, etc. with limitless possibilities contributing towards MNE complexity.

Looking into the future, it may be a better strategy to simply not rely on the strength of the value-chain activities (such as giants Unilever and Nestlé), that thrive on achieving economies of scale without serving all customers across all product segments. Instead, firm value should be a product of developing tighter networks that deliver a seamless global strategy catering for a broad consumer segment as if they exist in a singular context.

In the world of global business, achieving economies of scale and scope may not necessarily be better, hence any attempt to develop specific policies to assist executives lays itself to a futile exercise. For this reason, Rumelt (2011) who conceptualised strategy as not just "what" other managers have attempted to do but as to "why" and "how" it's done (see work by Pascale., 1999) may be right. This approach to strategising in a global context clearly aligns to the complexity theory of strategy as a relevant theoretical approach of strategy use in cross-border firms.

As organisations continue to span the globe to fulfil the needs of evolving consumers, equally strategic pressures increase with each additional market. Clearly, the discussion has shown that MNEs in their traditional divisional form largely dominant in domestic markets, must give way to modern complex structures that are continually adaptive, agile, and responsive to increasing complexity and scope of the operating environment.

The ever-straining geopolitical relationships between countries are beginning to slacken the foundations of globalisation of cross-border MNEs making it difficult for managers to articulate relevant strategies. For this reason, it may be naive to think there is one, if not more right strategy to adopt. In the absence of naivety, the authors are clearly aware that not all MNEs or firms for that matter succeed in all contexts. Where one firm fails, others may do well depending on a range of variables such as capabilities, resources, cultures of both the organisation and the context. Though there is no satisfactory contingent answer to what constitutes a 'good' strategy, global strategies of firms must reflect replicable capabilities, resources, innovations, etc., and non-replicable advantages that may be imbedded in the firm's ability to be flexible, adapt or situated in the culture within the context of the firm's location.

Any failures by firm managers to understand the complexity of global markets and the raison d'être of their internationalising will have wider strategic implications. Their choices may contribute to the decline of firm competitiveness in various global contexts and importantly in home countries in which their strength is based, a factor highlighted by the dual foundations' framework (Teece, 2020; 2022). In conclusion, an ideal strategy is one that co-evolves with the dramatic changes in the global economy, so that a plausible competitive advantage in the age of complexity may be sustained.

REFERENCES

Barney, J. (1991). Firm resources and sustained competitive advantage. *Journal of Management, 17*(1), 99–120. doi:10.1177/014920639101700108

Bartlett, C. A., & Ghoshal, S. (2002). *Managing across borders: The transnational solution*. Harvard Business Press.

Beamish, P. W., & Chakravarty, D. (2021). Using the resource-based view in multinational enterprise research. *Journal of Management, 47*(7), 1861–1877. doi:10.1177/0149206321995575

Billy, R. T. (2022). *The Winning Link: A Proven Process to Define, Align, and Execute Strategy at Every Level*. McGraw-Hill.

Bingham, C. B., Eisenhardt, K. M., & Furr, N. R. (2007). What makes a process a capability? Heuristics, strategy, and effective capture of opportunities. *Strategic Entrepreneurship Journal, 1*(1-2), 27–47. doi:10.1002ej.1

Buckley, P. J. (2022). Navigating three vectors of power: Global strategy in a world of intense competition, aggressive nation states, and antagonistic civil society. *Global Strategy Journal, 12*(3), 543–554. doi:10.1002/gsj.1444

Casadesus-Masanell, R., & Ricart, J. E. (2010). From strategy to business models and onto tactics. *Long Range Planning, 43*(2-3), 195–215. doi:10.1016/j.lrp.2010.01.004

Cattaneo, O., Gereffi, G., & Staritz, C. (Eds.). (2010). *Global value chains in a postcrisis world: a development perspective*. World Bank Publications. doi:10.1596/978-0-8213-8499-2

Chang, J., & Pillania, R. K. (2010). Internationalisation and global competitive advantage: Implications for Asian emerging market multinational enterprises. *International Journal of Business Environment*, *3*(4), 372–392. doi:10.1504/IJBE.2010.037597

Church, M. (1999). Organizing simply for complexity: Beyond metaphor towards theory. *Long Range Planning*, *32*(4), 425–440.

Clegg, J. (2019). From the editor: International business policy: What it is, and what it is not. Journal of International Business Policy, 2(2), 111-118.

Coase, R. H. (1995). The nature of the firm. In *Essential readings in economics* (pp. 37–54). Palgrave. doi:10.1007/978-1-349-24002-9_3

Connelly, B. L., Tihanyi, L., Ketchen, D. J. Jr, Carnes, C. M., & Ferrier, W. J. (2017). Competitive repertoire complexity: Governance antecedents and performance outcomes. *Strategic Management Journal*, *38*(5), 1151–1173. doi:10.1002mj.2541

Cunha, M. P., & Da Cunha, J. V. (2006). Towards a complexity theory of strategy. *Management Decision*.

Davis, J. A. S. O. N., & Eisenhardt, K. M. (2005). *Complexity, market dynamism, and the strategy of simple rules*. Working paper, Stanford University.

Davis, J. P., Eisenhardt, K. M., & Bingham, C. B. (2009). Optimal structure, market dynamism, and the strategy of simple rules. *Administrative Science Quarterly*, *54*(3), 413–452. doi:10.2189/asqu.2009.54.3.413

Dierickx, I., & Cool, K. (1989). Asset stock accumulation and sustainability of competitive advantage. *Management Science*, *35*(12), 1504–1511. doi:10.1287/mnsc.35.12.1504

Dunning, J. H. (2001). The eclectic (OLI) paradigm of international production: Past, present and future. *International Journal of the Economics of Business*, *8*(2), 173–190. doi:10.1080/13571510110051441

Dunning, J. H. (2014). Location and the multinational enterprise: a neglected factor? In *Location of international business activities* (pp. 35–62). Palgrave Macmillan. doi:10.1057/9781137472311_3

Dunning, J. H., & Lundan, S. M. (2008). Institutions and the OLI paradigm of the multinational enterprise. *Asia Pacific Journal of Management*, *25*(4), 573–593. doi:10.100710490-007-9074-z

Ferrier, W. J., Smith, K. G., & Grimm, C. M. (1999). The role of competitive action in market share erosion and industry dethronement: A study of industry leaders and challengers. *Academy of Management Journal*, *42*(4), 372–388. doi:10.2307/257009

Financial Times. (2022). *Google loses appeal against record EU antitrust fine*. Author.

Florida, R., & Adler, P. (2022). Locational strategy: Understanding location in economic geography and corporate strategy. *Global Strategy Journal*, *12*(3), 472–487. doi:10.1002/gsj.1456

Ghemawat, P. (2001). Distance still matters. *Harvard Business Review*, *79*(8), 137–147. PMID:11550630

Grant, R. M. (1991). Porter's 'competitive advantage of nations': An assessment. *Strategic Management Journal*, *12*(7), 535–548. doi:10.1002mj.4250120706

Grimm, C. M., Lee, H., Smith, K. G., & Smith, K. G. (Eds.). (2006). *Strategy as action: Competitive dynamics and competitive advantage*. Oxford University Press on Demand.

Hedlund, G. (2017). The Hypermodern MNC—A Heterarchy? In International Business (pp. 379-399). Routledge.

Holm, A. E., Decreton, B., Nell, P. C., & Klopf, P. (2017). The dynamic response process to conflicting institutional demands in MNC subsidiaries: An inductive study in the sub-Saharan African e-commerce sector. *Global Strategy Journal, 7*(1), 104–124. doi:10.1002/gsj.1145

Hoskisson, R. E., Hoskisson, R. E., Hitt, M. A., & Paul, M. (1994). *Downscoping: How to tame the diversified firm*. Oxford University Press on Demand.

Inkpen, A., & Ramaswamy, K. (2005). *Global strategy: creating and sustaining advantage across borders*. Oxford University Press. doi:10.1093/acprof:oso/9780195167207.001.0001

Jannace, W., & Tiffany, P. (2018). A new world order: The rule of law, or the law of rulers. *Fordham Int'l LJ, 42*, 1379.

Kafouros, M., Cavusgil, S. T., Devinney, T. M., Ganotakis, P., & Fainshmidt, S. (2022). Cycles of de-internationalization and re-internationalization: Towards an integrative framework. *Journal of World Business, 57*(1), 101257. doi:10.1016/j.jwb.2021.101257

Kobrin, S. J. (1991). An empirical analysis of the determinants of global integration. *Strategic Management Journal, 12*(S1), 17–31. doi:10.1002mj.4250120904

Landau, C., Karna, A., Richter, A., & Uhlenbruck, K. (2016). Institutional leverage capability: Creating and using institutional advantages for internationalization. *Global Strategy Journal, 6*(1), 50–68. doi:10.1002/gsj.1108

Mathews, J. A. (2006). Dragon multinationals: New players in 21st century globalization. *Asia Pacific Journal of Management, 23*(1), 5–27. doi:10.100710490-006-6113-0

Mathews, J. A. (2017). Dragon multinationals powered by linkage, leverage and learning: A review and development. *Asia Pacific Journal of Management, 34*(4), 769–775. doi:10.100710490-017-9543-y

Mckeown, M. (2019). The strategy book. Academic Press.

McNeilly, M., & McNeilly, M. R. (2012). *Sun Tzu and the art of business: Six strategic principles for managers*. OUP USA.

Melin, L. (1992). Internationalization as a strategy process. *Strategic Management Journal, 13*(S2), 99–118. doi:10.1002mj.4250130908

Mesquita, L. F. (2016). Location and the global advantage of firms. *Global Strategy Journal, 6*(1), 3–12. doi:10.1002/gsj.1107

Meyer, K. E., & Li, C. (2022). The MNE and its subsidiaries at times of global disruptions: An international relations perspective. *Global Strategy Journal, 12*(3), 555–577. doi:10.1002/gsj.1436

Meyer, K. E., Li, C., & Schotter, A. P. (2020). Managing the MNE subsidiary: Advancing a multi-level and dynamic research agenda. *Journal of International Business Studies, 51*(4), 538–576. doi:10.105741267-020-00318-w

Meyer, K. E., & Thein, H. H. (2014). Business under adverse home country institutions: The case of international sanctions against Myanmar. *Journal of World Business, 49*(1), 156–171. doi:10.1016/j.jwb.2013.04.005

Mintzberg, H. (1998). Covert leadership: Notes on managing professionals. *Harvard Business Review, 76*, 140–148. PMID:10187244

Mithas, S., Tafti, A., & Mitchell, W. (2013). How a firm's competitive environment and digital strategic posture influence digital business strategy. *Management Information Systems Quarterly, 37*(2), 511–536. doi:10.25300/MISQ/2013/37.2.09

O'Reilly, N. M., Robbins, P., & Scanlan, J. (2019). Dynamic capabilities and the entrepreneurial university: A perspective on the knowledge transfer capabilities of universities. *Journal of Small Business and Entrepreneurship, 31*(3), 243–263. doi:10.1080/08276331.2018.1490510

Parameswar, N., Dhir, S., & Sushil. (2020). Interpretive ranking of choice of interaction of parent firms post-international joint venture termination using TISM-IRP. *Global Journal of Flexible Systems Managment, 21*(1), 1–16. doi:10.100740171-019-00227-4

Pascale, R. T. (1999). Surfing the edge of chaos. *MIT Sloan Management Review, 40*(3), 83.

Patrick, C. (2016). Identifying the local economic development effects of million-dollar facilities. *Economic Inquiry, 54*(4), 1737–1762. doi:10.1111/ecin.12339

Penrose, E., & Penrose, E. T. (2009). *The Theory of the Growth of the Firm*. Oxford university press.

Porter, M. E. (1990). The competitive advantage of nations. *Harvard Business Review, 73*, 91.

Porter, M. E. (2000). Location, competition, and economic development: Local clusters in a global economy. *Economic Development Quarterly, 14*(1), 15–34. doi:10.1177/089124240001400105

Porter, M. E., & Kramer, M. R. (2006). The link between competitive advantage and corporate social responsibility. *Harvard Business Review, 84*(12), 78–92. PMID:17183795

Porter, M. E., & Kramer, M. R. (2019). Creating shared value. In *Managing sustainable business* (pp. 323–346). Springer. doi:10.1007/978-94-024-1144-7_16

Rugman, A. M. (1981). Research and development by multinational and domestic firms in Canada. *Canadian Public Policy, 7*(4), 604–616. doi:10.2307/3549490

Rumelt, R. P. (2012). Good strategy/bad strategy: The difference and why it matters. *Strategic Direction, 28*(8).

Ryan, A., Mitchell, I. K., & Daskou, S. (2012). An interaction and networks approach to developing sustainable organizations. *Journal of Organizational Change Management, 25*(4), 578–594. doi:10.1108/09534811211239236

Schumpeter, J.A. (1934). *The Theory of Economic Development*. Academic Press.

Scott, W. R. (1992). *Organizations: Rational, Natural, and Open Systems*. Prentice-Hall.

Shams, R., Vrontis, D., Belyaeva, Z., Ferraris, A., & Czinkota, M. R. (2021). Strategic agility in international business: A conceptual framework for "agile" multinationals. *Journal of International Management*, *27*(1), 100737. doi:10.1016/j.intman.2020.100737

Stalk, G. Jr, & Hout, T. M. (1990). Competing against time. *Research Technology Management*, *33*(2), 19–24. doi:10.1080/08956308.1990.11670646

Steinberg, P. J., Hennig, J. C., Oehmichen, J., & Heigermoser, J. (2022). How the country context shapes firms' competitive repertoire complexity. *Global Strategy Journal*, gsj.1458. doi:10.1002/gsj.1458

Stevens, C. E., Xie, E., & Peng, M. W. (2016). Toward a legitimacy-based view of political risk: The case of Google and Yahoo in China. *Strategic Management Journal*, *37*(5), 945–963. doi:10.1002mj.2369

Strachan, H. (2014). The lost meaning of strategy. In *Strategic Studies* (pp. 439–456). Routledge.

Teece, D., & Pisano, G. (2003). The dynamic capabilities of firms. In *Handbook on knowledge management* (pp. 195–213). Springer. doi:10.1007/978-3-540-24748-7_10

Teece, D. J. (2014). A dynamic capabilities-based entrepreneurial theory of the multinational enterprise. *Journal of International Business Studies*, *45*(1), 8–37. doi:10.1057/jibs.2013.54

Teece, D. J. (2020). Fundamental issues in strategy: Time to reassess. *Strategic Management Review*, *1*(1), 103–144. doi:10.1561/111.00000005

Teece, D. J. (2022). A wider-aperture lens for global strategic management: The multinational enterprise in a bifurcated global economy. *Global Strategy Journal*, *12*(3), 488–519. doi:10.1002/gsj.1462

Thompson, A.A., Strickland, A.J., Janes, A., Sutton, C., Peteraf, M. A., and Gamble, J.E. (2017). *Crafting and executing strategy*. McGraw-Hill US Higher Ed.

Thompson, J. D. (1967). *1967 Organizations in action*. McGraw-Hill.

Wang, J., Zhao, J., Ning, Y., & Yu, P. (2009). Transformation of Chinese State-Owned Enterprises: Challenges and Responses. *Multinational Business Review*, *17*(4), 99–122. doi:10.1108/1525383X200900029

Wernerfelt, B. (1984). A resource-based view of the firm. *Strategic Management Journal*, *5*(2), 171–180. doi:10.1002mj.4250050207

Womack, J. P., Jones, D. T., & Roos, D. (1990). The machine that changed the world. *Rawson Associates. New York*, *323*, 273–287.

Yip, G. S. (1989). Global strategy... in a world of nations. *Sloan Management Review*, *31*(1), 29–41.

ENDNOTE

[1] Strategic posture (i.e., where the firm wants to be with respect to the industry norm) (Mithas et al., 2013).

Chapter 12
Productive–Technological Capabilities, Development, and National Sovereignty:
Old and New Challenges for Brazil

Eliane Araujo
State University of Maringá, Brazil

Samuel Costa Peres
iD https://orcid.org/0000-0002-1278-8259
Brazilian National Council for Scientific and Technological Development (CNPq), Brazil

ABSTRACT

This chapter analyzes the industrial and technological capabilities of Brazil in the context of the social and economic losses caused by the COVID-19 global health crisis, and to what extent these capabilities highlight the need to rethink industrial and sciences, technology, and innovation (ST&I) policies in search of greater resilience to future crises, of an external insertion compatible with national sovereignty, and of better prospects for economic development. The evolution of Brazil's production-trade structure is explored, with emphasis on the health complex, followed by a discussion on the perspectives for economic development from the integration into global value chains and on the Brazilian technological and scientific capabilities in a comparative perspective. It concludes that the current crisis has exposed the ongoing process of weakening capabilities of Brazil and the urgency of intelligent and effective designs of industrial and ST&I policies, in a systemic, multidisciplinary, and multisectoral approach.

The global public health and economic crisis triggered by Covid-19 made clear the strategic importance of industrial and science, technology, and innovation (ST&I) policies for coping with crises of this nature and for national sovereignty. The industrial and technological competencies of the countries were abruptly tested by the interruption of links in global production chains and, especially, by the difficulty in obtaining essential medical and hospital equipment and materials, medicines, and chemical products,

DOI: 10.4018/978-1-6684-6845-6.ch012

both due to high international demand and competition and to the export restrictions imposed by several producing countries in order to ensure the availability of such equipment and materials to their populations.

Given the great shortage of medical-hospital equipment and instruments in several countries, the need for emergency industrial reconversion programs and collaborative efforts of government agencies, universities, companies, research institutes, and other organizations to repair and build similar low-cost devices from new products and processes has been imposed. Around the world, the work of researchers and scientists has been instrumental in estimating the health effects of Covid-19, its economic and social impacts, and the development of diagnostic tests and research into vaccines and treatments for the disease. Likewise, the need to develop innovations with the potential to contribute to responding to the social disconnect and the various ramifications of the pandemic, such as in communication, transportation, education, community assistance, etc., has reinforced the challenges to national innovation systems around the world.

The problems faced in foreign trade, in particular, have reignited the debate about the need for firms and countries to reduce international dependence, so that the expectation is that movements towards *reshoring* or relocation of production, diversification and regionalization will lead to the restructuring of global value chains (GVCs) and trade as a whole in the coming years (United Nations Conference on Trade and Development [UNCTAD], 2020b).

Japan, for example, from its economic stimulus package against the new corona virus crisis, has allocated approximately $2 billion in support in the form of subsidies and direct loans for its companies to transfer their industrial plants currently in China back to Japan (Reynolds & Urabe, 2020). France, on its turn, revealed its intention to regain the country's "technological, industrial and health independence", initially announcing the relocation of part of the production associated with the health complex, a 200-million-euro package to finance production infrastructures in the area, as well as research and development (R&D) centers (France...,2020). Also in search of reducing vulnerabilities exposed by the pandemic, in the United States, government statements and recent surveys signal a potentially significant movement toward reshoring the industrial production (Lawder, 2020; Hagerty, 2012; Ma, 2020).

Indeed, in terms of industrial and ST&I policies, the immediate lessons of the Covid-19 crisis are quite stark: lost time simply cannot be made up for by redoubled efforts when crises strike. That is, the capacity of each society to manage and quickly respond to threats and crises on several fronts depends, to a large extent, on a complex network of interactions and cooperation among the various agents that make up the productive-technological structure of the country, a system that, in turn, develops in long cumulative processes based on political and historical conditions.

Against this backdrop, it is imperative that the discussion about the productive, commercial, and technological transformations that condition Brazilian economic development and the country's resilience to future crises of various natures be brought to the forefront. According to a 2019 survey by the Institute for Studies in Industrial Development (IEDI), Brazil's industry was one of the world's largest retractors in nearly 50 years. Among 30 countries, Brazil presented the third largest retraction in the sector since 1970, behind only Australia and the United Kingdom, which in turn had already reached a high income when they naturally started their de-industrialization processes and continued to increase their income at a much higher rate than Brazil in the years that followed.

In this sense, the premature deindustrialization of the Brazilian economy is worrisome not only given the needs of the crisis context, but for the long-term development prospects themselves, due to several specificities of the manufacturing sector, among them: the capacity to generate and propagate technological change; to be the main driver of productivity growth; positive externalities and synergies between sectors and productive chains; greater dynamism in international trade and sustainability of the balance of payments and, in the case of developing countries, the fact that the manufacturing sector is the main driver of productivity growth. These benefits tend to be higher the greater is the participation of more technologically sophisticated activities (Palma, 2005, 2019; Szirmai, 2012; Tregenna, 2009; Tregenna & Andreoni, 2020).

Recently, with the process of international fragmentation of production underway in recent decades, opportunities for integration into GVCs by less developed countries have been enthusiastically embraced, especially within multilateral organizations. In this view, developing countries could take advantage of the industrial bases of the richer countries, instead of having to build entire industries from scratch. Therefore, they would accelerate their industrialization and development processes (Organisation for Economic Cooperation and Development [OECD], 2013; World Bank, 2020). Consequently, the current prospects for relocation of production and weakening or establishment of shorter GVCs triggered by the pandemic would set the stage for significant development challenges for low- and middle-income countries. On the other hand, some empirical evidence points out that a higher degree of integration in GVCs *per se* may not engender automatic and widespread benefits to countries and depending on the pattern of integration it may even be counterproductive (Fagerberg et al., 2018; Pahl & Timmer, 2019; Rodrik, 2018; UNCTAD, 2015).

Thus, in the context in which the health and economic crisis of Covid-19 affects Brazil and the global economy, the question that naturally arises is to what extent the industrial capabilities and the Brazilian national innovation system proved adequate to cushion the impacts of the crisis, or rather, to what extent the high social and economic losses of the pandemic forces us to rethink industrial policies and ST&I in search of greater resilience to future crises, an external insertion compatible with national sovereignty, and better prospects for the future of an external insertion compatible with national sovereignty, and of better prospects for economic development in the long term.

To shed light on this question, this article is divided into four sections in addition to this introduction. The first explores the evolution of Brazil's production-trade structure, with emphasis on the health complex. The following discusses more specifically the prospects for development from GVC integration, also considering the potential setback in the international fragmentation of production in the face of the Covid-19 crisis. The fourth section analyzes the Brazilian technological and scientific capabilities in a comparative perspective. The last section brings some final thoughts on the topic.

De-Industrialization and Sovereignty in Addressing COVID-19's Public Health Crisis

This section investigates how the productive and commercial transformations of the Brazilian economy condition its economic development and its resilience in the face of crises such as the Covid-19.

To this end, it is initially worth highlighting the declining trend in the participation of industry in the Brazilian economy. Manufacturing GDP, which accounted for 27% of GDP in the 1980s, was only 11% in 2018. In addition, there is also a tendency towards regressive specialization, that is, the industry producing medium-high and high technology goods continues to lose space to the non-manufactured and low and medium-low technology industry, which represented approximately 75% of the national industry production in 2017, as illustrated in figure 1.

This specialization of Brazilian industry in the production of low and medium-low technology goods is reflected in the country's exports and imports. Data from the United Nations Commodity Trade Sta-

Figure 1. Industrial production by technological intensity: 1996-2017 (% of total)
Source: Prepared by the authors based on data from the Brazilian Institute of Geography and Statistics, Annual Industrial Survey.
Note: Non-manufacturing constitutes the extractive activities, not included in the OECD classification by technological intensity.

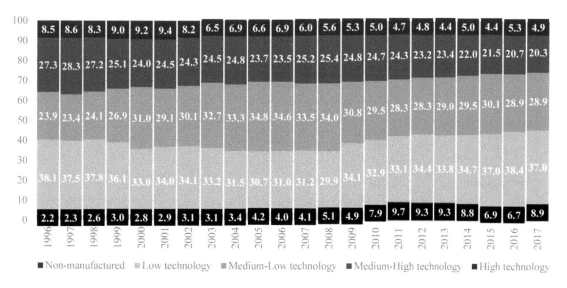

■ Non-manufactured　▧ Low technology　■ Medium-Low technology　■ Medium-High technology　■ High technology

tistics Database (UN Comtrade, 2020) reveal that, on the one hand, Brazilian exports follow the same direction as production, with exports of non-manufactured and low- and medium-low technology products accounting, in 2018, for 81% of the entire value exported by Brazil. On the other hand, imports follow the opposite path, as 60% of the value imported by the country has been allocated to medium-high and high technology goods.

In the context in which a health crisis affects Brazil and the global economy, a relevant question is how the health-related equipment and materials industry is represented within the production, export, and import of the Brazilian economy. To do so, data from the Brazilian Institute of Geography and Statistics (IBGE) will be used for industrial production and UN Comtrade with a higher level of disaggregation to capture exports and imports for two main groups of industries: 1) appliances and instruments for medical, hospital, precision, testing and control use and 2) pharmochemical, pharmaceutical and chemical products.

Regarding the first group, Graph 2 shows in the red line the Brazilian production of the industries of devices and instruments for medical, hospital, precision, test and control use, which in 2018 represented only 0.83% of the country's total industrial production. In the same graph, the gray bars show the percentage participation of exports (positive signs on the left axis) and imports (negative signs on the left axis) of these industries in the total exported and imported by the country, respectively, while the black line informs the trade balance (difference between exports and imports) of these industries.

The data show that the contribution of these industries to the country's total exports is practically insignificant, less than 1% throughout the entire period, while imports have a participation about 6 times higher, although they represent less than 2% of total imports. On the other hand, the trade deficit of these industries has been on an accelerated growth path since 1989, despite a slight recovery between 2014-2016, pointing down again and recording a major deficit of approximately $2.5 billion in 2018.

Graph 3 shows the same information (production and trade) for the pharmochemical, pharmaceutical and chemical industries. The red line reveals a downward trajectory in the relative output of these industries, which represented 11.08% of total Brazilian total output in 1996 and, in 2017, only 5.96%.

Figure 2. Productive-trade share of apparatus and instruments for medical-hospital, precision, test and control use industries: 1989-2018 (% of total)
Source: Prepared by the authors based on data from the Brazilian Institute of Geography and Statistics, Annual Industrial Survey, and the UN Comtrade Database, at the Harmonized System (HS) 6-digit product level.
Note: The relative shares of exports and imports are indicated by the positive and negative signs, respectively (left axis).

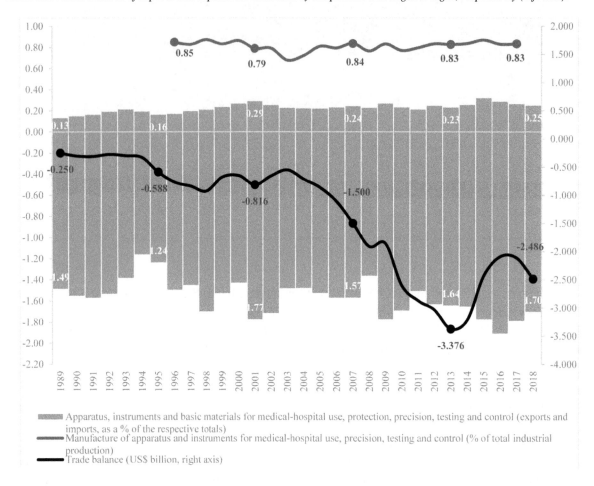

Apparatus, instruments and basic materials for medical-hospital use, protection, precision, testing and control (exports and imports, as a % of the respective totals)

Manufacture of apparatus and instruments for medical-hospital use, precision, testing and control (% of total industrial production)

Trade balance (US$ billion, right axis)

At the same time, a not very significant but still decreasing participation of exports from these sectors in the country's exports is noted, while imports are growing and currently account for about 20% of total imports, a very significant share. Naturally, the deficit of these industries followed a sharp growth trajectory, rising from 1 billion current dollars in 1989 to 26 billion at the end of 2018.

Therefore, the data discussed here reveal that the industry as a whole, and more specifically the health complex, is characterized by an important economic fragility, with high dependence on technology and basic industrial inputs, so that the supply of these products has long been incompatible with the national demand. Especially in the health complex, the new corona virus pandemic has clearly exposed these deficiencies, bringing important challenges to face the global health crisis, such as the difficulty of producing and even importing products that are essential in the fight against it. It can be seen, for example, shortages of alcohol gels in hospitals, gloves, masks and other personal protective equipment, mechanical respirators and other medical equipment, basic medicines and reagents for diagnostic tests, and various other items made from different chemicals.

In an attempt to supply the need for these products, the country has resorted to imports, in a market where China holds more than 90% of all world production. However, with the excess demand and international competition during the pandemic, Brazil has found it difficult to acquire these products. In addition to the health complex, a survey conducted by the Brazilian Electrical and Electronics Industry Association (Abinee) in March 2020 revealed that 70% of its member companies already had problems with the supply of components, mostly produced in China and other Asian countries (National Industry Confederation of Brazil, 2020). It is important to remember that the electronics industry is present from the transformation of natural resources into energy to the bit that is transformed into information in the access device. And in this highly constrained scenario, technology stands as a fundamental tool to connect people, businesses, and sustain the active economy, as well as provide entertainment, access to education, the supply needs of the food sector, etc.

Figure 3. Productive-trade share of the pharmochemical, pharmaceutical and chemical industries: 1989-2018 (% of total)
Source: Prepared by the authors based on data from the Brazilian Institute of Geography and Statistics, Annual Industrial Survey, and the UN Comtrade Database, at the Harmonized System (HS) 6-digit product level.
Note: The relative shares of exports and imports are indicated by the positive and negative signs, respectively (left axis).

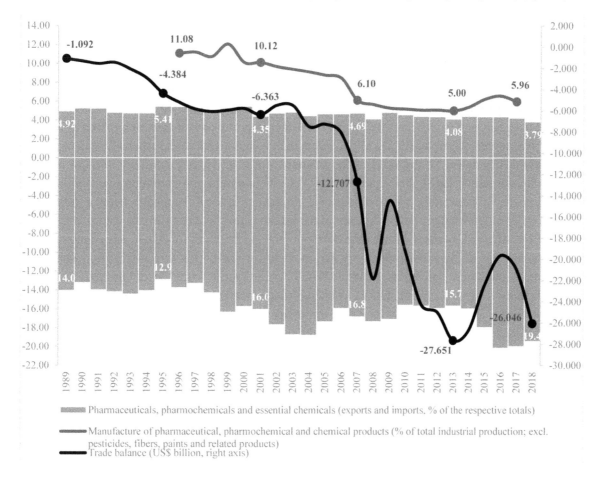

In short, the Covid-19 pandemic reveals another important virtue of the industry, which is to guarantee national sovereignty in the face of a public health crisis, and shows that for Brazil to recover from this deep plunge and resume a path of economic and social development, it is urgent to have a sophisticated national industry capable of connecting to the fourth industrial revolution already underway, and thus integrate itself in a sustainable way into the global economy. In this context, the development of public policies to encourage the industry and science and technology are, more than ever, indispensable.

Brazil's Insertion in Global Value Chains: Benefits, Risks, and the Post-Pandemic Future

Having highlighted the recent trends in the Brazilian industry, this section deals with the prospects for development based on the integration of the Brazilian economy into global value chains, especially in the face of a potential setback in the international fragmentation of production resulting from the Covid-19 crisis.

Global trade in modern agriculture, manufacturing and tradable services has been fundamentally transformed by GVCs, i.e., by the possibility of fragmenting production chains into specific tasks that may be dispersed around the world to take advantage of lower production costs. In this context, GVC integration has been enthusiastically seen as a pathway for the absorption of technology and knowledge by firms, and hence for the economic development of countries, so that deeper liberalizing policies have been strongly recommended (e.g., World Bank, 2020).

Some important advantages of this form of international trade integration are summarized by UNCTAD (2013). The first one refers to local value capture, highlighting that participation in GVCs can contribute to generating value added in domestic economies and to faster economic growth, which tends to be higher the lower is the import content of exports. Another important advantage highlighted is the ability of GVCs to generate income and create employment in developing countries, especially quality employment, which is dependent on the value added inherent to the activities carried out in these countries. Additionally, the authors highlight the potential of GVCs in disseminating technology and building skills, with the transfer of knowledge from multinational companies to local companies being conditional on the complexity of knowledge and governance in the relationships between the companies in the GVCs.

In other words, GVCs can offer long-term development opportunities for developing economies when local firms are able to increase productivity and move toward activities with increasing technological sophistication and higher value added within the GVC. However, the transfer of knowledge from multinationals to local firms operating in GVCs depends on the nature of inter-firm relationships and value chain governance, and the absorptive capacity of the firms. Therefore, GVCs can also act as barriers to learning for local firms or limit learning opportunities to a few of them. Local firms may also remain "stuck" in low-technology (and low value added) activities, with high dependence on the leading firms.

In this sense, among the various factors that can contribute to a country's entrapment in the so-called middle-income trap[1], the pattern of integration in GVCs is highlighted by UNCTAD (2015), because the linkage to GVCs can increase the risk of "domestic disengagement" and shrink the manufacturing sector in the process of concentrating on the production of specific parts and components rather than the final product. Thus, in addition to the risk of imprisoning domestic companies in low added-value stages with few prospects for technological *upgrading*, the integration profile also generates balance of payment difficulties and a further weakening of the macroeconomic conditions necessary for sustained industrial development.

Rodrik (2018) shows that while insertion in GVCs is expected to be beneficial for developing countries by facilitating the entry of these economies into global markets, these advantages tend to be offset by their disadvantages in terms of employment and trade. This is because GVCs require scarce skills and capabilities in developing countries, decreasing the contribution of these economies' traditional comparative advantages in unskilled labor, and their gains from trade. In addition, they make it difficult for low-income countries to use their labor cost advantage to compensate for their technological disadvantage, which occurs because of their inability to substitute unskilled labor for other production inputs.

A direct conclusion from this, according to Rodrik (2018), is that developing economies' strategies should focus less on international economic integration and more on so-called domestic integration. In this strategy, the main challenge is to spread throughout the economy the capabilities that already exist in the more advanced parts of the productive sector, improving the fundamentals of the economy through investment in human capital and governance, and more proactive government-private sector collaboration policies to strengthen the connection between highly productive global companies, potential local suppliers, and the domestic workforce.

Pahl and Timmer (2020) also investigated the relationship between participation in GVCs and long-term employment and labor productivity growth in developing countries. The evidence suggests positive effects of GVCs on formal labor market productivity growth in the manufacturing export sector, which is stronger when the distance to the global productivity frontier is greater. However, the authors find no evidence of positive effects in terms of job creation. On the contrary, the evidence points out that for high share industries in GVCs, export employment growth is slower than in the low share group. Furthermore, the association even becomes significantly negative for the productivity levels characteristic of middle-income countries, such as Brazil.

Interesting evidence was also obtained by Fagerberg et al. (2018). The results of the estimates made by the authors suggest that countries that increase their participation in GVCs do not grow faster than other countries, when other relevant factors are controlled for. In particular, the evidence suggests that the positive effects on economic growth are limited to advanced economies and those with well-developed national innovation systems.

Having made these considerations, the remainder of this section presents some indicators on the degree of Brazil's insertion in GVCs and some discussions related to the quality of this participation. Initially, Graph 4 shows the degree of integration in GVC of selected countries as percentages of total value added of exports. It is possible to observe that, since the 2007-2008 crisis, there has been a general decline and stagnation in the GVC integration process, especially in the case of Brazil, which has been overtaken by China and has the lowest degree of participation among the set of countries presented.

The participation of countries in GVCs can be decomposed between upstream (backward) linkages, measured by the value added of the foreign product used in their exports, and downstream (forward) linkages, given by the domestic value added incorporated in third party exports, both as a percentage of the total value added of the country's exports.

Graph 5 shows that Brazil's share of the upstream GVC is approximately 14%, a figure quite close to countries like China and the United States, but well below the OECD and South Korean average.

It is worth noting that the most upstream stages can be made up of both the processing of raw materials and the production of high-tech parts and components, as well as knowledge assets such as R&D, design, and brand building, which add very distinct values to the production process. The downstream stages are those related to the export of natural resources, product assembly, and the provision of after-sales or customer service. Some of these activities are more associated with generating high value added

Figure 4. Degree of integration into global value chains of selected countries (1990-2018)
Source: Prepared by the authors using data from Unctad-Eora Global Value Chain Database 2020. Note: Values as a percentage of the total value added of sports.

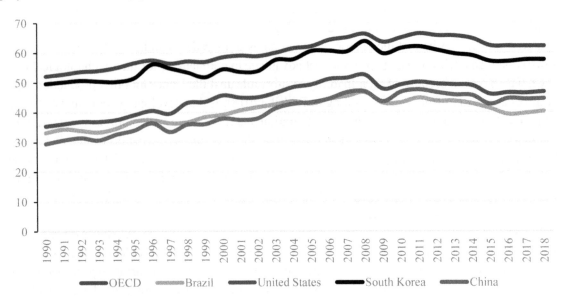

such as R&D, design and brand building (upstream) and other intangible services (downstream), while the production and export of raw materials, for example, adds little value.

The degree of participation or role that each country plays in international production networks is influenced by many different factors, including economy size, industrial structure and level of industrialization, export composition and positioning in value chains, political factors, and others. Thus, countries with very different characteristics can be very similar in terms of GVC participation rate. However, in general, large countries tend to have a higher degree of self-sufficiency in the production of final goods for export (so their products have less import content) and therefore tend to exhibit a relatively low degree of GVC participation. On the other hand, in economies where processing industries account for significant shares of exports, the share of foreign value added tends to be higher in developing economies than in developed economies. In industries such as textiles and electronics, developing countries supply the bulk of the semi-finished goods used by exporters in developed countries. In machinery and equipment, chemicals, and automotive industries, developing countries tend to import more foreign inputs, which are often technology- and capital-intensive to produce their exports (UNCTAD, 2013).

Graph 6 shows that the largest participation of Brazil in GVC occurs downstream, with 26% of the value added of total exports being incorporated as intermediate goods in exports from other countries. Although it has shown a downward trend and has been overtaken by China in recent years, it can be observed that in this form of integration Brazil is close to the OECD average, to China itself, and higher than South Korea. It is noteworthy that this higher degree of downstream participation of the Brazilian economy in GVCs is related especially to the large export of *commodities* and primary products, which are subsequently processed and exported by companies in other countries.

Importantly, the GVC participation rate, in addition to informing the extent to which a country's exports depend on GVCs, also indicates how much hypothetical "damage" to the GVCs and exports would occur if exports from another country were blocked, as well as the vulnerability of the GVC to

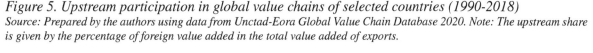

Figure 5. Upstream participation in global value chains of selected countries (1990-2018)
Source: Prepared by the authors using data from Unctad-Eora Global Value Chain Database 2020. Note: The upstream share
is given by the percentage of foreign value added in the total value added of exports.

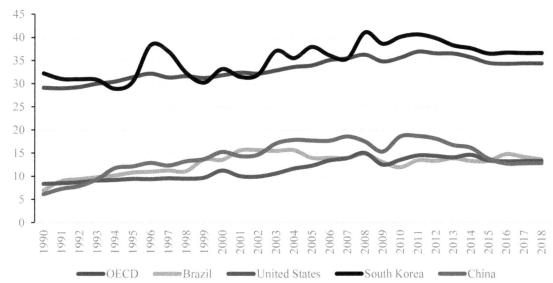

shocks in an individual economy along the value chain. More than that, as noted by the OECD (2020), the Covid-19 crisis has brought up the discussion of economic vulnerability during a pandemic or other crisis in which international trade is disrupted. The closure of factories in China at the end of January, and the subsequent blockades implemented around the world, have drawn attention to the high dependence of many input manufacturers on China and other countries.

This shakeup in GVCs has strengthened the debate about the risks associated with the fragmentation of production at the global level, and several researchers have begun to suggest that it is necessary to rethink GVCs in order to make them more resilient, for example by diversifying their supplier base or moving some activities based in different countries back to the original country.

In this context, the OECD research (2020) brings some propositions for increasing the resilience of international production networks and suggests policy options that can promote security of supply, mitigate disruptions in chains, and help promote economic recovery. To this end, the institution stresses the importance of strategies that improve risk management at the enterprise level, emphasizing awareness, transparency, and agility. Sourcing strategies may differ between activities, depending on the level of acceptable risk, with supplier diversification, especially in core activities. Governments can also support companies to create more resilient GVCs by collecting and sharing information about potential concentrations and upstream bottlenecks, developing stress tests for critical supply chains, and creating an enabling regulatory environment so that adopted policies are not a source of additional uncertainty.

However, as highlighted by UNCTAD (2020), the very effort for greater resilience of supply chains and greater autonomy in productive capacity by countries can have long-lasting consequences to the dynamics of international trade. The Covid-19 pandemic is not the only element of the cooling of GVCs, though, which had already been seen since 2010 in the wake of the global financial crisis. The new industrial revolution, the policy shift toward greater nationalism and economic protectionism, and sustainability trends will have far-reaching consequences for the shape of international production in the

Figure 6. Downstream participation in global value chains of selected countries (1990-2018)
Source: Prepared by the authors using data from Unctad-Eora Global Value Chain Database 2020. Note: The downstream
share is given by the domestic value added incorporated in third party exports as a percentage of the country's total value
added of exports.

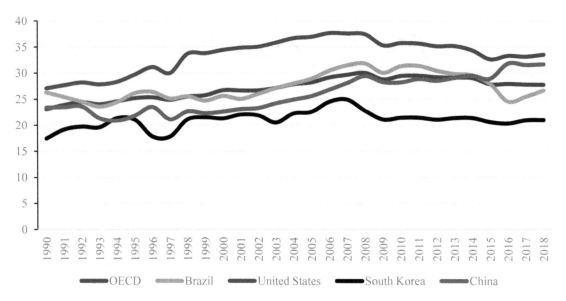

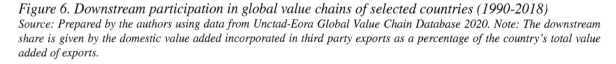

coming decade. The general directional trend in international production points to shorter value chains, greater concentration of value added, and reduced international investment in productive physical assets. This will bring enormous challenges for developing countries.

The expected transformation of international production also brings some development opportunities, such as promoting investments in search of resilience, building regional value chains, and entering new markets through digital platforms. However, capturing these opportunities will require a change in development strategies. Export-oriented investments will remain important, but some degree of rebalancing will be required for growth based on domestic and regional demand and the promotion of investments in domestic infrastructure and services.

This means promoting investments in sectors aligned with the Sustainable Development Goals for 2030, i.e., value-creating projects in infrastructure, education, renewable energy, water treatment and sanitation, food security and health care, climate change, cities, and sustainable consumption and production patterns, to name a few (United Nations, 2015).

Finally, in addition to the weaknesses and need to increase the resilience of global production chains (therefore, of countries) to exogenous shocks, the benefits seem to depend on several initial conditions, such as a well-developed industrial base and national innovation system, which contribute to better positioning and greater capture of added value by countries within production chains. Thus, the subject deserves further investigation, before being treated as an unequivocal economic policy recommendation, especially for developing countries, whose great heterogeneity of productive structures implies a closer look at the potential benefits and risks in each country.

National Science, Technology, and Innovation Policy: A Necessary Rethink During and After the COVID-19 Crisis

This part of the research analyzes the Brazilian technological and scientific capabilities in a comparative perspective and underlines the need to rethink ST&I policies, particularly in Brazil, both for the sustainability of its long-term economic growth and development, and to enhance the resilience of society in the face of turbulence and severe shocks. This is because, besides playing a fundamental role in determining the technological competencies and long-term international competitiveness of the industry in general, ST&I also has a key role in crisis situations, such as the Covid-19 crisis, either in the understanding of its origin and dynamics, or in the formulation of strategies to overcome it.

As a theoretical background, it is important to mention that in the technology and evolutionary economics literature, the systemic nature of innovation processes is highlighted, noting that companies usually do not innovate in isolation, but in collaboration and interdependence with other organizations. These organizations can be other companies or non-business entities, such as universities, research institutes, ministries, and governmental organizations. The behavior of organizations is also shaped by institutions, such as laws, norms, and the regulatory framework, which constitute incentives or obstacles to innovation. This system of organizations and institutions that contribute jointly and individually to the development and diffusion of new technologies, and which provides the framework within which governments design and implement policies to influence the direction and process of innovation, is called the National Innovation System (NIS) (Edquist, 2005; Nelson, 2009). From this perspective, the institutional arrangements and the industrial and science, technology and innovation (ST&I) policies that shape the NIS are key to explaining the different economic performances across countries, and their potentials for growth and development in the long run.

In this context, it is interesting to note that although the whole world is being hit hard by the pandemic of the new corona virus, recent estimates involving countries of the Association of Southeast Asian Nations (ASEAN) indicate that countries with more developed NIS pre-crisis performed better in health, as measured by the behavior of the ratio between Covid-19 recovery rates and deaths (Layos & Peña, 2020). Obviously, in the absence of adequate social distancing measures, the ability of a national innovation system to absorb the impacts of the pandemic becomes reduced.

The importance of ST&I in times of severe turbulence had already been exposed in the global financial crisis of 2008. A document produced by Unctad (2020a) highlights that, at the time, two different sets of trajectories were observed: on the one hand, countries with more developed NISs and more knowledge-intensive economies suffered less from the crisis and did not impose austerity on R&D spending. On the other hand, countries that entered the 2008 financial crisis with timid ST&I budget efforts and, consequently, with weaker NIS, showed less macroeconomic resilience, which led to a budget tightening in R&D expenditures that in turn further weakened their innovation systems, their capabilities for economic recovery, and their chances of shifting to more knowledge-intensive growth patterns. Moreover, countries that have reduced public spending on R&D have turned to alternative financing mechanisms and have carried out consolidation and rationalization of existing policies and programs, compromising the results of earlier investments and subsequently private investment in technology and innovation.

Thus, since the outcome of investments in research and innovation is particularly subject to uncertainties and risks, it is essential to maintain stability and a long-term perspective in public support for ST&I. When there is no certainty of continued government support, companies hesitate to invest in additional research and development. Predictability and long-term prospects in funding are also critical for research conducted by academic institutions. Likewise, investment in human capital can suffer *stop-and-go* policies and make it difficult to retain qualified human resources. Faced with unstable academic research systems and bleak career prospects, promising researchers and other skilled workers are likely to switch to other careers or migrate to countries where ST&I investments are stable or continue to grow.

In a race for leadership in the 4th Industrial Revolution (also called Industry 4.0 or advanced manufacturing), countries such as the US, Japan, Germany, South Korea, Israel, and China, have been investing heavily in complex systems of innovation and technological development to ensure leadership in the coming new paradigm. This issue gained much clearer dimensions in the midst of the pandemic, and points to the urgency of rethinking the industrial and ST&I policies in Brazil, so that the country can follow a sustained path of development, protecting national sovereignty.

What would be, then, the necessary investment for a country to effectively appropriate the benefits associated with ST&I? There is no exact answer, only projections, estimates, and goals, elaborated by the scientific community and other organizations that make up the NIS in each country. The results often depend on various initial conditions, macroeconomic policies, and the behavior of key variables (*e.g.* interest and exchange rates), hence the importance of coordination. In any case, R&D investment as a proportion of GDP is one of the most traditional and well-defined indicators internationally, allowing the comparison of countries' efforts to discover products and processes through science and engineering, and has been a central goal in the planning and strategies developed by governments.

Table 1 illustrates the behavior of R&D investment in Brazil, in perspective to the world's main technological centers, that is, the OECD countries (taken together) and, more recently, China. South Korea, although also an OECD member, is highlighted in the table as a striking example of accelerated economic development in recent decades. The table also shows the number of researchers dedicated to R&D activities. In this regard, studies point out that the social return from R&D activities becomes visible only when a certain fraction of the GDP (greater than 1%) is invested and a minimum "critical mass" of researchers per million inhabitants (between 1,000 and 1,200) are allocated to R&D activities on a full-time basis. When the NIS does not reach these minimum thresholds, there is unlikely to be a significant economic impact (United Nations Educational, Scientific and Cultural Organization, 2018).

These data show that although R&D investment in Brazil is slightly above the recommended minimum level, it is still well below that of the main international players, and growing at lower rates. Likewise, the number of researchers in the country is not only below the suggested threshold, but also far away from the countries in the table. The current mix between R&D investment and the number of researchers makes it very difficult to transform the country into a knowledge economy.

In terms of outcome variables, patents are a key measure of the R&D performance of countries, firms, industrial sectors, etc., and allow one to track the level of diffusion of knowledge produced, both nationally and internationally. Table 2 reveals that the number of patents granted per million inhabitants in Brazil is the lowest in the group of countries analyzed, especially in the areas fundamental to the control of the Covid-19 pandemic, that is, medical technology, biotechnology, optics, control and chemistry, chemical engineering, and pharmaceuticals.

Another important indicator of a NIS and that reflects the countries' efforts in ST&I is the publication of scientific articles. Table 3 shows that also in this aspect the country's performance is inferior to the other highlighted countries. Although it is slightly ahead of China in medicineand health professions, immunology, and microbiology, it is well below the other countries, and even lower than China, in total papers published and in chemistry, pharmacology, toxicology and pharmaceuticals, and engineering.

Table 1. Investment in R&D (% of GDP) and number of researchers per million inhabitants

		1990	1995	2000	2005	2010	2015	2018
Investment in R&D	OECD	2.16	1.95	2.12	2.14	2.28	2.33	2.40
	Korea	1.70	2.15	2.13	2.52	3.32	3.98	4.53
	China	0.72	0.57	0.89	1.31	1.71	2.07	2.19
	Brazil	…	…	1.05	1.00	1.16	1.34	1.26
Researchers in R&D	OECD	1882	2263	2619	2985	3244	3595	3767
	Korea	…	2228	2305	3732	5330	6987	7913
	China	410	433	550	858	905	1181	1340
	Brazil	…	…	295	509	686	888	…

Source: Prepared by the authors based on data from UNESCO Institute for Statistics (UIS), June 2020. Researchers defined in full-time equivalent (FTE) work.

Even in the medical field, it should be noted, the growth rate of Chinese publications has been much higher than the Brazilian ones, and should surpass them in the coming years.

Looking exclusively at the Brazilian industry, the Innovation Survey (PINTEC), conducted triennially by the IBGE, brings important results for the evaluation of ST&I in the country. Table 4 presents the innovative behavior of the Brazilian industry from 1998 to 2017. The innovative effort is decreasing in the general industry, in the industry of devices and instruments for medical-hospital use, precision, test and control, as well as pharmaceuticals, pharmochemicals and chemicals.

As for the innovation rate, it is higher in the medical devices and instruments, precision, testing and control, and pharmaceutical, pharmochemical, and chemical industries than in the general industry. However, with regard to the 2015-2017 period, this rate recorded lower values than those recorded in

Table 2. Patents granted by the US Patent and Trademark Office (USPTO), per million population

		1990	1995	2000	2005	2010	2015
Total	OECD	88.04	130.97	175.37	164.40	162.27	113.42
	Korea	17.74	77.26	101.65	251.05	280.45	238.56
	China	0.06	0.07	0.43	2.02	5.18	6.97
	Brazil	0.49	0.47	0.91	0.80	1.17	1.02
Medical technology, biotechnology, optics, control	OECD	16.70	27.11	34.43	32.80	30.45	18.40
	Korea	1.50	9.00	17.53	35.33	31.49	30.76
	China	0.01	0.01	0.04	0.25	0.56	1.11
	Brazil	0.05	0.09	0.13	0.13	0.17	0.12
Chemistry, chemical and pharmaceutical engineering	OECD	12.92	20.28	19.69	15.21	14.83	6.16
	Korea	1.23	3.01	7.21	11.16	14.49	9.89
	China	0.02	0.03	0.08	0.17	0.45	0.37
	Brazil	0.07	0.05	0.14	0.20	0.22	0.10

Source: Prepared by the authors based on OECD Statistics data, June 2020. About 90% of the grants at the USPTO are for "invention patents".

Table 3. Publications in scientific journals indexed by Scopus (per million population)

		1996	2000	2005	2010	2015	2018
Total	OECD	845.4	967.7	1346.5	1783.0	2183.8	2335.9
	Korea	226.6	387.5	775.2	1196.6	1537.4	1601.6
	China	25.2	40.6	130.5	253.8	327.7	422.9
	Brazil	55.0	87.2	141.0	247.5	322.7	371.8
Medicine and health professions, immunology and microbiology	OECD	369.0	412.0	506.7	623.1	758.9	819.6
	Korea	58.4	101.9	195.0	360.2	503.5	544.7
	China	4.2	7.4	24.3	44.0	76.9	93.5
	Brazil	24.9	34.4	54.5	91.8	114.1	132.0
Chemistry, pharmacology, toxicology and pharmaceuticals	OECD	149.1	162.1	206.8	248.6	301.8	316.0
	Korea	64.0	104.5	173.1	291.3	391.9	380.9
	China	6.6	12.3	29.8	50.7	89.3	114.3
	Brazil	10.5	17.3	26.7	35.4	46.6	55.5
Engineering, except chemical	OECD	111.8	138.0	239.4	286.3	352.4	394.2
	Korea	72.5	127.3	272.1	341.6	402.9	438.5
	China	7.8	12.3	49.1	92.7	103.3	136.0
	Brazil	6.6	12.0	21.6	30.9	40.9	48.4

Source: Prepared by the authors based on SCImago Journal & Country Rank [Portal] data, June 2020. These are considered to be the documents that can be cited.

previous periods, especially in health-related areas, which recorded the lowest values in the historical series. In general, after a relative growth between 2003-2008, there seems to be a downward trend in the number of firms that innovate, coupled with a drop in private investment in innovative activities.

Table 5, in turn, shows government support for innovation in Brazilian industry, in terms of the percentage of companies supported and the percentage of government support in the financing structure for innovations developed by companies. With regard to the first criterion, the increasing number of innovative companies that received some type of federal support until 2014 stands out in general, followed by a sharp drop in the three-year period 2015-2017, especially in the area of devices and instruments for medical-hospital use, precision, testing and control. As for the pharmaceutical, pharmochemical, and chemical products industry, an increase is observed in the last three-year period, although it is almost 10 percentage points lower than the number in the 2009-2011 three-year period, that is, in 2015-2017, 38.8% of innovative companies received government support, while in 2009-2011 47% of innovative companies received government support.

In terms of financing, it can be noted that after an important generalized reduction between 2001-2003 there was a strong recovery in federal financing for innovative companies, followed by a vertiginous one in the last triennium. The declines in funding for innovative companies in the health complex between the three-year periods 2012-2014 and 2015-2017 are striking: while companies in the pharmaceuticals, pharmochemicals and chemicals sector had to deal with a reduction in government support in the financing structure for their innovative activities from almost 20% to 9.4%, support for the medical-hospital, precision, testing and control devices and instruments sector plummeted from 20.7% to 2.7% in a short period of time.

Table 4. Innovative behavior in the Brazilian industry

Period	General Industry		Apparatus and Instruments for Medical-Hospital, Precision, Testing and Control Use		Pharmaceutical, Pharmochemical, and Chemical	
	Innovation Rate	Innovative Effort	Innovation Rate	Innovative Effort	Innovation Rate	Innovative Effort
1998-2000	31.5	3.8	59.1	5.0	46.1	4.0
2001-2003	33.3	2.5	45.4	3.1	43.6	2.2
2003-2005	34.4	3.0	68.1	5.3	50.0	2.5
2006-2008	38.3	2.8	51.2	...	62.0	2.9
2009-2011	35.7	2.6	49.2	3.7	58.5	2.7
2012-2014	36.0	2.5	53.1	2.8	49.9	2.2
2015-2017	33.6	2.0	47.4	2.6	45.3	2.4

Source: Prepared by the authors based on data from IBGE, Technological Innovation Survey. Note: Industrial companies with 10 or more people employed, which have implemented a technologically new or substantially improved product and/or process, were considered. Innovation rate is the percentage of innovative firms in relation to the total number of firms. Innovative effort refers to expenditures on innovative activities as a proportion of net sales revenues.

In summary, the PINTEC data point to a reduction in private investment in R&D and in the rate of innovation in Brazilian industry, a movement that accompanies the fall in government support for the innovative activities of companies, especially in recent years. In relation to the last edition of the survey, the biggest obstacles to innovation, indicated by the companies are: 1) excessive economic risks; 2) high innovation costs; 3) lack of qualified personnel, and, 4) scarcity of financing sources in the country.

Table 5. Government support for innovation in the Brazilian industry

Period	General Industry		Apparatus and Instruments for Medical-Hospital, Precision, Testing, and Control Use		Pharmaceutical, Pharmochemical, and Chemical	
	Supported Companies	Financing	Supported Companies	Financing	Supported Companies	Financing
1998-2000	16.9	8.0	7.5	19.0	14.9	3.0
2001-2003	18.7	5.0	16.1	3.0	14.1	1.0
2003-2005	18.8	8.0	24.1	2.0	18.2	8.0
2006-2008	22.2	19.0	20.2	6.0	30.8	9.0
2009-2011	34.2	10.9	24.7	10.9	47.0	12.9
2012-2014	39.9	14.3	33.9	20.7	33.2	19.9
2015-2017	26.2	7.4	13.1	2.7	38.8	9.4

Source: Prepared by the authors based on data from IBGE, Technological Innovation Survey. Note: Industrial companies with 10 or more people employed, which have implemented a technologically new or substantially improved product and/or process, were considered. Government support is the percentage of innovative firms that received some kind of support in relation to the total number of innovative firms. Support not broken down by type, such as tax incentive, grant, financing, public procurement, or other programs. Financing refers to the percentage share of government support in the financing structure of innovations developed by companies.

In line with what has been said so far, it is worth mentioning, finally, that in the latest edition of the 2019 Global Innovation Index (GII), prepared by the World Intellectual Property Organization (WIPO), which seeks to measure the level of innovation around the world, Brazil ranked 66th among 129 countries. In 2007, in the first edition of the GII, which included 107 countries, Brazil was ranked 40th, moving to 64th in 2013, among 149 countries. To put it in perspective, between the 2007, 2013, and 2019 rankings, South Korea's positions were 19th, 18th, and 11th, respectively. China's positions, meanwhile, from more recent ST&I efforts, was 29th, 35th and, incredibly, 14th in 2019.

Therefore, the data referring to ST&I in Brazil reveal a worrisome scenario of an important reduction in investments by the public authorities, as well as a performance well below the average of the major world economies in indicators such as the number of patents, scientific publications, and investments in research and development. This lack of investment and coordination around a NIS has an important impact on the economy and society in the long term, and especially in times like the Covid-19 health crisis, given the sharp reduction in resources allocated to health-related sectors in recent years.

Final Remarks

The Covid-19 crisis has made clear the great mismatch between the needs of the health field in Brazil and its economic base, in terms of production, investment, and trade of fundamental equipment and materials. The de-industrialization of the Brazilian economy appears precisely as one of the causes of this gap, which, together with the lack of robustness of its national innovation system, engender a process of multiple and growing reinforcement of the productive-technological capacities of the country, hence, of a dependent international insertion and extremely vulnerable to exogenous shocks, such as the Covid-19 pandemic.

While the global public health crisis highlights the need for smart and effective industrial and ST&I policies to deal with the immediate problems that may arise in the future with similar events in biomedicine and health infrastructure, a systemic, multidisciplinary and multisectoral approach is likely to be the most effective strategy to improve the resilience of Brazilian society against potential future threats.

In effect, the great attention currently focused on measures to increase the resilience of global production chains (and therefore of countries) to future exogenous shocks is obviously justified. However, the fundamental policy challenge for developing countries that is to ensure that participation in global value chains is only one among several complementary components of a development strategy that focuses on an accelerated pace of physical and human capital formation, economic diversification, technological sophistication, and social welfare enhancement.

In the future, therefore, the construction of a strong national innovation system that effectively contributes to the sustained development of the productive-technological capacities of the country will require strong coordination of economic policies and a significant flow of resources to support not only research and innovation in the health complex, but also in a wide range of scientific and technological knowledge and its practical applications. This includes the fields of data science, sociology, psychology, mass transportation systems engineering, supply chain management, digital and information and communication technologies, political science, and economics, just to name a few. Moreover, the public budget for ST&I needs to support not only the generation of new knowledge in this broad range of disciplines, but also the institutions and mechanisms that enable collaboration across sectors and between different organizations and markets.

However, considering the ongoing setbacks in recent years and the worsening fiscal conditions due to the Covid-19 crisis, the outlook is not at all optimistic. On the other hand, if it is true that the world is moving towards a post-pandemic "new normal," perhaps this is a unique opportunity to also re-evaluate the current accepted paradigms for the economic and innovation policy.

REFERENCES

Bresser-Pereira, L. C., Araújo, E. C., & Peres, S. C. (2020). An alternative to the middle-income trap. *Structural Change and Economic Dynamics, 52*, 294–312. doi:10.1016/j.strueco.2019.11.007

Edquist, C. (2005). Systems of innovation: Perspectives and challenges. In J. Fagerberg, D. Mowery, & R. R. Nelson (Eds.), *The Oxford Handbook of Innovation* (pp. 181–208). Oxford University Press.

Fagerberg, J., Lundvall, B.-A., & Srholec, M. (2018). Global value chains, national innovation systems and economic development. *European Journal of Development Research, 30*(3), 533–556. doi:10.105741287-018-0147-2

France moves to improve medical self-sufficiency. (2020). *Pressok*. Available at: https://pressok.org/2020/06/16/france-moves-to-improve-medical-self-sufficiency/

Hagerty, J. R. Some firms opt to bring manufacturing back to U.S. (2012). *The Wall Street Journal*. Available at: https://www.wsj.com/articles/SB10001424052702303612804577533232044873766

Institute for Studies in Industrial Development. (2019). *Desenvolvimento industrial em perspectiva internacional comparada* [Industrial development in comparative international perspective]. https://iedi.org.br/media/site/artigos/20190802_desind_intern_comp.pdf

Lawder, D. (2020). Exclusive: New U.S. development agency could loan billions for reshoring, official says. *Reuters*. Available at: https://www.reuters.com/article/us-usa-trade-reshoring-exclusive/exclusive-u-s-development-agency-could-loan-billions-for-reshoring-official-says-idUSKBN23U31F

Layos, J. J. M., & Peña, P. J. (2020). *Can innovation save us? Understanding the role of innovation in mitigating the Covid-19 pandemic in ASEAN-5 economies. MPRA Paper 100152*. University Library of Munich. https://mpra.ub.uni-muenchen.de/100152/

Ma, C. (2020). Manufacturer response to Covid-19 disruptions: Increased interest in automation, reshoring. *Thomas*. Available at https://www.thomasnet.com/insights/manufacturer-response-to-covid-19-disruptions-increased-interest-in-automation-reshoring/

National Industry Confederation of Brazil. (2020). *Crise do novo coronavírus promove desafios para a indústria e para o Brasil* [The new coronavirus crisis promotes challenges for the industry and for Brazil]. https://noticias.portaldaindustria.com.br/noticias/economia/crise-do-novo-coronavirus-promove-desafios-para-a-industria-e-para-o-brasil/

Nelson, R. R. (2009). Building effective 'innovation systems' versus dealing with 'market failures' as ways of thinking about technology policy. In D. Foray (Ed.), *The New Economics of Technology Policy*. Edward Elgar Publishing. doi:10.4337/9781848449169.00007

Organisation for Economic Cooperation and Development. (2013). *Interconnected economies: benefiting from global value chains.* OECD Publishing., doi:10.1787/9789264189560-

Organisation for Economic Cooperation and Development. (2020). *Covid-19 and global value chains: Policy options to build more resilient production networks. In OECD Policy Responses to Coronavirus (COVID-19).* OECD Publishing. doi:10.1787/04934ef4-

Pahl, S., & Timmer, M. P. (2020). Do global value chains enhance economic upgrading? A long view. *The Journal of Development Studies, 56*(9), 1683–1705. doi:10.1080/00220388.2019.1702159

Palma, J. G. (2005). Four sources of de-industrialisation and a new concept of the Dutch disease. In J. A. Ocampo (Ed.), Beyond reforms: Structural dynamic and macroeconomic vulnerability (pp. 71–117). Stanford, CA: Stanford University Press/Washington, DC: The World Bank.

Palma, J. G. (2019). Deindustrialization, "premature" deindustrialization, and "Dutch disease". *El Trimestre Economico, 86*(4), 901–966. doi:10.20430/ete.v86i344.970

Reynolds, I., & Urabe, E. (2020). Japan to fund firms to shift production out of China. *Bloomberg.* Available at: https://www.bloomberg.com/news/articles/2020-04-08/japan-to-fund-firms-to-shift-production-out-of-china

Rodrik, D. (2018). *New technologies, global value chains, and developing economies.* NBER Working Paper Series, 25164. Cambridge, MA: National Bureau of Economic Research. doi:10.3386/w25164

Szirmai, A. (2012). Industrialisation as an engine of growth in developing countries, 1950–2005. *Structural Change and Economic Dynamics, 23*(4), 406–420. doi:10.1016/j.strueco.2011.01.005

Tregenna, F. (2009). Characterizing deindustrialization: An analysis of changes in manufacturing employment and output internationally. *Cambridge Journal of Economics, 33*(3), 433–466. doi:10.1093/cje/ben032

Tregenna, F., & Andreoni, A. (2020). *Deindustrialisation reconsidered: Structural shifts and sectoral heterogeneity.* UCL Institute for Innovation and Public Purpose Working Paper Series (IIPP WP 2020–06). https://www.ucl.ac.uk/bartlett/public-purpose/wp2020-06

UNCTAD. (2013). *Global value chains: Investment and trade for development.* World Investment Report 2013. United Nations Publications. https://unctad.org/system/files/official-document/wir2013_en.pdf

UNCTAD. (2015). *Global value chains and south-south trade: economic cooperation and integration among developing countries.* (ECIDC), UNCTAD Report. https://unctad.org/system/files/official-document/gdsecidc2015d1_en.pdf

UNCTAD. (2020a). *The need to protect science, technology and innovation funding during and after the covid-19 crisis.* UNCTAD Policy Brief, 80. https://unctad.org/system/files/official-document/press-pb2020d4_en.pdf

UNCTAD. (2020b). *International production beyond the pandemic.* World Investment Report 2020. United Nations Publications. https://unctad.org/system/files/official-document/wir2020_en.pdf

United Nations. (2015). *Transforming our world: The 2030 Agenda for sustainable development* (A/RES/70/1). New York, NY: UN General Assembly. Retrieved from https://sdgs.un.org/2030agenda

United Nations Educational, Scientific and Cultural Organization. (2018). Mapping research and innovation in Lao People's Democratic Republic. In G. A. Lemarchand & A. Tash (Eds.), *GO SPIN Country Profiles in Science, Technology and Innovation Policy* (Vol. 7). UNESCO Publishing. https://unesdoc.unesco.org/ark:/48223/pf0000262884

World Bank. (2020). *Trading for development in the age of global value chains.* World Development Report 2020. Washington, D.C.: The World Bank. https://www.worldbank.org/en/publication/wdr2020

ENDNOTE

[1]   On this literature, see Bresser-Pereira et al. (2020).

Chapter 13
Strategic Sustainability in the Anthropocene

Eunice Tan

 https://orcid.org/0000-0002-1396-762X

Singapore Institute of Management, Singapore

Jürgen Rudolph

Kaplan Singapore, Singapore

ABSTRACT

This chapter discusses the critical value of integrating sound sustainability agendas into an organisation's strategic management strategies. Specifically, the authors debate the benefits, challenges, and counterpoints to authentic strategic sustainability alignment vis-à-vis an organisation's strategic value propositions in the Anthropocene. This perspective on sustainability shifts the paradigm of sustainability analyses from industry, sectoral, and financial indicators to proactive strategic guidelines that support human and societal development without compromising our planetary resources and ecological boundaries. In addition to discussing the implications of sustainable development agendas for strategic sustainability, the chapter also reviews two case studies of organisations that have successfully adopted sustainability into their strategic value propositions. Finally, it discusses Raworth's framework as a model for reinterpreting strategic sustainability management in the Anthropocene.

1. INTRODUCTION: SLEEPWALKING INTO CATASTROPHE?

Sustainability should be a key pillar of the strategy of every senior manager, irrespective of the company's location and industry. When the Apollo 8 astronauts filmed our beautiful blue planet for the first time, it became clear how small, isolated and vulnerable it is. To our knowledge, Earth is the only place in the universe where life exists. Despite climate change deniers – who are often unwittingly allied with super-rich elites who benefit from fossil fuel industries (Klein, 2014) – there is by now sufficient scientific insight into the destructiveness of the Anthropocene. Every record heatwave, flood, drought, storm and centimetre of sea level rise should remind us that "everything is environmental, from transportation to

DOI: 10.4018/978-1-6684-6845-6.ch013

taxes, work to love, cities to sex" (Schneider-Mayerson, 2020, p. 10). Increasingly, recent research and industry debates have highlighted the significance of integrating sustainability agendas into an organisation's strategic management strategies. As Robèrt et al. (2013) emphasise, companies need to proactively integrate strategic sustainability agendas and thinking into their business operations and strategies. Adopting a paradigm of strategic sustainability can epitomise a core driver for organisations to demonstrate their efforts to reduce their impacts on planetary boundaries as they aspire for competitiveness.

The Anthropocene is a period that started around the 1950s and is characterised by the dominant influence on climate and the environment of human activity. In the 1950s, the *Great Acceleration* began. Graphs for the rise of carbon dioxide, methane levels in the atmosphere, surface temperatures, factory farming, plastic pollution, ocean acidification, loss of fish populations and tropical forests all show a hockey stick shape from the mid-century onwards (Attenborough, 2020; Ripple et al., 2017; Wagler, 2011). This accelerating growth cannot continue forever, and the *Great Acceleration* is leading to the *Great Decline* (Attenborough, 2020). We are warming the Earth and adding carbon to the atmosphere at a rapid speed. Consequently, the Anthropocene as 'the epoch of humans' could end in the ultimate disappearance of our civilisation.

In the history of the Earth, a handful of mass extinctions have happened after each of which life had to be rebuilt. We are currently in the midst of the sixth mass extinction. For the past 10,000 years, we have been living in the Holocene, a relatively stable period in the history of our planet that has been compared to the Garden of Eden. During the Holocene, farming enabled civilisations. However, with the Anthropocene, the sixth mass extinction has begun. It is characterised by a current rate of biodiversity loss that is 100 – 1,000 times higher than natural extinction rates (Pimm et al., 1995; Pimm et al., 2014). We can, therefore, no longer continue with an unconsciousness of unsustainable living and business-as-usual.

Living unsustainably damages our whole ecological system to a point where it is bound to ultimately collapse. The shifting baseline syndrome, characterised by each generation defining what it experiences as 'normal', has distorted our perception of life. Attenborough (2020, p. 100) writes: "We have forgotten that once there were temperate forests that would take days to traverse, herds of bison that would take four hours to pass, and flocks of birds so vast and dense that they darkened the skies". He contrasts this with the situation only a few lifetimes later:

We have become accustomed to an impoverished planet. We have replaced the wild with the tame. We regard the Earth as our planet, run by humankind for humankind. There is little left for the rest of the living world. The truly wild world – the non-human world – has gone. We have overrun the Earth.

Likewise, Parker (2014) notes that sustainability concerns have become a key challenge in the 21st century. In this Anthropocene epoch, there needs to be a philosophical shift in managing humanity's impacts on the planet and its own fate. At present, almost four billion hectares or 80 per cent of farmland worldwide is used for meat and dairy production, with 60% of it dedicated to beef alone (Attenborough, 2020). The forcible transformation and destruction of the Earth by the human race have had damaging consequences, wherein human-induced changes have outpaced the natural processes (Dürbeck & Hüpkes, 2020; Parker, 2014). Consequently, there are great opportunities for rewilding the world through a healthier diet, vertical farming, and reduced emissions. Rewilding the world would reduce the carbon dioxide content in the air and lock it away in an expanding wilderness, leading to gains in carbon storage and biodiversity (Attenborough, 2020).

In the remainder of this chapter, we explore sustainable development as the nexus of sustainability and development by exploring the concept of sustainability, the triple bottom line (TBL) and sustainable business practices for our common future (section 2). Section 3 discusses indicators for sustainable development (including the United Nations sustainable development goals) and their implications for businesses' strategic sustainability. We then provide some case studies. The final section offers conclusions and recommendations for a sustainable future. The overall guiding question is: Once our eyes are wide open to the urgent need for sustainability in countries, businesses and our individual lifestyles, we must find answers to the question: *what actions can we take to avoid sleepwalking into catastrophe?*

2. SUSTAINABLE DEVELOPMENT: THE NEXUS OF SUSTAINABILITY AND DEVELOPMENT

2.1 The Concept of Sustainability

'Sustainability' is derived from the Latin verb *sustinere*, which means 'sustain' and refers to the ability to continue over a long period of time. The concept of sustainability (*Nachhaltigkeit*) can be traced back to German accountant Hans Carl von Carlowitz, who published a treatise on sustainable forest management in 1713 (Töpfer, 2013). The idea of sustainability is practised in many ancient cultures and contemporary indigenous societies, where human use of natural resources is restricted. In contemporary discourse, the term sustainability likewise generally refers to the efforts to ensure a dynamic equilibrium, such that the environmental impacts from human and economic activity are kept within the boundaries of Earth's carry capacity and finite resources (Pearce, 2014; Rezaee et al., 2019). Correspondingly, it can be said that sustainability is a dynamic, rather than static process (Huang et al., 2015). Thus, it is necessary to consider sustainability within the context of strategic management.

Broadly, sustainability can be subdivided into environmental, economic, and social sustainability. However, the extant discourse surrounding sustainability is not without its controversies. Whilst the general ideological concepts and sentiments of sustainability have been broadly accepted, there has yet to be "a set of universally applicable (and accepted) principles" which "define sustainability at all scales, disciplines and aspects of human endeavour" (Johnston et al., 2007, p. 62). Certainly, the term sustainability can mean different things to different people. In common usage, 'sustainability' usually refers to the environmental aspect, which is also how we primarily use the term in this chapter. This perspective and philosophical critique of 'sustainability fundamentalism' from an environmental, nature-centric and bioethics perspective has also been increasingly advocated in recent extant research (e.g., Parker, 2014; Richie, 2020; Sarkar, 2014). Within this context, Johnston et al. (2007) advise that sustainability discourse requires the reframing of the human-natural interaction towards an ethics of precautionary principles.

2.2 The Triple Bottom Line of Sustainable Development

The preceding section discussed the concept of sustainability and its broad categorisation into economic, social, and environmental dimensions. This is also commonly referred to as the triple bottom line (TBL) of sustainable development. Stoddard et al. (2012) explain that the TBL is fundamentally a philosophical orientation to extend an organisation's development agendas beyond its economic sustainable strategy, to also include its social and environmental sustainability strategies explicitly. In other words, it advocates economic, social, and environmental accountability of a firm's activities and performance. In contrast to prevailing notions about sustainability and its common emphasis on the environmental bottom line, the principles of sustainable development tend to focus on efforts to balance the overall equilibrium of the TBL. Thus, the two terms may not necessarily be the same (Pearce, 2014).

The definition of Sustainable Development (SD) has been widely attributed to the Brundtland Report: 'Our Common Future', presented at the World Commission on Environment and Development Conference (WCED, 1987), which defines sustainable development as "development that meets the needs of the present without compromising the ability of future generations to meet their own needs" (p. 8). Holden et al. (2014) revisited the discourse on SD and 'Our Common future' and observed that 25 years on, whilst SD remains an appealing and increasingly advocated strategy supporting all that is good, desirable, and socially responsible, it remains a highly debated ideological and political concept; and like its sustainability conceptual cousin, without a clear, universally agreed, or accepted definition. Nonetheless, despite this predicament, the pursuit of sustainable development agendas remains a priority. Fundamentally, the quest for SD and the TBL is important for the future of sustainability since it takes into account financial and non-financial aspects of sustainability relevant to supporting people, planet, and profit (Elkington, 2018; Huang et al., 2015; Rezaee et al., 2019). These three dimensions of the TBL are discussed below.

First, the environmental dimension of sustainability revolves around climate change, loss of biodiversity, land degradation and air and water pollution. Potentially catastrophic climate change results from rising greenhouse gas emissions from burning fossil fuels, deforestation, and agricultural production (Ripple et al., 2017). Second, the economic dimension of sustainability relates to the acknowledgement that economic growth and development matter for overall human and societal well-being (Pearce, 2014). This dimension of sustainability is controversial, as the notion of SD (and its inherent trade-off between economic prosperity for all and environmental conservation) can be used for whitewashing an ecologically destructive economic system (Daly, 1996; Redclift, 2005). As Johnston et al. (2007) suggest, the lack of a definitive conceptual definition and the proliferation of alternative definitions of SD has created an oxymoronic term that is increasingly considered self-contradictory, ambiguous, and even misleading.

Notwithstanding, economic growth is important for poverty reduction, especially in least-developed countries (United Nations, 2017). Finally, there is the social dimension of sustainability. Arguably, social issues are at the very heart of the sustainability discourse (Boyer et al., 2016). Sustainability depends on the relationship between the social and the natural domains, that is, human embeddedness in the environment.

2.3 Sustainable Business Practices for Our Common Future

Sustainable business practices strive to integrate the three dimensions of sustainability. The TBL attempts to balance people, planet, and profit (Elkington, 2018). Correspondingly, there has been increasing awareness and recognition of the strategic value of business sustainability and the significance of its strategic alignment and integration with an organisation's corporate culture, business environment, performance KPIs and decision-making processes (Rezaee et al., 2019). Sustainability thus remains a prominent multifaceted agenda in strategic business and management (Pearce, 2014). Accordingly, sustainable business practices should not merely be an accounting or balance scorecard tool and trade-off strategy to 'look good on the books'. There is a need to genuinely go beyond profits (capitalism and weak sustainability) to a stronger focus on people and planet (strong sustainability and socio-ecocentrism) *(*Elkington, 2018;

Getzner, 1999; Huang et al., 2015). To address this, sustainability initiatives have evolved to include related concepts such as the green economy and the circular economy in recent years.

In this respect, the circular economy attempts to decouple economic growth from environmental destruction. Nobre and Tavares (2021) posit that the circular economy has evolved beyond organisational hype to become a global tendency. In this respect, they define the circular economy as "an economic system that targets zero waste and pollution throughout materials lifecycles, from environment extraction to industrial transformation, and to final consumers, applying to all involved ecosystems" (p. 10). As Erdelen and Richardson (2019) suggest, there is an urgent need to enact a paradigm shift toward a green and circular economy to inspire strategic practices that keep humanity within the desired operating realms of the Anthropocene in the contemporary economy. In sum, the strategic and synergistic application of the TBL dimensions and sustainability principles can transform business sustainability practices that not only support the environmental and social sustainability agendas of present and future generations but are also economically appealing, practical, and profitable.

3. INDICATORS FOR SUSTAINABLE DEVELOPMENT: IMPLICATIONS FOR STRATEGIC SUSTAINABILITY

3.1 What Are Sustainable Development Indicators?

Sustainable development indicators are a key consideration when developing business sustainability agendas. While there may be variations in its articulation, SD indicators are commonly based upon the three dimensions of sustainability: the economic, social, and environmental bottom lines. Consequently, SD indicators are essential in the practice, science, and implementation of business sustainability since it represents key assessment and informational variables on the state and performance of an organisation's TBL dimensions and its contributions to human-environmental systems and well-being (Huang et al., 2015). Fundamentally, SD indicators set measurable parameters to assess, monitor and manage an organisation's sustainability efforts. Additionally, these measurable variables may also serve to reveal potential changes in conditions encountered. If properly developed, SD indicators can facilitate quantifiable assessment, management, monitoring, and reporting of sustainability performance from an organisation's business operations, based on crucial SD goals and targets (Bali Swain & Yang-Wallentin, 2020; Heras-Saizarbitoria et al., 2022; Warhurst, 2002). The United Nations global indicator framework for Sustainable Development Goals and targets of the 2030 Agenda for Sustainable Development (UN-SDGs) is one such example and is discussed in section 3.2 below.

SD indicators are part of a portfolio of sustainability quality control mechanisms, positioned along a spectrum of controls from internal, voluntary organisational mechanisms to external, regulatory (and obligatory) requirements. Sequentially, these include (1) codes of conduct (or code of ethics), (2) ecolabels (including specified indicators for certification and accreditation), and (3) awards (Weaver, 2013). Additionally, there has been a myriad of indices, balanced scorecards, benchmarking and other quality standards for measuring sustainability performance over the years. Whilst these are too extensive to review in detail within the confines of this chapter, suffice to say that such quality control measures and indicators of sustainability are necessary tools for managing an organisation's strategic sustainability efforts. Essentially, SD indicators provide quantifiable variables and informational sets that are formally selected for ongoing information gathering, monitoring, measuring and planning of all sustainability (i.e., its TBL) relevant activities at different operational and strategic levels (Bali Swain & Yang-Wallentin, 2020; Zeppel, 2015). Consequently, sustainability indicators interpret and report the state or changing condition(s) and performance standards of the organisation so that appropriate actions and decision-making can be decided. However, Weaver (2013) does caution that whilst ideologically appealing, strategic alignment of sustainability is complicated by the realities of selecting, measuring, monitoring and evaluating a practical set of relevant indicators. Thus, Zeppel (2015) suggests that to be effective, sustainability indicators must be: (1) observable, (2) measurable, (3) responsive to changing use conditions, (4) cover appropriate scales of measurement, (5) comprise a mix of measurement components, (6) address a range of indicator functions, and (7) relevant to an area's core management objectives. Finally, the above indicator provisions should be assessed against the fundamental factors of clarity, credibility, feasibility, relevance, and comparability with other enterprises over time.

3.2 The United Nations Sustainable Development Goals: Implications for Business

The United Nations Sustainable Development Goals (UNSDGs) were adopted in 2015 during the United Nations General Assembly and evolved from the previous Millennium Development Goals (MDGs). The UNSDGs are referred to as the 2030 Agenda for Sustainable Development and represent a plan of action and commitment to people, planet, and prosperity through 17 SD integrated, indivisible goal indicators and targets to balance the TBLs of economic, social, and environmental sustainability (Eisenmenger et al., 2020; UN, 2017). These 17 UNSDGs are summarised in Table 1 below.

While the UNSDGs have been ideologically and politically lauded for their intentions in forwarding socio-economic and environmental agendas and adopted as the global framework for SD, critiques have also deemed it to be too extensive, ambitious, universal, difficult to quantify, and inconsistent in harmonising socioeconomic and environmental outcomes (Bali Swain & Yang-Wallentin, 2020). As Eisenmenger et al. (2020) surmise, the UNSDGs face the same inherent challenges of SD prevalent since the definition was first coined in 'Our Common Future' (WCED, 1987), and is unlikely to achieve their "self-proclaimed goal...to transform our world" (Eisenmenger et al., 2020, p. 1102). The authors posit that real transformative change and outcomes necessitate social-economic, political, and cultural changes that exceed current modes of human consumption and production. Similarly, Heras-Saizarbitoria et al. (2022) observe that whilst the UNSDGs have been keenly advocated in organisational theory and practice as an opportunity for firms to rethink sustainable business practices and demonstrate their commitment to corporate social responsibility, there is limited real engagement, prioritisation, and progress to operationalise the SDGs. Likewise, Richie (2020) observes that most current efforts and initiatives in progressing sustainability are inadequate in their scope.

Notwithstanding articulated concerns about green-washing and superficial approaches to organisational commitments to the UNSDGs, sustainable development and sustainability agendas have universally become ubiquitous in the contemporary business lexicon. As Elkington (2018) reports, the UNSDGs may potentially generate some $12 trillion a year in market opportunities by 2030. However, the author also cautions that sustainability outcomes must go beyond just the narrow approach of the TBL as an accounting quid pro quo or trade-off to balance an organisation's sustainability accounting and reporting. To avoid such a trade-off mentality, van Zanten and van Tulder (2021) propose a nexus approach to corporate sustainability, wherein the interactions across all the 17 goals of the UNSDGs are monitored, assessed, and managed in an integrated manner to improve societal and environmental sustainability

Table 1. Goal indicator framework for the UNSDGs

Goal 1	End poverty in all its forms everywhere
Goal 2	End hunger, achieve food security and improved nutrition and promote sustainable agriculture
Goal 3	Ensure healthy lives and promote well-being for all at all ages
Goal 4	Ensure inclusive and equitable quality education and promote lifelong learning opportunities for all
Goal 5	Achieve gender equality and empower all women and girls
Goal 6	Ensure availability and sustainable management of water and sanitation for all
Goal 7	Ensure access to affordable, reliable, sustainable, and modern energy for all
Goal 8	Promote sustained, inclusive and sustainable economic growth, full and productive employment and decent work for all
Goal 9	Build resilient infrastructure, promote inclusive and sustainable industrialisation and foster innovation
Goal 10	Reduce inequality within and among countries
Goal 11	Make cities and human settlements inclusive, safe, resilient, and sustainable
Goal 12	Ensure sustainable consumption and production patterns
Goal 13	Take urgent action to combat climate change and its impacts
Goal 14	Conserve and sustainably use the oceans, seas and marine resources for sustainable development
Goal 15	Protect, restore, and promote sustainable use of terrestrial ecosystems, sustainably manage forests, combat desertification, and halt and reverse land degradation and halt biodiversity loss
Goal 16	Promote peaceful and inclusive societies for sustainable development, provide access to justice for all and build effective, accountable, and inclusive institutions at all levels
Goal 17	Strengthen the means of implementation and revitalise the Global Partnership for Sustainable Development

Source: UN (2017)

impacts. From this perspective, the various UNSDGs should not be selectively cherry-picked in silos but are synergistically and simultaneously progressed. As we have noted in section 2.2, there needs to be a more vigorous effort to centre the social and environmental domains at the heart of the sustainability discourse. After all, the well-being of our economy and society relies infinitely on our planetary well-being and biodiversity.

4. CASE STUDIES: GOING GREEN ON THE LITTLE RED DOT

Organisations play a vital role in contributing to global (un)sustainability, socio-environmental objectives, and the achievement of the UNSDGs (van Zanten & van Tulder, 2021). In this section, we review Singapore as a country case study with two small-and-medium-sized social enterprises, Crust Group and Unpackt, as mini-cases.

The reason for picking some Singaporean case studies is because both of us live in this beautiful island-city-state, with Singapore having a Green Plan and committed to sustainability targets (The Singapore Green Plan 2030, 2021). We also believe it is good to look beyond the usual WEIRD (Western, educated, industrialised, rich and democratic) countries (even if the main difference between them and Singapore is that the latter is Asian and not Western). Singapore is the "city with the highest density of greenery in the world" (Parfitt, 2018), and she is often referred to as the 'City in a Garden' or even 'City in Nature' (Tan, 2021). As a highly developed, heavily-populated and land-scarce city-state, Singapore faces considerable constraints when using renewable energy. There are no fast-flowing rivers that would enable hydro-power, and there is insufficient land for intensive use of solar energy or wind power. Nonetheless, between the declaration ahead of the Copenhagen Summit of 2009 and 2020, Singapore was able to reduce its emission of greenhouse gases by 32% (twice the targeted percentage: Wong, 2022). Prime Minister Lee Hsien Loong declared in 2019 that "everything else must bend at the knee" in order to confront the climate crisis (cited in Seah, 2020), and Singapore is also among the countries that have declared to pursue a so-called 'net-zero' strategy by 2050 (UN Climate Change Conference UK, 2021).

Net zero refers to a state in which the greenhouse gases (GHG) going into the atmosphere are balanced by removal from the atmosphere. It involves carbon neutrality, a state of net-zero, human-caused carbon dioxide (CO_2) emissions that can be achieved by balancing carbon dioxide emissions with its removal through carbon-offsetting or by eliminating emissions from society. CO_2-releasing processes are caused by transportation, energy production, agriculture, and industry. Carbon-offsetting refers to a reduction in GHG emissions or an increase in carbon storage (through land restoration or the planting of trees) that is used to compensate for emissions that occur elsewhere. Net zero is important because – for carbon dioxide at least – this is the state at which global warming stops (Pye et al., 2017). The term 'net zero' and its related goal are controversial. For instance, Dyke et al. (2021) warned that "the idea of net zero has licensed a recklessly cavalier 'burn now, pay later' approach which has seen carbon emissions continue to soar". By focusing on targets decades into the future, there is the danger of countries blowing their 'carbon budget' rather than concentrating on what we can do immediately to cut emissions sharply (Klein, 2020). You run out of road when you kick the can down the road enough times.

For Singapore, achieving net zero by 2050 is a stretch goal and will require paradigmatic behavioural changes for businesses and households alike. Both corporations and individuals need "to be more energy efficient, reduce energy consumption and carbon emissions, and adopt green energy alternatives" (Wong, 2022). Singapore's Deputy Prime Minister Lawrence Wong plans to use taxes as disincentives, both in the form of high carbon and high petrol taxes. This "will help to sharpen the impetus of shifting to cleaner alternatives" and send "the right price signals for the economy as a whole" (Wong, 2022). Other green policies include the decarbonisation of the power sector and a national strategy that focuses on low-carbon renewable energy (The Singapore Green Plan 2030, 2021). The Singapore government also plans to "make Singapore a green financial centre – to effectively channel green capital towards the development of transition projects and climate change solutions around the region" (Wong, 2022). Whilst these achievements and intentions are to be lauded, there are nonetheless counterpoints to its sustainability endeavours.

Whilst the Singapore government's plans are inspiring, and its technocrats have the justified reputation to get things done, it is noteworthy that the city-state has the highest per capita carbon footprint in the Asia-Pacific, and apparently, if everybody consumed like Singaporeans, we would need four planet Earths (Kim, 2020; *Climate Change Tracker*, 2021). Historically, Singapore has deep and long-standing ties with the highly problematic fossil fuel industry, and in 2015, the oil and gas industry made up a third of Singapore's manufacturing output, with Singapore being the world's third-largest exporter – and Asia's largest – of refined oil products (Mock, 2020). Thus, a complex picture emerges that paints Singapore neither as a green poster boy for sustainability nor as a global warming villain.

After having provided the overall context on Singapore, our first mini-case study focuses on Crust. In line with Elkington (2018), Crust Group has been identified as a Certified B-Corp Company (defined as not only 'best in the world', but 'good for the world') in Singapore. This is in line with increasing momentum in recent years for organisations to embrace a "middle ground view" of "doing well by doing good", wherein both financial and non-financial sustainability performances are strategically aligned to its core values (Rezaee et al., 2019, p. 24). The B-Corp certification aims to "measure a company's entire social and environmental impact", and certified companies are defined as "leaders in the global movement for an inclusive, equitable, and regenerative economy" (B-Lab, 2022). Crust upcycles by using surplus bread and other surplus ingredients from their restaurant and hotel partners to make sustainable, artisan beers. They have fun flavours like Beerguette and Kaya Toast Stout (kaya is a local jam made of coconut milk, eggs, sugar, and pandan leaf). Crust thus makes a small contribution to addressing the mountains of food waste by reducing bread waste. With the company cleverly advertising itself as the "beer that makes a difference" and "No crust left behind", they have also started Crop, a line of non-alcoholic beverages that is promoted with the slogan "No peel left behind" (Crust Group, 2022). These drinks include the corporation's naturally-essenced sparkling fruit water made from fruit waste and loss.

The second mini-case study is Unpackt, another Singaporean social enterprise. Whilst Crust is supplier-focused in its environmentalism, Unpackt focuses on the end consumer. As their name suggests, they offer package-free bulk food, products and daily necessities with the aim of a "zero waste lifestyle" (Unpackt, 2022). Their mission is to build a "green and mindful Singapore, one community at a time" (Unpackt, 2022). Unpackt provides retail, corporate and community and education services. In their retail outlet, they encourage customers to bring their reusable containers and buy package-free a curated range of local, sustainable brands and socially-conscious products. Given that a "refuse truck's worth of plastic is dumped into the ocean every minute" and that, "at this rate, by 2050 there will be more plastic than fish in the sea" (Raworth, 2022, p. 5), Unpackt is an important social enterprise trailblazer.

5. THE FUTURE OF STRATEGIC SUSTAINABILITY

The preceding sections of the chapter have emphasised the need to purposefully and proactively integrate an organisation's strategic sustainability into its strategic management agendas and actions to inspire competitive advantage. The future of strategic sustainability requires an authentic strategic alignment of an organisation's value propositions that support economic, social, and environmental goals within the boundaries of our finite planet. Within this context, the concept of planetary boundaries (Dürbeck & Hüpkes, 2020; Parker, 2014; Robèrt et al., 2013) has been proposed in the recent strategic sustainability discourse as an approach to critically manage our contemporary global sustainability and ecological challenges. This perspective on sustainability fundamentally shifts the paradigm of sustainability analyses from industry, sectoral and financial indicators to proactive strategic guidelines that support human and societal development that does not compromise our planetary resources and ecological boundaries. As we had noted at the start of this chapter, the Anthropocenic challenges lie in the planetary scale of human-environment interactions and their consequences on earth systems (Dürbeck & Hüpkes, 2020), and these challenges are likely to remain precarious. Likewise, Holden et al. (2014, p.130) suggest that the ethos of sustainability and sustainable development will remain "universally desired, diversely understood, extremely difficult to achieve, and won't go away". Thus, humanity must awake from its unsound sleepwalk into global environmental catastrophe and its own destruction before it is too late.

Kate Raworth (2022) has proposed a framework for sustainable development called the doughnut model, which is a reinterpretation of the planetary boundaries model. In essence, the doughnut model provides "a social foundation of well-being that no one should fall below, and an ecological ceiling of planetary pressure that we should not go beyond. Between the two lies a just and safe space for all" (Raworth, 2022, p. 11). The model contains two concentric circles. Its inner ring is its social foundation: the basic needs of people such as "sufficient food; clean water and decent sanitation; access to energy and clean cooking facilities; access to education and to healthcare; decent housing; a minimum income and decent work; and access to networks of information and to networks of social support" (Raworth, 2022, p. 45). These goals are to be achieved with "gender equality, social equity, political voice, and peace of justice" and they are all included in the UNSDGs (Raworth, 2022, p. 45). Below the inner ring lie critical human deprivations such as hunger and illiteracy. The outer ring is an ecological ceiling below which we must remain if we are to have a chance of maintaining a stable and safe planet. Beyond the outer ring lies critical planetary degradation which is defined by nine planetary boundaries: climate change, ocean acidification, chemical pollution, nitrogen and phosphorus loading, freshwater withdrawals, land conversion, biodiversity loss, air pollution, and ozone layer depletion. Many of these planetary boundaries have been quantified. For instance, the climate change boundary is at most 350 parts per million (ppm) of atmospheric carbon dioxide concentration – however, in 2015, it was already measured and described as 400 ppm and worsening (Steffen et al., 2015). The grand ambition of the doughnut model is a stable world in which everyone gets a fair share of its finite resources. We must keep below the ecological ceiling, but not at the expense of the well-being of people.

Figure 1. The doughnut model

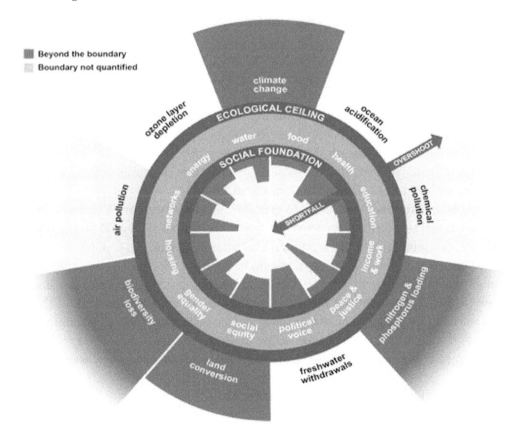

In Figure 1, the red wedges below the social foundation show the proportion of people worldwide falling short of life's basics. The red wedges radiating beyond the ecological ceiling show the overshoot of planetary boundaries. For the data, see Raworth, 2022, pp. 300-304. Image: Kate Raworth and Christian Guthier/The Lancet Planetary Health. Source: Raworth (2017).

The doughnut model provides us with a big picture of how a sustainable world may look like. We now discuss what governments, corporations and individuals can do in order to be more sustainable.

5.1 What Can Governments Do to Be Sustainable?

After much deregulation, calls for 'small government' and public austerity in the era of market fundamentalism and neoliberalism (that began with Reagan and Thatcher in the 1980s), it would appear that state leadership is now needed more than ever in order "to catalyse public, private, commons and household investments in a renewable energy future" (Raworth, 2022, p. 86). Thus far, most governments have not led by example and as regards the climate goals, there has been "a process of virtually uninterrupted backsliding" (Klein, 2014, p. 11). The UN Environmental Program, for instance, expects that by 2030 (as compared to 2010), global greenhouse gas emissions will have risen by 10% rather than be reduced by 45%. The latter would be necessary to be on track for net zero by 2050 (UNEP, 2022). Amongst many other things, reregulation of the corporate sector and "taxing the rich and filthy" (Klein 2020, p. 88) have been proposed.

5.2 What Can Businesses Do to Be Sustainable?

Milton Friedman (1970) (in)famously argued that "the social responsibility of business is to increase its profits", implying that the business of business is business. Thankfully, few people would agree with him on this today, with there being much emphasis on corporate social responsibility (CSR) and ESG (Environmental, Social, and Governance) investing becoming increasingly important (Halbritter & Dorfleitner, 2015). A popular approach is to "*do what pays*, by adopting eco-efficiency measures that cut costs, or boost the brand" (Raworth, 2022, p. 215). Other approaches can be "to *do our fair share*" or "*to do no harm*", with "*be generous*" the most far-reaching one (Raworth, 2022, pp. 216-218). True ESG companies are hard to find (Cornell & Damodaran, 2020).

Whilst most businesses have unsustainable practices, there has been much focus on the fossil fuel industry. Activists and scholars call for imposing severe restrictions on the oil and gas industry, "the richest and most powerful industry the world has ever known" (Klein, 2014, p. 63) and argue that the Western legal principle of 'the polluter pays' should be applied to fossil fuel companies. A whopping 71 per cent of total GHG emissions since 1988 can be traced to just 100 corporate and state fossil fuel corporations (Klein, 2020). Although fossil fuel companies have known for decades that their core product was warming the planet, many of them have lobbied politicians, funded decade-long campaigns of disinformation and obfuscation about the reality of global warming and actively blocked progress (Klein, 2020). For a climate catastrophe to be averted, fossil fuel companies may need to stop digging.

5.3 What Can Individuals Do to Be Sustainable?

Despite repeated exhortations by governments and businesses to individuals to save the planet by changing our habits, there is only so much that we can do. We can eat less or no meat (become vegetarians or vegans) – the carbon footprint of our food choices vastly differs (Greeneatz, n.d.). We can shop fair trade and local, boycott big, 'evil' brands, fly less, become anti-consumerist and end the cult of shopping, cultivate a home garden, save water, reduce, reuse and recycle. However, in Naomi Klein's words:

The hard truth is that the answer to the question 'What can I, as an individual, do to stop climate change?' is nothing... the very idea that we, as atomised individuals... could play a significant part in stabilising the planet's climate systems or changing the global economy is objectively nuts. We can only meet the tremendous challenges together, as part of a massive and organised global movement. (Klein, 2020, p. 133)

Hence, we could consider joining an environmentalist organisation such as Food and Water Watch, 350.org, Greenpeace, Rainforest Action Network, or Friends of the Earth.

What will the future look like? Science fiction author Kim Stanley Robinson stated that "the future isn't cast into one inevitable course. On the contrary, we could cause the sixth great mass extinction event in Earth's history, or we could create a prosperous civilisation, sustainable over the long haul. Either is possible starting from now" (cited in Brady, 2019). Climate change and other environmental destruction act as accelerants to many of our social ills (inequality, wars, racism, sexual violence), but they can also be accelerants for the forces working for economic and social justice (Klein, 2020). There is still hope that governments, businesses and individuals will do the right thing to avoid sleepwalking into catastrophe.

REFERENCES

Attenborough, D. (2020). *A life on our planet. My witness statement and a vision for the future*. Witness Books.

B-Lab. (2022). *About B-Corp certification*. https://www.bcorporation.net/en-us/certification

Bali Swain, R., & Yang-Wallentin, F. (2020). Achieving sustainable development goals: Predicaments and strategies. *International Journal of Sustainable Development and World Ecology*, 27(2), 96–106. doi:10.1080/13504509.2019.1692316

Boyer, R., Peterson, N., Arora, P., & Caldwell, K. (2016). Five approaches to social sustainability and an integrated way forward. *Sustainability (Basel)*, 8(9), 878. doi:10.3390u8090878

Brady, A. (2019, April 15). 17 writers on the role of fiction in addressing climate change. *Literary Hub*. https://lithub.com/17-writers-on-the-role-of-fiction-in-addressing-climate-change/

Climate Action Tracker. (2021). Singapore. https://climateactiontracker.org/countries/singapore/

Cornell, B., & Damodaran, A. (2020). Valuing ESG: Doing good or sounding good? *The Journal of Impact and ESG Investing*, 1(1), 76–93. doi:10.3905/jesg.2020.1.1.076

Crust Group. (2022). *Homepage*. https://www.crust-group.com/sg

Daly, H. E. (1996). *Beyond growth: The economics of sustainable development*. Beacon Press.

Dürbeck, G., & Hüpkes, P. (Eds.). (2020). *The Anthropocenic turn: The interplay between disciplinary and interdisciplinary responses to a new age*. Routledge. doi:10.4324/9781003037620

Dyke, J., Watson, R., & Knorr, W. (2021, April 22). Climate scientists: concept of net zero is a dangerous trap. *The Conversation.* https://theconversation.com/climate-scientists-concept-of-net-zero-is-a-dangerous-trap-157368

Eisenmenger, N., Pichler, M., Krenmayr, N., Noll, D., Plank, B., Schalmann, E., Wandl, M.-T., & Gingrich, S. (2020). The sustainable development goals prioritise economic growth over sustainable resource use: A critical reflection on the SDGs from a socio-ecological perspective. *Sustainability Science, 15*(4), 1101–1110. doi:10.100711625-020-00813-x

Elkington, J. (2018). 25 years ago I coined the phrase 'triple bottom line.' Here's why it's time to rethink it. *Harvard Business Review, 25,* 2–5.

Erdelen, W. R., & Richardson, J. G. (2019). *Managing complexity: Earth systems and strategies for the future.* Routledge.

Friedman, M. (1970). A Friedman doctrine: The social responsibility of business is to increase its profits. *The New York Times Magazine, 13,* 32-33.

Getzner, M. (1999). Weak and strong sustainability indicators and regional environmental resources. *Environmental Management and Health, 10*(3), 170–176. doi:10.1108/09566169910275022

Greeneatz. (n.d.). *Food's carbon footprint.* https://www.greeneatz.com/foods-carbon-footprint.html

Halbritter, G., & Dorfleitner, G. (2015). The wages of social responsibility—Where are they? A critical review of ESG investing. *Review of Financial Economics, 26*(1), 25–35. doi:10.1016/j.rfe.2015.03.004

Heras-Saizarbitoria, I., Urbieta, L., & Boiral, O. (2022). Organisations' engagement with sustainable development goals: From cherry-picking to SDG-washing? *Corporate Social Responsibility and Environmental Management, 29*(2), 316–328. doi:10.1002/csr.2202

Johnston, P., Everard, M., Santillo, D., & Robèrt, K. H. (2007). Reclaiming the definition of sustainability. *Environmental Science and Pollution Research International, 14*(1), 60–66. doi:10.1065/espr2007.01.375 PMID:17352129

Kim, H. M. (2020). Lovable lutrines: Curated nature and environmental migrants in the Ottercity. In M. Schneider-Mayerson (Ed.), *Eating chilli crab in the anthropocene: Environmental perspectives on life in Singapore* (pp. 241–268). Ethos Books.

Klein, N. (2014). *This changes everything.* Penguin.

Klein, N. (2020). *On fire. The burning case for a new green deal.* Penguin.

Mock, A. (2020). Singapore on fire. From fossil history to climate activism. In M. Schneider-Mayerson (Ed.), *Eating chilli crab in the anthropocene: Environmental perspectives on life in Singapore* (pp. 201–220). Ethos Books.

Nobre, G. C., & Tavares, E. (2021). The quest for a circular economy final definition: A scientific perspective. *Journal of Cleaner Production, 314,* 127973. doi:10.1016/j.jclepro.2021.127973

Parfitt, J. (February 7, 2018). A tale of two otters: settling in Singapore, suffering in China. *Mongabay.* https://news.mongabay.com/2018/02/a-tale-of-two-otters-settling-in-singapore-suffering-in-china/

Parker, J. (2014). *Critiquing sustainability, changing philosophy.* Routledge. doi:10.4324/9780203095577

Pearce, D. (2014). *Blueprint 3: Measuring sustainable development.* Routledge. doi:10.4324/9781315070414

Pimm, S. L., Jenkins, C. N., Abell, R., Brooks, T. M., Gittleman, J. L., Joppa, L. N., Raven, P. H., Roberts, C. M., & Sexton, J. O. (2014). The biodiversity of species and their rates of extinction, distribution, and protection. *Science, 344*(6187), 1246752. Advance online publication. doi:10.1126cience.1246752 PMID:24876501

Pimm, S. L., Russell, G. J., Gittleman, J. L., & Brooks, T. M. (1995). The future of biodiversity. *Science, 269*(5222), 347–350. doi:10.1126cience.269.5222.347 PMID:17841251

Pye, S., Li, F. G., Price, J., & Fais, B. (2017). Achieving net-zero emissions through the reframing of UK national targets in the post-Paris Agreement era. *Nature Energy, 2*(3), 1–7. doi:10.1038/nenergy.2017.24

Raworth, K. (2017, April 28). Meet the doughnut: The new economic model that could help end inequality. *World Economic Forum.* https://www.weforum.org/agenda/2017/04/the-new-economic-model-that-could-end-inequality-doughnut/

Raworth, K. (2022). *Doughnut economics. Seven ways to think like a 21st-century economist.* Penguin.

Redclift, M. (2005). Sustainable development (1987 – 2005): An oxymoron comes of age. *Sustainable Development (Bradford), 13*(4), 212–227. doi:10.1002d.281

Rezaee, Z., Tsui, J., Cheng, P., & Zhou, G. (2019). *Business sustainability in Asia: Compliance, performance, and integrated reporting and assurance.* John Wiley & Sons. doi:10.1002/9781119502302

Richie, C. (2020). Guest editorial: Sustainability and bioethics: Where we have been, where we are, where we are going. *The New Bioethics : a Multidisciplinary Journal of Biotechnology and the Body, 26*(2), 82–90. doi:10.1080/20502877.2020.1767920 PMID:32584209

Ripple, W. J., Wolf, C., Newsome, T. M., Galetti, M., Alamgir, M., Crist, E., Mahmoud, M. I., & Laurance, W. F. (2017). World scientists' warning to humanity: A second notice. *Bioscience, 67*(12), 1026–1028. doi:10.1093/biosci/bix125

Robèrt, K. H., Broman, G. I., & Basile, G. (2013). Analysing the concept of planetary boundaries from a strategic sustainability perspective: How does humanity avoid tipping the planet? *Ecology and Society, 18*(2), 5. doi:10.5751/ES-05336-180205

Sarkar, S. (2014). Environmental philosophy: From theory to practice. *Studies in History and Philosophy of Science Part C Studies in History and Philosophy of Biological and Biomedical Sciences, 45*, 89–91. doi:10.1016/j.shpsc.2013.10.010 PMID:24268932

Schneider-Mayerson, M. (Ed.). (2020). Eating chilli crab in the anthropocene: Environmental perspectives on life in Singapore. Ethos Books.

Seah, B. (2020). Another garden city is possible: A plan for a post-carbon Singapore. In M. Schneider-Mayerson (Ed.), *Eating chilli crab in the anthropocene: Environmental perspectives on life in Singapore* (pp. 241–268). Ethos Books.

Steffen, W., Richardson, K., Rockström, J., Cornell, S. E., Fetzer, I., Bennett, E. M., Biggs, R., Carpenter, S. R., de Vries, W., de Wit, C. A., Folke, C., Gerten, D., Heinke, J., Mace, G. M., Persson, L. M., Ramanathan, V., Reyers, B., & Sörlin, S. (2015). Planetary boundaries: Guiding human development on a changing planet. *Science, 347*(6223), 1259855. doi:10.1126cience.1259855 PMID:25592418

Stoddard, J. E., Pollard, C. E., & Evans, M. R. (2012). The triple bottom line: A framework for sustainable tourism development. *International Journal of Hospitality & Tourism Administration, 13*(3), 233–258. doi:10.1080/15256480.2012.698173

Tan, E. (2021). Wildlife tourism in urban destinations. Tan, E. (2021). Wildlife tourism in urban destinations: Singapore's urban otters and 'biodivercity' story. In J. Zhao, L. Ren, & X. Li (Eds.), *The hospitality and tourism industry in Southeast Asia: New growth, trends and development* (pp. 209–228). Apple Academic Press.

The Singapore Green Plan 2030. (2021). https://www.greenplan.gov.sg/

Töpfer, K. (2013). Nachhaltigkeit im Anthropozän. *Nova Acta Leopoldina NF, 117*(398), 31–40.

UN Climate Change Conference UK. (2021). *COP26 explained.* https://ukcop26.wpenginepowered.com/wp-content/uploads/2021/07/COP26-Explained.pdf

United Nations Environmental Programme. (2022). *Emissions gap report 2022.* https://www.unep.org/resources/emissions-gap-report-2022

United Nations (UN). (2017). Resolution adopted by the General Assembly on 6 July 2017. *Work of the Statistical Commission pertaining to the 2030 agenda for sustainable development.* A/RES/71/313.

Unpackt. (2022). *Homepage.* https://unpackt.com.sg/

Van Zanten, J. A., & van Tulder, R. (2021). Improving companies' impacts on sustainable development: A nexus approach to the SDGS. *Business Strategy and the Environment, 30*(8), 3703–3720. doi:10.1002/bse.2835

Wagler, R. (2011). The Anthropocene mass extinction: An emerging curriculum theme for science educators. *The American Biology Teacher, 73*(2), 78–83. doi:10.1525/abt.2011.73.2.5

Warhurst, A. (2002). Sustainability indicators and sustainability performance management. Mining, Minerals and Sustainable Development Report. Warwick: WBCSD & IIED.

Weaver, D. (2013). *Sustainable tourism: Theory and practice.* Routledge.

Wong, L. (2022, October 26). Singapore's strategy to net zero. *The Straits Times.* https://www.straitstimes.com/opinion/singapore-s-strategy-towards-net-zero

World Commission on Environment and Development (WCED). (1987). *Our Common Future: From One Earth to One World.* Oxford University Press.

Zeppel, H. (2015). Environmental indicators and benchmarking for sustainable tourism development. In C. M. Hall, S. Gossling, & D. Scott (Eds.), *The Routledge handbook of tourism and sustainability* (pp. 127–135). Routledge.

Chapter 14
Reinventing Strategic Execution in the Pharmaceutical Industry

Patrick Fatzer

CSL Vifor, Switzerland

ABSTRACT

The pharmaceutical industry's route to market had historically been based on sales teams interacting with key healthcare practitioners (HCPs) in their place of work. The COVID-19 pandemic forced an immediate reinvention of the pharmaceutical industry's entire sales strategy to protect multimillion dollar investments in new treatments and the essential feedback loop between the pharmaceutical industry and HCPs. Virtual and digital solutions were quickly put in place, demonstrating how such a radical strategic pivot is not only possible but can have unexpected benefits. The author is a pharmaceutical industry professional, and this chapter is based on his personal experiences of the industry's strategic response and the limited amount of published research available. The author concludes that leveraging new digital engagement strategies with the industry and optimizing external stakeholder relationships will be key to success in the industry's next normal.

INTRODUCTION

With an ever-increasing population, higher life expectancy, and the growing expectation that a cure will and should be found for every ailment, a successful pharmaceutical industry has become an essential pillar of any well-functioning society. To be able to continue to fulfil this foundational role, the industry must be capable of continued growth and development. This chapter looks at the ways in which the COVID-19 pandemic gave rise to new business models and sales execution strategies as a result of dramatic shifts in health care systems' day-to-day functioning caused by the global emergency.

With the onset of the pandemic, the industry was placed under severe pressure; hospitals were suddenly overwhelmed with patients in need of critical care, frontline healthcare staff faced shortages of vital equipment—from such apparent basics as Personal Protective Equipment to complex kit such as ventilators—and also of the resources needed to tend for unprecedented numbers of patients on life-support systems. At the same time, increased demand for medications came up against global supply

DOI: 10.4018/978-1-6684-6845-6.ch014

chain problems in the industry that stemmed from decreased manufacturing capacity, rising raw material prices and new transportation and logistics problems, all caused by the pandemic itself.

As the pandemic progressed, it became clear that pharmaceutical companies were operating sub optimally, struggling to meet the demands of the pandemic and to engage successfully with Health Care Practitioners (HCPs) to ensure the industry was effectively serving the needs of healthcare systems around the world. A McKinsey survey of European general practitioners, cardiologists, neurologists and oncologists showed a 70% drop in face-to-face interactions between HCPs and pharmaceutical reps in September 2020 compared with the pre-pandemic average (Mlika et al., 2020).

As a direct result, a number of complete strategy redesigns and pivots took place within the industry. New customer engagement models were devised and supply chains revisited in an attempt to cope with the 'new normal' that had so suddenly become a fact of life. HCPs themselves were making an equally sudden shift to remote ways of working, with a dramatic rise in remote ways of engaging with patients. A paper on the response of US academic medical centers to the pandemic noted that Yale New Haven Health Center performed 316 virtual video consultations with patients in 2019 and half a million video consultations in 2020 (Cohen, A.B. et al., 2022). An April 2020 survey reported by McKinsey & Company showed majorities of physicians experiencing a significant drop in numbers of patients visiting physicians, a corresponding growth of remote consultations ('telemedicine') and the expectation that the use of telemedicine would continue post crisis. The same April 2020 report noted that "[m]ost pharma companies have completely or partially pulled their reps out of the field" (Cohen, O. et al., 2020).

In the space of twelve months, the way the industry had operated for several decades was transformed. People working in the industry were forced to rethink working practices and find innovative ways of operating.

This chapter looks at how the pharmaceutical industry's established sales model, which relied heavily on face-to-face interactions with HCPs to promote the benefits of established products and introduce new products to the market, was forced to make a dramatic strategic shift, reinventing the way that it had traditionally done business in a very short timeframe. The industry had not, of course, ignored the possibilities of virtual meetings and, along with all other advertisers, was heavily invested in digital advertising prior to the pandemic. Virtual meetings had already become a significant part of the communications mix for interactions with HCPs, but were seen, not unreasonably, as inferior to face-to-face meetings. Nevertheless, the pharmaceutical industry had arguably been slower than other industries to adapt to the possibilities offered by rapidly evolving new technologies. In the industry's defense, this had been based on the premise that the industry's existing model was far from broken and was delivering healthy growth; it was not obvious that an urgent fix was needed. The onset of the pandemic changed that perception overnight.

Two key strategic areas have emerged as being vital to business success for the pharmaceutical industry in the post-pandemic world: transforming customer engagement strategies (field salesforce), and optimising external stakeholder management (governing bodies etc.) This chapter's objective is to offer examples of practical solutions that may be applicable to a range of industries and suggest ways in which organisations can remain agile, relevant, and success oriented in the post-pandemic environment.

The Pharmaceutical Industry Pre-Pandemic

Historically speaking, the pharmaceutical industry has operated in essentially the same way since the early twentieth century, when it first took on a recognizably modern form. Large pharmaceutical organisations invested heavily in research and development, looking for what we now tend to call new 'molecules' that had, or might have, a therapeutic effect. (There is currently a distinction between 'new molecular entities', 'new chemical entities', 'new biological entities' and 'new active substances' within what are classed as 'new therapeutic entities', but the author will use 'molecule/s' or simply 'drug/s' here as a shorthand) (Branch & Agranat, 2014).

In recent times, the process of bringing a new molecule to market as a therapeutic entity might take anywhere from seven to 15 years from start to finish and cost perhaps as much as $1 billion. A 2020 study by the London School of Economics and other instituitions used financial reports filed by pharmaceutical companies with the US Securities and Exchange Commission to estimate that the average cost of bringing a new drug to market was $1.3 billion. The study aimed to show that the cost was less than an average figure of $2.8 billion that previous studies had arrived at, and to suggest that the industry was using these higher figures as a justification for high drug prices (Wouters et al., 2020). That is not a debate that this chapter will address: the only point that needs to be established is that developing a new drug is usually extremely expensive and it is often a long time before any return on investment is seen. Each new molecule must be tested in a rigorous series of clinical trials. These typically start with studies involving a small group of volunteer subjects to establish that the molecule is safe. The next phase looks to establish its effectiveness along with any side effects; a third phase sets out to compare the new treatment to existing treatments; and a final phase looks for any long-term unwanted side effects. By this fourth stage of the process, clinical trials can involve tens of thousands of people.

In recent years, the industry's business model has shifted as small biotech companies emerged, purely focused on finding potentially useful molecules. Larger companies began to purchase these startups in the hope that perhaps one or two of these new molecules might turn into effective and profitable new drugs. The overall cost of this new way of operating was, in general, either the same or slightly less than the old 'in-house' model, but it considerably reduced the total time to market (Schumacher et al., 2013). New technologies using artificial intelligence to help identify or direct the search for molecules that may prove to be effective in various therapies have emerged, raising the prospect of higher success rates and a less expensive discovery process (Ayers et al., 2022). There is also a growing trend in outsourcing the clinical trial process (Adams, 2021). Whatever routes the pharmaceutical industry may use in the future to find new molecules and conduct clinical trials, the focus of this chapter is on the crucial next phase: bringing newly discovered drugs successfully to market.

In what we can refer to as 'the old days' (pre-2019), a new drug would be introduced to the organisation's salesforce which would be trained deeply on the drug's mode of action, efficacy, dosage, mode of application, potential side effects, which patients could potentially benefit most from it, and what differentiates it from other drugs in its class. Sales representatives would then communicate this information to HCPs, tailoring their presentation of the promotional information prepared by the pharmaceutical company's head office to suit what they had established were the most common and/or pressing needs of each HCP's patient group. Most pharmaceutical companies would expect their sales representatives to make anywhere between four and seven face-to-face interactions a day with senior HCPs—typically consultants (senior doctors), but also registrars (aspiring consultants), pharmacists and specialist nurses. High daily targets for face-to-face interactions would be set and the sales teams' compensation would be directly linked to this. These interactions were so essential to a successful sales operation that the number of daily face-to-face interactions was used as a proxy measurement of performance: a high call rate achieved by an effective sales team was a strong predictor of sales success.

The ability to achieve high volumes of face-to-face interactions required a particular set of skills. Experienced representatives would have built up a network of relationships on which they could draw to get access to HCPs. At its most straightforward, they would call the secretary of a senior physician and make an appointment in a way that would be familiar to salespeople in any similar, technical sales environment. This, in itself, might involve an element of salesmanship as the representative would need to explain why the physician should devote their limited time to this particular appointment; getting past the various 'gatekeepers' for senior HCPs is a skill in itself. Experienced representatives—who would be familiar faces in the hospitals they covered—would also be able to 'improvise' effective face-to-face interactions within hospitals, catching five minutes with a physician within the hallways or between clinics.

Hospitals are real communities of people and pharmaceutical representatives are a significant part of that community, providing essential information on new drugs to consultants and updating them on the latest developments with established drugs. Consultants, in turn, would talk about their own experiences of specific disease areas, which representatives would relay back to head offices. For the launch of new drugs, consultants' agreement that the data from clinical trials demonstrated its potential benefit to their patients—a process that would in itself typically require several interactions between representative and consultant—would be the green light to begin the complex process of adding a new drug to the hospital 'formulary': the list of drugs that doctors at that hospital are allowed to prescribe for patients. There are typically a handful of drugs on a hospital formulary for any specific disease area, and competition between drugs in the same disease area is fierce. The final decision on whether to accept a new drug onto the hospital formulary lies with a review board consisting not only of consultants but also of pharmacists, other physicians, hospital managers and others. The cost of the new drug will be a crucial factor in this decision.

When hospitals closed their doors to pharmaceutical representatives after the outbreak of COVID-19, a key route to market for new drugs that had cost millions of dollars to develop was closed off. Representatives also played a vital role in keeping established drugs in the forefront of HCPs' minds and encouraging continued prescription levels. The industry's long-established sales strategy had to be reinvented at speed, as the financial implications of failure are large.

With access to hospitals physically impossible, sales teams immediately resorted to phone calls, emails and virtual meetings. It is worth noting that senior consultants tend not to give their email addresses to everyone and to insist that representatives contact them via their office; only established representatives with strong personal relationships in place might have a consultant's email address. Sales interactions dropped from four to seven physical interactions per day to perhaps three to four virtual interactions of one kind or another *per week*. As the industry began to adjust to the ongoing realities of living with the pandemic, some face-to-face interactions resumed, but virtual interactions had already begun to establish themselves as a key part of the new landscape. . A 2021 survey by Accenture of HCPs in the USA, UK, France, Germany, China and Japan reported that a 64/36% ratio for in-person vs. virtual meetings with pharmaceutical company representatives pre-pandemic had reversed to a 35/65% ratio in mid-2020, a proportion that had changed only marginally by mid-2021 with a 39/61% ratio for in-person vs. virtual meetings. Accenture concluded that "all indications are that virtual meetings are here to stay." Only 12% of HPCs surveyed expressed a preference for exclusively in-person meetings with representatives; 46% for a mix of in-person and virtual meetings; 38% for all meetings to be virtual; and 4% for no meetings (Accenture, 2021, p. 15)

The key point to note here is that the unplanned and unforeseen strategic switch in favour of virtual interactions between pharmaceutical representatives and HCPs was carried out successfully and remarkably quickly. It has also opened up new opportunities.

In the rest of this chapter, the author will review the two key strategic areas the author believes will lead to future success for the pharmaceutical industry in the new virtual landscape: leveraging new customer engagement strategies and optimising external stakeholder management.

Leveraging New Customer Engagement Strategies

With the outbreak of the pandemic and the sudden, drastic restrictions on face-to-face meetings, a vastly different engagement model for both commercial sales teams and physicians was forced on the pharmaceutical industry. A flood of new digital activity ensued, and quick decisions had to be taken to find solutions that had the potential to be as effective as the old face-to-face model, not only in ensuring the continued flow of information between the pharmaceutical industry and HCPs but also—in hard business terms—in getting new drugs to market and continuing to encourage prescription levels for established drugs.

A first hurdle which quickly became obvious to all pharmaceutical sales operations was that physicians were suddenly being bombarded with phone calls and emails from the industry. To take the field of cardiology as an example, there is a very wide range of drugs that cardiologists might prescribe for their patients, and cardiology specialists need to stay abreast of the most recent developments in all of them. This could mean that they were used to having some level of interaction with perhaps as many as thirty different representatives on a regular basis. Physicians had developed a way of coping with this under the old face-to-face system by rationing their time—devoting more time to interactions with representatives for their most significant drugs, having brief conversations with others to ensure they were not missing anything new and important. With the switch to digital interactions, this rationing system proved challenging: all thirty representatives tried to interact with physicians all of the time. A phone call or email that says, in effect, "I only need a few minutes of your time", is as invasive as a communication to which a physician would normally be happy to devote half an hour. Physicians would open their computers each morning to find perhaps forty emails from pharmaceutical companies competing for their attention alongside the emails that were essential to them being able to function effectively in their role. HCPs, overwhelmed, began to 'switch off' from interacting with these communications.

Pharmaceutical companies also stepped up their use of digital advertising in specialist media—but the same effect quickly surfaced. As every company increased their volume of advertising messages, the fight for physicians' attention intensified. Where the industry had previously been able to devote most of its time to making its communications effective in terms of changing physicians' prescribing habits and getting new drugs accepted by the medical community, it suddenly found itself competing simply for physicians' time; trying to catch their attention sufficiently to begin the process of making a meaningful communication. Where, given access to an HCP's time and attention, the representative for any particular drug would previously be competing with the relatively small number of drugs in their specific area of medication, in the digital world, messaging about any particular drug was competing with messaging about every drug across every class of medication.

In this battle for physician's attention, it quickly became clear that opportunities for meaningful interactions were increasingly rare, and that it was essential to make those few meaningful interactions as effective as possible. In the author's experience, the following four factors proved to be the most critical for success: highly capable frontline employees; digital landscape leverage; personalised closed-loop execution; and adaptive organisational metrics.

1.   Highly Capable Frontline Employees

While many pharmaceutical sales representatives were already highly adept at virtual communication and all representatives needed at minimum to be able to run an effective virtual meeting, the sudden end to face-to-face interactions put the focus entirely on virtual interactions. The most important selling skills needed were suddenly very different. It is far easier to establish relationships and build rapport in the real world than it is in the virtual world. Knowing how to conduct a virtual meeting in the most basic sense was no longer enough; reps needed to familiarise themselves with and become experts in using every aspect of the functionality of the particular virtual platforms preferred by their physicians. Mundane technical aspects of the platforms became hugely important: being able to fluently share and unshare your screen to show presentation materials; using the laser pointer functionality to highlight important information; posting key information as a written comment so that attendees could copy and keep it for future reference.

Other core skills in presenting on virtual platforms became essential: looking directly into camera; having the face well lit; nodding and smiling to show the representative is listening; making sure that the background is not distracting and, better yet, reinforces the message. Other, more subtle, skills were needed: experienced representatives become good at 'reading the room' in a physical meeting—knowing who the most senior person in that room is, for example, because other people glance at them for approval when expressing an opinion; noting who is genuinely paying attention and who is disengaged; spotting—especially important for a salesperson—non-verbal buying signals. Many of these vital aspects of sales communication are easily lost in a virtual setting. It is also far easier for attendees to 'zone out' of a virtual meeting. It became essential for salespeople to be able to identify the key decision makers in a virtual meeting and get their attention, perhaps addressing them directly by name. Because 'attendance' is far easier in the virtual world, there was a tendency for meetings to include a higher proportion of people who would not play a part in any final decision.

It was also essential to check that the audience was aligned with the discussion points by asking if they agreed, or had any questions, or would like to talk about how this issue affects them or their patients. Finally, and perhaps most importantly, representatives had to ensure that every meeting ended with a clear call to action: to ask, for example, if they could send a package of materials electronically for decision makers to look at or follow up with a one-to-one meeting.

Many of the fundamental aspects of effective communication had to be relearned in the virtual landscape. Building highly capable frontline employees required representatives to rise to the challenge and learn new skills.

2.   Digital Landscape Leverage

Some aspects of the new digital landscape proved advantageous; virtual meetings made it easier to do important things that the pharmaceutical industry had already been doing but which were harder to execute when individuals needed to travel in order to come together in a physical space.

One of the most powerful tools in a pharmaceutical representative's toolkit—and one which is of great benefit to the health care community as a whole—is to encourage the spread of best practice. Sales representatives typically deal with a number of hospitals across large geographical areas, and different hospitals develop different ways of interacting with patients in various scenarios. Some of these are considerably more efficient and effective than others. Any process which is more efficient and effective in delivering care enables more patients to be treated, often reduces overall costs to the system, and is of benefit to all involved. However, hospitals rarely interact with each other. There are, in the author's experience, very few instances where there is a systematic sharing of best practice across hospitals. Although this may seem surprising, there is an understandable wariness in healthcare systems of control from a bureaucratic centre. Consultants are resistant to being told exactly how they must proceed in every situation, because this takes away their independence of action; there is the real risk that diktats issued from central sources may be inappropriate or unworkable under local conditions. In the same vein, senior professionals are resistant to suggestions from the pharmaceutical industry itself as to how they should treat their patients, no matter how well-informed and well-intentioned the industry may be. What hospitals and senior HCPs are very open to, however, is peer-to-peer education: hearing from a fellow professional how they found a particularly effective solution to a common problem. Pharmaceutical representatives are uniquely placed to facilitate this, persuading practitioners who have established especially effective ways of operating to share their experience with professionals from other hospitals in their area in meetings organised and facilitated by the pharmaceutical representative. The value of the networks built by the representatives allows them to understand complex issues across multiple hospitals and leverage their relationships to facilitate further communication.

In their role as facilitator, representatives are able to highlight the benefits of how account A is operating and to encourage account B to consider how that might be beneficial to them. It could also highlight what hurdles they might face in implementing the same way of operating. In a real sense, representatives become experts in various aspects of the hospitals' business, such as how the most effective clinics are run. This equips them to work with hospitals as a kind of business partner, helping hospitals find optimal solutions to various problems. It is this sort of 'value based' way of operating, where the pharmaceutical industry brings increasing value to its interaction with HCPs, that the author believes represents the future of pharmaceutical sales. The new digital landscape has made this way of operating easier.

Many examples of sharing best practice between hospitals can be as straightforward as logistical matters: looking at how one hospital deals with the flow of patients more efficiently than others. A good example would be the delivery of infusions – the intravenous administration of medications – in infusion suites within hospitals. The number of patients that the hospital or clinic can deliver an infusion to at any one time is a limiting factor that can become a bottleneck. Some hospitals have found an effective solution is the setting up of one central infusion suite, rather than having suites for individual departments (cardiology, nephrology etc.), creating efficiencies of scale. Some groups of hospitals have taken this a step further, creating a central fusion hub serving several hospitals in one area, creating an expert, specialist centre and freeing up rooms in each hospital. Patient throughput can increase two or threefold, reducing waiting times for patients and providing a better patient experience and level of care.

Pharmaceutical representatives can play a vital role in bringing together HCPs from various hospitals to discuss and share best practice in this way. With the spread of best practice, hospital processes become more efficient, funds are saved, patient waiting times are reduced and more patients are treated. The fact that the opening up of the digital landscape has made it far easier to convene such meetings is one of the key benefits of the new digital landscape—so much so that the convening of a certain number of such meetings per week is becoming a key target for sales teams and is beginning to replace face-to-face meetings as the key metric to reveal how effectively a sales team is operating.

Virtual meetings are, of course, only one small part of the new digital landscape for pharmaceutical representatives, though they were especially significant to an industry that had relied so heavily on face-to-face meetings. The increasing digitalization of the relationships between HCPs and patients and HCPs and pharmaceutical representatives began to create large amounts of new data stored in customer-relationship-management (CRM) databases, sales records and elsewhere, the analysis of which could deliver useful results (Mlika et al., 2020).

Personalised Closed-Loop Marketing

When face-to-face interactions were the main way of interacting with practitioners, it had been possible to supply representatives with quite broadly-based marketing information and rely on their understanding of each HCP's level of expertise in particular drug areas to direct the practitioners' attention to the most relevant and useful aspects of that material. With the move to digital communications, it became far more common for HCPs to be reading materials on their own, without such expert guidance. There was an urgent need to be able to supply practitioners with materials tailor-made for their current level of knowledge.

Another key benefit of digital communication is the ability to fine-tune messaging to small groups of individuals. In today's hypercompetitive pharmaceutical environment, the ability to capitalise on small nuances in messaging is key, supplying the most relevant and useful information to each practitioner. To take an obvious example, giving basic information to a practitioner who is highly experienced in a drug area is patronising; giving highly complex information to a physician who is relatively new to the field is unhelpful. In both contexts, there is a risk of losing a practitioner's attention--which, as we have seen, has become an increasingly precious commodity in the new environment. Providing information which is highly relevant to a practitioner's current circumstances is always valuable and attention-grabbing. During the course of the COVID-19 pandemic, this might include information on drug interactions with COVID-19 vaccines or, more generally, how other HCPs were dealing with issues such as the move towards telemedicine and reducing the risk of patient infection on healthcare premises (Mlika et al., 2020)

The move into a more thoroughly digital landscape helped marketers to personalise messages more precisely with the help of 'closed-loop' techniques, where growing amounts of information about individual customers are fed back into a customer database, allowing the delivery of marketing messages that are targeted with increasing accuracy to suit the recipient's needs and interests. Personalised, closed-loop marketing is akin to high levels of customer segmentation. In the pharmaceutical space, a simple segmentation might be to divide HCPs into 'non-believers', who have yet to be persuaded of the benefit of a drug to their patients; 'not-yet-sures' who, like swing voters in the world of politics, are a core target audience with great potential; and 'users'—practitioners who are currently prescribing the drug. This kind of segmentation would previously have relied on information gleaned from face-to-face interactions; it can now be inferred from digital interactions, along with a far more sophisticated level of awareness of an HCP's information needs. If, for example, a pharmaceutical company runs a digital campaign highlighting a relatively simple aspect of a drug area, and an HCP engages with that content, it can be inferred that they are in the early stages of a learning journey. The practitioner can then be offered appropriate materials as a follow up to move them forward on that journey. The same kind of segmentation can be achieved by posting online pages offering materials at various levels of depth and complexity, measuring who engages on which materials and, again, following up with the appropriate next level of information.

This applies to all forms of messaging: if a representative is convening a webinar, for example, it is far more effective to invite a group of participants with similar levels of knowledge and to deliver content appropriate to that group. A subsequent webinar later that year could pick up the thread and move the participants along the learning curve. The concept of a narrative journey is key. Where face-to-face interactions with individual practitioners would follow a natural progression in terms of an ideal journey from 'non-believer' to 'user', it is much easier to lose the thread in ongoing digital interactions. Pharmaceutical companies now plan their messaging in great depth, forward planning at perhaps a weekly level so that the content seen by HCPs at the beginning of a year and the content seen by the end of the year are linked throughout the entire process, telling a compelling story and providing a meaningful and effective learning journey.

With the loss of the 'personal touch' that was possible in face-to-face meetings, consistency of messaging across various platforms also became a key issue. Individual representatives could be relied on to deliver a consistent message over time to each individual practitioner. Where HCPs are receiving different messages over time from different media platforms, there is a risk of confusion. Whether a practitioner attends a virtual meeting, takes part in a webinar, listens to a podcast, or reads a promotional article, the messaging must remain consistent and clear and be precisely targeted to that practitioner's learning journey. Pharmaceutical marketers are increasingly learning the skills and techniques of online marketers and deploying data analytics based on CRM data, sales records and other data in their digital interactions with HCPs. As the September 2020 McKinsey report notes, this growth in data allowed pharmaceutical companies to refine what were essentially informed guesses about HCPs' reception of new drugs, based on pre-launch conversations and research, with real-life post-launch data, such as HCP feedback, field insight and prescription levels. Some unrelated data also proved surprisingly useful. Pharma companies in the US discovered that they could predict the extent to which an individual HCP was likely to be prepared to engage with pharma representatives with surprising accuracy from the general footfall and credit-card spend in the zip code of an HCP's office rather than any data gleaned from the HCPs themselves (Mlika et al., 2020).

Adaptive Organisation Metrics

One final note on the effects of the dramatic shift in sales strategy for the pharmaceutical industry brought on by the effects of the pandemic: it became necessary to measure performance in different ways. We have seen how the number of face-to-face interactions between representatives and HCPs used to function as a highly effective measure of likely success. The new virtual landscape is more complex. Although it was always that case that the quality of face-to-face interactions was as important as the sheer volume of interactions, in the virtual world it is far more possible for highly effective salespeople to have virtual interactions with HCPs that are actually sub optimal in terms of changing behaviour. There are new techniques to be learned and new forms of best practice to be taken on board. In a world where any form of personal interaction is a rare opportunity and virtual meetings can easily fail to live up to expectations, the focus must switch from volume to quality. As we return to a new kind of 'hybrid' interaction, predominantly virtual but with some face-to-face meetings, both kinds of interaction must be evaluated, using different metrics.

One clear disadvantage of the old face-to-face model is that it was time-consuming. Reps would spend large portions of their day traveling from one physical location to another. In today's hybrid world, it has become possible to be far more efficient, clustering physical meetings by proximity and using videoconferencing for others. The old concept of 'call rate' is now too blunt an instrument for effective evaluation of a sales team's performance. New metrics are needed to encourage the most efficient organisation of face-to-face meetings and the most effective use of virtual meetings. New measures—such as the number of best practice peer-to-peer meetings facilitated by representatives—need to be put in place.

Optimising External Stakeholder Management

The unusual complexities of the pharmaceutical industry stem in large part from the large networks of stakeholders that must be managed in order to carry out a successful product launch. In many healthcare systems, the end user of the product—the patient—is not the payer. The product is marketed to HCPs who can prescribe it, but whether or not the HCPs are able to prescribe the drug depends on its acceptance by the ultimate payers, who must agree that the drug offers a cost-effective solution to healthcare issues. Payers have finite budgets that cannot overrun and are drawn to drugs that offer the cheapest treatment of any disease. They may, quite understandably, reason that choosing a cheaper product would allow them to treat considerably more patients. However, less favourable products may have slightly undesirable side effects—for example, difficulty sleeping, gastrointestinal issues, or loss of appetite. A patient who would purchase their own medication might choose to pay a higher price to avoid such side effects, but a central payer who is obliged to treat the maximum number of patients from limited funds may argue that supplying a drug with fewer side effects may not be the best use of their budget. There are competing interests at play in the system: payers and governments are concerned about upfront and long-term costs, physicians are concerned with the efficacy and safety of the drug and patients are concerned with their overall well-being. Healthcare systems where patients have full control over their medication choice, such as private practices or clinics, would not face such an issue. Aligning these three priorities can be challenging, but there are effective strategies that companies can employ to reduce barriers and ensure optimal value is offered to payers, physicians and patients alike.

One of these strategies involves engaging with payers and government policy groups well in advance of drug availability—as early as twenty-four months in advance of a planned launch. Using a collaborative approach and looking to understand stakeholders' needs provides companies with the opportunity to address pain points and engage in solution-orientated discussions well before the actual 'sales campaign' begins. This could include, for example, reviewing and updating proposed guidelines to better detail key aspects of a drug's potential benefits; gathering further clinical evidence to reassure practitioners about important medical issues they raise in discussion; considering potential new pricing models to reassure payers about the cost-effectiveness of the treatment; and engaging with professional bodies and patient advocacy groups to discuss the benefits and address concerns ahead of the launch of a product.

Bringing Payers to the Front

On the traditional model, engaging with payers typically happens towards the latter end of the development process. Pharmaceutical companies research and create new molecules, get approval from the relevant regulatory bodies and launch them to market. The new drug is presented to HCPs and a discussion on why and how the drug could be of value ensues. Physicians may agree that they would like to prescribe the drug for their patients—but they must first contend with getting the drug accepted onto the hospital formulary which will ultimately be decided by a board that will take various factors, including and often especially cost, into account. This could be the first instance that the cost of a treatment has been actively discussed at a frontline level.

One issue that can arise at this point is that different payers within hospitals work in isolation and budgets are siloed. A pharmaceutical representative might be able to help a physician make the case that a drug should be included on the hospital formulary by helping demonstrate that the new drug will create an overall cost-saving for the hospital. The drug, for example, might be more expensive per dose than an immediate competitor, but if a patient were given the new drug, it may result in reduced hospitalisation admissions or length of stay. The reduced number of hospital visits reduces costs in hospital admissions—but the hospital admissions budget is typically separate from prescription drug budgets. It can be difficult for cash-strapped departments to be persuaded to spend additional funds from their own budget, even when there is a net benefit to the system as a whole.

If the drug is not accepted onto the hospital formulary at the first application—which it commonly is not—it is necessary to reapply, which could take anywhere between six and twelve months; even longer at times. It is often the case that a drug has been brought to market that physicians want to use, patients would like to be given, and which would reduce hospital spend, but due to complex funding issues, it is not accepted onto the formulary for several months to years. A more effective process might be to bring engagement with payers to the front of the process, raising awareness of disease areas and the relative costs associated in treating diseases. This approach not only puts the cost into perspective, but allows the payers to be a part of a solution oriented approach.

A complex area that is worth discussing briefly at this point is the relationship between the evidence generated from clinical trials that pharmaceutical companies use to demonstrate a drug's efficacy and safety, and the actual effect of a drug in the real world once prescribed to patients. Data from clinical trials will produce evidence that drug X can alleviate symptoms in sufferers of a particular disease by Y percent. When hospitals assess the overall benefits of a drug, they will factor in this figure: the Y percent reduction in symptoms might lead to cost reductions elsewhere—for example, reduced hospital admission and length of bed stay. These additional reductions for each patient play a significant role in the overall efficiency of a hospital. Fewer bed stays for a single patient allow more patients to be treated and possibly free up bed positions for those in greater need of them.

However, clinical trials are conducted, by definition, in very controlled conditions. The individuals that are selected to take part in the trials have been screened to fit the exact profile that the researchers conducting the trial are looking for, and during the trial those individuals' behaviours will be highly controlled: the precise amount of the drug that they take; when it will be taken; and what other medication they are currently prescribed. In all cases, patients who partake in clinical trials would have consented to do so. They are provided with unique opportunities to gain access to novel medications in disease areas which may be difficult to treat or where current treatments are not effectively working for them. They are acutely aware of their condition and are highly motivated to help the researchers discover if the drug is indeed effective. As a result of this awareness, patients tend to live a healthier lifestyle, and are more likely to remain compliant on treatment regimes, given there is the possibility that it could better their current situation. When a drug is being used in the 'real world' however, everything is far less controlled. Patients might not be as motivated. They forget to take their medication, or are exposed to different external factors and tend to lead less healthy lifestyles.

To take an historic example, drugs called statins are prescribed for patients who have high cholesterol levels. Statins are proven to reduce cholesterol levels in most patients, which in turn helps lower their blood pressure. In the course of the clinical trials for statins, patients taking part would have been acutely aware not only that they suffer from high cholesterol, but that they should lead a healthier lifestyle as a result of their participation. This is likely to have led them to follow a balanced, low cholesterol diet and perhaps to avoid alcohol or caffeine during the trial. In the real world, of course, people are less 'well behaved' and the level of cholesterol reduction achieved is less than in clinical trials. A 2019 study noted that many 'patient characteristics', such as sex, age, body weight, smoking status etc. had been reported to contribute to the different levels of cholesterol reduction, and stated that 'variations in individual patient genotypes, and probably non-adherence, may be an important explanation for this phenomenon'. (Akyea, 2019, p. 979).

The difference between a drug's proven effect in clinical trials and the effect of those drugs when taken in the real world can be significant (Blonde et al., 2018). This can have a large financial impact on healthcare systems. Over time, healthcare systems around the world have seen medicine budgets grow dramatically. Decisions had been taken based on technically correct claims about what drugs demonstrated in clinical trials, but the effect of those drugs in the real world have often turned out to be less impactful than the trial results had predicted. Total spending on drugs has skyrocketed while potential savings in other areas have been lower than originally forecasted. Payers in healthcare systems are increasingly looking for real world evidence of a drug's overall effects on the system and the subsequent total effect on budgets. This involves analysing large amounts of data from hospitals' accounts over several years to find evidence for the real overall costs and savings that have resulted from a particular drug's use. Pharmaceutical companies should embrace this reality, working with healthcare systems to provide more evidence about a drug's impact in real world conditions and looking for joint solutions that can improve the effectiveness of treatments from a holistic perspective—another example of a value-based sales approach where pharmaceutical companies can work as partners with healthcare systems to ensure delivery of the most cost-effective patient care.

Professional Associations and Patient Organisations

There are other stakeholders outside of HCPS, payers and hospital administrators who can be very influential in the acceptance process for any new drug. Individual physicians can and do speak up in support of a new drug. The traditional sales route has been for pharmaceutical reps to influence large numbers of HCPs and to build a groundswell of support, but the influence of individual practitioners is limited. Professional associations, on the other hand, carry more weight. If, for example, a cardiology drug had the support of the European Society of Cardiology, this would carry a great deal of influence. Investing more time in appropriate stakeholder management within these associations to demonstrate a drug's genuine value-add and gain their approval can provide powerful leverage towards convincing payers that the drug will help provide better care, move medicine forward, and potentially prove more cost effective when all relevant factors are taken into account.

Patient organisations and advocacy groups can also be important stakeholders. Often set up by people suffering from a particular condition, such organisations very successfully build a network of fellow sufferers, carers and well-wishers who lobby the pharmaceutical industry, governing bodies and governments to provide new treatments, better levels of care and approval for drugs that governing bodies have judged to be too expensive. The pharmaceutical industry cannot directly engage with patients, as promoting to the public is against the regulatory code, but engaging with patient associations who represent the group at large provides an effective communication tool to understand the needs and concerns of these patients. Patient organisations have the ability to voice their concerns with governments and payers alike, and through transparent dialogue with the pharmaceutical industry have considerable power to influence availability of medicines.

A guide to relationships between the pharmaceutical industry and charities was produced by the ABPI (the Association of the British Pharmaceutical Industry) and National Voices, a coalition of health and social care charities in England after initial meetings in 2014. The guide called for 'Clarity, Integrity, Independence and Transparency' in such relationships. (National Voices, ABPI, 2014)

All of these interactions with various stakeholders can help lay the ground for drug approval and avoid complete reliance on interactions between representatives and physicians at the very end of the development process. By engaging with stakeholders in a meaningful, two-way dialogue in the early stages of development, the pharmaceutical industry can better understand stakeholders needs and concerns and, hopefully, address them in advance to pave the way for an eventual successful launch.

CONCLUSION

The pharmaceutical industry was profoundly affected by the COVID-19 pandemic due to the sudden changes and stresses the healthcare system faced. Restrictions on physical interactions between practitioners and patients altered the ways in which practitioners provided health care; the same restrictions dramatically affected the way in which the pharmaceutical industry had traditionally communicated with practitioners via face-to-face meetings. The industry's entire sales strategy was forced to change overnight.

The industry coped with the strategic pivots remarkably well, discovering effective workarounds and unexpected benefits in new ways of working. Although face-to-face interactions will likely remain the most effective way of communicating, new skills and the optimised use of virtual meeting technologies allows virtual meetings to complement these interactions.

As the entire industry switched to communicating digitally with HCPs, the fight for HCPs' attention became even more intense, forcing the industry to become more focused in its communications, providing relevant and timely information to its key stakeholders.

The strategic shifts highlighted an over-reliance on the traditional sales model, which made the success or failure of multimillion dollar and multi-year-long development projects reliant on sales campaigns that began only when a drug was ready for market. This in turn highlighted the need to partner with all stakeholders throughout the development process to be able to better tailor the overall offering to the needs and concerns of healthcare systems, governing bodies and payers.

The shift reinforced the fact that the pharmaceutical industry is most effective at communicating with its customers when it adds value to their relationship, partnering with HCPs and hospitals to help them provide the most effective patient care. This is essentially the goal all stakeholders aim to achieve.

The pharmaceutical industry had arguably been guilty of strategic inertia, sticking to a highly effective sales strategy reliant on face-to-face interactions when new technologies had made other forms of digital and virtual communication possible. Although the industry had already been making extensive use of digital communications before the pandemic, the sudden focus on such communications drove a rapid learning experience and a more sophisticated use of digital marketing techniques. The success of the pivot confirms that businesses can and should be bold in making such strategic shifts earlier, jumping rather than waiting to be pushed.

REFERENCES

Accenture. (2021). The "new" rules of engagement: How pharmaceutical companies can give HCPs the new and meaningful interactions they want. *Accenture*. https://www.accenture.com/_acnmedia/PDF-167/Accenture-Life-Sciences-Healthcare-Provider-Covid-19-Survey.pdf

Adams, L. (2021, November 3). Outsourcing in clinical trials: A response to rising challenges. *Pharmafile*. https://www.pharmafile.com/news/594149/outsourcing-clinical-trials-response-rising-challenges

Akyea, R. K., Kai, J., Qureshi, N., Iyen, B., & Weng, S. F. (2019). Sub-optimal cholesterol response to initiation of statins and future risk of cardiovascular disease. *Heart (British Cardiac Society)*, *105*(13), 975–981. doi:10.1136/heartjnl-2018-314253 PMID:30988003

Ayers, M., Jayatunga, M., Goldader, J., & Meier, C. (2022, March 29). Adopting AI in drug discovery. *BCG*. https://www.bcg.com/publications/2022/adopting-ai-in-pharmaceutical-discovery

Blonde, L., Khunti, K., Harris, S. B., Meizinger, C., & Skolnik, N. S. (2018). Interpretation and Impact of Real-World Clinical Data for the Practicing Clinician. *Advances in Therapy*, *35*(11), 1763–1774. doi:10.100712325-018-0805-y PMID:30357570

Branch, S. K., & Agranat, I. (2014). "New drug" designations for new therapeutic entities: New active substance, new chemical entity, new biological entity, new molecular entity. *Journal of Medicinal Chemistry*, *57*(21), 8729–8765. doi:10.1021/jm402001w PMID:25188028

Cohen, A. B., Stump, L., Krumholz, H. M., Cartiera, M., Jain, S., Scott Sussman, L., Hsiao, A., Lindop, W., Ying, A. K., Kaul, R. L., Balcezak, T. J., Tereffe, W., Comerford, M., Jacoby, D., & Navai, N. (2022). Aligning mission to digital health strategy in academic medical centers. *NPJ Digital Medicine*, *5*(1), 67. Advance online publication. doi:10.103841746-022-00608-7 PMID:35654885

Cohen, O., Fox, B., Mills, N., & Wright, P. (2020, April). *COVID-19 and commercial pharma: Navigating an uneven recovery*. McKinsey & Company. https://www.mckinsey.com/industries/life-sciences/our-insights/covid-19-and-commercial-pharma-navigating-an-uneven-recovery

Mlika, A., Mong, J., Peters, N., & Salazar, P. (2020, December 15). *Ready for launch: Reshaping pharma's strategy in the next normal*. McKinsey & Company. https://www.mckinsey.com/industries/life-sciences/our-insights/ready-for-launch-reshaping-pharmas-strategy-in-the-next-normal

National Voices ABPI. (2014). *Working together, delivering for patients*. https://www.nationalvoices.org.uk/sites/default/files/public/publications/working-together-delivering-for-patients.pdf

Schuhmacher, A., Germann, P. G., Trill, H., & Gassmann, O. (2013). Models for open innovation in the pharmaceutical industry. *Drug Discovery Today*, *18*(23-24), 1133–1137. doi:10.1016/j.drudis.2013.07.013 PMID:23892183

Wouters, O. J., McKee, M., & Luten, J. (2020). Estimated research and development investment needed to bring a new medicine to market, 2009-2018. *Journal of the American Medical Association*, *323*(9), 844–853. doi:10.1001/jama.2020.1166 PMID:32125404

Chapter 15
Augmenting Performance Through Strategic Management and Leadership Capabilities:
Implications for Small and Medium–Scale Enterprises

Herman Fassou Haba
Université du Québec à Trois-Rivières, Canada

Omkar Dastane
 https://orcid.org/0000-0002-9921-859X
UCSI Graduate Business School, UCSI University, Malaysia

Muhammad Rafiq
 https://orcid.org/0000-0001-5037-6485
UCSI Graduate Business School, UCSI University, Malaysia

ABSTRACT

Small and medium-sized enterprises (SMEs) suffer persistent challenges due to global market competition, time limits to respond strategically, talent retention, productivity, and uncompetitive operational expenses. Enhancing employee performance (EP) then becomes critical in defining SME success. The purpose of this study is to evaluate the influence of strategic management (SM) and leadership capabilities (LC) on EP and recommend solutions to improve EP. The function of employee engagement (EE) as a mediator between interactions involving LC, SM, and EP is also investigated. A quantitative research method was employed by collecting empirical data of employees working with Malaysian SMEs. Analysis including reliability and normality assessments, confirmatory factor analysis, and structural equation modelling with AMOS 22 were carried out. According to the data, SM exerts a positive and substantial impact on EP. In the context of Malaysian SMEs, the novel findings provide a strong reason for the use of SM, emphasising the need to strengthen managers' knowledge in SM capabilities.

DOI: 10.4018/978-1-6684-6845-6.ch015

INTRODUCTION

Due to increased market rivalry and changeable market dynamics, a company's success is typically determined by the quality of its goods and services. As a result, human capital efficiencies have been identified as the most important factor in boosting the value of product delivery by a number of studies (e.g., Adesina, 2021; Kuzey, Dinc, Akin, & Zaim, 2021). According to Ali and Anwar (2021), EP is crucial to an organization's effectiveness, which in turn impacts the company's revenue. In hindsight, performance is the degree of accomplishment of a predetermined business objective (Bakker & de Vries, 2021). According to Ployhart (2021), human resources are the sole assets that must be developed and nurtured in plenty. Due to the fact that people are an organization's most valuable resource, talent management has been identified as a crucial performance indicator for HR practitioners. In a simple correlational example, the more the staff strives to exceed expectations, the higher the company's competitive advantages (Iqbal, 2018). Numerous studies showed that high-performing employees may contribute to the company's growth, increase customer happiness, and reduce employee turnover (Kuzey et al., 2021; Ployhart, 2021).

Without a question, strategy and organisational performance are becoming more significant than ever (Miller and Cardinal, 1994). Consequently, the outcome of an effective human management plan to accomplish organisational KPIs has become a leader's top priority (Deborah Schroeder-Saulnier, 2010). According to Kuriakose and Tiew, (2022), Malaysia, and specifically its SME sector, is often characterised as a workplace in which its executives have the most authority and control. The same set of leaders defines the rules and regulations and makes the decisions (Jayasingam & Cheng, 2009). According to Ansari et al. (2004), Malaysian employees are required to obey and carry out the directives of their superiors and disputing with them is not a common occurrence in the employee-employer relationship. As a result, the dominant impact of leadership qualities is a crucial denominator that must be well comprehended in light of the leadership's prominent position and great authority in Malaysia.

The SME sector is the subject of research since it is one of Malaysia's most important economic drivers, contributing more than 5.4% to the country's GDP through exports, investment gains, and employment indicators (Tham & Atan, 2022). Explaining the significance of the SME industry to Malaysia is the fact that without them, the country would suffer the "dual deficit" and trade deficit phenomenon, which would negatively affect the trust of foreign investors (Kuriakose & Tiew, 2022; Tham & Atan, 2022). Small- and medium-sized enterprises (SME) suffer persistent challenges due to global market competition, time limits to respond strategically, talent retention, productivity, and uncompetitive operational expenses (Ahmad et al., 2017). Recently, industry actors, notably business chambers, have begun to emphasise the calibre of Malaysian SME employees. According to Kuriakose and Tiew (2022), Malaysian employees' productivity rate of 1 PPP was the lowest among the selected major manufacturing nations. Productivity is the single most important factor in a country's long-term growth. The rise in productivity in Malaysia is flat and unequal (Haba & Dastane, 2019; Kuriakose & Tiew, 2022; Tham & Atan, 2022).

According to Mohamad, Mustapa, and Razak (2021), the most significant business challenge in Malaysia is a lack of talented employees to develop into "Next Gen" leaders and an inability to attract/retain top talent. Leaders have said unequivocally that top talent and effective leadership are essential for solving global issues and setting their organisation for future success, particularly in the face of digitalization needs and a borderless economy. EP is the megatrend that must be managed and advanced to the next level of market-driven economy and policy in order to achieve long-term competitive advantages. Four of the 10 components are associated with human capital, whilst five are associated with strategy management. Moreover, the shift to digital transformation and digital leadership identifies Malaysian human resource as a potential cause of worry (Mohamad, Mustapa, & Razak, 2021), highlighting the necessity to collaboratively enhance work force and associated EP. Malaysia's human resource is facing a significant gap in connection to LC, and the primary cause of management leadership failure in Malaysia is that its qualities, styles, and features are not aligned to increase staff productivity and efficiency, resulting in performance.

Despite the growing problem of leadership and management shortages in the Malaysian workforce, the Mercer EE Index indicated that 26 percent of Malaysian employees do not feel engaged at work. This is one of the highest rates in the Asia-Pacific region, and it has the potential to inhibit both managerial and financial progress. Malaysia's score on the EE Index suggests that there is a great deal of opportunity for improvement in how enterprises treat their employees and that there is much to be gained if human capital is cared for properly. In his analysis of Malaysian workers. Mohamad et al. (2021) observed that they have long been criticised for poor performance, a lack of flexibility, inefficiency, insufficient accountability, and bureaucracy. Consequently, the current study refines and expands our understanding of the impact of SM and LP on EP. This research makes a significant contribution to the body of knowledge as it is the first to evaluate the mediating effect of EE between SM and LC on EP in Malaysian SMEs. In terms of applicability, the recommended context and research findings are meant to provide guidance for the development of organization-specific policies to enhance EP. Therefore, this research would be an antidote to mitigate and treat the EP issue in SME from the leadership, management, and engagement viewpoints.

The purpose of this study is to explore the following in relation to Malaysian SME's. What is the impact of SM on EP? How do leadership abilities affect EP? How does EE function as a bridge between SM, LC, and EP? The remainder of the essay is organised as follows: literature review, methodology, analysis, and findings. The essay finishes with a discussion of its contribution, its consequences, its limits, and opportunities for further research.

REVIEW OF LITERATURE

Critical Review of Key Theories

Since inception of the resource-based perspective in SM by Barney (1991) and Wernerfelt (1984), the SM area has focused more on identifying significant business resources in order to achieve long-term competitive advantage and monetary success. Adoption of this theory was prompted by RBV's capacity to emphasise strategic activities for managers to plan and allocate resources to optimise returns. According to Barney (2001), resources are "the tangible and intangible assets that a corporation utilises to determine and implement its plans." Human, financial, organisational, and physical resources are all part of this. The valued human resources, on the other hand, are scarce and difficult to replicate and replace. Human resources, i.e., personnel, provide firms with a competitive advantage, according to RBV.

RBV supports variety of research has indeed determined the need of having a sound strategy to achieve competitive advantage from RBV theory. The RBV provides a platform for organisations to develop and execute their organisational strategy by measuring their internal resources' and capabilities' potential to achieve competitive advantages. A well-defined and implemented strategy increases the chance of achieving the competitive advantage level significantly (Porter & Kramer, 2006; Richard, 2000). However, its weakness outweighs its strength. According to Fahy (2000), the great majority of contributions within the RBV are conceptual rather than empirical in character. This indicates that many of the fundamental principle's results require confirmation in practise. Furthermore, there are criticisms and debates related to both the nature and determinants of competitive advantage, as well as its relationship to resource based. More crucially, the RBV has been chastised for exhibiting circular logics surrounding its essential component, namely, value that can only be assessed under specific conditions (Barney, 1991). Resources may provide a competitive advantage, but this in turn determines the relevant competitive structures, which raises the issue of the definition of a valued resource, a never-ending debate (Fahy, 2000). As a result, a thorough grasp of the dynamics of resource development is a vital dimension required to broaden competitive positioning. Without such knowledge, the problem of circular thinking cannot be resolved.

SM is designed to successfully connect a company to its environment, which includes political, social, technical, and economic components (Sharplin, 1985). According to Wheelan and Hunger (1989), SM is a rapidly expanding field of study that arose in response to increasing environmental issues. The breadth of research aimed at holistically managing the organisation while seeking to explain why certain organisations did better than others. The SM process's breadth encompasses organizational-wide concerns in the context of a wide variety of environmental variables. Wheelan and Hunger (2008) simplified SM by breaking it down into four essential components that interact with one another: (i) environmental scanning, (ii) strategy creation, (iii) strategy execution, and (iv) assessment and control.

Responsibilities at the corporate level include anything from environmental scanning to performance review. By monitoring the external environment, management identifies opportunities and risks. While assessing the internal environment, the strengths and weaknesses are highlighted. After identifying these strategic variables, management analyses their relationship and defines the corresponding business mission. The first stage of strategy development results in a mission statement, which directs the establishment of business objectives, missions and vision. Following that is the implementation and execution of mission and strategies that are backed by financial plans, programmes, and procedures. Finally, performance evaluation and feedback function as a control and closed loop mechanism for organisational operations. The strength of this model allows the manager to grasp a wide range of issues, including the capacity to control organisational culture. It also helps to highlight the talents required by the management to properly implement the plan (Mizanur, Kent, & Kopacek, 2021).

Leadership Skills Theory: Rather than qualities, this theory focuses on the leader's competences and skills for effective leadership (Dastane, 2020). Katz (1974) identified three key talents in relation to different managerial levels: technical, human, and conceptualization abilities. Mumford et al. (2000) proposed a better proposal that focuses on the leader's capacity to tackle difficult organisational problems. As a result, three ideas were developed based on the author's expertise, including problem solving skills, social-judgment competences, and knowledge mediation between person traits and leadership results.

Mumford, Campion, and Morgeson (2007) employ a 'leadership skill needs strataplex' to emphasise key talents that are critical to a leader's advancement to more senior job executive positions. As leaders advance in their careers, the development of strategic and business competences becomes more important as a performance facilitator than the learning of individual and social abilities. Mumford et al. (2007) elaborate on the cognitive skills that create the framework for the development of leadership qualities as follows: Communication abilities: how well the leader communicates and interacts with other leaders. Active listening is the capacity to distinguish whether information is vital and why particular information should be mitigated in a specific way. Communication via excellent writing: the capacity to clearly understand a message as well as grasp complicated written material.

Prioritization of resources and allocation of products, technology, and materials are examples of business talents (Mumford et al., 2007). Furthermore, the capacity of a leader to comprehend and prepare the fundamental competencies and abilities necessary to fulfil hard business goals was expected (Winston, 2007). Strategic talents include the leader's capacity to comprehend complexity, cope with ambiguity, solve substantial problems, and effect and influence change in the company (Mumford et al., 2007). Ling and Dastane (2022) designed thirteen generic leadership as a framework to train new generation leaders with organisational leadership skills, excellent business acumen, and commercial capabilities.

Research Gaps

Al-Qudah (2018) investigated the influence of SM utilising the balanced scorecard element on the business performance of a Jordanian pharmaceutical firm. Balanced scorecard elements include financial, customer, internal process, and learning perspectives. The findings revealed a substantial association between overall balanced scorecard performance and business performance, particularly in terms of learning and internal growth. Zaidi and Zawawi (2019) conducted research to explore the association of strategy execution process to EP in real-estate businesses among the contractors in greater Klang Valley region of Malaysia. This research includes three EP dimensions: employee commitment, employee retention, and employee growth. The findings revealed that the strategic implementation process has a considerable impact on staff retention and growth, but not on employee commitment. This study is constrained owing to extremely low sample given the size of Malaysia's construction sector, focuses solely on one grade of contractor, and does not utilise any specific SM models or theories comprehensively.

According to Toles (2020), more than half of the SMEs had strategic planning that is similar to the Wheelen and Hunger approach. Aside from the low sample size, the scope of this study does not represent the overall population of SMEs because it is limited to the northern region of Malaysia. Furthermore, the scope comprises just a portion of SM and does not quantify the impact on the business. Meresa (2019) found that SM improves business performance and sales growth. This study's limitations include limited sampling and a lack of adherence to a defined paradigm. Wahab, Mansor, Hussin, and Kumarasamy (2019) conducted an empirical study to determine the extent of SM practise among Malaysian school administrators. The findings of the 12 components component SM suggest that there are variances between the types of schools. The gaps in this study include a restricted number of schools and sampling, which limit the random distribution. This research compares the amount of SM in different types of schools rather than measuring the impact of SM on the organisation.

Against the stated background and review of relevant literature, there is a lack of thorough and localised research to assess the influence of leadership and management on EP in context of Malaysian SMEs. In Malaysian SME business, there is a lack of study on SM linked to human capital management and the relevance of these factors on EP. Inadequate research concentrating on leadership qualities as well as performance of framework type of behaviour measurement in Malaysian setting in general and SME sector in particular. There is a scarcity of academic research on EE as a mediating factor between leadership and management factors and EP.

Numerous academic studies have been conducted to assess the factors that influence EP. Common research that includes the favourable influence of company culture (Ibrahim & Ibrahim, 2015; Nazir et al., 2015; Njugi et al., 2014). Significant research has been conducted on the effects of motivation, empowerment, trust, and work satisfaction on EP (Khan Abdullah et al.2017; Singh, 2018). In conclusion, numerous studies frequently highlight the link between individual variables and organisational behaviour to EP, which supports some of the hypotheses developed in this study. However, relatively few studies have looked at the overall influence of leadership skill and SM on staff performance. More specifically, how does EE mediate the link between two independent factors ranging from LC and SM to EP?

Conceptual Framework

The conceptual model is thus presented based on aforementioned research gap. Figure 1 displays conceptual framework.

Figure 1. Conceptual framework

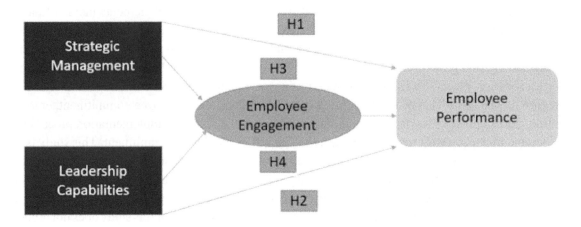

Hypothesis Development

Numerous academic studies have been conducted to assess the factors that influence EP. Common research includes favorable effects of company culture (Ibrahim & Ibrahim, 2015; Njugi et al., 2014; Nazir et al., 2015). There have been several research on the effects of motivation, engagement and work satisfaction on EP (Abdullah et al. 2017; Singh K, 2018; Syaidatul, 2013). In layman's terms, a well-performing employee is one who can achieve the results, goals, or KPIs stated by the firm. Performance is a multidimensional term that focuses on the behaviours or activities that people display in comparison to the expected outcome when completing a task (Tham & Atan, 2022).

According to Franco et al. (2002), performance is a result of intrinsic motivation; nevertheless, the availability of internal determinants such as suitable skills, intellectual capability, and resources necessitates the employer's provision of essential working circumstances. Many famous studies in this subject have determined that the expectation of job performance contains two critical perspectives: one as labour imposed by an organization's dedication to one's function, and the other as voluntary work behaviour (Kuzey et al., 2021). SM focuses on on formulation and implementation strategy while internal management, employee dedication, internal operations, and learnings are focused on organisational performance. The findings demonstrated that organisational culture and a subset of SM had a beneficial impact on the performance of government firms. Several academics, including Nmadu (2007) and others, have jointly solidified the benefits of SM. A clear conclusion can be formed that SM aids in the development of a proactive management posture that allows for a sustainable and changing company model. Against this background, following hypothesis is proposed:

H1: SM has significant and positive impact on EP

Iskandar et al. (2013) examined the validity of LC to EP and how organisational culture moderates performance confirmed the notion that embracing the correct leadership abilities will contribute to an organization's performance, and that organisational culture will further moderate this. Somaye (2012) conducted a study on the Malaysian electronics industry to investigate the link between organisational culture, participative leadership style, and employee job satisfaction. The study found a strong relationship between two independent factors and employee job satisfaction.

Several studies were undertaken by researchers to highlight the LC necessary for Malaysian leaders in the construction business, including the mediating role of leadership skills. The multiple regression analysis highlights nine essential leadership characteristics (e.g., coaching, mentoring, decision making) that have a strong link with six fundamental leadership qualities (e.g., customer focus, personal integrity, teamwork) to improve organisational performance (Wan Hanim et al., 2019). Ahmad (2014) evaluated the impact of leadership behaviours on the success of Malaysian SME service businesses. The dimension of behaviour resulting from transformational and transactional leadership, as well as the organization's success as measured by growth and profitability. According to the study, leadership and conduct are critical components in driving the success of SMEs, and various behaviours have diverse effects on performance.

The capacity to employ a collection of skills, knowledge, traits, and personal experiences at the right competency level across professional tasks is defined as capability (Bowles & Lanyon, 2016). It has a lot in common with competencies, which are sometimes referred to as a skill or ability (Boyatzis, 2008). Capabilities differ from technical or job-specific competences in that they are concerned with the talent and potential capacity necessary to execute within a certain context, quickly transfer that capability, and reproduce performance in a number of different roles or work situations. Transferability is measured not by job title or profession, but by contribution to the organization's core operations and contextual demands (Ployhart, 2021). Falk and Smith (2003) emphasised that a good leader would be able to adapt to internal and external changes, take risks, be extremely proactive and imaginative, and be able to foresee. However, Burgoyne (2004) asserted that not all of an individual's leadership and management qualities have been completely utilised in an organisational setting. Therefore, following hypothesis is proposed:

H2: LC has significant and positive impact on EP.

Ismail, Iqbal, and Nasr (2019) performed a study in Lebanon to look at the link between EE and work performance, as well as the mediation impact between the two variables. Iddagoda et al. (2020) empirically investigated the relationship effect of EE with the selected variables, namely high-performance work practises, religiosity, personal character, leadership, work–life balance, and EE mediating effects on the correlation between the selected dynamics and employee job performance. The study's major findings demonstrate that all dynamics, including leadership, have a favourable link with EE. Furthermore, leadership should play a constructive mediating function between EE and performance. Alias, Ezaili, et al. (2014) investigated the connection between talent management strategies and employee retention in a Malaysian IT business, as mediated by EE. The hierarchical regression analysis revealed that EE does, in fact, moderate the relationship between talent management strategy and employee retention. Job happiness, loyalty to the organisation, fewer employee turnover, noteworthy corporate citizenship behaviour, increased productivity, and greater customer satisfaction are all benefits of engaged employees. George, Omuudu, and Francis (2020); Vance, (2006) Personal disengagement, on the other hand, resulted in withdrawal from role performance defined by a loss of physical, cognitive, and emotional links to the specific work in an organisation (Kahn, 1990). Disengagement frequently leads in great tiredness and burnout, emotions of uncertainty, and a sense of inadequate performance and ability (Maslach et. al, 2001). Against this background, following mediation hypotheses are formulated.

H3: EE mediates the relationship between SM and EP.
H4: EE mediates the relationship between LC and EP.

RESEARCH METHODOLOGY

The type of research known as explanatory research is appropriate for this investigation. The objective here is to provide a depiction of a situation that is more distinct and truer to life. In this particular setting, it examines the connection between SM, LC, EE, and EP via the prism of SM, LC, EE, and EP respectively.

A positivist approach was taken since it was thought to produce more accurate results. The strategy of using questionnaires is utilised in order to obtain the required data in accordance with the goal of the study. The questions were derived from previously published journals and other sources of information that were then modified to fit the parameters of the current research. Through LinkedIn, the list of professionals working in SMEs was distributed with the questionnaire. This research takes use of a convenience sample method, as shown by (Keong & Dastane, 2019; Chen & Dastane, 2022;Pei & Dastane, 2022). The participants in this study are workers at SMEs who are completely aware of and understand their work environment. In addition, this method saves time, money, and resources while also having a cheap cost.

In order to build the questionnaire and use it as an interface for collecting input data in order to advance the study, the following approach was operationalized: Conduct a thorough review of the relevant studies as well as the relevant literature in search of items and questions that correlate to the objectives, questions, and variables of the research. A Likert scale with seven points was utilised by the researcher so that she could evaluate the results of the questionnaires. The first part provides an overview of the employees and responders in terms of their demographics. (Gender, age, amount of education obtained, number of years spent in the workforce, current employment level, and departmental function. The second part of the SM variable is comprised of two sub-dimensions, namely strategic planning and strategic assessment, and a total of seven questions are contained within this section. The third portion, entitled "leadership traits," is comprised of a total of six questions. These questions include personal, interpersonal, cognitive, and change-oriented capacities. The fourth phase of the examination is comprised of six questions that address the cognitive, emotional, and behavioural aspects of EE. EP from the standpoint of three dimensions, including task performance, adaptive performance, and contextual performance, with a total of seven questions in the fifth portion of the exam. The variables and their respective sources are presented in Table 1.

The initial step of the study was to clean the data, which consisted of checking for things like outliers and missing numbers, among other things. After that, we looked at how typical the data were and how reliable they were. Confirmatory factor analysis was used to arrive at the final version of the measure-

Table 1. Variables and Item sources

Study Variable	Foundational Framework	Source of Items
SM	Wheeler and Hungar (1995),	Ali et al. (2008); Schaufeli et al. (2006)
EE	Gallup Q12 Survey JD-R Model	Medlin and Green (2009)
LC	LC Framework (2013) CPE Instruments	Scott et al. (2008); Scott and McKellar (2012)
EP	The Triarchy Model of EP	Pradhan, Rabindra and Jena, Lalatendu (2016); Kazan et al., (2013)

ment model (CFA). A structural equation modelling (SEM) approach based on the AMOS 22.0 is used in this study to analyse the causal relationships and test the hypotheses between the observable and latent components in the suggested research model. This is done in order to ensure that the hypotheses are accurate. In addition, the process of structural equation modelling was broken down into two stages: validating the measurement model and adjusting the structural model to suit the data. The use of a two-step technique ensures that only constructs with excellent measurements (validity and reliability) are preserved in the survey and are therefore included in the structural model. This is accomplished by ensuring that only constructs with excellent measurements are preserved in the survey (Hair et al., 2014).

ANALYSIS, RESULTS AND DISCUSSIONS

Descriptive Analysis

A total of 240 employees from the SME sector participated in this survey. The majority of respondents are male (63.9%), between the ages of 26 and 45 yys, totaling 85%, with bachelor's of 65%, total experience ranging from 10 to 20 years 50.6%, a majority position level of first-line managers 26.6%, and a primary job role of engineering/technical 53.1%. The sampled population logically meets the research aim in terms of age, job level, and roles.

Reliability Analysis

The Cronbach alpha statistics are as follows: for the overall instrument of 26 elements, the alpha value is 0.979. SM1 consists of four components. 3 items in 938, SM2. 921 items, LC 7 things 959 items, EE 6 things 942 items in EP 6. It is critical to assess the dependability during statistical analysis to ensure the consistency of the overall data and consistent output. As a result, the data is regarded as extremely credible (Kothari, 2004). Cronbach's Alpha Test will be the most appropriate reliability technique in the context of several surveys with Likert type scales (Malhotra et al., 2017). According to the criterion, a Cronbach Alpha score of >0.9 for this study indicates good internal consistency.

Constructs Reliability

The recommended CR threshold value is 0.7 and the values in this study, as shown in table 3, exceeded the threshold, indicating the reliability of the measurements. The average variance expected (AVE) is a measure of the robustness of the latent concept, and the academically accepted threshold expectation is 0.4 and above (Hair et al., 2014). As a result, the AVE values reported in table 2 for this research support the claim that the research scales' dependability is highly acceptable, and so internal consistency is extraordinarily dependable.

Table 2. Accuracy analysis statistics

Construct	Items			Factor Loading	CR	AVE
EP	EP1	←	EP	0.857	0.933	0.777
	EP2	←	EP	0.882		
	EP3	←	EP	0.876		
	EP4	←	EP	0.909		
LC	LC6	←	LC	0.906	0.964	0.842
	LC5	←	LC	0.890		
	LC4	←	LC	0.935		
	LC2	←	LC	0.941		
	LC1	←	LC	0.915		
EE	EE5	←	EE	0.805	0.918	0.788
	EE3	←	EE	0.919		
	EE2	←	EE	0.934		
SM	SM4	←	Strategic Planning (SP)	0.910	0.956	0.784
	SM2	←	(SP)	0.845		
	SM1	←	(SP)	0.883		
	SM7	←	Strategic Evaluation (SE)	0.869		
	SM6	←	(SE)	0.897		
	SM5	←	(SE)	0.906		

Normality Test

The purpose of this test is to assess if a sample of data chosen from a population is normally distributed with a particular degree of tolerance. D'Agostino Test is computed using Skewness and Kurtosis values. Data is considered normal if Skewness is between 2 and +2 and Kurtosis is between 7 and +7, according to Hair et al. (2010). Because the kurtosis in this investigation was fixed at -/+3, all data points outside of this range were excluded from the CFA modelling. As a consequence, the univariate distribution assumption is accurate.

CFA

Any data points outside of this range were eliminated from the CFA modelling. As a result, the assumption of univariate distribution is correct. With this exclusion, the standard regression weight is now more than 0.8. Furthermore, redundancy was eliminated by linking the residual influence of SM1 and SM2. All fits are within limits except for the AGFI, which is mildly deviated (0.874 vs. the requirement of >0.90), but it is still acceptable. As an example, even if the GFI and AGFI values did not surpass 0.9 (the threshold value), they nevertheless satisfied the condition proposed by Baumgartner and Homburg (1995) and Doll, Xia, and Torkzadeh (1994), suggesting that acceptance is okay as long as the value is more than 0.8. Absolute indices, Chi-Square 0.000, RMSEA 0.062, GFI 0.908, Incremental indices, AGFC 0.874, CFA 0.977, NFI 0.954, Parsimonious Fit – Chi Sq / df = 1.923. The final fit measurement model as depicted in the figure 2. The model was then subjected to SEM as CFA obtained model fit.

Figure 2. Measurement model

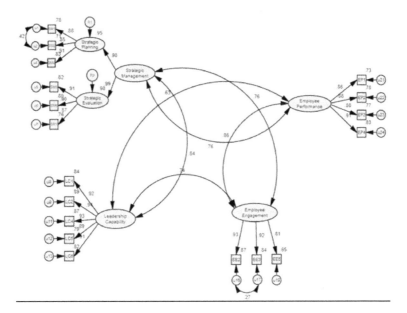

SEM

The structural model was used to examine the proposed causal link between the selected dependent and independent variables. The following reflects the hypothesis to be tested using this SEM: EE is included in the final fit model as a mediation factor between the two independent variables of SM and LC and the dependent variable of EP. As a result, the SEM analysis is divided into two sections: As a reference, the hypothesis was tested using a direct effect model with no mediation element. The goal is to identify the direct influence of both independent variables on EP, allowing for a more in-depth understanding and appreciation of the mediating effect, if any exists. As shown in figure 3, the hypothesis was tested using the final fit model with the mediating effect proposed in this study.

Hypothesis Testing: Direct Impact

Figure 3. Direct impact model without mediating effect

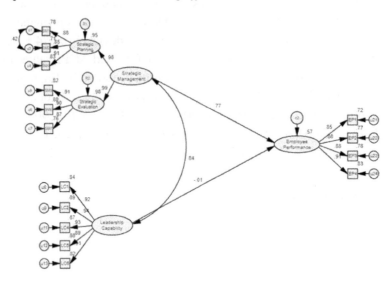

Table 3. Standardized regression weight of the model

Dependent Variables		Independent Variables	Beta Value	p-Value	Remarks
Strategic Planning	←	SM	0.977	0.000	Significant
Strategic Evaluation	←	SM	0.989	0.000	Significant
EP	←	SM	0.767	0.000	Significant
EP	←	LC	-0.011	0.911	In-significant

There were two exogenous constructs in this study, SM and LC and one endogenous component, EP. SM was formed as a second-order element by combining two components of SM (strategic planning and strategic assessment). The findings of the investigation revealed that SM has a substantial positive connection with EP (Beta = 0.767, p = 0.000). On the contrary, the capacity to lead has a minimal, negative, and insignificant relationship with EP. (Beta= 0.911, p= 0.011). The use of a SM approach will improve EP. However, management's emphasis on developing leadership abilities will stifle improvements in EP.

Hypothesis Testing: Mediating Impact

Figure 4. Model structure path diagram with mediating effect

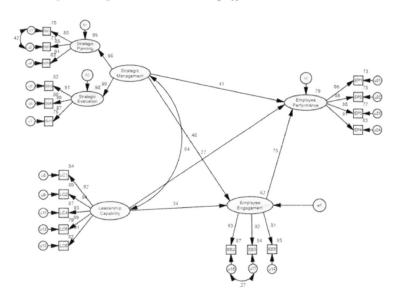

Results of Regression Analysis from SEM

Table 4. Standardized path coefficients

Dependent Variables		Independent Variables	Beta Value	p-Value	Remarks
EE	←	SM	0.477	0.000	Significant
EE	←	LC	0.342	0.000	Significant
Strategic planning	←	SM	0.977	0.000	Significant
Strategic evaluation	←	SM	0.989	0.000	Significant
EP	←	EE	0.749	0.000	Significant
EP	←	SM	0.414	0.000	Significant
EP	←	LC	-0.270	0.001	Significant

Mediation Analysis of EE Between SM and EP

The direct effect of SM to EP is greater than the indirect effect. Therefore, EE has no mediation effect between SM and EP

Figure 5. The hypothesized median model SM-EE-EP

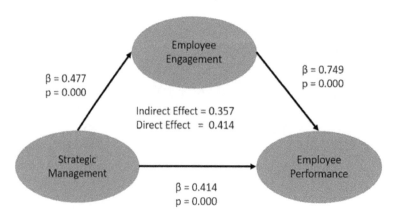

Mediation Analysis of EE Between LC and EP

As the indirect effect of LC on EP is greater than the direct effect, and because there is a significant path relationship between the independent and dependent variables, EE has a partial mediation effect between LC and EP.

Figure 6. The hypothesized median model LC-EE-EP

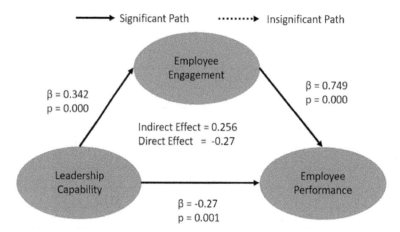

Discussion of Findings

Table 4 displays summary of hypothesis testing results and decisions.

This H1 is confirmed and proven by table 4, which show that implementing SM methods has a favourable and significant influence on EP (p=0.05, Beta = 0.414). This is true for both models that include and do not include a mediating element. The RBV theory supports the concept that most organisations operating and competing in the same business environment are presumed to have comparable sorts of resources, therefore they are challenged to compete with other businesses in their quest of increased performance through efficient resource management. As a consequence, this research found that SM practises such as strategic HR management, talent management, and performance management, among others, help businesses to perform better and build their competitive advantages and EP, leading in improved organisational performance (Sarminah et al., 2018). The results are similar to those of Nmadu (2007) and Akingbade (2007). (2007). They claimed that SM practise increases the quality of business-related decision-making, encourages proactive managerial posture, and helps a firm catalyse cooperation, all of which are important contexts and predictors of EP. The H3 hypothesis that EE will mediate the relationship between SM and EP, on the other hand, has been rejected since the direct effect of SM on EP is greater than the indirect effect. With the involvement of EE to enhance the performance of its workers, a strategic resource management throughout the organisation in which human capital is part of the management process may have no impact.

Table 4. Summary of hypothesis from the final fit model

Hypotheses	Relationship	Results
H1	SM positively and significantly impacts EP	Accepted
H2	LC positively and significantly impacts EP	Rejected
H3	EE mediates relationship between SM and EP	Rejected
H4	EE mediates relationship between LC and EP	Accepted

In both models with and without a mediating element, the H2 hypothesis that leadership skill positively effects EP was rejected. Leadership competence has a small, negative, and non-significant influence on EP in the model without the mediating component (Beta = -0.011, p>0.05). While the mediated model study revealed that leadership competence has a strong and negative association with EP. (P = 0.05, Beta = -0.27) This is an important point to emphasise: leadership qualities were unable to predict employee success. However, there is rising criticism in the literature that implies that leadership talents are sufficient to improve an individual's overall effort (Alimo-Metcalfe & Alban-Metcalfe, 2008a; Bolden & Gosling, 2006). Their key point was that skills and capacities are typically generic and expecting that they will operate regardless of the scenario or individual is not valid. Furthermore, the authors noted that because competences and skills are established based on previous performance rather than future objectives, this just reinforces old thinking rather than challenging for continual development. Clearly, the key respondents of this study are between the ages of 26 and 35, and they may have rejected the concept that conventional leadership qualities may assist them improve their work performance. Hollenbeck et al. (2006) stated that capacity frameworks defined in the single mode lacked adequate empirical evidence to predict validity.

However, when it comes to the H4 hypothesis, which states that EE mediates the relationship between LC and EP, the regression and mediation analyses show that EE does indeed have a significant, positive, and partial mediation effect between LC and EP; thus, the H4 hypothesis is accepted. Numerous literatures agree on the importance of EE in improving one's own performance, particularly given that engaged employees will gladly participate in producing and exploring new knowledge and skill sets, aggressively seeking chances, and going the additional mile. This is consistent with the findings Ong, Choon, and Hee et al. (2018) in the Malaysian public sector, which found that it is hard to separate EE from the leadership-EP connection in an organisation. Leadership alone in a single context will not improve EP unless individuals recognise their leader's talents, because the leader-employee connection is primarily driven by a belief and trust system, which only an engaging setting can deliver. According to Hughes and Rogs (2008), leaders that actively include employee involvement into their management styles can improve their workers' job performance by 10%.

CONCLUSION

The purpose of the study, which was to investigate the impact of SM and LC among Malaysian SME workers, including the mediating role of EE, was successful in achieving its stated aim. The following are some of the notable discoveries that were made. It is possible to improve an organization's efficiency and productivity by emulating and practising the SM model, which consists of the processes of environmental scanning, strategy formulation, strategy implementation, and finally evaluation and control across the organisation. This helps with the effective management of resources, which ultimately results in an increase in EP. The traits and capabilities of a leader do not stimulate the growth and development of their team members' performances. To put it another way, a capable CEO or department manager might not be able to increase his human capital alone by drawing upon his own skills and experiences. In addition to the characteristics that make up the framework, there are additional elements of leadership or organisational behaviour that are essential to practicality. Furthermore, relevance plays a more significant part.

It has been demonstrated time and time again that EE is an excellent instrument for the enhancement of EP. Participation on the part of workers is essential to the health, continued existence, and financial success of a company (Al-Qudah, 2018). The findings provided compelling evidence that an engaged employee strategy catalyses the power of talented leaders in significantly enhancing staff performance. Specifically, the findings suggested that an engaged employee approach The findings presented above were able to provide an answer to the questions that were posed by stakeholders in the SME sector and international research companies regarding the workforce competency and talent performance, stagnant leadership quality, chaotic management practises, and a worsening equal employment issue in Malaysia. The findings provided direction on prospective efforts for transformation and mitigation that an organisation ought to do as the industry transitions to Industry 4.0. [Citation needed] It is necessary to address the widespread misconception of what constitutes traits of a leader, as well as the organisational culture that emphasises selecting the most capable leader based on his or her track record of success. To state the obvious, human resource policymakers and business executives in Malaysia are required to address the significant accomplishment gap that exists in the field of equal employment opportunity (EE) more than ever before. In addition to successfully closing the loop between the findings and the aims of the study, these findings served to fill a significant void that existed in prior investigations (Ibrahim & Ibrahim, 2015; Nazir et al., 2015; Njugi et al., 2014).

IMPLICATIONS

On the basis of the findings of this study, a number of recommendations have been made to the senior management, policymakers, and human resource practitioners working in the SME business in Malaysia, including the following:

Reviewing, integrating, and applying systems thinking models to an organization's main result areas should be the primary focus of an organization's activities. To conduct risk assessments on the business processes of significant departments, departments that are not reaching KPI targets, or departments that are regarded crucial for employee and organisational performance, a task force team that is well-trained and specialised is deployed. If SM training is made required at a minimum job grade of first line managers, then this endeavour will have a better chance of being successful.

The results of the study revealed that organisations, while formulating and carrying out their leadership development programmes, had to give significant consideration to the institutional environment of the organisation. However, in order to adopt the engaging leadership concept, it should also place a stronger priority on approach. Leaders who engage their followers provide their organisations the ability to effectively deal with change and to take the initiative to shape their own destiny. This strategy was always implemented in a manner that was congruent with both the ethical standards as well as the spirit of co-creation and cooperation in order to accomplish a shared objective. As a consequence of this, favourable attitudes among workers will be fostered as a result of excellent perceptions of these engaged leaders, which will eventually lead to improvements in individual EP.

The final piece of guidance is for organisational leaders to make use of the findings of this study to design leadership and management techniques that will boost employee engagement and overall performance on the job. It is possible for the leadership to conduct employee surveys with the workers on a quarterly basis in order to have a better grasp of the workers' expectations as more time passes. In the process of getting ready to put efficient EE techniques into action, it may be advantageous to monitor and oversee an organization's various EE projects, in addition to benchmarking the organization's competitors. Efforts to increase employee engagement (EE) should always come before productivity enhancement initiatives when the goal is to increase the organization's profitability.

LIMITATIONS

Due to the fact that this research was carried out on a representative sample of Malaysian employees working for SMEs, the findings are likely to be applicable exclusively to workers in Malaysia and may not be relevant to employees in other countries. The term "generalizability" refers to the extent to which the findings of a research may be applied to situations that are not directly related to the one in which the study was conducted. The cross-sectional method that was used to collect the data for this study was another key factor that contributed to the problems that were found. Cross-sectional research has a lower degree of confidence overall when compared to research that utilises a longitudinal cohort technique (Hair et al., 2010). An examination known as a longitudinal cohort study is one in which responses are obtained over the course of numerous separate instances (Van et al., 2004). In the conclusions of the study, it was shown that employee participation was a partial mediator of leadership ability. In the future, research should concentrate on identifying additional potential mediating factors, such as trust in the manager, or moderating factors, such as the nature of the workplace, in order to gain a deeper comprehension of the underlying processes that influence direct correlations between EP and leadership ability. The construction of a library of predictive components for the relationship between SM and LC and EP will also benefit from the inclusion of a number of factors that act as mediators or moderators.

By expanding the scope of the study to include financially linked organisational performance-related outcomes as an independent variable, such as return on investment, profitability, and growth, or staff attrition, there is the potential to make this study more rigorous for stakeholders in SMEs as well as in the other sectors. The relational model was evaluated in the context of Malaysian small and medium-sized enterprises (SMEs) using a data collecting approach that consisted of a self-administered online questionnaire. As a consequence of this, if the same strategy can be verified in SME sectors in other countries such as China, Singapore, the United States, or European nations as part of a cross-comparison research, the breadth of these studies has the potential to deliver additional value to the company. In this study, leadership was examined from a singular vantage point, with the characteristics generated from the capabilities framework serving as the basis for the evaluation. As a consequence of this, next study will need to investigate the diverse implications that various leadership practises have on the results for employees. It is possible to do an analysis of value-based leadership in relation to the factors that are being looked into.

REFERENCES

Adesina, K. S. (2021). How diversification affects bank performance: The role of human capital. *Economic Modelling*, *94*, 303–319. doi:10.1016/j.econmod.2020.10.016

Al-Qudah, S. A. (2018). The influence of strategic agility & tackling competitive challenges toward improving performance among Jordanian pharmaceutical companies. *International Journal of Academic Research in Business & Social Sciences*, *8*(5), 762–774. doi:10.6007/IJARBSS/v8-i5/4175

Ali, B. J., & Anwar, G. (2021). Strategic leadership effectiveness and its influence on organizational effectiveness. *International Journal of Electrical, Electronics and Computers, 6*(2).

Alias, N. E., Nokman, F. N., Ismail, S., Koe, W. L., & Othman, R. (2018). The effect of payment, recognition, empowerment and work-life balance on job satisfaction in the Malaysia's oil and gas industry. *International Journal of Academic Research in Business & Social Sciences*, *8*(9), 639–656. doi:10.6007/IJARBSS/v8-i9/4645

Bakker, A. B., & de Vries, J. D. (2021). Job Demands–Resources theory and self-regulation: New explanations and remedies for job burnout. *Anxiety, Stress, and Coping*, *34*(1), 1–21. doi:10.1080/10615 806.2020.1797695 PMID:32856957

Barney, J. B. (2001). Resource-based theories of competitive advantage: A ten-year retrospective on the resource-based view. *Journal of Management*, *27*(6), 643–650. doi:10.1177/014920630102700602

Boyatzis, R. E. (2008). Competencies in the 21st century. *Journal of Management Development*, *27*(1), 5–12. doi:10.1108/02621710810840730

Chen, C. J. S., & Dastane, O. (2022). Advanced Technological Factors Affecting Digital Banking Usage Intention. In Handbook of Research on Green, Circular, and Digital Economies as Tools for Recovery and Sustainability (pp. 43-65). IGI Global. doi:10.4018/978-1-7998-9664-7.ch003

Dastane, O. (2020). Impact of leadership styles on EP: A moderating role of gender. *Australian Journal of Business and Management Research, 5*(12), 27–52. doi:10.52283/NSWRCA.AJBMR.20200512A03

Fahy, J. (2000). The resource-based view of the firm: Some stumbling-blocks on the road to understanding sustainable competitive advantage. *Journal of European Industrial Training, 24*(2/3/4), 94–104. doi:10.1108/03090590010321061

Falk, I., & Smith, T. (2003). *Leadership in vocational education and training: Leadership by design not by default*. National Centre for Vocational Education Research.

George, C., Omuudu, O. S., & Francis, K. (2020). EE: A mediator between organizational inducements and industry loyalty among workers in the hospitality industry in Uganda. *Journal of Human Resources in Hospitality & Tourism, 19*(2), 220–251. doi:10.1080/15332845.2020.1702869

Haba, H. F., & Dastane, O. (2019). Massive open online courses (MOOCs)–understanding online learners' preferences and experiences. International Journal of Learning. *Teaching and Educational Research, 18*(8), 227–242.

Hair, J. F., Gabriel, M., & Patel, V. (2014). AMOS covariance-based structural equation modeling (CB-SEM): Guidelines on its application as a marketing research tool. *Brazilian Journal of Marketing, 13*(2).

Hair, J. F., Ortinau, D. J., & Harrison, D. E. (2010). *Essentials of marketing research* (Vol. 2). McGraw-Hill/Irwin.

Ibrahim, M., & Ibrahim, A. (2015). The effect of SMEs' cost of capital on their financial performance in Nigeria. *Journal of Finance and Accounting, 3*(1), 8-11.

Iddagoda, Y. A., & Opatha, H. H. (2020). Relationships and mediating effects of EE: An empirical study of managerial employees of Sri Lankan listed companies. *SAGE Open, 10*(2), 2158244020915905. doi:10.1177/2158244020915905

Iqbal, A. (2018). The strategic human resource management approaches and organisational performance: The mediating role of creative climate. *Journal of Advances in Management Research.*

Ismail, H. N., Iqbal, A., & Nasr, L. (2019). EE and job performance in Lebanon: The mediating role of creativity. *International Journal of Productivity and Performance Management*. Advance online publication. doi:10.1108/IJPPM-02-2018-0052

Katz, S. (1974). The price and adjustment process of bonds to rating reclassifications: A test of bond market efficiency. *The Journal of Finance, 29*(2), 551–559.

Keong, L. S., & Dastane, O. (2019). Building a sustainable competitive advantage for Multi-Level Marketing (MLM) firms: An empirical investigation of contributing factors. *Journal of Distribution Science, 17*(3), 5–19. doi:10.15722/jds.17.3.201903.5

Khan, A., Ahmed, S., Paul, S., & Kazmi, S. H. A. (2017, July). Factors affecting employee motivation towards EP: A study on banking industry of Pakistan. In *International conference on management science and engineering management* (pp. 615-625). Springer.

Kline, T. (2005). Psychological testing: A practical approach to design and evaluation. *Sage (Atlanta, Ga.)*. Advance online publication. doi:10.4135/9781483385693

Koskei, R., Asienga, I., & Katwalo, A. M. (2013). *Analysis of the influence of strategic LC on performance of research institutions in Kenya*. Academic Press.

Kothari, C. R. (2004). *Research methodology: Methods and techniques*. New Age International.

Kuriakose, S., & Tiew, H. S. B. M. Z. (2022). *Malaysia-SME Program Efficiency Review*. Available at https://openknowledge.worldbank.org/bitstream/handle/10986/37137/P17014606709a70f50856d0799 328fb7040.pdf?sequence=1

Kuzey, C., Dinc, M. S., Akin, A., & Zaim, H. (2021). Does Innovation Capital Mediate the Link between Human Capital Investment and Financial Performance? An International Investigation. *Journal of East-West Business*, 1–28.

Ling, V. L. S., & Dastane, O. (2022). Impact of Organizational Culture on Performance during COVID-19 Pandemic: An Insight From the Malaysian Healthcare Industry. In *Handbook of Research on Challenges for Human Resource Management in the COVID-19 Era* (pp. 358–382). IGI Global. doi:10.4018/978-1-7998-9840-5.ch017

Malhotra, G. (2017). Strategies in research. *International Journal for Advance Research and Development*, 2(5), 172–180.

Maslach, C., Schaufeli, W. B., & Leiter, M. P. (2001). Job burnout. *Annual Review of Psychology*, 52(1), 397–422. doi:10.1146/annurev.psych.52.1.397 PMID:11148311

Medlin, B., & Green, K. W. Jr. (2009). Enhancing performance through goal setting, engagement, and optimism. *Industrial Management & Data Systems*, 109(7), 943–956. doi:10.1108/02635570910982292

Meresa, M. (2019). *The Effect of SM Practices on the institutional Performance; the case of Dedebit credit and saving institution in Eastern Tigray*. Academic Press.

Mizanur, M., Kent, M. D., & Kopacek, P. (2021). Techno-Economic Analysis of HRES in South-East of Ireland. *IFAC-PapersOnLine*, 54(13), 454–459. doi:10.1016/j.ifacol.2021.10.490

Mohamad, A., Mustapa, A. N., & Razak, H. A. (2021). *An Overview of Malaysian Small and Medium Enterprises: Contributions, Issues, and Challenges*. Modeling Economic Growth in Contemporary Malaysia.

Mumford, T. V., Campion, M. A., & Morgeson, F. P. (2007). The leadership skills strataplex: Leadership skill requirements across organizational levels. *The Leadership Quarterly*, 18(2), 154–166. doi:10.1016/j.leaqua.2007.01.005

Nazir, N., & Zamir, S. (2015). Impact of Organizational Culture on employee's performance. *Industrial Engineering Letters*, 5(9), 31–37.

Njugi, M. K. (2014). *Corporate governance and dividend payout-analysis of firms listed at the Nairobi Securities Exchange.* Academic Press.

Nmadu, T. M. (2007). SM in some Nigerian Businesses: A business reality. *Journal of Management Research and Development, 1*(7), 17–23.

Pei, T. J., & Dastane, O. (2021). Digital Technology in Retail: Impact on Shopper Satisfaction. In Handbook of Research on Disruptive Innovation and Digital Transformation in Asia (pp. 187-213). IGI Global.

Ployhart, R. E. (2021). Resources for what? Understanding performance in the resource-based view and strategic human capital resource literatures. *Journal of Management, 47*(7), 1771–1786. doi:10.1177/01492063211003137

Porter, M. E., & Kramer, M. R. (2006). The link between competitive advantage and corporate social responsibility. *Harvard Business Review, 84*(12), 78–92. PMID:17183795

Pradhan, R. K., Jena, L. K., & Kumari, I. G. (2016). Effect of work–life balance on organizational citizenship behaviour: Role of organizational commitment. *Global Business Review, 17*(3, suppl), 15S–29S. doi:10.1177/0972150916631071

Richard, O. C. (2000). Racial diversity, business strategy, and firm performance: A resource-based view. *Academy of Management Journal, 43*(2), 164–177. doi:10.2307/1556374

Schaufeli, W. B., Bakker, A. B., & Salanova, M. (2006). The measurement of work engagement with a short questionnaire: A cross-national study. *Educational and Psychological Measurement, 66*(4), 701–716. doi:10.1177/0013164405282471

Scott, G., Coates, H., & Anderson, M. (2008). *Learning leaders in times of change: Academic LC for Australian higher education.* Academic Press.

Scott, G., & McKellar, L. (2012). *Leading professionals in Australian and New Zealand tertiary education.* University of Western Sydney and Association for Tertiary Education Management.

Sharplin, A. D. (1985). Human Resource Planning: Low-Cost Strategies to Improve Worker's Job Security. *The Journal of Business Strategy.* Advance online publication. doi:10.1108/eb039077

Singh, S. K. (2018). Sustainable people, process and organization management in emerging markets. *Benchmarking, 25*(3), 774–776. doi:10.1108/BIJ-02-2018-0038

Stalk, G. (1992). *Time-based competition and beyond: Competing on capabilities.* Planning Review.

Tham, K. W., & Atan, S. A. (2021). SME Readiness Towards Digitalization in Malaysia. *Research in Management of Technology and Business, 2*(1), 361–375.

Toles, K., Jr. (2020). *Sustainability of Small Businesses Through Strategic Planning and Management* [Doctoral dissertation]. Capella University.

Vance, R. J. (2006). *EE and commitment.* SHRM Foundation.

Wahab, J. A., Mansor, A. Z., Hussin, M., & Kumarasamy, S. (2019). Headmasters' instructional leadership and its relationship with teachers performance. Religación. *Revista de Ciencias Sociales y Humanidades*, *4*(21), 202–206.

Wernerfelt, B. (1984). A resource-based view of the firm. *SM Journal, 5*(2), 171-180.

Wheelan, T. L., & Hunger, D. J. (1989). *SM and Business Policy*. Addison-Wesley.

Winston, C. (2007). *Government failure versus market failure: Microeconomics policy research and government performance*. Brookings Institution Press.

Zaidi, F. I., & Zawawi, E. M. A. (2019). Analysis of Strategy Implementation Process and Employees' Performance in Construction Companies. *Journal of Building Performance ISSN*, *10*(2), 2019.

Chapter 16
Types of Social Capital in the Context of Company Managers:
A Field Study for Policies to Maintain Competitive Advantage in Turkey

Mustafa Atilla Aricioğlu
Necmettin Erbakan University, Turkey

Yunus Emre Ertuğrul
Necmettin Erbakan University, Turkey

ABSTRACT

In the research, data were obtained from 200 different senior managers. As a result of the analysis, it was concluded that the attitudes of senior managers in Türkiye, the general level of trust similar to the general structure in Türkiye, and the rate of civic participation are low. In this respect, in the context of weak and strong ties, which is the first type of social capital, it is seen that senior managers in Türkiye have weak and strong ties at a low level. Finally, it was concluded that senior managers in Türkiye are higher than all other types of social capital in terms of structural social capital based on the existence of network structures between individuals and conceptual social capital, which is a more abstract part of social capital and is representative of trust, norms, and common discourses.

INTRODUCTION

While social capital is defined as "work of togetherness" for Tocqueville, (Singing, 2007: 73), it is defined as "goodwill, friend, closeness and social classes between family and family groups" for Hanifan (Hanifan, 1916). On the other hand, it is considered to be a better society and a better life as "awareness networks" for Loury (Loury, 1977). This historical development pointed out by the literature shows that next researchers also carried out the process in this context. As a matter of fact, while Field (2008) points out who he knows, not what he knows, Coleman (1988) emphasizes the way social networks work and Woolcock (2001) emphasizes who social networks will be with and how. While Bourdieu (1986) and

DOI: 10.4018/978-1-6684-6845-6.ch016

Fukuyama (2005) agreed that social capital means trust, Fukuyama emphasized that trust is actually necessary for class formations, and Bourdieu emphasized that it should be based on reciprocity and for everyone. Of course, social capital, which Putnam (1993; 1995) pointed out as the basis of cooperation, is actually a bond and this plays a leading role for development-growth. In addition, Nan Lin (1999) states that the network can be virtual, not just face to face. This is important in online relations. For inference about whether the network is weak or strong, the discussion on whether Coleman's understanding of "closed networks" or Granovetter's understanding of "weak networks" provides more benefits (Abay Alyüz, 2018; 21) has been concluded as being related to the individual's conditions and the purpose of using the relationship.

In this context, the existence of social capital should be examined within the framework of a series of questions such as for whom it is necessary, how it is formed and what its meaning is. In this context, the existence of social capital should be examined within the framework of a series of questions such as for whom it is necessary, how it is formed and what its meaning is. In this study, the answers to these questions were investigated in the context of the managers of companies operating in Türkiye. While the types of social capital examined in the research were questioned through the relationship styles of company managers, the meaning and formation of social capital for companies were also sought. On the other hand, although not the main purpose of the study, This study is expected to contribute to the search for the connection and meaning of Bourdieu's or Coleman's class relations with social capital..

THE CLASSIFICATION OF SOCIAL CAPITAL

Provide various classification studies of social capital have been carried out in order to find a meaningful response to the debates on what social capital means or what it should be understood, and to express the quality of its effect. Considering the studies conducted by Woolcoock (1973), Uphoff (1999), Nahapiet and Ghoshal (1997), Putnam (2000), Coleman (1988), and Burt (1992), social capital is classified into four parts as following:

- Bonding, Bridging and Unifying Social Capital,
- Strong Ties and Weak Ties,
- Solidarity, Intermediary and Connecting Social Capital,
- Structural, Conceptual and Relational Social Capital,

Putnam (2000) divides social capital into two as "bonding social capital and bridging social capital" according to its connections. "Unifying social capital ties" were defined by Woolcook (2001) and this was accepted as the third dimension of the previous distinction. In the second distinction, Granovetter (1973) and Nan Lin (1999) distinguish the relationship levels of social networks as strong and weak ties. Third, solidarity social capital based on Coleman's theory (1988), intermediary social capital created by Burt (1992) based on the theory of structural gaps, and Connecting Social Capital put forward by Woolcock's is the triple distinction. The last form of the distinction is structural and conceptual social capital made by Uphoff (1999). Nahapiet and Ghoshal (1997) added the relational social capital to this classification to increase the distinction to three.

Bonding, Bridging and Unifying Social Capital

Relationships between people who share the same socio-economic status as family, close friends and neighbors are defined as intra-community bonding social capital (Putnam, 1993). bonding social capital basically arises when relationships based on trust and reciprocity are developed between those who share something in common. In other words, they are private and introverted groups that can be given as examples of this type, such as family ties, religious affiliation, church membership, neighborhood committees (Graham, 2016). From this point of view, bonding social capital consists of horizontal relations between individuals with similar characteristics within the society and between individuals in these groups. While bonding social capital is generally seen among homogeneous and value-sharing groups, it can also be seen between only two individuals. But these people have to be members of the same community (Dolfsma and Dannreuther, 2003). Therefore, this type of social capital emerges from "strong" social relations on the basis of a "common identity" such as family, relatives, gender, ethnicity, religion, sect and organizational culture (Erselcan, 2009: 70).

Bridging social capital represents wider networks. It enriches network connections with versatile and diverse network relations established especially through civil society (Cersosimo and Nistico, 2007: 403). However, the similarities or differences of the people who are connected, in other words, the presence of people with whom a relationship is established in a narrow area and the presence of relationships that contain a rich variety of relationships force a distinction in terms of capital types. While the former is considered to be a bridge builder, it is understood that the latter is binding (Coffe and Geys, 2007: 123). In this respect, heterogeneity is perhaps the most important indicator of bridging networks. This diversity and richness also offers an important advantage in problem solving and alternative solutions (Kim, Subramanian and Kawachi, 2006). As a matter of fact, bridging weak links provides a capability-enhancing feature in knowledge transfer and innovation. (Leonard, 2004). In other words, personal ties and knowledge production emerge as an important element for the transfer of knowledge from individuals to industrial forms (Kitapçı, 2008: 124). In this regard, the existence of virtual networks and the Internet plays an important role. Thanks to these networks, getting together with people, groups and organizations with whom he has little or no chance to meet, has made a significant contribution to the development of bridged social capital (Ellison, Steinfield, and Lampe, 2007; Hofer andand Aubert, 2013).

Unifying social capital is defined through broken and weak relationships, and is expressed through the perception and network between citizens and central and local government institutions. The unifying social capital, which is handled through a private trust, is measured over the trust between individuals and the public individual (Cersosimo and Nistico, 2007). In other words, it express the relations between those who have power and those who do not and it is defined as a network of relations based on trust between people who interact between clear, formal or institutionalized power or authority distinctions in society (Szreter and Woolcock, 2004: 655). Lin emphasizes that this type of social capital is resources embedded in social structures beyond the society and in that society. He also emphasizes that it is important for individuals to be able to access and mobilize these resources (Lin, 2001: 12). In this respect, the norms approved by the general public throughout these relations are valid. Unlike other types of social capital, public trust should be necessary as well as interpersonal trust in unifying social capital theory.

Strong Ties and Weak Ties

The most obvious answers to the question of what are strong ties are: It is the situation that consists of a closed network structure and thanks to the harmony provided, change decreases, individuals rise in the internal hierarchy and ensure cooperation with others (Moran, 2005: 1130). For example, strong ties between companies reduce the risks and costs of opportunism as well as providing them with resources (Leenders and Gabbay, 1999: 10). These types of ties are indicators of trust, which is the most important prerequisite for trade in societies (Batt, 2008: 490). However, because its protection or sustainability is not very easy, it is necessary to maintain face-to-face communication and provide dynamic interaction (Hansen, 1999: 85).

According to Granovetter, weak ties allow people to reach their goals more effectively and easily. Thanks to the knowledge he has, he starts to bond and resemble the people in his frame in the social environment they are in. The standardization of information and the search for different information increase the need of this tie (Özdemir, 2008, p. 83).

It is possible to summarize the distinction between strong and weak ties as follows (Table 1):

Table 1. Strong ties vs. weak ties

Strong Ties	Weak Ties
Friendships, family relationships with similar characteristics such as social class, religion	Members of similar interests or social qualifications in voluntary associations
Close friends and family members of different social characteristics, such as age, gender, or ethnicity	Different social memberships and acquaintances in voluntary associations
Close working friendships; close co-workers in different hierarchical positions	Distance friendships in different hierarchical positions and ties between citizens and public servants.

Source: Felander (2007: 118)

While Coleman (1990) advocates the benefits of strong ties, Granavetter (1973), Uzzi (1997) and Burt (2000) argue that weak ties are a more effective and contributing feature so that the bond is rich and diverse. On the other hand, Hansen (1999) explains that the weak ties in project relations in organizations and the strong ties between departments should be considered as a whole, and this situation is necessary for each person. Many researchers such as Lin, Felander (2007), Kharkhardt (1992) and Harvey (2008) argue that weak and strong ties are equally important and necessary for individuals from different perspectives.

Solidarity, Intermediary, and Connecting Social Capital

Solidarity social capital emerges through the strong solidarity and familiarity of like-minded people, as well as the sharing of common values. This leads to the emergence of harmony (Carpiano, 2006). In this context, it advocates the emergence of individuals and affiliated groups with strong ties (Krackhardt, 1992; Granovetter, 1973). In other words, it defends Bourdieu's (2010: 60) thesis of "the sum of existing or potential resources associated with having a permanent network of more or less institutionalized relationships based on mutual recognition and recognition". At this point, Obstfeld (2014) defined mediation as "a behavior in which an actor influences, directs or facilitates interaction between other actors". Thus he expanded Marsden's (1982: 202) definition of "actors facilitate transactions between other actors who do not have access to or do not trust each other". Increasing studies on mediation also help to identify the institutions contributing to this issue and the policies they are trying to determine (Fernandez and Gould, 1994). Studies on mediation by Burt (Burt, 1997) argue that social capital can emerge by intermediary actors who bring together two disjointed remote parts of a network. In other words, he argues that disconnected ties can be formed through individuals who build bridges. Mediation offers great benefits in terms of access to information and control, just like weak ties in social capital. Burt interprets the advantage that the agent gains from this to the individual's position, while Granovetter attributes it to the strength of the network.

On the other hand, as it is known, this type of social capital was put forward by Woolcock in addition to the type of intermediary and solidarity social capital. It is a concept that generally defines the level of trust between individuals and social institutions (Lofors and Sundquist, 2007). More specifically, it is defined as "the ties that bind individuals or groups to each other in positions of political or financial power" (Aggera and Jensenb, 2015: 4). The most distinctive feature of this relationship is the existence of a hierarchical structure. That's why relationships take place vertically. Weakly contextual interactions are established between individuals because the relations in the connecting social capital are mostly in a formal or institutional context. The formation of these relations is mediated by state officials, nongovernmental organizations, voluntary organizations or businessmen (Szreter, 2002: 580). The social capital created through these intermediaries makes the micro-level social capital and social actions of individuals more productive politically and economically by allowing access to ideas, information and resources from institutions.

Structural, Conceptual, and Relational Social Capital

Structural social capital focuses mainly on the social interaction of individuals within both organizations and society. Thanks to this interaction, individuals act in direct proportion to the advantages that their position will offer them (Tsai and Ghoshal, 1998: 465). Establishing rules and procedures is considered the first step to reveal structural social capital (Uphoff, 2000: 228). While Structural forms of social capital relate to concrete social structures such as networks and associations, cognitive forms of social capital are related to more subjective or intangible elements such as trust and reciprocity norms (Zierschvd, 2005). Structural social capital, which causes cooperation between individuals, helps individuals to reduce transaction costs and achieve efficient results by reducing the time and investment they spend on any business. In addition, structural social capital contributes to collective action, both in the organizational and societal context. On the other hand, Collective action is an indicator of trust in society (Sampson, Raudenbush, and Earls, 1997). In other words, structural social capital indirectly provides social order by preventing violence in society.

Conceptual social capital is divided into two parts as cognitive and relational social capital. Cognitive social capital is briefly defined as a common code or a set of common values established between individuals to set a common goal (Tsai and Ghoshal, 1998: 465). These common views also create their own unique language and deeply embedded narratives and culture among individuals (Pearson, Carr, and Shaw, 2008: 957). This leads to the formation of trust in society or more specifically in companies, and this creates relational social capital, which is the second dimension of conceptual social capital. In other words, its relational dimension consists of resources that are revealed through personal relationships such as trust, norms, obligations and identity (Nahapıet and Ghoshal, 1998). While trust is accepted as a moral ability (Fukuyama, 2005: 42), it is perceived as a guarantee that individuals will not harm each other (Nahapıet and Ghoshal, 1998: 254). Moreover, in terms of the organization, it is considered as a leading player in establishing good relations with the people, institutions or organizations with which it does business (Fukuyama, 2005). Another factor that defines relational social capital is the norms that allow individuals to reach a consensus on what is right and what is wrong. Thanks to these rules, individuals gather themselves under an identity as a whole with another person or a group of people (Nahapıet and Ghoshal, 1998: 256). Finally, factors such as their attitudes towards each other, their ability to empathize and their appreciation of each other have a strong effect on establishing relationships (Yay, 2018).

METHOD

Sample and Scope of the Study

Purpose of the research; "It is to measure the social capital approaches of managers in large enterprises operating in the top 1000 in Turkey over types." In this context, an examination has been made on the types of the concept of social capital. In this study, first of the social capital types, bonding, bridging and unifying type of social capital, secondly, strong and weak ties social capital type, and lastly, structural and conceptual social capital types were included in the research. For this, the managers of the first 1000 companies operating in Turkey and published in 2018 by ISO were included.

Research Methodology and Hypotheses

The following scales were used for the survey questions:

- Structural and Cognitive Social Capital Scale (Nahapiet and Ghoshal, 1998; Moran and Ghoshal 1996; Tsai and Glohashal,1998)
- Bridged social capital scale (Pajak,2006)
- Weak bonds scale (Houser, 2007)
- Strong bond, connective and unifying scale of social capital (World Values Survey, Jenny Onyx and Paul Bullen and studies in local literature)

The fieldwork has been supported within the scope of the support of the Thesis Projects by Necmettin Erbakan University Scientific Research Projects Center. Due to the pandemic, the survey was carried out online and by the subcontractor company. The obtained data were analyzed with the help of SPSS 22 package program and the results were interpreted.

RESEARCH FINDINGS

Reliability Analysis

According to the findings of the reliability analysis, the trust scale and the social capital scale that bonding, bridges and unifying scale are between 0.60-0.80, which is quite good; The structural and conceptual social capital scale is greater than 0.80 and is highly reliable (see table 2).

Table 2. Reliability analysis

Scales	Cronbach Alpha
Trust Scale	0,781
Bonding, Bridging and Unifying Social Capital Scale	0,760
Structural and Conceptual Social Capital Scale	0,899

Source: Calculated by the authors

Factor Analysis

With the trust scale used in the research, it was tried to measure the trust level of the participants over 12 questions. As a result of the factor analysis, the factor load value of the 11th question was determined as 0.303 and it was decided to be excluded from the scale. In this context, according to the results of the factor analysis reconstructed; The KMO value was determined as 0.732 and it was decided that the sample size of the scale was sufficient for this analysis. As a result of Bartlet's test of sphericity, (see table 3) the p value being below 0.05 indicates that the scale is suitable for factor analysis.

In the scale, in which Varimax rotational factor analysis was applied, a four-factor structure with an eigenvalue above 1 was determined. Since the factor loads of the items were above 0.3 and there were no overlapping items close to each other, no questions were removed. With the a four-factor structure obtained, the total explained variance rate is 78.11%. The variance value explained by the factor of trust in institutions under the 1st factor was 29.88%; The variance value explained by the trust in the media under the 2nd factor was 18.93%; The variance value explained by the political trust under the 3rd factor is 16.71% and finally the variance value explained by the trust in people under the 4th factor is 12.5%. Cronbach's alpha values were 0.868, 0.981, 0.899 and 0.482 respectively. When the general reliability analysis of the scale was performed again, it was seen that this value increased to 0.797. Except for the factor of trust in people in the scale, all dimensions provide reliability in general. Even though factor was low at the level of 0.482, it was decided to to keep the trust factor in people on the scale because factor load values (see table 4) were above 0.6 and the congruence of the meanings of the items.

The 37th and 38th items were removed because of the factor loads were under more than one factor, and also the 28th and 31st items were removed because the values of items were below 0.3. As a result of the analysis, it was determined that there was a three-factor structure. The KMO value was determined as 0.761 and it was decided that the sample size of the scale was sufficient for this analysis. As a result of Bartlet's test of sphericity, the p value being below 0.05 indicates that the scale is suitable for factor analysis. Since the factor loads of the items were above 0.3 and there were no overlapping items close

Table 3. Trust scale

	Factors			
	1	**2**	**3**	**4**
Most people are trustworthy.				0,690
When we face any problem, I ask for support from my family or close friends.				0,858
I trust politics			0,936	
I trust TGNA (Turkish Grand National Assembly)			0,947	
I trust the Police Department	0,905			
I trust the justice system	0,870			
I trust Government Agencies	0,915			
I trust NGOs	**0,640**	**0,334**		
I trust universities	0,620			
I trust Visual Media		0,954		
I trust Social Media		0,961		
Sig.		0,001		
Bartlett Sphericity x2		1465,247		
KMO test		0,732		
Explained Variance	29,878	18,932	16,705	12,593
Total Explained Variance		78,107		
Cronbach Alfa	0,868	0,981	0,899	0,482
General Cronbach Alfa		0,797		

Source: Calculated by the authors

to each other, no questions were removed. With the three-factor structure obtained, the total explained variance rate is 50.89%. The variance value explained under by the bonding social capital factor under the 1st factor is 18.51%; The variance value explained under the bridging social capital under the 2nd factor is 18%, and the variance value explained under the Unifying Social Capital under the 3rd factor is 14.38%. Cronbach's alpha value was 0.800, 0.789 and 0.899 and 0.787 respectively. When the general reliability analysis of the scale (see table 5) was performed again, it was observed that this value increased to 0.780.

As a result of the analysis the factor loads of the 47, 48 and 55 items were excluded from the analysis because they were under more than one factor. It was determined that there was a three-factor structure. The KMO value was determined as 0.865 and it was decided that the sample size of the scale was sufficient for this analysis. As a result of Bartlet's sphericity scale, the p value being below 0.05 indicates that the scale is suitable for factor analysis. The factor loadings of the questions 46, 49 and 54, whose factor values are close to each other, are greater than 0.30. According to Tabachnick and Fidell (2007), items can be evaluated below the specified factor, provided that the difference in the load value between the two factors of the item is not less than 1 out of 10 of the factor with a high load value (overlay item). It was observed that the three identified items were not considered as overlay item for this reason.

Table 4. Bonding- bridging- unifying social capital scale

Factors	1	2	3
24. I meet my close friends very often			0,890
25. I often eat out with other people on the weekend.			0,915
26. I often do an activity with my colleagues at work.			0,880
27. Most of our employees in our business are relatives or acquaintances.			0,370
29. The people I know around me have a very different range of age groups than I do.	0,541		
30. The people I know around me have very different lifestyles from me.	0,616		
32. People I know around me watch different television programs than I do.	0,758		
33. People I know around me listen to different music than I do.	0,766		
34. People I know around me care more about writers than I care about.	0,661		
35. People I know around me read different newspapers and magazines than I do.	0,729		
36. The people I know around me have very different socio-economic status from me.	0,618		
39. Your company cooperates with institutions or organizations such as TUBITAK (The Scientific and Technological Research Council of Türkiye)		0,749	
40. Your company often engages in activities with universities to get support on any subject or to carry out a joint study.		0,738	
41. Our company operates with other groups or organizations that have different purposes with itself.		0,635	
42. Our company often receives support from the government or other institutions.		0,657	
43. Our firm is frequently involved in the planning, operation and maintenance of government-sponsored services.		0,734	
44. Our firm is frequently involved in various government development planning processes.		0,730	
45. In the last year, I have interviewed or corresponded with public institutions or political leaders on a topic for the benefit of society.		0,376	
Sig.		0,001	
KMO test		0,761	
Bartlett Glob. x2		1314,441	
Explained Variance	18,509	18,002	14,380
Total Explained Variance		50,89	
Cronbach Alfa	0,802	0,789	0,787
General Cronbach Alfa		0,780	

Source: Calculated by the authors

Since the items 52, 53, 51, 57 and 58 in the scale represent structural social capital in line with the literature by showing a structure together, this dimension is called "structural social capital". The ex-

Table 5. Structural and conceptual social capital scale

Factors	1	2
52. The common language we use in our company provides efficiency in obtaining, interpreting and understanding the information that is owned and shared.	0,779	
53. The common language we use in our company provides convenience in obtaining new information from existing information.	**0,754**	**0,301**
57. Organizational understanding in our company enables the formation of communication and relations based on different individual and cultural values.	0,748	
51. In our company, we use a language of common terms, expressions and phrases that will make it easier for us to understand and communicate with each other.	**0,691**	**0,315**
58. Success stories told in our company; It guides individuals and units in creating, sharing and storing information and values.	0,626	
54. Communication channels in our company allow access to information held by others.	**0,473**	**0,573**
50. In our company, the communication channel has a large amount of information and a large number of people and units that will share information.		0,841
56. The communication channel in our company allows individuals and units who want to share their knowledge to easily join the communication network.	**0,306**	**0,644**
46. Our company has communication channels where we can share our information with others.	**0,513**	**0,6**
49. The communication network in our company provides the people in the communication network with the opportunity to be aware of the possibilities of sharing and distributing their information.	**0,492**	**0,598**
Sig.	0,001	
KMO test	0,865	
Bartlett Glob. x2	855,505	
Explained Variance	35,532	23,395
Total Explained Variance	58,927	
Cronbach Alfa	0,815	0,755
General Cronbach Alfa	0,856	

Source: Calculated by the authors

planation rate of this factor is 35.53%, and the cronbach alpha value is 0.815. In the second dimension, since the items 54, 50, 56, 46 and 49 represent conceptual social capital in line with the literature by showing a common structure, this dimension is called "conceptual social capital". The explanation rate of this factor is 23.39%, and the cronbach alpha value is 0.755. When the general reliability analysis of the scale was performed again, it was determined that this value was 0.856.

Frequency Analysis

In the research, it was tried to determine the weak and strong ties structures of the participants through their membership to voluntary organizations. In this context, it is aimed to measure the relational attitudes of the participants towards voluntary organizations. As a result of the answers obtained (see Table 6), it was concluded that 14.5% of the participants (29 people) were members of any organization, while 85.5% (171 people) were not members of any voluntary organization. While 5 (2.5%) of the members who are

Table 6. Scale of strong and weak bonds

	Yes	No	Empty	Total
1.Do you voluntarily join any group?	29	171	-	200
2. How active are you in these organizations and associations?	5	13	182	200
3. Whether you are a member or not in the last three years in any workgroup or project did you take part?	5	13	182	200
4. In the associations you are a member of, do the members have a similar socio-economic structure?	6	12	181	200
5. In the associations you are a member of, the members of the association mostly have the same belief?	8	10	182	200
6. In the associations you are a member of, do the members of the association adopt the same political view?	-	18	182	200
7. I think that being a multicultural structure will make the environment I live in better?	15	3	182	200
8. Living together with people with different lifestyles makes me happy?	-	18	182	200
9. Have you spent time or money on a project that would benefit many people around you, even if it did not directly benefit you?	136	64	-	200
10. Does our company operate with other groups or organizations that have the same purpose as itself?	193	7	-	200

Source: Calculated by the authors

members are actively involved in activities, 13 (6.5%) of the members say that they are not active. In addition, 5 (2.5%) of the participants stated that they had been active in these voluntary organizations in the last three years, while 13 (6.5%) of the participants stated that they had not been involved in any activity in the last 3 years. Regarding the association structures to which they are members, 6 of the participants (3%) said that they were members of organizations with a similar structure, while 12 (6%) said that they belonged to organizations with different structures; While 10 (55.6%) of them said that they were made up of people with different religious beliefs, 8 (44.4%) of them said that they believed in the same religious view; All 18 (9%) people who are members of a voluntary organization and express their opinions stated that the associations they are members of consist of members with different political views.

While 15 (7.5%) of the participants believed that living together with various cultures would make their lives better, 3 (1.5%) said no because they thought it would be worse. Similarly, there are no participants who believe that living together with people with different lifestyles will bring happiness, while 18 (9.0%) of them give no answer.

While measuring the social responsibility attitudes of the participants, 136 (68.0%) of the participants answered yes to the question asked about spending their time and money for others, although it did not benefit them, 64 (32.0%) answered no. In fact, 193 (96.5%) of the participants answered yes, while 7 (3.5%) answered no to cooperation with people who share the same goal.

According to the distribution of voluntary, organizations of membership, the membership to sports clubs is 3 (1.5%), the membership of organizations with which they share similar beliefs is 13 (6.5%), the membership of organizations that contribute to commercial activities is 4 (2.0%), the membership of science, art and culture associations is 9 (4.5%) (see Table 7).

Table 7. Membership types of managers to voluntary organizations

	Sports Clubs	Organizations That Adopt Common Beliefs and Values	Institutions and Organizations That Support Commercial Activities	Science, Art, and Culture Associations	I Am Not a Member of Any	Total
Apart from the Chamber of Commerce and Industry you are a member of, which of the following associations or groups or NGOs are you a member of?	3	13	4	9	171	200

Source: Calculated by the authors

According to the results of the Pearson correlation analysis between the trust variables, it was determined that there was a more significant and positive relationship between media trust and other types of trust (r =, 321**,218**,317**,p<.01). In addition, a significant and positive relationship was found between strong ties and trust variables (r =, 662**,667**,599**,692**,p<.01). An increase in the level of trust of the managers in the media will cause a positive increase on all trust levels, while the level of trust in people will increase more than other types of trust. On the other hand, an increase in the strong ties of managers will cause a positive increase on all trust variables. Moreover, The positive correlation has been found between Trust in People with bonding social capital (r = .180**,p<.05), bridging social capital (r = .273**,p<.01), Unifying Social Capital (r = .152**, p<.01) and conceptual social capital (r = -.167*,p<.05), while there is a negative correlation with structural social capital (r = -.241*, p<.01). In addition, while there was a negative relationship between structural social capital and trust in institutions (-, 210**, p<.01), a positive and significant relationship was found between trust in media and social capital (,244**, p<.01). The increase in the trust level of managers towards people will cause an increase in their bonding, bridging, unifying and conceptual social capital, while it will cause a decrease in their structural social capital. Similarly, a decrease in structural social capital will cause an increase in the level of trust in institutions. Finally, combining managers with an increase in their level of trust in the media will also result in an increase in their social capital.

According to the Pearson correlation analysis, another result is that there is a positive and significant relationship between social capital that bridges strong ties (r =, 233**,p<.01) and unifying social capital (r =, 204**,p<.01). While there is a negative relationship between structural social capital (r = -,159*,p<.05) has been reached. An increase in the strong ties of managers will cause an increase in their levels of bridging social capital and unifying social capital, while a decrease in their level of structural social capital.

Finally (see Table 8), from the results of the correlation analysis, there is a positive and significant relationship between bridging social capital and unifying social capital (r =, 194**,p<.01), while both structural social capital (r = -,206**,p<.01). 01) and conceptual social capital (r = -.225*, p<.01). Similarly, while there is a negative relationship between conceptual social capital and unifying social capital (r = -, 225**, p<.01), it has a positive and significant relationship with structural social capital (r =, 638*,p<.01).

There is a statistically significant positive and weak relationship between the trust levels of the managers of the companies operating in Türkiye (r=0.161, p<0.05) and their trust levels in the media (r=0.231, p<0.05) and weak ties. In this case, hypotheses H1 and H4 were accepted. As their level of

Table 8. Correlation analysis

Variables	1	2	3	4	5	6	7	8	9	10
Trust in People	1									
Political Trust	,145*	1								
Trust in Institutions	,262**	,226**	1							
Trust the Media	,321**	,218**	317**	1						
Strong Ties	,662**	,667**	,599**	,692**	1					
Bonding Social Capital	,180*	,048	-,019	,033	,102	1				
Bridging Social Capital	,273**	,095	,106	,132	,233**	,129	1			
Unifying Social Capital	,152*	,063	,081	,244**	,204**	,103	,194**	1		
Structural Social Capital	-,241**	,035	,003	-,210**	-,159*	-,068	-,206**	-,069	1	
Conceptual Social Capital	-,167*	,108	,044	-0,12	-0,05	-,026	-,225**	-,225**	,638**	1

*$p < .05$. **$p < .01$
Source: Calculated by the authors

trust in people and their level of trust in the media increase, so will their weak ties. On the other hand, there is no statistically significant relationship between the political trust levels of company managers ($r=0.026$, $p>0.05$) and the level of trust in institutions ($r=0.056$, $p>0.05$) and weak ties. In this case, the H2 and H3 hypotheses are rejected. There is no correlation between the level of political trust of managers and their institutional trust and weak ties.

Another hypothesis result is between the managers' spending time with close friends and colleagues and bonding social capital ($r=0.870$, $p<0.05$), and between the bridging social capital with the diversity of people with different tastes around them ($r=0.640$, $p<0$)., 05) and between their perceptions of receiving support from the state or other institutions, with unifying social capital ($r=0.640$, $p<0.05$), there is a statistically significant positive strong relationship. In this case, hypotheses H6, H7 and H8 were accepted. As people's relationships with their close friends and colleagues increase, their bonding social capital, their bridging social capital as positive evaluations of people with different tastes around their diversity increase, and the unifying Social Capital that unites managers will become stronger as their level of relationship with the state or other institutions increases.

Finally, there is a moderately strong positive relationship between the perceptions of company managers regarding the existence of intra-company communication channels and their structural social capital ($r=0.586$, $p<0.05$) between their thoughts about the existence of organizational understanding within the company and their conceptual social capital ($r=0.422$, $p<0.05$). In this case, hypotheses H9 and H10 were accepted. As the perceptions of company managers regarding the existence of intra-firm communication channels increase, their conceptual social capital will become stronger as their structural social capital and their thoughts on the existence of intra-firm organizational understanding increase (see Table 9).

According to the table above regarding Hypothesis 5, there is a positive and significant relationship between the membership of the managers of companies operating in Türkiye to associations and volun-

Table 9. Hypothesis results

	Sub Dimensions	Hypotheses	Relationship Levels	Relationship Levels
	trust people	H.1	0,161*	not to reject
	Trust in institutions	H.2	*0,056*	Reject
Weak ties	trust the media	H.3	0,231*	not to reject
	political trust	H.4	*0,026*	Reject
Strong ties	Membership of a similar association	H.5	-	not to reject
Bonding Social Capital	Relationship with close friends	H.6	0,870*	not to reject
Bridging Social Capital	Diversity of people with different tastes around	H.7	0,640*	not to reject
unifying Social Capital	Getting support from different institutions	H.8	0,640*	not to reject
Structural Social Capital	Availability of internal communication channels	H.9	0,586*	not to reject
Conceptual Social Capital	Presence of organizational understanding within the firm	H.10	0,422*	not to reject

Source: Created by the authors

tary organizations with similar structures and their strong ties ($p<0.05$). In this case, the H5 hypothesis was accepted. Increasing the membership of managers to associations of similar nature will strengthen their strong ties.

SOLUTIONS AND RECOMMENDATIONS

According to the results of the trust scale, which represents the weak ties, which we accept as the first type of social capital, it has been shown that the trust levels of the managers in Türkiye are generally low. Although this result agrees with the low general trust level of people in Türkiye (Erdoğan, 2006; Ağıroğlu, 2008; OCDE, 2017, 2020), it seems to be slightly higher. It can be said that this is due to the higher education levels of the administrators (Gerçil and Araci, 2011; Keskin, 2008). In addition, the low level of trust in other types of trust can be cited among the reasons for the low level of trust in visual and social media due to political trust, pressure and control over the media due to Türkiye's economic and political turmoil.

Table 10. Hypothesis 5 consequences

Variable	Association Membership	N	X	SS	t	df	P
Strong Ties	Yes	29	3,0026	0,64241	2,361	198	0,026
	No	171	2,756	0,49695			

Source: Calculated by the authors

According to the results of the analysis we conducted on the memberships of voluntary organizations and associations for the analysis of strong ties, it was concluded that such civic participation rates in managers are very low (Çalışkan, 2010; Aydemir, 2011). The fact that many managers do not have a membership in other voluntary organizations other than being a member of a professional organization and chambers can be seen as a reason for the very low civic participation. It seems that these voluntary organizations that are members of are generally composed of fellow citizens such as communities and foundations with similar religious views (Devamoğlu, 2008; Akman, 2018; Coffe et al. 2007). The activity status of managers in voluntary organizations is divided into two. While the activity rates are very low in groups that do not have a common purpose with themselves, on the other hand, the activity status of voluntary organizations or groups with a common purpose is very high. In other words, while they are more comfortable spending their time and money for groups that are compatible with their own goals, they are not so comfortable with other groups. The activity status of the managers in voluntary organizations other than their own purposes shows us the difference between their actions and intentions. Moreover, while administrators have a positive view of groups that support cultural diversification, such as membership in voluntary organizations, they have a more negative view of groups that are more marginal and disrupt the social order.

It has been concluded that managers in Türkiye have the highest unifying social capital among the second types of social capital. This shows that the relationship of managers with public and private institutions and organizations is higher. This supports the fact that managers have the highest level of trust in institutions and the correlation between the unifying social capital and trust in institutions. In addition, the binding social capital was low. It has been shown that the ties of managers with other foreign people are better with the bridging social capital. However, just like in voluntary associations, it shows that binding social capitals are stronger, since the ties with these foreign people are either based on similar purposes, through similar belief structures or through fellow countrymen's unions.

Finally, it has been concluded that structural and conceptual social capital has the highest value among social capital types. The existence of internal communication channels and the effective and efficient use of these communication channels, as a result of the formation of common value judgments among employees, creates some advantages for the company. Therefore, it may have caused the type of structural and conceptual social capital to be so high. In addition, the fact that there are more studies on structural and conceptual social capital on business from both local and international literature supports this (Zhao et al. 2014; Turgut 2013; Yıldırım 2019). It can even be said that this type of social capital has a more important place in particular.

According to the results of the correlation analysis, it was concluded that there is a strong relationship between the connecting, bridging and unifying social capitals of the managers and the sub-dimensions of these capitals. It is noteworthy that the bonding social capital has a stronger relationship with its sub-dimensions. The high level of relationship between managers and close friends and colleagues is due to the general lack of trust in Türkiye, dominant cultural values and norms, and the difficulty of learning and finding solutions to social problems (Xiao, 2007; World Bank, 2020; OECD, 2017, 2020). While this caused managers to communicate with their close circles, the state's intervention in the economy, political and political crises forced the managers of the organization to establish more cordial relations with their close friends and colleagues and do business with them (Ergin, 2007; Yawson, 2018).

It has been concluded that there is a strong positive relationship between the bridging social capital type and the sub-dimension that measures the respect and tolerance of different tastes and preferences of managers. The fact that managers communicate more from different social, cultural, ethnic and economic environments shows that managers have a higher level of respect and tolerance. Established distant relations will strengthen the bonds of trust and cooperation between people and will lead to the emergence of respect and tolerance among them. Moreover, it helps him to establish bonds with different people (Shipilov; 2006; Suna, 2017) and access different information and resources (Alan, 2017). It supports that the value judgments formed are an important element in developing the bridging social capital. The reason for the high unifying social capital levels of the managers is related to the economic level of Türkiye. Although it is claimed that state intervention loses its importance in economies that have adopted the free market, this situation may differ in countries that follow similar economic policies. Managers in Türkiye choose to enter into vertical relations with the state in order to reach financial and technical resources (Acquaah, 2007; Li, 2014). This approach is a very valuable instrumental tool in terms of accessing resources and surviving, especially in times of crisis. For this reason, the increase in the relationship of managers with public and private institutions and organizations, which they have engaged in, will increase its unifying social capital.

FUTURE RESEARCH DIRECTIONS

It has been concluded that managers have a moderate relationship with their structural and conceptual social capital and their sub-dimensions. As a result, having communication channels within the company will improve their structural social capital. In other words, structural social capital, which represents both vertical and horizontal communication, will help to ensure communication between individuals at equal levels, on the one hand, and upper-level communication, on the other hand, in the organization. While this will solve the problem of collective action within the organization, it will help to create a common organizational understanding. Just as in conceptual social capital, the formation of a common vision, a common language and common values within the organization can enable employees to enter into mutual relations in line with the determined goals, helping them to solve their problems in collective action and to be more effective and efficient than their activities. Therefore, it can be understood that the two types of social capital complement each other.

As a matter of fact, the strong relationship between these types of social capital positively affects the performance of many employees, such as organizational learning, knowledge sharing, access to new information, implicit knowledge transfer, and innovation (Zhao et al. 2014; Turgut, 2013; Hamad, 2017; Gündoğdu, 2015; Büyüksaraç, 2015). In order to realize these, it is necessary to have a strong structural and conceptual capital.

Looking at the sub-scales that make up the trust scale, it has been determined that there is a positive relationship between the sub-dimensions of trust and general trust. In addition, there is a strong and positive relationship between strong ties and trust, and it is seen that there are more strong relationships that place trust in a central place in the connections established by managers. In addition, the trust sub-dimension has a relationship with all other types of capital except conceptual and structural social capital.

And:

-In order to develop the weak ties of managers in Turkey, the state, NGO, cooperation associations and industry studies to carry out studies in this field, It can be tailored and produced as such.

   ◦   A similar study across Turkey can be carried out on small and medium-sized enterprises.

    ◦   Explaining weak ties in terms of trust factor in our study weak ties due to insufficient can be measured over.

    ◦   In addition, in order to explain the relations of managers more in the organizational context, external social relations with suppliers, customers and competitor capital can also be measured.

CONCLUSION

In order to achieve their desired goals and objectives and provide a competitive advantage against other companies, businesses need a good level of social capital in addition to their physical and human capital. Firms with a high level of social capital enable them to gain competitive advantage by making positive contributions in many aspects, from accessing different sources to obtaining new information and contributing to the innovative activities of the firm, as well as helping the formation of common values within the organization and displaying more effective and efficient performances. Many studies have been carried out to support this in both local and international literature. However, there has not been a study covering the top 1000 large scaled enterprises managers on different types of social capital in Türkiye. Therefore, this study was conducted with the aim of measuring the social capital approaches of managers in large scaled enterprises operating in Türkiye over types.

In this context, in the study carried out, social capital is divided into three parts as structural, cognitive and relational. The results for each of the three species examined differ. In general, it seems that relational capitals encourage access to new information and innovative activities, while structural capitals offer the opportunity to communicate with different people and markets. In this respect, the study coincides with this general opinion in the literature. Looking at the results of the correlation analysis, it was concluded that there is a strong and positive relationship between the trust variables. It can be said that any increase in the trust levels of the managers will increase the other trust levels. Among these types of trust, trust in people is more remarkable in that it has a relationship with all other variables. While there seems to be a negative relationship between structural and conceptual social capital in this relationship, there seems to be a positive relationship between all other variables. In the results of the correlation analysis, the highest level of correlation was found in two places. First, it was found that there was a moderate relationship in the correlation analysis between trust variables and strong ties, and the second was a moderate relationship in the correlation analysis between conceptual social capital and structural social capital. In other words, an increase in the strong ties of managers will cause a moderate increase in positive direction on all types of trust, while an increase in structural social capital will cause a moderate increase in conceptual social capital. Finally, it is seen that the relationship between structural social capital and conceptual social capital is negative, except for the relationship between them and all other variables.

Finally, the findings of the study on senior company executives in Türkiye can be summarized as follows:

•   Managers' trust levels are low, which reduces the level of managers' interaction with different people.

- The low membership in voluntary organizations indicates the low level of civic participation of administrators. On the other hand, the similar structure of the associations to which they are members shows that their managers have stronger relations.
- In terms of bonding, bridging and unifying social capital, it seems that managers have higher levels of these three types of social capital, but their bonding social capital is higher.
- Structural and conceptual social capital was found to be higher than all other capital levels of managers.

ACKNOWLEDGMENT

This research was supported by the Necmettin Erbakan University [project number 201321001].

REFERENCES

Acquaah, M. (2007). Managerial Social Capital, Strategic Orientation, and Organizational Performance in an Emerging Economy. *Strategic Management Journal*, *28*(12), 1235–1255. doi:10.1002mj.632

Akman, A. Z. (2018). *Şehir Rekabetçiliğinde Sosyal Sermayenin Rolü Üzerine Bir Araştırma*. Necmettin Erbakan Üniversitesi Sosyal Bilimler Enstitüsü.

Alan, H. (2017). *Kadınların Kariyer Gelişimlerinde Sosyal Sermaye Edinme Biçimleri: Bağımsız Kadın Yönetim Kurulu Üyeleri Üzerine Bir Araştırma*. Başkent Üniversitesi Sosyal Bilimler Enstitüsü.

Aydemir, M. A. (2011). *Toplumsal İlişkilerin Sosyal Sermaye Değeri: Topluluk Duygusu ve Sosyal Sermaye Üzerine Bir Araştırma*. Selçuk Üniversitesi Sosyal Bilimler Enstitüsü.

Büyüksaraç, E. M. (2015). *Sosyal Sermayenin Bilgi Paylaşım Yönelimi Aracılığı ile Organizasyonel Performansa Etkisi*. İstanbul Teknik Üniversitesi Fen Bilimleri Enstitüsü.

Çalışkan, D. (2010). *Yenilikçi Oluşumlarda Sosyal Sermayenin Rolü ve Burdur İli Üzerine Bir Araştırma*. Süleyman Demirel Üniversitesi Sosyal Silimler Enstitüsü.

Coffe, H., & Geys, B. (2007). Toward an Empirical Characterization of Bridging and Bonding Social Capital. *Nonprofit and Voluntary Sector Quarterly*, *36*(1), 121–139. doi:10.1177/0899764006293181

Devamoğlu, S. (2008). *Sosyal Sermaye Kuramı Açısından Türkiye'de Demokrasi Kültürü Üzerine Bir Değerlendirme*. Pamukkale Üniversitesi Sosyal Bilimler Enstitüsü.

Erdoğan, E. (2005). *Sosyal Sermaye, Güven, Türk Gençliği*. www.urbanhobbit.net/PDF/ Sosyal%20 Sermaye_emre%20erdogan.pdf

Ergin, R. A. (2007). *Sosyal Sermayenin Yöneticiler Bağlamında Ölçülmesine Yönelik Konya Sanayisinde Bir Araştırma*. Selçuk Üniversitesi Fen Bilimleri Enstitüsü.

Gerçil, G. & Aracı, M. (2011). Sosyal Sermayenin Güven Unsurunun İşgörenlerin Performansı Üzerine Etkileri. *Çalışma ve Toplum, 1*.

Gündoğdu, N. (2015). *İş Ağlarının ve Sosyal Sermayenin Uluslararasılaşma ve Yenilikçilik Üzerindeki Etkisi*. Marmara Üniversitesi Sosyal Bilimler Enstitüsü.

Hamad, A. A. (2017). *The Effect of Social Capital on Operational Performance: A Research in Erbil*. Atılım Üniversitesi Sosyal Bilimler Enstitüsü.

Keskin, M. (2008). *Sosyal Sermaye ve Bölgesel Kalkınma: Erzurum Ticaret ve Sanayi Odası Üyelerinde Sosyal Sermaye Düzeyi ve Belirleyicilerinin Analizi*. Atatürk Üniversitesi Sosyal Bilimler Enstitüsü.

Li, C.-R., Lin, C.-J., & Huang, H.-C. (2014). Top Management Team Social Capital, Exploration-Based İnnovation, and Exploitation-Based İnnovation in SMEs. *Technology Analysis and Strategic Management, 26*(1), 69–85. doi:10.1080/09537325.2013.850157

Nahapıet, S., & Ghoshal, J. (1998). Social Capital Intellectual Capital And The Organizational Advantage. *Academy of Management Review, 23*(2), 242–266. doi:10.2307/259373

OECD. (2017). *How's Life? 2017: Measuring Well-being*. OECD Publishing. doi:10.1787/how_life-2017-

OECD. (2020). *How's Life? 2020: Measuring Well-being*. OECD Publishing. doi:10.1787/9870c393-en

Shipilov, A., & Danis, W. (2006). TMG Social Capital, Strategic Choice and Firm Performance. *European Management Journal, 24*(1), 16–27. doi:10.1016/j.emj.2005.12.004

Suna, B. (2017). *Otel İşletmelerinde Sahip ve Yöneticilerinin Sosyal Sermaye Unsurlarından Sosyal Ağlarının Müşteri Teminine Etkisi Gaziantep Örneği*. Hasan Kalyoncu Üniversitesi Sosyal Bilimler Enstitüsü.

Tabachnick, B. G., Fidell, L. S., & Ullman, J. B. (2007). *Using multivariate statistics*. Pearson.

Tsai, W., & Ghoshal, S. (1998). Social Capital and Value Creation: The Role of Intrafirm Networks. *Academy of Management Journal, 41*(4), 464–476. doi:10.2307/257085

Turgut, E. (2013). *Sosyal Sermaye ve Bilgi Paylaşımı Davranışının Yenilikçilik İklimine Etkisi*. Gazi Üniversitesi Sosyal Bilimler Enstitüsü.

World Bank. (2020). *Fy 2020 Türkiye Country Opinion Survey Report*. Retrieved April 24, 2022, from https://microdata.worldbank.org/index.php/catalog/3760

Xiao, Z., & Tsui, A. (2007). When Brokers May Not Work: The Cultural Contingency of Social Capital in Chinese High-tech Firms. *Administrative Science Quarterly, 52*(1), 1–31. doi:10.2189/asqu.52.1.1

Yawson, K. A. (2018). *Social Capital in İnstitutions of Higher Education: An Examination of The İnteraction Between Social Capital and Department Leadership*. Orta Doğu Teknik Üniversitesi Sosyal Bilimler Enstitüsü.

Yıldırım, E. (2019). *Sosyal Sermaye ve Bireysel Motivasyon Faktörlerinin Bilgi Paylaşma Niyeti Üzerine Etkisi*. Marmara Üniversitesi Sosyal Bilimler Enstitüsü.

Zhao, J., Wang, M., Zhu, L., & Ding, J. (2014). Corporate Social Capital and Business Model Innovation: The Mediating Role of Organizational Learning. *Frontiers of Business Research in China, 8*(4), 500–528.

KEY TERMS AND DEFINITIONS

Bonding Social Capital: The relationships a person has with friends and family, making it also the strongest form of social capital. Bridging capital: the relationship between friends of friends, making its strength secondary to bonding capital.

Bridging Social Capital: Bridging social capital is defined as the connections between individuals who are dissimilar with respect to socioeconomic and other characteristics.

Intermediary Social Capital: In intermediary social capital, which focuses on individual returns, the position of the individual in relations determines the advantages. In other words, those who are in the bridge position in the networks have more social capital due to their position in the network. Necessary prerequisites, structural gap, bridge role in intermediary social capital.

Linking Social Capital: Linking social capital is a type of social capital that describes norms of respect and networks of trusting relationships between people who are interacting across explicit, formal or institutionalized power or authority gradients in society.

Relational Social Capital: Relational social capital is a dimension of social capital that relates to the characteristics and qualities of personal relationships such as trust, obligations, respect and even friendship.

Solidarity Social Capital: Solidarity social capital network closure, high security, and strong bonds.

Strong Ties: Strong ties refer to intimate connections you have with family, friends, spouses, and coworkers. Nurturing these social relationships is a lot of work, but they're some of the most fruitful you will have in your life. That's because these strong-tie relationships have three important components to them.

Structural Social Capital: Structural social capital is a dimension of social capital that relates to the properties of the social system and of the network of relations as a whole. The term describes the impersonal configuration of linkages between people or units.

Trust: Trust is often mentioned specifically in definitions of social capital, for example, "connections among individuals—social networks and the norms of reciprocity and trustworthiness that arise from them". Some authors even equate trust with social capital, such as Francis Fukuyama.

Weak Ties: Weak ties are people you know but not very well. They're merely acquaintances. You interact with these people at work and in your personal life only as much as you need to.

Chapter 17
New Normal HEI:
Strategic Organizational Readiness Model

Teay Shawyun

(iD) https://orcid.org/0000-0001-6760-0930
South East Asian Association for Institutional Research, Thailand

Somkiat Wattanasap
MahaChulalongkorn University, Thailand

ABSTRACT

Existential crises question the organization's readiness to withstand uncertainties. Geopolitics and natural disruptions have changed human behavior into a "new normal." In improving business continuity, HEIs must strategically deal with operating models, resilience, and agility and be better prepared for disruptions. Typical HEI reactions of online home TLR lack addressing the human capacity/capability needs, technologies/infrastructure, academic/student services support, and TLR evaluation/assessments that cover the HEI broader approach of education values, systems, mechanisms and pedagogies, and student outcomes assurance. It includes HEI human, infor, and organizational capital capacities and capabilities of these systems. Being resilient and agile calls for faster decision-making focused on HEI priorities. This chapter addresses the HEI strategic readiness through a strategic organizational readiness model (SORM) managing the HEI organization readiness. The SORM evolves around the HEI six thematic systems, with resilience and agility as vital analytical and assessment parameters.

INTRODUCTION: ORGANIZATION STRATEGIC READINESS

Since 2000, global uncertainty and natural disaster frequencies have grown manifold, including a 24% point increase in cyber incidents since 2013, with the 2020 COVID-19 pandemic and Ukrainian crisis being the turning point (Nauck et al., 2021) in the backdrop of other geopolitical adversities and natural calamities of past decades. These have affected all human life, moving from the "normal" to the "new normal." Human life has revolved around the "real normal" that has been around, downplayed, and greatly ignored for decades due to its acceptance as part and parcel of life. This normal is the human life "real

DOI: 10.4018/978-1-6684-6845-6.ch017

normal" Diversity-Discrimination-Displacement-Divide multifaceted variables of age, gender, sexual orientation, nationality, language, race, color, ethnicity, socioeconomic status, cultural, religious and political beliefs and ideologies, physical and mental ability interplayed and impacted by four human-centered personal-personifications, psycho-pretense, political-pretense, and power-posture dimensions (Teay and Wattanasap, 2020). Succeeding in natural or uncertain times through strengthening institutional resilience and being agile enough to adapt to disruptive changes and challenges has never been more critical to all profit & non-profit enterprises or academic institutions (Tomlinson et al. 2021).

The FERMA–McKinsey (Federation of European Risk Management Associations) research of 200 senior executives and risk and insurance professionals (Natale et al. 2022) from various industry sectors and countries showed that risk is still mainly involved in crisis response. It highlighted that previous risk management practices focused on a few well-defined risks, primarily financial ones. Two-thirds of responding companies acknowledge that the global pandemic has made risk and resilience significantly more critical to their organizations. The respondents said that resilience is central to their organizations' strategic process. It calls for secure and flexible organizational and technical infrastructure at the potent intersection of digitization within other resilience areas, including work-from-home strategies. It also indicated that a better risk governance model is vital for efficient and effective decision-making. Crisis management with foresight capabilities (scenarios and stress testing) emerged as one of the core areas for improvement. Natale et al. (2022) surmised that "resilient organizations develop business models that can adapt to significant shifts in customer demand, the competitive landscape, technological changes, and the regulatory terrain."

As the world, human life, and organizations are undergoing increasingly rapid, unpredictable, and unprecedented changes, Nauck et al. (2021) called for broad-based resilience imperatives. This resilience should go beyond financials into operational, technological, organizational, reputational, and business-model resilience by embedding resilience in the organizations that address and mitigate these changes (Tomlinson et al. 2021). In moving forward, they highlighted the organization's need to (a) describe how resilient the organization is today, (b) determine the degree and nature of resilience the organization needs for the future, and (c) design the organization's approach to building the organization resilience needs and to future-proof their organizations (Mankin et al., 2021). Mankin et al. (2021), recommended some critical practices in future-proofing the organization as (1) thinking ahead when defining business-critical roles, as supported by Bain Research and others indicating that fewer than 5% of an organization's roles account for more than 95% of its ability to execute its strategy and deliver results and the organization needs to rethink which skills will be most important in an increasingly tech-enabled future, develop them in the current workforce, and actively recruit for them, (2) redefining what a great organization looks like that allows organizations to devise talent development and recruiting strategies to help meet their needs, (3) not cutting back on management development as reskilling well done does help and reskilling is also cheaper than the "fire and hire" model for filling new business-critical roles, and (4) figuring out the organization's future aspirations by rediscovering the importance of meaningful jobs, supportive colleagues, and flexible employers. In addition to being resilient, the organization needs to be agile through faster decision-making, better interdepartmental coordination with a sharper focus on organization priorities through (1) alignment and conviction on mission, goals, values, and prerogatives, (2) culture and change management that underscore the organization's mindsets and value system, (3) organization structure, core values processes, and people capacities and capabilities, and (4) adaptation and evolution to address, meet and go beyond the new requirements (Álvarez et al., 2022).

Brasca et al. (2022) highlighted some critical implications of technology use during the Covid-19 pandemic (1) Cost, Availability & Access to Technology, (2) Faculty, Staff, Students & Technology Designers, developers & implementers *(educators, administrators & students)* Capacities & Capabilities, Culture & Mindset, and Commitment & motivations, (3) Leadership, Governance & Administration repositioning or new business modelings, approaches, and deployments; and (4) Organizations Systems, Mechanisms, Tools & Techniques requirements, workforces, students, stakeholders & technological changes.

As a synopsis, Natale et al. (2022), Tomlinson et al. (2021), and Nauck et al. (2021) place resilience categorically as (1) *Operational resilience* dealing with operational and supply chain challenges, (2) *Technological resilience* focusing on technological challenges, (3) *Organizational resilience* addressing organizational challenges of governance, leadership, administration personnel capacities & capabilities, culture, values & mindsets, (4) *Financial resilience* addressing financial challenges, (5) *Reputational resilience* of institutions aligning values with actions and words to stakeholders (employees, customers, regulators, investors, and society) who hold firms accountable for their actions, and (6) *Business-model Resilience* of repositioning or reinventing business capacities & capabilities to adapt to significant shifts in customer demand, competitive landscape, technological changes, and the regulatory terrain. As such, being resilient would mean the organization is strategically agile and resilient to these competitive changes, new needs, and requirements. These organization & technology implications raise a fundamental question of the HEI strategic & operational readiness and the need for a new HEI Business Model.

Given the organization's requirements to meet and address dynamic changes, it is recognized that any HEI, an organization in the education industry, is also faced with and affected by dynamic and volatile changes and uncertainties. While most researchers have dealt with business-oriented organizations, a key question is what and how the HEI can be strategically ready to address and meet these uncertain, unpredictable challenges and changes. In meeting and mitigating these challenges and changes, this paper proposes a Strategic Organization Readiness Model (SORM). This SORM encompasses two significant dimensions of resilience and agility of its strategic direction performance and assessment that the HEI should address and assess to determine its organizational strategic readiness.

Organization Strategic Journey: Resilience and Agility

Organization Strategic Readiness Journey

Rey (2019) analogized the organization's strategic journey's faltering and failure or success as "the intent and decision to participate in a competition and the execution on the day of the actual marathon," i.e., its strategic readiness. Organizational failures or mediocre achievements are mainly due to overlooking the strategy development and execution gap and not recognizing the organization and human capacities and capabilities as critical capital requirements. It fundamentally lacks organizational and individual learning and sharing mindsets and the Institutionalization of the execution readiness culture. Stone's (2021) Institute for Corporate Productivity (i4cp) Accelerating Workforce Readiness research reported 5 top workforce readiness issues. These being insufficient data about current workforce capacities and capabilities (53%), unclear workforce definitions and communications of workforce readiness (52%), lack of clarity of new skills or upskills needed for moving forward (47%), no clear understanding by leaders of workforce readiness (42%), and no analysis of workforce readiness (42%).

Within the social cognitive theories, organizations are hemmed by humans with social, behavioral, and psychological attributes that underscore the organization and individual readiness to change and be resilient and agile. It is supported by Weiner et al. (2008 and 2009)'s research noting that the term 'readiness' implies a psychological and behavioral state of organizational and individual preparedness, willingness, and ability to take action. It connotes that organizational readiness can mean the organizational members' change commitment and implementation of organizational change efficacy. Bandura's (1997) notion of goal and change commitment highlights the organizational members' shared resolve to pursue or change the courses of action. Bandura (1997) notes that cognitive and motivational aspects of readiness, fear, and other negative motivational factors (Maddux, 1995) can underestimate or downplay one's capability judgments and confidence levels in action executions. It weakens one's motivation to engage in specific or changing courses of action. These can affect the organizational readiness for change in more structural terms of the organization's financial, material, human, and informational resources, organizational structures, and resource endowments (Bloom et al., 2000), with organizational features affecting the receptive context for innovation and change (Pettigrew et al., 1992).

Jones et al. (2005) contend that an organizational culture that embraces innovation, risk-taking, and flexible organizational policies and procedures with a positive organizational climate and learning supports organizational readiness for change (Pettigrew et al., 1992). Gist and Michell (1992) noted that efficacy is a "comprehensive summary or judgment of perceived capability to perform a task." Change efficacy is a function of the organizational members' cognitive appraisal of three determinants of implementation capability: task demands, resource availability, and situational factors. When organizational readiness for change is high, organizational members are likelier to initiate change by instituting improved or innovative policies, procedures, or practices. They exert more effort in supporting and executing changes with more remarkable persistence in facing obstacles or setbacks during implementation (Bandura, 1997; Gist and Mitchell, 1992). In conclusion, the organizational readiness for change depends on the organizational members' individual and psychological state (Holt et al., 2006) and their capacities and capabilities as attuned to the organization's culture and values within the governance and structural context.

Organizational Resilience

This day's highly dynamic, changeable, and competitive environment brought about by technology and globalization has led to a hyper-competitive environment (D'Aveni et al., 2010), calling for organizations to be more resilient and agile. Organizations need to nurture and develop a resilience capacity that enables them to adequately and actively react to unanticipated events and capitalize on possibilities that could threaten the organization's survival (Lengnick-Hall et al., 2011) with an adaptation aspect (Madni and Jackson, 2009). Doing so allows the organization to emerge from a crisis or calamity stronger. Additionally, the organization must be agile, which is the "ability quickly to recognize opportunities, change direction, and avoid collisions" (McCann 2004) and be successful (Christopher, 2000; Heckler and Powell, 2016). To successfully maintain and sustain achievements, Kouzes and Posner (2007) noted that vision, mission, courage, trust, leadership, knowledge, learning capacity, and change capacity and capability (Najrani, 2016) are essential elements. These are critical for developing strategies to improve the organization's performance (Anwar et al., 2019) through its organizational characteristics and resources and core value-addition processes significant for resilience (Weick et al., 2005; Kendra and Wachtendorf, 2003; Gittell et al., 2006).

Generally, resilience happens when the people and systems bounce back from negative experiences, happenings, and disturbances and survive after being knocked around and about whether the organization can recover to its previous status or stable state. The extent of successful change is measured by its organizational resilience over time to reflect the strength of any organization to withstand "sudden blows" (Lengnick-Hall and Beck, 2005). Resilience is vital in enabling the organization to (1) anticipation of adversities, develop mechanisms for fortification or mitigation against experiences and events that could be overwhelming (Rerup, 2001; McManus et al., 2008; Somers, 2009), and resist and recover (Robert, 2010) to a state of "normalcy" (Boin and Eeten, 2013), (2) maintain balance in the organization's life during challenging or stressful epochs through organizational functionality restoration by focusing on organizational processes, capacities, and capabilities advancement (Robb, 2000; Lengnick-Hall and Beck, 2005; Lengnick-Hall et al., 2011; Ortiz-de-Mandojana and Bansal, 2015), and (3) protect the organization and human capitals from developing mental and physical inertia and issues.

Linnenluecke's (2017) summary review showed that organizational resilience research covers organizational responses to external threats, organizational steadfastness and trustworthiness, employee assets, business model adaptability, and design principles that reduce vulnerabilities. Some research has indicated that resilient organizations should not be led or managed hierarchically. Instead, they should rely on decentralization, self-organization, and shared decision-making (Mallak, 1998; Denhardt and Denhardt, 2010; Lengnick-Hall et al., 2011). It involves a high degree of people involvement and empowerment at all levels of the organization (Cheese, 2016; McManus et al., 2008; Lampel et al., 2014). Comfort (1999) proposes connecting people through enhanced communication and imaging technology whereby communication and face-to-face dialogues are rooted in trust, honesty, and self-respect (Weick, 1993). It supports the researchers calling for an open, trustful, and learning-oriented organizational culture (Teixeira and Werther, 2013; Mafabi et al., 2015; Pal et al., 2014; Sawalha, 2015). Ginsburg and Jablow (2020) highlighted seven integral and interrelated resilient components: competence, confidence, connection, character, contribution, coping, and control. These are critical to human and organizational capability of withstanding surprises and shocks without lasting or permanent alteration or falling out, with the ability to recover or adjust easily to misfortune or changes. In retrospect, some main factors accentuating organizational resilience are organizational strategy, resources & capabilities, communication & relationships, organizational learning & work passion, and social capital.

Organizational Agility

Organizational agility began in manufacturing organizations' production departments in the early 1990s (Lopes, 2009; Zhang and Sharifi, 2000). Organizational agility allows organizations to be more flexible, adapt, and respond rapidly to uncertainty and risk (Sherehiy et al., 2007; Hoyt et al., 2007). It is by adjusting to environmental variation quickly according to external changes (Kumkale, 2016; Shin et al., 2015; Braunscheidel and Suresh, 2009) and crises (Grewal and Tansuhaj, 2001) to increase the organization's performance (Tallon and Pinsonneault, 2011). Therefore, agility is a crucial driver of an organization's competitive advantage in an uncertain environment (Ganguly et al., 2009). Other vital studies covered sustainable competition (Mason, 2010), human resources (Shafer, 1997; Ahammad et al., 2020; e Cunha et al., 2020), management, including finance (Uğurlu et al., 2019), and educational establishments (Doğan and Baloğlu, 2018). Most of these agility studies looked at the organizational level of analysis, conceptualizing organizational agility as an organizational capability. The studies include agility growth, job satisfaction, organizational achievement, efficiency, quality of service, leadership roles and styles in management within organizational agility, capability to recognize and seize opportunities rapidly, strategic direction changes initiation and capitalizing on changes, and risk avoidance (Jamrog et al., 2006).

Organizational agility can be defined as the ability of the organization to (1) adapt to external and internal changes (Kumkale, 2016; Shin et al., 2015), (2) rapidly meet customer demands and expectations, and (3) lead change by improving culture, practices, and outcomes (Tallon and Pinsonneault, 2011; Anwar et al., 2019). It is built on a foundation of mutually enforcing elements of organizational agility of leadership and governance, organization culture and architecture, and infor and human capital (Kouzes and Posner, 2007; Ahammad et al., 2020; e Cunha et al., 2020). In the background, there is the constant dynamic interplay of individuals (self), organizations (system), and their context (situation) that adds value to all stakeholders who operate in uncertain, complex, and ambiguous environments. Menon and Suresh (2021) identified eight structural enablers of agility as the ability to sense the environment, organizational structure, adoption of ICT, organizational learning, human resource strategies, leadership, readiness to change, and collaboration with the stakeholders with leadership as the most crucial enablers followed by human resource strategies and organizational structure.

Sharifi and Zhang (2001) organizational agility model identified three agility components (1) agility drivers underscoring the organization's operation, (2) agility capabilities, which are the organizational abilities that make it agile; and (3) agility providers that are the managers' abilities to practice agility capabilities. Other vital studies by Sharifi and Zhang (1999 and 2001); Sharifi et al. (2001); Crocitto and Youssef (2003); Shahaei, (2008); Nejatian and Zarei (2013); Mohammadi et al. (2015), and Nwanzu and Babalola (2019) suggest that there are four fundamental skills required of organizational agility as (1) responsiveness that covers awareness, receptiveness and reactions (Sharifi, 1999; Lin et al., 2006; Shahaei, 2008; Mohammadi et al., 2015); (2) flexibility of organization to respond to environmental changes (Sanchez, 1993), finding the best possible or optimal scope and to react constantly to unpredicted changes (Kundi and Sharma, 2015); (3) speed as organizational imposing decisions quickly after deciding to respond to the changes (Gunasekaran and Yusuf, 2002; Jain et al., 2008) rapidly (Christopher, 2000) or responding quickly to changing environment (Hoyt et al., 2007; Shahaei, 2008), and (4) competency with the organizational and human capacity to up-skills in order to adapt and respond to environmental changes (Teece et al., 1997) and the capacity to achieve the organization objectives efficiently and effectively (Sharifi and Zhang, 1999 and 2001). In summary, agility is the ability of an organization to adapt quickly to internal and external environmental changes to be at a competitive advantage continuously. It includes developing comprehensive organizational and individual working solutions to respond rapidly and flexibly to organization and customer needs productively and cost-effectively without compromising quality.

HEI Strategic Resilience and Agility Readiness

Strategic Organization Readiness Model (SORM)

Like any business entity, the HEI as an organization constantly faces changing business, stakeholders, and governmental environments, whereby organizational resilience and agility are crucial. To take advantage of the HEI's opportunities and make the most competitive challenges, the HEI must be able to protect itself from unforeseen or unpredictable circumstances and adapt, improve, innovate, and implement quickly. Institutional resiliency is related to the mind and settings and the capacity for resisting, absorbing, and responding to sudden changes to institutional directions and operations. However, agility is the physical response and power to move quickly, flexibly, and decisively. As such, institutional agility is the ability to adapt and sustain its education products and services in a continuous and dynamic change context with crucial characteristics of flexibility, strength, and speed and stretching the faculty and staff human capacities and capabilities and leadership and governance organizational mindsets, structure, and systems. The agile HEI aims to develop new education systems and learn new skills or upskill by exploring new knowledge that minimizes short-term shot-gun solution approaches and maximizes long-term student, stakeholders, and organizational HEI outcomes. Thus, this study aims to develop an HEI Strategic Organization Readiness Model (SORM), its readiness components and sub-components, and an assessment framework based on resilience and agility, with its evaluation factors and scoring using the MBNQA Performance Excellence ADLI (Approach, Deployment, Learning, and Integration) for Process items and LeTCI (Level, Trend, Comparison, and Learning) for Results items (NIST, 2022). The SORM applies equally to any profit or non-profit enterprise, as they all face similar external factors attributable to environmental, societal, political, and natural calamities. Mitigations highly depend on the internalized human, infor, and organization capital's abilities and resilience. The SORM can be the basis for further research into profit and non-profit enterprises.

As foundational capitals, the SORM strategic readiness (Figure 1) is adapted from Kaplan and Norton's (2004) BSC (Balanced Scorecard) Learning and Growth Perspective's three sets of critical foundational intangible assets vital for realizing organizational strategies successfully of (a) Human Capital (HC) of the skills, talent, and knowledge, namely the capacity and capabilities that organization people possess, (b) Information Capital comprising of databases, information systems, networks, and technology infrastructure, that needs to be upgraded to Infor Capital (IC), as these are highly dependent on human cognitive, behavioral and psychological utilization and interpretation to move from data to information to wisdom in support of informed decision making, and (c) Organization Capital (OC) of the organization's culture and values, leadership and governance, people alignment with organization and operation strategic goals, and learning and sharing of knowledge (Teay, 2022).

Organization capital enables tangible and intangible resources to be productive, such as machines, patents, brands, and human capital. The elements that constitute the organization capital or capital of the firm, namely, its culture, structure, and organizational learning, can be a source of competitive advantage (Martín-de-Castro et al., 2006). As such, organization capital is the prime intangible asset of businesses. Enterprise resources, such as equipment, labor, patents, etc., are inert. Prescott and Visscher (1980) defined Organization capital as the accumulation and use of private information to enhance production efficiency within a firm. This capital can be a significant source of the organization's value (Carlin et al., 2011). It is an interconnected set of qualitative features, including education, skills, and culture, which creates value-added products and services for the organization.

Organization capital can be decomposed into three firm-specific capital (Bourdieu, 1986) (i) human managerial capital, which denotes managerial skills that mix all internal capabilities intelligibly through the absorption and application of new ideas that promote growth and value of the firm, (ii) process capital, which includes production decisions on quality management, employee programs, efficiency in operations and organizational flexibility, and (iii) innovation capital that measures the ability of a firm in creating and nurturing new products and services for the competitive advantage (Carlin et al., 2011; Bruhn et al., 2010; Edvinsson and Malone,1997). Chiu et al. (2021) indicated that the leader could influence an organization's value by controlling the organization's capital. It includes the organizational knowledge that can be institutionalized or codified through some instruments, like databases, routines,

Figure 1. Strategic organization readiness model (SORM)

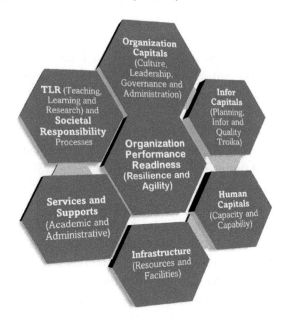

manuals, patents, and so forth, culminating in intellectual capital (IGI Global, 2022). This intelligence capital is based on the organization's information capital, which is applied to specific business or organization problems to lead the organization to better decisions or how the information will lead to a better flow, streamlining processes between different systems. Thus, the infor capital includes human-created knowledge within the knowledge management systems, enterprise policies and procedures, software applications, R&D programs, patents, and training courses.

In addition to the three foundational strategic capitals of the integrated and inseparable OC, IC, and HC, the other critical components of strategic readiness cover the core processes of (1) Teaching, Learning, and Research (TLR), (2) Services and Supports that include societal responsibility, Academic and Administrative Support to all students and stakeholders, and (3) infrastructure that comprises the facilities and equipment, and financial, library and IT resources (whereby human resources is assessed under the human capitals that include capacity and capabilities, and infor capitals that cover the interpretation and usage of information that is human-centered cognitive, psychological and perceptive interpretations).

Strategic Organization Readiness Assessment Framework

In the SORM, longer-term performance sustainability revolves around the critical foundational factors of OC, IC, and HC (Teay and Wattanasap, 2022), as they are human-centered system drivers that create and deliver the educational products driving the core processes. These other value-creating process components are the core processes driven by the OC, IC, and HC capital assets, as prescribed by and subscribe to different IQAs and Accreditation requirements, and dependent on the maturity of the HEI.

The other aspect is the assessment framework, two main frameworks for performance excellence assessment of the MBNQA's ADLI and LeTCI (NIST, 2022) and EFQM's RADAR. RADAR is Results aiming to achieve as part of its strategy through its Approaches that will deliver the required results,

Figure 2. SORM evaluation factors and assessment framework

Readiness Components	Readiness Sub-Components	Readiness Criteria (in terms of Effectiveness & Efficiencies) Scoring Bands: Band 1 of 0-5%, Band 2 of 10-25%, Band 3 of 30-45%, Band 4 of 50-65%, Band 5 of 70-85%, Band 1 of 90-100%		
		Resilience (weight of 60%)	Agility (weight of 40%)	Overall Readiness Score
Organization Capitals	Leadership	Score * 0.20	Score * 0.20	
	Cultural Web & Values	Score * 0.20	Score * 0.10	
	Governance & Admin	Score * 0.10	Score * 0.05	
	Org. Structure	Score * 0.10	Score * 0.05	
Organization Capitals Readiness (OCR) Score				
Infor Capitals	Planning System	Score * 0.20	Score * 0.15	
	Infor System	Score * 0.20	Score * 0.15	
	QA System	Score * 0.20	Score * 0.10	
Infor Capitals Readiness (ICR) Score				
Human Capitals	Academic Capacity	Score * 0.20	Score * 0.10	
	Academic Capability	Score * 0.20	Score * 0.15	
	Staff Capacity	Score * 0.10	Score * 0.05	
	Staff Capability	Score * 0.10	Score * 0.10	
Human Capitals Readiness (HCR) Score				
Infrastructure	IT Resources	Score * 0.20	Score * 0.15	
	Facilities	Score * 0.20	Score * 0.10	
	Financial Resources	Score * 0.10	Score * 0.10	
	Library	Score * 0.10	Score * 0.05	
Infrastructure Readiness (IR) Score				
Services & Supports	Academic	Score * 0.20	Score * 0.20	
	Administrative	Score * 0.20	Score * 0.10	
	Societal Responsibility	Score * 0.20	Score * 0.10	
Services & Supports Readiness (SSR) Score				
Teaching, Learning & Research	Curriculum Mgt	Score * 0.20	Score * Weight	
	Pedagogies	Score * 0.20	Score * Weight	
	Assessment	Score * 0.10	Score * Weight	
	Research Management	Score * 0.10	Score * Weight	
Teaching, Learning & Research Readiness (TLRR) Score				
Organization Readiness	Organization Capitals Readiness (OCR) Score			
	Infor Capitals Readiness (ICR) Score			
	Human Capitals Readiness (HCR) Score			
	Infrastructure Readiness (IR) Score			
	Services & Supports Readiness (SSR) Score			
	Teaching, Learning & Research Readiness (TLRR) Score			
Overall Organization Readiness Score				

Resilience and Agility Assessment (RAA) Factors: Key Process Components and Sub-Components systems, mechanisms, tools & techniques (SMTT)

- **WHAT** SMTT **Approaches** (A) are in place and deployed for a resilient & agile organization"
- **HOW** resilient & agile is the SMTT **Deployed** (D) efficiently and effectively, and by WHO for WHAT purpose"
- Analysis and **Learning** (L) of **WHY** the SMTT resilience & agility is performing for improvement and innovation"
- In the SMTT resilience & agility fully **Integrated** (I)"

both now and in the future, with the Deployment of these approaches appropriately culminating in Assessment and Refinement) (EFQM, 2021) assessment criteria. As such, in its readiness assessment of its resilience and agility, there are two main aspects that the HEI must determine as follows:

1. **Evaluation Factors:** In the SORM Evaluation and Assessment Framework (Fig. 2), the evaluation factors proposed are the critical foundation comprising the strategic capital assets of OC, IC, and HC, as these are primarily human-centered drivers of excellence unique and specific to the HEI. It is the basic SORM Scorecard that the organization should develop to assess their resilience and agility components. The degree of success of the HEI is highly related to and dependent on these

critical capitals. The stronger they are, the more advantageous the HEI is in attaining and sustaining competitive advantage. They are primarily intangible and reside only within the HEI that employs or empowers them. Other than these fundamental evaluation factors, the other three can be expanded or collapsed depending on the IQA or Accreditation requirements. They address and cover most aspects of the core education processes academically and administratively according to the key pillars of education as enshrined in the HEI mission.

2. **Performance Assessment Scoring (PAS):** The SORM uses the MBNQA ADLI and LeTCI assessment methodology as it is more robust and in-depth. Still, it is the HEI's choice to opt for the EFQM RADAR assessment. The weighted PAS comprises two main components of scoring from 0% to 100% based on the chosen MBNQA or RADAR criteria and an assigned weight for each Readiness sub-component, set based on the "degree of importance" to the HEI based on its stated mission and goals. The proposed vital Readiness Components and Sub-components, with the PAS and its assigned weights, meet most of the generic HEI pillars of education. Additionally, each Readiness sub-component is assessed based on crucial construct measures, mostly from key theoretical concepts or fundamentals, as illustrated by the sample Sub-Component of the Leadership Readiness Assessment Criteria in the next section. Whatever construct measures are used depends again on the HEI's unique and specific needs and requirements. The PAS for Leadership Resilience and Agility assessment and scoring is used as part of the computation of the Overall OC score, contributing to the Overall Organization Readiness Score. Resilience is given a 60% weight as it is deemed that the HEI should do its utmost in being resilient before being agile, as agility is based on most of what and how the HEI has executed to be resilient.

Based on the two key aspects above, the SORM Evaluation Factors and Assessment Framework, as proposed, meets the generic needs and requirements of HEI success. Still, as noted, it can be adapted to meet the strategic and operational context of the HEI specificity. The critical essence is that the SORM is an adaptable Strategic Readiness Framework that any HEI can use. Still, the bottom line is that all HEI should review and assess their organizational resilience and agility readiness to address and anticipate the uncertainties of the internal and external environmental changes and challenges.

Sample Sub-Component of Leadership Readiness Assessment Criteria

The proposed construct measures of leadership as one of the critical components of the OC (Figure 3) and its Leadership Resilience and Agility Assessment (Figure 4), whereby the Leadership Readiness subcomponents are used as a sample of detailed identification of the components of Leadership resilience and agility readiness assessment. The organization can adapt the "Leadership Resilience and Agility Scorecard" depending on the leadership system. It means that the various components of other resilience and agility scorecards can be adapted and reconfigured to meet the organization's perspectives. The construct measures are focused on the generic attributes interpreted as "generally accepted management principles or fundamentals" to avoid specificity or narrowly interpreted or fewer researched constructs. Based on the widely accepted and practiced leadership attributes, the critical construct measures for the Leadership PAS are generally applicable across the board. Still, they depend more on the HEI mission, goals, and unique or specific attributes. Some of the critical leadership literature is discussed below. This illustration is applicable in determining each readiness sub-component of OC, IC, HC, and the other components of SORM (Figure 2) and its resilience and agility readiness assessment (Figure 4).

For the SORM, leadership is a critical component of the Organization's Capital and is illustrated here to determine and assess the leadership component of the OC. An organization leader's purpose is to enhance the organization's performance; without good leadership skills and efficacy, an organization could be significantly affected (Dabke, 2016; Knies et al., 2016). Effective leadership is about executing the company's vision and mission (or redefining and improving it) and setting the tone and culture for that organization to achieve its targeted goals and SMART Objectives (Yukl, 2013). Organizational leadership builds and clarifies the organization's direction through the credibility of its mission, sets the correct values, and provides momentum through its culture and value system, and that helps people focus on and improve their abilities and develop future leaders.

Typically, a good leader can hit metric targets, but most leadership evaluations are based on the previous year's financial achievements or disappointment, which can only show past performances. A tool that can measure past performance and use it to predict a leader's performance in the future is critical to the organization. They can look at profits and metrics, promote and measure overall workplace attitude, ignite growth, check individual development by providing sufficient support, and delegate responsibility. In summary, measuring leadership is not a one-size-fits-all model. It means putting various approaches together to measure an effective leader across the board, not just in metrics or personality traits. Leadership effectiveness reflects excellent hard and soft performance measures, not just complex numbers.

Some indicators of an effective leader (Procházka and Smutný, 2011) are (a) their self-awareness, leadership attitudes, and development through self-reflection and spending time evaluating their performance and continually seeking ways to improve (Ioan, 2014; Frackenpohl et al., 2016), (b) translating learning into action with a drive to succeed, (c) creating opportunities for feedback, so people learn and hear about new findings and trends, (d) equipping and demonstrating effective personality traits of self-confidence, responsibility, energy, innovation, the ability to solve interpersonal tensions, accept the consequences of their decisions, have the audacity, and take the initiative in a social situation. In the SORM, leaders' effectiveness (Cakir and Adiguzel, 2020; Cooper and Nirenberg, 2004; Frackenpohl, et al., 2016; Knies, et al., 2016) are demonstrated through (a) clarity of vision, mission, goals and values by leading a team, managing people, as well as tasks to hit challenging targets, which means creating plans and securing resources through offering a great organizational culture, (b) credibility and commitments to promises through unselfish integrity attitude of servant leadership to build positive perceptions among the team members, and looking out for and improving errors to effectiveness in enhancing workplace culture, leading by example, and developing and improving the skill sets of others, (c) competence by shifting intentional efforts to increasing leadership competence, capacity and capability, emotional intelligence (Dabke, 2016), and (d) communication and relationship through spending time with team members to learn more about them as a person, not more about what they are doing for the team, and be genuinely curious about your team members by being approachable and accessible, yet not too friendly, and knowing how to provide feedback and ask for it in return brings out the best in people.

Based on the literature discussed above, the proposed generic leadership readiness sub-components as part of the OC readiness components are concentrated on the HEI 4 Leadership "Cs " attribute of (1) clarity and credibility of thoughts, vision, goals, and value and Performance Measures (2) commitment-integrity, (3) Competence Capacity-Capabilities, and (4) frank, open, and two-ways Communication-Relationship, (Figure 3). Again, these actual attributes can be replaced with attributes important to the HEI based on its leadership maturity, specificity, or uniqueness. The Leadership Resilience and Agility Readiness score is also weighted with the process efficiency and results in effectiveness assigned a proportionate 70% and 30% weight, respectively. The assessment uses the MBNQA evaluative factors

Figure 3. Leadership readiness process components and evaluation factors

	Process Components	Evaluation Factors	Performance Scoring
Leadership Readiness	Clarity & Credibility of Thoughts, Vision, Goals & Values, and Performance Measures Commitment-Integrity Competence Capacity-Capabilities Communication-Relationship that is Frank, Open, and Two-way	• **A (Approach)** measures of system, mechanisms, tools & techniques effectiveness, and efficiency • **D (Deployment)** of approach to relevant work units throughout the organization • **L (Learning)** through cycles of evaluation and improvement, innovation, and sharing with all relevant work units • **I (Integration)** by aligning approach with organizational needs, harmonizing plans, processes, information, resource decisions, actions, analyses of organization-wide goals	There are 6 bands of scoring: 0-5%, 10-25%, 30-45%, 50-65%, 70-85%, and 90-100% (all in progressing level of maturity of the ADLI and Results Outcomes with evidence). *See assessment guidelines of Baldrige Performance Excellence for Processes & Results*
	Leadership Results	**Le (Levels); T (Trend); C (Comparison) & I (Integration)**	
	Overall Leadership Readiness Score		

Source: NIST (2022). *The 2021-2022 Baldrige Excellence Framework (Education)*. NIST, MD: Department of Commerce, National Institute of Technology and Standards. http://www.nist.gov/baldrige

Figure 4. Leadership resilience and agility readiness performance assessment

	Leadership Process Components (Efficiency)	Weights	Performance Scoring				Process Evaluation Scoring: A (Approach), D (Deployment), L (Learning), I (Integration)
			Resilience		Agility		
			Score	Overall	Score	Overall	
Leadership Readiness	Clarity & Credibility of Thoughts, Vision, Goals & Values, and Performance Measures	0.20					
	Commitment-Integrity	0.20					**Results Evaluation Scoring:** Le (Levels), T (Trend), C (Comparison) & I (Integration)
	Competence Capacity-Capabilities	0.15					
	Communication-Relationship that is Frank, Open, and Two-way	0.15					
	Leadership Process Efficiency	**0.70**					
	Leadership Results Effectiveness	**0.30**					
	Leadership Resilience & Agility Score						
	Overall Leadership Readiness Score						

Note: While there might be other Leadership requirements, these 4 Leadership components are presumed to comprehensively cover key leadership traits, values, and performance.

of ADLI for processes and LeTCI for results (NIST, 2022), in line with the overall SORM Assessment Framework. The overall Leadership Readiness Score is then posted to the complete SORM assessment tabulations to derive an overall Organization Readiness Score. As noted, identifying and defining the sub-components of each OC, IC, HC, and other readiness component factors will not be covered here. Their parameters follow the discussion of the sample "Leadership readiness factors" determination and assessment based on literature specificity or uniqueness of the HEI or the college or programs.

IMPLICATIONS

The COVID-19 Pandemic, the Ukraine crisis, and other geopolitical disruptions and natural disasters have caught the world off guard and have taken the world by storm. They have affected all sectors of human life but have hit hardest on the disadvantaged and non-privileged, forming the most extensive human life group on earth. These have made governments across the globe make "pretentious" efforts to ask their people to move from the "normal" to the so-called "new normal." The reality has been and will still be the "real normal" due to pervasive and inherent displacement-discriminations-divides attributable to socioeconomic, geopolitical, and socio-cultural-demographic inequalities that have existed and have persisted over the decades if not centuries. It is hoped that the COVID-19 pandemic has provided a clarion and wake-up call for the HEI to check for and assess its strategic and operational readiness organizationally to face these challenges and changes head-on. While this paper proposes the SORM as an organization readiness and assessment framework, it depends on some key issues that the HEI needs to address and its willingness to realistically address the implications called for to check its strategic organization readiness in terms of its resilience and agility as the following:

1. **Foundational OC-IC-HC Strategic Capital Troika Readiness:** The success of the HEI is highly dependent on the basic foundations of its OC-IC-HC uniqueness, which are human-based drivers of the processes through their appending systems specific to each HEI. As such, the stronger these foundational capital assets are, the better and more significant the chances for the HEI to meet and address the dynamic and fluid internal and external environmental challenges and changes required for its success and sustainability. It questions the degree of resilience and agility of the HEI leadership, Governance, and Management. It includes their mindsets, attitudes, value, and culture that further and drive the human capital of its faculty and staff's motivations and commitments throughout the organization's vision, missions, goals, and values that underscore their meeting and address the challenges and changes through their resilience and abilities. The essential requirements are communication and commitment to their beliefs and value systems to achieve student and stakeholder outcomes. The leaders and organizational cultural vibes across the workforce must be united, related, and committed to the same ideologies and values mindsets to achieve and sustain their strategic and operational advantages and successes. It includes learning and sharing information supporting informed-decision making and actions through its IC capacities and capabilities, which are human-based judgmental and cognitive usage and interpretation of the IC. To illustrate the importance, two private universities, University A, owned by a Chinese businessman, and a leading Catholic-based university B in Thailand, and one leading public University C in the Middle East did not demonstrate (1) strong OC-IC-HC capacities and capabilities, (2) any risk management system in place, and (3) classical and traditional leadership systems of patronage and respect, rather than proactive management. These are also demonstrated in business enterprises that fold easily when in crisis, going into "knee-jerk" reactions and not displaying the resilience and agility expected of performance excellence.

2. **Core Value Addition Processes Readiness:** The second set of resilience and agility prerequisites is in the core value addition processes of the systems and mechanisms of (1) Teaching, learning, and Research (TLR), (2) Services and Supports that include Societal responsibility, Academic and Administrative Support to all students and stakeholders, and (3) infrastructure and facilities. These are the critical resilient and agile systems and mechanisms, tools, and techniques used by the human-based OC-IC-HC Troika to create and deliver educational value to the students and stakeholders. As such, these core value-addition processes are only as good as the capacities and capabilities of the OC-IC-HC Troika. These systems should be assessed for resilience and agility to meet and address the volatile and changing needs and requirements. The HEI should be agile

to change over effortlessly by the whole HEI to meet and address micro issues through its macro resilient and agile organizational readiness. Again, in the three universities above, the core values are not walked, with the core processes and corresponding TLR, or marketing, operation, human resources, and finances in business enterprises, weakened through a weak OC-IC-HC Toika foundation.

CONCLUSION

The COVID-19 Pandemic, the Ukraine war, and socioeconomic, genocidal-tribal, geopolitical, and natural disasters have brought about displacement-discriminations-divides that have disrupted or destroyed the children's education from the normal to the so-called "new normal" that is, in fact, the "real normal." It is the natural human life that people and so-called governments have attempted to alleviate their people's livelihoods over the decades. During the 2020–2021 pandemic and warring episodes, most HEIs have tried showing education continuity through online distance learning technologies. These are affordable to some but not all, as these high-tech pedagogical approaches are still beyond the "real normals" acquired by the disadvantaged who continue to be impoverished.

While most countries have looked at teaching-learning through technological supports, there are still doubts about the effectiveness or efficiencies of these approaches, albeit the fact that the organization, human and infor capital are strategically and operationally equipped and ready to undertake these changes and challenges. In other words, there is a vital question of the strategic and operational readiness of the HEI itself, with its faculty and staff capacities and capabilities, the academic and administrative systems, and especially the leadership, governance, and management capacities and capabilities that drive the success of HEI. While looking at the micro-level pedagogical teaching-learning, this paper proposes that the HEI tends to its macro-level resilience, agility, and strategic and operational readiness

In addressing this strategic and operational readiness, this paper has developed the Strategic Organizational readiness Model (SORM) by defining two main aspects of its resilience and agility as part of its SORM performance and assessment. The SORM is expected to prepare the HEI to be readier to face changes and challenges if its existing readiness components are resilient and agile. The SORM has provided a performance assessment scheme by identifying (1) the readiness component of the OC, IC, and HC, in addition to the three system components required of an HEI, and (2) identifying the subcomponent of each principal component by using the Leadership component as an illustrated example, and (3) a resilient and agility performance assessment methodology by adapting the MBNQA's Process ADLI and Results LeTCI to derive the overall organizational readiness score. It is hoped that the SORM can assist and support the HEI in determining its resilience and agile readiness and develop mitigating plans and approaches to strengthen the HEI's resilience and agility to meet and address dynamic changes and challenges. As noted earlier, the SORM works equally well for the profit and non-profit enterprises, as they have the OC-IC-HC Troika foundations that need strengthening and sustainable resilience and agility. Most components in HEI exist in these enterprises that need to be re-created and aligned within the organization's contexts.

REFERENCES

Ahammad, M. F., Glaister, K. W., & Gomes, E. (2020). Strategic agility and human resource management. *Human Resource Management Review*, *30*(1), 100700. doi:10.1016/j.hrmr.2019.100700

Álvarez, A., Suárez, S. F., Joaristi, N., Lee, V., Tam, M., & Woodcock, E. (2022). *How can corporate functions become more agile?* McKinsey and Company, https://www.mckinsey.com/business-functions/operations/our-insights/how-can-corporate-functions-become-more-agile

Anwar, A., Azis, M., & Ruma, Z. (2019). The integration model of manufacturing strategy competitive strategy and business performance quality: A study on pottery business in Takalar regency. *Academy of Strategic Management Journal*.

Bandura, A. (1997). *Self-efficacy: The exercise of control*. W.H. Freeman.

Bloom, J. R., Devers, K., Wallace, N. T., & Wilson, N. (2000). Implementing capitation of Medicaid mental health services in Colorado: Is "readiness" a necessary condition? *The Journal of Behavioral Health Services & Research*, *27*(4), 437–445. doi:10.1007/BF02287825 PMID:11070637

Boin, A., & van Eeten, M. J. G. (2013). The resilient organization: A critical appraisal. *Public Management Review*, *15*(3), 429–445. doi:10.1080/14719037.2013.769856

Bourdieu, P. (1986). The Forms of Capital. In J. G. Richardson (Ed.), *Handbook of Theory and Research for the Sociology of Education* (pp. 241–258). Greenwood.

Brasca, C., Krishnan, C., Marya, V., Owen, K., Sirois, J., & Ziade, S. (2022). *How technology is shaping Learning in Higher Education. In McKinsey's Education Practice*. McKinsey & Company.

Braunscheidel, M. J., & Suresh, N. C. (2009). The organizational antecedents of a firm's supply chain agility for risk mitigation and response. *Journal of Operations Management*, *27*(2), 119–140. doi:10.1016/j.jom.2008.09.006

Bruhn, M., Karlan, D., & Schoar, A. (2010). What capital is missing in developing countries? *The American Economic Review*, *100*(2), 629–633. doi:10.1257/aer.100.2.629

Cakir, F. S., & Adiguzel, Z. (2020). Analysis of Leader Effectiveness in Organization and Knowledge Sharing Behavior on Employees and Organization. *SAGE Open*, 1–14.

Carlin, B. I., Chowdhry, B., & Garmaise, M. J. (2011). Investment in organization capital. *Journal of Financial Intermediation*, 16–17.

Cheese, P. (2016). Managing risk and building resilient organizations in a riskier world. *Journal of Organizational Effectiveness: People and Performance*, *3*(3), 323–331. doi:10.1108/JOEPP-07-2016-0044

Chiu, J., Li, Y. H., & Kaos, T. H. (2021). Does organization capital matter? An analysis of the performance implications of CEO power. *The North American Journal of Economics and Finance*, 59.

Christopher, M. (2000). The agile supply chain: Competing in volatile markets. *Industrial Marketing Management*, *29*(1), 37–44. doi:10.1016/S0019-8501(99)00110-8

Comfort, L. K. (1999). *Shared risk: Complex systems in seismic response*. Pergamon.

Cooper, J. F., & Nirenberg, J. (2004). Leadership effectiveness. In G. R. Goethals, G. J. Sorenson, & J. M. Burns (Eds.), *Encyclopedia of leadership* (pp. 450–457). Sage.

Crocitto, M., & Youssef, M. (2003). The human side of organizational agility. *Industrial Management & Data Systems*, *103*(6), 388–397. doi:10.1108/02635570310479963

Cunha, M. P., Gomes, E., Mellahi, K., Miner, A. S., & Rego, A. (2020). Strategic agility through improvisational Manageentcapabilities: Implications for a paradox-sensitive HRM. *Human Resource Management Review*, *30*(1), 100695. doi:10.1016/j.hrmr.2019.100695

D'Aveni, R. A., Dagnino, G. B., & Smith, K. G. (2010). The age of temporary advantage. *Strategic Management Journal*, *31*(13), 1371–1385. doi:10.1002mj.897

Dabke, D. (2016). Impact of leader's emotional intelligence and transformational behavior on perceived leadership effectiveness: A multiple source view. *Business Perspectives and Research*, *4*(1), 27–40. doi:10.1177/2278533715605433

Denhardt, J., & Denhardt, R. (2010). Building organizational resilience and adaptive management. In *Handbook of Adult Resilience*. The Guilford Press.

Doğan, O., & Baloğlu, N. (2018). *Organizational agency and its reflections in some educational institutions*. The 13th International Educational Administration Conference.

Eby, L. T., Adams, D. M., Russell, J. E. A., & Gaby, S. H. (2000). Perceptions of organizational readiness for change: Factors related to employees' reactions to the implementation of team-based selling. *Human Relations*, *53*(3), 419–442. doi:10.1177/0018726700533006

Edvinsson, L., & Malone, M. S. (1997). *Intellectual capital: Realizing your company's true value by finding its hidden roots*. HarperBusiness.

EFQM. (2021). *The EFQM Model*. European Forum for Quality Management.

Frackenpohl, G., Hillenbrand, A., & Kube, S. (2016). Leadership effectiveness and institutional frames. *Experimental Economics*, *19*(4), 842–863. doi:10.100710683-015-9470-z

Ganguly, A., Nilchiani, R., & Farr, J. V. (2009). Evaluating agility in corporate enterprises. *International Journal of Production Economics*, *118*(2), 410–423. doi:10.1016/j.ijpe.2008.12.009

Ginsburg, K. R., & Jablow, M.M. (2020). *Building resilience in children and teens: giving kids roots and wings*. American Academy of Pediatrics.

Gist, M. E., & Mitchell, T. R. (1992). Self-Efficacy: A Theoretical Analysis of Its Determinants and Malleability. *Academy of Management Review*, *17*(2), 183–211. doi:10.2307/258770

Gittell, J. H., Kim, C., Lim, S., & Rivas, V. (2006). Relationships, layoffs, and organizational resilience airline industry responses to September 11. *The Journal of Applied Behavioral Science*, *42*(3), 300–329. doi:10.1177/0021886306286466

Global, I. G. I. (2022). *Organizational Capital*. IGI Global. https://www.igi-global.com/dictionary/organizational-capital/21465?

Grewal, R., & Tansuhaj, P. (2001). Building organizational capabilities for managing economic Crisis: The role of market orientation and strategic flexibility. *Journal of Marketing*, *65*(2), 67–80. doi:10.1509/jmkg.65.2.67.18259

Heckler, J., & Powell, A. (2016). IT and organizational agility: a review of major findings. *Eleventh Midwest Association for Information Systems Conference*.

Holt, D. T., Armenakis, A. A., Harris, S. G., & Field, H. S. (2006). Toward a Comprehensive Definition of Readiness for Change: A Review of Research and Instrumentation. In *Research in Organizational Change and Development* (pp. 289–336). JAI Press.

Hoyt, J., Huq, F., & Kreiser, P. (2007). Measuring organizational responsiveness: The development of a validated survey instrument. *Management Decision*, *45*(10), 1573–1594. doi:10.1108/00251740710837979

Ioan, P. (2014). Leadership and emotional intelligence: The effect on performance and attitude. *Procedia Economics and Finance*, *15*, 985–992. doi:10.1016/S2212-5671(14)00658-3

Jain, V., Benyoucef, L., & Deshmukh, S. G. (2008). What's the buzz about moving from "lean" to agile integrated supply chains? A fuzzy intelligent agent-based approach. *International Journal of Production Research*, *46*(23), 6649–6677. doi:10.1080/00207540802230462

Jamrog, J., Vickers, M., & Bear, D. (2006). Building and sustaining a culture that supports innovation. *People and Strategy*, *29*(3), 9–19.

Jones, R. A., Jimmieson, N. L., & Griffiths, A. (2005). The Impact of Organizational Culture and Re-shaping Capabilities on Change Implementation Success: The Mediating Role of Readiness for Change. *Journal of Management Studies*, *42*(2), 361–386. doi:10.1111/j.1467-6486.2005.00500.x

Kaplan, R. S., & Norton, D. P. (2004). *Measuring the Strategic Readiness of Intangible Assets*. https://hbr.org/2004/02/measuring-the-strategic-readiness-of-intangible-assets

Kendra, J. M., & Wachtendorf, T. (2003). Elements of resilience after the World Trade Center disaster: Reconstituting New York City's Emergency Operations Center. *Disasters*, *27*(1), 7–53. doi:10.1111/1467-7717.00218 PMID:12703151

Knies, E., Jacobsen, C., & Tummers, L. (2016). Leadership and organizational performance. In J. Storey, J. Hartley, J.-L. Denis, P. 't Hart, & D. Ulrich (Eds.), *The Routledge companion to leadership* (pp. 404–418). Routledge.

Kouzes, J.M., & Posner, B. Z. (2007). The five practices of exemplary leadership. *The Jossey-Bass Reader on Educational Leadership*, 63-74.

Kumkale, İ. (2016). Organization's tool for creating competitive advantage: Strategic agility. *Balkan and Near Eastern Journal of Social Sciences*, *2*(3), 118–124.

Kundi, M., & Sharma, S. (2015). Efficiency analysis and flexibility: A case study of cement firms in India. *Global Journal of Flexible Systems Managment*, *16*(3), 221–234. doi:10.100740171-015-0094-0

Lampel, J., Bhalla, A., & Pushkar, P. (2014). Does governance confer organizational resilience? Evidence from UK employee-owned businesses. *European Management Journal*, *32*(1), 66–72. doi:10.1016/j.emj.2013.06.009

Lengnick-Hall, C. A., & Beck, T. E. (2005). Adaptive fit versus robust transformation: How organizations respond to environmental change. *Journal of Management*, *31*(5), 738–757. doi:10.1177/0149206305279367

Lengnick-Hall, C. A., & Beck, T. E. (2009). Resilience capacity and strategic agility: Prerequisites for thriving in a dynamic environment. In Resilience Engineering Perspectives, Preparation and Restoration. Ashgate Publishing.

Lengnick-Hall, C. A., Beck, T. E., & Lengnick-Hall, M. L. (2011). Developing a capacity for Organizational Resilience through Strategic Human Resource Management. *Human Resource Management Review*, *21*(3), 243–255. doi:10.1016/j.hrmr.2010.07.001

Lengnick-Hall, C. A., Beck, T. E., & Lengnick-Hall, M. L. (2011). Developing a capacity for organizational resilience through strategic human resource management. *Human Resource Management Review*, *21*(3), 243–255. doi:10.1016/j.hrmr.2010.07.001

Lin, C. T., Chiu, H., & Chu, P. Y. (2006). Agility index in the supply chain. *International Journal of Production Economics*, *100*(2), 285–299. doi:10.1016/j.ijpe.2004.11.013

Linnenluecke, M. K. (2017). Resilience in business and management research: A review of influential publications and a research agenda. *International Journal of Management Reviews*, *19*(1), 4–30. doi:10.1111/ijmr.12076

Lopes, K. J. (2009). *Organizational agility: Exploring how the US coast guard chooses and implements effective courses of action*. ProQuest.

Maddux, J. E. (1995). Self-efficacy theory: An introduction. In Self-efficacy, adaptation, and adjustment: theory, research, and application. Plenum Press.

Madni, A. M., & Jackson, S. (2009). Towards a conceptual framework for resilience engineering. *IEEE Systems Journal*, *3*(2), 181–191. doi:10.1109/JSYST.2009.2017397

Mafabi, S., Munene, J. C., & Ahiauzu, A. (2015). Creative climate and organizational resilience: The mediating role of innovation. *The International Journal of Organizational Analysis*, *23*(4), 564–587. doi:10.1108/IJOA-07-2012-0596

Mallak, L. A. (1998). Measuring resilience in health care provider organizations. *Health Manpower Management*, *24*(4), 148–152. doi:10.1108/09552069810215755 PMID:10346317

Mankins, M., Garton, E., & Schwartz, D. (2021). Future-Proofing Your Organization. *Harvard Business Review*. https://hbr.org/2021/09/future-proofing-your-organization

Martín-de-Castro, G., Emilio, J., Lopez, N., & Salazar, E. A. (2006). Organizational capital as competitive advantage of the firm. *Journal of Intellectual Capital*, *7*(3), 324–337. doi:10.1108/14691930610681438

McCann, J. (2004). Organizational effectiveness: Changing concepts for changing environments. *Human Resource Planning*, *27*, 42–50.

McManus, S., Seville, E., Vargo, J., & Brunsdon, D. (2008). A facilitated process for improving organizational resilience. *Natural Hazards Review*, *9*(2), 81–90. doi:10.1061/(ASCE)1527-6988(2008)9:2(81)

Menon, S., & Suresh, M. (2021). Factors influencing organizational agility in higher education. *Benchmarking*, *28*(1), 307–332. doi:10.1108/BIJ-04-2020-0151

Mohammadi, M., Nikpour, A., & Chamanifard, R. (2015). The relationship between organizational agility and employee productivity (Case study: Ministry of youth affairs and sports, Iran). *Fourth International Conference IT in Education, Research and Business-ITERB.*

Najrani, M. (2016). *The effect of change capability, learning capability, and shared leadership on organizational agility.* Theses and Dissertations. 687. https://digitalcommons.pepperdine.edu/etd/687

Natale, A., Poppensieker, T., & Thun, M. (2022). *From Risk Management to Strategic Resilience, Risk & Resilience Practice, March 2022.* McKinsey & Company.

Nauck, F., Pancaldi, L., Poppensieker, T., & White, O. (2021). *The resilience imperative: Succeeding in uncertain times Strengthening institutional resilience has never been more important.* McKinsey and Company.

Nejatian, M., & Zarei, M. H. (2013). Moving towards organizational agility: Are we improving in the right direction? *Global Journal of Flexible Systems Managment*, *14*(4), 241–253. doi:10.100740171-013-0048-3

NIST. (2022). *Baldrige Excellence Framework (Education).* National Institute of Standards and Technology. https://www.nist.gov/baldrige/publications/baldrige-excellence-framework/education

Nwanzu, C. L., & Babalola, S. S. (2019). Impact of organization ownership and strategy on organizational sustainable practices. *Academy of Strategic Management Journal.*

Ortiz-de-Mandojana, N., & Bansal, P. (2016). The long-term benefits of organizational resilience through sustainable business practices. *Strategic Management Journal*, *37*(8), 1615–1631. doi:10.1002mj.2410

Pal, R., Torstensson, H., & Mattila, H. (2014). Antecedents of organizational resilience in economic crises: An empirical study of Swedish textile and clothing SMEs. *International Journal of Production Economics*, *147*, 410–428. doi:10.1016/j.ijpe.2013.02.031

Pettigrew, A. M., Ferlie, E., & McKee, L. (1992). *Shaping strategic change: Making changes in large organizations: The case of the National Health Service London.* Sage Publications.

Prescott, E. C., & Visscher, M. (1980). Organization Capital. *Journal of Political Economy*, *88*(3), 446–461. doi:10.1086/260879

Procházka, J., & Smutný, P. (2011). Four indicators of effective leadership. In E. Letovancováand & E. Vavráková (Eds.), Psychology of work and organization. University Library in Bratislava Digital Library.

Rerup, C. (2001). Houston, we have a problem: Anticipation and improvisation as sources of organizational resilience. *Comportamento Organizacional e Gestão*, *7*, 27–44.

Rey, S. (2019). *Readiness: The Missing Key Between Strategy and Execution.* https://trainingindustry.com/articles/strategy-alignment-and-planning/readiness-the-missing-key-between-strategy-and-execution/

Robb, D. (2000). Building resilient organizations. *OD Practitioner*, *32*, 27–32.

Robert, B. (2010). Organizational Resilience: Concepts and evaluation Method. *La Presse*, 1.

Sanchez, R. (1993). Strategic flexibility, firm organization, and managerial work in dynamic markets: A strategic options perspective. *Advances in Strategic Management*, *9*(1), 251–291.

Sawalha, I. H. S. (2015). Managing adversity: Understanding some dimensions of Organizational Resilience. *Management Research Review*, *38*(4), 346–366. doi:10.1108/MRR-01-2014-0010

Shafer, R. A. (1997). Creating organizational agility: The human resource dimension. In Dissertation Abstracts International Section A: Humanities and Social Sciences. Cornell University.

Shahaei, B. (2008). *A paradigm of Agility definitions, features, and concepts*. Tadbir Publication.

Sharifi, H., Colquhoun, G., Barclay, I., & Dann, Z. (2001). Agile manufacturing: A management and operational framework. *Proceedings of the Institution of Mechanical Engineers. Part B, Journal of Engineering Manufacture*, *215*(6), 857–869. doi:10.1243/0954405011518647

Sharifi, H., & Zhang, Z. (1999). A Methodology for achieving agility in manufacturing organizations: An introduction. *International Journal of Production Economics*, *62*(1-2), 7–22. doi:10.1016/S0925-5273(98)00217-5

Sharifi, H., & Zhang, Z. (2001). Agile manufacturing in practice: Application of a methodology. *International Journal of Operations & Production Management*, *21*(5/6), 772–794. doi:10.1108/01443570110390462

Somers, S. (2009). Measuring resilience potential: An adaptive strategy for organizational crisis planning. *Journal of Contingencies and Crisis Management*, *17*(1), 12–23. doi:10.1111/j.1468-5973.2009.00558.x

Stone, T. (2021). *What is Workforce Readiness? And Why Aren't You Measuring It?* https://www.i4cp.com/briefs/what-is-workforce-readiness-and-why-arent-you-measuring-it

Tallon, P. P., & Pinsonneault, A. (2011). Competing perspectives on the link between strategic information technology alignment and Organizational Agility: Insights from a Mediation Model. *Management Information Systems Quarterly*, *35*(2), 463–486. doi:10.2307/23044052

Teay, S. (2022), Leadership for Organization Performance: Organization, Infor and Human Capitals Troika Requisites. In Key Factors and Use Cases of Servant Leadership Driving Organizational Performance. IGI Global.

Teay, S., & Wattanasap, S. (2020). Multifaceted Diversity-Discrimination-Divide Disparities Dilemma of 20|20 Education Agenda. *Journal of Institutional Research South East Asia, 18*(2).

Teece, D. J., Pisano, G., & Shuen, A. (1997). Dynamic capabilities and Strategic Management. *Strategic Management Journal*, *18*(7), 509–533. doi:10.1002/(SICI)1097-0266(199708)18:7<509::AID-SMJ882>3.0.CO;2-Z

Teixeira, E. de O., & Werther, W. B. Jr. (2013). Resilience: Continuous renewal of competitive advantages. *Business Horizons*, *56*(3), 333–342. doi:10.1016/j.bushor.2013.01.009

Tomlinson, D. C., Nauck, F., Pancaldi, L., Poppensieker, T., & White, O. (2021). *The resilience imperative. Risk & Resilience Practices. May 2021.* Mckinsey and Company.

Weick, K. E. (1993). The collapse of sensemaking in organizations: The Mann Gulch disaster. *Administrative Science Quarterly, 38*(4), 628–652. doi:10.2307/2393339

Weick, K. E., Sutcliffe, K. M., & Obstfeld, D. (2005). Organizing and the process of sensemaking. *Organization Science, 16*(4), 409–421. doi:10.1287/orsc.1050.0133

Weiner, B. J., Amick, H., & Lee, S. Y. (2008). Conceptualization and measurement of organizational readiness for change: A review of the literature in health services research and other fields. *Medical Care Research and Review : MCRR, 65,* 379–436. doi:10.1177/1077558708317802 PMID:18511812

Weiner, B. J., Lewis, M. A., & Linnan, L. A. (2009). Using organization theory to understand the determinants of effective implementation of worksite health promotion programs. *Health Education Research, 24*(2), 292–305. doi:10.1093/her/cyn019 PMID:18469319

Yukl, G. (2013). *Leadership in organizations* (8th ed.). Pearson Education.

Zhang, Z., & Sharifi, H. (2000). A methodology for achieving agility in manufacturing organizations. *International Journal of Operations & Production Management, 20*(4), 496–513. doi:10.1108/01443570010314818

Zhou, K. Z., & Wu, F. (2010). Technological capability, strategic flexibility, and product innovation. *Strategic Management Journal, 31*(5), 54.

About the Contributors

Ailson J. De Moraes is the Deputy Director for Kaplan and Royal Holloway Undergraduate Programme, Singapore. He has a Bachelor's and Master's degrees from Andrews University, Michigan, USA and an MA in Business and Culture Studies from City University, London; a Postgraduate Certificate from Fundacao Getulio Vargas, Brazil, and University of California, Irvine. Ailson has also a Postgraduate Certificate in Skills of Teaching to Inspire Learning (Accredited programme by the Higher Education Academy) from Royal Holloway Educational Department. Ailson has attended a number of executive and non-executive programs along his career as an academic and professional in management and business. He has extensive management and business experience, having been worked in a variety of industrial and commercial sectors in international organisations in Brazil, Portugal, Switzerland and the UK. With a profound interest in globalisation and cultures, Ailson travels extensive around the world teaching and attending/presenting in international conferences and seminars; and he speaks fluent three main international languages – Portuguese, English and Spanish. Ailson is an adjunct professor for the iMBA UCL, University College London and Peking University China, and he is a guest lecturer for the MBA for HELBUS, Helsinki Business School in Finland. Ailson was previously a guest lecturer for the MBA at the SPACE, University of Hong Kong, and for the executive programme, St Martins Institute, Malta.. Ailson is a Fellow of three prestigious British institutes, The Higher Education Academy (FHEA), the Chartered Management Institute (FCMI) and the Institute of Administrative Management (FInstAM). He is also a member of the British Academy of Management (BAM) and the Center for Public Services Organisations (CPSO).

* * *

Michael A. Altamirano, Ph.D. Professor, Researcher, Motivator, is a full graduate professor for the King Graduate School of Monroe College where he also serves as a proud member of Monroe College's Board of Trustees and the Alumni Board. He has over 25 years of experience leading and transforming organizations. Dr. Altamirano has a distinguished record of accomplishment as an entrepreneur as well as leadership success with organizations such as Campbell's Soup, Pepperidge Farm, Coca-Cola, and Procter & Gamble. He is a published researcher with interests in leadership development, diversity, inclusion, multiculturalism, and ethics. Dr. Altamirano is the VP of Strategic Management for the Communication Institute of Greece where he also serves as the annual presentation panel leader on international leadership and strategic management. He is an ardent supporter of community involvement and serves as a member of the Board of Directors for Meals on Wheels of New Rochelle, New York. Dr. Altamirano holds a PhD from Carolina University in Winston-Salem, North Carolina, where his research focus was on organizational leadership and urban education, with a discipline in theological studies. He also holds an MS degree from Manhattanville College in Leadership and Strategic Management, and undergraduate degrees from Concordia College and Monroe College in Business Management and Accounting.

Eliane Araujo is a Professor at Department of Economics of State University of Maringá (UEM), Paraná, Maringá, Brazil, and Researcher at Brazilian National Council for Scientific and Technological Development (CNPq), Brasilia, Federal District, Brazil.

Mustafa Arıcıoğlu got his undergraduate degree in Business Administration at İzmir Dokuz Eylül University, his master's degree and PhD in Department of Management and Organization at Selçuk University. He worked in private sector for 7 years. Then, he worked at Selçuk University until 2012. Now, he is Professor at Necmettin Erbakan University.

Jesús Barrena-Martínez, PhD, is an associated professor in the Department of Business Management, Faculty of Economics and Business, at the University of Cádiz (Spain). His lines of research cover Human Resources Management (HRM), Organizational Behavior and Sustainability. He teaches undergraduate and postgraduate students in subjects such as, Business Management, Managerial Skills, and Organizational Behavior. Specially, he has been teaching "management of emotions" for more than 10 years in the Master Program in Human Resources Management.

B. Anthony Brown received his Ph.D. in Management With an Emphasis in Leadership and Organizational Change from Walden University in 2020. In 2021 he was hired as a Maritime Consultant at Blue Ocean Marine (BOM) Limited based on his over 30 years in the Maritime Industry where he also served as Captain on passenger and cargo ships, as well as Marine Superintendent and Chief Operations Officer for land-based corporations.

Venkateswarlu Chandu is working as assistant professor at KL University, Vijayawada and has more than 10 research publications.

Beatriz Clarinha has a Bachelor's degree in Languages and Business Relations. She is finishing her Master's degree in Languages and Business Relations, at the University of Aveiro, Portugal.

Diana Cunha has a Bachelor's degree in Languages and Business Relations. She is finishing her Master's degree in Languages and Business Relations, at the University of Aveiro, Portugal.

Georgi Danov is a finance professional with years of experience in investment banking. Having graduated with a business degree from University of London, he began his professional career as a financial consultant. Through his career to date, he has managed multiple projects across Tier 1 investment banks and different regions, including the United Kingdom, continental Europe, and South Africa. He is a dedicated lifelong learner, holding professional qualifications in investment management, risk management and project management. He is also an avid social psychology enthusiast and a self-published author.

Omkar Dastane obtained his Ph.D. in Business from Curtin University and is working as an Assistant Professor and Head of Program (MBAs) at the UCSI Graduate Business School, UCSI University,

Kuala Lumpur, Malaysia. Dr. Omkar's research mainly emphasizes digital consumer behavior, consumer perception and values, technological impact on businesses, and scale development studies in the marketing domain. His research has been published in several international journals and books including the Journal of Retailing and Consumer Services, Marketing Intelligence & Planning among others. Dr Omkar is appointed as as an Editor of Arab Gulf Journal of Scientific Research (Emerald, Scopus, WoS). He is also an active reviewer for Web of Science and Scopus Indexed Journals.

Mojca Duh is a professor of Governance and Strategic Management at Faculty of Economics and Business at the University of Maribor where she teaches courses in the bachelor, master and doctoral study programmes. She is head of the Department of Strategic Management and Enterprise's Policy. She participated with research papers at several national and international conferences and (co)authored several scientific and professional articles, and chapters in books. Research areas of her interest include: Strategic management; Corporate governance; Integral management; Start-up and developmental management; Business planning; Governance and management of family businesses, Developmental particularities of family businesses; Dynamic enterprise.

Yunus Ertuğrul graduated from Necmettin Erbakan University, Faculty of Political Sciences, Bachelor of Business Administration. He completed his master's degree in the Social Sciences Institute of the same university, Department of Business Administration. He works as a customer representative in an international company's store in Konya.

Patrick Fatzer is a commercial director within the pharmaceutical industry. He has held various commercial roles within country affiliates, regional positions and running Global brands. His expertise in business optimization and product launches has helped him garner respect within the industry as leader of the future. Patrick holds a BSc in Molecular Biology and a Masters in International Business Management.

Amala Gangula is working as a Faculty Research Associate having 8years of teaching experience and 7years of Banking experience and about 10publications.

Herman Fassou Haba is an analyst for BMO financial group and researcher who does research studies in management, marketing, project management and finance. Having BSC in accounting and finance and an MBA from Anglia Ruskin University. I am currently doing MSC in project management research studies at L'université du Québec à Trois-Rivières.

Keri L. Heitner is a research psychologist, consultant, and contributing faculty in the PhD in Management Program at Walden University. Her work involves applied research, evaluation, and program development about diversity and inclusion; career advancement and re-entry; service delivery research and development in health, mental health, and the government and nonprofit sectors; and entrepreneurship. She is also a writer, editor, methodologist, and curriculum developer.

Seda Işgüzar is an assistant professor in the Management Information Systems field at Turgut Özal University in Malatya, Turkey. She received her Master's degree from the Computer Systems department of Fırat University's Electronic Computer Education program. She completed her Doctoral program in the

Technology and Information Management department of the Social Sciences Institute at Fırat University. Her research interests include management sciences, artificial intelligence, digital transformation, and graphics programming.

Chan Kah Chee has had over 30 years of senior management experiences. He is a specialist in international management consulting & organizational development. His highest role was Chief Operating Officer (COO) of a US$3.2b integrated resort project. His corporate track record was to turnaround a conglomerate, during the Asian Crisis with US$14b debt, to becoming the 2nd richest company in Indonesia. Professor Chan has trained over 10,000 managers in transformational & servant leadership courses throughout Asia. He conducts organizational behaviour & leadership, and agile entrepreneurship modules at Bachelors, Masters, and Doctorate levels as a global visiting professor during the past 20 years. Recently, he is awarded "Academic Fellow of The International Council of Management Consulting Institutes" and "1st Fellow of Strategy Implementation Institute". He is also the founder of Wholistic Institute of Lifelong Learning (WILL).

Erdinc Koç completed his PhD in Business Administration at Ankara University in 2017. He continues his academic activities as an associate professor in Department of Business Administration at Bingöl University. He works in the fields of supply chain management, innovation management and operations management.

Bhavana Likhitkar is a research savvy having more than 20 publications and 1 text book

Macarena López-Fernández, PhD, is a professor in the Department of Business Management, Faculty of Economics and Business, at the University of Cádiz (Spain). She has undertaken various courses specializing in Management competences, HRM and Business Organizations. She also teaches undergraduate and postgraduate students in subjects such as, HRM, Managerial Skills, and Organizational Behavior. Her research interest covers different aspects of Human Resource Management in organizations and Socially Responsible HRM. She is also Coordinator of the Postgraduate Program in Human Resource Management on the Faculty of Economics and Business of the University of Cádiz.

António C. Moreira obtained a Bachelor's degree in Electrical Engineering and a Master's degree in Management, both from the University of Porto, Portugal. He received his Ph.D. in Management from the University of Manchester, England. He has a solid international background in industry leveraged working for a multinational company in Germany as well as in Portugal. He has also been involved in consultancy projects and research activities. He works as Associate Professor with Habilitation at the Department of Economics, Management, Industrial Engineering, and Tourism, University of Aveiro, Portugal. He is a member of the GOVCOPP research unit.

Samuel Peres is a Researcher at Brazilian National Council for Scientific and Technological Development (CNPq), Brasilia, Federal District, Brazil.

Muhammad Rafiq, PhD is working as an Assistant Professor HRM at UCSI Graduate Business School, UCSI University, Kuala Lumpur, Malaysia. He obtained his PhD in Business Administration from Harbin Institute of Technology, Harbin, China. His research interests include Employee Job Insecurity, Employee Wellbeing, Personnel Resources, Job Stress, Job (Re)design, and Cross-cultural Studies in Psychology and Organizational Behaviour fields. He has published research articles in well reputed international journals such as *Career Development International, International Journal of Environmental Research and Public Health, WORK: A Journal of Prevention, Assessment, and Rehabilitation, and Frontiers in Psychology*. He has presented papers at several international conferences.

K. Pradeep Reddy is working as associate professor at SAGE University Bhopal and has more than 15 research publications.

Pedro M. Romero-Fernández, PhD, is a professor in the Human Resources area of the Business Management Department, Faculty of Economics and Business. His teaching experience (over 20 years) covers an extensive background: Strategy, Human Resources, Organizational Behaviour, and Personnel Management. He has published in the field of Human Resource Management in highly prestigious journals like the International Journal of Human Resource Management, British Journal of Management, and the Journal of Business Research.

Jürgen Rudolph is presently Director of Research, Kaplan Singapore. He is also Editor in Chief, Journal of Applied Learning & Teaching (an open-access journal that neither charges its authors nor its readers). Jürgen has four postgraduate degrees; a PhD from the University of Erlangen-Nuremberg (Germany); an MBA from the University of Louisville (Kentucky, USA); and an M.Ed. from the University of Adelaide (Australia). Jürgen has 30 years of Higher Education teaching experience and has taught a wide variety of subjects, ranging from Knowledge Management to Innovation & Entrepreneurship. He has published numerous journal articles, and he is the author/co-editor of three books (on the social history of the Peranakan Chinese in Singapore; and the Asian crisis in the late 1990s).

Margarita Ruiz-Rodríguez, PhD, is a lecturer in the Department of Business Management, Faculty of Social Sciences and Communication, at the University of Cádiz. Her lines of research and teaching experience cover Strategic Management, Business Management and Human Resources. She has participated in several teaching innovation projects about managerial skills and competences. Some of them have obtained awards and mentions of excellence. She is also Coordinator of the Strategic Management module in the Master in Tourism Management (UCA) for more than 11 years.

Francisca Sá has a Bachelor's degree in Languages and Business Relations. She is finishing her Master's degree in Languages and Business Relations, at the University of Aveiro, Portugal.

Teay Shawyun is Associate Professor in Strategic Management, Consultant to King Saud University's electronic Performance Management System linking quality-information-planning. He was President of SEAAIR (2005-2017), Editor of JIRSEA (2018 to present) & member of the TQA (Thailand Quality Award) Board of Assessors for 15 years. He has ten years of business experience, 38 years of academic experience, and research interest in MIS, IT, and Strategic Management, with research interest covering Management of Technology, Strategic Management, Quality Management, and Performance Management.

Ameil A. Sloley is the Director of Human Resources of World Wide Holdings Corp., where she is a part of the company's core team that focuses on acquisitions, development, venture capital investments and charitable/political endeavors. Prior to World Wide Holdings worked at Trilogy Sportswear/North Bay Apparel in the Menswear Manufacturing industry as a Senior Executive Assistant/Assistant Salesperson. For 8 years, she worked intricately with designers, importers, distributors and manufacturers gaining tremendous insight and experience in the industry. She served as liaison between the warehouse and factories in the Orient and coordinated all arrangements for MAGIC, the Men's Convention in Los Angeles which is a biannual event and where companies present their new line to all the major outlets, retailers etc. Ameil is a graduate of Manhattanville College in Purchase, NY she holds a Master's in Organizational Behavior/Management & Human Resource Development; and a B.B.A. in Business Management from Monroe College. She has been a faculty member in the School of Business & Accounting for 12 years, and she currently serves as a member of the Monroe College Board of Trustees and the Alumni Association Advisory Board. She also serves on the Corporate Educational Advisory Board at Manhattanville College.

Tjaša Štrukelj is an associate professor in the field of governance and strategic management at the University of Maribor, Faculty of Economics and Business (UM EPF), Department of Strategic Management and Company Policy, Institute for Corporate Governance and Strategic Management. She is the (co) author of articles in various (inter) national journals, monographs and conferences (, 16338). She was (2015–2018; 2016–2017; 2018–2019) and is (2019–2022) a member of the international research team, leads the faculty part of Erasmus+ project Economic of Sustainability (2019–2022) and bilateral international research project (2019–2022), actively participates in the research program Entrepreneurship for Innovative Society (2016-), is a member of the program committee of the journals Oeconomica Jadertina, Croatia (2017-), Journal of Research and Innovation for Sustainable Society, Romania (2019-), Acta Economica, Bosnia and Herzegovina (2020-), is a certified Leader for Social Responsibility and Sustainable Development (2019-), Path to integrity (P2I) community leader for Slovenia (2020-), Commissioner for Sustainable Development from the ranks of FEB employees (2022-) and member of the UM Pedagogical Network (2022-). She is a senator at the Faculty of Economics and Business, University of Maribor.

Eunice Tan is Head of Programme, Academic Support at SIM Global Education, Singapore Institute of Management. Eunice is passionate about sustainable development, social equity, and climate agendas in the Anthropocene. Thus, she is a keen proponent of equitable education, compassionate teaching, humanizing the academy and eco-pedagogical approaches within sustainability education, teaching, and learning. A committed Asian researcher, her research interests include sustainable development, sustainability education, culinary and heritage tourism, gender research in tourism and destination resilience and recovery in the Asia Pacific region.

Somkiat Wattanasap has been a Purser with Thai International Airways for 35 Years, whereby he retired in 2020. He attained his Ph.D. in Buddhist Psychology from MahaChulalongkorn University in 2010 and has since been an active academic and researcher at the same university.

Index

A

Agile 76, 78-80, 82, 87, 89, 100, 102, 123, 170, 220, 227, 230, 234, 272, 327-330, 332-333, 336, 339-341, 343, 346
Agility Framework 327
Anthropocene 256-257, 260, 268-270

B

Board of Directors 1-2, 4-11, 48, 58
Bonding 307-309, 312-314, 318-319, 321, 324, 326
Bonding Social Capital 308-309, 314, 318-319, 321, 324, 326
Born Globals 12-13, 15, 30, 32
Born Regionals 12-13, 15
Brazilian Economy 236-239, 242, 244, 252
Bridging and Unifying 307-309, 312, 321, 324
Bridging Social Capital 308-309, 314, 318-319, 321-322, 326
Business Model 35-36, 38, 48, 53, 75, 103, 106, 137, 139, 143, 168, 170-172, 178, 180-182, 185-188, 196, 273, 325, 329, 331

C

Capability 17, 76-77, 82, 84, 86, 95, 97, 122, 124, 126, 128, 136, 188, 221, 226, 230, 232, 290-291, 327, 330-332, 337, 345, 347
Capital Structure 33, 105-107, 110-115, 117-120
Challenges 9-10, 30, 35, 39, 45, 55, 59, 64, 123, 128, 139, 145, 156-157, 160, 163, 165, 171, 179, 189-191, 196, 199-201, 204, 206-207, 209-210, 212, 220, 222-223, 225-226, 229, 234, 236-238, 240, 246, 253, 256, 261, 264, 267, 284-286, 302, 304, 328-329, 332, 336, 339-340
Child Labor 34, 38-39, 42, 44-45, 47, 49-50, 54, 56-57, 61, 68, 71-72, 74-75
Climate Change 34-38, 41-42, 46, 53, 55-56, 59, 61, 63, 65-66, 69, 74-75, 202, 246, 256, 259, 263, 265, 267, 270
Compensation 1-2, 6-11, 273
Competitive Advantage 17-18, 34, 78, 82, 84, 86, 97, 103, 105-106, 118-119, 121-129, 132-137, 151, 171, 174, 176, 179, 187, 189, 191-192, 195, 197-198, 200, 203-204, 210-213, 217, 220, 222, 225-227, 229-233, 264, 287-288, 302-303, 305, 307, 323, 331-333, 336, 343-344
Competitiveness 10, 31, 112, 114, 122, 124, 126, 129, 168, 170, 172, 174-177, 179-182, 184-188, 199, 210, 220-224, 227-230, 247, 257
Complexity 1, 80, 84-85, 119, 168-169, 171, 173, 201, 207, 219-224, 227-231, 234, 242, 268, 278, 289
Complexity Theory 219, 223-224, 227, 229, 231
Conceptual and Relational 308
Corporate Governance 1-2, 5, 8-11, 55, 69-70, 74, 93, 215, 305
Cost Of Capital 105, 107, 109, 111-112, 114, 116, 118-119, 303
COVID-19 21, 38, 40, 43-44, 52, 54, 60, 71, 74, 76, 93, 123-124, 126-127, 134-137, 148, 158, 164-165, 168-169, 172, 184, 218, 236-238, 242, 245, 247-248, 252-254, 271, 274, 278, 283-284, 304, 327, 329, 338-340
Crisis 4-5, 45, 59, 67, 69, 80, 84, 93, 109, 123-124, 126, 128, 134-137, 148, 168-170, 172-174, 180-182, 184-188, 215, 236-240, 242-243, 245, 247, 252-254, 263, 272, 322, 327-328, 330, 338-339, 343, 346
Cross Border 221, 227
CSR, Triple Bottom Line, Environmental, Social, and Governance 34
Customer Segmentation 278

D

Debt 84, 105-119, 173
De-Industrialization 236-238, 252

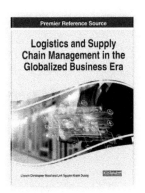

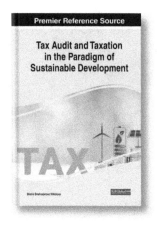

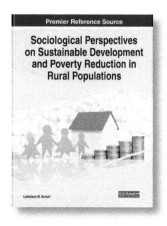

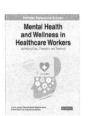